Jesus the Bridegroom

Jesus the Bridegroom

The Origin of the Eschatological Feast as a Wedding Banquet
in the Synoptic Gospels

Phillip J. Long

☛PICKWICK *Publications* · Eugene, Oregon

JESUS THE BRIDEGROOM
The Origin of the Eschatological Feast as a Wedding Banquet in the Synoptic Gospels

Copyright © 2013 Phillip J. Long. All rights reserved. Except for brief quotations in critical publications or reviews, no part of this book may be reproduced in any manner without prior written permission from the publisher. Write: Permissions, Wipf and Stock Publishers, 199 W. 8th Ave., Suite 3, Eugene, OR 97401.

Pickwick Publications
An Imprint of Wipf and Stock Publishers
199 W. 8th Ave., Suite 3
Eugene, OR 97401

www.wipfandstock.com

ISBN 13: 978-1-62032-957-3

Cataloguing-in-Publication data:

Long, Phillip J.

Jesus the bridegroom : the origin of the eschatological feast as a wedding banquet in the synoptic gospels / Phillip J. Long.

xvi + 282 pp. ; 23 cm. Includes bibliographical references.

ISBN 13: 978-1-62032-957-3

1. Jesus Christ—Parables. 2. Bible. Gospels—Criticism, interpretation, etc. I. Title.

BT375.2 L85 2013

Manufactured in the U.S.A.

To Lori, Amy, and Caroline

Contents

Preface | ix
List of Abbreviations | xi

1 Introduction | 1
2 The Use of Hebrew Bible Imagery in the New Testament | 10
3 Eschatological Banquet in Isaiah | 43
4 A Banquet in the Wilderness | 68
5 Israel as the Wife of the Lord | 103
6 From the Hebrew Bible to the Historical Jesus: Banquet and the Marriage Metaphor in Second Temple Period Judaism | 148
7 The Wedding Banquet in the Synoptic Gospels | 184
8 Conclusions and Suggestions for Further Research | 241

Bibliography | 245

Preface

THIS BOOK IS SLIGHTLY revised version of my dissertation. My study of the eschatological banquet began in a seminar on exegesis of metaphors taught by John McVay. About the same time I read a great deal on intertextuality in the book of Revelation as a part of an Advanced Studies in Revelation class taught by Jon Paulien. Steve Moyise was visiting Andrews University at that time and held several lectures on the topic of intertextuality, although the application at the time was only to the book of Revelation. My intention was to apply this methodology to the metaphor of a wedding banquet in the teaching of Jesus. I originally conceived of this as a kind of Historical Jesus project, intentionally working with the words and actions of Jesus rather than the Gospel writers as authors.

I want to thank my faculty adviser P. Richard Choi for his helpful insights as the project was taking shape. Robert M. Johnston offered many helpful suggestions on early drafts of the dissertation and I appreciate his encouragement to continue. Old Testament Professors Jacques B. Doukhan and Jiri Moskala offered many comments on the Hebrew Bible portions of the book. My external reader Mark Whitters of Eastern Michigan University provided many helpful comments and criticisms. Professor Roy E. Gane was chair of the PhD committee when I began the project and was a constant encouragement. All shortcomings of this work are of course my own, but the book is much better as a result of the contributions of these scholars.

I owe a debt of gratitude to my institution, Grace Bible College, for support during my coursework and dissertation research. I could not have completed this project without the generous support of the Faculty Development Fund. Dale DeWitt was a mentor to me first as his student and later as a colleague. Dale is the ideal model of humble scholar; I can never repay the debt I owe to his wisdom over the years. I appreciate the assistance of Paul Sweet as Academic Dean and Linda Siler as Registrar in arranging my classes so that I could attend classes full time while maintaining a full teaching load at the College. The faculty and staff of Grace Bible College were constantly supportive during those difficult years. I thank my students during those years that had to endure me as I worked "messianic banquet" into every lecture. Bob and Jerry helped me through several difficulties along the way, I appreciate their support.

Preface

Most of all I want to express my thanks to my wife, Lori, and especially my two daughters Amy and Caroline for their patience on those many nights when I was off working on my dissertation. It is to them that this book is dedicated.

Abbreviations

AAT	Agypten und Altes Testament
AB	Anchor Bible
ABD	Anchor Bible Dictionary
ABRL	Anchor Bible Reference Library
AJSL	*American Journal of Semitic Languages and Literature*
AnBib	*Analecta biblica*
ANTJ	*Arbeiten zum Neuen Testament und Judentum*
AOAT	*Alter Orient und Altes Testament*
AsSeign	*Assemblées duSeigneur*
ASTI	Annual of the Swedish Theological Institute
AThR	*Anglican Theological Review*
AUSDS	Andrews University Dissertation Series
AUSS	*Andrews University Seminary Studies*
BA	Biblical Archaeologist
BBB	Bulletin de bibliographie biblique
BBR	Bulletin for Biblical Research
BECNT	Baker Exegetical Commentary for the New Testament
BETL	Bibliotheca ephemeridum theologicarum lovaniensium
BGBE	Beiträge zur Geschichte der biblischen Exegese
Bib	*Biblica*
BibInt	*Biblical Interpretation*
BibOr	*Biblica et orientalia*
Bijdr	*Bijdragen: Tijdschrift voor filosofie en theologie*
BIS	Biblical Interpretation Series

Abbreviations

	BJRL	*Bulletin of the John Rylands University Library of Manchester*
	BJS	Brown Judaic Studies
	BKAT	Biblischer Kommentar, Altes Testament. Edited by M. Noth and H. W. Wolff
	BNTC	Black's New Testament Commentaries
	BR	*Biblical Research*
	BRev	*Bible Review*
	BRLJ	Brill Reference Library of Judaism
	BSac	*Bibliotheca sacra*
	BTB	*Biblical Theology Bulletin*
	BZ	*Biblische Zeitschrift*
	BZAW	Beihefte zur Zeitschrift für die alttestamentliche Wissenschaft
	CB	*Cultura bíblica*
	CBET	Contributions to Biblical Exegesis and Theology
	CBQ	*Catholic Biblical Quarterly*
	CBQMS	Catholic Biblical Quarterly Monograph Series
	CC	Continental Commentaries
	ConBNT	Coniectanea neotestamentica
	ConBOT	Coniectanea biblica: Old Testament Series
	COS	*The Context of Scripture.* Edited by W. W. Hallo. 3 vols. Leiden, 1997–
	CTJ	*Calvin Theological Journal*
	CTR	*Criswell Theological Review*
	DJD	Discoveries in the Judaean Desert
	DSD	*Dead Sea Discoveries*
	EBib	*Etudes bibliques*
	ECC	Eerdmans Critical Commentary
	EvQ	*Evangelical Quarterly*
	EstEcl	*Estudios eclesiásticos*
	ETL	*Ephemerides theologicae lovanienses*
	ETR	*Etudes théologiques et religieuses*
	ExpTim	*Expository Times*
	FAT	Forschungen zum Alten Testament

Abbreviations

FOTL	Forms of the Old Testament Literature
HALOT	Koehler, L., W. Baumgartner, and J. J. Stamm, *The Hebrew and Aramaic Lexicon of the Old Testament*. Translated and edited under the supervision of M. E. J. Richardson. 4 vols. Leiden, 1994–1999
HBT	*Horizons in Biblical Theology*
HeyJ	*Heythrop Journal*
HKAT	Handkommentar zum Alten Testament
HS	*Hebrew Studies*
HSM	Harvard Semitic Monographs
HUCA	*Hebrew Union College Annual*
HvTSt	*Hervormde teologiese studies*
ICC	International Critical Commentary
IEJ	*Israel Exploration Journal*
Int	*Interpretation*
IB	*Interpreter's Bible*. Edited by G. A. Buttrick et al. 12 vols. New York: Doubleday, 1951–1957
IDB	*The Interpreter's Dictionary of the Bible*. Edited by G. A. Buttrick. 4 vols. Nashville: Abingdon, 1962
IDBSup	*Interpreter's Dictionary of the Bible: Supplementary Volume*. Edited by K. Crim. Nashville: Abingdon, 1976
ISBE Rev.	*International Standard Bible Encyclopedia*. Edited by G. W. Bromiley. 4 vols. Grand Rapids: Eerdmans, 1979–1988
ITC	International Theological Commentary
JAOS	*Journal of the American Oriental Society*
JBL	*Journal of Biblical Literature*
JBR	*Journal of Bible and Religion*
JETS	*Journal of the Evangelical Theological Society*
JJS	*Journal of Jewish Studies*
JNES	*Journal of Near Eastern Studies*
JNSL	*Journal of Northwest Semitic Languages*
JQR	*Jewish Quarterly Review*
JRT	*Journal of Religious Thought*
JSJ	*Journal for the Study of Judaism in the Persian, Hellenistic, and Roman Periods*

Abbreviations

JSNT	*Journal for the Study of the New Testament*
JSNTSup	Journal for the Study of the New Testament: Supplement Series
JSP	*Journal for the Study of the Pseudepigrapha*
JSPSup	Journal for the Study of the Pseudepigrapha: Supplement Series
JSOT	*Journal for the Study of the Old Testament*
JSOTSup	Journal for the Study of the Old Testament: Supplement Series
JSS	*Journal of Semitic Studies*
JTS	*Journal of Theological Studies*
KAT	Kommentar zum Alten Testament
LD	Lectio divina
LEC	Library of Early Christianity
LNTS	Library of New Testament Studies
LOTS	Library of Old Testament Studies
LTP	*Laval théologique et philosophique*
MNTC	Moffatt New Testament Commentary
NAC	New American Commentary
NCB	New Century Bible
Neot	*Neotestamentica et Semitica*
NewDocs	New Documents Illustrating Early Christianity
NIB	The New Interpreter's Bible
NICNT	New International Biblical Commentary on the New Testament
NICOT	New International Biblical Commentary on the Old Testament
NIDOTTE	*New International Dictionary of Old Testament Theology and Exegesis*. Edited by W. A. VanGemeren. 5 vols. Grand Rapids: Eerdmans, 1997
NIGTC	New International Greek Testament Commentary
NovT	*Novum Testamentum*
NovTSup	Novum Testamentum Supplements
NSBT	New Studies in Biblical Theology
NTM	New Testament Monographs
NTS	*New Testament Studies*
OTB	Overtures to Biblical Theology
OTL	Old Testament Library

OTP	*Old Testament Pseudepigrapha*. Edited by J. H. Charlesworth. 2 vols. New York, 1983
PEQ	*Palestine Exploration Quarterly*
PRSt	*Perspectives in Religious Studies*
PSB	*Princeton Seminary Bulletin*
RB	*Revue biblique*
ResQ	*Restoration Quarterly*
RevQ	*Revue de Qumran*
RevScRel	*Revue des sciences religieuses*
RHPR	*Revue d'histoire et de philosophie religieuses*
RNT	Regensburger Neues Testament
SBLDS	Society of Biblical Literature Dissertation Series
SBLMS	Society of Biblical Literature Monograph Series
SBLSP	*Society of Biblical Literature Seminar Papers*
SBT	Studies in Biblical Theology
ScEccl	*Sciences ecclésiastiques*
Sem	*Semitica*
SHBC	Smith & Helwys Bible Commentary
SJLA	*Studies in Judaism in Late Antiquity*
SJOT	*Scandinavian Journal of the Old Testament*
SJT	*Scottish Journal of Theology*
SNT	Studien zum Neuen Testament
SNTSMS	Society for New Testament Studies Monograph Series
ST	*Studia theologica*
STDJ	*Studies on the Texts of the Desert of Judah*
STRev	*Sewanee Theological Review*
STVP	Studia in Veteris Testamenti Pseudepigrapha
SVQT	*Saint Vladimir's Theological Quarterly*
SwJT	*Southwestern Journal of Theology*
TDOT	*Theological Dictionary of the Old Testament*. Edited by G. J. Botterweck and H. Ringgren. Translated by J. T. Willis, G. W. Bromiley, and D. E. Green. 14 vols. Grand Rapids: Eerdmans, 1974–2003

Abbreviations

TDNT	*Theological Dictionary of the New Testament.* Edited by G. Kittel and G. Friedrich. Translated by G. W. Bromiley. 10 vols. Grand Rapids: Eerdmans, 1964–1976
THNT	Theologischer Handkommentar zum Neuen Testament
TJT	*Toronto Journal of Theology*
TLOT	*Theological Lexicon of the Old Testament.* Edited by E. Jenni, with assistance from C. Westermann. Translated by M. E. Biddle. 3 vols. Peabody, MA: Hendrickson, 1997
TLZ	*Theologische Literaturzeitung*
TQ	*Theologische Quartalschrift*
TSK	*Theologische Studien und Kritiken*
TynBul	*Tyndale Bulletin*
TZ	*Theologische Zeitschrift*
USQR	*Union Seminary Quarterly Review*
UUÅ	*Uppsala Universitetså rskrift*
VT	*Vetus Testamentum*
VTSup	*Vetus Testamentum* Supplements
WBC	Word Biblical Commentary
WUNT	Wissenschaftliche Untersuchungen zum Neuen Testament
ZAW	*Zeitschrift für die alttestamentliche Wissenschaft*
ZBBCOT	*Zondervan Illustrated Bible Backgrounds Commentary on the Old Testament.* Edited by J. H. Walton. Grand Rapids: Zondervan, 2009.
ZNW	*Zeitschrift für die neutestamentliche Wissenschaft und die Kunde der älteren Kirche*
ZTK	*Zeitschrift für Theologie und Kirche*

1

Introduction

Background to the Problem

Frequently New Testament commentaries will state that the image of a banquet, or more specifically, a wedding banquet, was a common messianic image in the first century.¹ However, other than Isa 25:6–8, sources for the image of a banquet for the messianic age in the Hebrew Bible are sparse, and there is very little to support the view that a wedding banquet was a widespread image of the messianic age in Second Temple period Judaism. E. P. Sanders therefore doubts the symbolic value of the messianic banquet as a wedding celebration in the first century.² Jesus used imagery that was designed to recall Jewish messianic hopes current in the first century. For example, Sanders cites Jesus' selection of twelve disciples as re-creating Israel in his

---

1. For example, "Jewish apocalypticism envisioned the coming messianic age as a great wedding day" (Batey, *New Testament Nuptial Imagery*, 60). "A wedding banquet frequently depicted the fellowship of the Messiah with his people at the eschatological consummation" (Blomberg, *Matthew*, 326). Commenting on Matt 22:3, Hultgren says "The wedding banquet is a metaphor for the eschatological messianic kingdom and its joys" (*The Parables of Jesus*, 344). Stock comments that "the marriage feast was a well-known Jewish image for the joy of the last days" (*Saint Matthew*, 334). Stein says, "The portrayal of the age to come as a great messianic banquet where the redeemed would sit and feast with the Messiah is a common one in Judaism" (*Luke*, 199). According to Smith, the messianic banquet at the end of time was "a theme widely reflected in biblical and extra-biblical tradition" (*From Symposium to Eucharist*, 157).

2. Sanders, *The Historical Figure*, 185; see especially n15 on Isa 25:6–7. While Sanders states here that the Christian interest in meals based on the Last Supper has led to an over-interest in Jewish meals, he does not deny the image of a messianic banquet in the Second Temple period. In an earlier work Sanders stated that it is "almost beyond a shadow of a doubt" that Jesus depicted the kingdom of God as a messianic banquet. Sanders, *Jesus and Judaism*, 307. Likewise, Jeremias denies any presence of bridegroom-as-messiah imagery in the Second Temple period (Jeremias, "νύμφη," 4:1102). On the other hand, Stauffer claimed that "Jesus moves wholly within the circle of ideas of His contemporaries when He expresses the meaning and glory of the Messianic period in the images of the wedding and wedding feast" (Stauffer, "γαμέω," 1:654).

followers. A Jew living in Palestine in the first century would be able to understand the point of a Jewish teacher who talked about a kingdom and selected twelve men as his disciples.[3] Similarly, Davies and Allison deny that there are any Second Temple period sources for the idea of a messianic feast as a wedding banquet.[4]

Yet the image of a banquet clearly appears in the Synoptic Gospels in both the actions of Jesus as well as his teaching. In his table fellowship Jesus invites all people to eat and drink with him (Matt 8:11–12). In his teaching through parables Jesus describes his ministry as an invitation to a feast. Those who respond to this invitation are participating in the banquet, but those who do not respond will never be admitted to the banquet (Matt 22:1–14, Matt 25:1–12). This ongoing banquet is described as a wedding feast and Jesus himself claims to be the bridegroom (Mark 2:19–20). Because the metaphor of a wedding banquet is not found in the literature of the Second Temple Period, scholars frequently assume that this sort of language was created by the Gospel writers and that Jesus himself did not claim to be a bridegroom.

It is the contention of this book that Jesus did indeed claim to be a bridegroom and his ministry was an anticipation of the eschatological banquet. While there is no single text in the Hebrew Bible or the literature of the Second Temple Period which states the "messiah is like a bridegroom," the elements for such a claim are present in several traditions found in this literature. Jesus created this unique image by clustering three traditions drawn from the Hebrew Bible and applying them to his ministry. First, the eschatological age is inaugurated by a banquet eaten in the presence of God (Isa 25:6–8). Second, the end of the exile is often described as a new Exodus and a new journey through the wilderness (Isa 40–55). Third, the relationship of God and his people is often described as a marriage (Hosea, Jer 2–4). Like any other teacher of the Second Temple Period, Jesus intentionally alluded to traditions drawn from the Hebrew Bible in order to describe a new situation. Jesus claims that his ministry is an on-going wedding celebration that signals the end of the Exile and the restoration of Israel to her position as the Lord's beloved wife.

Statement of the Problem

The problem this book seeks to address is the origins of the wedding banquet imagery in the teaching of Jesus. In this dissertation I will argue that Jesus combined several related eschatological traditions drawn from the Hebrew Bible in order to depict his

---

3. Sanders, *The Historical Figure*, 172–73, 185. The reassembly of Israel is a focal point of Jewish messianic hopes. They expected the Diaspora to end and to return to a free Palestine. The re-gathered people would rebuild the cities of the Land and populate it as they should have done after the Exodus. The land will be central to the true worship of God. God will gather the twelve tribes, *Sirach* 35:11; Elijah will restore Jacob, *Sirach* 48:10; Jerusalem's children will come from the east and west, *PsSol* 11.2f.; The people will be divided according to tribes, *PsSol* 17:28–31, 50, cf. *Temple Scroll*, 11QT 8:14–16, 57.5 and Philo, *Rewards* 164, where there is an expectation of the return of the Diaspora Jews to Palestine.

4. Davies and Allison, *Matthew*, 3:199n27.

ministry as an on-going wedding celebration. This combining of traditions may be described as intertextual, but the term will need to be more broadly defined to include traditions as well as texts. While these traditions are present in the Hebrew Bible and the literature of the Second Temple Period, the combination of traditions was unique to historical Jesus. The main thesis of this dissertation is that Jesus himself combined the tradition of an eschatological banquet with a marriage metaphor in order to describe the end of the Exile as a wedding banquet.

Previous Scholarship on the Messianic Banquet

No single monograph has been devoted to the messianic banquet in Second Temple period Judaism, nor has there been a comprehensive study of the idea of a messianic banquet in the Hebrew Bible. Several articles and a few dissertations have examined the topic, although from different perspectives than proposed by the present study. Prior to 1990, most studies on parables simply repeated information found in Strack and Billerbeck[5] or G. F. Moore.[6] For example, J. C. O' Neill contributed a short note on the origin of the bridegroom metaphor which listed a number of texts which he assumes are "background" for the idea.[7] This list is given with no critical evaluation and includes items which may be dated well after the time of Jesus. R. A. Batey briefly surveyed possible sources for the image of a wedding banquet in the New Testament as part of his dissertation and subsequent monograph but paid very little attention to the development of what he called nuptial imagery in the Second Temple period.[8]

Two articles appeared in the early 1990s which sought to address the lack of serious study of the theme of messianic banquet in New Testament studies.[9] Citing the common assumption that the idea of a messianic banquet is pervasive in the Second Temple period, J. Priest's article proposed to re-evaluate the evidence for messianic banquet in the Second Temple period.[10] Gathering virtually every text which might

5. Strack and Billerbeck, *Kommentar zum Neuen Testament*, 4:1154–65.

6. Moore, *The Age of the Tannaim*, 2:364–65.

7. O'Neill, "The Source of the Parables," 485–89.

8. Batey, *New Testament Nuptial Imagery*. This revision of his 1961 PhD dissertation is condensed greatly. The study provides only minimal background material, limiting the usefulness greatly. Lack of scholarly interest in the wedding banquet metaphor is evident in Batey's literature review. Only a handful of articles can be listed, most of which concern Paul's use of a marriage metaphor, for example, Murihead, "The Bride of Christ," 175–87. The only monograph cited by Batey is Chavesse, *The Bride of Christ*.

9. One other monograph appeared in this period. Vögtle's monograph studied the parable of the Great Banquet and concluded that the original parable was a prophetic speech (*Drohwort*) against Israel. Jesus' ministry presented salvation to Israel at the end of time, but they refused this offer and therefore salvation is offered to "pagans from all over the world." Vögtle, *Gott und seine Gäste*, 16. Since Vögtle's study does not trace the origins of messianic banquet in the Hebrew Bible or Second Temple period, it is of limited value for this dissertation.

10. Priest, "A Note on the Messianic Banquet," 222–38. In the introduction to the article, Priest states his intention to expand the article in later research. It appears that he never completed this goal.

be read as a banquet in the Apocrypha and Pseudepigrapha, he finds two contrasting themes which are constantly present: the joy of the redeemed and the judgment and destruction of the enemies of God.[11] While there is a great deal of variation in the description of the banquet in these texts, a renewal of nature resulting in abundant food and drink is consistent.

D. Smith contributed a short article on the messianic banquet in which he sought to demonstrate several motifs which make up the messianic banquet in biblical and Second Temple period literature: a joyous banquet, the presence of the messiah, judgment, and a pilgrimage of the nations.[12] Smith suggested that Jesus' wedding banquet metaphor was a "variation on the messianic banquet theme" which combined the common image of marriage to describe God's relationship with his people with mythological traditions.[13] He specifically cites Isa 55:1–5 as foundational for this combination.

Both Priest and Smith mention the presence of a communal meal in the *Messianic Rule* found at Qumran but do not provide a detailed analysis.[14] L. Schiffman's monograph on the *Messianic Rule* indicates that a messianic banquet idea was present in the Qumran community.[15] Commenting on the so-called *Messianic Rule* (1QSa), Schiffman argues the community believed the advent of the messianic age would include a banquet over which the priestly messiah himself would preside.[16] While the conclusion is controversial, Schiffman argues the meal shared by the Qumran community was a daily re-enactment of the future messianic banquet.[17] This meal may be based on Ezek 44:3, a passage which describes a meal which the Davidic prince will initiate at the time of the renewal of the temple.[18]

---

11. Priest, "A Note on the Messianic Banquet," 227.

12. Smith, "The Messianic Banquet Reconsidered," 64–73. Much of this material is available in Smith, "Messianic Banquet," 4:788–91, and his more recent *From Symposium to Eucharist*.

13. Smith, "The Messianic Banquet Reconsidered," 68.

14. While Priest and Smith suggested the idea of messianic banquet to Jesus' practice of table fellowship at Qumran, Cho's dissertation developed this idea by comparing the practice of the Qumran community and table fellowship in Q. At Qumran, the "daily communal meal . . . is the messianic meal in advance" and the daily table fellowship at Qumran became a way of adapting Temple worship to the messianic banquet. Cho, "The Son of Man Came Eating and Drinking (Matthew 11:19)," 89, 123. After examining the meal at Qumran, Cho draws appropriate connections to table fellowship as practiced by Jesus. Since Cho is studying table fellowship specifically in Q, there are a number of assumptions concerning the nature of Q and the Q community which inform the study. For example, the Q community is similar to the Qumran community since they are both apocalyptic.

15. Schiffman, *The Eschatology of the Dead Sea Scrolls Community*. Schiffman's study was published prior to the articles by Priest and Smith. On 1QSa as a messianic banquet see Cross, *The Ancient Library of Qumran and Modern Biblical Studies*, 77.

16. Schiffman, 67; cf. Hosein, "The Banquet Type-scene in the Parables of Jesus," 183–85.

17. Schiffman, 70; cf. Priest, "A Note on the Messianic Banquet," 228. Priest modified his earlier view that the meal in 1QSa was purely eschatological agreeing that the communal meals were an anticipation of the eschatological banquet.

18. Russell, *The Method and Message of Apocalyptic*, 322. This text has many messianic associations. Ezekiel describes an outer gate of the sanctuary facing east. The gate is shut because the glory of the Lord has entered through it (Ezek 10:1–22; 11:22–25). Only the "prince himself" may eat in the

D. Steffen's 2001 dissertation on the messianic banquet in Matthew charts a different course than this study.[19] Steffen's interest is in Matthew's use of the messianic banquet to explain Gentile inclusion in present age rather the use of the image by Jesus. For example, in dealing with Matt 8:11–12, Steffen identifies the "many who will come from the east and the west" as Gentiles rather than Diaspora Jews, pointing out that scholars such as Davies and Allison are more interested in reconstructing the words of the Jesus than Matthew's theological use of the saying.[20] While Steffen will occasionally recognize the possibility of an allusion in the text, he has no interest development of traditions since his focus is on Matthew as a theologian rather than the historical Jesus.[21]

F. Hosein surveyed references to banquets in ancient literature as part of his 2001 dissertation on banquet type-scenes in the parables of Jesus.[22] This collection of material is quite detailed, covering Ancient Near Eastern banquets through the Greco-Roman symposium. Hosein has provided an excellent collection of references to banquets in Second Temple period Jewish literature, including references to the messianic banquet. Remarkably, however, the dissertation is lacking in coverage of the Hebrew Bible. While he sees Passover as a potential banquet scene, he does not include covenant meals in general in his survey. Exodus 24 and Isa 25:6–8 are only briefly mentioned alongside Esther's double banquet and the invitations of Folly and Wisdom in Prov 9. There are quite a number of additional texts in the Hebrew Bible to be examined if one allows for a covenant meal as an example of a banquet. This lacuna in Hosein's research is a result of his interest in banquet as a literary *topos* rather than tracing the development of traditions in Jesus' teaching. Methodologically, my research is distinct from Hosein by proposing to study the messianic banquet from the perspective of tradition history or intertextuality. Rather than examine the texts which Jesus might have used in developing his teaching on the messianic banquet as a wedding feast, Hosein focuses on how the gospel writers employ the type-scene of a banquet in describing Jesus' activities.

---

presence of the Lord in this location. "The privilege is reminiscent of the place reserved for the worshiping king in the pre-exilic temple (2 Kgs 11:14; 23:3)" (Allen, *Ezekiel 20–48*, 260). Some scholars identify this prince with the Messiah and the meal eaten in the gate as a communal meal. For example, Cooper states "The prince of Ezekiel's temple is a godly representative of the messianic King" (Cooper, *Ezekiel*, 390).

19. Steffen, "The Messianic Banquet as a Paradigm for Israel-Gentile Salvation in Matthew."

20. Ibid., 134. Steffen cites Davies and Allison, *Matthew*, 2:17–32 as well as Allison, "Who Will Come from East and West?," 158–70. Contra Steffen, Davies and Allison suggest that the text does not specifically mention Gentiles and is likely an allusion to Ps 107:3, which is a reference to the return of Jewish exiles from the Diaspora (Davies and Allison, *Matthew*, 2:27).

21. For example, when commenting on the second part of the wedding banquet parable in Matt 22, he simply observes that the additional part of the parable may be an allusion to Zeph 1:7–8. No arguments are given for the possibility of an allusion in the text of Matthew.

22. Hosein, "The Banquet Type-scene in the Parables of Jesus."

Jesus the Bridegroom

J. McWhirter studied the image of a wedding banquet in the Gospel of John.[23] She applies the insights of D. Juel[24] and R. Hays[25] to the final form of the gospel of John and proposes that author of the gospel of John has constructed his gospel in order to highlight Jesus as a bridegroom. Since her task is tracing John's theology, she does not examine the messianic banquet motif in the Hebrew Bible or Second Temple period in any detail. In addition, my study concerns the synoptic gospels, while McWhirter is only concerned with the Gospel of John. However, McWhirter's interaction with intertextual studies is often insightful and her observations concerning the marriage metaphor will be examined closely.

K. Snodgrass includes a detailed section on the parable the wedding banquet in Matt 22 and Luke 14 as part of his larger work on the parables of Jesus in which he gathers most of the relevant texts from the Hebrew Bible through the rabbinic period.[26] He believes that the evidence shows that "many ancient Jews, particularly those who considered themselves pious, assumed that they as God's elect would be at the messianic banquet."[27] Snodgrass provides a wealth of rabbinic material along with the typical texts from intertestamental literature to demonstrate that the idea of a messianic banquet was common in the first century. Snodgrass discusses the metaphor of a bridegroom as current in the first century, citing two texts from 1QIsa which imply that the metaphor of the messiah as a bridegroom may have been current in the Second Temple Period.[28] The significance of Snodgrass' study for my dissertation is that he attempts to read both parables as the words of Jesus rather than allegories written by the early church.[29]

---

23. McWhirter, *The Bridegroom Messiah and the People of God*.
24. Juel, *Messianic Exegesis*.
25. Hays, *Echoes of Scripture*.
26. Snodgrass, *Stories with Intent*, 299–325.
27. Ibid., 317.
28. Snodgrass, *Stories with Intent*, 514.
29. For example, with respect to the bridegroom in Matt 25, Snodgrass states that the image is a self-reference by Jesus (*Stories with Intent*, 514). While he does not refer to any "criteria of authenticity," he argues persuasively that there is nothing in these parables that is out of touch with the historical Jesus. Jeremias represents scholars who assign messianic banquet language to later additions to the text of the Synoptic Gospels and deny that Jesus intended to describe himself as a bridegroom. Commenting on Mark 2:18–20, Jeremias cites several relevant Second Temple period texts and concludes that there is little in the literature to equate a bridegroom with the messiah: "None of the passages cited contains a clear instance of the Messiah/bridegroom allegory" (Jeremias, "νύμφη," 4:1103). That the disciples of Jesus are the guests at the wedding is likely, but Jeremias may have stated his case too strongly when he says Jesus did not see himself as a bridegroom. He denies that the second line of the saying goes back to the historical Jesus and that Mark 2:19b–20 has been added in the tradition in order to make the "messiah as bridegroom" identification more clear. Similarly, Bultmann denied that bridegroom language went back to the historical Jesus. For Bultmann, Jesus did not present himself as a "heavenly bridegroom" nor is there any reference to an eschatological community in the gospels. Bultmann, *The Gospel of John*, 173n11. But if 2:19b–20 is authentic, then Jesus is clearly referring to himself as a bridegroom despite the paucity of evidence from the Second Temple period. This point is made by Guelich, *Mark 1–8:26*, 110. Similarly, France states that Jesus is the "only plausible

In summary, there seems to be an understanding in scholarship that at least some streams of Second Temple period Judaism did understand the Messiah's activity in terms of a banquet and there is an assumption that the "wedding banquet" theme in the gospels has something to do with that messianic banquet. But there has been no detailed study of the traditions Jesus used when he combined the messianic banquet with marriage language so that he could say "the kingdom of heaven is like a king who made a wedding banquet for his son" (Matt 22:1). This dissertation will attempt to fill this gap in the literature on the messianic banquet.

Justification For This Research

Recent studies on the Synoptic Gospels have increasingly used the language of intertextuality to describe allusions to the Hebrew Bible. But because of imprecise nature of the term "intertextuality," it is necessary to re-evaluate the value of intertextual methods used by scholarship to study the Synoptic gospels. In this dissertation I will develop a methodology which seeks to carefully define intertextuality and use it as a tool to explore the words and deeds of the historical Jesus. In doing so, I will show that Jesus developed his wedding banquet parables from well-known tradition clusters by combining these traditions in a new and surprising way as he applied to his present ministry. This process is no different than other Second Temple Period writers (Sirach, for example) and bears similarities to midrash as practiced by Jewish teachers of the period. Since these traditions are so well-integrated into every layer of the Synoptic Gospels, I will argue that sayings often dismissed by scholars as secondary additions of the gospel writer are in fact authentic creations of Jesus.

I will argue that Jesus combined the image of an eschatological banquet with the marriage metaphor to describe the end of the Exile as a new Exodus. The idea that Jesus styled his ministry as a New Exodus is not new,[30] but connecting table fellowship and the image of a banquet in Jesus' teaching to the covenant and wilderness meals has not been considered in detail before.[31] There is a need for a fresh study of the messianic banquet because much that is assumed in scholarship concerning the nature of Jewish messianic expectations is cannot be sustained. For example, the idea of a messianic banquet is assumed rather than demonstrated. Once assumed, the messianic banquet has very little influence on understanding the teaching of Jesus with respect to Jewish

identification of the 'present' bridegroom" (*The Gospel of Mark*, 139). Stauffer sees Jesus as moving "within the circle of ideas of his contemporaries" in this text. Stauffer, "γαμέω," 1:654.

30. For example, Wright, *Jesus and the Victory of God*, 292–94; Watts, *Isaiah's New Exodus in Mark*; Pao, *Acts and the Isaianic New Exodus*. Following Wright on the Lord's Prayer, Pitre connects the "give us this day our daily bread" to manna, which was only given daily (Exod 16). He finds such a view helpful in making sense of the messianic banquet texts as well as the Passover context of the Last Supper. Pitre, *Jesus, the Tribulation, and the End of the Exile*, 144n31.

31. Blomberg has written a monograph on the topic of table fellowship and argues that table fellowship is an obvious allusion to the messianic banquet. Blomberg, *Contagious Holiness*, 113.

messianic expectation in the first century. For example, N.T. Wright states that table fellowship is a "symbolic evocation of the coming messianic banquet."[32] In addition, Wright considers Jesus' "bridegroom" language as evocative of the messiah and that his "kingdom-banquets" were foretastes of the "messianic-banquet."[33] Although he recognizes the presence of banquet and marriage metaphors, there is little in the rest of Wright's work which makes use of the messianic banquet to interpret the words or deeds of Jesus. I will argue in the final chapters of this dissertation that the messianic banquet as a wedding feast provides a powerful tool for understanding Jesus' preaching and especially his actions in presenting himself to Israel.

Although the eschatological banquet tradition appears in the Second Temple period, it is not particularly prominent. Some messianic imagery drawn from the Hebrew Bible was developed in the Second Temple period (eating Leviathan in *2 Baruch*, for example), but there was such a broad range of messianic expectations in the period that it is difficult to categorically state "all Jews" believed the messianic period to be like a banquet. It seems clear that the image of a messianic banquet was one of several motifs for the eschaton in the Second Temple period literature and that Jesus was innovative in his re-use of wilderness traditions and the marriage metaphor to describe what he was doing in his ministry. What is curious is that early Christian literature picks up on banquet and bridegroom language quite early. By the time of the Gospel of John and the book of Revelation are written, the image of the end as a wedding banquet is established. How can this theological reflection in the earliest forms of Christianity be explained if the wedding banquet as a metaphor for the end of the age was not part of the words and deeds of Jesus?

Plan of the Study

Since intertextuality is a thorny issue in contemporary scholarship, chapter 2 will deal at length with hermeneutical issues and methodology. In this chapter I will argue that Jesus interacted with traditions drawn from the Hebrew Bible in ways similar to other first-century teachers. This interaction with scriptural traditions can be described as intertextual, although I will define the term carefully in order to avoid confusion with typology, midrash or other interpretive methods. The method I propose in chapter 2 is relevant for historical Jesus studies since it can be used to measure the historical value of the sayings of Jesus.

I will then examine the three overlapping traditions used to describe the restoration of Israel: the messianic banquet in Isa 25:6–8 (chapter 3), the return from the

---

32. Wright, *Jesus and the Victory of God*, 322. Wright cites Isa 25, *1 En.* 62, and *2 Bar.* 29 as evidence of the currency of this theme without comment. The *Messianic Rule* (1QSa) may also include a messianic banquet idea, but as Wright admits, this is more controversial.

33. Wright, *Jesus and the Victory of God*, 645. Wright connects this messianic banquet with "a new wilderness wooing" as in Hos 2:14–15, Ezek 16, but he does not expand on this idea.

Introduction

wilderness in Isa 40–55 (chapter 4), and marriage metaphor in Hosea (chapter 5). Chapter 6 will trace these metaphors in the literature of the Second Temple period. This chapter will also argue that the idea of the covenant as Israel's marriage to the Lord developed, at least in some texts, into the view that the eschatological age will in some sense be a reuniting of former marriage partners. In chapter seven I will examine how Jesus combined these interrelated traditions in both his actions and teaching. In this chapter I will show that the actions and teaching of Jesus is consistent with similar developments of these traditions in the Second Temple Period. Furthermore, I will demonstrate that wedding-banquet sayings and parables are authentic sayings of historical Jesus.

2

The Use of Hebrew Bible Imagery in the New Testament

Introduction

THE SYNOPTIC GOSPELS PRESENT Jesus in his public ministry functioning as a first century Jewish teacher who interacted with the Hebrew Bible using accepted methods of Second Temple Judaism. Jesus knew the Hebrew Bible well and drew on both texts and images that were well-known to his listeners. When Jesus described the Kingdom of God as like "a king who made a wedding banquet for his son" (Matt 22:1), he consciously drew on imagery well-known from the Hebrew Bible. When he described himself as a bridegroom (Mark 2:19–20), he evoked a traditional metaphor for God's relationship with his people. In order to understand Jesus' use of the Hebrew Bible, it is necessary to deal with several methodological matters in this initial chapter.

First, I will examine the evidence that Jesus was a teacher who used pedagogical methods familiar to his listeners. The fact that Jewish teachers of the first century interacted with the Hebrew Bible is obvious, but how they used texts from the scriptures must be carefully examined since they often combined texts creatively in order to apply those texts to a contemporary situation. Likewise, Jesus combined scripture in ways not necessarily anticipated by the original context of his allusions. This method has been described as both midrash and intertextuality, terms which are quite popular in scholarly writing yet rarely defined with respect to the words of Jesus. Second, I will survey recent attempts to describe how the writers of the gospels used the Hebrew Bible. While these studies are less concerned with Jesus than the exegetical maneuvers of the gospel writers, they provide a useful foundation for the present study of the use of the Hebrew Bible in the New Testament and deserve special attention.

Following this chapter I provide a brief excursus on terminology. A study of this sort needs to be clear on what constitutes a quotation, an allusion, or an echo of the

Hebrew Bible. In addition, it is often argued that the presence of an allusion signals to the reader that the original context is of importance for understanding the new context. This interaction is sometimes described as "intertextuality," a term which must be carefully defined if it is to be used at all. Since several scholars have challenged the use of the term, I describe intertextual methodology in comparison to typology, midrash, and tradition history.

Jesus and First-Century Teachers

Although studies on the use of the Hebrew Bible in the New Testament are common, few have focused on the words of Jesus.[1] This omission is not without good reasons. First and foremost is the problem of sources. When studying quotations or allusions to the Hebrew Bible in the undisputed Pauline letters, there is little question that Paul is the author of the quotation or allusion. The same is true for the Johannine material. But the Synoptic Gospels are more complicated than work of other New Testament authors because it may be that the Gospel writers themselves who are alluding to the Hebrew Bible when they report the words and deeds of Jesus. Most studies concerned with the use of the Hebrew Bible in the Gospels focus on this level of the tradition.[2] But the historical Jesus may be the source of the quote or allusion to the Hebrew Bible. For example, a case could plausibly be made that Luke 6:20–21 alludes to Isa 61:1–2,[3]

---

1. Early studies on the use of the Hebrew Bible in the New Testament focused on quotations found in Acts and Paul as a window into the development of Christology in the early church as well as the exegetical method of these early Christians. Dodd, examined the speeches found in Acts. *According to the Scriptures*. Lindars took a similar approach, focusing primarily on clear citations of the Hebrew Bible as signaled by some introductory formula. *New Testament Apologetic*. Neither Dodd nor Lindars were particularly interested in less formal allusions to the Hebrew Bible. Building on this foundation, several studies in the mid-twentieth century studied Christological exegesis of New Testament writers. See, for example, Hanson, *Jesus Christ in the Old Testament*, and France, *Jesus and the Old Testament*. Several studies focused on the method of exegesis found in the biblical materials. See, for example, Longenecker, *Biblical Exegesis* and Juel, *Messianic Exegesis*. While Fishbane is concerned with exegesis within the Hebrew Bible, many of his observations are applicable to the New Testament writers as well. Fishbane, *Biblical Interpretation in Ancient Israel*. The same can be said for Kugel and Greer, *Early Biblical Interpretation* and many of the essays in Mulder, *Mikra*. The most recent wave of studies on the use of the Hebrew Bible in the New Testament has sought to apply principles of intertextuality, building on the foundation of Hays, *Echoes of Scripture* and the collected essays in S. Draisma, *Intertextuality in Biblical Writings*. Finally, not a few studies seek to describe the exegesis of the biblical writers as midrash. For example, Miller and Miller, *The Gospel of Mark as Midrash*. Boyarin combines the idea of intertextuality and Midrash in his *Intertextuality and the Reading of Midrash*. For a brief review of several "Jesus as a Jewish teacher" studies, see Chilton, "Jesus within Judaism," 179–201.

2. For example, Stendahl is interested in the use of scripture in Matthew as part of his thesis that Matthew was produced as a textbook or discipleship manual. That Jesus himself may have alluded to the Hebrew Bible is not of importance to his work. Stendahl, *The School of St. Matthew*.

3. Allison, *The Intertextual Jesus*, 214. Stein sees a possible allusion to Isa 29:19, 49:13, and 61:1–2 in the four Lukan beatitudes. *Luke*, 199. Likewise, Bovon lists this as a possible allusion but also detects an allusion to Isa 40:29–21. *Luke 1*, 223.

49:10 or 65:13.⁴ The text is considered as "likely authentic" by the often skeptical Jesus Seminar,⁵ Crossan⁶ and Lüdemann,⁷ and can be shown to be authentic by several of the criteria of authenticity used by these scholars. If it can be shown that there is an allusion to Isaiah in this saying, who is making the allusion? Did Jesus turn a text from Isaiah into a beatitude, or does Luke report Jesus' words using Isaiah as a model? If it can be shown with some confidence that the saying comes from the historical Jesus and it is indeed an allusion, then it must be admitted that Jesus is the source of the allusion.

One recent attempt to take allusions in the teaching of the historical Jesus seriously is D. Allison's work on allusions in Q.⁸ After describing his criteria for detecting an allusion, he proceeds to examine dozens of proposed allusions to the Hebrew Bible in Q in order to demonstrate that the earliest layer of tradition available to scholarship was already an intertextual document. Allison wonders how much of this intertextuality goes back to the historical Jesus. He selects seven texts accepted as authentic by Crossan, all of which clearly allude to the Hebrew Bible.⁹ In each case there is no way in which the allusion could be extracted and still leave a meaningful saying. Even with such a small sample of texts which likely go back to Jesus himself, Allison concludes that Jesus knew the scriptures well: The "intertextual Jesus of Q is not a misleading representative of the historical Jesus."¹⁰

Another recent study which takes the words of Jesus seriously is B. Pitre's study of the eschatological sayings of Jesus.¹¹ He chides scholars such as N. T. Wright who accept the words of Jesus uncritically, accepting everything in the synoptic Gospels as historical.¹² Following his mentor J. Meier,¹³ Pitre uses several well-defined criteria of authenticity to show that the words of Jesus are likely authentic. Using this methodology, Pitre believes he has distinguished the *ipssima vox* of Jesus. He then provides a

---

4. Green, *Luke*, 267. Both Green and Marshall see this line as a reference to the messianic banquet. Marshall, *Commentary on Luke*, 250–51.

5. Funk and Hoover, eds., *The Five Gospels*, 289. Luke 6:20 is the second highest ranked saying by the Jesus Seminar, indicating strong support for the line as coming from the historical Jesus.

6. Crossan, *The Historical Jesus*, 270–73.

7. "The earliest stratum of the beatitudes goes back to Jesus" (Lüdemann, *Jesus After 2000 Years*, 297). Bovon agrees: The "first three Lukan beatitudes . . . presumably go back to Jesus himself" (*Luke 1*, 221).

8. Allison, *The Intertextual Jesus*. With reference to the passion narratives, Moo has observed that more allusions to the Servant songs and sacrificial language in the gospels come from Jesus rather than the evangelists. Moo, *The Old Testament in the Gospel Passion Narratives*, 357.

9. Allison, *The Intertextual Jesus*, 214. Of the seven selected texts, five appear in the Jesus Seminar's *Five Gospels* as pink or red.

10. Allison, *The Intertextual Jesus*, 215. Similarly, Zimmerman concluded that the combination a marriage metaphor and the eschatological banquet "is obviously an achievement of early Christianity" and that the source of the combination was banquet tradition in Q. Zimmermann, "Nuptial Imagery in the Revelation of John," 166–67.

11. Pitre, *Jesus, the Tribulation, and the End of the Exile*.

12. Ibid., 22. His reference is specifically to Wright, *Jesus and the Victory of God*.

13. Meier, *A Marginal Jew*, vol. 1.

detailed exegesis of the saying in question with a special interest in placing the saying in the context of the Hebrew Bible. Pitre is not interested in the nature of an allusion nor Jesus as a teacher, therefore he simply reports scholarly consensus for the presence of an allusion in the sayings of Jesus.[14] Pitre's methodology is an important guide for this study since he takes seriously the words of Jesus as a reader and interpreter of the Hebrew Bible who stands in the tradition of early Jewish pedagogy.

If Jesus was in fact a Jewish teacher who was familiar with the Hebrew Bible, it is possible that Jesus was the source of any given allusion. But that Jesus was literate is a very difficult problem among scholars of the historical Jesus.[15] Luke 4:16-30 would seem to demonstrate that Jesus could read from a synagogue scroll and therefore seems to support some level of literacy in Hebrew.[16] However, the historicity of this text is often questioned as it is part of Luke's special material and is "loaded with Lucan motifs" and appears as a "programmatic statement" in the third gospel.[17] That Jesus was raised in a relatively small and obscure village in Galilee is usually given as evidence for his lack of education. Since Luke wishes to describe Jesus as an educated teacher to his Gentile readers, he portrayed Jesus as reading in the synagogue.

This view overlooks several facts. First, Josephus points out that the education of children was of great importance to Jews even in the first century (*Apion* 1.60), probably based on the command of scripture to teach children in Deut 4:9, 6:7, and 11:9.[18]

14. For example, when dealing with the saying in Matt 10:34-26, Pitre states that this saying is a "clear allusion" to Mic 7:5-6, citing several scholars as examples of the consensus opinion (*Jesus, the Tribulation, and the End of the Exile*, 208). When treating Elijah typology in Mark 9:11-13, Pitre observes that anything which appears to be difficult in this saying "makes sense if the Old Testament and early Jewish eschatology are allowed to inform our reading" (ibid., 188).

15. Meier, *A Marginal Jew*, 1:268-78. For a general overview of education in the Second Temple period, see N. Drazin, *History of Jewish Education from 515 B.C.E. to 220 C.E.*; Safari, "Elementary Education, Its Religious and Social Significance in the Talmudic Period," 11:148-68; Townsend, "Ancient Education in the Time of the Early Roman Empire," updated as "Education (Greco-Roman)," 2:312-17; Boomershine, "Jesus of Nazareth and the Watershed of Ancient Orality and Literacy," 7-36; Winger, "Why Didn't Jesus Write?," 259-61; Vegge, "The Literacy of Jesus the Carpenter's Son: On the Literary Style in the Words of Jesus," 19-37.

16. Two other texts imply that Jesus was literate although both are fraught with questions of historicity. In John 7:14-15, presumably literate hearers of Jesus ask how it is that "he knows letters" (γράμματα οἶδεν), a phrase normally associated with reading and writing (*BDAG* 205). In Luke 2:52 Jesus is described as a "mature student who listens, poses questions and shows insight through his questions and answers" (Vegge, "The Literacy of Jesus," 25).

17. Meier, *A Marginal Jew*, 1:270. Crossan and Reed dismiss the whole pericope as a Lukan invention which foreshadows Paul experience in the synagogue in Acts 13 and 17. Crossan and Reed, *Excavating Jesus*, 29. Stuhlmueller suggests that there are as many as three visits to Nazareth are combined here by Luke. Stuhlmueller, "The Gospel According to Luke," 131. Lüdemann comments that Jesus could not have spoken these verses since they have been "dogmatically manipulated" the whole story is based on a "crude distortion of Jesus' view of himself." Lüdemann, *Jesus after 2000 Years*, 284-85. Marshall, on the other hand, observes that while there are no "simple solutions" to the problems presented by the section, there is no reason to assume that Luke created this story out of material found in Mark 6:1-6. *The Gospel of Luke*, 179.

18. For the Second Temple period, Sir 51:23, Philo, *Mos.* 2.216; *Spec. Leg.* 2.62. In both texts Philo calls the Synagogue gathering διδασκαλία.

Jesus the Bridegroom

R. Riesner has argued that even in a village as small as Nazareth the synagogue would have provided an elementary education.[19] Second, recent archaeological surveys of Galilean villages seem to indicate that literacy was more widespread than previously thought.[20] It is therefore plausible that Jesus knew the Hebrew Bible well, either from reading it personally or hearing it regularly.

Whether Jesus read the Hebrew Bible or not, he used the Hebrew Bible in a way similar to other Jewish interpreters of his day, including the manner in which he alluded to texts drawn from the Hebrew Bible.[21] For example, Jesus clearly employs hermeneutical rules developed by Hillel. In Matt 7:11/Luke 11:13 Jesus employs the rule of *qal wahomer* (light to heavy).[22] In Mark 2:25–28 Jesus uses an analogy based on a scriptural precedent which follows Hillel's rule of *gezerah shawah*.[23]

The parables provide another example of Jesus as a Jewish teacher.[24] Parables are considered part of the work of an educated scribe. The man who devotes himself to the study of the Law of the Most High "is at home with the obscurities of parables" (Sir 39:2).[25] Modern study of the parables has shown that Jesus' parables are in many ways

---

19. Riesner, "Jesus as Preacher and Teacher," 185–210; Riesner, *Jesus als Lehrer*, 123–206. With reference to Acts 4:12, Riesner comments that the low-level of education of the Galilean disciples is only in comparison to the relatively high level of education among the elite in Jerusalem. When compared to the educational level of the rest of the empire, Galilean Jews are more educated. Allison emphasized the performance of Scripture in the synagogue as an explanation for the scriptural literacy of Second Temple period Jews. *The Intertextual Jesus*, 16–18.

20. This is the point of Millard who argues that Galilee is not the cultural backwater earlier studies assumed it to be. Evidence from Hellenized cities indicates that the residents of these places were as "cultured" as Jerusalem. For example, *mikvoth* like those found in Jerusalem are found in Sepphoris and Gamla; stoneware found in Jerusalem is found in Galilean cities as well, indicating opulent lifestyles. In fact, Khirbet Reina, a town just north east of Nazareth, appears to have been a factory for stoneware. Other material evidence indicates a fairly high level of society in Galilee which supports the assertion (for Millard) that many people in Galilee were generally literate and could write receipts, mark jars or ossuaries, and make personal notes. Millard, *Reading and Writing in the Time of Jesus*, 179–12. Head's brief note on excavations in Tel Kedesh in Upper Galilee indicate that what was once thought to be a farming village had a Hellenistic administrative archive, as evidenced by the discovery of 1,800 *bullae* in 1999. Head, "A Further Note," 343–45.

21. Gergardsson, *Memory and Manuscript*; Ellis, *Prophecy and Hermeneutic in Early Christianity*; Riesner, *Jesus als Lehrer*. Hengel, *The Charismatic Leader*. Sanders strongly warns that Jesus cannot be considered "simply a teacher." *Jesus and Judaism*, 173. It is true that he cannot be only a teacher, but he is nonetheless portrayed in the Gospels as teaching.

22. Longenecker, *Biblical Exegesis*, 68, cf. Matt 10:25 and Luke 12:28. For Mark 2:9 see France, *The Gospel of Mark*, 127.

23. Guelich, *Mark 1–8:26*, 121; Longenecker, *Biblical Exegesis*, 69; cf. Matt 21:3 and Luke 6:3–5. Bock considers the combination of texts in Luke 4:18–19 as an example of *gezerah shawah*, based on the use of the word "release" in Isa 61:1 and 58:6. Bock, *Luke 1:1—9:50*, 404. See also Doeve, *Jewish Hermeneutics*.

24. In fact, it is generally agreed that in the parables of Jesus represent the true *ipsissima vox Jesu*. See Joachim Jeremias, *The Parables of Jesus*, 16–17. See also Gerhardsson, "Illuminating the Kingdom: Narrative *meshalim* in the Synoptic Gospels," 266–309.

25. Vegge uses this section of Sirach to argue that parables were not at all "popular literature" but rather the method of a trained teacher who commands "knowledge of the use and function of text

The Use of Hebrew Bible Imagery in the New Testament

similar to those preserved in later rabbinic literature. Since the work of C. Bugge[26] and P. Fiebig,[27] scholars have been aware of parallels between Jesus' parables and rabbinic parables (מָשָׁל). In a more recent survey of the rabbinic parallels, McArthur and Johnston collect some 115 rabbinic parables.[28] Likewise, Flusser studied the parables by identifying the motifs which are consistent between Jesus and the rabbinic parables.[29] For example, the theme of "wise and foolish" is found in the New Testament (Matt 25:1–13) as well as in rabbinic parables concerning wise and foolish servants of a king (*b.Shabbat* 152b).[30]

In summary, it is axiomatic that Jewish texts written in the Second Temple period were in constant dialogue with the Hebrew Bible. If the historical Jesus had any sort of dialogue with the religious leadership of Judaism on theological points, he would have had to know the Scriptures well and allude to them regularly. The synoptic gospels portray Jesus as doing exactly that. The main problem here concerns how to describe Jesus' exegetical method. Since Jesus did not create a literary document as an exposition of the Hebrew Bible, his method cannot be intertextuality in a strict sense. But the fact remains that his allusions function in very similar ways to literary allusions in written documents. Does Jesus' teaching simply reflect typical intertextual

---

forms in communication." This is in contrast to the pronouncement of Bultmann, who saw Jesus as a wisdom teacher in the "popular form" (as cited by Vegge, "The Literacy of Jesus," 28–29).

26. Bugge, *Die Haupt-Parabeln Jesu*.

27. Fiebig, *Altjüdische Gleichnisse und die Gleichnisse Jesu*. Fiebig's second volume was written in a large part to counter the work of A. Drews, who used the rabbinic parables as evidence that Jesus of Nazareth was a complete fiction and that the early church had used the rabbinic parables as models for the sayings of Jesus (Drews, *Hat Jesus gelebt?*). Other scholars found similarities with rabbinic literature: Feldman, *The Parables and Similes of the Rabbis*; Oesterley, *The Gospel Parables*.

28. McArthur and Johnston's chief contribution is their description of the general form of the *mashal*. First is an illustrand, or the thing which will be illustrated. Sometimes these illustrands are historical or legal, but more often they are problem texts or theological points. There is usually an introduction to the parable using the word *mashal* both as a noun and a verb ("they parabled a parable.") Then the parable proper followed by an application point. The application is almost always signaled by the Aramaic *kak*, "even so, likewise." After this application point scripture is cited to "clinch the point," using the phrase "as it is said . . . ." McArthur and Johnston, *They Also Taught in Parables*.

29. Flusser, *Die rabbinischen Gleichnisse und der Gleichniserzähler Jesus*.

30. Flusser's work was extended by his student Young. Young asserts that the Gospels are the earliest witness to parables as a literary form. This includes the frequent use of three characters, two of which are the point of conflict in the story, often resolved in a dramatic fashion. (*The Parables*, 57) Most of Young's examples are parables functioning as *midrash*, or an interpretation of scripture. Since many of his examples are drawn from midrashic texts, this is not surprising, but these examples differ greatly from Jesus' parables. With the exception of the conclusion to the parable of the Wicked Husbandmen, Jesus does not explicitly refer to scripture in the parables. In his more recent monograph, Young begins by describing parables as part of Jewish *haggadah*, which he defines as "storytelling with a message" which "bridge(s) the gap between the common people and the highly educated" (ibid., 7–8). "All parables fall within the realm of *haggadah*, even though *haggadah* encompasses much more than parables" (ibid., 11). Neusner severely criticized *Jesus and His Jewish Parables*, pointing out that this study ignores the critical problems associated with rabbinic names and attribution of parables as well as the well-known problem of dating the material found in rabbinic literature. Neusner, *Rabbinic Literature and the New Testament*, 185–90.

patterns common to all discourse, or did he intentionally allude to texts in a manner which Jewish teachers often did in the first century? The following section surveys several studies of intertextuality as applied to the New Testament, and specifically the synoptic gospels.

Intertextuality and the New Testament

Intertextuality is a literary approach, often applied to allusions to the Hebrew Bible by New Testament writers, which seeks to examine how texts are adapted and placed into a new context. The term "intertextuality" was introduced as a highly technical term in literary studies by J. Kristeva in 1967 to describe the play between texts which creates new meaning when encountered by a reader.[31] To understand any text one must recognize that it draws on other texts and contexts, whether consciously or not.[32] While this insight has had a major impact on literary studies of the New Testament, not all are agreed that this has been a positive development. What is more, many of the studies which use the term "intertextuality" do so uncritically and perhaps confuse a modern literary method with ancient hermeneutical strategies. It is therefore important to survey previous studies which apply methods of intertextuality to the New Testament in order to avoid either extreme.

Richard Hays

The term intertextuality is found in New Testament studies as early as 1989 in R. Hays's work on echoes of the Hebrew Bible in the Pauline letters.[33] For Hays, intertextuality appears more or less equivalent to an allusion or echo of an older text.[34] Following the lead of literary critic J. Hollander,[35] Hays proposes to study allusions to the Hebrew Bible in Paul using a few methodological assumptions on how to detect allusions as well as recognizing that the critic needs to have a "sense" for detecting allusions.[36]

---

31. Kristeva, *Desire in Language*. Compare to the work of Z. Ben-Porat on allusions in literature, "The Poetics of Literary Allusion," 105–28. For an assessment of intertextuality in Ricour, see Vanhoozer, *Is There a Meaning in this Text?*

32. Hays cites the early comments of T. S. Eliot who recognized his debt to earlier poets in his own "The Waste Land," calling it a "bricolage" of fragments from other poems. Hays, *Echoes of Scripture*, 17. Bloom says that "every poem is a misinterpretation of a parent poem." See Bloom, *Anxiety of Influence*, 94.

33. Hays, *Echoes of Scripture in the Letters of Paul*. See also O'Rourke, "Possible Uses of the Old Testament in the Gospels: An Overview."

34. Hays, *Echoes of Scripture*, 15.

35. Hollander, *The Figure of Echo*.

36. Like Mickelsen's famous definition of hermeneutics, detecting allusions can be seen as both an "art and a science." Mickelsen, *Interpreting the Bible*, 3.

Hays develops Hollander's thesis that "the revisionary power of allusive echo generates new figuration."[37] When an older text appears in a new context there is an "echo" or reverberation which can go both directions, creating a new meaning. Hollander calls this metalepsis or transumption.[38] When an allusion functions in this way, the new text is to be understood not only in the light of the specific allusion, but also in the light of the context of the older text. As Hays explains, "the poet's imagination seizes a metaphor and explicitly wrings out of it all manner of unforeseeable significations."[39] In the case of Paul, the citations of older texts often "produce unexpected correspondences" which "suggest more than they assert."[40] But where does this production of "unexpected correspondences" happen? Is it only in the mind of Paul, the mind of the original reader, or even in the mind of a later individual reader or "community of interpretation"? Alternatively, is the meaning created in the "intertextual fusion" found in the text itself? For Hays, the answer is "all of the above."[41] Meaning is found in the original communication as well as the original and subsequent readings of the text, but the text itself is the only thing to which readers have access.

Hays is careful to guard against the charge of employing a reader-response hermeneutic in which "anything goes."[42] A critic must hear an echo or allusion and then convince others that the proposed allusion is in fact an intertextual echo. Hays therefore proposes seven questions which indicate the possibility of an allusion.[43] First, is the proposed allusion available to the author as well as the original readers? The Hebrew Bible can be assumed as a source for all New Testament writers, but any proposed allusion to a non-biblical source would require careful dating of the materials in order to show the text could have been used.[44] Second, what is the "volume" of the echo? Here Hays looks at elements in the text which suggest a literary relationship, including explicit repetition of words and themes. Third, how often is the proposed

---

37. Hollander, ix, cited by Hays, *Echoes of Scripture*, 19.

38. Bloom described metalepsis in *A Map of Misreading*, 101–2. See also Quintilian, *Inst. Orat.* 8.6.37–39.

39. Hays, *Echoes of Scripture*, 20.

40. Ibid., 24.

41. Ibid., 26–27.

42. For example, Crossan's *Cliffs of Fall*.

43. Hays, *Echoes of Scripture*, 29–32. Many have followed Hays's methodology. For example, Thompson developed a definition of allusion and eleven-point rubric for determining the presence of allusions to the Jesus tradition in the writings of Paul. While his first three points are similar to Hays (verbal, conceptual and formal agreement), his fourth criterion is important for the present study. Since Thompson is interested in detecting allusions to the Jesus tradition in Paul, he must weigh the authenticity of any given saying of Jesus by using the frequently cited criteria of authenticity such as multiple attestations. Thompson, *Clothed with Christ*. More recently, Wagner has worked with Hays's criteria in order to study allusions to Isaiah in Romans, although with more interest in the text form Paul employed. Wagner, *Heralds of the Good News*.

44. This is a more serious problem when proposing intertextual relationships within the Hebrew Bible. For example, Amos may allude to the book of Numbers, but this assumes Amos was written after Numbers.

source used by the author? Hays suggests that since Paul often alludes to Isaiah and Deuteronomy, a proposed allusion is more likely if it is drawn from these contexts. Fourth, how well does the allusion fit into the overall themes of the writer? Hays looks for a "thematic coherence" of the allusion within the overall argument Paul develops. Does a proposed allusion illuminate Paul's argument? If not, the proposed allusion is less likely (since it is pointless). Fifth, is it historically plausible that Paul might allude to a particular text? Similar to his criterion of availability, Hays states that an allusion needs to be grasped by the original readers.[45] Sixth, Hays looks to the history of interpretation for clues to a possible allusion. Has this allusion been noticed before? While he admits this is the least reliable guide, it does guard against arbitrary readings of the text. It is true, however, that earlier interpreters sometimes hear echoes which are not as obvious to us. Hays's last criterion is the most subjective but also the most important: does the proposed allusion satisfy the reader? Does the reader really "hear the echoes" in the text?

In summary, what Hays provides is a set of principles for identifying allusions and echoes to earlier texts. His seven guiding principles provide for some objectivity which will prevent the excesses of a reader-oriented hermeneutic since these principles assume that the writer intended the allusion in the first place and expected their readers to understand the allusion. But these principles are sufficiently broad enough to account for the subtle, artistic echoes which a writer may employ in order to hint at other texts and contexts. Because Hays attempts to include both objective and subjective criteria, he has faced criticism for being too open to postmodern hermeneutics. On the other hand, some scholars fail to see what the difference is between his suggested method and other long-established methods.

Responses to Hays

Since the publication of Hays's study the use of the term "intertextuality" has become common in New Testament studies almost to the point that it no longer means anything. New Testament scholars have used "intertextual" to describe anything from the simple search for sources of allusions to midrashic exegesis.[46] The question needs to be asked: can methods of intertextuality be used without adopting some form of reader-response criticism? If intertextuality "creates meaning," is the critic on insecure hermeneutical ground? S. Porter has warned against the use of the term for New Testament studies simply because most scholars who use the term do not intend to import the postmodern baggage which the term originally carried.[47] T. Hatina believes that

---

45. Hays refers to readings of Paul which are overtly Lutheran or deconstructionist, or any other modern category. Preference, he says, ought to be given to proposals which allow Paul to "remain a Jew" (*Echoes of Scripture*, 31).

46. Miscall, for example, defines intertextuality as "covering all the possible relations that can be established between texts." Miscall, "Isaiah: New Heavens, New Earth, New Book," 44.

47. Porter, "The Use of the Old Testament in the New Testament: A Brief Comment on Method

since the term arose in a poststructuralist context it cannot be used as part of historical-criticism and therefore he does not use the term, despite engaging in study which is termed "intertextual" by others.[48] Hatina shows that Kristeva's original agenda when she introduced the term in 1967 was to subvert author-oriented hermeneutics, since she did not believe meaning exists apart from a reader.[49] For Hatina, this alone makes the term incompatible with the aims of historical criticism, which is author and text based. In reviewing Hays's work, Hatina points out that his method never abandons the historical-critical method nor does he seek meaning outside of the text. Simply put, what Hays does is to "seek the limits of Paul's sphere of influence."[50] Whatever the method is, for Hatina, it is not intertextuality.

C. Evans has also responded to Hays's method of intertextuality by pointing out that what Hays does is not intertextuality as practiced by poststructuralism, but rather a kind of implicit typology.[51] In fact, what Hays describes is not that far from rabbinic interpretation. Evans sees Paul as standing within the tradition of Judaism, even when he provides a "scandalous inversion" of the scriptural story in Romans 9–11.[52] Paul is interpreting scripture in virtually the same way the prophets did in the Hebrew Bible. Evans does not share Hays's aversion to the use of the term midrash as a description of how Paul dealt with scripture.

S. Moyise is also wary of the implications of the term as found in literary studies, but realizes that the term has "taken on a life of its own" and therefore might very well need to be abandoned.[53] Moyise therefore suggests three nuances of intertextuality found in New Testament studies. First, he describes "intertextual echo" as typical in most studies of the "Old Testament in the New."[54] The goal of studies of this type is finding the source or origin of quotation or allusion, if present. In Moyise's second category of intertextuality, the communication is two-way. As he describes it, "dialogical intertextuality" establishes a connection between two texts which intentionally operates in

---

and Terminology," 84. For a discussion of intertextuality and the New Testament which is interested in the original meaning of the term, see Moore, *Poststructuralism and the New Testament*; Vanhoozer, *Is There a Meaning in This Text?*, 131–32. Because the term is so commonly used in hermeneutical discussions it is retained in this study without any overtones of reader-response criticism.

48. Hatina, *In Search of a Context*, 5. This position is argued in detail in Hatina, "Intertextuality and Historical Criticism in New Testament Studies: Is There a Relationship?," 28–43.

49. Hatina, "Intertextuality and Historical Criticism," 30.

50. Ibid., 37.

51. Evans, "Listening to Echoes," 43–44.

52. Ibid., "Listening to Echoes," 51, citing Hays, *Echoes of Scripture*, 67.

53. Moyise, "Intertextuality," 41.

54. Ibid., 18. For example, Moyise examines Romans 8:20 as a possible allusion to Ecclesiastes. What is at stake here is whether Paul intended to draw the reader's attention to the idea of vanity in Ecclesiastes. If this connection can be established, then one may be able to make some exegetical point based on Paul's allusion to the earlier text. The older text sheds light on the new text and perhaps broadens our understanding of Paul's point.

both directions.⁵⁵ The third category of intertextuality as defined by Moyise also sees an interaction between texts but includes the reader as an active participant in the creation of meaning.⁵⁶ This "postmodern intertextuality" is precisely the method which evokes strong objections. In the first two types of intertextual reading, the reader's goal is to determine the meaning of the text as intended by the author. In the postmodern version, the reader creates meaning by interacting with the author. While Moyise recognizes that "no text is an island" and that the reader brings assumptions to the text, he feels that for many exegetes the postmodern project will seem "a pointless exercise."⁵⁷

Moyise's categories are helpful for distinguishing the difference between older studies interested only a writer's method of citing Scripture from the excesses of reader-response criticism. In fact, Moyise's middle category is the most fruitful for the study of the words of Jesus. Jesus occasionally cites the Hebrew Bible in a more or less formal sense, such as his reading of Isaiah in Luke 4:14–21. Yet in the same context he also alludes to the biblical story of Elijah (Luke 4:24–27) without a formal citation. Does the reader's awareness of the original context have an influence on understanding Jesus' point in the use of these texts? To use Ben-Porat's term, does Jesus intend to activate the texts by alluding to them? Conversely, does Jesus' use of these texts change our understanding of the former texts? A moderate intertextual method suggests that the context of the allusion is important and the later writer is interpreting

---

55. The extent to which the New Testament author "respects" the Hebrew Bible text has been the subject of no little debate between Moyise and Beale in the context of the book of Revelation. The essential problem concerns how John used the Hebrew Bible and to what extent he expected his readers to understand his allusions with respect to the context from which the allusions have been drawn. Beale argues that John used the Hebrew Bible in a "contextual" manner. By this Beale means that John knew what the texts meant to say and he intentionally imports that meaning into his own work. Beale, *John's Use of the Old Testament in Revelation*. Bauckman agrees, noting that hardly a word appears in Revelation which has not "been chosen without deliberate reflection on its relationship to the work as an integrated, interconnected whole." Bauckham, *Climax of Prophecy*, x. This book shows a pattern of "disciplined and deliberate allusions to specific Old Testament texts." Bauckham, *Climax of Prophecy*, xi. These allusions are intended to signal to the reader that something in the context of the Hebrew Bible passages alluded to is important to the meaning of the text of Revelation. Moyise, on the other hand, is more open to the idea of dialogical intertextuality in reading John's quotations. There is interplay and conversation between the two contexts; meaning may very well come from this interplay of texts. Although this opens a door for a reader-response hermeneutic, one wonders whether Moyise steps through the door in quite the way Beale thinks he does. Moyise, *The Old Testament in the Book of Revelation*, 23; Beale, *John's Use of the Old Testament in Revelation*, 51. Beale is right to be wary of reader response hermeneutics, but it is not clear from Moyise that he advocates a full-blown reader-response criticism of Revelation (or any other New Testament text for that matter). See also the summary of the conversation between Paulien, Moyise, and Beale in Paulien, "Dreading the Whirlwind," 5–22; Moyise, "Authorial Intention and the Book of Revelation," 35–40; Moyise, "Does the Author of Revelation Misappropriate the Scriptures?," 3–21; Beale, "A Response to Jon Paulien," 23–34.

56. Moyise, "Intertextuality," 33.

57. Ibid., 37. An example of sort of intertextual study is Brawley, *Text to Text Pours Forth Speech: Voices of Scripture in Luke-Acts*. Brawley develops the ideas of Barthes and Riffarterre in his treatment of intertextual allusions in Luke. See also the articles in Aichele and Phillips, *Intertextuality and the Bible*.

the earlier text in the light of present circumstances. Close attention should be paid to the original context of eschatological banquet and marriage metaphors drawn from the Hebrew Bible. Since these traditions appear in the Hebrew Bible in contexts which describe the end of the Exile of Israel, the New Testament exegete ought to bring that context to bear when Jesus uses this language.

Since Hays's criteria for detecting an allusion are helpful for controlling a study, they will be adopted when this study examines Jesus' use of the Hebrew Bible. While I recognize the problems in using the term intertextuality, it seems unavoidable at this point because the term has become so common in New Testament studies. I will use the term with the reservations expressed above. While Hays worked in the Pauline epistles, many of his insights have been applied to the study of allusions in the Gospels.[58] The next stage in this chapter therefore is to briefly survey the recent studies on the use of the Hebrew Bible in the Gospels in order to see how Hays's criterion (or similar methodology) have been applied.[59]

Scripture in Mark

Studies on the Scripture in the Gospel of Mark typically focus on writer's use of scripture as an insight into the Christology of Mark. As such, these studies are looking at the writer of the gospel as a creative exegete who drew together texts from the Hebrew Bible which find their fulfillment in the events recorded in the Gospel. Typically these studies are interested in the prologue[60] or the passion narrative.[61]

J. Marcus' monograph on Mark's use of the Hebrew Bible is primarily interested in Christological exegesis in the second Gospel.[62] He begins with a critique of A. Suhl's study in which he argues that Mark does not use scripture as part of a promise-fulfillment scheme, as Matthew and Luke do.[63] For Suhl, according to Marcus, the Hebrew Bible is used to show that the same God who spoke in the scriptures now

---

58. Studies on allusions in the book of Revelation have perhaps been the most fruitful for developing methodologies for detecting allusions and echoes of earlier texts. As such, this literature will be surveyed only with respect to their contributions to a method for determining allusions. Methodological problems associated with Revelation and the Hebrew Bible are in many ways more complex than in the Gospels and therefore this vast literature cannot be surveyed in detail.

59. For the most part the scholars surveyed in the next section focus on the second level of the Gospels, that of the author of the gospel, rather than how Jesus might have functioned as a teacher in Second Temple period Judaism.

60. Guelich, "The Beginning of Mark's Gospel," 5–15. Marcus, "'The Time Has Been Fulfilled; (Mark 1:15),'" 49–68.

61. Matera, *The Kingship of Jesus*; Moo, *The Old Testament in the Gospel Passion Narratives*; Kee, "Function of Scriptural Quotations and Allusions in Mark 11–16, " 165–88; Ahearne-Kroll, "The Suffering of David and the Suffering of Jesus."

62. Marcus, *The Way of the Lord*.

63. Suhl, *Die Funktion der alttestamentlichen Zitate und Anspielungen im Markusevangelium*. For a penetrating critique of Suhl's conclusion, see Anderson, "The Old Testament in Mark's Gospel," 280–306.

speaks through Jesus.[64] Mark's gospel cites and alludes to the Hebrew Bible, often on the lips of Jesus.[65] In contrast to Suhl, Marcus does not see Jesus himself as the source of any given allusion or citation. For example, commenting on the use of Ps 110 in Mark 12:35-37, Marcus correctly notes that the use of Ps 110 is based on a tradition earlier than Mark's gospel since Barnabas 12:10-11 is an independent witness to the tradition. But Marcus does not think this tradition necessarily goes back to Jesus.[66] In treating Jesus' parable of the vineyard and the citation of Ps 118 in Mark 12:10-11, Marcus comments that the citation of the Psalm is optimistic, while the parable is pessimistic, leading to the suggestion that they were not intended to be read together.

While T. Hatina's study on the Hebrew Bible in Mark strongly resists the use of the term "intertextuality," his method is similar to others in this survey.[67] As Hatina observes, allusions are important because the author implies the importance of a text to a present situation or audience.[68] One of his stated goals is to "propose a model for reading scriptural quotations and allusions that is sensitive to both the narrative of Mark's gospel and the historical setting with which it was written."[69] In order to achieve this goal, Hatina uses a narrative-critical approach which by-passes historical-critical questions in favor of the "story world" of Mark.[70]

Since most critics do not assign allusions or quotations to the *Sitz im Leben Jesu*, references to the Hebrew Bible are not described in any particular context. Hatina's goal, therefore, is to place quotations and allusions into the context of the "story world" of Mark's gospel based on the idea of Kingdom of Heaven—an ideological

---

64. Marcus, *The Way of the Lord*, 2.

65. Marcus, *The Way of the Lord*, 1. In practice, little of Marcus's examples are "on the lips of Jesus." He studies the introduction to Mark (Mark 1:2-3), the voice from heaven at the baptism and transfiguration (Mark 1:9-11; 9:2-8) and the Passion Narrative (Mark 14-16, with special emphasis on Zech 9:9, Dan 7:13 and Isaiah's servant songs). His chapter on Mark 9:11-13 does not trace the allusion to the Hebrew Bible to Jesus, but rather early Christian thinking about the forerunner of the Messiah.

66. Marcus, *The Way of the Lord*, 131-32. According to Marcus, Mark has provided a frame for the tradition (12:35ab, 37bc). He goes on to suggest that the original form of Jesus' parable is to be found in *GThom* 65-66 to which the citation of Psalm 118 was added in order to emphasize the vindication of the son. At a later time, Mark adapted the parable along allegorical lines to make the connection between the son and Jesus clear and to make the parable into a judgment on Israel. This view of the development of the parable was part of Marcus' earlier work, *The Mystery of the Kingdom* and Fitzmyer, *The Gospel According to Luke*, 2:1278-81. In treating Jesus' parable of the vineyard and the citation of Ps 118 in Mark 12:10-11, Marcus comments that the citation of the Psalm is optimistic, while the parable is pessimistic, leading to the suggestion that they were not intended to be read together. In any case, according to Marcus, the quotation of Ps 118 does not come from Jesus.

67. Hatina, *In Search of a Context*.

68. Ibid., 1.

69. Ibid., 3.

70. For example, the troublesome citation of Isa 6 in Mark 4 is understood within the narrative context of the entire Gospel rather than using Isa 6 as a key to understanding Mark 4. If one "stays within the story world of Mark," then the original context of Isa 6 does not matter. Hatina, *In Search of a Context*, 238.

viewpoint shared by the author of Mark and Jesus. In practice, then, Hatina does not place any allusions into the context of Jesus, but rather the context of Jesus in the literary creation of Mark. For the most part, Hatina is concerned with citations of the Hebrew Bible, he offers no rubric for detecting an allusion.[71]

Marcus and Hatina contribute much that can aid the goals of this study. While Hatina in particular provides a strong warning against using intertextual methods, methodologically he is not far from Moyise's second category of intertextual studies described above. Neither Marcus nor Hatina deal with the sayings of Jesus as historical but rather as sayings embedded in a specific literary environment, or the "story world of Mark." What is remarkable is that both studies take seriously the historical and literary evidence drawn from Second Temple period Judaism without considering the possibility that Mark records something that can be considered the *ipsissima vox* of Jesus.

Scripture in Matthew

While R. Gundry's classic study of Matthew's use of scripture does not attempt a study of allusions nor is it at all interested in intertextuality, it is still valuable for the present study since it takes seriously the historical Jesus' citation of scripture.[72] He dismisses "radical form criticism" as being too skeptical concerning the sayings of Jesus on the basis of several false premises.[73] First, the assumption that one can only accept material that differs from both Judaism and Christianity as authentic cannot be maintained since Jesus must have shared something with his contemporaries. Second, radical form criticism is anti-supernaturalist, disallowing *a priori* the possibility that Jesus' words might be preserved in the New Testament. This is not to say that the gospel writers were not creative in their application of scripture to Jesus. Yet even in this monograph Gundry does not argue the authenticity of every saying he addresses. In his commentaries on Matthew and Mark however, he does critically evaluate the sayings of Jesus.

Y. S. Chae examined potential intertextual relationships in Matthew and the motif of the Eschatological Shepherd.[74] While Chae is careful to define intertextuality

---

71. The exception is Mark 13:24–27 which contains a series of allusions. He offers no criteria for identification, although he agrees with the majority of scholarship in seeing allusions to Isa 13:10, 24:4, Dan 7:13, Zech 2:10 and Deut 30:4. He begins with an evaluation of the citation, then surveys historical-critical readings of the text. Finally, he offers an alternative narrative-critical reading which places the citation in the overall context of Mark's plot. Here Hatina considers both historical and literary factors. For example, he includes a lengthy excursus on Pharisees in treating Isa 29:13 in Mark 7:6–7 and a survey of the importance of Ps 118:26 in the Second Temple period and beyond when commenting on Mark 11:9. Hatina asks whether a scriptural quotation determined the meaning of Mark's narrative, or the reverse (*In Search of a Context*, 46). Mark's gospel could be interpreted in the light of a quoted text, or the quoted text could be interpreted in the light of Mark's gospel.

72. Gundry, *The Use of the Old Testament in St. Matthew's Gospel*.

73. Ibid., 191–92.

74. Chae, *Jesus as the Eschatological Davidic Shepherd*.

in order to guard against any postmodern baggage associated with the term outside of New Testament studies, he observes that allusions go "beyond citations" and give insight into the author's interaction with the Hebrew Bible.[75] Most intertextual studies trace the use of a particular book from the Hebrew Bible in a later document, but Chae proposes to study a motif in Matthew. As such, his method is the closest to that proposed for this study of a tradition such as the eschatological banquet in the Synoptic Gospels. Like this study, Chae employs Hays's criterion for detecting allusions along with the standard tools of the grammatical-historical method. He begins by surveying the motif of an eschatological shepherd in the Hebrew Bible[76] and Second Temple period literature,[77] developing a database of potential texts to which Matthew may refer when he uses the eschatological shepherd motif. He then turns to the text of Matthew and demonstrates that Matthew interacted with this tradition. Where appropriate, Chae evaluates the words of historical Jesus, although his main interest is in Matthew as an author.[78] Chae does not argue that the shepherd motif originates in Jesus' own teaching.

Scripture in Luke

Studies on the use of the Hebrew Bible in Luke tend to focus on Luke as a theologian and are especially interested in his use of the Hebrew Bible to develop a christological

---

75. Chae attempts to balance historical, literary and theological methods under the rubric of intertextuality. He observes that by privileging one of these three methods over the others, much is lost when approaching a text like Matthew's gospel. Chae, *Jesus as the Eschatological Davidic Shepherd*, 6–7.

76. Chae begins with a brief survey of shepherd imagery in the Ancient Near East before his detailed examination of the Hebrew Bible. Like the messianic banquet motif, these cultural images are not particularly useful for understanding the Hebrew Bible or Matthew since the shepherd motif is substantially re-imagined in the biblical material because of the Exodus event. Chae, *Jesus as the Eschatological Davidic Shepherd*, 25. Like this study, Chae covers several major texts in the Hebrew Bible which use shepherd imagery and develops a few key elements of this motif which he then can trace in the Second Temple period literature.

77. In this section Chae surveys various examples of the shepherd motif in Second Temple period literature in more or less chronological order. Using the revived messianic hope of the Maccabean period as background, he is able to show that the re-use of the shepherd motif in the Animal Apocalypse (for example) is a reaction against the failure of the Hasmoneans to establish a davidic kingdom. Chae, *Jesus as the Eschatological Davidic Shepherd*, 112–13.

78. For example, "Matthew is conversant with the OT Davidic Shepherd tradition from the vantage point of the Jesus event." Chae, *Jesus as the Eschatological Davidic Shepherd*, 173. This is likely the case for the two quotations (Matt 2:6 and 26:31) and perhaps the allusion to the shepherd motif in 9:36. Chae evaluates the "lost sheep of Israel" sayings in Matt 10:6, 16 and 15:24 as authentic words of Jesus. What is more important is that the event of sending the twelve out to the "lost sheep of Israel" is historically plausible as well. As I will argue later, the actions of Jesus should be given more weight in evaluating the sayings of Jesus. If, as Chae says, Jesus sent out the Twelve to the "lost sheep of Israel" in order to demonstrate his own authority as the eschatological shepherd (ibid., 219), then that event gives more weight to Chae's claim that Jesus used the shepherd motif in his teaching.

theology. D. Bock's study is a good example of this tendency.[79] He is less interested in Jesus as an interpreter of the Hebrew Bible than Luke as an interpreter of the events of Jesus' life. Luke's redactional activity is a window into his theology. As an interpreter of Jesus' life, Luke is often described as employing a "proof-from-prophecy" hermeneutic. That is, Scripture is cited in order to show that the Christ must suffer or that Jesus is Lord.[80]

Bock concludes that the use of the Hebrew Bible in Luke reflects exegetical techniques current in Second Temple period Judaism.[81] What is more, Bock sees Jesus as the "guiding figure" in developing the Christological exegesis that is later found in the apostolic teaching.[82] Bock therefore treats the words of Jesus seriously as evidence of Jesus' messianic self-awareness. Jesus applied well-known messianic texts to himself during his ministry in order to indicate that the events of his life were a fulfillment of those prophecies.[83] Since the messianic banquet motif is muted in Luke's gospel, it is not a concern of Bock's study.[84]

79. Bock, *Proclamation from Prophecy and Pattern*. Bock is in dialogue with Martin Rese, who denies that Luke's motivation was "proof-from-prophecy." Rese, *Alttestamentliche Motive in der Christologie des Lukas*. Rese saw Luke reinterpreting the Scripture in light of a christological agenda. Paul Schubert, on the other hand, argued that Luke used scripture primarily as proof-texts. Schubert, "The Structure and Significance of Luke 24," 165–86. Compare Schubert to Bovon, *Luke the Theologian*.

80. Franklin, *Christ the Lord*. Compare this approach to that of Litwak, who examined "Luke's intertextual use of the Scriptures of Israel" with full attention to more subtle "echoes" often ignored in typical studies of the use of the Hebrew Bible in Luke. Litwak, *Echoes of Scripture in Luke-Acts*. For example, Litwak rejects the common "proof-from-prophecy" hermeneutic and demonstrates that Luke uses Scripture as a framing device for Luke-Acts. He therefore is concerned with the birth narratives and Paul's preaching in Acts 28:16–31, but also the "middle of Luke/Acts," Luke 24:44–Acts 1:12, along with Acts 2:16–21. The use of Scripture at these critical points in the story serve to show that there is continuity between the Scriptures of Israel and Jesus and his followers (ibid., 32). Here Litwak is indebted to Green, "The Problem of a Beginning: Israel's Scriptures in Luke 1–2," 61–85. As such, Litwak does not treat texts in which Jesus draws texts together in order to interpret the Hebrew Bible, only Luke's editorial activity is in view. Litwak argues that "all the intertextual echoes in Luke's infancy narrative can be account for as part of Luke's framing in discourse" (ibid., 111), all the texts covered in the "middle section" who "Luke using intertexts from Israel's sacred texts for framing in a discourse" (ibid., 173) and "Luke uses the Scriptures of Israel. . . . to frame his discourse about Paul's message" (ibid., 199).

81. Bock, *Proclamation and Prophecy*, 271–72. Specifically, the birth narratives are "very close to haggadah," contra Brown's suggestion that the birth narrative is a midrash. Brown, *Birth of the Messiah*, 235.

82. Bock, *Proclamation and Prophecy*, 274. Bock specifically has in mind is Jesus' use of Psalm 118, 110, Isa 53 and Dan 7 in the temple teaching during his final week in Jerusalem. He is aware that his view of Jesus is dependant on the historicity of the sayings, which he attempts to defend as authentic. However, the historicity does not affect his thesis that Luke was doing christological exegesis (ibid., 153–54).

83. This includes new Exodus typology found in Ps 118 and Zech 9:9 at the Triumphal entry and Dan 7:13–14 at his trial. Bock, *Proclamation and Prophecy*, 116, 117, 132. Bock assumes this material is from the historical Jesus as mediated through tradition. He does not attempt to prove the authenticity of any saying in this study.

84. The parable of the Great Banquet in Luke 14 should be considered as a messianic banquet since it is preceded by a clear allusion to the idea of the "feast in the kingdom of God" (Luke 14:15). It would

Jesus the Bridegroom

C. Kimball compares the exegetical method of Jesus in the gospels with known hermeneutical patterns in the Second Temple period.[85] After a chapter sketching Jewish exegetical techniques,[86] Kimball surveys eight passages in Luke in which Jesus engages in a discussion of the Hebrew Bible.[87] He concludes that Jesus used several Jewish exegetical techniques, including typology and *pesher*-like statements involving meanings of words (especially in the parable of the Vineyard and the Son of Man saying).[88]

The significance of Kimball's work for my study is his insistence on Jesus as the source of the exposition of scripture in Luke. He dismisses form critical assumptions as biased against the historical value of the synoptic gospels. He reviews the criteria of authenticity used in most historical Jesus studies and finds them lacking since they do not tell us much about the historical Jesus. In fact, the criterion of double dissimilarity frames the question backwards in Kimball's view. If Jesus says something that is more or less in line with contemporary Judaism then it is more likely to be historical. Ultimately, Kimball is willing to accept the sayings of Jesus in the gospel of Luke as historical unless there is some other reason to reject them as later creations.[89]

Scripture in John

While my study concerns only the synoptic gospels, there are several recent monographs which focus on the intertextual use of the Hebrew Bible in the gospel of John which may be helpful. A. Brunson contributed an intertextual study of the use of Ps 118 as part of the new Exodus pattern in the theology of John.[90] Brunson recognizes that the Gospel of John is part of the larger intertextual culture which "extends back to the writing of the OT itself."[91] Following the work of Hays, Brunson understands the applications of the Hebrew Bible as moving along a spectrum from quotations, which

---

not be included in Bock's study since the statement comes from a fellow-banqueter, not Jesus or Luke. The parable in 14:15–23 seems to address the topic of humility (14:7–14) rather than the blessing of 14:15.

85. Kimball, *Jesus' Exposition*.

86. Kimball includes in his survey quotations and allusions, introductory formulas, Hillel's exegetical rules, and a lengthy description of midrash. He finds some 525 allusions to the Hebrew Bible in Luke, to every book except Song of Solomon, Obadiah and Zephaniah. See page 49 and appendices A and B for a table of occurrences.

87. The temptation (4:1–13), the Nazareth sermon (4:16–30), discussions with the lawyer (10:25–37), the rich young rule (18:18–30), expositions of Isaiah 5 (20:9–19), resurrection (20:27–40), Messiah as David's Lord (20:41–44), and the Son of Man saying in the eschatological discourse (21:25–28).

88. Kimball, *Jesus' Exposition*, 163–64; 196.

89. Kimball's approach is similar to that of B. Pitre, who argues that teachings of Jesus which are like Judaism are not to be rejected as inauthentic since Jesus functioned as a Jewish teacher. B. Pitre, *Jesus, the Tribulation and the End of the Exile*. I find more value in the so-called criterion of authenticity than Kimball.

90. Brunson, *Psalm 118 in the Gospel of John*.

91. Ibid., 9.

can be determined with certainty, to allusions, which are by nature more subjective, to an echo, which might very well be subliminal. Brunson affirms authorial intention in citations and allusions of the Hebrew Bible, arguing that the author of the alluding text meant something specific by the use of an earlier text.[92] His methodology consists of a rubric for identifying allusions similar to Hays', although he recognizes this method can only result in the probability of an allusion in any given text.[93] Brunson adds a second methodological step which is a helpful contribution to intertextual studies. Citing the observations of Charlesworth and Fishbane, Brunson observes that Judaism always sought to interpret and apply scripture to new contexts. The intertestamental literature, therefore, ought to be examined in order to understand how a particular text was re-read in Second Temple period Judaism. Allusions are not simply to the Hebrew Bible, but they are echoes of interpreted texts.[94]

G. T. Manning studied the use of Ezekiel in the Gospel of John.[95] Manning's methodology as "intertextual" and quite similar to that of Hays in that he is interested in constructing a rubric for detecting allusions. Of importance to Manning is John's original reason for making an allusion.[96] Similar to Brunson, an important contribution to the discussion of allusions in this work is Manning's emphasis on how an image may be used in other Second Temple period literature. Rather than tracing a trajectory of usage from the Hebrew Bible through the Second Temple period as "background" to the New Testament usage, he suggests that Second Temple period writers may have picked up imagery from the Hebrew Bible and adapted the images for their own use in ways that are not found in the New Testament. He cites the messianic texts in *PsSol* 17:28, 41 as examples of a messianic king drawn from Ezek 45:8. While Ezekiel sees a future in which the nations are adopted into Israel, *PsSol* sees a future when the nations are no longer present at all in Israel.[97] Manning therefore argues that it is important not only to trace allusions through the Second Temple period literature, but also to notice how the imagery is adapted within that literature itself. The assumption that Jesus or the any of the New Testament writers used images from the Hebrew Bible in the exact same way other Second Temple Period used these texts is misleading.

---

92. Ibid., 13. Here he specifically disavows a reader-response style intertextuality. An echo, however, may be unintended and therefore is of no interest to his study.

93. In summary, Brunson cites verbal coherence; a reasonable chance the author could know the alluded text, the use of the alluded text elsewhere by the author, and "structural correspondence" such as similar context of circumstances. Brunson, *Psalm 118 in the Gospel of John*, 14–15.

94. Brunson, *Psalm 118 in the Gospel of John*, 18. In practice this includes texts from the Apocrypha and Pseudepigrapha as well as the LXX. In the case of Zech 9:9, Brunson's thesis that the image of a donkey is that of a king at the time of his enthronement rather than a meek and gentle king turns on the translation of Zechariah in the LXX, see ibid., 272.

95. Manning, *Echoes of a Prophet*.

96. Ibid., 14.

97. Ibid., 15.

Jesus the Bridegroom

J. McWhirter adapted Hays's methodology to study the motif of the Bridegroom Messiah in the Gospel of John.[98] McWhirter adds an additional layer to Hays's seven criterion by including in her discussion "representative figures" as potential allusions. A representative figure is a symbol which is recognized by an audience because it conforms to familiar conventions.[99] These figures may be common Jewish conventions, such as light to symbolize God and darkness to symbolize evil, but may also be well known characters from the Hebrew Bible. For example, McWhirter suggests that John 1:47 is an allusion to Jacob since there are verbal clues (Hays's method) as well as a reference to a well known, "premier" representative character from the Hebrew Bible.[100] John is answering a theological question (was Jesus the Messiah?) by drawing together a few texts from the Hebrew Bible which describe the messiah with non-royal images.[101] John's technique, as McWhirter describes it, is in the tradition of a Jewish midrash. McWhirter's study is similar to the methodology I will propose since her "representative character" is not far from what I will call a "tradition."

With respect to wedding banquet imagery, McWhirter contends that John used texts such as Jer 33:10–11, Gen 29:1–20, and the Song of Solomon, drawing connections via Psalm 45, a well-known messianic psalm, in order to show that John presents the messiah as a bridegroom. This thesis is important for the present study since it attempts to show that early Christological exegesis was structured around the metaphor of a marriage and wedding banquet and that the basis for that imagery is the Hebrew Bible itself. McWhirter is not interested in the origin of John's thinking, i.e., why did the writer of the fourth gospel draw these particular texts? Why would John choose to describe Jesus in terms of a bridegroom or his ministry in terms of a wedding banquet? Perhaps the origin of this collation of texts is Jesus himself. In addition, it is possible to understand allusions like the "messianic banquet" in general along the lines of a representative character or idea.[102]

---

98. McWhirter, *The Bridegroom Messiah and the People of God*.

99. Ibid., 31–36. McWhirter is following the lead of Wendell Harris, "Symbol," in *Dictionary of Concepts in Literary Criticism and Theory*, 398–405, and Koester, *Symbolism in the Fourth Gospel*.

100. McWhirter, *The Bridegroom Messiah*, 36. Allusions and representative characters are employed by John as part of messianic exegesis.

101. Here McWhirter cites *4 Ezra* and *PsSol 17* as examples of a more or less militaristic messiah.

102. What makes McWhirter's work unique is her use of texts from the early church which have already "heard echoes" in the text of John to the Hebrew Bible. While Hays's methodology does look to confirm allusions by asking if others have heard these allusions before, McWhirter begins with Origen of Alexandria's *Commentary on John* which connects the story of the Woman at the Well in John 4 to Jacob and Rebekah's meeting at a well in Genesis 24 and Moses meeting Zipporah at another well in Exod 2:15–22. While rejecting the allegorical exegesis of Origen, she suggests that Origen heard a genuine echo in the text of John when he connected these three "woman at the well" contexts. What is more, John has combined these scenes around the theme of marriage in order to present Jesus as a bridegroom-messiah. Allison also begins his list of criteria with the history of interpretation, distancing himself from Hays's view that history of interpretation is less reliable. See Allison, *The Intertextual Jesus*, 10, especially n30 where he points out that Marcion encouraged the search for First Testament parallels.

The Use of Hebrew Bible Imagery in the New Testament

In some ways studies in the gospel of John are the best models for working an intertextual method using Hays's seven guidelines. Each of the studies represented above begin with discussions on how to detect allusions and provide Hays-like criteria which are then applied to the gospel of John. In addition, these studies work very hard to ground the allusions in the Hebrew Bible or literature of the Second Temple period.

Summary: Toward an Intertextual Method

In this study, intertextuality refers to an exegetical strategy which seeks to give full weight to the rhetorical value of an author's use of texts or traditions drawn from existing sources. If Jesus used a traditional metaphor drawn from the Hebrew Bible, then he did so intentionally to communicate with an audience. But Jesus did not simply quote traditions, he combined traditions intertextually in order to draw out new applications of that tradition to his present situation. In order for this rhetorical strategy to be effective, the audience would have to not only "hear the echo" of earlier traditions, but also hear the developments of the traditions. In fact, this study will argue that Jesus combined the eschatological banquet with a marriage metaphor in order to apply it to a new situation, his own proclamation of the Kingdom of Heaven. According to Jesus, the anticipated "kingdom of heaven" is like a "marriage feast" and that he is in fact the bridegroom, celebrating the restoration of Israel's marriage at the end of the Exile.[103]

The method proposed in this section differs from most intertextual studies by recognizing that the Second Temple Period was an oral culture which quite literally "heard" Scripture. When Jesus alluded to an eschatological banquet, he would not have necessarily alluded to a text (Isa 25:6–8, for example), but to a cluster of oral tradition which included Isa 25:6–8. His audience may not have ever read Isaiah, but they had heard Isaiah read to them and therefore would be familiar with the traditional use of the eschatological banquet in Scripture. This approach to intertextuality is admittedly not far from Tradition History, although this method tends be more concerned with pre-literary forms and original *Sitz im Leben* of a tradition.[104] I am interested in the

---

103. These first two stages are essentially what Hays suggested in his first three questions summarized above. These first two steps naturally inform each other. Since I am concerned with metaphor as much as text, the more evidence which is gathered from the Hebrew Bible and Second Temple period, the more resonate the echo may become in the New Testament. Naturally one can only hear an echo if the previous text is known and understood. For example, the more texts which genuinely contribute to the metaphor of a wedding banquet, the more the echo will sound clearly. This clustering of texts from the Hebrew Bible and Second Temple period literature will help gauge the strength of the metaphor for a first-century listener as well as increase the likelihood that Jesus would employ such a metaphor in the first place.

104. For example, Gese proposed three elements of tradition history: individual texts with their pre-literary antecedents, the development of those texts a literature, and the growth of the textual tradition as a "whole." Gese, "Tradition and Biblical Theology," 323. The methodology I am describing is only concerned with the third element, specifically, how a tradition (eschatological banquet) came

canonical form of a tradition as it appears in the Hebrew Bible and the development of that tradition in the teaching of Jesus. I suggest that Jesus functioned as any Second Temple Period teacher did when he alluded to clusters of Scriptural traditions and applied them to his current situation.[105]

An intertextual relationship exists when an author or speaker intentionally draws texts or traditions together based on some warrant in the early text, even if the modern exegete is puzzled by the connection. When an author or speaker combines two or more texts or traditions, there is a development of the idea and an intentional application of the tradition to the present situation. There are many examples of this in the Second Temple Period, such as Sirach's unique combination of Wisdom and the Torah. It is possible to track the development of a tradition from the earliest available texts to the later, but also the application of the tradition to the situation of the author. The intertextual methodology suggested here is beneficial for interpretation because it focuses on this development and application of earlier traditions and texts and will therefore highlight the unique contribution of Jesus as an interpreter of Scripture. This method will illuminate the earlier tradition by showing how the tradition was understood by a later generation. In this sense the intertextual method suggested here seeks to interpret traditions in "both directions."

By applying this definition of intertextuality to the words and deeds of Jesus as reported in the synoptic gospels,[106] I will assume that Jesus stands within the tradition of the Hebrew Bible and the rich discussion of Scripture in the Second Temple Period. In his teaching he alluded to scripture frequently in dialogues with his contemporaries, and his method of using scripture was consistent with the methods illustrated by the literature of the Second Temple Period. Yet he uniquely developed the concept of an eschatological banquet by combining it with another common tradition drawn from the Hebrew Bible, the marriage metaphor. The resulting cluster of traditions is a unique development of the eschatological banquet which Jesus applies to his own ministry. He is the bridegroom, his ministry is the eschatological banquet, and he is inviting Israel to participate in that banquet in anticipation of the end of the age.

---

to be used by a Jewish teacher (Jesus) to describe a new situation (his ministry). In addition, I am aware of the fact that Jesus and his audience may not necessarily have had access to actual texts. Gese accounts for oral communication in the pre-history of a tradition, but not in the development of the tradition. In this study I will assume the historicity of Jesus as oral teacher and argue that the traditions he developed were well-known to his audience.

105. Zimmerman employs a similar method in his discussion of Rev 14:1–5. He detects several elements of the virgin-metaphor in this text, including Jungfräulichkeit, Makellosigkeit, and Nachfolgeversprechen. These elements are combined with redemption and firstfruit metaphors to create a "complex picture." Zimmerman's observations are important since Rev 14 clearly employs what I am calling a marriage metaphor ("geschlechtermetaphorischer" for Zimmerman) to talk about the eschatological age. Zimmermann, "Die Virginitäts-Metapher," 45–70. While Zimmermann's work is more or less *religionsgeschichte*, he is does employ some modern literary methods. For a full development of his method, see Zimmermann, *Geschlechtermetaphorik und Gottesverhältnis*.

106. I will discuss the value of the various criteria of authenticity in chapter 7.

Jesus is looking back at a traditional way of describing Israel's relationship with God and applying now to his own followers by creating new connections between related eschatological traditions. This observation will help to interpret several difficult texts in the Synoptic gospels, such as the burning of the city in Matt 22:7.

In order to track this development and application of a text or tradition, an intertextual study must pass through several steps if it is to be successful. First, following Hays's criteria for detecting an allusion, one must first "hear an echo" within the text. By this I mean one recognizes something in the words or deeds of Jesus that sounds like a text or tradition from the Hebrew Bible. When Jesus claims to be a bridegroom in Mark 2:19–20, the reader may hear echoes of previous texts such as Hos 1–3, Ps 45, or the Song of Solomon. The same is true of Matt 8:11–12, where Jesus says "many will come from the east and west to recline at the table with Abraham." The reader may hear echoes of texts in which the restoration of Israel is described in terms of a banquet, such as Isa 25:6–8 or Ps 23:5. Unlike methods surveyed above which focus only on verbal citations or allusions, my method seeks to hear echoes of traditional metaphors which may not be bound to any one particular text in the Hebrew Bible but exist as a cluster of traditions.

Second, having heard the echo of an earlier text or tradition, one must then determine which texts and traditions may have been used by the author. Since allusions to tradition are not direct citations, a wide range of texts must be gathered with linguistic and thematic links to the later text. The eschatological banquet is a tradition which developed out of a variety of texts in the Hebrew Bible. Jesus may have had only one text in mind, but it is more likely that he invokes a cluster of tradition by describing the kingdom as "reclining at the table with Abraham." This step therefore requires the exegete to collect all of the texts which may be part of the metaphor of a banquet for the eschatological age in a more or less chronological order. This stage of the research will show how a tradition (a covenant meal) develops into a metaphor for end of the age (an eschatological banquet). By the Second Temple Period this eschatological banquet is combined with the developing idea of a messiah, resulting in a "messianic banquet" which inaugurates the coming new age. Chapter 3 therefore begins by examining the eschatological banquet in Isa 25:6–8 as a baseline for writers who expanded and applied the eschatological banquet to new situations. For example, the idea that the eschatological age as inaugurated by a meal in Zion is developed in Isa 40–55 to include an ongoing meal in the wilderness as the Exile comes to an end. Chapter 4 tracks this development a banquet motif as it was combined with wilderness traditions and applied to the end of the Exile in Isa 40–55 and Jer 31.[107] Chapter 5 examines

---

107. While this study could include the whole of the latter prophets, I am limiting myself to these two portions of the Hebrew Bible since they are often alluded to in the Synoptic Gospels. This satisfies Hays's first and third criteria for detecting an allusion, since these are not only texts the authors could have known, they in fact regularly allude to both Isaiah and Jeremiah. While I will refer to the Psalms at several points, to thoroughly survey banquet and wilderness traditions in the Psalms is not possible to survey them in detail in the present study.

Jesus the Bridegroom

the marriage metaphor since this metaphor overlaps at key points with banquet and wilderness traditions, especially in Hosea. Chapter 6 then tracks the development and application of these motifs in the Second Temple Period. These four chapters form a database of traditions which were available to teachers such as Jesus in the first century. These strands of tradition were woven and adapted in various combinations to address new situations such as the anticipated end of the exile (Qumran) or the fall of Jerusalem in AD 70 (*2 Baruch*, *4 Ezra*).[108]

Third, these observations drawn from the Hebrew Bible and Second Temple Period literature must be applied to the texts in the Synoptic Gospels which contain banquet or wedding imagery. Many studies which use some sort of intertextual method fail to use the insights gained to interpret the words and actions of Jesus since they are concerned with the source of an allusion more than its application. But if Jesus developed banquet traditions, it was as intentional as any other such combination in the literature of the Second Temple Period. This third step can potentially be used as a test of the authenticity of the sayings of Jesus. As described above, Pitre rightly rejects the criterion of double dissimilarity which argues that Jesus' authentic teachings are unlike both Second Temple Period Judaism and early Christianity. Pitre argued for a "criterion of historical congruence" which sees the sayings of Jesus which are congruent with the historical setting of Second Temple Period Judaism as authentic.[109] What I propose here is a "criterion of tradition congruence." If it is shown that a saying of Jesus stands within well-known traditions from the Hebrew Bible, then that saying is more likely to be authentic.

Chapter 7 is a historical and exegetical study which deals with Jesus' sayings and actions that can be described as wedding texts (Mark 2:11–12) or banquet texts (Matt 8:11–12). In some texts the marriage metaphor is combined with the eschatological banquet (Matt 22:1–12, 25:1–14). In other texts banquet and wilderness traditions are combined and developed (Mark 6:30–44). This stage of the research is an intertextual study in that I will be using the texts and traditions surveyed in chapters three through six to understand Jesus' claim to be a bridegroom and his description of his ministry as an on-going banquet. Increasing familiarity with the texts from the Hebrew Bible and Second Temple Period literature will enable us to "hear their echoes" in Jesus' sayings. I will therefore argue that Jesus' combination of eschatological banquet and

---

108. Could Jesus have used this kind of metaphor or alluded to a particular body of texts? That Jesus "could not have used this metaphor" is sometimes used to declare a text like Mark 2:11–12 as inauthentic. It is assumed that the early church thought of Jesus as a bridegroom and the gospel writer placed the saying into the mouth of Jesus to support this later theological view. For example, the Jesus Seminar takes Mark 2:20 as a "Christian expansion" which "justifies the return of the subsequent Christian community to the practice of fasting." Funk and Hoover, *Five Gospels*, 47. This study will show that this unique clustering of traditions is traceable to the historical Jesus. Showing that a motif "could have been used" is more or less Hays's fourth and fifth questions as described above.

109. Pitre, *Jesus, The Tribulation, and the End of the Exile*, 29. Pitre alludes to the "contextual plausibility" (*Kontextentsprechung*) suggested by Theissen and Winter. Theissen and Winter, *The Quest for the Plausible Jesus*.

marriage metaphor constitutes a development of traditions present in the Hebrew Bible and that he re-applies these images to his own ministry in order to define its nature and his mission. Since this artful intertextual blending of scriptural traditions in all layers of the Synoptic Gospels (Mark, Q, M, L), this dissertation will argue that the historical Jesus is responsible for this unique combinations of traditions.

Excursus: Defining Quotation, Allusion, Echo

A serious problem encountered in studies on intertextuality in the New Testament is a lack of precision with respect to definitions of terms. While defining a quotation is fairly straightforward, there seems to be serious differences between these studies with respect to defining intertextuality, allusion, echo, typology and midrash. In some cases, these terms are left undefined, leading to confusion. By defining these terms as carefully as possible and placing them in contrast with one another I hope to avoid this confusion.

Quotation, Allusion and Echo

A quotation is a conscious reference to an earlier text, usually using some sort of introductory formula in order to signal the citation.[110] For the most part, citations of scripture in the synoptic gospels come from the hand of the Evangelist, often as a commentary on some action within the story of the Gospel. For example, Mark's Gospel begins with a set of quotations drawn from Isa 40:3, Exod 23:20 and Mal 3:1. The quotes are introduced by a clear formula (Καθὼς γέγραπται). Jesus uses a similar formula in Mark 7:6, 9:12–13, 11:17, 14:21, and 27 to introduce a quote from the Hebrew Bible.[111] Scholarly interest in quotations tends to center on the form of the text cited rather than on literary issues.

As defined by Z. Ben-Porat, an allusion is "the simultaneous activation of two texts" which "results in the formation of intertextual patterns whose nature cannot be predetermined."[112] Rather than a direct citation of a source, an allusion subtly refers to another text by verbal, syntactical, and thematic hints. The interpreter finds a "marker," or identifiable element in the text which evokes another text (a marked text). The interpretation of the marker should be modified on the basis of the marked text. What is more, one may need to "activate" the marked text in order to fully interpret

---

110. Moyise, "Intertextuality and the Study of the Old Testament in the New Testament," in *The Old Testament in the New Testament*, 18. Fekkes defines a formal quotation as "any portion of the OT text accompanied by *any* additional word or phrase which the author uses to introduce the text" while an informal quotation omits the introductory formula. Fekkes, *Isaiah and Prophetic Traditions*, 63–64.

111. The formula is used by scribes in Matt 2:5 and by the devil in Matt 4:4. Matthew also uses πληρωθῇ τὸ ῥηθὲν ὑπὸ κυρίου to introduce a citation in 1:22, 2:15, 2:23, 4:14, 8:17, 13:35, and 21:4. Similarly, John uses similar introductory phrases in 12:38, 13:18, 15:11, 25, 17:12, 19:9, 32, 19:24, 36.

112. Ben-Porat, "The Poetics of Literary Allusion," 105–28.

the allusion, although this last step is optional. Ben-Porat also defines an "allusion in general" as a "hint to a known fact" or biblical motif. This might be described as an "echo" of a biblical theme, such as the judgment or holiness of God. While the presence of a quotation is usually quite objective and usually explicit, the presence of an allusion is a subjective inference which a reader must make. As a result, scholars will disagree with respect to the presence of an allusion in a particular text.

If an allusion is present, it is intentional and the author expected his readers to understand the allusion. But if an allusion is very subtle, it is better described as an echo, or a "faint trace" of another text which may very well be unconscious on the part of the author.[113] These sorts of traces in the text are less useful since they are at best speculative and possibly coincidental. Potentially an echo can signal something which is tangential to the author's main point.

Studies on allusions in the New Testament usually develop a working definition of an allusion which distinguishes it from a formal quotation.[114] In addition, they typically create a set of criteria to detect allusions, such as Hays's seven-point rubric examined above. G. Beale, for example, describes allusions in three categories.[115] If there is "almost identical wording" as well as a shared "core meaning," then the New Testament text can be described as a "clear allusion." When the wording of the proposed allusion is not as close as a clear allusion, but there is still some idea or structural element in common with the text of the Hebrew Bible, then the proposed allusion can be labeled as "probable." Beale's final category is more or less the same as an echo as defined above. The "possible allusion" has some general similarity in wording or concepts, but it is not obvious that the allusion is intended. If a "possible allusion" is to be accepted, there must be an argument for why an author might have chosen to echo the text in question. As Jauhiainen observes, these are not tight categories and are therefore not particularly useful for detecting allusions.[116]

After surveying several proposals for the detection of allusions, Jauhiainen concludes that any pursuit of a scientific rubric for determining allusions is misguided

---

113. Moyise, "Intertextuality," 19.

114. See also Paulien, *Decoding Revelation's Trumpets: Literary Allusions and Interpretation of Revelation 8:7–12*. See also "Dreading the Whirlwind," 5–22. While the focus of Paulien's dissertation was primarily allusions in Revelation, he proposed a useful three-part method for weighing the evidence for the likelihood of a proposed allusion: verbal, thematic, and structural parallels. With respect to verbal parallels, Paulien looks for at least two significant words in the allusion which conform to the text of the LXX. Thematic parallels may use only a single word, thought or theme. Paulien, *Decoding Revelation's Trumpets*, 182. A structural parallel is based on another complete literary context, such as the plagues or experience of Israel in the wilderness. With respect to the words of Jesus, this method of weighing evidence is not as helpful because Jesus did not cite the LXX. Any similarity in wording to a Greek version must therefore come from the tradition which translated the words of Jesus into Greek. On the other hand, the criterion of structural and thematic similarity may be very helpful in showing that Jesus stands within the tradition-history of the Hebrew Bible as it was interpreted in the first century.

115. Beale, *The Use of Daniel*, 306–9.

116. Jauhiainen, *The Use of Zechariah*, 21.

from the start and "ought to be laid to rest."[117] While rejecting the irresponsible "parallelomania" of studies with no methodology for determining allusions, no criteria will be able to detect all allusions because of the complexity of the allusion itself. D. Allison concurs, arguing that any list of criteria for detecting allusions is merely suggestive—there is no scientific method for detecting allusions.[118] Nevertheless, some objective criterion is needed in order to suggest that a text is intentionally evoked by the words and deeds of Jesus. Hays's seven criteria remain a useful basis for analyzing potential allusions to earlier texts.

Intertextuality, Typology and Midrash

Older studies which focus on the use and re-use of scripture and tradition do so under the rubric of typology.[119] In these studies, typology assumes that the earlier text is a veiled reference to some new theological reality, usually Christological.[120] This is based on Paul's comment in 2 Cor 3:14–16 and describes Paul's typological method in 1 Cor 10 and Gal 4 as well.[121] While definitions for typology vary, B. Ramm emphasized the "preordained representative relation" of persons or institutions from the Hebrew Bible with persons or events in the New Testament.[122] As G. E. Wright commented, "typology is more of an attitude than a method."[123]

---

117. Ibid., 33.

118. Allison, *The Intertextual Jesus*, 13. Allison continues: "The best reader is, not one who mechanically or dogmatically observes indices, but one who has gained an instinct of artistry, who can delve below a text with a delicate and mature judgment, bred of familiarity with the tradition to which it belongs." He specifically separates himself from the confidence of Paulien who declares a few allusions in Rev 8 as "certain." For Allison, there is always some room for doubt.

119. The classic text on typology is Fairbairn, *The Typology of Scripture*. Most modern works on typology build on Fairbairn: Goppelt, *Typos*; Bultmann, "Ursprung und Sinn," 205–12; Ramm, *Protestant Biblical Interpretation*, 197–219; Lampe, and Woollcombe, *Essays on Typology*; Rad, "Typological Interpretation of the Old Testament," 17–39; Wolff, "The Hermeneutics of the Old Testament," 160–99; Eichrodt, "Is Typological Exegesis an Appropriate Method?," 224–45; Gundry, "Typology as a Means of Interpretation: Past and Present," 233–40; Baker, "Typology and the Christian Use of the Old Testament," 137–57; Achtemeier, "Typology," 926–27; Davidson, *Typology in Scripture*; Aageson, "Typology, Correspondence, and Application of Scripture in Rom 9–11," 51–72; Alsup, "Typology," 6:683–85; Ninow, *Indicators of Typology within the Old Testament*.

120. In fact, the motivation in recent manifestations of typology has been to show the unity of the Bible. Rad comments that his view of typology attests to "the belief that the same God who revealed himself in Christ has also left his footprints in the history of the Old Testament covenant people-that we have one divine discourse, here to the fathers through the prophets, there to us through Christ." Rad, "Typological Interpretation," 36.

121. Alsup, "Typology," *ABD* 6:683–85, esp. 683. Other biblical examples of typology include Acts 7:44 and Hebrews 8, where the tabernacle is described as a type of the heavenly sanctuary. In Rom 5:14 Paul uses the term τύπος to describe Adam as a type of Christ. In 1 Peter 3:21 the experience of Noah is linked to Christian baptism.

122. Ramm, *Protestant Biblical Interpretation*, 208. Ramm is very careful to distinguish typology from allegorical methods of interpretation.

123. Wright, *The God Who Acts*, 64. See also Lampe, "Typological Exegesis," 202.

It is possible, however, to describe some texts within the canon of the Hebrew Bible itself as typological. For example, Isa 40–55 can be described as using an Exodus typology to explain the future (or present) restoration of Israel to the land.[124] Similarly, the use of Exodus imagery in Ps 77 can be described as typological.[125] In this sense, however, typology is restricted to the reuse of a common motif in the Hebrew Bible, including key vocabulary. Since these texts do not use a formal "type / antitype" structure like Hebrews or Philo, it might be better to describe the relationship of the Exodus and Second Isaiah as "inner-biblical exegesis" (Fishbane) or intertextuality (Boyarin).[126]

It is possible to see intertextual methods as a sort of implicit *Traditionsgeschichte*, but there are significant differences. Intertextual methods study the development of texts from the earliest written texts to the later written texts. For example, Fishbane begins with an early law and shows how later writers attempted to deal with ambiguities or perceived problems in this earlier text. This may take the form of scribal corrections or legal interpretations, but in either case the goal was to apply the text to issues current at the time of the writer. Boyarin follows the same method, but extends his investigation into *midrashim*. Fishbane separates himself from *Traditionsgeschichte* by confining his investigation to the "received scripture," or "stabilized literary foundation," and the interpretations based upon it.[127]

Tradition History, on the other hand, developed from form criticism and looked to the development of traditions that led up to the text as they appear in the Hebrew Bible.[128] This includes the development of the oral traditions that eventually became stabilized and canonized.[129] Both von Rad[130] and Noth[131] used *Traditionsgeschichte* to describe the development of oral tradition into canonical forms and then into theology. This development of theology begins in the pre-canonical form of the Pentateuch,

---

124. Anderson, "Exodus Typology in Second Isaiah," 177–95. The two most common typologies on the Hebrew Bible are creation and the Exodus. In a section entitled "intertextuality," Waltke comments that "allusions commonly merge with typology." Waltke and Yu, *Old Testament Theology*, 133. This blending of intertextuality, allusion, and typology is indicative of the overlapping nature of the terms.

125. Stevenson, "Communal Imagery and the Individual Lament," 215–29.

126. Similarly, Rabbinic Judaism turned other unique events into a series of recapitulating events. Neusner points out that the destruction of the Temple in 586 and 70 were linked through (real and imagined) correspondences so that the past took place in the present as well. See Neusner, *The Halakah*, 155–56; cf. Neusner's description of "paradigmatic time" in the same volume, 118–24 and *The Presence of the Past, the Pastness of the Present*. This book appears in a revised form in Neusner, *The Idea of History in Rabbinic Judaism*, 115–46.

127. Fishbane, *Biblical Interpretation*, 7.

128. Knight, "Tradition History," 6:634. Osborne has described *Traditionsgeschichte* as one of the "stepchildren" of form criticism. Osborne, "The Evangelical and *Traditionsgeschichte*," 117–30.

129. Catchpole, "Tradition History," 165. Catchpole's emphasis is on the ongoing process of development of traditions.

130. Rad, *The Problem of the Hexateuch*; Idem, *Old Testament Theology*.

131. Noth, *A History of Pentateuchal Traditions*.

in the J and E documents. The end of that development may be either the formation of a canonical document (Knight),[132] the canon of the Hebrew Bible (Gese),[133] or even the New Testament (Stuhlmacher).[134]

Typology is to be distinguished from allegory or allegorizing, which simply assigns new meanings to older words in a one-to-one fashion. For example, one would be allegorizing an older text if one were to identify Moses as Zerubbabel. A type may be thought of as one step removed from allegorizing: Moses is "like" Zerubbabel in some ways, but perhaps not like him in other ways. In this respect, a proper typological method functions something like a metaphor.[135] The re-use of a motif highlights certain aspects of that motif without necessarily making every possible connection active at the same time. What is important in a type is the general motif, not necessarily the words of the earlier text. In addition, a motif from the Hebrew Bible may appear in many different specific contexts, all of which can be invoked by the typology. For example, Isaiah refers to the "wilderness" in general without citing any particular text.

Typology is also to be distinguished from intertextuality, although some recent writers list typology as a species of "intertextuality."[136] Intertextuality refers to the practice of a writer in which an earlier text is consciously invoked and re-employed in a new context, while typology normally deals with persons or motifs. Moses is often described as a "type of Christ" by citing the broad outlines of Moses' history as an analogy. Intertextuality functions more on the level of words from a specific text. Still, it is difficult to draw the line between typology and intertextuality. Several recent studies have attempted to show that what many scholars call intertextuality is quite similar to rabbinical exegetical method. Critics who use the term "intertextuality" often point out that, in practice, the method described is more or less like a rabbinic midrash than

---

132. Knight, *Rediscovering the Traditions of Israel*.

133. Gese, "Tradition and Biblical Theology," 301–26. Gese begins with the individual forms of the text, seeking a *Sitz im Leben* for those forms which in itself is a development of theology (p. 308), but he is careful not to privilege these earliest units (ibid., 325). He then proceeds to the texts as they appear in the Hebrew Bible. Later texts open new theological questions and therefore expand on the earlier texts: "through apocalyptic additions a complex of prophetic texts can acquire an altogether new character, representing old truth on a new ontological level" (ibid., 313). Finally, Gese shows that there is development within the Hebrew Bible. As an example, Gese points to the development from the Davidic king to the idea messiah-king in Isa 9 and 11, then to the "messiah of peace" in Zech 9 and the "heroic messiah" of Zech 13 (ibid., 315). While this sounds like Fishbane's "inner biblical exegesis," there is no exegesis in Gese's development of tradition. In this short essay he simply cannot expand on how a tradition developed from a Davidic king to a "heroic messiah." Fishbane is interested in the hermeneutics employed by later texts, Gese, like von Rad, is interested in the development of theology.

134. Stuhlmacher, *Historical Criticism and Theological Interpretation of Scripture*. Since Stuhlmacher is a New Testament theologian his interest is in bridging the Testaments.

135. Lakoff and Johnson, *Metaphors We Live By*.

136. Waltke places typology under the heading of intertextuality as a "unique species of promise and fulfillment" which is "concerned with comparative historical events, persons and institutions in the Bible." As Waltke observes, types are only recognized as patterns in retrospect. Waltke, *Old Testament Theology*, 136.

postmodern intertextual studies.[137] This may very well be a valid criticism since what midrash does at the very least is to bring various texts into dialogue on the basis of some verbal or syntactical clue.[138]

There are several challenges for anyone who wishes to describe exegesis in the New Testament as midrash. First, like intertextuality, defining midrash is extremely difficult.[139] Scholars offer a range of definitions which could either include or exclude exegesis in the New Testament depending on the goals of the study in which the definition appears.[140] In addition, midrash is frequently described as a creative act on the part of the evangelist with little or no connection to a historical Jesus.[141]

Second, many examples of midrash are drawn from rabbinic material dating from well after the first century. While it is virtually certain that Hillel's seven rules pre-date Jesus, it is unclear that the type of midrash often cited as "backgrounds" to Jesus' methods were current in the first century. It is therefore important to critically assess the midrash genre before applying it to the method of Jesus.

---

137. This point is made by Childs in a different context. Childs, "Critique of Recent Intertextual Canonical Interpretation," 173–84. For example, Derrett has suggested that the parable of the Great Supper (Luke 14:15–23) is a midrash on Zeph 1:1–16. Zephaniah 1 itself can be described as a midrash on several Holy War passages including Deut 20. According to Derrett, Jesus has constructed his parable from these texts in the style of the *midrashim*, calling up biblical passages which "reillustrate and document the parable, as it were, by invisible footnotes." Derrett, "The Parable of the Great Supper," 126–55. The Targum on Zeph 1:7–9 found in *Targum ps-Jonathan* reads as follows: Derrett renders the Targum as follows: "Be silent before the Lord God, for the day of the Lord is at hand; the Lord has prepared a sacrifice/feast and sanctified/consecrated his guests/persons-who-have-been-summoned. I shall visit/punish the officers and the sons of the king and all who are clothed in strange clothing." Derrett argues that Jesus combined the words of Zephaniah and the laws concerning war (the excuses given for not attending the banquet) and Isa 65:21–22. Deut 20 is interpreted in the *haggadah* as referring to the war with the Amalakites, the prototypical enemy of the people of God (ibid., 132). Isaiah 65 describes the chosen of God living in an ideal environment, which includes "feasting" after their enemies have been utterly destroyed. For Derrett, Jesus has "availed himself of the interpretation of Deut 20:10–12 found in *Targum ps-Jonathan*" and used the same technique in developing his own parable. Derrett therefore sees nothing in the parable which is "unrealistic." Whether or not there is merit to Derrett's complex analysis of the Great Supper parable, the point here is what he describes as midrash, other (more recent) scholars call intertextuality. Jesus is drawing together various threads from the Hebrew Bible which, when combined, create new interpretations of the original texts unanticipated by the original context.

138. A particularly idiosyncratic attempt at describing Mark as a midrashist is Miller and Miller, *The Gospel of Mark as Midrash*. Many of the alleged midrashic texts in Mark's gospel are based on superficial similarities between Marks' narrative and the Hebrew Bible.

139. Quarles attempts to clarify the definition of midrash to preclude creation of stories by the evangelists. Quarles, "Midrash as Creative Historiography: Portrait of a Misnomer," 457–64. In his monograph, *Midrash Criticism*, Quarles surveys a large number of definitions of midrash offered in the last hundred years.

140. For example, Kimball, *Jesus' Exposition of the Old Testament*, 61, defines midrash as broadly as possible in order to include what Jesus does in Luke under the umbrella of midrash. On the other hand, Chilton does not consider anything which Jesus does as midrash since there is no "plan of commentary evident in his sayings." Chilton, "Jesus within Judaism," 191.

141. For example, Goulder, *Midrash and Lection*; Drury, *Tradition and Design*.

A third problem involves the origin of a given example of midrash as it appears in the Synoptic Gospels. For example, Mark 12:1-22 // Matt 21:33-44 // Luke 20:9-19 is a text which can be described as a midrash. The parable is based on Isa 5:1-7 and includes a citation of Ps 118:22. There is a clear allusion to Dan 2:34, 44, as well as possible allusions to Isa 28:16 (a precious cornerstone) and 1 Kgs 21:2-3,16 (the death of Naboth).[142] What is more, there is a subtle word-play in Isa 5:2 built around the Aramaic or Hebrew for "stone / to stone" (סקל)[143] and son / stone (בֵּן and אֶבֶן).[144] C. Evans collects an impressive number of rabbinic parallels to this parable which also make use of midrashic techniques.[145] While many commentaries see this collation of texts as going back to the historical Jesus,[146] others see the whole parable as an allegorical creation of the Evangelist,[147] or perhaps an allegory built on an original parable of Jesus.[148]

E. Ellis has contributed several monographs and articles on midrash in New Testament studies.[149] Ellis attempts to clarify the definition of midrash by broadening it into two sub-categories. When a text is cited, the midrash is explicit, but when older texts are only alluded to, the midrash is implicit. As evidence for this, Ellis cites both forms of midrash in the Qumran literature. The *pesherim*, for example, are explicit in that they cite a text and make clear and specific interpretation.[150] On the other hand, texts like *Jubilees* and the *Genesis Apocryphon* never specifically cite a source

---

142. Snodgrass, "Recent Research on the Parable of the Wicked Tenants," 196. Snodgrass develops this position in his *Stories with Intent*. Compare also Evans, *Mark 8:27—16:20*, 235.

143. Ellis, "Midrash, Targum, and New Testament Quotations," 67n34. The piel of סקל can be used for clearing stones from the ground (cf. Isa 62:10) as well as to throw stones (2 Sam 16:13, 1 Kgs 21:14).

144. Hagner, *Matthew 14-28*, 622.

145. Evans, *Mark 8:27—16:20*, 220-22; cf. Kimball, "Jesus' Exposition of Scripture in Luke 20:9-19," 85: "In its literary form the Luke 20:9-18 pericope is a proem-like midrash on Isa 5:1-2, its opening text, which is expounded by a parable...."

146. Ellis, "Midrash, Targum, and New Testament Quotations," 67; cf. Ellis, *The Gospel of Luke*, 232; Evans, *Mark 8:27—16:20*, 216; Snodgrass, *Stories with Intent*, 287.

147. Jülicher saw the parable as an example later church allegory, 2:385-406. More recently, Lüdemann states the tradition behind the parable is the Markan community and "its degree of authenticity is nil," *Jesus After Two Thousand Years*, 235. Kloppenborg takes Mark 12:1-8 as authentic, but the addition the quotation in verses 9-11 was added by Mark. Kloppenborg, *The Tenants in the Vineyard*, 335-47. Marcus sees the use of the Hebrew Bible in this section of Mark as reflecting the theology of the Evangelist and "displays discontinuity with its Jewish forbears." Marcus, *The Way of the Lord*, 122.

148. Jeremias related the parable to Jesus' offer of the gospel to the poor. Jeremias, *Parables*, 70-77. Mann read the parable as a vindication of John the Baptist. Mann, *The Gospel According to Matthew*, 462-63. Crossan argued the parable was "a commendation of resolute opportunism." Crossan, "The Parable of the Wicked Husbandmen," 451-65. Newell and Newell apply the parable to the political activity of the Zealots. Newell and Newell, "The Parable of the Wicked Tenants," 226-37. More recently, Hester applied a sociological model to the parable. Hester, "Socio-Rhetorical Criticism and the Parable of the Tenants," 27-57.

149. Ellis, "Midrash, Targum and New Testament Quotations," in *Neotestamentica et Semitica*, 61-69.

150. Examples of explicit midrash at Qumran include 4Q Flor, 1QHab, and CD 4.14.

and therefore should be described as implicit midrash.[151] With respect to the material found in the Gospels, Ellis would identify the Parable of the Vineyard (Matt 21) as an implicit midrash on Isa 5:2f. But Ellis still warns that "in the absence of a clear allusion or an explicit quotation it is, in the nature of the case, difficult to establish a midrashic background for a New Testament passage."[152]

M. Fishbane describes this method of interpretation as "inner-biblical exegesis."[153] Fishbane argues that Israel was a "reading community" in general and contends that even within the Hebrew Bible there is evidence of exegesis of earlier texts.[154] To use Fishbane's terms, older *traditium* are revitalized by newer *traditio*. In some cases this is little more than a parenthetical gloss by a scribe or an application of specific law in a new situation.[155] Of interest to the present study is what Fishbane calls "aggadic exegesis" which is neither scribal nor legal, but homiletical in nature.[156] While legal exegesis focuses on a single text, "aggadah is interested in the whole inherited tradition" for the purpose of making new theological connections and insights.[157] While there are a handful of texts which explicitly cite their source (Jer 5:16–17, 16:14–15, for example), the majority of aggadic exegesis is in the form of implicit citations. As with studies on allusions surveyed above, these implicit citations are difficult to detect. For Fishbane, there is little to be gained in calling aggadic exegesis "midrash," as many studies do.[158]

Perhaps the most thorough application of intertextuality to Jewish exegesis is to be found in the work of D. Boyarin.[159] Boyarin argues that biblical narrative is "gapped

---

151. Defining *Jubilees* as midrash can be found as early as Charles, xiii. *The Genesis Apocryphon* is occasionally described as a midrash, but can also be described as a targum. Fitzmyer refused to describe it as either in his publication of the text. Fitzmyer, *The Genesis Apocryphon of Qumran Cave I*. Rev. Ed. 8.

152. Ellis, "Midrash, Targum, and New Testament Quotations," 69.

153. Fishbane, *Biblical Interpretation*. Fishbane's work is followed closely by Waltke in his section in intertextuality in the Hebrew Bible. Waltke, *Old Testament Theology*, 125–42.

154. Fishbane, *Biblical Interpretation*, 34.

155. Scribal exegesis is "meager" (ibid., 78), although Fishbane lists a number of examples of euphemisms and corrections to the text in his third chapter.

156. Ibid., 281.

157. Ibid., 283. In legal exegesis, Fishbane points out that most often there is some problem or gap in the text which needs to be addressed. But in aggadic exegesis, it is assumed that the scriptures are comprehensible as they are. The goal, therefore, is to draw forth a new meaning or an unsuspected meaning, but drawing together texts in new ways.

158. Fishbane has been criticized for relying on assumptions from higher-critical studies which limit the usefulness of his study. Eslinger points out that Fishbane assumes a diachronic relationship between texts which may not in fact be valid. For example, Amos may allude to the Pentateuch, but this cannot be proven since there is no direct quote. It is therefore equally possible that the Pentateuch alludes to Amos or some other source known to both. Elsinger therefore suggests calling this sort of study an "inner-biblical allusion" and examines the texts on a literary level without assumption of priority. This criticism of Fishbane is valid, but it is not particularly a problem for observing how Jesus might have used the Hebrew Bible since there is no question of priority. Eslinger, "Inner-Biblical Exegesis and Inner Biblical Allusion," 47–58.

159. Boyarin, *Intertextuality and the Reading of Midrash*.

and dialogical" and that midrash is a method by which those gaps are filled.[160] Midrash exploits gaps in the text by filling them with quotations and allusions from other texts. It is therefore not an exegesis per se, but rather an exposition of the gaps. For Boyarin, this "gap-filling" is not wholly controlled by the text, but it is not unconstrained, either. It is the "product of strong intertextual motivations and constraints."[161] Of major importance in Boyarin's view is the blending of texts in the genre *mashal* in order to overcome textual difficulties and create new meaning. Using a midrash on Exod 14:21 as an example ("and Moses stretched out his hand over the sea"), he show that several texts are combined which show that the wind is a weapon of God (Hos 13:15, Ps 48:8, 114:3, Isa 27:8, Jer 18:17).[162] In this example, the "story" of the *mashal* does not directly comment on the texts being discussed but provides an illustration which "fills the gap" intertextually. Like Fishbane, Boyarin sees this process of intertextuality as present in the text of the Hebrew Bible. The Bible itself is "characterized by a degree of self-reflexivity, self-citation, and self-interpretation."[163]

Applying the foregoing discussion to the words of Jesus, it must be admitted that it is not appropriate to describe Jesus as producing midrash in the sense that he created a coherent commentary on scripture or even that he sought to explain textual difficulties or legal problems by means of midrash. However, since Jesus combined scripture by means of allusion and echo in order to apply it to the present situation, his method can be described as at least akin to midrash as described by Fishbane and Boyarin. Jesus stood within the tradition of the Hebrew Bible when combined related traditions and applied them to his own messianic ministry. If this is the case, then the prophets of the Hebrew Bible are more appropriate as models for Jesus than later rabbis.

Summary and Conclusions

Is there any value for determining allusions? Certainly an interpreter wants to use whatever tools will assist in explicating a text, but studies of allusions in other parts of the Bible sometimes descend into a long list of vague parallels which do not illuminate

---

160. Ibid., 16. Boyarin describes the Bible as "fraught with background," by which he means that if the reader is going to make sense of the text he will have to "fill-in the gaps" with historical data, or other texts (ibid., 41).

161. Ibid., 45. The material used to fill gaps is not a subjective creation of the reader but rather the product of intertextual allusions. The Torah is explained by using the "tradition" of the Prophets and Writings. While this may constrain the meaning in some ways, often the new meaning is quite creative and even antithetical to the original text itself. As an example, Boyarin uses a midrash on Exod 15:22, "And Moses removed them." Eliezer used both Jer 2:2 and Neh 9:17–18 to explain the meaning of this phrase. Both texts concern the testing in the wilderness, therefore there is thematic warrant for connecting the texts as well as some common vocabulary (to "return").

162. Boyarin, *Intertextuality*, 94–95.

163. Ibid., 128. For Boyarin, the rabbis themselves were acute readers of scripture who were more aware of the intertextual self-interpretations than modern readers. This observation is not far from Hays's final principle which takes into account the history of interpretation when suggestion an allusion.

the text in the least. Care should be taken to avoid finding allusions where there are likely none intended, but attention should be given to the allusions which do genuinely appear in the text. Jewish writers in the first century did not allude to the Hebrew Bible simply as ornaments, but rather to add meaning to their texts.[164] Therefore if an allusion exists it is important for understanding the text at hand.

This study is an attempt to apply the strengths of so-called intertextual studies without being distracted either by radical reader-response methods, which produce very little of value for understanding the historical Jesus, or the pedantic "search for sources," which produce long lists but fail to address the text as it appears in the Gospels. Since I have expanded the concept of "intertextual" to include streams of tradition, it is possible to detect these non-textual sources in a later written text. A judicious intertextual method employing the criteria of Hays to the words of Jesus will highlight traditions from the Hebrew Bible which were important to Jesus and interpreted by him as describing his own messianic calling. The goal of using an intertextual method therefore is to illuminate the teaching of Jesus as a representative of Second Temple period Judaism and to authenticate a saying or action of Jesus. When a saying of Jesus is congruent with commonly understood traditions drawn from the Hebrew Bible, that saying is more likely to be authentic. By narrowing the study to wedding and banquet imagery, I will demonstrate that Jesus functions within the world of first-century exegesis by combining texts for good reasons in order to tease out of these texts new applications to his present ministry as a messianic wedding banquet.

---

164. Allison, *The Intertextual Jesus*, 19.

3

Eschatological Banquet in Isaiah

Introduction

The prophets of the Hebrew Bible frequently describe a coming age of prosperity in terms of eating and drinking. The event is called a "eschatological banquet" in scholarly literature whether this is an inaugural meal at the beginning of a future age (Isa 25:6–8) or an ongoing Edenic feast in an idealized age (Isa 32:15–20, Ezek 34:25–31, Ps 23:1–5).[1] That the eschatological age will be inaugurated by a victory banquet is found initially in Isa 25:6–8. Isaiah 25:6–8 describes the eschatological age as beginning when the Lord himself deals decisively with the enemy of humanity (death). All people celebrate with excellent food and wine on Mount Zion. Isaiah 40–55 uses the Exodus and the Wilderness Tradition to describe the end of the Exile as an on-going banquet. At the end of the exile, the captives will return to Zion in a new Exodus and journey through the wilderness. Instead of a struggle through a terrifying desert, the journey will be easy and safe with plenty of good food and water. In fact, the wilderness will be transformed into Eden. In this chapter I will be concerned with the banquet as an inauguration of the eschatological age, in the next chapter I will examine the texts in Isaiah 40–55 which describe the on-going nature of the eschatological banquet.

---

1. Despite the fact that vocabulary for a banquet is not found in Isa 31:15–20, it is clear from the context that the messianic age is a time of abundant food and wine. Isaiah 32:15–20 describes a messianic age in which prosperity returns to the land. "It is hard, in the midst of plenty, to imagine hunger" (Watts, *Isaiah 1–33*, 418). Likewise, Ezek 34:25–31 describes a time of peace and tranquility in the land and an increase in produce in the land which banishes hunger. Eichrodt compared this to the "return to Eden" found in several other prophetic books. Eichrodt, *Ezekiel*, 483–84. Cooper agrees, commenting that Ezek 34:25–31 is a "restoration of the Edenic ideals." Cooper, *Ezekiel*, 303. Psalm 23 is often overlooked as a messianic text, but it is one of the few which combine the image of a shepherd with that of a victory feast prepared by the Lord himself. The Psalm may therefore be described as both a victory banquet and ongoing feast in the presence of the Lord.

Jesus the Bridegroom

The first step in the intertextual method described in chapter 2 is to "hear the echo." Jesus says in Matt 8:11 that "many will recline at the table" in the Kingdom. Likewise, Jesus states that his disciples will eat at his table in the coming kingdom, just as they will judge the twelve tribes of Israel (Luke 22:29). The reader may hear echoes in texts like these of any number of descriptions of an eschatological banquet in the Hebrew Bible. For example, in Ps 23:5 the author says that God prepares a table for him in the presence of his enemies. In Ps 78:19 God's provision after the Exodus is described as "spreading a table in the wilderness." With respect to a banquet at the beginning of the eschatological age, the most likely "echo" would been to Isa 25:6–8.

The rationale for beginning with Isa 25:6–8 is that this is the earliest reference to an eschatological banquet in the Hebrew Bible. This text is the foundation for later reflections on the beginning of the new age in Jeremiah or Second Isaiah as well as the literature of the Second Temple Period. The book of Isaiah is particularly important since the goal of this study is to provide the foundation for studying the messianic banquet in Jesus' teaching and practice. It is clear that Isaiah was a highly influential book in the Second Temple Period, but especially so in the teaching of Jesus.[2]

An additional reason for beginning with Isa 25:6–8 is that this text is an example of clustering two types of tradition in order to form a new related image. As is well know, Isa 25:6–8 contains elements of a victory banquet common in the Ancient Near East.[3] But it also has elements of a wilderness tradition. As I will show in this chapter, Isa 25:6–8 alludes to the original gathering at Sinai and the covenant meal eaten on the mountain. In Isa 25:6–8 there is a gathering of people at the mountain of God and a covenant meal is shared in God's presence. This clustering of traditions in Isaiah forms a foundation for the new Exodus motif which will be used extensively in Isa 40–55 (chapter 4 of this study).[4]

Before turning to a review of the vocabulary for banquets in the Hebrew Bible, it is important to clarify what I mean by eschatology from the perspective of the Hebrew Bible. The prophets of the Hebrew Bible responded to two major crises in the history of Israel. First, prophets such as Amos, Hosea, Micah, and Isaiah respond to the invasion of Israel by Assyria and the subsequent destruction of Samaria in 722 B.C. and exile of the people of Israel. The prophets explained that covenant unfaithfulness was the reason for the invasion and exile. In fact, exile into the nations was a clear threat

2. Jesus cites the book of Isaiah as describing his messianic ministry in Luke 4:18–21 and as a rationale for his teaching in parables (Mark 4:10–13, Matt 13:14–15, Luke 8:10). Numerous other allusions to Isaiah can be found in Jesus' teaching. In addition, Isa 40:3–5 is foundational for the ministry of John the Baptist (Mark 1:3, Matt 3:2–3, Luke 4:4–6) and the Qumran Community.

3. For a collection of these texts see Hosein, "The Banquet Type-Scene."

4. A new Exodus in Isa 25:6–8 is rarely recognized by scholars. While O'Kane recognizes the use of Exodus material in Isaiah 40–55, he omits the gathering of the nations to Zion as a potential use Exodus tradition. O'Kane, "Isaiah: A Prophet in the Footsteps of Moses," 46–47. Despite the title of the article, Otzen contributes little to this discussion since he is more interested with the date of Isaiah's apocalypse and the identity of the city in Isa 24. Otzen, "Traditions and Structures of Isaiah 24–27," 196–206.

of the Deuteronomic covenant (Deut 28:64–68). Second, by the time of Jeremiah and Ezekiel, the Babylonian empire threatened Judah. Jerusalem and the Temple were destroyed and the people of Judah were taken into captivity. This exile was also interpreted as a failure on the nation's part to keep the covenant (Jer 31:31–32, Ezek 37:16–19). In the case of both Israel and Judah, the exile was assumed to be God's judgment for their covenant unfaithfulness.

But the prophets did not see the exile as permanent. Jeremiah, Ezekiel and Isaiah 40–66 each looked forward to a time when the Lord will make a "new covenant with the house of Israel and with the house of Judah" (Jer 31:31–33). It is remarkable that both the house of Judah and the house of Israel are mentioned in this promise of restoration. Jeremiah saw an end to the Judean exile after seventy years, but there is no such limit given for the exile of Israel.[5] At the end of the exile the Lord will recall his people from the nations and re-gather them in the Land once again. In Isa 25:6–8, that gathering is described as a banquet of rich foods prepared by the Lord on Mount Zion. The future hope of the prophets was a return of Judah and Israel to Zion where the Lord would rule over them. In this eschatological time people of Israel would be united and enabled to keep the Law so that they would enjoy the blessings of the Deuteronomic Covenant.[6] The eschatological banquet in Isa 25:6–8 is the inauguration of that future restoration.

מִשְׁתֶּה in the Hebrew Bible

מִשְׁתֶּה as a Joyous Banquet

The Hebrew term used for the banquet in Isa 25:6 is מִשְׁתֶּה, a word which refers to a banquet or a festive meal especially related to a joyous occasion.[7] Since all of the texts in which מִשְׁתֶּה has a connotation of a more or less wild festival are post-exilic, this nuance of meaning may not be present in the occurrences in earlier texts. Of the forty-six occurrences of the term in the Hebrew Bible, nearly half are found in Esther where they refer to royal banquets of the Persian Empire and would presumably include rich food and abundant drink.[8] The same word is used to describe the feasting of the Jews at the end of the book (9:17–19). The feast of Purim which is based on this text has

---

5. This point is made by Pitre, *Jesus, the Tribulation, and the End of the Exile*, 31–40.

6. These prophetic expectations of a time of fantastic banqueting may be driven by the "blessing and cursing" aspect of the covenant. The positive aspect of the conclusion to the covenant in Deuteronomy was that the people would be blessed if they kept the words of the covenant. These blessings are all quite material and could very well be summarized as describing such prosperity that people could regularly eat banquet-like meals.

7. See HALOT מִשְׁתֶּה cognate to the verb שתה, "to drink." The word does not mean "only drinking," contra H. P. Smith, *The Books of Samuel*, 279.

8. Esth 1:3 describes a lengthy 180 day מִשְׁתֶּה for the purpose of displaying the riches of the kingdom. Many commentators cite the descriptions of Persian banquets from Herodotus. Breneman, *Ezra, Nehemiah, Esther*, 304.

a reputation for feasting and drunkenness. The word occurs in Dan 1:5, 8, 10 in the context of royal banqueting. The young men are assigned rich foods and wine from the king's מִשְׁתֶּה. The word is parallel to פַּתְ־בַּג, a phrase found only in Dan 1 and 11:26 which likely means "rich food."[9] In Ezra 3:7 the word is used for drink in parallel to food (מַאֲכָל), although it is not clear that the food and drink provided to the people of Sidon and Tyre to work on the new temple constitutes a "festive" environment or a covenant meal.

The connotation of a festive banquet appears in the prophets as well. The term appears in Isa 5:12 to describe to the drunken revelry of Israel. Jeremiah is told that he is not to enter into a "house of feasting" (בֵּית־מִשְׁתֶּה, Jer 16:8). In the previous verses he was forbidden to enter a house of mourning (16:5–7), implying that the "house of feasting" is a joyful celebration which is in contrast to a house of mourning. This is confirmed in verse nine where Jeremiah is told that God will bring an end to the sounds of joy or the voices of the bride and bridegroom. It is therefore likely that בֵּית־מִשְׁתֶּה is a "wedding banquet."[10]

The use of מִשְׁתֶּה in Jer 51:39 serves to demonstrate that the image of a feast was not strictly used as a metaphor of salvation. The Lord judges Babylon by making the city a ruin (שַׁמָּה, v. 37) and a dry heap of rubble (גַּל, v. 37). The people of Babylon are described as "young lions" who are aroused, but when the Lord sets out a banquet, they will become drunk and sleep forever. So too in Isaiah's Apocalypse an unnamed city is made into a ruin (שַׁמָּה, 24:12) and a rubble heap (גַּל, Isa 25:2). The point of the banquet laid out by the Lord seems different since those who eat of it have the "shroud" removed from their face and tears wiped away (25:6–8, although these details can be disputed). Since the text of Jer 51:37–39 is remarkably close to Isa 25:6–8, we cannot assume that the imagery of the banquet in Isaiah is strictly positive. A banquet may be set before a people as an image of judgment.

מִשְׁתֶּה as an Enthronement Meal

The term מִשְׁתֶּה is used in a number of covenant and enthronement contexts with or without the implication of a "festive" meal.[11] For example, in 2 Sam 3:13 David makes

---

9. Miller, *Daniel*, 63; Goldingay lists several reasons why this food may have been unacceptable to Daniel, including the idea that the food was "festive," sacrificed to a Babylonian god, etc., Goldingay, *Daniel*, 18. The same meaning is found in Job 1:4–5. Clines understands מִשְׁתֶּה in this context as "irregular, occasional festivities rather than an unceasing round of high living." Clines, *Job 1–20*, 15.

10. See Eccl 7:2 where the two phrases are also used in contrast. Craigie, Kelley, and Drinkard, *Jeremiah 1–25*, 217.

11. Anointing a king and a communal meal appear together frequently in the Ancient Near East. For example, in the Armana letters, Alashiya writes to apologize for missing the Pharaoh's coronation feast and ends instead perfumed oil. In the Mari text ARM VII 13, a business transaction is sealed with a communal meal and anointing with oil; in a Middle Assyrian legal text (ANET 183) a bride is anointed in connection with a feast. Mettinger, *King and Messiah*, 212–20. In 2 Sam 9:22 Samuel prepares a meal for Saul and invites guests, culminating in the anointing of Saul as king (10:1). Like

a treaty (בְּרִית) with Abner, the commander of Saul's army, with the stipulation that his wife Michal should be returned to him. While this is not David's enthronement, it is certainly the treaty which enables him to rule over all Israel. Abner and twenty of his men come to Hebron where David "prepared a feast" (מִשְׁתֶּה . . . וַיַּעַשׂ) for them (v. 20). Following the feast Abner goes to assemble Israel to meeting their "lord and king" in order to make a covenant with David and Abner's men have gone away in peace (v. 21, בְּשָׁלוֹם). Anderson calls this meal a "feast marking the end of successful negotiations," but he does not consider this a covenant meal because it is a private covenant between David and Abner.[12] However, there are enough elements in the text to argue the meal is part of making the covenant between Abner and David. Key vocabulary is present (בְּרִית, שָׁלוֹם), two warring parties, a re-establishment of a marriage, etc. When the northern tribes accept David as king, they gather at Hebron and David eats a plentiful meal with his soldiers (in 2 Sam 5:1–5 there is no meal, but see 1 Chr 12:38–40, 40–41 MT).[13] The Chronicles passage is sometimes described as having "strong messianic overtones," although they are not always noticed.[14] This meal included fig and raisin cakes,[15] wine and oil, cattle and sheep, all in abundance and with "great joy." All of Israel is united under a single king and gather from all over the land with supplies and food in order to anoint David king. David then conquers Jerusalem (2 Sam 5:6–16) and subdues the enemies of Israel, the Philistines (2 Sam 5:17–25).

In the next pericope of 2 Samuel, David calls for the Ark of the Covenant to be restored to Israel by bringing it into the city of Jerusalem and "set in its place" for the first time. This is a text which has both covenantal and enthronement overtones since it is the first time the Ark has been installed at Jerusalem.[16] This procession is accompanied by great worship (2 Sam 6:12–15) and sacrifice (2 Sam 6:13, 17–18).[17] After

---

David in 2 Samuel 6, Saul participates in a form of worship after this meal and anointing. Mettinger 113 describes this as a "royal banquet," although מִשְׁתֶּה does not appear in the text. For a survey of covenants in the Hebrew Bible, see McCarthy, *Old Testament Covenant*, 41–54.

12. Anderson, *2 Samuel*, 60. Anderson cites McCarthy, "Social Compact and Sacral Kingship," in *Studies in the Period of David and Solomon*, 79, and Mettinger, *King and Messiah*, 138, as supporting the presence of a covenant in this passage. Compare Birch, "First and Second Samuel," 2:1224.

13. Hooker highlights the joyous celebration as people and abundance "flow into Hebron for the party." *First and Second Chronicles*, 61. Japhet comments that this is a secular celebration, in contrast to Solomon's enthronement in 1 Chr 29:22 (they "ate and drank before the Lord"). Japhet, *I & II Chronicles*, 269. So, too, Klein, *1 Chronicles*, 325, although Klein calls this meal an "enthronement festival at Hebron."

14. Smith, "Messianic Banquet," 4:788–90.

15. The cakes are צִמּוּקִים, a word only found four times in the Hebrew Bible. In 1 Sam 25:18 and 2 Sam 16:1 they are part of a "peace offering" given to David (Abigail and Mephibosheth).

16. Mowinckel, *The Psalms in Israel's Worship*, 2:62, cited by Gray, *2 Kings*, 90 with tacit approval. Morganstern argues that David chose to bring the Ark to Jerusalem as part of a New Year's celebration. Morganstern, "A Chapter of the History the High Priesthood," 1–24. Compare this to Seow, *Myth, Drama, and the Politics of David's Dance*, 131–36; Birch, "First and Second Samuel," 2:1249.

17. 1 Chr 16:1 describes the sacrifice as "burnt offerings and peace offerings." Peace offerings were shared by the worshipers, indicating a time of feasting. Curtis and Madsen, *The Books of Chronicles*, 219.

the sacrifice, David distributes "a loaf of bread, a cake of dates and a cake of raisins" to all the people, both men and women. This is a unique event in the Hebrew Bible: it "has no real parallel in the Old Testament but coronation rites in the ancient Near East are commonly accompanied by a banquet and the distribution of food to all and sundry."[18] While most commentators do not find any evidence for an "enthronement of the Lord" in this text,[19] it is possible to see this as a celebration of the Lord's arrival at Zion in the form of the Ark and his servant David.

The foods distributed in v. 19 are significant. "Date cakes" (אֶשְׁפָּר) and "raisin cakes" (אֲשִׁישָׁה) are expensive foods made of dried compressed fruit.[20] The meaning of אֲשִׁישָׁה (raisin cakes, NIV) in this context is difficult as indicated by the LXX and some rabbinic texts which take the word as referring to "a jug of wine." While "date cakes" are only found here in the Hebrew Bible and the parallel in 1 Chr 16:3, "raisin cakes" are mentioned in Song 2:5 and Hosea 3:1, both wedding contexts. In the Song 2:5 the bride has entered into the banquet hall (probably the "wedding hall" in this case)[21] and is overwhelmed with love and asks to be "strengthened with raisins, refreshed with apples."[22] Like 2 Sam 6:19, it is possible "raisins" ought to be "a jug of wine," given the context of the banquet hall. If so, then this text describes King David gathering people to Jerusalem for the installation of the Ark and celebrating with bread and wine given to all people. Perhaps the author is intentionally using the language of a wedding in order to highlight the relationship of Israel with her God. While the placement of the

---

18. Porter, "The Interpretation of 2 Samuel 6 and Psalm 132," 168. On the other hand, Klein, *1 Chronicles*, 358, declares that this distribution of food is a "symbolic banquet to celebrate the accession of Yahweh to his home in Jerusalem." Seow draws attention to an Akkadian royal inscription which describes Sargon II ushering the gods into the city and conducting a feast. Seow, *Myth, Drama, and the Politics of David's Dance*, 194–95. Several examples from the Ancient Near East of procession and feasting are collected in Barnett, "Bringing the God into the Temple," 10–20. On the meaning of David's ritual dance, see McCarter, "The Ritual Dedication of the City of David in 2 Samuel 6," 276–77; Wright, "Music and Dance in Second Samuel Six," 201–25.

19. For example, Anderson, *2 Samuel*, 107. Bergen makes this meal a gift in exchange for a blessing, as with Abraham and Melchizedek in Genesis 14. Bergen, *1, 2 Samuel*, 332. One might be able to argue this is David's "enthronement" in Jerusalem, although he has been king for seven years at this point.

20. In a lengthy footnote Morgenstern cites Isa 16:7 as an indication that the use of these cakes was associated with religious activities at the harvest season, or perhaps the cakes used to honor the Queen of Heaven in Jer 7:18, 44:19. Morgenstern, "The High Priesthood," 7n22. The second term is translated with ἀμορίτην, "sweet cake" in LXX 1 Chr 16:3.

21. Literally the "house of wine," but Garrett translates the phrase as "wedding hall." Garrett, *Proverbs, Ecclesiastes, Song of Songs*, 391. Pope comments that the House of Wine was taken by the Targum as the Academy and the banner of love was the study of the Torah. Pope, *Song of Songs*, 377.

22. The translation of both of these verbs can be contested; Garrett suggests the bride is asking to be placed in a bed of raisins and apples, both symbols of love in the Ancient Near East. Garrett, *Proverbs, Ecclesiastes, Song of Songs*, 392. Pope surveys several attempts to explain verb סמך, concluding the word has the connotation of a eating a meal; the raisin-cakes themselves are well-known from Ancient Near East fertility cults as aphrodisiacs. So too, apples and apple juice were used in anti-impotency incantations. The verb רפד may be related to an Ugaritic root used for sexual activity between Baal and Asarte. Pope, *Song of Songs*, 378–80; Snaith, *Song of Solomon*, 31.

Ark is not exactly "on Zion," the association of this meal with the Ark of the Covenant is significant in the context of the later association of the Ark and Zion.

1 Kings 1:5–31 is another example of a banquet in an enthronement context. In this pericope Adonijah celebrates what he believes will be his enthronement with a sacrifice at a sacred stone[23] (v. 9) and invites all of the king's sons to eat with him (vv. 19, 25). The term מִשְׁתֶּה is not used for this meal, the description of "eating and drinking" at the enthronement of a king is parallel to Solomon's מִשְׁתֶּה in 1 Kgs 3:15. That Adonijah's action is an enthronement feast is clear from the reaction of Bathsheba and Nathan who persuade David to have Solomon named as heir in order to prevent Adonijah from taking the throne. In addition, the text states that three times that Adonijah sacrificed מְרִיא, "fatted calves," a fairly rare word in the Hebrew Bible (1 Kgs 1:9, 19, 25).[24] The only other place in Samuel-Kings where a מְרִיא is sacrificed in 2 Sam 6:13, during the procession of the Ark of the Covenant into Jerusalem for the first time.

While Adonijah is feasting with his allies, Solomon is coronated with the blessing of David. While there is no feast served at this point,[25] there are a number of other elements of an enthronement which are important to notice. Solomon is placed on a mule and lead to the Gihon spring where both the priest Zadok and the prophet Nathan anointed him as the king. That he should be riding a mule recalls David's return to Jerusalem in 2 Sam 19.[26] A "horn of oil," likely the same one Samuel used to anoint David,[27] is brought from the Tabernacle and the crowds acknowledge him as the king. In v. 40 there is music and "great rejoicing" (חָלִיל).[28] Solomon's feast occurs after his

---

23. The Stone of Zoeleth, or the "Serpent's Stone" was likely a sacred stone dedicated to some deity. The location of the stone is near En Rogel, at the confluence of the Kidron and Hinnom valleys. Opposite the Gihon spring there is a modern Arabic location *ez-Zehweleh*, a rocky outcrop in the village of Siloam, south of the Old City. Mare, "Serpent's Stone," 5:1116; Gray, *1–2 Kings*, 83–84. Swanson connects the stone to Jebusite worship. Swanson, "Serpent's Stone," 1188; Masterman, "Serpent's Stone," 4:419.

24. The word is used in Amos 5:22 for the finest of sacrifices and in Ezek 39:18 the word designates the fattest animals from Bashan. The first item in the list of slaughtered animals is שׁוֹר, an ox or bull used for sacrifices (cf. Lev 17:3 for example). The third item is a sheep, צֹאן, a similarly common sacrificial animal. Since all three are collective terms, it is possible only one of each animal is meant. But given the context of a large celebration, it is possible several animals of each category were used in order to enhance Adonijah's prestige.

25. 1 Chr 29:21–25, on the other hand, indicates that Solomon was enthroned with a sacrifice of "a thousand bulls, a thousand rams and a thousand male lambs, drink offerings and other sacrifices." In addition, the Chronicler emphasizes the fact that the people "eat and drink before the Lord." This compares to Exod 24:7 where the elders of the people saw the Lord and ate and drank.

26. Anticipating Zech 9:9, see the suggestion of Mowinckel, *The Psalms in Israel's Worship*, 2:62. See also Amsler, "Des visions de Zacharie à l'apocalypse d'Esaïe 24–27," 263–73.

27. Provan, *1 and 2 Kings*, 29.

28. Music is frequently associated with a banquet. The verb חלל III ("to play the flute") appears in Isa 5:12 in the context of those who revel at banquets and become drunk with wine. Playing flutes are also part of royal procession of the Lord in Isa 30:29 as the people go up to the mountain of the Lord. Isaiah 30:29, however, uses the noun חַג is used for festival in this verse rather than מִשְׁתֶּה. Watts associates this verse with "the festal drama of Zion's New Year." Watts, *Isaiah 1–33*, 405. חָלִיל is not

dream at Gibeon (1 Kgs 3:1–15). Solomon returned to Jerusalem and stood in front of the Ark of the Covenant and made a large sacrifice of both burnt and fellowship offerings. He then prepared a feast for his officials (3:15, וַיַּעַשׂ מִשְׁתֶּה). While this is after his official enthronement, the Lord confirms Solomon's kingship by means of a vision from God. Solomon responds to the vision with a massive sacrifice and feast.[29]

From this survey of texts, it is clear than a meal is often associated with the enthronement of a king. Although the presence of the noun מִשְׁתֶּה is not required for a meal to be a celebration of an enthronement, the term often appears. This meal is a celebration and usually is described as excellent food. The king is the host of this meal, distributing the food to those invited to the enthronement feast. But when David brought the Ark of the Covenant to Jerusalem excellent food was distributed to all people as a celebration of the enthronement of the Lord in Zion. It is therefore possible to describe Isa 25:6–8 as an enthronement since there is a gathering of all people to Zion to share a meal served by the Lord as King.

מִשְׁתֶּה as a Covenant Meal

In the context of a treaty or covenant, two parties often ate and drank together in order to finalize an agreement.[30] While the term מִשְׁתֶּה is used in the context of a covenant in the Hebrew Bible, it is not the only element found when a covenant is finalized. For example, a cultic stone may be set up, an altar may be built and offerings made, the covenant itself may be read aloud or a scroll of the covenant may be prepared for the occasion.[31] Sometimes the location of the covenant is given a new name or the participant in the covenant is re-named. Many of these elements are present in Gen

---

exclusively associated with joy, Jer 48:36 uses the noun in the context of a lament. LXX 1 Kings 1:40 has renders the noun as dancing (χορός). This noun is used in LXX Judg 11:34 to describe the dancing of Jepthah's daughter and in 21:21 for the dancing of young girls who are to be taken as wives for the Benjaminites. The final useof the noun in the LXX describes the joyous dancing of the women who greeted David after the defeat of the Philistines in LXX 1 Kgs 29:5.

29. Meals as part of an enthronement are commonplace apart from those surveyed here. These are included because of the use of key vocabulary (primarily מִשְׁתֶּה). Patai describes Saul's anointing in 1 Sam 9:22—10:1 as an enthronement meal which included a sacrifice and communal meal with the elders of the people. Patai, "Hebrew Installation Rites," 160. When Saul is reaffirmed as king in 1 Sam 11:14–15, the people make fellowship offerings and "rejoice greatly." The verb שׂמח does not have the same range of meaning as מִשְׁתֶּה, although feasting is likely involved here. *TWOT* 2:828–35.

30. A meal is not always part of a covenant ceremony, as in Josh 24. There is a review of the covenant relationship (2–15), the people swear an oath to keep the covenant (16–18), a pronouncement of curses for disloyalty with additional oaths (19–24), a recording of the covenant into a "book" along with a notice of the deposit of the document at a shrine (25–26), a setting up of a sacred stone as a witness (26–27). These are all elements of covenant ceremony, although there is no meal at the conclusion of the ceremony.

31. This list derives from Hagelia, "Meal on Mount Zion," 73–95. Compare Hagelia to the description of covenant found in Mendenhall and Herion, "Covenant," 1:1179–1202; and Mettinger, *King and Messiah*, 212–28.

31:43–54 where Jacob and Laban make a covenant which includes marriage. Jacob sets up stones as a reminder of the covenant; he recites the stipulations of the covenant and pronounces a curse upon anyone who breaks the covenant. The two parties make a sacrifice and Jacob invites all his relatives to eat a meal together (although the verb אכל appears rather than מִשְׁתֶּה). What is important about this covenant in Gen 31 is that the typical word for covenant, בְּרִית, is not used. As H. Hagelia argues, the word בְּרִית does not have to be present for a passage to be considered a covenant—there is variation in vocabulary and in the elements of covenant in various covenant passages in the Hebrew Bible.[32] Similarly, the term מִשְׁתֶּה does not need to be present in every covenant context (i.e., Josh 24).[33]

Polaski has argued that the use of מִשְׁתֶּה in the Hebrew Bible is often associated with "extending boundaries."[34] In the case of Jacob and Laban the covenant expands the territory of both men by uniting their herding efforts (Gen 29, 31). The case of Samson's marriage to the Philistine woman in Judg 14 is an example of uniting two warring factions. Solomon's מִשְׁתֶּה in 2 Sam 3 is an example of political arrangement which brings two parties together as well. Polaski therefore argues that the use of מִשְׁתֶּה in Isa 25:6–8 along with the universal language ("all nations", etc.) implies this mountain-top meal is an "ethnic meeting ground."[35] Isaiah is describing an international pilgrimage to Mount Zion. What this sort of pilgrimage means is not as clear—do the nations come to Zion for salvation or for judgment? In at least two of the examples Polaski uses the benefits of the treaty is obtained by deception (Jacob deceives Laban; Joab assumes Abner has deceived David, Samson's wedding banquet is laced with deception). Perhaps there is an hint of deception in Isa 25 as well—the nations have come to the mountain to eat and drink expecting peace with the Lord (25:6–8), but instead find judgment waiting (25:9–11, cf. Jer 51:37–39 where the meal is a deception).

In summary, the noun מִשְׁתֶּה often appears in covenant or treaty texts as an indication that the covenant has been accepted by both sides. It is remarkable that many of these covenant meals are marriage covenants. As we will see in chapter 5, a wedding contract is a type of covenant which was often concluded with a joyous meal celebrating a marriage. Hosea, for example, will use the marriage contract as a metaphor for the relationship of God and his people. The noun מִשְׁתֶּה therefore can refer to joyous meal eaten to celebrate a wedding.

32. Hagelia, "Meal on Mount Zion," 84. Similarly, Pedersen, *Israel, Its Life and Culture*, 2:305.

33. Mettinger calls attention to another potential treaty or covenant in 1 Kgs 5:1 (LXX 1 Kgs 5:15). In the LXX reading, Hiram of Tyre sends a delegation to anoint Solomon since Hiram had "always loved David." Mettinger points out that the verb אהב is used as a contractual term in both biblical and Ancient Near East comparative material. Hiram is therefore renewing a covenant agreement with the new monarch Solomon. The terms of this covenant involve the provision of food for Hiram's royal household. Mettinger, *King and Messiah*, 226–27.

34. Polaski, *Authorizing an End*, 165–66.

35. Ibid., 166.

Covenant Meal on Sinai / Zion

Although this brief scene is often overlooked as a banquet scene, Exod 24:1–11 is perhaps the most important text for understanding the idea of an eschatological banquet.[36] In this text Moses and the seventy elders of Israel ascend Mt. Sinai to swear an oath to keep all which was written in the book of the covenant. Then the elders "saw God, and they ate and drank" (24:9, NIV). This "eating and drinking" is occasionally seen as a covenant meal since it takes place on the mountain of God and in his very presence.[37] As such, it is the climax of the whole sequence of Exodus events and the conclusion to the first half of the book. As J. Durham comments, "a more appropriate conclusion to the Sinai narrative sequence could hardly be imagined."[38] The relationship between God and Israel therefore begins with a covenant meal on the mountain of God. The theme of eating the excellent food and drink which God has provided on the "heights of the land" returns in the song of Moses (Deut 32:13–14).[39]

On the other hand, E. W. Nicholson has argued against the notion of a covenant meal in Exod 24:11.[40] Rather than a covenant meal, the fact that the people "ate and drank" ought to be taken as in the context of "seeing God." Moses and the elders of Israel experience a theophany in v. 9–10 yet they live. "Eating and drinking" is therefore simply an indication they were not struck dead when they went up the mountain. Nicholson argues that there is no sacrifice, setting aside vv. 3–8 as stemming from

---

36. Stallman, "Divine Hospitality in the Pentateuch: A Metamorphical Perspective on God as Host"; cf. Hosein, "The Banquet Type-scene," 170–71; Blenkinsopp, *Isaiah 1–39*, 358. Lieber understands this as a covenant meal and cites parallels to the covenant between Jacob and Laban in Gen 31:54. Lieber, "I Set a Table before You," 77. Johnson says that the image of Moses and the elders of Israel eating in the presence of God was "worked out by the prophets," citing Isa 25:6–8 and 1 QSa 2:15–22. Johnson, *The Gospel of Luke*, 217.

37. Rad calls this meal a "very primitive communion sacrifice." *Old Testament Theology*, 2:254. McCarthy separates the covenant meal by itself (found only in J) from a covenant meal as part of a sacrifice, (found only in E), in *Treaty and Covenant*, 163–64n26. Dumbrell thinks more should be made of this mean and he explicitly connects this covenant meal to "eschatological meals" in Is 25:6–8 and Rev 7–9. Dumbrell, *Covenant and Creation*, 94. Smith considers the meal in Exod 24 as a covenant meal and explicitly connects Exod 24 and Isa 25. Smith, "The Psalms as a Book for Pilgrims," 161.

38. Durham *Exodus*, 347. See also Goldingay, *Old Testament Theology: Israel's Faith*, 825.

39. "This can only be a covenant meal" (Noth, *Exodus*, 196). "The final description 'they ate and drank' places the whole account into the context of a covenant meal" (Childs, *Exodus*, 507). "Walking on the high places" is often a metaphor for victory, cf. Hab 3:19. Christensen, *Deuteronomy 21:10—34:12*, 797; Cassuto understands the meal as a sacred meal of peace offerings (vv. 3–8) which they ate when they returned to camp. Cassuto, *A Commentary on the Book of Exodus*, 315; Merrill, *Deuteronomy*, 415.

40. Nicholson, "The Interpretation of Exodus XXIV 9–11," 77–97. While Dozeman denies this is a covenant meal, he does think that it is a "festival of worship" and draws a parallel to Isa 25:6. Dozeman, *God on the Mountain*, 114–15. Ruprecht makes a similar comment. Ruprecht, "Exodus 24:9–11 als Beispiel lebendiger Erzähltradition aus der Zeit des babylonischen Exils," 104n3. More recently, C. Houtman understands "eating and drinking" as a statement "that they went on living as before . . . there is no meal here with God or in the presence of God." Houtman, *Exodus*, 3:296.

another tradition,[41] and there is no indication that "eating and drinking" is sharing of food from a sacrifice. For Nicholson, vv. 9–11 "neither knows nor implies the existence of a covenant."[42] He cites the difficulty the rabbinic literature had explaining this text because of the clear prohibition on going up the mountain. Those who look upon the glory of God are under a death penalty.[43] The fact they went up the mountain and lived is expressed as "they ate and drank." He also shows that the phrase "eat and drink" is frequently used to mean "live life," perhaps with the connotation of prosperity (1 Kgs 4:20, Eccl 5:16, Jer 22:15).

Nicholson is correct in his connection of the "eating and drinking" with the theophany, but he fails to take the whole passage into consideration. Separating the sacrifice of 3–8 from the elders "eating and drinking" on the mountain seems to be as damaging to the point of the section as removing the "eating and drinking" from the theophany.[44] The real problem for seeing Exod 24:9–11 as background for an eschatological banquet is the lack of the key term מִשְׁתֶּה. However a covenant can have any number of elements different elements (invitations, "eating and drinking," sacrifice, etc.), but not every element must be present.

If both Exod 24:9–11 and Isa 25:6–8 can be described as "covenantal," can it be shown that Isa 25 looks back to Exod 24 as an inspiration? While it must be admitted that there are few lexical connections between the two texts, employing the criteria for detecting an allusion described in my second chapter will indicate that there may in fact be an intertextual connection.[45] The traditions found in the book of Exodus are clearly foundational for the book of Isaiah since new Exodus and Wilderness motifs are common in both halves of the book. That both texts are covenantal indicates thematic coherence. It is certainly historically plausible that a prophet in the eighth century BCE would evoke the first covenant meal at Sinai in order to describe the inauguration of a future new covenant. Both texts describe a gathering of people on

---

41. Nicholson, "The Interpretation," 86–87. This is a common view in the commentaries.

42. Ibid., 96.

43. Ibid., 89–91.

44. Durham suggests that Exod 32:1–6 was originally attached to chapter 24 and there is an intentional contrast between the elders on the mountain and the people at the foot of the mountain. Whether the texts were originally attached or not, the contrast is clear: the elders on the mountain eat and drink in the presence of God, the people eat and drink and profane the presence of God. Durham, *Exodus*, 421.

45. Even the few similar words are more of a "contrast" than true parallels. For example, "people" (עַם) is used in both contexts, but Isaiah is plural, referring to all the peoples of the earth, while in Exodus the word appears four times in the singular, clearly referring only to the Israelites. Both contexts concern a mountain, but in Exodus the mountain is Sinai, while in Isaiah it is clearly Zion in Jerusalem. This could be an example of the transference of Sinai to Zion as Israel's centrally important mountain. If Isa 25:6–8 describes a new Exodus, then the mountain on which the covenant is made in the new Exodus is Zion rather than Sinai. In Isaiah the meal is described in detail, in Exodus they simply "eat and drink." The key term מִשְׁתֶּה is missing from Exodus as are all of the descriptive terms from Isa 25:5. To use Hays's terminology, if vocabulary is the sole criterion, then the "volume" of the allusion is low.

a mountain where they eat in God's presence. While commentators have not seen a connection between these two texts, Isa 25:6–8 is occasionally described by scholars as a prophetic reflection on the first covenant meal in Exod 24:11.[46]

The motivation for the allusion to the covenant meal in Exod 24 in the apocalyptic Isa 25 may be to connect the beginning of the coming age and the beginning of the old. An important element of an intertextual relationship is the possibility of activating the earlier text to illuminate the later. At the beginning of God's relationship with Israel, he overcame his enemies in the plagues, triumphing over Egypt and bringing his people out of slavery to Mount Sinai where he establishes his covenant on the mountain. At the beginning of the eschatological age, God will overcome his enemies once again and recall his people to his mountain (Sinai or Zion) and renew his covenant with them. In both cases there is a meal which celebrates the covenant. Rather than restricting the meal to only the elders as representatives of the people, in Isa 25:6–8 God is inviting all people to the mountain to eat a royal banquet as a symbol of universal salvation. This "universal" element of the meal in Isaiah is not unlike David's distribution of food to all people when he first took possession of Jerusalem and Zion. The time of the restoration of Israel will be like a New Exodus and will include a New Conquest as well. God will call all people to "the mountain" (now Zion) and enact a new covenant with them. While his people eat the banquet the Lord himself prepares, the Lord will "swallow up death forever" and "wipe away all tears forever." The banquet of Isa 25:6–8 therefore represents the ultimate vindication of the people of Israel since God will "remove their disgrace from all the earth." I conclude, therefore, that the there is an allusion to Exod 24 in Isa 25:6–8 and by activating the earlier text we are able to understand Isa 25:6–8 more clearly.[47]

---

46. For example, Berges considers Isa 25:6–8 an expansion on the meal eaten by Moses and the elders on Sinai. Berges, *Jesaja 13–27*, 189. Compare to Welten, who sees the covenant "universalized" in this text to include the whole world. Welten, "Die Vernichtung des Todes und die Königsherrschaft Gottes," 145. Moyter agrees, although with little discussion. Motyer, *Isaiah*, 202.

47. There are a number of other texts in the prophetic material which can be related to the messianic banquet motif. The servants of the Lord are contrasted with those who "spread a table" for Fortune and Destiny in Isa 65:13–14. When the judgment comes, the servants of the Lord will eat and drink in joy, while those who practice divination go hungry and thirsty. Ezekiel describes a horrific anti-banquet when the Pharaoh of Egypt is judged—the birds will gorge themselves after the great battle (32:4). This image is repeated in Ezek 39:17–20 in the description of the gore following the invasion of God and Magog. The emphasis of both passages in Ezekiel is on animals feasting on the flesh of great men until they are fat and drunk. Cf. Rev 19:17–18, where this image is called the "great supper of God." Compare these horrific scenes to the Feast of Anat (KTU 1.3.II.20–23, 27–29), who invites heroes to her feast but instead gorges herself on their flesh. Stern, "The 'Bloodbath of Anat' and Psalm xxiii," 120–25. In a clearly apocalyptic context, Zech 9:15–16 describes the intervention of the Lord who will appear over the warriors like lightning to destroy the armies of Israel's enemies. The survivors will "drink and roar with wine." In a depiction of the messianic age, Joel 2:24–26 and describes those says as abundant in material blessing, grains, and wines will abound and people will have plenty to eat. In Joel 3:18 the mountains will "drip with new wine and the hills will flow with milk." The rest of the world, however, will not experience this bounty—Egypt will be desolate and Edom a desert waste.

Conclusions on מִשְׁתֶּה in the Hebrew Bible

To conclude this survey of the usage of מִשְׁתֶּה in the Hebrew Bible, it is clear that there are numerous passages in the Hebrew Bible which describe eating and drinking as part of a covenant celebration and some passages which use eating and drinking at a wedding or enthronement celebration.[48] These scenes may or may not use the term בְּרִית but nonetheless have covenantal overtones since they share a number of common features including eating and drinking. Likewise, these covenant scenes may or may not use the term מִשְׁתֶּה to describe the eating as a "banquet."

The problem in Isa 25:6–8 is the exact nuance of מִשְׁתֶּה. Is the word used to simply emphasize the meal served on the mountains as a "sumptuous banquet," or is there a covenant motif present? Even if this is a covenant meal, it is hard to conceive of this text alone as foundational for a wedding banquet in the teaching of Jesus, as many New Testament interpreters do. Is this a universalist passage in which all the nations of the world are gathered for a royal feast,[49] a re-enactment of the covenant on Mt Sinai, or is Israel the only nation to benefit from this gathering? Given the negative use of the מִשְׁתֶּה of Jer 51:37–39, it might be possible to argue this meal on Zion is a judgment on the nations rather than a scene of universal salvation. At the very least, salvation for Israel will mean judgment of the nations which have shamed God's people. The next section of this chapter will therefore examine the most-often cited text for messianic banquet, Isa 25:6–8. This text has all of the elements of a covenant meal and describes the ultimate מִשְׁתֶּה on the mountain of the Lord.

Eschatological Banquet in Isa 25:6–8

This section of Isaiah has been described as a "Little Apocalypse" or "Isaiah's Apocalypse."[50] The pericope is structured using the phrase בַּיּוֹם הַהוּא "in that day."[51] In

---

48. Perhaps another line of evidence that feasting and covenants are frequently linked in the ancient world would be the use of oil for anointing in nearly every example surveyed above. Mettinger's examples of anointing in the Ancient Near East indicate that a feast or meal of some sort accompanies the anointing of a king, the use of oil in contractual agreements and a bride at a wedding feast. Mettinger, *King and Messiah*, 185–232, especially 212.

49. For example, Gray comments on Isa 25:6–8: "But there seems no reasonable room for doubt that we have here one of the most catholic passages in the entire Old Testament" (Gray, *Isaiah I-XXXIX*, 429).

50. Johnson, *From Chaos to Restoration*; Vermeylen, "Composition Littéraire De L' 'Apocalypse D'isaïe' (Is 24–27)," 5–38; Ringgren, "Some Observations on Style and Structure in the Isaiah Apocalypse," 107–15; Millar, *Isaiah 24–27 and the Origin of Apocalyptic*; Sweeney, "Textual Citations in Isaiah 24–27," 39–52.

51. The phrase occurs 13 times in Isaiah, almost always in an eschatological context (7:18, 21, 23; 10:20, 27; 11:10, 11; 17:4; 22:20; 23:15; 24:21; 27:12). It introduces the apocalyptic Oracle against Egypt (Isa 19:1) as well as in the conclusion to Isaiah's Apocalypse (26:21). The only example in Isaiah of a non-eschatological use is 7:20. There the phrase refers to a political event in the near future which will be the salvation of the nation (the fall of Rezon of Damascus). Neither of the two phrases appears in Isa 40–66. There are an additional 45 occurrences of בַּיּוֹם הַהוּא (as in 26:1) in Isaiah, frequently in

Jesus the Bridegroom

this Apocalypse, the phrase signals a new section in the structure of the unit. In the first section (24:1–20) the Lord "lays waste" the earth in apocalyptic fashion, culminating in the destruction of a great city.[52] A second section of the Apocalypse begins with the words "in that day" (24:21—25:8). The kings of the earth are judged and led off as prisoners, their fortified cities are made rubble heaps. Even the sun and moon are ashamed at the enthronement of the Lord Almighty on Mount Zion. Isaiah 24:23 indicates location of the enthronement (Zion) as well as the presence of the elders of Jerusalem. As argued in the previous chapter, these are significant hints that Isaiah has a re-enactment of the covenant of Exod 24 in mind. The small unit of 25:6–8 is a description of the victory banquet on Mount Zion at the enthronement of the Lord. In this eschatological context there is an invitation to eat a great and joyous banquet where the Lord himself is the host. This victory restores the people to God's favor by removing their disgrace and tears. Climatically, the Lord himself consumes death, swallowing it up forever. Alternatively, this is an eschatological context where the nations are invited to meet their Lord on Zion not as savior, but as judge.[53]

---

eschatological contexts. This is not surprising since the phrase "in that day" is found in these sorts of passages throughout the prophets. While this is especially true in Zeph (4 times in a short book) and Zech (22 times), nearly all of the prophets employ this phrase to speak of the future salvation of the nation by the hand of the Lord.

52. Millar lists several possibilities for identifying this city. Millar, *Isaiah 24–27*, 15–21. More recently, Biddle suggests the city is intentionally ambiguous, but there may be clues in the larger structure of Isaiah. Chapters 24–27 are a conclusion to the oracles of the nations, and in many ways the destruction of the city is a generic version of the specific judgments in the preceding oracles. But chapters 24–27 can also be taken as prologue to the judgment on Jerusalem in 28–33 or 40–66. For Biddle, in these sections Jerusalem is clearly under judgment. Biddle concludes the Apocalypse of Isaiah contains "two polar opposites / alter egos" and in intentionally ambiguous in order to serve as a transition between these two sections of the book. He cites several "unique features" in Isaiah 24–27 which can be found in Isaiah 13 (a childbirth motif in 26:17–18 // 13:6–16). This same motif is present in the latter part of Isaiah (54:1, 66:12). Biddle, "The City of Chaos and the New Jerusalem: Isaiah 24–27 in Context," 5–12.

53. The phrase "in that day" appears in 25:9, but it possible 25:9–12 does not constitute a "new unit" in the overall structure of the apocalypse. First, the phrase appears without הָיָה as it does in 24:21. This is not a critical point since וְהָיָה is not always present in the prophetic formula "in that day." More important is the fact that בַּיּוֹם הַהוּא does not begin the line, but rather וְאָמַר, a qal perfect with a vav-consecutive, implying that the "action" is continued over from the previous section (*GKC* §112). The verb here is a generic singular, "it will be said." 1QIsa has ואמרת, "you will say." Each of the other boundary markers in the Apocalypse has בַּיּוֹם הַהוּא at the beginning of a line in order to create a disjunction. This is also does not totally disqualify 25:9–12 as a new section since Isa 12:1 and 12:2 use a form of אָמַר and בַּיּוֹם הַהוּא. If this is a new section, it is extremely brief in the overall structure Isaiah's Apocalypse and commentators typically struggle with what to make of the violent judgment specifically on Moab after such a universalist text as 25:6–8. Frequently the solution is to jettison the verses as a later addition, but this is not necessary. It is possible this is a specific instance of the judgment of the kings found in 24:21–22. The trampling of Moab could form an inclusio for the unit 24:21—25:12. Oswalt makes 25:1–12 a unit, although he understands that Moab is a more "generalized picture" of the universal city if 25:2, 26:5, and 27:10. Oswalt, *The Book of Isaiah. Chapters 1–39*, 467. Compare this to Watts who attempts to identify various voices in the text to the effect that the speaker of the condemnation of Moab is "Jerusalem demanding the humiliation of Judah's former vassal" (Watts, *Isaiah 1–33*, 335).

This study will define the unit as beginning in 24:21 ("in that day") through 25:8 ("the Lord has spoken.") This is not unlike Watts who makes 25:6-8 the climax of 24:23—25:8 on the basis of the enthronement motif in 24:23 and 25:6-8, framing a thanksgiving song in 25:1-5.[54] The final words of v. 8 serve as closure for the unit, "for the Lord has spoken." Verse 9 begins with the stereotypical "in that day," beginning a short oracle against Moab. In addition, there is a repetition of the mountain in 23:21-23 and 25:6-8 (Mount Zion and "this mountain").[55] Isaiah 25:6-8 is therefore a climax within the larger unit of Isa 24-27 and describes the enthronement of the Lord on Zion.[56] The pericope has three units; each beginning with a verb plus vav-consecutive. The Lord will prepare a banquet (6a), he will engulf the veil (7a), and he will wipe away tears (8b). In v. 6 there is a description of the banquet prepared for all people. The section uses alliteration in the description of the foods served at this meal. In v. 7-8a the Lord engulfs death forever. This description also makes use of repetition and alliteration to describe the Lord consuming the veil and destroying death. The key verb בלע is repeated in the first and last line of this section as a frame. In v. 8b-d the Lord removes tears and disgrace from all people.

---

54. Watts, *Isaiah 1–33*, 329. Chapter 26 begins a third movement of the apocalypse, once again beginning with the phrase "in that day." This chapter is a song of praise with very little of the apocalyptic material which was found in chapter 24. Verse 19 may very well describe resurrection and v. 20-21 refer to the wrath of the Lord, albeit with virtually no description. Chapter 27:1-11 begins another new section with the phrase "in that day." This chapter returns to the apocalyptic language found in 24. The final section of the apocalypse (27:12-13) repeats the phrase "in that day" twice as a summary of the previous chapters. This coming time includes the gathering of Israel from the lands of two enemies of Israel, Egypt and Assyria. These dispersed people of Israel will return to Zion (the holy mountain) to worship their Lord.

55. Wildberger, *Isaiah 13–27*, 454, 525. Polaski argued that the meal on Mount Zion is the centerpiece of an ABA' pattern. The chapter begins in 25:1-5 with a hymn praising the Lord for his acts (25:1-5) and concludes with a hymn praising the Lord for his salvation (25:9-10a). While the section describing judgment on Moab (25:10b-12) is often dismissed as a later addition, Polaski attempts to 24:21-25-12 a unit including the judgment of Moab in the section. There is a parallel between the judgment of the kings in 25:21-23 and the more specific judgment on Moab in 25:10b-12. In this view, the blessings of verses 6-8 are enhanced by the judgment of a prototypical enemy of God's people, Moab. The richness of the enthronement banquet in verses 6-8 stands is stark contrast to the degradation of Moab, which "swims in filth." As attractive as it is, there is not enough evidence in the text itself to sustain Polaski's chiastic structure. For example, a break between 10a and 10b is unwarranted since there is a vav-conjunction on the nifal perfect of דוש which begins 10b. This links the threshing of Moab to the hand of the Lord resting "on this mountain," presumably Zion for 6-8. In addition, verse 9 begins with "in that day," a phrase which seems to function as a unit-marker in the larger structure of the Apocalypse. For details of his argument, see Polaski, *Authorizing an End*, 162.

56. Day, *God's Conflict With The Dragon And The Sea*, 148, cf. Williamson, "The Messianic Texts in Isaiah 1–39," 240.

Jesus the Bridegroom

The Lord Prepares a Banquet for All People (25:6)

The title יְהוָה צְבָאוֹת "LORD Almighty" (25:6) is a common title for the Lord in the Hebrew Bible, but especially so in Isaiah who associates it with Zion.[57] The Lord Almighty gathering the nations to Zion is plausibly an image of judgment since the title is not common in contexts of universal salvation. That there will be peace in Zion is a common theme (Ps 46:10, Isa 2:4, Mic 4:1–4), but the price of the peace is often the destruction of the enemies of Zion. That enemy, however, may not be people or nations. Psalm 46 may be taken within the context of the conflict between God and primeval Chaos, making the title Lord Almighty one of majesty rather that associated with battle.[58] In Isa 25:6–8, Death is the enemy which is destroyed.

The LORD Almighty will prepare a מִשְׁתֶּה, "banquet."[59] In the survey of enthronement passages above the king himself prepares the banquet for those invited to celebrate the enthronement. Both David and Solomon prepared and distributed food for those invited. In this case, the meal is served to all peoples. The repeated phrase, עַל־כָּל, includes the people (vv. 6, 7), the nations (v. 7), faces (v. 8), and the earth (v. 8). This is usually taken looking forward to universal salvation. When Messiah establishes his kingdom, he will draw all the nations to himself and they will acknowledge him as their Lord. In popular Christian commentaries, this is connected to the ministry of Jesus. Jeremias specifically associated Isa 25:6–8 with the "decisive hour of redemption . . . Gentiles accepted as guests at God's Table . . ."[60] Kissane calls

---

57. Half of the dozen times in the Hebrew Bible where the LORD Almighty and Zion appear together are in Isaiah, with an additional example in 1 Kgs 19:31, a parallel passage to Isa 37:32. The other occurrences are in Zech 1:14, 17; 8:2, 3 and Jer 26:18. The title emphasizes the Lord as enthroned before his heavenly council (the "host"); Strong, "Zion: Theology of," 4:1316; Hartley, *TWOT* 2:749–50. Isaiah has 62x of the 260x in the Hebrew Bible. Only Jeremiah uses the phrase more often (77 times), although Hag (14 times), Zech (53 times) and Mal (24 times) use the phrase more frequently than Isa or Jer. The title does not appear in Ezek or Dan. It is associated with the victorious Lord who will reign from Zion after he subdues the nations. Isaiah 13:4 the Lord Almighty fights against the nations (cf. 24:21–23, 29:5–8). Isaiah 31:4 describes the Lord Almighty descending from Zion to protect Jerusalem from invading armies of the nations. In Isa 34:1–12 describe the Lord Almighty's vengeance and wrath against the nations (specifically Edom, v. 11).

58. For this warning, see Ross, "Jahweh Sebaôt in Samuel and Psalms,"88.

59. "Prepare" is the common verb עשׂה, Qal Perfect, 3MS. It is used in the context of food preparation in Gen 18:7, 19:3, 21:8; Judg 6:19, 13:15, Ezek 4:9. Childs suggests this refers to meals purchased with tithes (Deut 14:26), but this fails to take into account that the meal is provided by the Lord on Zion. Childs, *Isaiah*, 184

60. Jeremias, *Jesus' Promise to the Nations*, 75. Typical of this Christological interpretation is Birks, who connected this passage with the wedding banquet parable of Matt 22: "[T]he blessings of the gospel are described under the figure of an ample feast as in Isa 55:1–6, Matt 22:1–4, Luke 14:15–20." (Birks, *Commentary on the Book of Isaiah*, 134). Delitzsch states that the banquet in Isa 25:6–8 symbolizes "the full enjoyment of blessedness in the perfected kingdom of God." Delitzsch, *Old Testament Commentary*, 7:286.

Eschatological Banquet in Isaiah

this section the "conversion of the nations," noting that in the future, "all the nations" are invited to Zion and are included in this feast.[61]

But this text may be taken as a judgment of the nations who have gathered to face their Lord and Judge rather than scene of universal salvation. This interpretation is found in several Jewish sources, although taking this section as a judgment is not confined to Jewish exegetes. Kimhi glosses the key text as "death will destroy them," that is, the nations of the earth. "Removing the veil" makes the nations vulnerable to death.[62] Slotki cites Rashi as saying "For they will think that it will be easy for them to conquer Israel, much like fat, which is smooth and soft. Instead, it will be converted for them into a feast of bitter dregs."[63] Both Ibn Ezra and Kimhi cite two clear judgment texts (Zech 12:12 and Obad 16) as parallel to Isa 25:6–8.[64] It is possible to take each of the elements of the meal as signifying a judgment rather than a rich meal. Caquot argues that if one sets aside the New Testament interpretation of Isa 25:6–8, one will read this banquet as a judgment scene rather than a description of universal salvation.[65]

Since this banquet on Zion could be understood as universal salvation or judgment on the nations, it is not surprising that there are some later texts which use the eschatological banquet as a symbol of salvation (Jer 31:1–14) and some which use the eschatological banquet as a symbol of judgment (Ezek 39:17–20, Rev 19:17–21). This is an example of how traditions such as the eschatological banquet are developed and applied to new situations. For Jeremiah, the eschatological banquet was a positive image he applied to the future restoration of Israel after the Exile. For Ezekiel, the eschatological banquet was developed as a judgment on the nations. These two applications of the eschatological banquet are the result of some ambiguity on the point of the meal in Isaiah.[66] Isaiah 25:6–8 is the foundational text for both the glorious banquet on Zion for Israel and the nations, but it is equally the foundation for the hellish descriptions of total judgment on those who opposed the Lord.

---

61. Kissane, *The Book of Isaiah*, 1:285. In verse 7 the distinction between Jew and Gentile is abolished, the veil is not a sign of mourning, but rather "symbolizes the revelation of Jahweh to the Gentiles." Kisanne does not think it likely that the prophet had in mind the type of immortality Paul did by the phrase "destroying death." Kisanne, *The Book of Isaiah*, 285. Oswalt connects Isa 25:6 to Rev 22:2 in describing the deliverance of the whole world. Oswalt, *Isaiah 1–39*, 463.

62. Ibn Ezra, *The Commentary of Ibn Ezra on Isaiah*, 115; cf. Slotki, *Isaiah*, 116.

63. Slotki, *Isaiah*, 116, citing Rashi. On lees, Rashi says that this will be in the war of Gog and Magog. Kimhi sees a parallel to Obadiah 16, a poisoned cup.

64. Cited by Caquot, "Remarques," 113.

65. Caquot, "Remarques," 109–19. However, most commentaries do not even reference the Targum's negative view. Of the few who do, the universalist view predominates. For example, Berges, *Das Buch Jesaja*, 190n250. Berges does not think that the banquet is totally universal—Moab is excluded. See also Davies, "The Destiny of the Nations in the Book of Isaiah," 100.

66. It is entirely possible that Jeremiah predates Isa 25, but I think it is more likely that the ambiguity in Isa 25:6–8 is the source for divergent developments in the eschatological banquet. Why would the author of Isa 25 make the banquet less clear than it is in Jeremiah or Ezekiel?

Jesus the Bridegroom

The Lord will prepare this banquet בָּהָר הַזֶּה, "on this mountain."⁶⁷ The antecedent of the demonstrative pronoun appears in 24:23, Mount Zion, from which the "LORD Almighty will reign." That Mount Zion is antecedent seems clear because of the repetition of the title of God as well as the word הָר, but also because the elders of Jerusalem mentioned in 24:23 may refer to the elders of Israel in Exod 24, who ate the covenantal meal on Sinai. Zion occupies a particularly important place in enthronement contexts, appearing frequently in enthronement contexts in the Psalms (2, 46, 48, etc.)⁶⁸

The people are to dine on שְׁמָנִים, "rich foods." The root שֶׁמֶן is typically translated "fat" or "oil" but came to be used as a metaphor for prosperity, as in Deut. 32:13.⁶⁹ Food described as "fat" has the idea of rich, high quality food or drink.⁷⁰ The fat portions of the sacrifice were to be for the Lord (Lev 3:3, 4:8, cf. Gen 4:4). One ought not think of the meal as fatty meats only, but as any rich food prepared with oil.⁷¹ Fat, however, does not always convey a positive image. In Isa 6:10 the word is has the connotation of "calloused," indicating spiritual insensitivity.⁷² Both Deut 32:15 and Jer 5:28 describe the nation as people who have grown rich and complacent as "fat." A feast of rich food can even be a metaphor for judgment, as in Jer 51:39: Babylon will eat a great feast but will fall asleep, never to rise again.

The "rich foods" are modified in the parallel line by מְמֻחָיִם, "flavored with marrow." This pual participle is from a root found only here in Isaiah. Most commentators relate to the verb מחה III, "to suck out marrow"⁷³ or the noun מֹחַ, "marrow." In 25:8 a similar root is used, מחה I, "to wipe," the object being tears from the faces of those who have had the shroud removed. Sweeney has argued the verbs are the same root, and the first occurrence ought to be read as "smeared with fat" rather than "flavored with marrow," attempting to connect this meal with a peace offering⁷⁴ since "fatty

---

67. The preposition בְּ indicates location in a spatial sense (Waltke and O'Conner, 11.2.5b). The use of בְּ with הַר is rare; the combination only appears four times in the Hebrew Bible. Deut 1:6 is sole example outside of Isaiah's Apocalypse. The phrase הָהָר הַזֶּה is not common either, referring only to Sinai (Exod 3:12).

68. Levenson, "Zion Traditions," 6:1099.

69. For example, Gen 27:28, 39; Job 29:6. Isa 61:3 and Ps 45:7 describe the person especially blessed by God as having "oil of gladness" rather than "oil of mourning."

70. A cognate מַשְׁמַנִּים is used only in Neh 8:10, for a sacred meal of "richly prepared food" and "sweet drinks" prepared after the reading of the Law. Cf. *GKC* 124e for this expression as superlative. Wildberger observes that for Ancient Arabs the fatty hump of a camel was the "choicest part of the slaughtered animal." Wildberger, *Isaiah 13–27*, 531. This sense is found in *4QAdmonitory Parable* (4Q302 f2ii) where a man has a good tree which produces "juicy fruit." Martinez and Tigchelaar, *The Dead Sea Scrolls Study Edition (Translations)*, 2:667.

71. Wildberger, *Isaiah 13–27*, 531.

72. See also *4QSapiential Text* (4Q424f3), describing the sorts of people not allowed to be a judge: do not send "a man with a fat heart."

73. Based on the Arabic *mahha*, see *HALOT*.

74. Sweeney, *Isaiah 1–39*, 355.

foods" are associated with a sacrificial feast."[75] Perhaps Delitzsch is correct when he comments that the word is chosen for its "musical quality."[76]

The drink at this meal is described as שְׁמָרִים, "aged wine." This root is only used in three other passages in the Hebrew Bible, always to express a judgment of the Lord. Both Jeremiah 48:11 (Moab) and Zeph 1:12 (Jerusalem)[77] compare a complacent nation to "wine left on its dregs" (NIV). Wine that is left undisturbed to age becomes a good wine, but if it is left too long it becomes undrinkable.[78] In Ps 75:9 (75:8 ET) dregs are clearly a judgment motif: the Lord the earth by making them drink a cup of spiced wine "down to the very dregs" (NIV). In Jer 25:15 a "cup of strong wine" is used as an image of judgment on the nations.[79]

There is a difference between the wine in this verse and the others cited above which may imply that this is not an image of judgment after all. The wine has been left to age on the lees then very carefully strained, resulting in a clear and strong wine.[80] Isaiah modifies שְׁמָרִים with a pual participle of זקק "to refine, filter, purify" (HALOT). In nearly every other case, the word is used for refining gold or silver.[81] The implication then is that the wine served at this banquet has been purified as carefully as one might purify gold or silver in order to make it of such a high quality it is acceptable at the Lord's banquet table. Therefore is it inappropriate to take this meal as a judgment on the nations since "all these phrases contribute to underline the excellency of the banquet."[82] The idea that those who worship in the house of the Lord participate in a wonderful meal is found several Psalms (23:5, 22:27, 36:9).[83]

75. Briggs and Briggs, *Psalms, II*, 73, commenting on Psalm 63:6 (63:5 ET). Briggs also associates the meal in Ps 36:9 ("feasting on the fatness," דֶּשֶׁן) in the house of the Lord) with a "messianic banquet."

76. "It is as if we heard stringed instruments played with the most rapid movement of the bow." Keil and Delitzsch, *Old Testament Commentary*, 7:286.

77. Zeph 1:12 combines שְׁמָרִים with קפא "to congeal, thicken." Selms compares this word to the Ugaritic *zmr*, van Selms, *Marriage and Family Life in Ugaritic Literature*, 101, but COS 1.103 (KTU 1.17:1:26–21.17:1:33) translates *zmr* as "song" rather than wine.

78. Typically commentaries will describe this wine as excellent, although the other two times "wine on lees" appears in the Hebrew Bible it is a negative image. For example, Young, *The Book of Isaiah*, 2:192.

79. Cf. *PsSol* 8:14. God judges Rome for Pompey's invasion by mixing them a drink of "wavering spirit" and a "cup of undiluted wine to make them drunk." This line is influenced by Isaiah 19:14 where the Lord gives Egypt a spirit of dizziness (NIV).

80. Oswalt, *The Book of Isaiah*, 464.

81. Job 28:1, Mal 3:3, Ps 12:7, 1 Chr 28:18, 29:4. The word appears also in Job 36:27 in the qal for filtering rain into water, although this is a difficult passage to interpret. In the DSS the word appears nine times, always in the pual. 1QHa 13:16 the words is used for refining gold, but it is clearly a metaphor for spiritual purification. In 1QHa 14:8 the word appears in the context of purifying a righteous remnant (cf. 1QHa 6:3). Spiritual purification is the meaning of the word in 1QS 4:20, 4Q429 f1ii:2, 4Q511 f35:2; 4Q427 f8i:17 (4QHa, *4QHodayota*). 4Q177 Col 2 uses the word in a citation of Psalm 12:7, which is applied to the Qumran community in 2:11. The community used the word to describe the process by which the remnant would become acceptable to God.

82. Hagelia, *Coram Deo: Spirituality in the Book of Isaiah*, 198.

83. Caution is still required. A description of judgment on the Gentiles is found in *2 Bar.* 13:8–11

The Lord Engulfs Death Forever (25:7)

After the description of the meal, Isaiah repeats the phrase "on this mountain" from v. 6 and extends the action of the Lord with the piel imperfect verb בלע: The Lord will "swallow up the shroud" (26:7). This word is never used for eating a meal in the Hebrew Bible; it is usually used to describe a spectacular judgment.[84] Unfortunately most English translations obscure this colorful metaphor by using more literal language such as "to destroy" (as in the NIV). Often the word appears with the Lord as subject (Lam 2:2, 5, 8, with Israel as the object; Hab 1:13, the wicked as object), although there are several examples of an enemy engulfing Israel (2 Sam 20:19, Isa 49:19; Lam 2:16, Hos 8:8). This word appears at both the beginning and ending of the line, but the object in each case is different. In the first case the object is the veil or shroud which covers all people, in the second case the object is death. This parallel structure suggests the veil or shroud should be interpreted in the light of "death," although "death" in 8a can be taken several ways.

The Lord is the subject of בלע, but the object is not something which is typically consumed. לוֹט has the sense of a covering or a wrap, hence the translation usual "shroud, sheet or veil."[85] Both לאט and לָט have the connotation of secrecy, hence a "veil." לָט has a particularly negative connotation as it is associated with sorcery in Exod 7:22, 8:3, 14. The word is modified, פְּנֵי־הַלּוֹט. The noun פְּנֵי is often left translated (NIV) or translated "the surface of the veil" (KJV) as if it referred to a cloth which covers a face. Alternatively, one might translate "veiled faces," as if the author was emphasizing the covered face, rather than the covering.[86] Wildberger comments that all of the various suggestions are "nothing but random attempts to make some sense of a perplexing phrase."[87] Nevertheless, he translates the word "mask" based on an Arabic cognate, *latia*.

There are a number of suggested solutions to the problem of the repetition of the word לוֹט. It is possible one occurrence is a participle from the same root, although this

---

which contains number of thematic and verbal similarities to Isaiah 25:6–8. The nations once drank "clarified wine," but now they will drink the dregs of wine. The excellent, aged wine becomes bitter dregs at the time of judgment. The Lord gave Israel a "cup of unmixed wine" so that they would greet Pompey as they might have greeted the Messiah (*PsSol* 8:14–17, with obviously parallels to Isa 40:3–5).

84. Lam 2:2, 5, 8; Isa 3:12; 49:19. The Red Sea swallows Egypt's army (Exod 7:12); the earth swallowed Korah rebellion (Nu 16:30–24). For literal swallowing see Gen 41:7, 24 (the swallowing of grain heads in Pharaoh's dream), Exod 7:12 (Aaron's snake swallowing the others, perhaps an implication of judgment), Jonah 2:1 (1:17 ET). As Wildberger notes, it is important to study who does the swallowing in the Hebrew Bible, Sheol (Exod 15:12, Num 16:32, 34), and Nebuchadnezzar is described as a monster who "swallows" the nation (Jer 51:34). Wildberger, *Isaiah 13–27*, 532.

85. The word appears in only three other contexts. In 1 Sam 21:10 for the wrappings in which the sword of Goliath was stored in Nob; in 2 Sam 19:5 David covers his face in mourning when he hears Absalom has been killed. In 1 Kgs 19:13, Elijah wraps his head when he leaves the cave on Sinai, having heard the "gentle whisper."

86. Caquot, "Remarques," 115–16.

87. Wilderbger, *Isaiah 12–27*, 524.

requires repointing the second appearance (הַלּוֹט becomes הַלּוּט, a passive participle in parallel with the passive participle, הַמַּסֵּכָה "to entwine").[88] It seems simpler to see this as another repetition to enhance the sound of the poetry, as with the description of the foods in the previous verse.[89] In addition, it is parallel to the next line which repeats a similar sounding word for "covering."

This shroud or veil is often taken as a symbol of mourning[90] although there is little lexical evidence to support this claim. It is also common to see the veil as an image of spiritual blindness, although the word is not used as a metaphor for blindness elsewhere in the Hebrew Bible.[91] The veil might also refer to the "vast destruction which God has wreaked on all the nations and peoples but is about to be removed."[92] Rather than the complete annihilation of all people, God has reversed his actions and is now inviting the nations to a great banquet where they will experience salvation. This suggestion too fails to provide linguistic evidence and is motivated by a New Testament perspective.[93]

The root for "entwine" is נסך II, a qal passive participle, "to entwine, to plait." The form is cognate to מַסֵּכָה, "a covering." Both words are only found in Isa 25:7, but מַסֵּכָה is also found in 28:20. נסך I is a more common verb which means "to pour, to pour out a libation." The action of pouring out a drink offering on an altar occurs primarily in the hifel, as in Gen 35:14. There Jacob sets up a stone pillar, pours out a drink offering, pours out an oil offering (שֶׁמֶן), and renames the location Beth-el because "God talked with him" in that place.[94] Since all of these are elements of a covenant, Hagelia suggests reading נסך in Isa 25:7 as "pouring out a drink offering" rather than "the sheet that covers" the nations" (NIV).[95] However, it is hard to see how this brings much light to Isa 25:7. Since this word is parallel to לוֹט, it seems better to read the root as referring to a veil or shroud as well.[96]

---

88. Kimhi, cited by Watts, *Isaiah 1–33*, 328, *GKC* 72p lists לוֹט as an active participle. The passive form appears in 1 Sam 21:10 (21:9 ET).

89. Cf. Delitzsch, *Old Testament Commentary*, 7:286, it is "written in this form, according to Isaiah's peculiar style, merely for the sake of the sound."

90. Brueggemann, *Isaiah 1–39*, 199.

91. This view is motivated by the use of "veil" in the New Testament. Kissane, for example, refers to 2 Cor. 3:15, a "veil of ignorance" which prevents gentiles from coming to salvation. Cf. Delitzsch, *Old Testament Commentary*, 7:268.

92. Seitz, *Isaiah 1–39*, 190.

93. Another possible connection to Ancient Near East ritual is the veiling of an idol during a Festival. During the Zukru Festival, Lord Dagan was brought out in a procession, his face uncovered, and then the people ate and drank. The face was then covered once again and the procession returned to the temple. ANET 387–89.

94. Compare this to Jacob in Gen 28:18–22. He anoints a stone with oil and enters a contractual agreement with the Lord. Mettinger, *King and Messiah*, 224–25.

95. Hagelia, "Meal on Mount Zion," 91.

96. Another possibility is to take נסך as referring a political leader, one who has been "consecrated." Caquot lists Theodotion, the Targum, Rashi as reading this word as a political authority, and

Jesus the Bridegroom

What does it mean that the Lord will "swallow" the veil? What is the "veil"? Perhaps it is best to stick with what the text tells us. The Lord consumes the veil and death. Therefore the "thing which enshrouds all people" is death (8a). The nations have come to Zion and have been served a banquet with their faces veiled. Now the Lord removes the veil by destroying it. As with the elements of the banquet, it is possible to take the removal of the veil as a positive image indicating salvation,[97] or as a negative image indicating impending judgment.[98] Once again, there is just a bit of ambiguity in the text which will be exploited by later readers as they apply this to new situations.

The text reaches a climax with the repetition of בלע, "to swallow" in 8a. This time the object is מָוֶת, "death." While this translation is accurate, it does not fully do justice to the idea of מָוֶת in the Hebrew Bible.[99] While anything which causes trouble in this life can be described as מָוֶת, this use of the word appears to go beyond "life's troubles."[100] That the Lord consumes the shroud and death by swallowing naturally suggests a connection to the Canaanite god Mot, well know from Ugaritic texts as the god of death, drought, disease, and wickedness, the god who swallows up all life. Since Isa 27:1 mentions Leviathan, a primordial chaos-monster and a later banquet text refer to Rahab (2 Bar. 29), it is likely that Isa 25:8 should be understood as an allusion to Mot. Mot is destroyed in the way he has destroyed all others, he is swallowed up לָנֶצַח, "forever."[101]

Symmashus as a "manifestation of authority." HALOT lists this as a function of the nifel, although a qal passive would have the same meaning. Psalm 2:6 is the only example in the Hebrew Bible of נסך as a consecrated leader, although the related noun נסך means a chief of a tribe, or a prince (Josh 13:21, Ezek 32:30, Mic 5:4, Ps 83:12). Caquot, "Remarques," 114. If this is the case, then the line would refer to the Lord destroying the veil or covering which is over the "princes of the people." These princes would therefore be parallel to the הַגּוֹיִם, "the nations," in the next line. This in and of itself does not suggest that the "princes of the people" are under judgment unless one understands לוֹט as a reference to judgment.

97. Oswalt, *The Book of Isaiah*, 464.

98. Caquot, "Remarques," 116.

99. Barth, *Die Errettung vom Tode in den individuellen Klage- und Dankliedern des Alten Testamentes*; Pardee, "As Strong as Death," 65–69; Bailey, *Biblical Perspectives on Death*; Watson, "The Death of 'Death' in the Ugaritic Texts," 60–64; Wakeman, *God's Battle with the Monster*, 106–8; Richards, "Death, Old Testament," 2:108–10; Lewis, "Mot," 4:922–24.

100. Wildberger, *Isaiah 13–27*, 533, citing Barth, *Die Erretung vom Tode*.

101. Wakeman, *God's Battle with the Monster*, 108. Wakeman cites Sarna, who comments that "Isa 25:7 may well mean that Mot shall be hoisted by his own petard!" That the devourer himself should be devoured is also found in Jer 51:34–44, although the language is applied to Babylon rather than Egypt. Both Aquila and Theodoton have εἰς νῖκος, in victory" rather than εἰς τέλος "forever," as in Symmachus. Most commentaries on the Hebrew Bible follow the MT (with the support of the Targum and Syriac), although matters are complicated by Paul's citation of this text in 1 Cor. 15:54, which has "in victory." Verse 8a is often thought to be a later interpolation because it seems to be a clear reference to resurrection and therefore a rather unique idea in the Hebrew Bible. If our understanding of the structure of the middle section of the unit is correct, then "death is swallowed forever" intentionally mirrors the first phrase, "the veil is destroyed" and is therefore critical to the understanding of the text. Cf. Millar, *Isaiah 24–27*, 41–42.

The defeat of Death is often described as "universal salvation" since these verses repeat four times that all people will have the veil removed and all people will have their tears wiped away. But as Wildberger points out, the idea of a festive meal in which all people will participate in salvation is unique in the Hebrew Bible, perhaps originating with the author of Isaiah.[102] In addition, v. 8c qualifies the people as "his people." This text is neither universal salvation nor is it exclusively Israel which is saved. All the nations come to Zion and all the nations participate in the banquet, but the removal of "reproach" refers only to "his people" and "the land" (8c). The nations will be invited to the banquet and some will in fact turn to the Lord, but not all experience salvation.[103] Universalism in this pericope is at best ambiguous.[104]

The Lord Removes Disgrace from All People (25:8b-d)

The Sovereign Lord will "wipe clean" the tears from all the faces. The root מחה, "to wipe" is normally associated with "blotting out" names or memories as a result of sin (Exod 32:32f, Deut 9:14, 29:19, 2 Kgs 14:27, Ps 9:6) or the destruction of life in the flood (Gen 6:7, 7:4, 7:23). In 1 Kgs 21:13 the word appears in a figure of speech for the destruction of Jerusalem as a result of Manasseh's sin. In Isa 5:17 the word is used for "ruins" which are the result of judgment. The word can also be used positively for the "blotting out" of sins (Isa 43:25, 44:22, Ps 51:3, 11, Zech 3:9). Isa 25:8 is the only

---

102. Wildberger, *Isaiah 13–27*, 525.

103. Seitz disagrees with this, pointing out that "his people" is now inclusive of both Israel and the nations, although he recognizes the tension between particularism and universalism present in this text (as well as in the New Testament). Seitz, *Isaiah 1–39*, 191–92. But not all will participate as guests—some are under the judgment of the Lord. Verses 10–12 indicate Moab will not be at the banquet eating the best of meats and finest of wines, they will be "trampled down in the manure." Berges suggests that the noun לוט has suggested to the author Lot, the father of the Moabites. *Jesaja 13–27*, 190. Like the first Exodus and the Passover meal, this invitation goes out to all, yet only those who respond will experience salvation, the rest will experience humiliation and judgment. It is generally accepted that there is universalism in this section of Isaiah. Johnson, for example, states that "The universalism could scarcely be more evident...." although he regards the Moab section a later interpolation. Johnson, "Devastation and Restoration," 189–90. There are some who argue the exclusion of Moab indicates this victory banquet is an elevation of Israel over its enemies. Redditt, "Isaiah 24–27: A Form Critical Analysis," 213–14.

104. This ambiguity is picked up in Second Temple period texts as well. Some writers do look forward to a conversion of the gentiles (especially Paul in the New Testament), but others see a complete destruction of the enemies of Israel, including most of unfaithful Israel (*4 Ezra*, the Qumran community). Gentile exclusion in *4 Ezra* stands in stark contrast to Isa 25:6–8. The saved in *4 Ezra* are exclusively the Jews who keep the law; the damned are the gentile nations. When they are destroyed, they are described as an "innumerable multitude" (13:5, 11, 34), a description which seems to say there are no "righteous gentiles" who will survive the final judgment. What is remarkable is a return of the ten tribes (13:40–45). That the ten tribes might be saved at the time of the final judgment may be an indication of mercy, since in the Hebrew Bible there is little good to be said for the northern kingdom. This does not help the discussion much at all since the salvation of anyone in the northern ten tribes can only be considered merciful in 100 CE!

example of מחה in the context of wiping tears.[105] The word is in parallel with סור in the hifel. While סור is used for simply removing something (such as clothing, Gen 38:14), when God is the subject there is an implication of judgment. In 2 Kings the Lord "removes" Israel, Judah or Jerusalem from his presence or from his sight.[106] The noun דִּמְעָה (tears) is consistently used in the context of mourning. The cause of the mourning is either one's personal sin (Ps 42:4, 56:9) or in response to judgment from the Lord.[107]

In parallel to the wiping of tears, the Lord will "take away the reproach of his people." The noun חֶרְפָּה, "reproach," is often associated with breach of covenant law[108] or some sort of shameful condition (childlessness Gen 30:23, uncircumcision, Gen 34:14, physical mutilation 1 Sam 11:2). In Isaiah the word is used five times outside of this context. In 4:1 it refers to a disgrace caused by childlessness and in 47:3 the nation of Babylon will be shamed when God judges them. But Isa 51:7 and 54:4 describe the shame of Israel in the context of a promise of restoration—the nation will no longer be shamed, there will be no more fear from the reproach of the nations.

Summary and Conclusions

In Isa 25:6-8 the prophet describes a covenant meal and / or enthronement scene at the time of the Lord's ascension to Zion. There are several key features of this eschatological banquet. First, there is an invitation to Israel to return to the mountain of God, now Zion, where all the people will participate in a meal prepared by their God. Second, the nations will be invited to participate in this banquet as well. For some of the participants the banquet is salvation but for others it is a judgment. Third, the meal inaugurates a time when Israel's shame is removed and her enemies are judged. Fourth, the meal is characterized by joy. The Lord wipes away every tear from the eyes of his people. Last, this image of a meal served on the Mountain of God evokes a wilderness tradition and anticipates a new Exodus of people to Zion.

As I will demonstrate in the next chapter, these traditional elements of an eschatological banquet are transformed in Isa 40-55 to describe the end of the Exile as a return to Zion. Israel is invited to participate in a new Exodus and a new journey through the Wilderness where they will participate in an on-going meal provided by God himself. The reproach of the nation will be reversed. In these chapters, Zion is

---

105. In Num 5:23 the word is used for erasing words from a document, although this is in the context of the punishment of an adulterous woman. Prov 30:20 uses the word for wiping a mouth. This too has a negative connotation since the verse refers to an adulteress who "wipes her mouth and says 'I have done nothing wrong'" (NIV).

106. 2 Kings 17:13, 23; 23:27; 24:23, Jer 32:31. Cf. Deut 38:37, Josh 5:9, Jer 6:1, Ezek 5:14-15.

107. Jer 8:23, 9:17, 13:17; Lam 1:2, 2:11, 18. In Isa 38:5 the word is used for Hezekiah's grief when he hears he is about to die and in 16:9 in an oracle against Moab.

108. Oswalt, *The Book of Isaiah*, 465.

personified as a woman who has lost her husband and children and the return from exile changes her tragedy into joy as her husband and children are restored to her.

These elements are found in other eschatological texts in the Second Temple period as well as in the teaching of Jesus. While there are no clear citations of Isa 25:6–8 in the teaching of Jesus, the invitation to join him in table fellowship resonates with this banquet of rich foods on Zion at the end of the age. Jeremias, for example, understood all of Jesus' use of feast and wedding imagery as standing on the foundation of Isa 25:6–8.[109] Like the eschatological banquet in Isa 25:6–8, Jesus' invitation to join his table fellowship was inclusive and open to all. These meals are described as joyful celebrations of salvation (Mark 2:18–20, Matt 9:10–13). Jesus stands within a long tradition of interpretation of the eschatological banquet. Just as other biblical and Second Temple Period writers developed the eschatological banquet and re-applied it to a new situation, so too Jesus develops the banquet by combining it with a marriage metaphor and applying that new version of the eschatological banquet to his on-going ministry.

I will now turn to a detailed examination of how Second Isaiah picks up the idea of Israel returning to the mountain of God at the end of the age and develops the journey back to Zion in chapter 40–66. In the next chapter will demonstrate that the banquet is not only on Mount Zion, but God invites his people to a continuous banquet as they come out of exile and return to the Land.

---

109. Jeremias, *Jesus' Promise to the Nations*, 63. While I will disagree with many of Jeremias' conclusions in chapter 7, this statement nevertheless summarizes well the point of this dissertation. Compare Sanders's comment that the Great Banquet (Luke 14) the riff-raff sharing table fellowship with Jesus are analogous to the Israelites as slaves eating in God's presence at Sinai. Sanders, "Banquet of the Dispossessed," 362.

4

A Banquet in the Wilderness

Introduction

In the previous chapter I argued that Isa 25:6–8 describes a covenant meal at the beginning of the eschatological age. The key word used for the meal in Isa 25:6 is מִשְׁתֶּה, a word which refers a banquet or a festive meal especially related to a joyous occasion, but also appears in a number of enthronement or covenant contexts with or without the implication of a "festive" meal. Isa 25:6–8 describes the beginning of the eschatological age as a time when God will overcome his enemies and recall his people to his mountain in order to renew his covenant with them. Just like the first Exodus, God will once again overcome his enemies as he did in the plagues and the defeat of Egypt at the Red Sea. Like Exodus 24, God will bring his people out of captivity in order to establish his covenant with them on the mountain. Rather than Sinai, this time Zion will be the mountain of God. Rather than restricting the meal to only the elders as representatives of the people, God will invite all people to the mountain to eat a royal banquet as a symbol of universal salvation. Rather than defeating Egypt, Assyria, or Babylon, the Lord will defeat the ultimate enemy, Death. Death itself will be consumed as Rahab was in the Exodus (cf. Ps 74). The tradition of the Exodus is used to describe the expectation of a return from exile.

The task of this chapter is to survey the development of the eschatological banquet motif in Second Isaiah by tracing the New Exodus tradition found in these chapters.[1] In addition to the Exodus, the writer of Isa 40–55 develops the Wilderness tradition in order to describe the present "messianic" possibility of a return from exile.[2] There is

---

1. The concern here is the use of Exodus and Wilderness language in Second Isaiah. That Isaiah used other scripture is a complex topic which goes well beyond the present study. See Sommer, "Allusions and Illusions," 156–86 as well as his more detailed *A Prophet Reads Scripture*.

2. These texts are messianic in that they refer to a future time in which God will act by gathering Israel and returning them to their Land. To what extent they are "future" or "eschatological" will vary

a pool of vocabulary and themes which re-occur throughout the Wilderness tradition which the author of Isaiah 40–55 crafted into a plea to his audience to return to the Land. These themes include plentiful provision of food and water by the hand of the Lord, and a re-entry into the Land of the Promise. I will first describe what I mean by a Wilderness tradition and then set the context of Second Isaiah. I will then survey these passages as they appear in Second Isaiah for the purpose of demonstrating that the author thought of the return from exile not simply as a new Exodus, but as a new Wilderness journey. The return is a described as a "banquet in the wilderness." As such, the writer developed the earlier Exodus and Wilderness traditions by combining them with the tradition of an eschatological meal in order to apply them to his present circumstance, the end of the exile.

While Isa 40–55 describes the end of the exile as an on-going banquet in the wilderness rather than an inaugural banquet, elements of the banquet from Isa 25:6–8 appear. The section begins and ends with an invitation to participate in the journey from the place of exile to Zion (40:1–5, 55:1–5). Throughout these chapters the Lord provides food and water for the returning exiles, culminating in an entry into a restored Land which as fertile as Eden (55:10–13). The shame of the participants in this on-going meal will be removed. Zion is personified as a woman who mourns her lost husband and children. She will be comforted (51:1–3) and her children restored (54:1–3). Zion's shame is reversed and once again she will be dressed as a glorious bride (52:1–2, 54:10). Isaiah 40–55 develops the idea of an eschatological banquet not only by combining it with wilderness traditions but also with a marriage metaphor in order to apply the banquet to the end of the exile.

This section is limited to Isa 40–55 for several reasons. First, the Exodus motif dominates these chapters. As will be shown below, language drawn from both the Exodus and wilderness travels is repeated throughout the chapters. Since there are clear verbal and thematic links between many of these texts and book of Exodus, this is an example of the intertextual process as described in chapter 2. While there are clear references to the Exodus and wilderness in other sections of the Hebrew Bible, Isa 40–55 is the primary example. Second, the use of the wilderness as a positive experience in Isa 40–55 is perhaps unique. In Hosea, for example, the wilderness is primarily a place of punishment. In Isa 40–55, however, the prophet calls the people back through the wilderness and back to Zion in a joyous procession. Third, the point of this study of the Exodus and wilderness in Isa 40–55 is to provide the foundation for a study of Jesus' image of a wedding banquet for his ministry. As such, material from Isa 40–55 is especially important since these chapters were not only known by Second Temple period Judaism, but they were discussed extensively by Jewish teachers contemporary

---

based on theological presuppositions. Schoors, for example, sees no eschatology or messianism in Second Isaiah. Schoors, "L'eschatologie dans la prophéties du Deutéro-Isaïe," 107–28. Since Second Isaiah has includes an anointed servant of God, it is proper to describe the eschatological age as a "messianic age."

to Jesus. While Jesus does not allude to Isa 25:6–8, the key banquet text in the Hebrew Bible, he does allude in both his actions and teaching to Isa 40–55.

What is the Wilderness Tradition?

Studies which focus on the New Exodus theme have a ready-made pool of texts from which the Exodus motif is drawn. It is the same case with the Wilderness tradition. A study of Isa 40–55 provides an opportunity to observe intertextual relationships described in chapter two at work as the author develops the events of the Red Sea and the entry into the Land of the Promise and applied them to his own view of the return from Exile. This typological pattern will continue to resonate into the Second Temple period, as observed by U. Mauser in his monograph tracing the development of a New Exodus / Wilderness tradition in the Gospel of Mark.[3] Mauser finds this material "very heterogeneous" since the New Exodus motif called to mind the whole wilderness period from the eighth-century prophets onward.[4] The Wilderness tradition is important since it is in the wilderness that Israel was born as a nation.[5]

Contents of the Wilderness Tradition

Clearly the book of Exodus must be included as the foundation to the tradition. It is in Exodus when God first provides food and water for his people in the wilderness (Exod 16–17). In response to complaints from the people, the Lord provides both food and water, but only just enough to survive in the wilderness. This provision of food is described as a good and miraculous provision in Num 24:6–7. Portions of Deuteronomy

---

3. Mauser, *Christ in the Wilderness*. See also Galling, *Die erwählungstraditionen Israels*; Bonnard, "La Signification du desert, selon le Nouveau Testament," in *Hommage et reconnaissance*, 9–18; Sahlin, "Zur Typologie des Johannesevangeliums"; Mánek, "The New Exodus in the Books of Luke," 8–23; Schmauch, *Orte der Offenbarung und der Offenbarungsort im Neuen Testament*; Anderson, "The Role of the Desert in Israelite Thought," 41–44; Funk, "The Wilderness," 205–14; Smith, "Exodus Typology in the Fourth Gospel," 349–52; Riemann, "Desert and Return to Desert in the Pre-exilic Prophets"; Fritz, *Israel in der Wüste*; Coats, "Conquest Traditions in the Wilderness Theme," 177–90; Addinall, "The Wilderness in Pedersen's Israel," 75–83; Kallai, "The Wandering-Traditions from Kadesh-Barnea to Canaan: A Study in Biblical Historiography," 175–84; Burden, "The Wilderness Traditions in the Hebrew Bible"; Levine, "The Land of Milk and Honey," 43–57; Leal, *Wilderness in the Bible: Toward a Theology of Wilderness*; Douglas, *In the Wilderness: The Doctrine of Defilement in the Book of Numbers*; Leveen, *Memory and Tradition in the Book of Numbers*.

4. Mauser, *Christ in the Wilderness*, 17. Similarly, "In Deutero-Isaiah we encounter an extraordinary blending of exodus and Zion traditions" (Clements, *Prophecy and Covenant*, 115).

5. Mauser, *Christ in the Wilderness*, 23. Mauser also points out that it is in the wilderness that God reveals his name and his law, beginning the religions life of Israel (ibid., 29). He finds the three major elements of Israel's theology initiated in the wilderness: covenant and law, election, and rebellion. The Covenant is established at Sinai, confirming Israel's election. Immediately, however, there is rebellion against God in the golden calf incident. Compare to Ochs who states that the wilderness "provides the single most informative experience in the creation of the Jewish people." Ochs, "The Desert, Biblical Spirituality, and Creation," 493–508, 493; cf. Ochs, "The Presence of the Desert," 293–306.

should be included in the Wilderness Tradition as well, since there is a review of the wilderness sojourn in the prologue to the book (Deut 1–3). Mauser comments that by the time Deuteronomy was written, the "wilderness period has become a text for a sermon."[6] In fact, it is in these wilderness stories that Israel's religious life begins. It is in the wilderness that God reveals his name and establishes his covenant with his people.[7] The wilderness is also the place of Israel's initial and continual rebellion against God. Complaints about food and water in Exod 16–17 indicate the people are unsure of the Lord's intentions and idolatry is a problem as early as Exod 32. This twin theme of revelation and rebellion reoccurs in development of the Wilderness tradition in the prophets and psalms.

Joshua 1–5 forms a conclusion to the historical Wilderness tradition. In fact, the beginning of the provision of manna and its cessation provide a framework for the wilderness narrative.[8] Manna ceased with entry into the land (Josh 5:12), but only after the celebration of the first Passover in the land. This celebration in Joshua therefore looks back at the history of the nation but also forward to the entry into the Land. The context of the cessation of manna is critical. When the people cross the Jordan following the lead of the Ark of the Covenant (Josh 3:14–17), they set up twelve stones at Gilgal as a memorial (4:1–9). The Ark is removed from the river and the people are only then officially "in the land" (4:18–24). The report of this event is laced with references to the Exodus and the crossing of the Red Sea. Once in the land, Joshua commands circumcision of those who had traveled in the wilderness (5:1–9), parallel to the circumcision of Moses' sons, born while he was in the wilderness for forty years (Exod 4:26). After the people celebrate the first Passover in the land and begin to eat of the produce of the land, the manna ceases.

Development of the Wilderness Tradition

Chronologically, Amos represents one of the earliest uses of the Wilderness tradition in the Hebrew Bible.[9] Writing in the eighth century, Amos 2:9–12 and 3:1 employs

---

6. Mauser, *Christ in the Wilderness*, 20, assuming a sixth-century date for Deuteronomy.

7. Ibid., 23, citing Bright, *History of Israel*, 113.

8. Wagenaar, "The Cessation of Manna: Editorial Frames for the Wilderness Wandering in Exodus 16,35 and Joshua 5,10–12," 192–209. Burden also makes this observation, although he places Josh 5 outside the original collection of Wilderness texts. Joshua 5 represents the kerygma of the Wilderness tradition rather than the tradition itself. Burden, "The Wilderness Traditions in the Hebrew Bible: Kerygma and Community of Faith," 197.

9. Based on the historical references in the book itself, Hubbard states that "scholarly consensus" has settled on a date of 760–55 BC for the ministry of Amos, see Hubbard, *Joel and Amos*. On the date of Amos, see Stuart, *Hosea-Jonah*, 294; Hayes, *Amos*, 31–39; Andersen and Freedman, *Amos*, 141; Hasel, *Understanding the Book of Amos*, 77; Terrien, "Amos and Wisdom," 108–15. Finley, *Joel, Amos, and Obadiah*, 106. Wolff has developed a complex six-stage development of the book of Amos in which chapters 3–5 are the oldest layers of the text. Wolff, *Joel and Amos*. Compare this to Willoughby, "Amos, Book of," 1:211. In either scheme, the Wilderness tradition is embedded in the earliest strata of the book.

the Wilderness tradition (Num 13:32–33, Deut 1:28; 9:2) and the Exodus (Exod 20:2) in order to pronounce impending judgment on the northern kingdom of Israel. Amos draws attention to the delay between the salvation event and the entry into the land, implicitly recalling God's patience with the Israelites in the wilderness.[10] Amos' method can be described as inner-biblical or intertextual exegesis, even if there are no actual texts for Amos to use. Amos reflects a well-known tradition that Israel was "in the wilderness" for some time before they entered the land. He is able to recall that tradition and use this language as part of his own prophetic speech. While this tradition is found in the book of Numbers, it is impossible to know whether Amos knew Numbers or the same traditions which are found in the canonical book of Numbers.

Amos' contemporary Hosea employs similar imagery in 2:16–20 (ET 14–16). Within the overall metaphor of a marriage, Hosea describes the period of the wilderness testing as "alluring a lover," resulting in a restoration of the marital relationship.[11] There is some ambiguity in the wilderness image in Hosea: was this first time in the wilderness a good or bad experience?[12] As demonstrated by S. Talmon, the wilderness normally has a negative connotation in the Hebrew Bible as a place of judgment.[13] However, it is possible to see the wilderness as a time of preparation before entry into the land. In this sense, it could be a positive image. Yet it is also possible to read

10. This text explicitly refers to the Amorites as "tall as cedars" and the 40-year sojourn in the wilderness. What is more, verses 11–12 refer to the Nazarites, original described in Numbers 6:1–21. This point is made by Jeremias, *The Book of Amos*, 41. Wolff takes verse ten as a deuteronomistic redaction, explaining the reverse order of wilderness—exodus. Wolff, *Joel and Amos*, 112. Andersen and Freedman evaluate the arguments for and against an insertion, concluding the evidence is far from conclusive, and note that it is "gratuitous to declare that Deuteronomic traditions did not exist in any form before the seventh century." Andersen and Freedman, *Amos*, 328–29.

11. This is a particularly interesting passage since there is a combination of wilderness tradition with the metaphor of a marriage. If the Lord is a bridegroom for Israel, then the wilderness period is the courtship or the invitation to the marriage. The marriage metaphor in Hos as well as Isa and Jer will be detailed in chapter 5. As Brueggemann states, "Wilderness, that is exile, is for remember and seducing and covenant making." Brueggemann, *The Land*, 125.

12. Davies, "The Wilderness Years: Utopia and Dystopia in the Book of Hosea," 163.

13. Studies on the "wilderness motif" usually focus on both the geographical and "socioreligious" aspects of the concept. Talmon, "The 'Desert Motif' in the Bible and Qumran Literature," 57, cf. Talmon, "Wilderness," 946–49. For similar assessments, see Davies, "Wilderness Wandering," 6:912–14; Fox, "Jeremiah 2:2 and the Desert Ideal," 441–50. These studies are evaluated by DeRoche, "Jeremiah 2:2–3 and Israel's Love for God During the Wilderness Wanderings," 364–76. Leal concludes a survey of Talmon and his critics by saying that there is "no definitive resolution" to the problem, although his monograph argues that the wilderness motif is overwhelmingly positive. Leal, *Wilderness in the Bible*, 192. Childs concludes that the tradition itself is neither positive nor negative, but that later writers adapted it to be either an ideal time (Hos and Jer) while for others it was negative (Ezekiel). Childs, *Exodus*, 263. While Goldingay realizes that the word "wilderness" itself does not have an inherently negative connotation, the experiences of Israel in the wilderness were negative since the people themselves were rebellious. Goldingay, *Israel's Gospel*, 458. Propp, detects a negative and mythological use of the wilderness traditions. Propp, *Water in the Wilderness*. Levine studied the phrase "milk and honey" and concluded that a land "oozing with milk and honey" is neither a "desert ideal" nor a "nomadic ideal." The emphasis of the phrase is on covenant loyalty which God rewards with prosperity in the land. Levine, "The Land of Milk and Honey," 43–57.

A Banquet in the Wilderness

Hosea's use of Wilderness tradition as negative since it was a time of testing and failure for Israel. As A. Leveen argues, the wilderness is a critical transition between the previous age in Egypt and God's future plan in the land of the promise.[14] Just as Israel needed to be cleansed of Egypt before entering the land of the promise, so too in the future Israel must be once again purged of her idolatry and rebellion during a time in the wilderness. A text like Hosea 13:4–6 may be taken as evidence that the wilderness image was used by Hosea to point to the sinfulness of the nation from its origins. Hosea 9:10, however, seems to hint at an original innocence of the nation since the Lord found Israel like new grapes in the wilderness. The nation was innocent, "in their first season," until they came to Baal-Peor.[15] Israel is therefore pictured in Hosea as an innocent bride who becomes a prostitute during the wilderness sojourn, but she is promised restoration by way of a return to the wilderness to start her marriage anew. The next chapter will examine the wilderness imagery in Hosea.

In Jer 31 the image of a return from exile and the wilderness journey is used as a metaphor for the predicted return form Exile.[16] Jeremiah is told that those who survive the sword will find favor in the wilderness (31:2) and will be gathered back to Zion as a shepherd gathers his sheep (31:10–11) where they will "rejoice in the bounty of the Lord" (31:12). The people will live in a well-watered land which has abundant produce (31:13, 15) and joy will once again return to the Land (31:14). Like Isa 40, Jeremiah refers to the highway on which the Virgin Israel will return to Zion (31:21). In fact, this New Exodus is described as a "new thing" (31:22, cf. Isa 43:19). The climax of this vision in 31:23–25 makes explicit both the motifs of New Exodus and Wilderness journey which resonates with Isa 25:6–8: the Lord will bring his people back to the sacred mountain and they will be satisfied.[17]

Ezek 20 uses the wilderness tradition as well, although he develops it as an image of judgment rather than hope.[18] When the Lord brought the people up out of Egypt, he commanded them to leave their idols (20:7) but they chose to retain them (20:8–9). The people in the wilderness rebelled against the Lord, yet a remnant survived (20:13–

---

14. "The people carry the vestiges of their lives in Egypt into the wilderness. To destroy Egypt, God must destroy the generation." Leveen, *Memory and Tradition*, 94. This is the conclusion of P. Riemann, who argued that the pre-exilic prophets saw the wilderness as a threatening place filled with judgment. Riemann, "Desert and Return to Desert in the Pre-exilic Prophets," 60–61.

15. Davies, "The Wilderness Years," 168. There is an implication in Hos 9:10 of marriage infidelity as well, since the sin at Baal-Peor was men going to cultic prostitutes. On a physical level this is marital infidelity, on a spiritual level this is idolatry.

16. This well-known text is cited by Jesus at his final meal with his disciples also has an Exodus motif. In 31:32 Jeremiah clearly sets the new covenant in contrast with the old made with the people after they have come up out of Egypt. It is perhaps significant that the old covenant is described here in terms of a marriage contract. Israel broke the covenant "though I was a husband to them." This text will be covered in more detail in chapter 5.

17. The verb רוה in the hifel has the idea of watering thoroughly and appears in Isa 55:10. Isaiah 43:24 is ironic: the Lord has been "thoroughly filled up" with the sins of the people.

18. Mauser comments that this chapter describes the wilderness period as "the odious impression of futile repetition." Mauser, *Christ in the Wilderness*, 49.

20). So too in Ezekiel's day (fall of Jerusalem), a generation of Israel will be cut off while a remnant survives to be gathered from the nations and brought back into the wilderness (20:34). The language is reminiscent of the Exodus ("a mighty hand and outstretched arm"), but this time the wilderness will be place of judgment (20:37–38). Those who survive will return to the holy mountain in Jerusalem and will worship the Lord properly (20:39–44). Once again, this return to Zion recalls Isa 25:6–8.

Several psalms develop the wilderness tradition. Of primary importance are Psalms 78[19], 105[20] and 106[21] because they re-apply the Exodus and Wilderness tradition to later contexts. Ps 95:8–10 describes the failure at Meribah and describes the whole period as a time of "testing." Whether these Psalms are pre-exilic or written during the exile, they provide a pool of vocabulary for the Wilderness tradition from which Isa 40–55 may have drawn.

Nehemiah's prayer in Neh 9:12–23 is a clear representative of a post-exilic wilderness tradition. The vocabulary and themes of this section represent the state of the Exodus and Wilderness tradition in the fifth century BCE. Nehemiah refers to the Exodus, the Lord's leadership to Sinai, the gift of the Law, and the rebellion of the people in the wilderness. Like the Psalms, this prayer of the elders of Israel reviews the history of Israel in order to recall the goodness of God in his past rescue and provision for the people as well as his patience during the rebelliousness of the Israelites in the wilderness.[22] That Neh 9 is a celebration of the Feast of Booths should not be missed. The people are replaying the wilderness journey after they have returned from exile and are therefore enacting the biblical story. It is even possible that the prayer in Nehemiah 9 is a reflection on Isaiah 41.[23]

An important feature of Nehemiah's prayer is that the foundation for God's provision for his people in the wilderness is his compassion (9:19). The noun רַחֲמִים has the connotation of strong, even visceral emotion.[24] The word is always used of a superior

---

19. Rad describes Psalm 78 a meditation on history which becomes "a somber confession of Israel's failures." Rad, *Old Testament Theology*, 1:357. As such, it may be dated as early as the Assyrian crisis of the early eighth century. The description of the plagues in 78:49–51 with Exod 12:29–30 and Isa 27:36–37 are quite similar. Lee, "The Context and Function of the Plagues Tradition in Psalm 78," 83–89. The Psalm could plausibly date to the tenth century according to Campbell, "Psalm 78: A Contribution to the Theology of Tenth Century Israel," 51–79.

20. Terrien argues for a pre-exilic date based on the lack of reference to Assyrian or Babylonian invasions. Terrien, *The Psalms*, 725. Fensham, however, treats Psalms 105 and 106 along with the prayer in Nehemiah 9 as post-exilic. Fensham, "Neh 9 and Pss 105, 106, 135 and 136: Post-exilic Historical Traditions in Poetic Form," 35–51.

21. Terrien dates Psalm 106 to the "latter part of the exile" when Babylon was giving way to Persia on the basis of verse 46. Terrien, *The Psalms*, 733. Weiser declines to date the psalm, however. He applies the captivity of verse 46 only to the northern kingdom. Weiser, *The Psalms*, 680.

22. Van Wijk-Bos, *Ezra, Nehemiah, and Esther*, 81.

23. For a chart detailing an impressive number of allusions to the rest of the Hebrew Bible, see Meyers, *Ezra—Nehemiah*, 167–69.

24. Stoebe, "רחם," in *TLOT* 3:1225–30; Dahmen, "רחם," *TDOT* 13:437–54. In general, the LXX translates רחם and cognates with ἔλεος, οἰκτιρμός, and σπλάγχνον. Fishbane argued that the verb is

toward an inferior, such as a father toward a child (Ps 103:13, for example), but most often God is the subject.[25] This is not sentimentality, but rather the suspension of wrath and restoration of a relationship. The verb is used in Isa 55:7, for example, to describe the restoration of relationship after a person has repented of sin and turned toward God: he receives a "pardon." This statement of God's love and compassion stands at the center of the prayer, between descriptions of the rebellion of the people of Israel in the wilderness.[26] The word is often coupled with חֶסֶד in the Hebrew Bible (Hos 2:21, 11:8). Hosea 2 is a clear use of the term as part of the marriage metaphor. In fact, when חֶסֶד is in the singular and it precedes רַחֲמִים, then the two terms are to be understood together as a "demonstration of mercifulness."[27] Because of his compassion, the Lord did not abandon his people in the wilderness. The verb עזב ("abandon") is common in the Hebrew Bible, but is related to the Akkadian *ezêbu*, to divorce. The word has this sense in Isa 54:6, 60:15 and 62:4. Combined with the presence of רַחֲמִים, Neh 9:19 might be described as employing a marriage metaphor for the wilderness period. Both words appear again in the climax of Nehemiah's prayer (9:31).

Isaiah 40–55 therefore stands within this Wilderness tradition regardless of an eighth- or sixth-century date, although the author uses the Wilderness to describe the restoration of Israel to Zion. This "positive" use of the Wilderness tradition is perhaps unique in the Hebrew Bible. This development of traditions found continues in the Second Temple period and into the teaching of Jesus, who invites Israel to join him in the wilderness to celebrate the restoration of their relationship with their God.

Isaiah 40–55: Unity and Themes

While it is certain that Isa 40–55 is a literary unit, the authorship of the section is far less certain.[28] Since B. Duhm's commentary on Isaiah was published, the designation

---

used in as a treaty formula in Amos 1:11 on the basis on the Vassal Treaties of Esarhaddon ("you will love [the king] as yourself") as well as the treaty between Jonathan and David. In both examples אבד or cognate is used, but in the Aramaic of *The Wisdom of Ahikar*, lines 11 and 51, the root נחם is used to describe the love of the Assyrian king for Ahikar. What is more, the Akkadian *râmu* ("to love") is etymologically relate to רחם and appears in treaty formulae. Fishbane therefore argued that Amos 1:11 used רחם to describe a treaty relationship between Judah and Edom which the Edomites broke. Coote agreed that Fishbane's suggestion that Amos 1:11 is a treaty is "surely correct," although he disagreed with Fishbane's proposal that רחם is related to *râmu*. Fishbane, "Treaty Background of Amos 1:11 and Related Matters," 313–18. Coote, "Additional Remarks on *rhmyh* (Amos 1:11)," 206–8; Fishbane, "Additional Remarks on *rhmyh* (Amos 1:11)," 391–92.

25. Four-fifths of the occurrences and in no case is the word used to describe the love of a human towards God. Stoebe, "1229 ",רחם. In a similar penitential prayer, 4QDibHama (*4QWords of the Luminariesa*) uses רחם in at least two lines (frag 4, line 5; frag 7, line 11).

26. Williamson, *Ezra, Nehemiah*, 314.

27. Stoebe, "1230 ",רחם, see Jer 16:5, where the withdrawal of love and pity makes Israel like a funeral.

28. Goldingay and Payne, *Isaiah 40–55*, 1:4. Goldingay and Payne rightly point out that there is no such thing as a "book of Deutero-Isaiah" which simply lacks a heading. However canonical Isaiah came together, chapters 40–55 are well integrated into the overall design of the sixty-six chapters of

"Deutero-Isaiah" for chapters 40–55 has become almost universal among scholars.[29] Duhm divided the book into three units on the basis of clear stylistic differences between chapters 1–39, 40–55, and 56–66. Despite modifications to Duhm's thesis, these divisions are retained in virtually every discussion of Isaiah since the first section of the book is primarily condemnation and imminent judgment on Judah within the context of the eighth-century Assyrian crisis. As Bruggemann describes it, the first half of Isaiah is a "critique" of the ideology of Judah in the light of the fall of the northern kingdom.[30] The second half of Isaiah seems primarily concerned with comfort, redemption and the end of the Babylonian exile. The fact that Isa 44:28 and 45:1 mention the name of the Persian king Cyrus is often considered proof that the section was written after Cyrus conquered the Babylonians and released the Jews from captivity. In general, chapters 40–55 are associated with the sixth-century hope for a return from Exile in the light of the fall of Babylon. Chapters 56–66 are associated with the early fifth century, although proposals for a historical context for Third-Isaiah are much less confident.[31] It is possible the third section (chapters 56–66, or "Trito-Isaiah") expresses a frustration with the lack of return from Exile.

But as Bruggemann says, Isa 40–55 "seems to take the Exodus as a type and urge that the deliverance now supercedes the old event."[32] Did the "old traditions" of the Exodus fail? Is the exile proof that the hopes of Moses and David were cancelled? Isaiah 40–55 indicates that the Exodus event is the pattern on which the new Exodus is built. N. Snaith describes the author of Isa 40–55 as the prophet of the return from exile since, as he reads the book, the return from exile is the prophet's only theme.[33] W. Zimmerli considered the allusions to the New Exodus in these chapters as so striking that they are central to the prophecy of unit.[34] J. Muilenburg also sees Isa 40–55 as describing the Lord's new work "in language drawn from the Exodus."[35] G. W. Buchanan sees the New Exodus as "obvious, even to the casual reader."[36] A. Schoors points out that since the fundamental theological basis for Israel's election and salvation is historical, the Exodus must be the primary historical event for the author of Isa 40–55.[37] The New Exodus theme seems predominant in all of Second Isaiah with the possible exception of the Servant Songs. But even in this section A. Ceresko has traced suf-

---

the book. For a defense of a single author for the whole book of Isaiah, see Archer, *A Survey of Old Testament Introduction*, 329–51; and Harrison, *Introduction to the Old Testament*, 764–95.

29. Duhm, *Das Buch Jesaia*.

30. Brueggemann, "Unity and Dynamic in the Isaiah Tradition," 102.

31. Ibid., 89.

32. Bruggemann, "Unity," 97.

33. Snaith, *Studies on the Second Part of the Book of Isaiah*, 147. See also Stuhlmueller, *Creative Redemption in Deutero-Isaiah*, 59.

34. Zimmerli, "Le nouvel 'exode' dans le message de deux grands prophètes de 'exil," 221.

35. Muilenburg, "Introduction to Isaiah Chapters 40–66," 399–400.

36. Buchanan, "Isaianic Midrash and the Exodus," 101.

37. Schoors, *I Am God Your Saviour*, 172.

fering language to the enslavement of Israel in Egypt.[38] Suffering in Egypt serves as a "proximate preparation for a (new) exodus and return to the promised land."[39]

Isaiah 40–55 goes beyond the events of the Red Sea, however. The writer is less interested in the "salvation event" than the journey in the wilderness. In Isa 25:6–8 the prophet was interested in an eschatological re-interpretation of Sinai as Zion. But in Isa 40–55 this same eschatology is now realized. Salvation has already come in the person of the Lord's anointed (Cyrus). The battle against Babylon has been won, all that remains is to undertake the journey back to the promised land. This second journey will be similar to the first, but there is no description of hardship since the Lord's provision will be so grand that the wasteland of the wilderness will become like the Garden of Eden. The wilderness journey becomes a "triumphant, miraculous procession."[40]

Beginning with B. Child, studies on Isaiah began to look at the book as a whole rather than three separate books artificially placed together by some late editor.[41] Childs saw the final form of all 66 chapters as the work of a conscious editorial process, suppressing the historical context of 40–55 and 56–66 as well as editing the original book in order to bring the three units together theologically.[42] Given the insights of Childs, the date of Isa 40–55 may not be critical to the overall point of this study since the interest of this study is in the development of the New Exodus / Wilderness tradition. If this development is only within the lifetime of an eighth-century prophet or over the course of the two-hundred years between the eighth and sixth century, it should not detract from the overall argument of this proposal. In tracing these themes, it is assumed that the early sections of Isaiah are foundational to the writer of Isa 40–55. Like Isa 25:6–8, Isa 40–55 takes up the language of Exodus but applies it to the return from Exile after the fall of Babylon.[43] Once again God defeats his enemies and once again he will lead his people through the wilderness and back to the Land. Missing in this new Exodus is a gathering at the mountain for a renewal of the covenant. There is no victory banquet on the Mountain of God to celebrate the destruction of Babylon.

38. Ceresko, "The Rhetorical Strategy of the Fourth Servant Song (Isaiah 52:13—53:12): Poetry and the Exodus-New Exodus," 47.

39. Ceresko, "The Rhetorical Strategy of the Fourth Servant Song," 51.

40. Diamond, "Desert," 4:524.

41. Childs, *Introduction to the Old Testament as Scripture*.

42. Childs, *Introduction*, 325–30. This observation was the starting point for R. Heskett's study of Messianism in Isaiah. Heskett examines messianism in the final form of Isaiah rather than tracing potential trajectories or developments of messianic thought from pre-exilic traditions (Isa 1–36) to the later post-exilic interpretations of the "school of Isaiah" (ibid., 40–55, 56–66). In emphasizing the way in which Isaiah "functions as a scriptural book" Heskett applies Childs' method, although he makes contributions which go beyond the "canonical criticism" of Childs as well as the "scriptural approach" of Juel, his dissertation advisor. Beginning with what he calls "pre-biblical" traditions, Heskett attempts to show that the final form of Isaiah has worked within the bounds of scripture to reread earlier texts as expressions messianic hope even if these texts had historical referents or were originally ambiguous. Heskett, *Messianism within the Scriptural Scroll of Isaiah*. Heskett does not deal with the messianic banquet in his monograph and does not treat chapters 24–27 at all.

43. Soggin, *Introduction to the Old Testament*, 316.

The writer of Isa 40–55 is more interested in drawing from the Wilderness tradition rather than the Exodus event. As such, the provision of food and water in the wilderness come to the forefront. The journey from exile to restoration is not simply a return to the land of Israel, it is a return to Eden. As such, the provision of food and water is described in terms of abundance freely provided by the Lord himself.

As B. W. Andersen has commented, what characterized the worship of ancient Israel was the "remembrance and rehearsal of a real past."[44] This is not a recycling of the past, but rather the idea that the Lord has already planned and prepared for the future in similar ways to his past acts of salvation. This re-use of Exodus and Wilderness traditions seems to be the clear thematic element in Isa 40–55. For the writer of this section, the "former things" are about to become "new things." The new saving activity of God will be so grand that it will cause the people to forget the "old things" of the first Exodus.

What of the meal on Sinai / Zion which was central to 25:6–8? While there is no covenant meal scene in Isa 40–55, the Lord's provision of food and water during the journey to Canaan is developed in Isa 40–55. Like Isa 25:6–8, the whole people eat and drink from the hand of the Lord. The bountiful provision is described in creation-like terms. Just as the Lord provided for humans in the Garden of Eden, so too will he provide again in the return from exile. One might object that the provision of food and water is not a "banquet" in the traditional sense of a Mesopotamian victory banquet or a spectacular wedding feast. But eating in the wilderness was eating in the presence of God and it was eating the food which he provided. While water and manna seem to be a slight fare for a "banquet," the food is less important than the symbolism of eating food provided by the hand of God in the very presence of God.

The Wilderness Tradition in Second Isaiah

In order to survey the Exodus and Wilderness texts in chapters 40–55, it will be helpful to identify what smaller units are most directly connected to the "new Exodus" motif. The following texts represent my own reading of Isa 40–55, supplemented by

44. Anderson, "Exodus Typology," 193. For other studies on the Exodus motif in Second Isaiah, see Zillessen, "Der alte und der neue Exodus," 289–304; Fischer, "Das Problem des neuen Exodus in Isaias c. 40–55," 111–30; Harvey, "La typologie de l'Exode dans les Psaumes," 383–405; Daube, *The Exodus Pattern in the Bible*; Beaudet, "La typologie de l'Exode dans le Second-Isaïe," 11–21; Childs, "Deuteronomic Formulae of the Exodus Traditions," 30–39; Anderson, "Exodus and Covenant in Second Isaiah and Prophetic Tradition," 339–60; Kiesow, *Exodustexte im Jesajabuch: literarkritische und motivgeschichtliche Analysen*; Coats, "The Sea Tradition in the Wilderness Theme: A Review," 2–8; Simian-Yofre, "Exode en Deuteroisaias," 530–53; Bienaimé, "Un retour du Paradis dans le désert de l'Exode selon une tradition juive," 429–49; Watts, *Isaiah 34–66*, 80–81; Barstad, *A Way in the Wilderness*; Blenkinsopp, "Scope and Depth of the Exodus Tradtion in Deutero-Isaiah, 40–55," 41–55; Berges, "Der zweite Exodus im Jesajabuch: Auszug oder Verwandlung?," 77–95. For a survey of the Exodus tradition in the Second Temple period literature and New Testament, see Snodgrass, "Streams of Tradition Emerging from Isaiah 40.1–5 and Their Adaptation in the New Testament," 149–68. Finally, Baltzer's commentary on Second Isaiah thoroughly employs the idea of New Exodus.

the work of Andersen,[45] Stuhlmueller[46] and Watts.[47] It is possible this list might be expanded to include a few verses embedded in larger contexts (the servant-songs are under-represented, for example), but the following pericopes will suffice to demonstrate the pervasiveness of the New Exodus / Wilderness theme in these chapters.[48] Some texts are not as clearly part of the wilderness motif (43:1–15)[49], while others are undoubtedly to be included.

Isaiah 40:1–5

Isaiah 40:1–5 forms an introduction to the second half of Isaiah and as such introduces a number of important themes which resonant throughout the section. Vocabulary drawn from the Exodus and wilderness journey is crafted into an invitation for the exiles in Babylon to return in the Land. These opening verses also demonstrate how the wilderness tradition can blend with a marriage metaphor. While the marriage metaphor will be examined in detail in the next chapter, it is important to observe at this point that the invitation found in the opening verses of Isa 40–55 anticipates the invitation of Isaiah 55 to join a wedding celebration.

In the New Testament, Isa 40 becomes the foundation for the ministry of John the Baptist. The passage is cited in all three synoptic gospels and may therefore be seen as paradigmatic for the gospels, especially Mark's gospel. This text is also important for the Qumran community, demonstrating at least two groups with messianic

---

45. Andersen, "Exodus Typology," 181–82.
46. Stuhlmueller, *Creative Redemption in Deutero-Isaiah*.
47. Watts, *Isaiah's New Exodus in Mark*.
48. It is tempting to include Isa 49:26 as an "anti-banquet" in which the enemies of God are food for birds and animals. Holmgren included Isa 52:7–12 as a New Exodus text, although the motif is muted at best. Holmgren, *With Wings as Eagles*, 101; Leslie, *Isaiah*, 193. The clearest reflection of the first Exodus is 52:11–13. The exiles are urged to return, but they will not have to "leave with haste" as with the first Exodus. As with previous texts, the writer describes the new Exodus as a joyous procession to Zion characterized by bursts of joy (פצח). Other than Ps 98:4 and Isa 14:7, the word only appears in Second Isaiah (44:23, 49:13, 54:1, each time used with רנן, "to rejoice loudly"). Verse 9 returns to the theme of comfort and redemption (40:1), but now it is redemption is accomplished.
49. Isaiah 43:1–15 is a unit framed by a description of God as the creator of Israel. ברא is used (for Jacob, v. 1; for Israel, v. 15; as well as the center of the passage in v. 7). This rather unique word for God's creational activity grounds the imagery in creation, but it also recalls Isa 41:20. Because God has created Israel, he redeemed them (גאל, vv. 1, 14) and called them by name (קרא, v. 1). These two verbs appear together in Gen 48:16, Jacob's blessing of Ephraim and Manasseh. While גאל is a common verb in the Hebrew Bible, it is used only twice in the book of Exodus, both times with reference to bringing the nation out of their slavery in Egypt (Exod 6:6, 15:13). Like גאל, נחם appears frequently in Isa 40–55 (16 times). This text describes the redemption as passing through waters and through flame, a possible reference to the Exodus events. Kissane argues that the perfect verb כָּפַרְדָּ in v. 3 refers to the past ("the Lord gave Egypt") rather than present, making the Exodus motif more clear. Kissane, *The Book of Isaiah*, 50.

interest found Isa 40:1–5 applicable to their present context.[50] It is therefore not an exaggeration to describe this text as critically important in both the Testaments.

Frequently Isa 40–55 is called a "book of comfort" based on the use of נחם in Isa 40:1. נחם appears some 51 times in the Hebrew Bible and frequently in Isa 40–55.[51] Exodus 13:17 uses the verb in the nifal to describe the Israelites after they crossed the Red Sea: if they face war, "they may change their mind and return to Egypt." Here, however, the verb appears in the piel and has the connotation of encouragement rather than sympathy.[52]

Isaiah 40:2 hints at a marriage motif which will be picked up in chapter 55. While "speak to her heart" (דַּבְּרוּ עַל־לֵב) does not always connote romance or "love-talk," it does begin to create the marriage metaphor which will re-occur throughout Second Isaiah.[53] The phrase occurs in the context of reconciliation with an unfaithful wife (Judg 19:3) and Hos 2:14 (ET) as well as in Gen 34:3 where Shechem "speaks tenderly" to Dinah after he has raped her. Hos 2:14 is important since there is a combination of tender speech at the end of a time of punishment in the wilderness. It is not insignificant that Isa 40:1 comfort for עַמִּי "my people," since Hosea used the name of his child to declare that God no longer considered Israel as "my people." Like the book of Hosea, Isaiah describes Jerusalem / Zion as a wife who is separated from her husband. Jerusalem is like an unfaithful wife who must be called back to a proper relationship with her husband, the Lord (cf. 54:1–5).

The description of the exile as "hard service" in Isa 40:2 may also be an echo of the wilderness tradition. צָבָא is most often translated "divisions" in the Pentateuch, primarily in the book of Numbers where it refers to divisions of the people in the census (seventy-seven out of ninety times in the Hebrew Bible). The verb מלא is used for completion of a time period, in this case a period of servitude.[54] Goldingay and Payne suggest this translation is a "loose rendering of the slightly enigmatic Hebrew."[55] This time of hard service is a "double-payment for her sin." While this phrase may refer to the duration of

---

50. For example, 1QS 8.14, 9.17–21, 4Q176. Brooke, "Isaiah 40:3 and the Wilderness Community," 117–32; Goldingay and Payne, *Isaiah 40–55*, 2:75–76.

51. Isa 40:1, 49:13, 51:3, 12, 19, 52:9; 61:2, 66:13.

52. Koole, *Isaiah III*, 50; Elliger, *Biblischer Kommentar*, 11:13, cited in HALOT.

53. Goldingay and Payne, *Isaiah 40–55*, 2:66; cf. Koole, *Isaiah III*, 51: "God restores the bond with Lady Jerusalem." Whether this is love-talk or not, the phrase does in fact highlight the "intimate gift" of comfort to his people, see Merendino, *Der Erste und der Letzte: eine Untersuchung von Jes 40–48*, 27. Baltzer also at least allows for the possibility that the phrase is part of the "language of love." Baltzer, *Deutero-Isaiah*, 51.

54. HALOT lists Isa 40:2 as a unique usage of the מלא glossing the phase as "her warfare has come to an end." Significantly, Exodus uses צָבָא four times to refer to how the Israelites were to come out of Egypt, "by divisions" (7:4, 12:17, 41, 51). The word is used for compulsory labor in only three verses (Job 7:1, 10:17, 14:14, none of which have anything to do with slavery). The LXX translates צָבָא as ἡ ταπείνωσις, "humiliation of abasement" (LSJ), a word which was used by the translator in the Servant Songs (53:7–8, cf. the citation of this verse at Acts 8:33).

55. Goldingay and Payne, *Isaiah 40–55*, 1:70.

the exile,[56] Baltzer suggests that the judgment is twofold: widowhood and loss of children.[57] These are the two items which are reversed in the climax of Second Isaiah (54:1, 4) and they are also the two ways in which Babylon itself is judged in 47:8–9. What is more, Isa 51:18–20 emphasizes the judgment on Jerusalem is equivalent to the loss of a husband and sons. Since Jerusalem's time of hard service in the wilderness is over, she will be restored to her marriage and her children will return.

That God is about to redeem (רצה) his people is certainly an allusion to the Wilderness tradition. In Isa 40:2, רצה has the idea of the payment of a price, to redeem or to ransom. Other than Isa 40:2, the word is found only in Lev 26 and 2 Chr 36:2. Commenting on the word in Lev 26:34, J. Milgrom says "scholars are at their wits' end to render this word."[58] Milgrom suggests that the word was used as a virtual synonym for כפר on the basis of Num 35:33 and Deut 32:43 (the land requires atonement).[59] Both passages are in the context of the curses associated for breaking the commands of the Law. Leviticus promises that after the nation sins, it will go into exile and the land will "have rest." After the exile is over, the land will be restored.[60] Isaiah 40:2 is intentionally connecting the return from exile to the curse text in Leviticus, just as the author of 2 Chr did.[61] What is remarkable is the context of 2 Chr 36:21. The author cites Jeremiah, but the words used are from Leviticus. The Chronicler immediately refers to the decree of Cyrus, the anointed one of Isa 44:28—45:1. The redemption from sin, then, is an end of the curse of the Law which resulted in the exile (Lev 26:41). Isaiah therefore shares the view of the Chronicler that the exile is over and that Cyrus is God's anointed one.

Isaiah 40:3 describes the invitation to participate in the return from Exile. "A voice of one calling in the wilderness," combines two common words from the wilderness, מִדְבָּר and עֲרָבָה.[62] While Jer 2:6 combines the two terms to describe the

56. Taking the punishment of the faithless generation as a guide, the exiles were punished with two generations in the "wilderness," approximately 70 years. For this view, see Phillips, "'Double for all Her Sins,'" 130–32.

57. Baltzer, *Deutero-Isaiah*, 53.

58. Milgrom lists several options for translation in Lev 26:33. Based on Rashi, the word may mean "to appease" God's anger, or alternatively the land may need to be appeased for the missed Sabbath years. Based on Job 14:6, the word may be "be completed," possibly the meaning in Isa 40:2. Lastly, the word may mean to "accept as payment," as first suggested by Driver and White in 1894. Milgrom, *Leviticus 23–27*, 2323.

59. Ibid.

60. The word appears in the piel in Job 20:10 with the meaning of returning money the poor.

61. Williamson calls this a "clear allusion" to Lev 26:43. Williamson, *1 and 2 Chronicles*, 417. Dillard makes this point as well. He comments that Chronicles tells the story of Israel from Adam until the end of the exile, as if to say "God has loved us from the foundation of the world; we are a prepared people brought to a prepared land. It is a new day." Dillard, *2 Chronicles*, 301. Citing the Leviticus text, Jacob Myers describes this verse in 2 Chr as showing that the "exile was a purifying process carried out in line with the law." Myers, *II Chronicles*, 223.

62. While thirty of the sixty times עֲרָבָה appears in the Hebrew Bible it is in combination with מִדְבָּר, it does place the context of allusions to the wilderness traditions of Numbers.

wilderness journey, the terms usually are used to describe a totally barren dry region, a "wasteland."[63] It is significant that the voice cries out that a "way" must be prepared and a highway must be built for the procession returning from exile. This is travel language associated with the first Exodus from Egypt. The "way" is the common דֶּרֶךְ, and in every other case in the Hebrew Bible the דֶּרֶךְ יְהוָה refers to ethics (following the "way of the Lord" Prov 10:29, for example).[64] But the bulk of the non-figurative uses of דֶּרֶךְ in the Hebrew Bible are in the Wilderness tradition (Exod 13:17–18, 23x in Numbers). In these earlier traditions the word דֶּרֶךְ refers to the road traveled by the Israelites after they left Egypt, here the author picks up that language and applies it to a new Exodus out of Babylon.[65]

There are other allusions to Exodus and Wilderness traditions here as well. While the "highway" (מְסִלָּה) is less important in the Wilderness tradition (only Num 20:19),[66] the presence of the word in 40:1–11 is an important echo of earlier passages in Isaiah. In Isa 11:16 the highway is for the remnant of Israel who will return from exile in Assyria, making an explicit connection to Israel's journey out of Egypt. In the conclusion to the first half of Isaiah, the prophet declares that the Lord will establish a highway (מְסִלָּה) and a way (דֶּרֶךְ) in the wilderness (35:8–10). This wilderness is described as a new creation in verses 35:1–2, 5–7.[67] A highway motif with imagery drawn from the first Exodus is found in Isa 14–15 as well. Israel passed through the Red Sea on dry ground (Exod 14:29, 15:19), on a way prepared by the Lord's mighty power (Exod 14:31, 15:1–8). When the author of Isa 40:3 describes the straight path in the wilderness, he is invoking the language of the founding and defining moment for Israel—what God has done in the past he will do again in the present.[68] Finally, the paths are made clear for the

---

63. Isaiah 35:1–6 uses this combination in a New Exodus context, cf. 41:19, 51:3. These texts refer to the flowering of the עֲרָבָה as the people move towards Zion. This theme appears in Isa 33:9 and 35:1 as well. In both of these verses the wilderness streams with water and flowers blossom.

64. The majority of the uses of דֶּרֶךְ in the Hebrew Bible are figurative. Merrill draws attention to the covenantal aspect of following the "way of the Lord," found in Isa 48:17. Merrill, "דֶּרֶךְ" in *NIDOTTE*, 989.

65. According to Muilenburg, the prophet "constantly refers" to the Exodus and it is the "primary element of his eschatology." Muilenburg, "Isaiah 40–66," 427.

66. See also Jer 31:21, very much a new Exodus text, also in the context of a return from Exile. On this word, see Tidwell, "No Highway!," 251–69. This article is a somewhat negative review of Dorsey, *The Roads and Highways of Ancient Israel* with respect to the term מְסִלָּה.

67. The land will burst forth with new life, it will become like Lebanon where water gushes forth and grasses and plants grow. Verse 9 describes the wilderness as being free of wild animals. This new highway leads to Zion (v. 10) and only the righteous will travel this road to the mountain of God (vv. 8, 10). Tidwell therefore describes the use of מְסִלָּה in Isaiah as *via sacra*, a holy road leading to a place of worship. Tidwell, "No Highway!," 257.

68. While warning the reader from jumping too quickly to the assumption of a New Exodus theme, Seitz comments that the way does not lead from Babylon to Zion, but "erupts in the desert," where God makes the wasteland into Eden. See Seitz, "Isaiah," 335.

glory of the Lord to be revealed. The phrase כְּבוֹד יְהוָה appears in Exod 16:7, 10 as well as in the context of the theophany at Sinai (Exod 24:16–17).[69]

In summary, it is difficult to overestimate the importance of Isa 40 to the eschatological thinking of Second Temple period Judaism and especially the synoptic Gospels. All three directly cite Isa 40 and identify John as the "voice crying in the wilderness." In each this is an invitation to prepare the coming Messiah's ministry. Just as Israel was once invited to return to her God in Isa 40, so too the ministry of John invited people to join with Jesus in his on-going ministry. Taken along with Isa 54–55, Isa 40 is an invitation for Israel to re-unite with her husband of old and to travel once again through the wilderness to the land given to her. The themes of redemption and consolation appear in the actions and teaching of Jesus as well. While John's preaching focused on judgment, Jesus invited Israel to join him in an on-going "banquet in the wilderness" which culminates in the groom's arrival at Jerusalem. By gathering true Israel to himself in a journey marked with provision of food, Jesus is enacting the event envisioned in Isa 40–55.

Isaiah 41:17–20

In Isa 41:17–20 there is a contrast between the condition of the land as a result of the curses of the covenant and the land in the new Exodus. Many commentators include this text as an example of New Exodus motif. Whybray, for example, simply states that the imagery ought to be taken literally as referring to the homeward march from Babylon after the exile.[70] Stuhlmüeller describes this text as "the exceptionally glorious way of the new exodus along which Yahweh leads his people from exile to the surprising paradise of their promised homeland."[71]

There is, however, some question however as to whether this pericope is part of the New Exodus motif. B. Spencer argued that the material in 41:17–20 lacks the travel imagery found in the other unequivocal New Exodus texts and therefore it should be read as employing "fertility motif."[72] Spencer makes an excellent point, although fertil-

---

69. Typically a theophany is associated with the Lord "drawing near in battle," see Baltzer, *Deutero-Isaiah*, 56. In this case, "all flesh" witnesses the glory of the Lord. In Exod 16, after the people have complained about food in the wilderness, the glory of the Lord appears in the wilderness in the cloud. It is the next day when the Lord first provides manna and quail for the people to eat.

70. Whybray, *Isaiah 40–66*, 66–67. Keisow also sees this text as describing the concern of the Lord for the returnees as they suffer in the heat of the sun. Kiesow, *Exodustexte im Jesajabuch*, 127. Kiesow cites Elliger, *Deuterojesaja*, 167. Ellinger connects the "comfort" of providing water to the returning exiles to Isa 40:1.

71. Stuhlmüeller, *Creative Redemption*, 67. Compare to Hessler, "dessen 'Wüstewanderung' diesmal ein reines Vergnügen." Hessler, *Das Heilsdrama: der Weg zur Weltherrschaft Jahwes (Jes. 40–55)*, 67–68; Bonnard compares this text with Exod 17:1–7 and Num 20:1–10 in *Le second Isaïe, son disciple et leurs éditeurs: Isaïe 40–66*, 115.

72. Spencer "The 'New Deal' for Post-exilic Judah in Isaiah 41,17–20," 583–97. But Baltzer suggests the author using a typical *topos* drawn from the exodus story. Baltzer then connects Isa 41:17–20

ity may very well be included in a "new wilderness" journey. The "new journey" will be like the old in that the Lord will provide food and water, but it will be much more than the old journey in that creation will burst forth with life as the people return from exile. The land becomes fertile because the curse of the covenant has been lifted and (perhaps) the curse of sin has been reversed. Land which was barren and cursed because of the sin of Israel will once again teem with life. Likewise, E. F. Navarro argues that this text is better seen as part of Second Isaiah's new creation motif, rather than New Exodus.[73] He argues that the meaning of desert never refers to a concrete geographical location in the prophets (with the exception of Jer 2:6). The desert is the place where Israel finds itself because the Lord has hidden his face.[74] Since creation language is used in this section (ברא, for example), the re-creation of the desert into the Garden of Eden is an "allegory for the regeneration of Israel" when they are freed from Assyrian rule.[75] More recently, U. Berges treats 41:1–20 as a dispute over God's power.[76] The use of creation language is intended to point the reader toward a more internalized faith in the holy one of Israel. The contrast in 41:1–20 is not between the first Exodus and the new Exodus, but rather between the power of Cyrus and the power of the Lord. It is the Lord who provided water in the wilderness and grew the trees which would one day be used for his worship. What is more, Berges argues that the creation motif if often used to indicate the "social transformation" of the poor.[77] Perhaps this is not a case of either a New Exodus motif or a Creation motif. The text itself seems to be working both metaphors at the same time. In fact, when one studies Exodus imagery, creation language is never far from mind. There are several examples in Isa 40–55 of a merging of creation and Exodus language. In fact, this clustering of traditions occurs in the Exodus story itself.[78]

---

to Isa 5:8–15, 10:1–4 and Jer 2:6–7. Baltzer, *Deutero-Isaiah*, 108.

73. Navarro, *El desierto transformado*, 213.

74. Ibid., 209. This is not far from Kisanne, *The Book of Isaiah*, 2:32: "The exile is compare to wretches dying of thirst, its land to a barren wilderness."

75. "La conversión del yermo en parque es una alegoría (metáfora continuada) de la regeneración de Isarel, El pueblo castigado, moribundo bajo la dominación asiria 'desierto,' será resucitado por su Hacedor a una vida lujuriante, inmarcesible 'Eden'" (Navarro, *El desierto transformado*, 213).

76. "Die Transformation der Wüste in ein wasser– und baumreiches Terrian soll nicht nur gesehen, sondern als schöpferische Tat Gottes wahrgenommen und verinnerlicht werden . . . Die Wortwahl zeigt, dass diese Transformation der Wüste kein Tun wie jedes andere ist, sondern ein exquisiter Beweis der schöpferischen Kraft YHWH." Berges, *Jesaja 40–48*, 204–5.

77. Berges, *Jesaja 40–48*, 201. On the other hand, Baltzer suggests that these verses are in fact a "midrashlike exposition of Exod 15:15–20." After the song of Miriam there is a brief narrative describing the movement from the Reed Sea to the wilderness where there is no water, just as in Isa 41:17 ("the needy seek water, but there is none.") When the people arrive at Elim, there are twelve springs and seventy palm trees. Baltzer draws a parallel to the *Exagoge of Ezekiel*. The arrival at Elim is a foreshadowing of entry into the land itself, plenty of water and trees of every kind, not unlike Isaiah's description here (cf. LXX Jer 38:12). Baltzer, *Deutero-Isaiah*, 112.

78. Isa 41:17 also sets the New Exodus within the curses of the covenant. The verb עזב, "to forsake," is used in Deut 29:24 (29:25 ET) to describe the Lord forsaking the covenant as part of the curses and

A Banquet in the Wilderness

There are a number of clear allusions to a Wilderness tradition in this pericope. Those who "thirst" (v. 17, צָמֵא) will find water in dry places. Both the verb and the noun form appear in the first complaint (Exod 17:3) and a related term (צִמָּאוֹן) is used in Deut 8:15 and Ps 107:33 to describe the land through which the Lord leads the people of Israel. In Isa 41:18 a parallel term is used (צִיָּה, cf. Isa 49:8, 53:2, Ps 78:17). The implication here is that those who return from exile will no longer thirst physically or spiritually.[79]

Traditional wilderness language continues in 41:18. The land is described as a "barren height" (שְׁפִי), a valley plain (בִּקְעָה), a wilderness (מִדְבָּר), and parched-earth (אֶרֶץ צִיָּה). The first item (שְׁפִי) is a "bare plain, without trees" (HALOT) בִּקְעָה refers to a valley plain, such as the valley of Jericho (Deut 34:3) and the Valley of Lebanon (Josh 11:17, 12:7). This is the same word used in Isa 40:3, "every valley shall be raised." Since the word for wilderness (מִדְבָּר) is the most common word in the Hebrew Bible for wilderness, it is not surprising that it appears in Numbers and Deuteronomy quite frequently. The adjective צִיָּה in the last phrase is associated with several wilderness texts.[80] Finally, Isa 35:1 begins with the "the dry land will rejoice."

These barren places were turned into rivers (נָהָר), springs (מַעְיָן), a reed-pool (אֲגַם), and springs of water (מוֹצָאֵי מָיִם). While נָהָר is a common word in the Hebrew Bible, it is used nine times in Isa 40–55 either in the context of the drying up of rivers as a judgment (42:15, 44:27, 50:2) or provision of water in a dry place (41:18, 43:19–20). In 43:2 it refers to passing through a river, a reference to either the Red Sea or the crossing of the Jordan. The less common מַעְיָן is associated with the wilderness tradition (Ps 74:15 and 114:8).[81] The word אֲגַם refers to swampy water such as the

---

blessings. The word appears with the same meaning in Lev 26:43, but the subject is the land rather than the people. The land will be deserted (using the nifel of עזב) as a result of the covenant disobedience of the people. In 1 Kgs 19:10, 14 Elijah states that the Israelites have forsaken the covenant, words which frame the theophany of 19:11–13. This is significant since the theophany takes place on Mt. Horeb and is therefore reminiscent of Exod 19:16–20, 24:1–18, and 33:18–22. The author of Second Isaiah picks up on this theme again in 42:18 and 49:14: despite a history of unfaithfulness, the Lord will not abandon his people or Zion.

79. Thirst is often used as a metaphor for spiritual longing in the Hebrew Bible, see Ps 42:3 MT, 36:8–9 MT, 63:2–3 MT, 143:5–6, and more importantly for the present context, Isa 41:17–18, 44:3 and 55:1. While it is difficult to show that the saying John 7:37 comes from the historical Jesus, that he declares himself to be "living water" in the wilderness should be seen as an allusion to this motif.

80. Both Pss 78:20 and 105:41 clearly have the provision of water in the wilderness in mind, although Ps 107:35 ("parched ground into flowing springs") is less obvious. Given the presence of several verbal parallels to Ps 107 in this verse it can be concluded that this word has a "wilderness association" as well. It is quite possible Ps 107 echoes Second Isaiah. Allen sees this psalm as echoing the same sorts of themes as Second Isaiah. The psalmist is "repackaging" the traditions for a new generation Allen, *Psalms 101–50*, 91. Snaith detects elements of wilderness tradition in the Psalm in verses 4–9, as does Dahood, in verses 33–43. See Snaith, *Five Psalms*, 17–21; Dahood, *Psalms III 100–150*, 80–91. Because any date suggested for Psalm 107 is tentative it is impossible to know with certainty which direction the tradition runs. It is equally possible that Second Isaiah "repackages" Psalm 107, or that both rely on an earlier, unknown source.

81. Joel 4:18 (3:18 ET) uses מַעְיָן to describe the wonders of the messianic age, when a "fountain"

Nile (Exod 7:19, 8:1). This word appears in Ps 107:35 in describing a return from exile and is repeated in Isa 42:15 in the context of judgment (the reed-pool will be dried up). The final phrase in the list (מוֹצָאֵי מָיִם, literally "appearing of water") is used in Ps 107:33, 35.[82] The imagery is hyperbolic: God does not simply provide water as he did in the original wilderness story; he turns the desert into a "great sheet of water."[83]

Isaiah 41:19 lists a number of trees and plants which the Lord will plant in the wilderness (מִדְבָּר). While many of these plants are associated with the construction of the Tabernacle and the Temple,[84] the point of the collection here is the utter fertility of the desert after the Lord sends the waters.[85] The cedar (אֶרֶז) is associated with Lebanon and not at all the type of tree one expects to find in the barren wilderness, the acacia (שִׁטָּה),[86] myrtle (הֲדַס)[87] and "fat trees" or "oil trees" (עֵץ שָׁמֶן).[88] While there are several suggestions other than the olive tree, it may be preferable to understand this reference as "rich trees" or "fruitful trees." The overall impression of the two lines of poetry is that the Lord himself will cultivate a most unviable land and make it a fertile, useful land.

The point of all of this activity is that people may see and know that the restoration from exile is by the hand of the Lord, the "Holy One of Israel" (Isa 41:20). The phrase "hand of the Lord" in Isa 41:20 appears in Exod 9:3 with reference to the plagues, but more significant is Josh 4:24. This verse is in the final section of the Wilderness tradition and occurs at the moment that the Israelites cross the Jordan

---

will flow from the house of the Lord.

82. The phrase is also found in 2 Kgs 2:21 and 2 Chr 32:30 to refer to a spring of water. Isaiah 58:11 uses the phrase to describe the land after the Lord restores it to its former glory.

83. Koole, *Isaiah II*, 180. This is not a description of desert people finding water at desert wells or springs, but rather a reversal of the desert into a vast water source. Similarly, Reymond states "Ce qui est possible a l'homme, en petit, quand il creuse un puits et qu'il atteint, grace a lui, l'eau du monde inférieur, Dieu le fait sur une beaucoup plus vaste échelle lorsqu'il fait jaillir l'eau des sources." Reymond, *L'eau, sa vie, et sa signification dans l'Ancien Testament*. See also Rütersworden, "Erwägungen zur Metaphorik des Wassers in Jes 40ff," 1–22.

84. Berges comments, "Diese Bäume stehen weder für Schatten und schon gar nicht für Nahrung, sondern zumindest teilweise für die exklusive Qualität ihrer Hölzer, die zur Herstellung des Tempels und seiner Kultgegenstände dienten" (Berges, *Jesaja 40–48*, 204).

85. The verse gives the impression of a garden and trees which are firmly rooted, a "pleasure garden." Koole argues that this cannot be a "return to paradise" since none of the trees are, in his view, fruit trees. The identification of each tree, however, is fraught with difficulties which make it at least possible that some are fruit-bearing (the olive, for example.) Koole, *Isaiah II*, 181.

86. Jacob and Jacob, "Flora," 2:804. Merendino suggests that these trees are a hint of the rebuilding of the temple since they decorate the Sanctuary in Isa 60:13. Merendino, *Der Erste und der Letzte*, 182.

87. This is a rare word, used only here and in 55:13, Zech 1:8, 10 (the night vision of a man among the myrtle trees) and Neh 8:15 (describing the Feast of Booths). The tree is associated with "peace and divine blessing" and is the Babylonian term for a bride, See Jacob and Jacob, "Flora." 2:807. The fruit of the myrtle the berry was used as a food flavoring and could be made into a wine.

88. The phrase is only used here and in Neh 8:15, along with the myrtle, and in the construction of the temple (1 Kgs 6:23, 31–33). One additional use is Sir 50:10, which is also translated as an olive tree "laden with fruit" (NRSV).

and enter into the land for the first time. Joshua says that God has done to the Jordan what he did to the Red Sea, so that all the people of the earth might know the "hand of the Lord" is powerful. The image of the hand of the Lord therefore frames the Exodus events. Second Isaiah declares that when exiles return to the Land God will once again do amazing things "by his powerful hand," just as he has done in the past.

Isaiah 41:20 also declares that the Holy One of Israel has "created" this new fertile land. This is an important theological statement because it grounds the flourishing of the desert not only in the Wilderness tradition, but in the story of creation itself. The verb ברא is used primarily in the creation story and Isa 40–55.[89] While it is stated that God is the creator in 40:28, 41:20 introduces the "court case" on false gods beginning in 41:21. The Holy One of Israel is the Creator of the heavens and earth, while the gods of the nations are themselves creations of humans.

In summary, this section is an example of intertextual exegesis by the prophet. There are clear linguistic and thematic connections to an earlier well-known tradition (Creation, Exodus) which are consistent with the themes of the larger unit (Isa 40–55). It is entirely plausible that the author knew and intentionally used the Exodus tradition and the creation narrative, combining them in order to speak about a new situation, the return to the Land after the exile. In fact, Isa 41:17–20 so well-satisfies all the suggested criteria for determining an allusion that it is a model of intertextual exegesis in the prophets. Texts and traditions are clearly invoked and combined in order to create a new idea which speaks to the present situation of the prophet. This development and application of an earlier motif continues in other reflections on the Exodus in the Hebrew Bible (Psalm 105, 106) as well as the Second Temple Period. It will not, therefore, be a surprise to find that Jesus stands within this rich tradition when invites people to share in the new Exodus by eating and drinking in celebration of the end of the exile.

Isaiah 42:10–17

G. W. Buchanan has drawn attention to the fact that this section closely parallels the Song of the Sea (Exod 15),[90] although some scholars disagree.[91] The Song of the Sea is a poetic reflection on the crossing of the Red Sea, but also looking forward to the conquest of Canaan (v. 13–16) and the establishment of Israel in the Land as well as

---

89. Of the forty-eight occurrences in the Hebrew Bible, eleven are in Genesis and twenty-one are in Isaiah. In Isaiah, all but 4:5, 57:19, 65:17, 66:18 are in Isa 40–55.

90. Buchanan, "Isaianic Midrash and the Exodus," 104–5. Cf. Muilenberg, "Isaiah 40–66," 471; Kissane, *The Book of Isaiah*, 2:42–52; Koole, *Isaiah II*, 258; Bonnard, *Le second Isaïe*, 130 (citing Exod 15:3 in parallel with 42:13).

91. Berges, *Jesaja 40–48*, 257. E. Beaucamp sees this text describing a theophany in general, not necessarily the Exodus ("Il décrit simplement l'éclat d'une théophanie"). Beaucamp, "'Chant nouveau du retour' (Isa 42:10–17): un monstre de l'exégèse moderne," 145–58, 152. Like Spencer above, this text is describing God's power through creation language (Beaucamp, 153).

the establishment of a sanctuary (v. 17). Certainly the opening lines of both texts are similar: in Exod 15:1, Moses leads all of Israel in "singing a song," in Isa 42:10 there is a command to "sing to the Lord a new song." In the Wilderness tradition, the next time all Israel sings is Num 21:17, celebrating the Lord's provision of water in the wilderness. However, the vocabulary of Exod 15 and Isa 42:10–17 is not particularly close. Aside from the opening line, there are only superficial similarities involving common vocabulary.[92] However, the two passages may be thematically linked. In both texts the Lord is described as a mighty warrior who triumphs over his enemies (15:3, 42:13) and both refer to the enemy going down under the sea (15:4–5, 42:10). Both refer to the people of Canaan,[93] although 15:14–15 describe them as fearful at the news of the victory of the Lord. In 42:11 the people of the desert[94] rejoice at the New Exodus.

Verse 16 may also invoke Exodus language, although the evidence is slender. The Lord will lead his people on level pathways is a theme throughout Isa 40–55 (40:3–5, 50:14, 27). The Lord "brought them out," using a hifel of הלך. While הלך is very common in the Hebrew Bible, the hifel only appears 45 times, frequently with reference to the Exodus and wilderness period.[95] In Hos 2:16 MT, the word is used for restoring Gomer to her husband and returning from the wilderness. On the other hand, the subject of the verb is the blind who would require a guide. Scholars who see a New Exodus motif here prefer to see this as the spiritual blindness of Israel in captivity.[96]

Once again there are verbal and thematic clues which make it likely that the prophet is evoking the Exodus events in general as well as to a particular text, Song of the Sea (Exod 15). While the "volume" of the allusion is low, taken along with the other allusions throughout Isa 40–55, it is likely that the author is once again playing on the idea of the Exodus to describe the return from exile.

---

92. Common vocabulary between Isaiah and the Song of the Sea includes the following: Isa 42:10 תְּהִלָּה, praise, 15:11; ירד, go down, 15:5; יָם, sea, 15:1,4,8,10,19,22; ישב, to dwell, 15:14,15, 17; in 42:11, מִדְבָּר, desert; הַר, mountain; in 42:13, מִלְחָמָה, war; אֹיֵב, enemy.

93. Philistia, Moab, Edom, and Canaan are listed in Exodus, foreshadowing the struggle with these nations later in the history of Israel.

94. The two nations mentioned are Kedar and Sela. Kedar refers to bedouin tribes of the Negev and is used in this text as a synonym for Edom. Knauf, "Kedar (Person)," 4:9.

95. Lev 26:13; Deut 8:2, 15; 29:14; Ps 106:9, 136:16, cf. Am 2:10; Isa 42:16, 63:12–13, Jer 2:6, 17. Of the twenty-three uses of the term in Isaiah, all but 35:9 are in the second half of the book. Isa 35:9 is an important text because it combines several themes which are foundational in Second Isaiah: redemption, ransom, a joyous return to Zion, gladness, etc.

96. Schoors, *I Am Your God*, 92.

A Banquet in the Wilderness

Isaiah 43:16–21[97]

This section clearly uses Exodus language to describe the return of the exiles from Babylon.[98] In fact, Baltzer describes this text as a model for the function of biblical tradition.[99] Travel vocabulary is present once again. Roads or paths (דֶּרֶךְ and נְתִיבָה in v. 16 and 19) are to be built in the wilderness (מִדְבָּר and יְשִׁימוֹן in v. 19) just as they were built in the seas (יָם and מַיִם in v. 16). Verse 17 references the first Exodus (horses, Exod 14:9, 23; 15:1, 19, 21; chariots, Exod 14 (8x), 15:19; an army, 14:4, 9, 17, 28, 15:4).[100] Verses 19b–21 refers to the provision of water in the wilderness. While the word יְשִׁימוֹן for the wilderness is not found in Exodus,[101] it appears in the Psalms which describe the period of wilderness testing (Ps 68:8, 78:40, 106:14, 107:4). An additional clue that this text looks back to the Exodus is the use of עַם and the rare relative pronoun זוּ, found only in 43:21 and Exod 15:13 and 16.[102]

While the writer is invoking the great tradition of Exod 14 and 15, he admonishes his listeners to "not remember the past" because the Lord is about to do a new thing (43:18–19). It is ironic that the prophet describes new things by means of an old thing (the first Exodus.)[103] This new Exodus will be something which recalls not just the Exodus, but also Creation. The author uses creation language to describe this new thing: it is sprouting up (צמח v.19, cf. Gen 2:5). The animals which rise up to honor the Lord in verse 20 are חַיַּת הַשָּׂדֶה (wild animal, cf. Gen 2:5, 19).[104] Once again the wilderness becomes a well-watered plain. That God provided water for his people in the Exodus is already a common theme in Isa 40–55, but the word בָּחִיר (chosen) is associated with the wilderness traditions as well. The word is used in Ps 105:6, 43 as a literary frame for the Exodus events. In addition, Ps 106:5 describes the nation as בָּחִיר (chosen) as an introduction to a historical review of the wilderness period.[105]

---

97. This section is marked off by indentations in the MT and 1QIsa and 4QIsb. Goldingay and Payne suggest chiastic arrangement for these verses, balancing the Lord's provision through the water (verses 16–17) with the Lord's future provision with water in the wilderness (19b–21). *Isaiah 40–55*, 1:293.

98. "Unmistakable here is the exodus prediction" (Seitz, "Isaiah," 6:378); Berges: "Das Wortwahl in V 17 lässt keinen Zweifel daran, dass heir massiv auf die Tradition von Exod 14–15 zurückgegriffen wird" (*Jesaja 40–48*, 298). Cf. Bonnard: "L'Exode nouveau sera tel, qu'il eclipsera l'ancien" (*Le second Isaïe*, 146).

99. Baltzer, *Deutero-Isaiah*, 175.

100. Goldingay and Payne, *Isaiah 40–55*, 1:297. The noun עֱזוּז is not found in Exodus, but appears in the context of the mighty acts of God in Ps 78:4 and 145:6.

101. The word appears in Num 21:10 and 23:18 as part of a place name. The noun only appears in the Hebrew Bible in parallel with מִדְבָּר.

102. Goldingay and Payne, *Isaiah 40–55*, 1:300. This is a clear verbal parallel which may be a clue that the writer knew the book of Exodus as a literary document rather than an oral tradition.

103. Merendino, *Der Erste und der letzte*, 334.

104. It is highly unlikely that the animals in this verse refer to the gentiles, contra Hessler, "Die Struktur der Bilder bei Deuterojesaja," 362.

105. In the same Psalm, Moses is described as the chosen one of God who "stood in the breach"

Jesus the Bridegroom

Isaiah 48:20–21

In this conclusion to Isa 40–48, the writer implores people to come out of Babylon by invoking the Wilderness tradition.[106] It is possible these lines are an editorial marker since there is a return to the "trek through the wilderness" motif from 40:3–4.[107] Isa 52:11–12 has a similar injunction to depart, although the wording is not quite the same. Unlike 40:3–4, there can be no question that the imagery is drawn from the Exodus. While the verb יצא (v. 20, come out) is extremely common in the Hebrew Bible, it is the word used to describe the Exodus in Exod 13:3 and Ps 114:1. The verb ברח (v. 20, flee) in verse 20 is used in Exod 14:5 as well to describe the departure from Egypt. The hifel of הלך (v. 21) is particularly associated with the Exodus tradition. The writer commands that this new Exodus be proclaimed with רִנָּה (shouts of joy), a term used in several Exodus contexts.[108] The content of the announcement is that the Lord has "redeemed" his people, using the verb גאל. As in the previous texts surveyed, there is a close connection of a redeemer and the Exodus in the Song of Moses (Exod 15:13, cf. 6:6). The verb צמא (thirst) is fairly rare in the Hebrew Bible but appears in Exod 17:3 (cf. Isa 49:10). That the Lord caused water to gush out of the rock is a clear evocation of the Wilderness tradition, using the term צוּר for rock.[109] Baltzer suggests that the word for ruins (חָרְבָּה) was chosen in order to echo the place name Horeb, the mountain associated with the first provision of water in Exod 17:6.[110]

Isaiah 49:8–13

More than any other of the texts surveyed thus far, Isa 49:8–13 looks forward to a future new age inaugurated by a new Exodus. This is the beginning of a new section in Isa 40–55 which focuses on Zion beginning in 49:14. The new Exodus, or better, the

---

between an angry God and his rebellious people (vs. 23). The word is used also in Isa 45:4, 1 Chr16:1 and Sir 46:1 for the nation of Israel. Koole comments that the use of "chosen" in this context indicates expresses the "covenantal relationship with God. Koole, *Isaiah II*, 334.

106. Assuming a post-exilic date, Baltzer comments that the author is reversing Jer 50:8 when he implores Israel to flee from the Babylonians. Now that Babylon itself has fallen, Israel ought to come out of the city are return to Jerusalem. The writer may very well be blending Ps 78:15–20 and Num 20 as well. Baltzer, *Deutero-Isaiah*, 301, but compare Goldingay and Payne, *Isaiah 40–55*, 1:149. Similarly, Bonnard states that "Ainsi le premier exode est-il une fois de plus le gage assuré du second: les Israélites libérés seront aussi protégés dans le désert syrien qu'ils le furent dans le désert sinaïtique." Bonnard, *Le second Isaïe*, 201.

107. Blenkinsopp, *Isaiah 40–55*, 285.

108. Isa 49:13, 51:11, 54:1, 55:12; Ps 105:43 The noun is used in a very similar context Ps 126. Three times this short psalm proclaims that the return to Zion is an occasion of great joy. Verses 4–6 describe tears changing to joy and the Negev becoming fertile.

109. Exod 17:6, Deut 8:15, cf. Exod 32:13, Ps 78:15, 20, 105:41, 114:8.

110. The first vowel in חָרְבָּה may be pointed with a qames-hatuf and therefore pronounced very close to the name Horeb. HALOT suggests following a variant reading, חֳרָבוֹת, deserts.

new Wilderness journey, serves as a transition between these two sections.¹¹¹ Because of the nature of the Servant songs (Isa 49–53), they have generated a massive secondary literature, most of which is not of interest to this study. While this pericope serves as a bridge between Isa 40–48 and the Servant Songs, the Exodus and Wilderness motifs nearly drop out in chapters 49–53.

There are several elements of this pericope which may be described as part of the new Exodus and Wilderness tradition, although they can also be described as a shepherd metaphor. In verse 8, the time of the restoration of Israel is described as the time of the Lord's favor. The noun רָצוֹן is used infrequently in the Pentateuch, often used for "acceptable offerings" (Lev 19:5, 22:19–29). Here in Isa 49 it is the time of the Exodus that is a time of God's favor. The only places in the Hebrew Bible where רָצוֹן and יְשׁוּעָה are used in combination are this text and Ps 106:4. The Psalm proceeds to contrast the present generation with the generation of the wilderness who rebelled despite witnessing the great miracles of the Exodus and wilderness (vss. 6–43). The day of the Lord's favor is also described as a day of salvation. יְשׁוּעָה is frequently used in Exodus contexts, such as in Exod 14:13 where Moses declares that God would in fact deliver his people in the wilderness.¹¹²

The day of favor and salvation is the time when the Lord will re-establish his covenant with his people. He will make a covenant with the people and restore the land (vs. 8cd). The hifel of the common verb קום is frequently used for the confirmation of a covenant.¹¹³ Exodus 6:4 combines this same vocabulary (hifel of קום plus בְּרִית). That it is the land that will be "confirmed" is important since אֶרֶץ does not refer to the land of Israel in the other 25 occurrences in Isa 40–55.¹¹⁴

The journey of the captives is described in terms of a shepherd leading his flock and recalls the language of Isa 40. The journey will be easy since mountains and valleys will be leveled and the dangers of desert travel will be eliminated. The nouns דֶּרֶךְ and מְסִלָּה are repeated from Isa 40:3. In verse 9b the flock will feed beside the road. The verb רעה is normally used to refer to livestock, but it is used here as a metaphor for the people of Israel being shepherded back to the land.¹¹⁵ This recalls Isa 40:11, which used the same verb to describe the return from exile.

---

111. Baltzer, *Deutero-Isaiah*, 304.

112. Although the verb אסר is used here and Isa 61:1 for "captives," it never is used for the captivity in Egypt. In 2 Chr 36:6 it describes Jehoiakim's captivity at the hand of Nebuchadnezzar. The verb is often used in a literal sense for imprisonment (being bound with chains) and in a figurative sense for being bound by an oath (Num 30).

113. The Noahic covenant: Gen 6:18, 9:9, 11, 17; The Abrahamic Covenant: Gen 17:7, 19, 21; between individuals: Gen 21:32; 2 Sam 3:21. The Mosaic covenant is in view in Exod 6:4, Lev 26:9, Jer 34:18 and Ezek 16:60, 62.

114. Goldingay and Payne, *Isaiah 40–55*, 2:174.

115. Compare to Zeph 2:7, 3:14, Hos 13:6; Jer 50:19; Ezek 34:8–9. Presumably a shepherd would only pasture his sheep beside a road during a time of peace or prosperity.

As they travel, the flock will find pasture in every שְׁפִי (barren hill). In 41:18 the Lord causes water to flow in these lonely places. A "barren place" is where one would not expect to find sufficient pasture, but the Lord will lead his flock there because he has turned the wilderness into fertile pastures. מַרְעִית (pasture) is often a metaphor for the people of Israel as the "sheep of his pasture."[116] Hos 13:6 is a pre-exilic negative use of the image. The Lord will feed the people in their pasture but they became arrogant and satisfied and turned away from their shepherd.[117]

The verbs רעב (to hunger) and צמא (to thirst) appear in several other Wilderness tradition contexts.[118] Much like Isa 49:8, Ps 107:5 describes the return from exile in terms of the hungry and thirsty being led on straight paths. Later in the psalm, the Lord turns the desert into water and the hungry are brought into the land (vss. 33–38). It is no surprise by this point to find this sort of vocabulary in the Song of Moses. Like Isa 49:10, Exod 15:13 describes the compassion (רחם) of the Lord who leads (נהל) his people in strength into a "holy pasture."[119]

Verse 13 concludes this introductory section of Isa 49 with a cry of joy. Once again the verb רִנָּה appears, this time in parallel to גיל, a verb which appears in a number of texts which describe the gathering of the people to Zion in the eschatological age.[120] For example, Ps 53:7 looks forward to salvation coming out of Zion, a time when God restores the fortunes of his people. In Isa 49:13, it is creation which rejoices because the time has come for God to comfort his people (using the important verb נחם, cf. Isa 40:1) and to have compassion upon them, using רחם. This verb was used to describe the tender compassion of the shepherd in the wilderness in 49:10, and will re-occur in 54:8, 10 and 55:7.

There are a number of reasons why this text particularly is important for the goals of this study. First, many of the themes and images found here are picked up again in Isaiah 61, an important text for understanding Jesus' ministry in the context of the Second Temple period. Luke 4:18:19 cites Isa 61:1–2 as paradigmatic for Jesus' ministry in Galilee. Second, when Jesus feeds the 5000 he has compassion on the people of Israel because they are "sheep without a shepherd." In chapter 7 I will argue that Mark 6:30–43 intentionally echoes this passage and the event is described as an anticipation of the eschatological banquet described here. Third, the idea of the "year of the Lord's favor" figures significantly in other Second Temple Period texts such as 11QMelchizedek.[121] Last, this allusion to Exodus and Wilderness tradition is

---

116. Ezek 34:31; Ps 74:1, 79:13, 95:7, 100:3.

117. נהל in the piel, to provide livestock with food (Gen 47:17, Ps 23:2).

118. Ps 78:26, the wind was lead in order to feed the people quail; Ps 78:52, exodus context, lead like a flock; Ps 80:2, lead Jacob like a flock; Isa 63:14, lead this people like cattle.

119. Exodus 15:13 uses the noun נָוֵה, which has the connotation of a destination place or stopping point for a semi-nomadic people, hence pasture.

120. Isa 65:18–19; 66:10; Joel 2:21, 23; perhaps Ps 97:1, 8 ought to be included here as well.

121. The text combines the Jubilee year with the return of captives. 11QMelchizedek does not directly cite Isa 49:8–13 or 61:1–2.

significant because the very next verse in Isaiah personifies Zion as a woman who has been forsaken by her husband (Isa 50:1). This combination of Wilderness tradition and marriage metaphor will be examined in the next chapter.

Isaiah 51:9–11

Isa 51:1–3 and 9–11 appear to be related in that they refer to two foundational episodes from Israel's history. In verses 1–3 the writer urged his readers to recall Abraham and Sarah; in vss. 9–11 the generation of the Exodus is invoked. While it is likely that the reference in verse three to fertility in the desert refers to Sarah bearing a child after her barrenness, the reference to the Exodus is unmistakable in verses 9–11. Keisow is correct to state that 51:9–11 is "exactly parallel" to 43:16.[122] Three times in 51:9 the writer calls the Lord to awaken and act as he did in the first Exodus, when he "bared his holy arm." This anthropomorphism is uniquely connected to the Exodus (15:16), especially in the Deuteronomic history.[123] As in several previous examples, the redeemed enter into Zion with great joy.[124] The ransomed are those who are now released from the exile, just as the former generation was released from Egypt. The noun used in v. 11 is פדה, a term often associated with the Exodus especially in Deuteronomy.[125]

While subtle, this is the only possible reference to the banquet scene in Isa 25:6–8 in Isa 40–55. In Isa 25:6–8 the Lord summoned both his people and the nations to his mountain for a banquet of fine foods, but the Lord himself consumed the mythological creature Mot, or Death. In Isa 51:9 the Lord cuts[126] the mythological creature Rahab to pieces. Rahab, Leviathan and the "sea monster" are associated with Egypt in various

---

122. The differences are far from superficial. In that context there are several clear verbal parallels to the Exodus stories as they appear in Exod 14–15 as well as a call from the writer to recall the things of the past. As Keisow observes, "Gerade auf dem Hintergrund der aufgezählten Gemeinsamkeiten beider Texte zeichnet sich aber eine keineswegs nur oberflächliche Verschiedenheit ab." Keisow, *Exodustexte*, 169.

123. Van der Woude, "זְרוֹעַ," in *TLOT* 1:392–93; Deut 4:34, 5:15, 7:19, 11:2, 26:8, Jer 32:21, Ps 136:12. Similarly, Dreytza, "זְרוֹעַ" in *NIDOTTE* 1:1146–47; Ginsberg, "The Arm of YHWH in Isaiah 51–63 and the text of Isa 53:10–11," 152–56. Hoffmeier argued that the phrase is a parody of an Egyptian description of the power of Pharaoh, see "The Arm of God Versus the Arm of Pharaoh in the Exodus Narratives," 378–87.

124. Compare this text to Isa 35:8–10. There are a number of clear verbal parallels between the texts. For example, jubilation (רִנָּה) and joy (שִׂמְחָה) appear in both contexts. They only appear together in these two verses, Isa 55:12, and Zeph 3:17. The nouns grief (יָגוֹן) and groaning (אֲנָחָה) appear in Isaiah only in 35:10 and 51:11.

125. Deuteronomy 7:8, 9:26, 13:6, cf. Mic 6:4. In addition, the verb is used in the Davidic Covenant (2 Sam 7:23, 1 Chr 17:21).

126. The verb חלל II in the polel only appears elsewhere in the Hebrew Bible in Job 26:12–13 where it also refers to cutting up a mythological creature in parallel to Rahab. The term is related to cutting or hewing stone rather that eating a meal. The 1QIsa has מחץ, a more typical word for crushing an enemy's head (cf. Num 24:8, 17, Judg 5:26). In Ps 89:11 (89:10 ET), however, Rahab is crushed (דכא). The related term דוך appears in Num 11:8 with reference to beating manna with a mortar to prepare it for a meal.

versions of the Exodus story.[127] Ezekiel 32:2–8 describes Egypt as a sea monster drawn up out of the sea by the Lord and eaten by birds and animals. Goldingay and Payne observe that the writer describes the Exodus in terms reminiscent of creation, including the creation of these sea creatures.[128]

Isaiah 51:10 refers to the Exodus in language which is reminiscent of Ps 74. Psalm 74 also refers to the enemies of the Lord as sea monsters who are crushed and given to animals as food, although they are creatures of the desert in 74:13–14. Bonnard, for example, considers this "l'excellente connexion entre les rachetés d'Égypte et les affranchis de Babylone."[129] The verb חרב is normally associated with judgment (especially in the hifel), but appears in the qal in Isa 44:27, Ps 106:9 with reference to the drying of the Reed Sea in the Exodus. The Lord dried the "waters of the deep," מֵי תְהוֹם, a phrase also found in Exodus traditions (Exod 15:5, 8, Isa 63:13, Ps 106:9). Ps 77:16–20 is a significant parallel since there is a clear reference to the crossing of the sea, the "waters of the deep convulsed" when they saw the Lord, perhaps recalling Exod 15:14 when the nations who witnessed the Exodus trembled in fear. But Isa 51:11 refers to the new Exodus at the time of the return from exile.[130] The redeemed will return to Zion with joy (רִנָּה, cf. Isa 44:23, 48:20, 49:13) and jubilation (שִׂמְחָה, cf. Isa 51:3, 61:7, 66:5).[131] Those who return to Zion will have joy (שָׂשׂוֹן)

---

127. Rahab appears as a metaphor for Egypt in Ps 87:4, Ps 89:11 MT, Isa 30:7. The sea monster or Leviathan appears in Ps 74:13–14. Ps 87:4 refers to Egypt as Rahab in the context of the nations coming to Zion to acknowledge the Lord. In Ps 89:10 MT Egypt is described as Rahab in the context of the crossing of the Red Sea. The name רַהַב is associated with the mythological chaos monster represented by the sea (יָם). The Lord cuts this monster to pieces and feeds it to the animals (see Isa 30:7; 51:9–10; Job 9:13; 26:12). This imagery also includes Leviathan (Isa 27:1, Ps 74:14) and "sea monsters" of Gen 1:21 (תַּנִּין, Ezek 29:3; 32:2, applied to Egypt; Jer 51:34, applied to Nebuchadnezzar, Job 7:12; Ps 148:7). See Day, "Rahab (Dragon)," 5:610; Day, *God's Conflict With The Dragon And The Sea*. The substance of this monograph is summarized in Day, "Dragon and Sea, God's Conflict With," 228–30.

128. Goldingay and Payne, *Isaiah 40–55*, 2:236, citing the well-known parallels between Gen 1 and *Enuma Elish* (the *tannim* and Tiamat, cutting the sea creature, etc.). This is to be expected since the writer has consistently described the return to Zion through the wilderness as not only a new Exodus but a new Creation.

129. Bonnard, *Le second Isaïe*, 253.

130. Baltzer sees this text as a link between the Exodus and Zion traditions in Second Isaiah. He compares this text to Dan 7, four beasts rising from the sea, eventually destroyed by the representative of the Ancient of Days (*Deutero-Isaiah*, 357). He also sees this as a far more mythic version of the Exodus events than Exod 14. *Deutero-Isaiah*, 355. Cf., Day, "Rahab," 5:610.

131. The noun שִׂמְחָה is associated with joyous feasting in Judg 16:23, Neh 8:12, 12:27, 2 Chr 30:23. This last text is particularly interesting since it is associated with a seven day feast in celebration of Passover at the beginning of the reign of Hezekiah. The sacrifices are enormous and the joy is compared to the days of David and Solomon (30:26). The Chronicler intentionally patterns Hezekiah after David and Solomon by emphasizing his spectacular sacrifice and festive celebration near the time he became king. What is more, Hezekiah invites the northern kingdom to participate in an attempt at restoring the kingdom to the time of David. Dillard, *2 Chronicles*, 245. Neh 12:27 is the dedication of the rebuilt walls of Jerusalem. Musicians and singers make up a joyous procession to the walls of Jerusalem, accompanied by great sacrifice (v. 43). By the rabbinic period, שִׂמְחָה was synonymous with מִשְׁתֶּה, banquet. Fabry, "מַרְזֵחַ," in *TDOT* 9:14.

upon their heads.[132] Like Isa 25:6–8, grief and mourning are banished and replaced with everlasting joy.[133]

Isaiah 51:9–11 is another example of the prophet drawing on earlier Wilderness traditions and applying these traditions to his present situation. There are sufficient verbal and thematic parallels in these verses to indicate that the author intentionally evokes Exod 15, but there is more here than just that text. The use of Rahab and the chaos of the sea is part of the same mythological world as Isa 25:6–8. When he liberated his people, the Lord not only fought with the human enemies of Israel but also their spiritual enemies. This destruction of the real enemy (Rahab) is a cause for great joy and celebration like that of the banquet (Isa 25:6–8). If the enemy is defeated and the exile is over, joy and celebration is the only response possible.

Isaiah 55:1–5[134]

That Isa 54–55 is the conclusion to Isa 40–55 is clear and as such it ties together a number of threads found throughout these chapters. The new "way" has been prepared and traveled and Israel has returned to Zion so that the eternal covenant made with David can be renewed. In fact, Isa 55 is often described as broadening the Davidic covenant. The Lord re-affirms the covenant, but applies to it all of the people rather than only the Davidic line forever. As André Caquot comments, "L'oracle d'Isaïe 55:1–5 announce le triomphe universel et définitif d'Israel, définitif parce que Dieu concluera une 'alliance éternelle.'"[135] Isaiah 55:1–5 describes the beginning of the eschatological age in terms of a banquet to which all of the people are invited to participate.[136] The meal

---

132. Four times in Jeremiah שָׂשׂוֹן describes the joy of a wedding. The word appears in two other wedding contexts. In Ps 45:8 and Isa 61:3 the word refers to anointing with "an oil of gladness."

133. Grief (יָגוֹן) is ssociated with the death of a child in Gen 42:38 and 44:31 and the day of mourning in Esther 9:22. Elsewhere it appears in the context of great calamity or disaster. The noun אֲנָחָה and verb אנח are associated with great distress, see Lam 1:4, 8, 11, 21, for example. Significantly, the word is used in Ex 2:23 for the "groaning" of Israel while in slavery in Egypt.

134. Since 1QIsa divides the section at 54:17b, Goldingay and Payne begin the section at that point, *Isaiah 40–55*, 2:363. Virtually all scholars divide the chapter after v. 5. 4QIsaiahc has a blank line after v. five. Given the fact that 54:17 concludes with "thus says the Lord" and 55:1 beings with an interjection which normally begins a pericope, it is best to divide the section at 55:1. Verses 1–5 are parallel to vv. 6–9, with vv. 10–13 functioning as a set of concluding promises. Some commentators divide vv. 1–5 and 6–13 into two separate sources, others sub-divide vv. 1–5.

135. Caquot, "Les 'grâces de David' à propos d'Isaïe, 55/3b," 57.

136. This fact is not always noticed in the commentaries. Muilenburg follows the earlier suggestion of Delitzsch that this invitation as "reminiscent of the water seller." Muilenburg, "The Book of Isaiah," 5:643; Keil and Delitzsch, *Old Testament Commentary*, 7:325; Melugin, *The Formation of Isaiah 40–55*, 172. As Clifford, "Isaiah 55: Invitation to a Feast," 27, points out, there is no literary evidence of ancient water-sellers. In fact, Delitzsch only refers to modern water sellers. This view is adopted by Goldingay and Payne, *Isaiah 40–55*, 364, citing Waldow, *Anlass und Hintergrund der Verkündigung des Deuterojessja*, 22. Cf. his *Der traditionsgeschichtliche Hintergrund der prophetischen Gerichtsreden*. However, Blenkinsopp points out that a vendor who refuses payment will not be in business long! Blenkinsopp, *Isaiah 40–55*, 369. Volz imagines a wealthy man who buys up all the food in a famine

is described in terms which resonate with Isa 25:6–8, although there is virtually no similar vocabulary.

R. Clifford surveyed ancient Near Eastern banquet material and concluded that the chapter describes the Lord's invitation to the exiles to leave Babylon and return to Zion to enjoy a rich feast.[137] Clifford then draws the analogy to Isaiah 25:6–8 since exiles are invited back to Zion.[138] C. L. Seow has connected the installation of the Ark in Jerusalem and David's dance and festive meal to this passage. The eschatological banquet is associated with David as a divine warrior who leads a procession to Zion.[139] S. Starbuck follows the suggestion of O. Eissfeldt and connects Isa 55:1–5 with Ps 89.[140] The meal in Isa 55:1–5 is therefore an expansion on the Davidic enthronement scene in 2 Sam 6–7.[141]

Others have pointed out that the invitation is not unlike that of Lady Wisdom in Prov 9, who invites all to eat rich foods and drink aged wines at her table.[142] The imperative of הלך is used in Prov 9:5, Sir 24:19, and Isa 55:1 and in all three cases there is a promise of food which will lead to life (Prov 9:6, Isa 55:3). In addition, the people in Isa 55 are chided for having spent their money on food which does not satisfy rather than accepting the rich food which is freely given. This is not far from the theme of Prov 9 in which Wisdom and Folly are portrayed as contrasting women offering their hospitality to all. Isa 55:1–5 cannot be described as a Wisdom text, however, because of the presence of royal language. The people are not invited to sit at Wisdom's table, but rather to celebrate the renewal of the Davidic covenant. This invitation is therefore an enthronement image, recalling the original enthronement of David in Jerusalem.

---

then redistributes it to the poor. Volz, cited by Whybray, *Isaiah 40–66*, 191. But all of this seems to be an unfounded speculation based on modern practice. Some scholars, however, do understand Isaiah 55 as a messianic banquet. For example, Wilson, *The Nations in Deutero-Isaiah*, 218, 246. Koole connects this text back to the banquet in Isa 25:6–8 as well as forward to Matt 22:1–12 and Rev 19:7, Koole, *Isaiah III*, 2:400.

137. Clifford, "Isaiah 55: Invitation to a Feast," 27–35 and Clifford, *Fair Spoken and Persuading: An Interpretation of Second Isaiah*. Clifford first examines CTA 23 ('UT 52 ' KTU 1.23), often thought to be a *heiros gamos*. In this short text a royal party greets guests by inviting them to partake of bread and wine. Like Isa 55:1, this text begins with *'ay*, similar to the Hebrew הוי. Compare Zech 2:10–11 MT, הוי is repeated twice in an invitation to leave Babylon and return to Zion. A second text has an almost identical invitation (KTU 1.17), but the sections ends by offering her guests eternal life. Clifford, "Isaiah 55," 29.

138. Compare to Begrich, *Studien zu Deuterojesaja*, 59–60.

139. Seow, *Myth, Drama, and the Politics of David's Dance*, 135–36. Seow cites Fisher, "From Chaos to Cosmos," 191–94, cf. Freedman, *Canaanite Myth*, 144, 263.

140. Starbuck, "Isaiah 55:1–5, Psalm 89, and Second Stage Traditio in the Royal Psalms," 247–65; Eissfeldt, "Promises of Grace to David in Isaiah 55:1–5," 196–207. Eissfeldt thought it possible that Ps 89 was known to the writer of Isa 55, but thought the royal ideology was quite different.

141. Starbuck, "Isaiah 55:1–5," 251. Koole, *Isaiah III*, 401, looks back the original covenant meal in Exod 24:11.

142. Prov 9:1–5, cf. Sir 24:19, 51:24. Westermann, *Isaiah 40–66*, 281; Whybray, *Isaiah 40–66*, 190; Blenkinsopp, *Isaiah 40–55*, 369. This was first suggested by Begrich, *Studien zu Deuterojesjea*, 52–54.

A Banquet in the Wilderness

The invitation to the feast appears in the first two verses. The interjection הוֹי is normally at the beginning of an announcement of woe, although occasionally it is used to attract the attention of the listener.[143] Are these the "wretched and poor," people who cannot support themselves? Koole for example sees the invited guests as the poor from 41:17, the exiles in Babylon who are far from the course of real water (Zion) and in both physical and spiritual want.[144] But this comment seems to ignore the fact that the Babylonian captivity was comfortable for most people and many became quite prosperous in the exile. Starbuck therefore argues that the phrase אֵין־לוֹ כָּסֶף implies that those addressed do not have silver for food because they have spent it on other things.[145] Compare this to verse 2a where the people are described as having spent money and labor on things which cannot satisfy.

Besides bread and water, the text invites people to buy milk without cost. Milk (חָלָב) was part of a good meal in the ancient world. In Judg 5:25 Jael brings Sisera milk in a bowl worthy of a Canaanite prince.[146] Ezek 34:3 the bad shepherds "eat the curds" and dress in fine cloths but do not tend for the flock. Milk is the drink of wealthy priests who live lives of opulence.[147] As is well known, Joel 4:18 describes the coming age as a time when hills drip with milk, new wine and water.[148] In Num 18:12, for first-fruits of the harvest, and in Deut 32:14, both חָלָב and חֵלֶב appear in a parallel construction. Deuteronomy 32 is a retrospective of the wilderness period and describes Israel as arriving in a land "flowing with milk and honey." Israel is nourished by bountiful provision from the hand of the Lord: oil, milk, honey, fattened and choice animals.[149] In either case, this description of rich food is reminiscent of the banquet scene in 25:6–8.[150]

---

143. Something like "Hey!" (Goldingay and Payne, *Isaiah 40–66*, 2:367) or "Ho!" (Blenkinsopp, *Isaiah 40–55*, 369), although he chooses to leave the particle untranslated.

144. Koole, *Isaiah III*, 2:404. Koole points out Lam 5:4 as proof for the high cost of water after destruction of Jerusalem.

145. Starbuck, "Isaiah 55:1–5," 249, "Their poverty is a poverty of wisdom."

146. The bowl of milk was a "lavish expression of hospitality." Block, *Judges and Ruth*, 240n441; Gray briefly comments on parallels at Ras Shamra, *Joshua, Judges, Ruth*, 280. Although anachronistic, Moore comments that this was "a grateful and refreshing drink, the best the Bedawin had to give." *Judges*, 163.

147. In Job 21:24, a wealthy person is described as "full of milk, Isa 60:16 the phrase "drink the milk of nations" refers to taking the "wealth of nations." In 1 Sam 17:18, Jesse sends a gift worthy of King Saul, ten portions of cheese, literally "slices of milk."

148. Milk is used as a metaphor for beauty as well. In Gen 49:12 the heir of Judah has "eyes are like wine and his teeth are like milk," (cf. SoS 4:11, 5:12). It is possible to repoint חָלָב, milk, as חֵלֶב, fat. There are at least two other texts which represent a confusion of the two words (Ps 73:7, Ps 17:10, possibly Job 21:24). חֵלֶב as the connotation of the "best parts" of something (a sacrifice, Lev 3:17 or the land, Gen 45:18).

149. Merrill, *Deuteronomy*, 414. This language appears in Amos 6:4 in a negative sense. The wealthy of Samaria lounge on ivory couches and dine on fattened animals. By the Second Temple period, this list becomes typical of the "good things in life," Sir 39:26. Levine, "The Land of Milk and Honey," 43–57.

150. Although this is rarely noticed in the commentaries, see Wilson, *The Nations*, 228.

Isaiah 55:3 contains something of an interpretive conundrum. The construct relationship of חַסְדֵי דָוִד ("faithful love of David") can be taken either as an objective (faithful love which has David as its object, "faithful love for David") or subjective (faithful love which David demonstrated, "David's faithful love"). Prior to Caquot's 1965 article,[151] most translations and commentators took the construct as objective. Caquot argued that the ancient translations of Isaiah 55:3 took the phrase as subjective, although Williamson points out the evidence from the LXX can be read differently.[152] Caquot also argues that in each of the 18 occurrences of חֶסֶד as a plural construct, all but one governs a genitive relationship and all except this text and Gen 32:11 are clearly subjective. Williamson points out that in each of the texts which precede Isaiah 55 chronologically, God does חֶסֶד on behalf of man.[153] If one includes the singular occurrences of חֶסֶד in a construct relationship, the evidence is even more ambiguous and context must guide.[154]

Finally, when the covenant is renewed, the nations will acknowledge the Holy One of Israel as God because he has endowed his people with splendor (v. 5). Each of the five times the verb פאר appears in the piel, God is the subject. He glorifies his temple (Isa 60:7, 13; Ezra 7:27) and Zion (Isa 60:9), and the lowly (Ps 149:4). The related noun תִּפְאֶרֶת is used occasionally for beauty or beautiful ornaments (Ezek 16:17, 39; 23:26, 28:2, 40, Isa 3:18, 4:2, 2 Chr 3:6). "Blossoming of the wilderness" (vv. 12–13) is by now familiar metaphors employed by the author to describe the new Exodus. The way through the desert is made fertile and the deserts bloom wildly.

---

151. Caquot, "Les 'grâces de David.'" The same construction and interpretive difficulty appears in 2 Chr 6:42. In addition to the commentaries, see Beuken, "Isa. 55, 3–5: The Reinterpretation of David," 49–64; Williamson, "Sure Mercies of David: Subjective or Objective Genitive," 31–49; Bordreuil, "Les 'graces de David' et 1 Maccabees 2:57," 73–76.

152. Williamson, "Sure Mercies of David," 32. The LXX renders חַסְדֵי דָוִד as τὰ ὅσια Δαυιδ τὰ πιστά. Caquot takes the neuter plural of ὅσιος, appearing only here and in Deut 29:19, as "les actes saints de David," "the holy acts of David". But the neuter plural ὅσια can include the idea of a "good gift" expected from a deity, implying an objective genitive. Commenting on the citation of this text in Acts 13, Lövestam demonstrates from other texts in the second century BCE that the neuter plural is associated with general blessings. Lövestam , Son and Saviour, 75. Compare Dupont, Études sur les Actes des apôtres, 337–59.

153. Williamson, "Sure Mercies of David," 36.

154. The most Williamson is willing to admit is that when חֶסֶד governs a genitive, it is often subjective. But this cannot be taken as a rule. Williamson, "Sure Mercies of David," 39. The context of the חַסְדֵי דָוִד is an articular nifel participle הַנֶּאֱמָנִים from the root אמן. Caquot takes this participle as modifying חַסְדֵי דָוִד, with the sense of "stable" or "durable" faithful acts of David. Caquot, "Les 'grâces de David,'" 53. These three words appear in the Davidic covenant (1 Kgs 7:26, 2 Chr 6:17). In addition, Ps 78:37 and Neh 9:8 are negative examples of this same vocabulary since Israel did not remain faithful to the covenant. It is not a surprise to find that both of these examples are part of the "wilderness tradition" developed in Second Isaiah. As Williamson concludes, these three words "point most plainly to the oracle of Nathan upon which the Davidic dynasty was founded." Williamson, "Sure Mercies of David," 43, citing Ps 139:29 as additional evidence. Clifford considers Williamson to have proven his case against Caquot and Beuken. Clifford, "Isaiah 55," 34n9.

Isaiah 55:1–5 has a number of thematic similarities to the eschatological banquet of Isa 25:6–8. In both texts there is an invitation to participate in a meal served by the Lord himself. In both, the food is excellent and available to all. Isaiah 55 makes explicit that this meal celebrates a new, everlasting covenant of David. Taking this pericope along with chapter 54, the shame of the nation is reversed (54:1–4) and the nations which oppressed Israel will be punished (54:15–17). The invitation to participate in the on-going feast which characterizes the new age is found in the sayings of Jesus as well. The beatitude in Matt 5:6 pronounces blessing on those who hunger and thirst, a potential allusion to Isa 55:1. The miracles of miraculous meals in Matt 14:13–20 and 15:32–39 are enactments of this passage. Jesus invites people into his ministry and he provides them "food without cost." In Matt 10:28 Jesus invites the weary to find rest in him. As I will show in chapter 7, Jesus' invitation to participate in meals is an invitation to celebrate in the end of the Exile in anticipation of God's renewal of his (marriage) covenant with Israel.

Summary and Conclusions on Isaiah 40–55

After surveying Isa 40–55 it is clear that the prophet chose to describe the return from Exile as a new Exodus. The Lord is inviting his people to join in the procession back to Zion (40:3–5, 55:1–2). The shame of the nation will be removed as they are restored to their place in the Land promised to Abraham. Like the first entry into the Land, the Lord himself will provide food and water along the way. Like Isa 25:6–8, there is an invitation to return to Zion and a reversal of shame to joy. But Isa 40–55 also describes the return from exile as an ongoing time of joyous fellowship with the Lord. This section of Isaiah was intended as an encouragement to the people living in Exile to return to Jerusalem and end the Exile. As such, the writer has developed of the idea of an eschatological banquet by combining it with the Exodus and Wilderness traditions and utilized this developed tradition as a call to end the Exile.

This development and application of tradition may continue in the Isaiah corpus. The third section of the book may express dissatisfaction with the response to Isaiah's call to end the exile and return to Zion. The literature of the Second Temple Period also occasionally expresses frustration with a continued exile and foreign rule (1 Maccabees, *PsSol.* 17). When Jesus invites people to celebrate "because the bridegroom is with them," he stands in this tradition of developing the Exodus and Wilderness traditions and applying them to a contemporary situation. In the case of Jesus, he is calling people to follow him as God's representative at the end of the Exile.

Jeremiah 31:10–14 As Banquet

This section will briefly trace features of a banquet found in Isa 25:6–8 and Isa 40–55 in another passage which can be described as an eschatological banquet. In Isa 25, the people of God will be gathered to Zion where they participate in a joyous festival characterized by feasting. There are a number of other texts which describe the gathering of the redeemed nation (Ezek 20:34, Zech 10:8, Zeph 3:19–20) or a joyous celebration on Zion (Isa 56:7, Zech 3:14–15). Likewise, some texts combine eating and drinking in the presence of God without obvious eschatological interest (Ps 36:9). My interest at this point is in the combination of all of the features found in Isa 25:6-8. I will therefore limit this section to Jer 31:10–14.[155] Two factors make this text important for this study. First, it is likely that Jeremiah stands between Isa 25:6–7 and Isa 40–55 chronologically and can therefore be seen as a test case for how intertextual relationships develop. Second, Jer 31–33 is highly significant for reading banquet metaphors in the New Testament. There is no question that Jer 31 is critically important in the Synoptic gospels, appearing in each of the Synoptic Gospels during the Last Supper.

Jeremiah 31:10-14 describes an eschatological banquet on Mount Zion.[156] This passage might be described an intertextual reflection of Isa 25:6-8 since there are few words which appear in Isa 25:6-8. There are also a remarkable number of thematic similarities as well as a few verbal parallels to Isa 40–55.[157] For example, the noun אִי (coastland, 31:10) appears only 36 times in the Hebrew Bible, but 9 times in Isa 40–55. More significantly, Isa 41:1 and 49:1 begin an oracle with the Lord addressing the coastlands (אִי), as in Jer 31:10. Jeremiah uses a shepherd metaphor for the gathering of the nation to Zion. While the verb קבץ is common in the Hebrew Bible, it appears in Isa 40:11 in nearly the same context as Jer 31:10. Isaiah 40:9–11 describes the Lord gathering the nation to the high mountain, Zion.[158] The nation is able to return from exile because the Lord as ransomed (פדה) and redeemed (גאל) them. Both words are important in Isa 40–55. In Isa 51:11 the ransomed of the Lord return to Zion with joyous singing, just as in Jer 31:11–12.[159] In Jer 31:12 the people will live in a well-watered garden, a place of abundance.[160] In Jer 31:13 the Lord will turn mourning into joy (שָׂשׂוֹן), comforting (נחם) his people. This is thematically akin to Isa 25:8 ("wiping every tear"), although the vocabulary is not the same. Isaiah 51:3 combines שָׂשׂוֹן with

---

155. Ezekiel 34:11–24 sounds many of these same themes although the text uses the image of a shepherd gathering his sheep and leading them to "mountains of Israel" (vv. 13–14) where the Lord will feed them himself in a "rich pasture."

156. For example, Keown observes that this passage has much in common with both a pilgrimage (Ps 84) and an eschatological banquet (Isa 25:6–8). Keown, *Jeremiah 26–52*, 114.

157. A problem for any intertextual allusion in the Hebrew Bible is the relative dating of the texts. Isa 25:6–8 may date after Jer 31, in which case the intertextual relationship would be reversed. This is not a serious problem for this study since I am considering all of these texts as a whole as the intertextual database used by Jesus.

158. The word appears in Isa 11:12, 43:5, 54:7 and 56:8 as well to describe the gathering of the exiles from the nations. Isaiah 54:7 uses a marriage metaphor.

159. In Isa 51:11 the redeemed "enter Zion singing" (וּבָאוּ צִיּוֹן בְּרִנָּה). In Jer 31:12 they "enter and sing on the heights of Zion," (וּבָאוּ וְרִנְּנוּ בִמְרוֹם צִיּוֹן).

160. The verb רוה appears in Isa 55:10; Jer 31:12 has the cognate noun, cf. Isa 58:11. The verb has the sense of being satisfied with drink, similar to the Arabic *riyy* (HALOT).

comforting (נחם) the personified Zion. All people will participate in this feast in Zion: young women will dance and both young and old men will be merry (Jer 31:13). In the same context, the feast will include the blind and lame. This too is similar to the expectation of Isa 40–55 (42:7, 16, 18, 43:8). While the word translated "feast" in Jer 31:14 is not מִשְׁתֶּה, the verb רוה usually has the sense of giving abundant rains or well-irrigated. Combined with "fatness" (דֶּשֶׁן) and the priesthood (the object of the verb is הַכֹּהֲנִים נֶפֶשׁ), the image is of an abundant sacrifice shared by the priests and people. Given the number of connections between Jer 31:1–14 and Isa 40–55, it is not surprising to find the food described in Isa 55:2 is בַּדֶּשֶׁן נַפְשְׁכֶם, "rich foods." This is a clear verbal allusion since the combination of נֶפֶשׁ and דֶּשֶׁן is rare.[161] This time of joyous feasting stands in stark contrast to the affliction of the fall of Jerusalem.[162]

Jeremiah 31:10–14 looks forward to a time when the nation of Israel will be gathered out of the nations and returned to Zion where all of the people will celebrate joyfully and share a meal. Like Isa 25:6–8, Zion is the location this joyful meal and like Isa 40–55, this shared meal is described in Eden-like terms. There will come a time, Jeremiah says, when God will restore his people from Exile and deal with the real problem behind their covenant unfaithfulness. That Jeremiah 31 should refer to the gathering of the nation to Zion as a grand meal shared by young and old alike is important for the goal of this study. In each of the synoptic Gospels, Jesus eats and drinks with all the people of Israel, celebrating in his Kingdom. What is more, Jesus refers to the New Covenant described in Jer 31:31–33 in the context of a special meal eaten with his closest supporters. Combining traditions like Isa 25:6–8, 40–55, and Jer 31:10–14, Jesus enacts the end of the Exile by eating, drinking, and joyful celebration.

Summary and Conclusion:
New Exodus as Eating and Drinking in the Eschatological Age

This survey has shown that the pervasive metaphor for end of the Exile in Isa 40–55 is the New Exodus. However, it is not simply the decisive events at the Red Sea which are reused for the return from exile. Israel's experience in the Wilderness is invoked and applied to a new problem, the return from exile after the fall of Babylon. Just as the nation was protected and fed in the wilderness when they were first bought out of slavery, the Lord will again provide abundant food and water as a sign of his salvation. The eschatological age is therefore characterized by continuous provision of abundant

---

161. The only other occurrence is Ps 63:5, "my soul will be satisfied with fat and rich foods." The usage is not exact since נֶפֶשׁ is the subject of the verb and דֶּשֶׁן is coupled with חֵלֶב.

162. "Their period of mourning will be brought to an end by their encounter with the LORD's goodness. While feasting on the abundance of Zion and drinking from the river of divine 'delights' (Ps 36:9–10). They will experience the joyful abundant life of the eschatological banquet (cf. Isa 25:6–10)." Keown, *Jeremiah 26–52*, 115–16.

food and water. This is in contrast to Isa 25:6–8, which described the eschatological banquet as an inaugural meal. In Isa 40–55, the meal is on-going.

The coming age will be inclusive since all people will participate in this new covenant meal. Isaiah 55 especially highlights the invitation to join in the eschatological age. All people are called to respond to the invitation to "come, eat and drink." What is more, the eating and drinking is part of a joyous procession to Zion. When the Lord leads the exiles back to Zion, the Lord will restore all things. The people will have returned to Eden itself. The whole of Isaiah 40–55 therefore can be described as a new application of Wilderness tradition in which eating and drinking before the Lord is a sign of inclusion and salvation.

Isaiah 40–55 also merges the Wilderness tradition with a marriage metaphor, especially in chapters 54–55. Israel's return from exile is a return from the wilderness to the Land of Promise, but it is also a restoration of the relationship that the nation once enjoyed with the Lord. This is of importance to the overall argument of this study since Jesus does not simply describe his ministry as an eschatological banquet, but rather as a wedding banquet. Further, he claims that he is the bridegroom who hosts the banquet. The relationship between God and his people is described as a restoration of a marriage in 54–55, but Isaiah is not the originator of this metaphor. Since Hosea was the first to describe the relationship of Israel and their God as a marriage, the next chapter will examine Hosea's unique blending of marriage and wilderness motifs.

5

Israel as the Wife of the Lord

Introduction

FROM THE FOREGOING SURVEY, it is clear that the image of the eschatological age as a feast is an important metaphor in Isaiah. But there is little support in this data for the idea that this time would be like a wedding feast. When the eschatological age is described in terms of eating and drinking, imagery is drawn from either a victory or enthronement banquet (Isa 25:6–8) or the wilderness experience of Israel (Isa 40–55). If a first-century Jewish teacher described the eschatological age as a wedding banquet, he could not be consciously invoking any single text that describes the eschaton in terms of a wedding banquet. This is why some scholars have rejected the possibility that the historical Jesus described himself as a bridegroom or thought of his ministry as a "wedding feast." These images are thought to have come from later Christian writers and reflect the developing theology of the Church as the bride of Christ.

There are, however, an impressive number texts in the Hebrew Bible which describe the relationship between God and Israel in terms of a marriage. This marriage ended in separation or divorce because of the infidelity of the wife, Israel. The eschatological age will be a time when the marriage between God and Israel will be renewed. The unfaithful wife will be restored to her former position because her sins have been forgiven and the marriage covenant has been renewed. As E. Ben Zvi commented, the marriage metaphor became "a way to shape, imagine, express and communicate" an understanding of the nature of God's relationship with his people.[1] If the coming age is a restoration of that marriage relationship, then it is natural to combine the imagery of a joyous celebration (an eschatological banquet) with the marriage metaphor. Commenting on the messianic banquet in 1QSa, Cross describes "a whole kaleidoscope

---

1. Ben Zvi, "Observations on the Marital Metaphor of YHWH," 363.

of ideas . . . was woven into an apocalyptic fabric."[2] Cross has in mind the nations streaming to Zion to join Israel as they are fed and nourished on "the height of Israel." I would suggest that the restoration of marriage between Israel and God is another element of that "apocalyptic fabric."

There is a connection between a covenant relationship and a marriage relationship which may account for the overlap of metaphorical fields in the biblical material. That a marriage is a form of a covenant is important, but more critical to the development of the metaphor of a marriage is the fact that the covenant between God and Israel was based on חֶסֶד, covenant faithfulness. The Lord will certainly be faithful in keeping the covenant, but his partner has been unfaithful. The covenant between God and his people is called a "covenant of love" in Deut 7:7–16.[3] As R. P. Carroll comments, the marriage metaphor "works very well for describing the history, however imaginary, of a community because marriages often start well and then turn sour."[4]

Since it is natural for a covenant relationship to be understood in terms of a marriage, a broken covenant relationship is easily understood in terms of marital unfaithfulness and divorce. Israel's lack of חֶסֶד is portrayed as a woman who breaks her marriage vows to become a prostitute. Given the practices of ancient patriarchal cultures, the reaction of the faithful spouse to the breach of marriage vows is often brutal and frequently described in scholarship as misogynist. The force of the metaphor is the horror of Israel's unfaithfulness and says nothing about the way women ought to be treated.

What is remarkable is the amount of overlap between the marriage metaphor and the new Exodus / wilderness motif as described in the previous chapter.[5] At the time of the new Exodus, Israel will return to the wilderness where the Lord will treat the nation as he did in the first Exodus.[6] The return from exile is therefore both a New Exodus (chapter 4) and a restoration of a marriage relationship (this chapter). It is therefore

---

2. Cross, *The Ancient Library of Qumran*, 78.

3. This is a hendiadys: "a loving covenant" or "a gracious covenant." Merrill, *Deuteronomy*, 181. Compare also Neh 9:32, God keeps "his covenant and his steadfast love" (חֶסֶד).

4. Carroll, *Jeremiah*, 120.

5. Carroll observes that the historical narrative of the Wilderness tradition is routinely negative, yet the prophetic use of that period is positive. Deut 32:10–14 is in fact positive, but for Carroll it is a late addition to the text of Deuteronomy. The positive view of the wilderness found in the prophets "holds promise for the future" (Hos 2:14–23). Carroll, *Jeremiah*, 121.

6. Deuteronomy 32:13–14 is a description of the care the Lord has provided for Israel. She has been fed with plentiful food, a list which includes meats and wine. Both Manna and quail were seen as "miraculous" food provided by God for his people in the wilderness. Claassens collects summaries from the rabbinic literature on the idea of manna. Claassens, *The God Who Provides*, 1–22. John 6:31–34 is another important text since a Jewish audience asks Jesus for a sign, such as manna. The return of manna is found in *2 Bar.* 29:8 ("the treasury of manna will come down again from on high, and they will eat of it in those years because these are they who have arrived at the consummation of time") and *Sib. Or.* 7.149 ("they will eat dewy manna with white teeth"). *The History of the Rechabites* 13:2 refers to a return of manna in a clearly Christian context. Jewish writers also looked for "the bread of the age to come" (*Gen. Rab.* 82.8 on Gen 35:17, cf. *Qoh. Rab.* 1:9, *Num. Rab.* 11.2 on Num 6:22). Aune, *Revelation 1–5:14*, 189.

possible to find a few texts that combine these two metaphors in order to describe the eschatological age as a wedding celebration. God in fact does a miracle by restoring the faithless bride to her virgin state and re-wedding her in the coming age.[7]

This chapter maps out the metaphor of a marriage in the Hebrew Bible as a foundation for understanding Jesus' use of that metaphor in his actions and teaching, especially as he blends imagery for the coming age. In order to understand the metaphor as clearly as possible, it is necessary to begin with a brief section surveying marriage customs in ancient Israel. While this section is worthy of a monograph, the goal here is merely to provide background for understanding the marriage metaphor as fully as possible. I will then examine the more important texts employing the marriage metaphor (Hos 1–3, Jer 2–3, 31).[8] I will then return briefly to Isa 40–55 and apply what is learned from these texts to "the end of the exile" and Wilderness tradition. In the final section of this chapter, I will examine the wedding song Ps 45. This is the only text in the Hebrew Bible which includes both the idea of an "anointed one" and a marriage.

---

7. There are two unusual elements in the book of Numbers which may point to a convergence of the marriage metaphor and the Wilderness tradition. Douglas has called attention to the presence of two sets of commands concerning women in Numbers. In Num 5:11–29 there is an elaborate set of instructions for determining an unfaithful wife and in Num 30:1–16 there are a series of commands on vows, the bulk of which concern the vows of woman, whether a virgin, a wife or a divorced woman. Douglas argues that these texts are intentionally placed in the book of Numbers in order to highlight Israel's status as the "mystic bride" of the Lord. The ritual described in Num 5 is connected to idolatry and re-used by Ezekiel in his condemnation of the spiritual adultery of the nation and can easily be seen in Hos 2:14–15. Douglas sees a connection to Hos 2:15 and Ezek 23:1–4, both of which describe Israel in the wilderness as "in the days of her youth" (*In the Wilderness*, 171). Israel made vows to the Lord in the wilderness which are binding. Any vows she makes to "other husbands" will be cancelled. Douglas, *In the Wilderness*, 160–71.

8. Clearly Ezekiel 16 portrays Israel's relationship with God in terms of a marriage covenant, but there is a different emphasis than one finds in the Isaiah use of the metaphor. Since the use of the metaphor in Ezekiel is negative and has little bearing on the teaching of Jesus, I will not examine Ezekiel in detail. In Ezekiel, Israel has clearly violated her marriage vows and been wholly unfaithful. Marriage is a metaphor for past election and there is no hope for a future renewal of the marriage in the future. Yet even in Ezekiel, the time in the wilderness as positive. Thompson comments that despite the overall negativity of the marriage metaphor in Ezekiel, the wilderness period is still a time of close fellowship with God (Ezek 16:8–16). Thompson, *The Book of Jeremiah*, 164n10. The parable of the Two Adulterous Sisters in Ezekiel 23 makes use of the marriage metaphor in and equally disturbing fashion. There are strong similarities between the Jer 3:6–11 and Ezekiel 23. So close that McKeating comments that they cannot possibly be independent of each other. McKeating, *The Book of Jeremiah*, 37. Perhaps the most disturbing image from Ezekiel concerns the death of own his wife in 24:15–27. After the siege of Jerusalem begins, Ezekiel tells the nation that they are impure "because of their lewdness" and that they will not be cleansed again until the Lord's wrath us over. After this prophecy, Ezekiel's wife dies. She is described as the "delight of his eyes." The noun מַחְמָד is used for Zion as a "precious thing" to the Lord (Isa 64:10; 2 Chron 36:19), but also of the Lover in SoS 5:16. Ezekiel may not mourn publically for his wife, just as the exiles will not be able to mourn for the delight of their own heart when the city is finally destroyed.

Ancient Marriage, Weddings and Feasts

Introduction

The search for details of marriage customs in ancient Israel is complicated by a number of methodological factors. Should we use other ancient Near Eastern material to illuminate Israelite practice? Sociologist D. Mace has no problem with the practice on methodological grounds given the common culture across the ancient Near East.[9] A classic example of this method is A. van Selm's study of marriage in the Ugaritic literature which provides a wealth of details on ancient Canaanite wedding practices.[10] While some Ugaritic practices (polygamy, for example) are not particularly helpful for fleshing out the biblical marriage metaphor, others shed considerable light on marriage traditions in the biblical period. For example, Ugaritic marriages were arranged through a matchmaker by paying a price to the father of the bride[11] as well as a gift to the bride. The beauty of the bride is notable: "The pupils (of whose eyes) are of pure lapis-lazuli, whose eyes are like alabaster bowls" (*COS* 1.102). The main element of the ceremony of the wedding itself occurs when the bridegroom escorts the bride into the house.[12] After she arrives, blessings are given to the couple and there is food and wine in abundance.[13] These elements of ancient marriage arrangement appear in the Amarna Letters as well. In a lengthy letter from Tusratta, the king of the Mittani to Naphureya there is a discussion of an arranged marriage via a third party (a servant) (EA 29 lines 16–27).[14] Once the king accepted the bride price (gold and jewelry), he

---

9. Mace states that he will "frequently . . . refer to these outside cultures which have influenced Hebrew marriage and family ideas and ideals." Mace, *Hebrew Marriage: A Sociological Study*, 44–46. Other examples include Parker, "The Marriage Blessing in Israelite and Ugaritic Literature," 23–30; Yamauchi, "Cultural Aspects of Marriage in the Ancient World," 241–52; Roth, *Babylonian Marriage Agreements*; Zeman, "Le statut de la femme en Mesopotamie d'après les sources juridiques," 69–86. Falk, *Hebrew Law in Biblical Times*.

10. Selms, *Marriage and Family Life in Ugaritic Literature*. Selms uses Ugaritic texts describing the marriage of gods and argues that these practices would reflect the culture which created the myths. Among others, Selms employs the *Kirta Epic* (COS 1.102, KTU 1.14), in which the bride is captured by force. Selms surveys biblical marriage in "The Best Man and the Bride: From Sumer to St John with a New Interpretation of Judges, chapters 14 and 15," 65–75.

11. Selms, *Marriage and Family Life*, 22–23. The Ugaritic word *mhr*, compensation gift, which Selms takes as related to the Hebrew מור, "to exchange."

12. Selms, *Marriage and Family Life*, 37. The bride may have been accompanied by companions. Selms comments that the entry into the groom's house is the legal moment of the marriage, even if the marriage is not immediately consummated (ibid., 39).

13. These blessings concern the fertility of the couple: "The woman you take, Kirta, the woman you take into your house, the girl who enters your courts, She shall bear you seven sons, even eight shall she produce for you." (COS 1.102). In the context of Kirta's wedding, the assembly of the gods attends the feast he prepares; perhaps implying sacrifices were made when the bride arrived, KTU 1.15, 2:1–11. This section is badly damaged and there is no description of the feast, but KTU 1.3, Ba'lu's feast of meat and wine.

14. Moran, *The Amarna Letters*, 92–99. For a transcription with translation, see Mercer, *The Tell el-Amarna Tablets*, 1:165–81.

anointed his daughter and sent her to Nimmureya, the father of the groom. Lines 28–54 describe the meeting of the bride and groom as a "festive occasion." Her dowry is delivered and inspected by the groom, but it was found to be incomplete. The rest of this tablet is a plea to complete the arrangements so that the marriage can proceed. EA 31 is a record of marriage negotiations conducted by a servant of the king. The woman was to be inspected, anointed with oil and a bride-price paid. EA 31 contains the response to this arrangement: the father gives his daughter in marriage. Both of these marriages follow the pattern described by Selms.[15]

Many of these elements also appear in biblical stories of betrothal and marriage, such as Jacob bartering with Laban for Rachel as a wife (Gen 29:13–30) or the rather negative story of Dinah and Shechem (Gen 34). The payment of a price at the time of the wedding may explain some details in Hosea as well. Since there are few examples of marriages in the narrative portions of the Hebrew Bible, it is almost impossible not to refer to the practice of contemporary cultures. Emphasis ought to be given to the descriptions found within the Hebrew Bible, but these texts may be illuminated by other ancient Near Eastern texts.

Another potential source for illuminating marriage practices is the various laws found in Deuteronomy. But as Hamilton warns, the biblical law codes are no "marriage manual."[16] In addition, a law code describes what ought to happen, not necessarily what did happen. Stienstra, for example, wonders about using Law to illustrate practice.[17] This is less of a methodological choice for the present project since there are no laws which illustrate a wedding celebration. Only Deut 24:1–4 can be considered a legal statement on divorce, but this is a rather troublesome text to say the least. Nevertheless, Law may be used to explain practice as we survey the development of the marriage metaphor in the prophets, especially with respect to the "faithless wife."

Frequently post-biblical wedding practices from the Mishnah and Talmud are used on the assumption that Jewish marriage practice is more or less the same from the biblical period through the time of the Rabbis. This anachronistic method has been rightly criticized in other contexts, but rarely does a scholar object when a description of a wedding of medieval European Jews is used to illuminate the chronologically diverse of weddings of Jacob, Samson or the parables of the Wedding Banquet and Ten Virgins (Mt 22 and 25).[18] While it is possible that there are some elements of Jewish wedding and marriage practice in these sources which date to antiquity, it is impossible to know this for certain. This study will therefore consciously avoid using these

---

15. Perhaps the Akkadian document entitled "Installation of the Storm God's High Priestess" (COS 1.122) ought to be included here.

16. Hamilton, "Marriage, Old Testament," 4:560–69,

17. Stienstra, *YHWH is the Husband of His People*, 71.

18. Törnkvist warns against using the Mishnah and Mekhilta to illustrate practices in the Hebrew Bible. Törnkvist, *The Use and Abuse of Female Sexual Imagery in the Book of Hosea: A Feminist Critical Approach to Hos 1–3*, 76.

sources to illustrate practices in the biblical material. Biblical law and narrative will be compared with and illuminated by other ancient practices, but the biblical material will be given preference.

Marriage

Of the process of courtship and marriage itself we can know only a little.[19] Perhaps the best example of a marriage arrangement is Gen 24. In this text Abraham sends his servant to his brother's family in order to obtain a bride for his son Isaac. After the Lord gives a sign that Rebekah is the woman, the servant contacts Laban her brother and negotiates the terms of the marriage, including a rather substantial gifts to both Rebekah and her family (24:53). After the arrangements are complete, the servant stays in Haran for three days and "eats and drinks" with Laban's household. After this time, Rebekah consents to go with the servant (24:57–58) and her family pronounces a blessing as they leave (24:59). It is not until Isaac takes Rebekah into the tent of his mother that they are married (24:67a).[20]

To what extent does the Hebrew Bible understand marriage as a covenant? J. Milgrom argues marriage is not a covenant in the biblical material,[21] but Hugenberger disagrees.[22] Perhaps illustrations drawn from narrative are helpful here, despite the methodological problems it presents. When Jacob marries the daughters of Laban in Gen 29:21–30, Laban makes a feast, מִשְׁתֶּה, a word I have already shown is often used to describe a covenant meal. Jacob's marriages will be part of an expanded covenant in Genesis 31. In Judg 14 there are several occurrences of the word מִשְׁתֶּה in the context of a wedding celebration. As the bridegroom, Samson is the one who hosts the feast (מִשְׁתֶּה וַיַּעַשׁ שָׁם, 14:10). In each of these examples there some sort of a contract and a meal associated with the consummation of the covenant. But E. Yamauchi disagrees that these are examples of covenants since he finds no references to marriage contracts in the Hebrew Bible.[23] While it is true that the language of a marriage contract comes

---

19. The family unit is the most basic element of Israelite society. In fact, all of Israel is structured around the extended family unit: a father's house, a clan, a tribe, even "the sons of Israel" is a family metaphor. Stienstra, *YHWH is the Husband of His People*, 75. Family is expanded through the marriage of sons. There are a remarkable number of stories in the Hebrew Bible which center on childlessness and marriage, illustrating the importance of family in ancient Israel. Many of the traditions which developed concern the distribution and preservation of family wealth. Guenther, "A Typology of Israelite Marriage: Kinship, Socio-Economic, and Religious Factors," 388. It is well known that the Levirate marriage preserved the family name, but more so, it preserved the property of a son who died without an heir. For a helpful summary of the importance of family in ancient Israel, see Blenkinsopp, "The Family in First Temple Israel," 48–103.

20. Sarah is dead by this point in the story, so presumably this is his tent now. There is no word for "married" in this verse; the text reads: "Isaac took her and she was with him as wife and he loved her."

21. Milgrom, *Cult and Conscience*, 134.

22. Hugenberger *Marriage as a Covenant*, 280.

23. Yamauchi, "Cultural Aspects of Marriage," 246. The earliest he is willing to accept is Tobit 7:14. For this warning, see also Meier, *A Marginal Jew*, 4:140–41.

from a much later date, the process taking a wife as illustrated by Gen 24 and the presence of vocabulary describing a covenant meal (מִשְׁתֶּה) indicates that even in the earliest biblical marriage was thought of as a contract or covenant.[24]

Many scholars have approached ancient Jewish weddings by examining contemporary customs and practices in the Middle East. For example, J. G. Wetzein examining Syrian customs in the nineteenth century, describes a bride and groom being carried to a great wedding feast on the day after the marriage is consummated by means of a decorated threshing sledge.[25] The bride and groom are treated like royalty during the week-long feast while the groom's companions act as a sort of honor guard. Such a method is fraught with difficulties since it is almost impossible to argue that marriage customs have not changed considerably over thousands of years. Even if it can be established that Middle Eastern culture has changed little, such studies often ignore the impact of Islamic culture on the Middle East. Are we to believe that a thousand years of Islamic culture have left no mark on marriage practices?

With this warning in mind, it is therefore remarkable that many of these practices (negotiation of a bride price, entry into the groom's home as consummation, celebration with drink) are found at Ugarit and in the Hebrew Bible, as well as post-biblical descriptions of Jewish marriage practice. Studies of marriage contracts confirm that the form of the covenant has changed little from ancient times.[26] Such studies typically cite as evidence the Babata marriage contract found in the so-called Cave of Letters.[27] M. Friedman surveys about 65 marriage contracts from the Cairo Geniza concludes that while they have many similar elements, there is also a great deal of variety in formula.[28] What remains consistent, however, is the bride price and transfer of the bride to the home of the groom. In several examples in Friedman, the signing of the contract is

---

24. Both Ps 45 and the Song of Solomon ought to be considered as a reflection of Israelite marriage practice, although neither of these royal weddings can be seen as describing an ordinary practice. R. Gordis argues that at least SoS 3:6–11 is a wedding song composed in honor of one of Solomon's marriages. Gordis, "A Wedding Song for Solomon," 263–70. That Ps 45 was taken as messianic perhaps even in the Second Temple period should signal the importance of this text.

25. Wetztein, "Die Syrische Dreschtafel," 270–302. Wetztein contributed an appendix to Delitzsch's commentary on Song of Solomon which summarizes much of this article. Delitzsch comments that Wetztein's article "contains not a few things that serve to throw light on the Song." Delitzsch, "Song of Solomon," 6:616. Wetztein's comments are not included in the English translations of the commentary, but Delitzsch provides a brief review of the points he found most illuminating. Compare also Oesterley, *The Gospel Parables in the Light of Their Jewish Background*, 134; Tasker, *The Gospel According to St. Matthew*, 232–33.

26. Epstein, *The Jewish Marriage Contract: A Study in the Status of the Woman in Jewish Law*; Epstein, *Marriage Laws in the Bible and the Talmud*; *Sex Laws and Customs in Judaism*; Davidovitch, *The Ketuba: Jewish Marriage Contracts through the Ages*.

27. The Babata contract is commonly dated 117 CE. See Yadin, "Expedition D—The Cave of the Letters," 227–57; Benoit and Milik, *Discoveries in the Judean Desert 2*; Yadin, *The Documents from the Bar Kokhba Period in the Cave of Letters*.

28. Friedman, *Jewish Marriage in Palestine: A Cairo Genizah Study*, 12–13. These texts date from 933 CE to the early twelfth century (see ibid., 30–33 for a table of geographical and chronological distribution of the Geniza fragments).

celebrated with a cup of wine.[29] After delivery a dowry, the father of the bride Tamar dresses his daughter in beautiful clothes and he makes her pour out wine at a feast.

The most obvious element of a wedding is a joyous celebration which takes the form of a feast. Since feasting was surveyed in chapter two, only a few brief notes are necessary here. In addition to the marriage covenant of Jacob described above, the book of Tobit describes a wedding in the Second Temple period. In Tobit 7 a contract is made "according to the decree of Moses" (7:13) and a blessing is given (7:11). In this case, Tobias refuses to eat or drink until the contract is signed, then they ate and drank. There is nothing here to suggest the meal was a marriage celebration, since there is a strong possibility the groom will die his first night with his new bride! Since Sarah has a demon which has already killed seven husbands on her wedding night, Raguel, the father-in-law, digs a grave for his new son-in-law (8:10–11). It is only after Tobias survives his first night with his bride that Raguel makes a wedding feast (8:19–21).[30]

In summary, we can know some things about ancient Jewish marriage practices, but other elements of the festivities remain obscure. What is important for this study is the view of the marriage as a legally binding contract with stipulations and responsibilities. As such, a marriage contract is a sub-form of a covenant. Like a covenant, the marriage contract is confirmed with eating and drinking.

Adultery

Given the fact that marriage was intended to produce legitimate heirs for the husband, adultery was a crime against the family and therefore a grave offense indeed.[31] While adultery is punishable by stoning (Deut 22:22–23, Lev 20:10), there are no narratives in the Hebrew Bible which illustrate the application of this law. The story of David and

---

29. *T.Jud* 13.5 is an additional illustration of this practice. A Palestinian marriage liturgy dating to the eleventh century ends the betrothal by having the groom drink from a cup of wine, who then gives the cup to the bride who drinks indicating her agreement. Friedman, *Jewish Marriage in Palestine*, 2:103; cf. *m.Qid* 2.2. The story in *T.Jud* 13 is a warning against drunkenness and sexual promiscuity and is considerably different than Gen 38. Like Tobit, Tamar is widowed in the bridal chamber when Er is struck dead (10:4). After Onan dies a year later she dresses in her bridal array and sits, according to Amorite custom, "in public like a whore" (12:1–2). Judah is overwhelmed by her beauty because he is drunk (12:3–5), and eventually marries Tamar (13:4–8).

30. The description of a wedding in *Joseph and Aseneth* will be covered in the next chapter.

31. Any extramarital sex on the part of the woman was considered adultery, while the man was only an adulterer if he has sex with a married woman. Stienstra points out that the reason for this inequity is that the woman's sexuality was not her property, it belonged to her husband. Conversely, the woman did not have the right to exclusive sexuality with her husband. Stienstra, *YHWH Is the Husband*, 85. A husband who visits a prostitute is not committing adultery, although there are clear statements concerning the folly of going to the prostitute (Sir 9:6, 19:2 for example). Although the text belongs to the Second Temple period, Sir 23:22–27 provides a vivid description of the grave nature of a woman's adultery. In this text a woman has committed adultery and presented her husband with "an heir by another man." This woman has sinned against God and her husband, and ought to be brought before the assembly for public punishment, her children cut off and her she will "leave behind an accursed memory" from which she can never recover.

Bathsheba is the only example of an adultery story and there is no punishment given to the woman in that case. In Gen 38 Tamar is presumably caught in adultery since she is found to be pregnant while waiting for a levirate marriage arrangement. While the punishment ought to have been death, she is not executed when she proves that Judah her father- in-law was in fact the father of her children. Older studies usually point out that in ancient Near Eastern law adultery was a crime against the husband, but in the biblical law adultery is a crime against God requiring the death penalty.[32] Westbrook however challenged this assumption since they are based on silence rather than statements of law.[33]

Other cultures practiced stripping the adulterous wife and driving her from the home.[34] But this may not be used as evidence of the practice in Israel. Stienstra warns that metaphors from Hosea and Ezekiel may not reflect real daily life.[35] It is possible, however, that Stienstra protests this point too much. The fact is that there are a number of texts which describe a faithless woman as being stripped and driven from her home.[36] If these texts do not reflect some sort of real-world situation, their rhetorical impact is blunted.

Divorce[37]

Aside from Deut 24:1–4, there few provisions for divorce in the Law. A husband might divorce his wife for any reason, but in practice childlessness and adultery are the two chief causes of divorce. In most cases in the Hebrew Bible, childlessness is dealt with through a second wife or a concubine rather than divorce.[38] Divorce was not commonplace in Israel and there are no examples of divorce in the narrative portions of the Hebrew Bible.[39]

32. For example, Kornfeld, "L'adultère dans l'orient antique," 92–109; Phillips, "Another Look at Adultery," 3–25. A text like Prov 6:32–35 seems to indicate that the adulterous wife should be prosecuted without pity.

33. Westbrook, "Adultery in Ancient Near Eastern Law," 542–80.

34. Ibid., 559. Westbrook cites an Old Babylonian tablet which states: "And if his wife Bitti-Dagan says to her husband Kikkinu: 'You are not my husband,' she shall go out naked, they will cause her to go up to the roof of the palace." Other texts refer to shaving the head of the adulterous wife in order to humiliate her. For a similar use of this material, see Whitt, "The Divorce of Yahweh and Asherah in Hos 2:4–7,12ff.," 36.

35. Stienstra, *YHWH is the Husband of His People*, 86. Contra Phillips, "Some Aspects of Family Law in Pre-Exilic Israel," 353.

36. Hos 2:3, Ezek 16:39, 19:13. In Isa 47:1–4 Babylon is described as a stripped woman, cf. Nah 2:10, describing Assyria.

37. For an extensive bibliography on divorce, see Meier, *A Marginal Jew*, 4:128–39.

38. For example, Abraham and Hagar (Gen 16), Jacob and Bilah (Gen 30:1–8), Elkanah and Penniah (1 Sam 1).

39. One possible example is David and Michal. In 1 Sam 25:44 we are told that Saul gave David's wife Michal to Paltiel of Laish, presumably annulling her marriage with David. She is returned to David in 2 Sam 2:12–16. In neither text is divorce mentioned, but commentators often wonder if David

Malachi 2:14–15 describes a marriage in terms of בְּרִית with the Lord himself as a witness of that marriage covenant. This is a difficult text to interpret, but for our purposes it is only important that the idea of covenant can be expanded to a wedding covenant.[40] It is possible to see this wedding covenant not as a prohibition on literal adultery and divorce, but rather a description of the nation in the most general sense. A. C. Welch, for example, argued that this text describes Judah as having married "the daughter of a strange god."[41] Judah has forgotten that she has already been married to the Lord therefore she has committed adultery by worshiping other gods. This is certainly the point of other prophets in the Hebrew Bible who describe the covenant between Israel and the Lord as a marriage (Ezek 16, Jer 31:32, Hos 1–3). While the initiation of the marriage is not fully described as a wedding or a wedding banquet, the idea of God's relationship with his people as a marriage is common enough in the Hebrew Bible. The Lord develops this relationship with provision of food in the wilderness, especially manna.

Once divorced, a woman could marry another man. If that happened, the first husband was prohibited from taking her back (Deut 24:1–4).[42] Stienstra connects this prohibition to Jer 3:1 and states that the second marriage renders the woman "unclean" and no longer a proper marriage partner.[43] Jeremiah describes Israel as a divorced wife who has taken other lovers, but now wants to return to her first husband. The Lord states clearly that she is defiled and has no right of return to her first husband.[44]

---

was not in violation of Deut 24. As Anderson comments, David's situation does not quite match that of Deut 24 since he did not divorce his wife. Anderson, *2 Samuel*, 57. Similarly, Bergen suggests that Michal was an adulteress since David did not divorce her. Bergen, *1, 2 Samuel*, 309.

40. For the difficulties found in Malachi 2:15, see Smith, *Micah-Malachi*, 322.

41. Welch, *Post-Exilic Judaism*, 120.

42. A potential exception to this is David's remarriage to Michal in 2 Sam 3:13–14. See Ben-Barak, "The Legal Background to the Restoration of Michal to David," 15–27. It is possible that Michal never consummated the second marriage (she was childless) and the law in Deut 24:1–4 would not have applied. On the other hand, David seems to have ignored marriage laws on several occasions.

43. Stienstra, *YHWH is the Husband of His People*, 89. Perhaps the prohibition concerned property the woman might obtain in her new marriage. Frymer-Kensky, "Deuteronomy," 51–62. Cf. to Anderson and Freedman, *Hosea*, 222.

44. Divorce was discouraged in the wisdom tradition. Sir 7:19 is usually taken as a warning to not quickly divorce a "wise and good wife." Sir 7:26 is a more clear warning against a hasty divorce. The verb ἀστοχέω is extremely rare in the biblical materials and elsewhere does not have the meaning of divorce. In the LXX it is used only here and in Sirach 8:9, where it has the sense of "rejecting" the wise traditions of the elders. The word appears only three times in the New Testament with the same sense of rejecting a traditional teaching (1 Tim 1:16, 6:21, 2 Tim 2:18). Cf. *Did.* 15:3 and *2 Clem.* 17:7.

Israel as the Wife of the Lord

Marriage and Kingship

Another avenue of research is the Royal wedding, although only Ps 45 and the Song of Solomon contain descriptions of such weddings.[45] While these wedding texts are idealized regal weddings and should not be taken as descriptions of common wedding practices in ancient Israel, they may very well be the sort of wedding practices which were used as metaphors in the prophetic texts we will examine. At the very least they provide the pool of vocabulary which the marriage metaphor employs. That Ps 45 and Song are royal weddings is especially interesting since it is at least possible that royal weddings were used as a chance to celebrate the covenant between Israel and the Lord.[46]

Summary and Conclusion

While it is difficult to be conclusive about typical wedding rituals and marriages in ancient Israel, it is possible to state the following with some confidence. First, marriage was a covenant relationship. In the earliest texts marriages were arranged via a contract between the family of the bride and the groom. A price was paid to the family and the bride was considered to belong to the groom and his family from that time onward. Second, a marriage could be ended if the wife displeased the husband in any way. Without taking a side in the rather thorny issue of the "shameful thing" of Deut 24, at the very least an unfaithful wife was a blow to the honor of the husband and his family. We cannot know much if anything about the practice of divorce in the First Temple period, but the very fact that divorce can be used as a metaphor in the Hebrew Bible indicates that it was a known practice. Third, a marriage could be restored, albeit with some prohibitions and restrictions. Again, we cannot know how often this occurred; other than David and Michal there are no restoration stories in the Hebrew Bible. Fourth, it is the nature of a metaphor to both highlight some aspects of reality but also to hide others. Each writer may highlight a different aspect of marriage to describe Israel's relationship with God. How Hosea employs the marriage metaphor is different than Ezekiel, both of which are in turn much different than Isaiah. It is therefore important to observe how each writer uses the metaphor.

---

45. Mettinger, *King and Messiah*, 185–232, especially 218–21. Parker, connects the marriage blessing in Ruth 4:12 to genealogy and suggests this is a royal wedding blessing. Parker, "The Marriage Blessing in Israelite and Ugaritic Literature," 23–30; cf. Seow, *Myth, Drama, and the Politics of David's Dance*, 136–39.

46. A royal wedding accompanies "enthronement" of a king in several cases in the Hebrew Bible. "Thirty men" accompany Saul at his enthronement meal; a state wedding ceremony may have included thirty men. Patai, "Hebrew Installation Rites," 161. Patai connects this to Matt 9:15, sons of the bridegroom (οἱ υἱοὶ τοῦ νυμφῶνος). When Saul is enthroned in 1 Sam 9:22—10:1, they eat a meal and then Samuel takes him to the roof for the evening—why? Patai suggests a connection to Absalom's rebellion (2 Sam 16:20–21). When he was enthroned he spent the evening in a tent with his father's concubines (cf. Adonijah's request for Abishag in 1 Kgs 2:22). When a king was enthroned, he marries the widow of the previous dynasty (David married widows of Saul, 2 Sam 12:8). Patai draws together several parallel texts from Egyptian and Modern African practice. Patai, "Hebrew Installation Rites," 165.

Finally, and despite this warning, there is remarkable consistency in prophets in the use of the marriage metaphor, especially in the combination of the marriage metaphor with the wilderness traditions surveyed in the previous chapter. That Hosea and Isa 40–55 both blend the marriage metaphor and the wilderness tradition seems to argue in favor of the popularity of the wilderness as the beginning of a relationship between God and Israel that can be described in marital terms. The remaining sections of this chapter attempt to gather the relevant texts in the prophets which employ a marriage metaphor.

Marriage Metaphor in Hosea 1–3

Introduction

Commenting on Hos 2:16–17 [14–15],[47] Clements states that the future restoration of Israel would be like a new bride, taken into the wilderness "where the marriage bond was first sealed."[48] Hosea 1–3 both looks back at the past relationship of the Lord and his people and forward to a time of restoration. The burden of Hosea is to describe the sin of Israel as a spiritual adultery. Often Hosea is described as the originator of the metaphor of a marriage for the relationship between Israel and the Lord,[49] but as Ben Zvi points out, the use of a metaphor presupposes a readership which is familiar with that metaphor.[50] Whether Hosea created the image or not, the marriage metaphor was designed from the beginning to look forward to the time of restoration of the relationship of God and his people after a period of estrangement.[51]

For the purpose of studying the marriage metaphor in Hosea, this section is limited to Hosea 1–3. As G. Eidevall has shown, the metaphor of Israel as the wife of the Lord is absent from chapters 4–14.[52] While it may be possible to argue that wilderness imagery found in these chapters of Hosea are tangentially related to the marriage metaphor, they are not critical to the argument being made here.[53] In addi-

---

47. References are to the MT of Hosea, English references are in brackets.

48. Clements, *Prophecy and Covenant*, 110–11. Cf. Friedman, who sees a future everlasting covenant between God and his people depicted as the "Lord's marriage" in Hos 2. Friedman, "Israel's Response in Hosea 2:17b: 'You are My Husband,'" 199. More recently, Winkel states that Hosea sees both the original covenant and the "renewal of the covenant in terms of a marriage." Winkel, *Jeremiah in the Prophetic Tradition*, 179.

49. Kruger, "Israel, the Harlot (Hos 2:4–9)," 107. Kruger also points out that there is no other ancient Near Eastern example the metaphor for the relationship of a god to its people. There are some similarities to Deut 32:10–14, but in that text the Lord finds Israel as an abandoned child in the wilderness rather than a bride.

50. Ben Zvi, "Observations on the Marital Metaphor," 363.

51. "The goal of a prophetic book is to provide hope," specifically that the sinful deeds which lead to a harsh punishment will be forgiven, leading to a restoration in the future. Ben Zvi, "Observations on the Marital Metaphor," 369.

52. Eidevall, *Grapes in the Desert: Metaphors, Models, and Themes in Hosea 4–14*, 229.

53. Hosea 9, for example, refers to the Lord finding Israel as 'finding grapes in the wilderness" and the Lord declares that their children will not be his—he will drive Israel out of his house and no longer love

tion, well-known debates concerning the reliability of the story of Hosea 1–3 are not important to this study.[54] It is best to stay within the "world of the story" in order to fully appreciate the metaphor. Gomer was a prostitute from the beginning of their marriage just as Israel was idolatrous from the very beginning. Hosea 2 describes Gomer's adultery in language which recalls the Exodus and Wilderness traditions. Hosea gave her good gifts and she had everything she needed to be happy and prosperous. He gave her grain, new wine and oil, silver and gold (2:8), indicating that he was a good husband to his wife. But Gomer did not recognize Hosea as the source of these gifts, but used them as part of her worship of Baal. This is a willful act on the part of Israel to worship Baal. She has chosen to ignore the very core of her religion (God is One) in the hopes of easy blessings from the worship of Baal (2:8, 13). Gomer's prostitution therefore refers to sin which occurred as early as the golden calf incident in Exod 32. The Lord brought the nation of Israel out of slavery, fought their enemies and established a covenant with them at Sinai, but they chose to credit this victory to a golden calf. The material used for the god was the gold they brought with them out of Egypt, the worship given to the god was the worship owed to the Lord.

In chapter 3, Hosea is commanded to love his wife again despite the fact she is an adulteress. Hosea purchases his wife and tells her that she is to live with him many days without being intimate with any man; afterwards Hosea will live with her again. This re-marriage is immediately interpreted in 3:4–5 as a long period without king or prince, sacrifice or idols. If this refers to the coming exile, then Hos 3 is an eschatological promise that after this long exile, Israel will "seek the Lord their God and David their king."

Previous Studies of the Marriage Metaphor in Hosea

There have been a number of important studies of Hosea's marriage metaphor in recent years, although some a driven by sociological agendas which limit their usefulness for this study.[55] Most of these studies work with a literary approach, beginning with a survey of how metaphors function in literature. One of the first studies on the marriage metaphor was a monograph N. Stienstra. She devoted a chapter to the metaphor in Hosea and another to the development of the metaphor in the rest of

---

them (vs. 15). This resonates with the marriage metaphor from chapters 1–3, especially divorce language such as "driving from the house." Here Eidevall recognizes the possibility of erotic language. See *Grapes in the Desert*, 150; cf. Rudolph, *Hosea*, 185. Nwaoru comments that there is "something virginal" about the simile of grapes in the wilderness. Nwaoru, *Imagery in the Prophecy of Hosea*, 170. Even the image of a prostitute at the threshing floor in 9:1 recalls the unfaithful wife of chapters 1–3.

54. For a survey of the options for understanding the plot-line of Hosea 1–3, see the standard commentaries and introductions, especially Harrison, *Old Testament Introduction*, 861–68.

55. In addition to the literature survey below, Oestreich, *Metaphors and Similes for Yahweh in Hosea 14:2–9 (1–8)*. Oestreich includes a chapter on love in Hos 14:5 and provides a great deal of material on the verb אהב. Kakkanattu, *God's Enduring Love in the Book of Hosea*. Kakkanattu studies the metaphor of God's parental love in Hos 11, including a significant section on the Exodus motif in Hosea (ibid., 101–10).

the Hebrew Bible.⁵⁶ For Stienstra, the marriage metaphor emphasizes God's desire for his people to respond to him "as when she was young" (Hos 2:16–17[14–15]).⁵⁷ This relationship is supposed to be the tender love and passion of a young married couple, but it has changed because of the unfaithfulness of the bride. This leads to divorce and public humiliation.⁵⁸ The marriage metaphor entails the sub-metaphor that the Lord can divorce his people and humiliate them in ways analogous to cultural traditions concerning the humiliation of an adulterous wife. But in the case of the Lord and his people, the humiliation is intended to draw the unfaithful wife back to her husband. The Lord desires to bring his people back to the place "where they once spent their honeymoon," the wilderness (2:17 [15]).⁵⁹ The Lord will re-woo his wife and bring her out of the wilderness and erase the memory of her unfaithfulness. Stienstra points out that the verb ארש ("to betroth," 2:21 [19]) is certainly not the word one would use for reconciling with an adulterous wife, rather, it is the word used for marrying a virgin.⁶⁰ The Lord is not simply wooing his old wife back; he is restoring her to her status as a virgin: her sin is forgiven and wiped out completely.

E. O. Nwaoru's 1999 monograph on Hosea's imagery treats the marriage metaphor as foundation for all which Hosea has to say throughout the book, specifically that "love, not punishment is the basic ingredient for restoration."⁶¹ It is the love of the husband which restores the marriage and enables the wife to be restored. Within the metaphor, then, the love of God restores the relationship of the Lord and Israel and enables the nation to receive the blessings of the covenant. Nwaoru points out repeatedly that it is the Lord who takes the initiative for this restoration.⁶²

56. Stienstra, *Yahweh Is the Husband of His People*.

57. Ibid., 100. According to Stienstra, the marriage metaphor emphasizes the love and trust which ought to characterize the relationship between god and his people (ibid., 96).

58. It is this humiliation which usually is the focus of studies on the marriage metaphor in Hosea. The brutality of the husband toward his adulterous wife is shocking. As in other ancient Near Eastern cultures, the husband strips his wife and publically humiliates her (Hos 2:4a [3a)]) then drives her from the community; the children of the adultery are also sent away as unloved. Humiliation is also found in Isa 47:2–3 (Babylon), Jer 13:26, Ezek 16:37, 23:29 (Judah or Jerusalem), Nah 2 (Assyria).

59. Stienstra, *Yahweh Is the Husband of His People*, 119. Hosea 2:17 refers to the valley of Achor. This was the location where Aachen was executed because he broke the ban on Jericho. This is the first incidence of unfaithfulness in the conquest of the land and the first defeat of the armies of Israel as a result of their unfaithfulness. This "place of trouble" will become a "doorway of hope." Nwaoru sees this as another example of Hosea's view that the wilderness was the ideal time in Israel's life, *Imagery in the Prophecy of Hosea*, 171. For Rashi and Kimhi, the valley of Achor represented the lowest point of the misery of the exile. Macintosh, *Hosea*, 74. On the other hand, Nyberg argues that לְפֶתַח תִּקְוָה ought to be translated as a place name. The phrase then would define the boundaries of the vineyards, "from the valley of Achor to Petah Tiqwa." See Nyberg, *Studien zum Hoseabuche*, 23. While this is possible, few commentaries have followed the suggestion (Törnkvist, for example). Josh 15:7 lists the valley of Achor as the northern border of Judah, usually identified as El Buqeah (little valley), north of Qumran. This is the only location near Jericho that might be called a valley. Pressler, "Achor," 1:56.

60. Stienstra, *Yahweh Is the Husband of His People*, 121.

61. Nwaoru, *Imagery in the Prophecy of Hosea*, 65.

62. This initiative is what sets Hosea apart from the so-called sacred marriages found in other

A. A. Keefe takes this further and argues that the common assumption that Hosea is a polemic against fertility religions of Canaan lacks textual evidence and is based on a false dichotomy that saw Canaanite religions as "seductive and feminine."[63] For Keefe, Hosea attacks the avarice of Israel's cult rather than the practice of Canaanite fertility cults[64] and that the "lovers" after which the wife chases are the nations.[65] Further, she argues that the covenant in Exodus was a covenant of love (Exod 20:6, Deut 4:37) and that violations of that covenant are described as provoking the Lord's jealousy (Exod 20:5, Deut 4:24, for example).[66] Whether Keefe has read the evidence concerning Canaanite cults correctly or not, her argument that the covenant was described in terms of a marital relationship even in the Torah is extremely helpful.

Since the early 1990's there have been a series of feminist interpretations of Hosea. Many of these in-depth studies build on the foundation of P. Bird's article challenging the conventional view that Gomer was a sacred prostitute.[67] In fact, Bird argues that "sacred prostitution" is not cultic sex at all, but rather polemic against Canaanite religion.[68]

---

ancient Near Eastern cults, "it is YHWH who calls Israel to a marital relation. We find no other deity making an insistent marital claim over his people." Nwaoru, *Imagery in the Prophecy of Hosea*, 131. Adler study of the origins of the marriage as a metaphor of God's covenant with his people confirms this conclusion. She concludes that the marriage metaphor as a description of the relationship between Israel and her god is unique in the Ancient Near East. Adler, "The Background for the Metaphor of Covenant as Marriage in the Hebrew Bible."

63. Keefe, *Women's Body and the Social Body in Hosea*. Contra Moseley, who describes Baal worship as a "licentious *hieros gamos*." Moseley, "A Critical Evaluation of the Methods and Motifs in the Polemic against Baalism in Hosea," 203.

64. Ibid., 103.

65. Ibid., 125–27. Keefe is following Hayes unpublished SBL paper "Hosea's Baals and Lovers: Religion or Politics?" There are number of texts which serve as evidence that nations could be described as "lovers" (Jer 4:30, 22:20–22, Lam 1:2, Ezek 16, 23). In 1 Kgs 5:1 states that Hiram has "always loved David," meaning that he had enjoyed a longstanding treaty relationship with David. The relationship of David and Jonathan is described with the language of love, although here too we may be reading the language of a treaty. The verb חפץ is used in 1 Sam 18:22 when Saul invites David to return to his service. This may be read as an "offer of peace" or a return to a former personal covenant between David and Saul. See also Albertz, *A History of Israelite Religion in the Old Testament Period*, 1:312, commenting on Elijah's polemic against "diplomatic syncretism."

66. In addition, apostasy is described as spiritual fornication (Exod 34:15–16, Deut 31:16, Lev 20:5). Keefe stops short of stating that the Pentateuch is the foundation of Hosea's marriage covenant since she cannot prove that Hosea is later than the Pentateuch. Keefe assumes that Deuteronomy itself comes from at least 100 years later, so the references she gives from that book might be influenced by Hosea. This recalls the criticism of inner-biblical exegesis from chapter 1; it is difficult to decide the direction of influence. She is willing to suggest, however, that Hosea may have coined the "political terminology of covenant-making as a theological concept. Keefe, *Women's Body and the Social Body in Hosea*, 108

67. Bird, "'To Play the Harlot': An Inquiry into an Old Testament Metaphor," 75–94. See also Fisher, "Cultic Prostitution in the Ancient Near East? A Reassessment," 225–36. For a statement of the standard view, see May, "The Fertility Cult in Hosea," 73–98 and Rowley, "The Marriage of Hosea."

68. Likewise, Wacker's 1996 monograph sought to de-patriarchalize Hosea. Wacker, *Figurationen des Weiblichen im Hosea-Buch*. Sherwood presents a thoroughly deconstructionist reading of Hosea. Sherwood is critical of other feminist approaches to Hosea which deal with the prophet's marriage

Jesus the Bridegroom

R. Törnkvist denies that cultic prostitution is in the background of Hosea and challenges the common understanding of זָנָה, prostitute.[69] She is shocked and offended by the image of God as a "wife-battering" husband and takes fellow feminist interpreters to task for trying to "save the reputation of Yahweh" by dealing with the imagery as metaphorical.[70] While these studies can contribute to our understanding of Hosea, they often miss Hosea's point by getting bogged down in the sociological details of the metaphor. The key to understanding Hosea is the love which the Lord has for his nation. Hosea uses the term חֶסֶד to describe the love and covenant loyalty which the Lord has for his nation, in spite of the nation's disloyalty. The term חֶסֶד intentionally evokes covenant language

---

as metaphor. Sherwood, *The Prostitute and the Prophet*. She describes her study as "an intersection between reader-response theory, deconstruction, and feminist criticism" (ibid., 321). Weems is especially under fire for accepting the violence of the text (God has a right to punish people) but not the sexual abuse of Gomer. Weems, "Gomer: Victim of Violence or Victim of Metaphor?," 87–104. In Sherwood's view, Weems tries to use metaphor to "protect Yahweh from taint." Sherwood, *The Prostitute and the Prophet*, 284.

69. Törnkvist, *The Use and Abuse of Female Sexual Imagery in the Book of Hosea: A Feminist Critical Approach to Hos 1–3*. In addition, she finds no evidence for a *hieros gamos* ritual in ancient Israel (p. 85), contra Rallis, "Nuptial Imagery in the Book of Hosea: Israel as the Bride of Yahweh," 198–200. Rallis, who is indebted to Wolff throughout her article, believes that Hosea chose the image of a marriage because of the Israelite practice of Canaanite fertility cults.

70. Törnkvist, *The Use and Abuse of Female Sexual Imagery in the Book of Hosea*, 64–65. Yee is critiqued in this section. There are other studies on the marriage metaphor in Hosea that can only be briefly noted here. Abma studies Hosea 1–3 as part of her survey of the marriage metaphor in four specific prophetic texts. Abma, *Bonds of Love*. She takes issue with scholars such as Setel ("Prophets and Pornography: Female Sexual Imagery in Hosea," 86–95), who describes Hos 1–3 as "pornographic" because female sexuality is depicted as an object of male control (Abma, *Bonds of Love*, 27). She goes on to point out that there is a difference between "understanding these texts" and "adopting their values." No reader of Hosea should adopt his treatment of his wife as a model for modern (Christian) behavior. Abma attempts to deal with the text by commenting on the violence, but recognizing that the violence described is not in and of itself the interpretation of the text. To describe a biblical text as pornographic is "anachronistic" and judges an ancient culture by modern standards.

Baumann produced a comprehensive study of the marriage metaphor in scripture, including significant contributions on the development of the metaphor in Hosea, Jeremiah, Ezekiel, and Isaiah. While each chapter has a brief section concerning the feminist view on the text treated, the study is not dominated by ideological concerns which distract from understanding the marriage metaphor. Baumann, *Love and Violence: Marriage as a Metaphor for the Relationship between YHWH and Israel in the Prophetic Books*. This is a translation of *Leibe und Gewalt: Die Ehe als Metaphor für das Verhältnis JHWH-Israel in den Prophetenbuchein*. Yee devoted a chapter to Hosea in her 2003 monograph on women as images of evil in the Hebrew Bible. She understands Hosea as the originator of the marriage metaphor. Yee, *Poor Banished Children of Eve*, 81–110. Another chapter is devoted to Ezekiel's use of the marriage metaphor. For Yee, Hosea must be understood within the context of the "YHWH-only" movement of the eighth century (Elijah, Elisha, and Jehu). Of importance for Yee is the fact that the marriage metaphor feminizes the ruling male hierarchy; it is the ruling men who are the promiscuous wife in order to shame and humiliate them for their unfaithfulness to their covenant with the Lord (ibid., 98). She describes this as "symbolic castration." It is in the wilderness that the Lord will seduce the nation again, "speaking tenderly" to her. This seduction is a covenant renewal (ibid., 107). The metaphor "finding grapes in the wilderness" recalls Israel's exclusive relationship with the Lord in the wilderness. In fact, Yee argues that 9:10–17 was recited as part of the celebration of Sukkoth, which is a combination of fertility and wilderness.

within Hosea's marriage metaphor.[71] Within the marriage relationship, both partners are to be loyal. In the case of the Lord's marriage to Israel, the Lord himself cannot break the marriage covenant, it was Israel who was disloyal.[72]

In summary, it seems obvious, then, that the marriage metaphor in Hosea describes the relationship of God and his people. As Keefe commented, when "Hosea's readers read marriage as a metaphor of the covenant in Hos 1–2, they assume the model of covenant which is proffered in Exod 19–20."[73] Friedman connects the marriage metaphor in Hos 1–3 to Exod 19:5–8. The prophet "allegorically connects" the initial proposal of marriage in Exod 19 to Israel's response in Hos 2.[74] The key word in 2:17 is ענה, "to answer." When the adulterous wife is restored, then she will "answer as in the days of her youth." When the Lord offered the covenant to the people in Exod 19:5–6, he promised that they would be a treasured possession of the Lord if they obeyed the covenant. In verse 8, the people answer (ענה) the Lord saying that they will do all that the Lord has asked. It is the next day that the great clouds settle on Mount Sinai and the people consecrate themselves before the Lord.

Restoration of Marriage in Hosea

There are a series of items in Hosea 2 which indicate that Israel's restoration is a renewed marriage. First, in 2:16–17 [14–15], the Lord declares his intent "to allure" wife. The verb פתה in the piel can have the connotation of seduction (Exod 22:15, for example), but more often it is a gentle persuasion.[75] Second, the Lord will "speak tenderly to her heart." This phrase is found in other contexts containing "romantic speech."[76] A similar phrase appears in Isaiah 40:2 in the context of comforting Israel

---

71. Fensham, "The Marriage Metaphor in Hosea for the Covenant Relationship between the Lord and his People (Hos 1:2–9)," 71–78. "Hosea is a book thoroughly covenant based" (Dumbrell, *Covenant and Creation: An Old Testament Covenantal Theology*, 170).

72. In Hos 1:6 the Lord states that he will no longer love (רחם) nor forgive (נשא) the house of Israel. Both words appear in God's self-declaration in Ex 34:6–7, along with חֶסֶד. Fensham, "The Marriage Metaphor," 75. Dumbrell, *Covenant and Creation*, 200.

73. Keefe, *Women's Body and the Social Body in Hosea*, 110.

74. Friedman, "Israel's Response," 202. Compare this to Deut 26:17–19 where the Lord declares that Israel is "his treasured people."

75. Clines and Gunn, "You Tried to Persuade Me," 20–27. Clines and Gunn argue that the word has no sexual overtones nor is there any deception involved in the persuasion. While the state that the use of the verb in Judg 15:15 and 16:5 lack deceit and should rather be translated "coax" or "cajole," in both cases the women persuade Samson to tell them a secret for a reason other than what they have claimed. Nwaoru points out that there is no place in the Hebrew Bible where this verb has a connotation of unlawful "leading away" or forceful abduction. While it is used for a deceptive sexual enticement (Judg 14:15, 16:5, 1 Kgs 22:2–22), there is no sense of violence in the word. Nwaoru, *Imagery in the Prophecy of Hosea*, 29n124. Andersen and Freedman take this word as indicating the "artful wooing of a simple girl." Andersen and Freedman, *Hosea*, 272.

76. In Ruth 2:13 the phrase describes Boaz's words to Ruth. Commenting on the Genesis passage, Mathews sees the same meaning as Ruth 2:13 and Isa 40:2. Mathews, *Genesis 11:27—50:26*, 593.

and the end of the exile. The point of this coaxing is to bring the bride back "into the wilderness," the place where Israel began her relationship with God.[77] Third, when the relationship is restored the wife no longer will call her husband בַּעְלִי, "my baal," but אִישִׁי "my husband" (2:18[16]).[78] Looking to the future (in that day), a new covenant will be made which includes all of creation and a return of peace (2:20[18]).[79] Fourth, the verb ארשׂ ("to betroth") is used twice in 2:21[19]. She is to be betrothed in righteousness, justice, faithfulness, mercy, and knowledge of the Lord. These terms of betrothal are the theme of the rest of Hosea. Because there is no real knowledge of God in Israel, there is no righteous, justice and mercy. The eschatological age of the consummated marriage is still future; the present is not like what the future will be.

Does this restoration of the marriage constitute a "divorce and remarriage"? Anderson and Freedman argue strongly that Hos 2:4–22 does not constitute a divorce because the events described are not consistent with the biblical adultery laws and the fact that the husband continues to have some sort of a relationship with the wife after the pronouncement of divorce.[80] Westbrook believes that his study marshals sufficient evidence to show that there could be reconciliation after a divorce in the biblical law.[81]

In Gen 34:3 the phrase is used to described the words of Shechem to Dinah. That this is romantic speech is troubling since the man raped Dinah first, but the verse states that he his "soul was drawn to her" and that "he loved her" (אהב). Törnkvist therefore takes this phrase as sexually manipulative. Törnkvist, *Use and Abuse*, 157; cf. Diaz, "I Will Speak to Their Hearts," 271–76.

77. Fischer argues that there is no romantic connotation to the phrase at all. Rather, the phrase means "to persuade someone who has an opposing (negative) attitude." Fischer, "Die Redewendung דִּבְּרוּ עַל־לֵב im AT—Ein Beitrag zum Verständnis von Jes 40, 2," 244–50.

78. For a detailed review of the used of בעל in Semitic languages, see Nwaoru, *Imagery in the Prophecy of Hosea*, 140n648.

79. Roche, "The Reversal of Creation in Hosea," 400–409. The noun בֶּטַח is associated with the messianic age (Jer 32:37, Ezek 34:27; Zech 14:11).

80. Anderson and Freedman, *Hosea*, 218–90. Older studies tended to take the statement "Not my wife" as a legal statement of divorce, but virtually all modern studies reject this view. Kelle surveys literature on Hos 2:4 and concludes that there is no divorce formula in 2:4, but rather "a situation where the wife refuses to comply with the marital relationship." Kelle, *Hosea 2: Metaphor and Rhetoric in Historical Perspective*, 58.

81. Westbrook, "Adultery in Ancient Near Eastern Law," 577. Westbrook points out that Jer 3:8 clearly describes God as divorcing his people, although the fact that Jeremiah saw the destruction of Israel as a divorce may not effect a reading of Hosea. On the other hand, Whitt argues that the language of Hos 2 clearly describes a divorce, but it is the divorce of Yahweh and Asherah. In Whitt's view, Asherah was worshiped in Israel as Yahweh's consort at Gilgal (cf. Hos 9:15, p. 64). Hosea is a fanatical Yahwehist who could not accept the Asherah worship practiced in Gilgal. Whitt, "The Divorce of Yahweh," 56, 67. Schmitt offers another view in response to Whitt, suggesting that the woman is Samaria since there are a number of texts in the Hebrew Bible which describe the Lord's marriage to a city. In fact, Schmitt argues, Israel is never described as the "wife" of the Lord, nor is Israel described as a mother. Schmitt, "Yahweh's Divorce in Hosea 2—Who Is That Woman?," 119–32. Setting aside the obvious objection that Hosea can describe Israel as a wife even if it does not appear anywhere else in the Hebrew Bible, Schmitt fails to see that even if Samaria is the wife, the city of Samaria represents the nation of Israel in the same was Jerusalem/Zion represents Judah. This is certainly the case in Ezek 23. Schmitt is correct that Hos 2 announces the destruction of Samaria, whether the wife represents Samaria or Israel.

In fact, that idea that Hosea must follow biblical law as recorded in Deuteronomy implies that the adultery laws were known and enforced in the northern kingdom in the eighth century. Perhaps it is instructive to remember that the marriage and separation take place in the metaphorical world of an enacted parable. This is especially true of Anderson and Freedman's second argument, since the whole point of the enacted parable is that the Lord desires to be reconciled with his adulterous wife (Israel) and in fact will be at some point in the future. The Lord promises to do a miracle in reconciling with Israel, not to follow the commands of the law with respect to adultery.

The restoration of Israel's marriage will take place in the wilderness (2:16, [2:14]).[82] This constitutes a blending of the wilderness tradition with a marriage metaphor. Like Isa 40–55, Hosea sees the restoration of Israel as happening in the wilderness. While the time in the wilderness is a separation from the husband for a long time, Hosea sees a certain restoration of the marriage in the future. There will be the time when the Lord calls his bride out of the wilderness and restores her to himself as her original husband.

Summary and Conclusion

Hosea represents the earliest example of the marriage metaphor in the Hebrew Bible and employs the metaphor to describe both the past (the sins of Israel), the present (Israel is estranged from their God), and the future (the restoration of Israel to their former relationship with God). Even more important, the marriage metaphor is combined with the new Exodus and Wilderness traditions.[83] The time of Israel's estrangement is described as a new wilderness period. Only after this period will the wife be recalled from the wilderness and the marriage restored. For Hosea, Israel is currently in the wilderness and can only look forward to the time when God will restore her to her place as the bride of the Lord.

A problem for the present study is that Jesus does not allude to Hosea extensively. Where there are clear allusions to Hosea, they are not to the marriage metaphor or even to the first three chapters of the book. While there are few linguistic connections to the marriage metaphor of Hosea, Hos 1–3 is foundational for the marriage metaphor as found in Isaiah 1–5, Jeremiah and Ezekiel. The idea that Israel was an adulterous wife to the Lord is pervasive in these prophets. As we will see in the final section of this study, Jesus described himself as a bridegroom on a number of occasions and he invites people to enter into his marriage celebration. In addition, on at least three

---

82. Friedman, "Israel's Response," 200, who compares this to Jer 2:2.

83. Vannorsdall comes to a similar conclusion in his unpublished dissertation. He argues that Hosea functions as a covenant mediator who developed an eschatology based on a return to the desert where God would re-establish his covenant of love with his people. That Gilgal and Bethel are prominent in Hosea is, for Vannorsdall, significant. In his view, these cultic centers were associated with the Exodus events, Passover, and the wilderness wanderings. Vannorsdall, "The Use of the Covenant Liturgy in Hosea," 356–57.

occasions Jesus describes the present generation as adulterous (μοιχαλίς, Matt 12:39, 16:4, Mark 8:38). Jesus therefore is consciously evoking traditions drawn from Hosea which describe God as a loving husband to his people despite their unfaithfulness. What is more, Hosea enacted his metaphor. Hosea's experience in chapters 1–3 is not simply a literary creation vividly describing Israel's sin, he lived out a parable of Israel's unfaithfulness. Enacting a parable is not uncommon in the prophets in either the Hebrew Bible or the New Testament. Isaiah, Jeremiah and Ezekiel each perform their prophecies, as does Agabus in the New Testament. Like Hosea, Jesus enacted a marriage metaphor by performing the role of the groom in the restoration of the marriage from Hosea.

Marriage Metaphor in Isaiah 1–5

Following Hosea, the eighth-century prophet Isaiah employs the marriage metaphor as part of the introduction to his prophecy. In the restoration of Zion, the Lord will once again provide a cloud as he did in the wilderness (4:5). That the cloud is described as a חֻפָּה (canopy) is not insignificant since the noun חֻפָּה refers to a "nuptial chamber" in Joel 2:16 and Ps 19:6. While many commentators notice the association with a wedding canopy, this nuance is routinely dismissed in favor of a more general meaning of protection.[84] But in the context of Isa 4–5, it is likely that the canopy ought to be taken as part of a marriage metaphor for several reasons. First, the immediate context is the washing of the "daughters of Zion." The "daughter of Zion" is a common metaphor for Jerusalem.[85] From the beginning of the book Jerusalem has been pictured as an unfaithful woman who will be judged for her sins (1:21). In Isa 3:16–17 the "Daughters of Zion" represent the nation's arrogance and are judged as adulterous. Their fine clothing and jewelry will be removed (vss. 18–23) and they will be humiliated with their heads shaved and dressed in stinking rags (3:24–26). In 4:1 seven women will petition one man to marry them, forgoing the usual dowry.[86] Yet 4:4 the Lord himself restores the daughters

---

84. Gray cites Duhm, "As the king sites under, as the bride and bridegroom go under, a canopy, so the Temple Mount as a king's throne, the religious community as bride of a heavenly bridegroom, must have a canopy over it." Gray, *Isaiah I-XXXIX*, 80. Dillard observes that although the term eventually came to mean the canopy under which marriage ceremonies were conducted, in the biblical period it was the chamber in which the consummation took place. Dillard, "Joel," 283; cf. Garrett, *Hosea, Joel,* 348. Smith also notices the similar language, but concludes that the imagery points to "the divine protection of all the holy people in Zion." Smith, *Isaiah 1–39*, 158–59.

85. The phrase appears 30 times in the Hebrew Bible as a metaphor for Jerusalem. For example, in Isa 37:22 (par. 2 Kgs 19:21) Isaiah describes nation as the "virgin daughter of Zion" who mocks the power of the Assyrians. As Stinespring points out, the Hebrew construction is an appositional genitive and therefore a title. Stinespring, "No Daughter of Zion: A Study of the Appositional Genitive in Hebrew Grammar," 133–41.

86. When a man takes a wife he is required to care for her (Exod 21:10) and pay a bride-price (Deut 22:29). These women will "eat their own food" and "wear their own clothes," indicating that they are willing to waive their rights in order to be married and remove their shame. When the women ask to be "called by your name" they are confirming a marriage contract. Watts, *Isaiah 1–33*, 47.

of Zion to their original purity and holiness, evoking language of the theophany at Sinai, except this time the cloud covers Mount Zion. While the "daughters of Zion" are not specifically said to be wedded to the Lord, they are treated in the same way as Hosea's unfaithful wife. They are brought back to Sinai and the wilderness and they are restored to their original purity and relationship with their Lord.

Second, the "daughters of Zion" appear in another very significant marriage text, Song 3:11.[87] In this passage the daughters of Zion are to go out and look upon Solomon arriving in all his glory.[88] Like Isa 4, this arrival is "from the wilderness" and is accompanied by "columns of smoke" (Song 3:6). The column (תִּימָרָה) is sometimes taken as a reference to the column of smoke which accompanied Israel in the wilderness[89] but some dismiss the possibility since the word תִּימָרָה is not used in the Wilderness tradition for the column of smoke.[90] The word only appears in elsewhere in MT Joel 3:3 [2:30 ET], an apocalyptic description of judgment.[91]

Third, the next pericope in Isaiah is the Song of the Vineyard (Isa 5).[92] This parable is regularly thought to have been some sort of a wedding song,[93] although there is some difference of opinion as to who is singing the song and to whom it is addressed.[94] While it is possible that the singer is the bride and she is addressing her

---

87. The "daughters of Zion" and the "daughters of Jerusalem" appear frequently in Song. Pope discusses several possible identifications of these women, ranging from the wedding party (in the "naturalist" hypothesis) to the royal harem (in the so-called dramatic theory). He cites Robert, who argued persuasively that the "daughters of Zion" should be understood as the population of Jerusalem. Pope, *Song of Songs*, 318. This view is based on the personification of the city of Jerusalem as a woman (and the royal bride). This view makes sense here in Isaiah 5 as well since the prophet is describing the unfaithfulness of the population of Jerusalem. In addition, Hos 2 describes the children of Gomer pleading with their mother to return from her adulteries. In that context, the children of Gomer are the inhabitants of Israel.

88. "The portrait of the man making a dramatic arrival is perhaps drawn from a wedding custom, in which a groom makes a grand entry at his wedding feast" (Garrett, *Proverbs, Ecclesiastes, Song of Solomon*, 401).

89. For example, Pope concludes that there is in fact a reference to the wilderness wandering in SoS 3:6, but the choice of the noun תִּימָרָה indicates a theophany. Pope, *Song of Songs*, 426.

90. Garrett, *Proverbs, Ecclesiastes, Song of Solomon*, 400.

91. LXX SoS 3:16 translates תִּימָרָה with στέλεχος, a word normally referring to trees or tree-trunks.

92. If the vineyard is a metaphor for the bride in the song (cf. SoS 1:6, 8:12), then the vineyard is the bride of the Lord. Pope gathers a great deal of evidence from Ancient near eastern Literature which confirms the use of a vineyard as a common metaphor for sexual encounters and marriage. Pope, *Song of Songs*, 323–26. An additional example of a vineyard for Israel is found in Isa 27:2–5. There the Lord declares that he is the keeper of the vineyard. He watered it both night and day, but it does not give him wine. The noun חֵמָה (wrath) could be emended to חֶמֶר, wine, as suggested by 1QIsa, some manuscripts of the LXX and the Targum.

93. Although the word אהב ("to love") does not appear, the song is introduced with the words "I will sing to the one I love," using the noun יָדִיד and דּוֹד. דּוֹד is used frequently in SoS (33x) to describe the bride as "my beloved." The LXX uses ἀγαπητός to translate דּוֹד.

94. See Watts, *Isaiah 1–33*, 53–54 for a useful summary. In addition to confusion over who is speaking, some commentators take Isa 5:1–7 as addressed to the northern kingdom of Israel (Watts, Blenkinsopp) and others to the southern kingdom of Judah (Gray, Childs, Wildberger, Smith).

groom (Schmidt and Föhrer), most scholars understand the singer as the prophet as a "friend of the groom." Junker argued that the singer is an intermediary who negotiated the marriage contract.[95] Wildberger suggested that the song is sung by the "friend" of the groom in order to call attention to the bride's unsuitability.[96] It is more likely that the singer is the prophet describing the love between the groom (the Lord) and his bride (Israel). The song begins positively as the groom does all that he can to prepare the vineyard for his beloved (vv. 1–2), but turns in to a lament because the vineyard has not produced fruit (vv. 3–4). As a result, the vineyard will be uprooted and suffer waste and drought (vv. 5–6). In verse seven the parable becomes clear: the "vineyard of the Lord," the house of Israel and Judah.

Isaiah 1–5 is critically important for the argument of this study since Jesus' teaching in Matt 21:33–44 (Mark 12:1–12, Luke 20:9–19) is clearly based on the prophet's parable of the vineyard.[97] This parable is an important climax to Jesus' teaching in the Temple his final week and it is virtually certain that Jesus has this passage in mind when he describes the leaders of Israel of the first century as "wicked tenants." Looking ahead to the teaching of Jesus, we have a clear echo of an earlier text which describes the restoration of Israel as a restoration of a marriage relationship. The echo is clear on linguistic and thematic grounds and is historically plausible that Jesus knew this text and consciously alluded to it in his parable of the Vineyard. This will be examined more closely in the final chapter, but it is important at this point to see that the marriage metaphor is used in Isa 1–5 to describe the present, estranged relationship of the Lord and Israel as well as the future hope of a renewed relationship. The renewed relationship is not simply another marriage but a restoration of Israel to a pure and virginal state ("washed") so that she can enter into a marriage as a holy bride.

In summary, Isa 1–5 takes up the marriage metaphor from Hosea which originally described the northern kingdom of Israel and applies it to Judah and Zion. In Isaiah the daughters of Zion are the faithless bride (3:16–17), but they will be made pure again when the Lord cleanses them and they return to Zion and gather under the wedding canopy (4:4–5). This anticipates the eschatological banquet Isa 24:6–8: the nations will gather to Zion and enjoy the presence of the Lord.

Marriage Metaphor in Jeremiah

Jeremiah 2–4

Like Hosea and Isaiah, the book of Jeremiah opens with a vivid description of Jerusalem as a bride who has forgotten her past devotion. As such, Jer 2–4 can be described as

---

95. Junker, "Die literarische Art von Isa 5:1–7," 259–66.

96. The prophet appears "as a minstrel singing a love song on behalf of his best friend, perhaps his best man." Goldingay, *Isaiah*, 52; cf. Seitz, *Isaiah 1–39*, 47.

97. Bruggemann, *Isaiah 1–39*, 49.

Israel as the Wife of the Lord

an intertextual reading of Hosea.[98] As W. Holladay has overwhelmingly demonstrated, there are clear linguistic and thematic links to the book of Hosea which go well beyond basic vocabulary.[99] But as Untermann says, while Jeremiah certainly knew Hosea, "he was no imitator but a true student" who used and extended Hosea's thought by applying it to situations which went beyond the original intent.[100] What is significant for the present study is that Jeremiah applied the marriage metaphor to a new situation. In Hosea the unfaithful wife was Samaria and Israel. Jeremiah begins with Israel, but by 3:6 the metaphor is extended to include to Jerusalem and Judah. Judah too is adulterous and pollutes the land with half-hearted devotion to her first husband (3:6–10). In fact, Jeremiah claims that Judah is more unfaithful than Israel. Jeremiah is therefore re-applying the marriage metaphor in the new context of his present situation as a warning to Judah. What is more, the use of the marriage metaphor in Jer 2–4 and 31 points ahead to a future restoration of the marriage.[101] However, Jeremiah's eschatological use of the marriage metaphor is more fully developed than Hosea.

In these chapters we encounter a problem with the use of the marriage metaphor. In what appears to be a cohesive unit of related poems, there is shifting between male and female metaphors.[102] Diamond and O'Connor show that there are four poems in Jer 2–4, alternating between male and female images to describe the crimes of Israel.[103]

---

98. As Fensham has observed, "Hosea has exercised a profound influence on Jeremiah." Fensham, "The Marriage Metaphor," 76. Bright agrees, commenting that "similarities to Hosea are striking. Not only is the dominant theme (the adulterous wife) borrowed from that great prophet of northern Israel there are verbal similarities-perhaps even quotations-as well." Bright, *Jeremiah*, 26. While this observation is true, there are few studies of the marriage metaphor in Jeremiah. Hall, "The Marriage Imagery in Jeremiah 2 and 3: A study of Antecedents and Innovations in Prophetic Metaphor"; Hall, "Metaphor," 169–71; Deissler, "Das 'Echo' der Hosea-Verkundigung im Jeremiabuch," 61–75; Roche, "Jeremiah 2:2–3 and Israel's Love for God During the Wilderness Wanderings," 364–76; Diamond and O'Connor, "Unfaithful Passions," 288–310; Bauer, *Gender in the Book of Jeremiah: A Feminist-Literary Reading*; Shields, *Circumscribing the Prostitute*.

99. Holladay collects "at least fifty points at which Jrm draws on the diction of Hosea," although these allusions are mostly confined to Jer 2–10 and 31. Holladay, *Jeremiah 2*, 45–47. Diamond and O'Connor list five major common thematic elements between Jeremiah and Hosea. In their view, Jeremiah "adopts narrative structure... and an authoritative tradition that he remolds." Diamond and O'Connor "Unfaithful Passions," 141–42. See also the data collected by Dieissler, "Das 'Echo' der Hosea" 61–75. McKeating comments that the wilderness period in Hosea and Jeremiah is a period of "young love," in contrast to the pessimistic use of the image in Ezekiel. McKeating, *The Book of Jeremiah*, 28. Most commentators notice the use of Hosea in these two chapters. For example, see Thompson, *The Book of Jeremiah*, 163; Carroll, *Jeremiah*, 119; Lundbom, *Jeremiah 1–20*, 252.

100. Untermann, *From Repentance to Redemption: Jeremiah's Thought in Tradition*, 178. Based on chapter 2, Untermann's description of Jeremiah's method can be described as an intertextual hermeneutic.

101. Mackay suggests that "Jeremiah draws on the message of Hosea to set out the love of the Lord." He includes in this summary Jer 31:3. Mackay, *Jeremiah*, 1:73.

102. Compare the shift in gender to Malachi 2:11. O'Brien, "Judah as Wife and Husband," 241–50. On 2:1—4:4 as "a self-contained unit," see Holladay, *Jeremiah 1*, 62.

103. Diamond and O'Connor, "Unfaithful Passions," 128–30. Elsewhere O'Connor comments that the two literary figures (male and female) are intended to indicate one entity. Both the male and

Clearly Jeremiah uses the image of a marriage in 2:1–3, but in 2:4–13 the prophet addresses the nation as a whole, using masculine forms to describe the rebellion of the wilderness generation. But in 2:17–25 Jeremiah refers to the nation in the feminine once again, returning to the image of Israel as an unfaithful woman. In 2:26–31 the pronouns shift to masculine as the prophet uses the metaphor of a thief to describe the nation's sins. In 2:32 he returns to Israel as a bride. In 2:33—33:5, the pronouns are once again feminine singular and describe Israel's sin as adultery. This inconsistency in pronouns is a problem for the marriage metaphor since the vocabulary which is used to construct the metaphor is necessarily feminine (bride, cities), but the target (Israel, Jacob, Ephraim, Judah) is usually described with masculine vocabulary.

In Jer 2:1–3 the Lord "recalls the time in the wilderness as a honeymoon period in the relationship."[104] This period is described as the "devotion of your youth," using a noun drawn from Hosea, חֶסֶד (covenant faithfulness).[105] This devotion is in her youth (נְעוּרִים), a noun appearing in a number of marriage metaphor texts describing a virgin bride (Hos 2:17 [15], Ezek 16:22, 43, 60).[106] The woman is described as a young bride[107] "walking after" her husband.[108] The relationship of God and his people was ideal and the new bride unquestioningly trusts her groom, even following him into the wilderness.[109] The wilderness is described as a "land not sown." The passive participle of זרע (to "sow") may refer to the virginity of the bride. At the time of the wedding, the bride

---

female characters turn away from the Lord, therefore the same rhetorical device can be used for both. O'Connor, "The Tears of God and Divine Character," 389. Mackay also observes this phenomenon and explains it as reflecting Jeremiah's use of two metaphors of God's relationship with his people, a vassal treaty (requiring a masculine pronoun) and marriage (requiring a feminine pronoun). Mackay, *Jeremiah*, 123–25. As I observed in an earlier chapter, these are not unrelated metaphors since a vassal treaty and a marriage are both types of covenants and חֶסֶד is used for both relationships.

104. Goldingay, *Israel's Gospel*, 459. Thompson agrees that "the Sinai relationship is depicted in terms of a marriage where the bride accepts her husband in full confidence and trust and follows him into a new life." Thompson, *The Book of Jeremiah*, 163. Since Sinai is not mentioned, Fretheim suggests that the wilderness period was a "pre-Sinai reality" since God calls Israel his people from the beginning of Exodus. Fretheim, *Jeremiah*, 63. "In the days of the wilderness-wandering Israel was Yahweh's bride, devotedly loyal to him" (Bright, *Jeremiah*, 14).

105. Roche, "Jeremiah 2:2–3 and Israel's Love for God," 374. Roche recognizes that the positive use of the wilderness tradition in Jer 2 is different than the negative use found in Ezek 20, Ps 78 and 106. Cf. Holladay's comment that "the word resonates strongly both with marriage and political imagery. No one English word is adequate, but 'loyalty' will have to do." Holladay, *Jeremiah 1*, 83.

106. Holladay suggests that Jeremiah's choice of words was based on Hos 2:17. Holladay, *Jeremiah 1*, 84, cf. Lundbom, *Jeremiah 1–20*, 252.

107. The noun כְּלוּלֹת in Jer 2:2 can refer to both a betrothed woman and a married woman. Lundbom rightly observes that "metaphorical usage may not require such exactness." Lundbom, *Jeremiah 1–20*, 252. The LXX and Rashi take the phrase as a reference to a consummated relationship. McKane, *Jeremiah*, 28.

108. A young woman would walk behind her husband. Holladay, *Jeremiah 1*, 84. Holladay cites examples from Gen 24:5, 1 Sam 25:42. See also Bracke, *Jeremiah 1–29*, 24.

109. "Hosea and Jeremiah depict God's love for his people in the wilderness as the love of a husband for his wife" (Rubenstein, *The History of Sukkot in the Second Temple and Rabbinic Periods*, 258).

loved her husband using the common verb אהב. There is a hint of covenant loyalty in this verb as well since the word can be used to describe a treaty relationship as well as a marriage relationship.[110]

Jeremiah applies the marriage imagery of verses 2–3 directly to Israel in verses 4–8. The bride Israel was brought up out of Egypt, fed rich foods and cared for in every way by a good and loving husband, yet she was unfaithful. The ancient hearer of this text would have sympathized with the husband since he has been wronged by the unfaithful wife.[111] Reflecting on the wilderness period, B. Levine comments that Jeremiah "reasoned that Israel must have been devoted to God at some time in the past so as to have been the recipient of his *hesed*."[112] The wilderness period was that time when the nation enjoyed the loving kindness of her husband. Jeremiah shows that the nation had a period of innocence in the wilderness, but that innocence quickly turned to sin when the nation turned from the "love of a new bride."[113]

The young bride became polluted when she entered the good land the Lord gave to her by committing adultery. In 2:13 the sin of Israel is describe in terms of forsaking the Lord, a fountain of living water, in exchanged for their own cracked cisterns. In the light of Prov 5, this should be taken as a metaphor for adultery. Her adultery is most explicit in 2:20–22; she has acted as a prostitute in every high place.[114] Despite her denials, the bride the unfaithfulness of the bride is obvious to all (2:23–25).[115] Rather than turn to her husband and God, the nation claims that the gods represented by trees and standing stones are her parents.[116] Finally, she is described as a bride who has forgotten her wedding day (2:32).[117] The ornaments described are similar to examples

---

110. Thompson, *The Book of Jeremiah*, 163, citing 2 Kings 16:10–16 as evidence.

111. In fact, in an ancient context, the wife would not have been given a chance to defend herself. O'Connor, "The Tears of God," 390.

112. Levine, *Numbers 1–20*, 45. The young bride is described as "devoted" to the Lord, once again using חֶסֶד.

113. "The implied reader construes the marital metaphor of the dramatic situation as an allegory of the national myth, linking a specific period of the 'marriage' to a specific period in national history" (Diamond and O'Connor, "Unfaithful Passions," 136).

114. Verses 20–22 are a particularly vivid description of Judah's spiritual adultery. Thompson associates this hilltop prostitution with Baal worship. Thompson, *The Book of Jeremiah*, 177.

115. In fact, Israel is so unfaithful that even prostitutes could learn from her! McKeating, *The Book of Jeremiah*, 35. While a camel in heat is mild, a she-ass actively seeks the male. Thompson, *The Book of Jeremiah*, 169; Bailey and Holladay, "Young Camel and Wild Ass in Jer 2:23–25," 256–60. Israel is not just a prostitute; she is "an energetic whore." Carroll, *Jeremiah*, 130.

116. Ironically, the male image (the standing stone) is called "my mother" and the female image (the tree) is called "my mother." Thompson, *The Book of Jeremiah*, 180.

117. As Holladay observes, "in the Israelite context the high moment of a woman's life is her wedding day, and her mode of dress proclaims her status: virginity, bridehood." Holladay, *Jeremiah 1*, 109. Lundbom describes a knotted cord carried by the bride which was used to count down the days until her wedding. If this is the intended meaning of קִשֻּׁרִים, then the line has the sense of "a bride to be does not forget her wedding day." Lundbom, *Jeremiah 1–20*, 292. The word appears in Isa 49:18 for a bride's ornaments and in Isa 3:20 for some sort of jewelry.

of the marriage metaphor (Isa 3:20, Ezek 16:10–13) and are likely part of her wedding dress which indicated that the woman was married.[118] These items ought to have been cherished, but not they are forgotten because of her adultery.

Since Israel has been unfaithful she is "divorced" by the Lord (3:1–5). This text is modeled on divorce law found in Deut 24:1–4.[119] Since the whole of Jer 2–4 can be described as a lawsuit speech, it is not surprising to encounter divorce language at this point.[120] The verb שלח is used as a technical term for divorce.[121] The point of citing the legal text from Deuteronomy is that according to the Law, if the Lord has divorced his wife, they could never reconcile and remarry; Judah can never return to the Lord.[122] While it is possible to argue that the Lord has not divorced his people,[123] it is better to see this as the extreme graciousness of the Lord in accepting back his adulterous wife in a manner which would not be legally or socially acceptable in contemporary culture.[124] As we saw in Hosea, the Lord does a miracle by restoring the virginity of the bride when he returns to the original relationship. So too here, the Lord creates a new situation in which he can be reconciled with his wife once again.

What is surprising is that the text asks if the husband would return to the wife—as if he is the one who has been unfaithful![125] A gracious offer of reconciliation is made in 3:11–14. It is God who is loyal to his covenant[126] and it is God who now offers to

---

118. Thompson, *The Book of Jeremiah*, 184. For a further description of a bride's ornaments, see Moran, *The Amarna Letters*, 93.

119. Fishbane, "Revelation and Tradition: Aspects of Inner-Biblical Exegesis," 343–61. Holladay suggests that since Hos 2:9 also employs Deut 24, it is likely that Jeremiah is using both texts here. Holladay, *Jeremiah 1*, 112. The relationship of Deut 24 and Jer 3 is most fully developed in Shields, *Circumscribing the Prostitute*, 21–50. She thinks that it is possible that the reference to the wife's return could be an allusion to Hos 2:9, but points out (contra Holladay) that there are no other verbal allusions to Hos 2 in Jer 3:1—4:4. She therefore decides "not to discuss Hos 2 as an intertext," while indicating that further study maybe fruitful. Carroll states that the metaphor of divorce is "inherited from the Hosea tradition" and the "Deuteronomistic writers." Carroll, *Jeremiah*, 143.

120. That this is a lawsuit speech seems to be a consensus view even though the verb ריב appears only in 2:9. Just as a marriage is a specific form of a covenant, so too is divorce a specific kind of lawsuit. See, for example, Holladay, *Jeremiah 1*, 73; Thompson, *The Book of Jeremiah*, 159.

121. Westbrook, "Adultery in Ancient Near Eastern Law," 560n68; McKeating, *The Book of Jeremiah*, 38. Holladay, on the other hand, comments that שלח in the piel "does not quite mean divorce, but implies it." Holladay, *Jeremiah 1*, 112.

122. Carroll, *Jeremiah*, 143.

123. Anderson and Freedman argue this with respect to Hosea, *Hosea*, 218–19. Bruggemann makes the unlikely suggestion that God's love is so great for his people that he is willing to risk breaking the Torah. Brueggemann, *To Pluck Up, to Tear Down*, 41.

124. "God is not simply open to restoration; God moves to make restoration possible, even through and beyond judgment." Fretheim, *Jeremiah*, 75. Cf. McKane who comments that in such a case as this, the bride has no power to come back to her original husband. God is not bound by legal protocol. McKane, *Jeremiah*, 1:64, 66

125. Holladay, *Jeremiah 1*, 113. The LXX renders this line as referring to the wife returning to the offended husband.

126. The noun חָסִיד in v. 12 refers to someone who does חֶסֶד. Thompson, *The Book of Jeremiah*, 197n3.

Israel as the Wife of the Lord

renew his relationship with his people. Like Hosea 2:4 [2:2] and 2:18 [2:16], the Lord reminds his people that he is their master, בעל, not Baal (Jer 3:14).[127] Sadly, when this restoration occurs, only a few from the North will return to Zion.[128] It is significant that any of the exiles from the northern kingdom will return to form a united kingdom under the leadership of true shepherds who will feed them with "true wisdom" (3:15).[129] In 3:18 the "house of Judah shall join with the house of Israel," a clear anticipation of the New Covenant in 31:31.[130] While the MT simply uses הלך to describe this reunification, the LXX renders the verb with συνέρχομαι, a verb used to describe a marriage.[131] As in Isa 25:6–8, all the nations will acknowledge the Lord (3:17).

In conclusion, as Diamond and O'Connor observe, Jer 2–3 employs the marriage metaphor to describe the Lord as "brokenhearted and bitter, angry and ashamed," yet ultimately faithful despite the unfaithfulness of his wife, Israel.[132] In short, "Jeremiah reads an old metaphor and writes a new narrative."[133] The exile ends when Israel is united at Zion and led by true shepherds. Despite the absence of an eschatological banquet in Jer 2–3, it is clear that the restoration of Israel can be imagined as a restoration of marriage.

---

127. Since the line begins with the image of a rebellious child, it is unlikely that בעל refers to husband, although Jer 31:32 may certainly use this word in the sense of husband.

128. Carroll, *Jeremiah*, 149. Lundbom, however, thinks that 3:18 implies a great multitude. The wording of 3:14 is in the x, x+1 format found in Amos 1:3 and therefore intends to show that "the returnees will increase and their numbers will swell." Lundbom, *Jeremiah 1–20*, 313. There is in fact a common theme in the Hebrew Bible of a small righteous remnant (Isa 6:13, Amos 3:12), but in Jer 31:7–8 there is a multitude who return, including the blind and the lame. This is perhaps an example of eschatological tension in Jeremiah. After the exile there was a small remnant which returned, but in the future gathering, there will be an uncountable multitude.

129. The verb רעה means "to shepherd," but in the Qal it can also mean "to graze." There may be a hint of an eschatological banquet here. When God restores his sheep, they will be shepherded into green pastures. For example, in Jer 50:19 Israel will be restored and they will graze (רעה) in Bashan and Gilead. In Mic 7:14 the true shepherd will shepherd his flock (רעה) in a "garden land." Psalm 23 is a clear example of grazing sheep as a metaphor for eschatological victory. This shepherd image recalls David, a shepherd who was also "after God's own heart."

130. This restoration of the united kingdom appears in Jer 50:4, Isa 11:13, Ezek 37:11–12, and Hos 1:11. "With this prose collection of future hopes about Jerusalem and the reunification of Judah and Israel, with the other nations in attendance, the direness of the discourse is temporarily arrested and the book of Consolation (30–31) is anticipated." Carroll, *Jeremiah*, 151.

131. The word appears in marriage contracts as a synonym for γαμέω. See MM for several examples from the papyri.

132. Diamond and O'Connor, "Unfaithful Passions," 134. As Bruggemann comments, "the metaphor of a broken marriage is intimate and domestic, but its importance is public and historical." Brueggemann, *To Pluck Up, to Tear Down*, 35.

133. Diamond and O'Connor, "Unfaithful Passions," 142.

Jesus the Bridegroom

Jeremiah 31

Holladay pointed out that the Jeremiah's use of Hosea is confined to chapters 2–10 and 30–31.[134] Likewise, McKeating notes strong connections between Hosea and Jer 31, a "fresh betrothal" rather than a "new covenant."[135] As I argued at the beginning of this chapter, a marriage is a specialized form of covenant. It is therefore not surprising to see the metaphor return in Jeremiah's famous description of the New Covenant. The language of a new covenant appears in Hos 2:22–25 [2:20–25] and Jer 31:27–28, 31–34. The metaphor is appropriate since the establishment of a New Covenant with the House of Israel and Judah will be an occasion for great joy and celebration, qualities normally associated with a wedding. In addition, Jer 31 contains a clear "return from exile" theme which can be described as a new Exodus.[136]

Jeremiah 31 is an extremely important text for understanding Jesus' teaching since it is cited directly by Jesus during his final meal with his disciples (1 Cor 11:25, Luke 22:20).[137] Jeremiah 31 also contains familiar themes from Hosea's marriage metaphor and the Wilderness traditions to describe the time when God will renew his covenant with all his people, both Israel and Judah.[138] In 31:1 the end of the exile is described as a return to the wilderness.[139] Like Hosea and Isa 40–55, Jeremiah describes Israel as returning to the wilderness and "finding grace." In the wilderness the Lord once again declares his love (אהב) and his loving-kindness (חֶסֶד). Both of these words appear in Jer 2:2, but now they are expanded. God's love for his people is an "everlasting love" and he "draws them with loving-kindness."[140]

---

134. Holladay, *Jeremiah 2*, 47.

135. McKeating, *The Book of Jeremiah*, 156. Ezekiel can describe this new covenant in terms of a new heart, Ezek 18:31. The influence of Hosea on the New Covenant text has been noticed as early as Giesebrecht, *Das Buch Jeremia*.

136. Van der Wal, "Themes from Exodus in Jeremiah 30–31," 559–66. Becking disagrees that there the New Exodus is the "basic element" in Jer 30–31, arguing instead that the "passionate and changeable God" is the foundation for understanding the pericope. Becking, *Between Fear and Freedom*, 273–83. These two theses are not necessarily opposed to one another if one recognizes elements of a marriage metaphor in Jer 30–31. God can be described as a "passionate God" as he recalls his people from the wilderness in a New Exodus because the overall metaphor is a restoration of a marriage relationship. The metaphors of the wilderness and marriage combine even here in Jer 30–31.

137. The parallel passages in Matt 26:27–28 and Mark 14:24–24 do not include the word "new," it is simply the cup of wine is the "blood of the covenant."

138. Carroll considers the parallels with Hosea and Second Isaiah so strong that they "point in the direction other than the author of the bitter denunciations of Judean life." Carroll, *Jeremiah*, 588.

139. Holladay suggests repointing חֶרֶב to חֹרֵב in 31:2 making the connection to the Exodus events stronger. Instead of "people who escaped the sword" we would then read "people who escaped to Horeb." Holladay, *Jeremiah 2*, 181

140. The verb משׁך has the sense of drawing someone along or pulling someone along. It is used in Hos 11:4 to describe God's guidance of Israel in the wilderness, he "drew them along with cords of human kindness" (NRSV). What this seems like a strong verbal connection between Jeremiah and Hosea, caution is necessary because the text of Hosea is difficult. The noun translated faithfulness is not חֶסֶד but אָדָם, although these is a strong possibility the text is corrupt and חֶסֶד is missing. English

In verse 4, the virgin daughter Israel will adorn herself with a "timbrel," an instrument which is exclusively played by a woman.[141] To "adorn" is עדה, a root used several times for the jewelry of a young bride.[142] The dance described is מָחוֹל, a root which implies whirling and is associated with joyous dancing.[143] The virgin will dance with the "merrymakers." The piel participle of שׂחק is used for joyous singing and dancing (Jer 30:19). When David brings the Ark of the Covenant into Jerusalem for the first time he and all of Israel are described as "making merry" (again, the piel participle of שׂחק) with all manner of musical instruments (2 Sam 6:5). As observed in chapter 3, this time of joyous worship is followed by a meal which included all of Israel. The piel participle of שמח (rejoicing) is found only in wedding contexts in Jeremiah outside of chapter 31.[144] If Jer 31:7 and 12 follow the same usage as elsewhere in Jeremiah, then perhaps the re-gathering from exile in chapter 31 is using a marriage metaphor.[145] If the Old Covenant could be described in terms of a marriage, then it is not a surprise to find that the New Covenant in Jer 31 uses similar language to describe a God's restoration of his relationship with his people. Fensham sees Jer 31 as describing the broken covenant as infidelity, although there is a "new covenant" given in Jeremiah.[146]

In v. 5 the virgin will plant a vineyard in Samaria and enjoy the fruit. While most commentators see this as an image of a long period of peace,[147] the statement that virgin Israel will plant vineyards may recall Hos 2:16–18 [14–15]. There the Lord called his wife out of the wilderness, and when she returned he gave her vineyards in the valley of Achor. The virgin Israel will receive a vineyard from her husband and she will have peace long enough to enjoy the fruit from the land. It is possible that the

---

translations may be influenced by the LXX Jer 38:3, εἰς οἰκτίρημα "with mercy" or "with compassion." LXX Hos 2:21 the related word οἰκτιρμός to translate רַחֲמִים, mercy. It is tempting to see this word as meaning something like "woo" (as the piel participle פתה in Hos 2:16 MT). משך has this sense only in SoS 1:4. While the LXX uses ἕλκω in both Jer 31:3 (LXX 38:3) and SoS 1:4 to translate משך, it is not clear if SoS 1:4 has the connotation of seduction.

141. Meyers, "Of Drums and Damsels: Women's Performance in Ancient Israel," 16–27.

142. Isa 61:10, Ezek 16:11, 13, 23:40; Hos 2:15 (MT).

143. While the root hast the connotation of dancing in a circle, we should resist the temptation to draw parallels to post-biblical Jewish wedding traditions, specifically the Hora, since this tradition can be dated to 1924!

144. Jer 7:34; 16:9; 25:10; 33:11, cf. 4Q502, see chapter 6.

145. McCarthy sees a relationship between Jeremiah's New Covenant and Hosea's idea of the covenant as a marriage. McCarthy, *Old Testament Covenant*, 33, 76. Coppens understands the New Covenant in Jeremiah as a marriage metaphor as well. Coppens, "La nouvelle alliance en Jer 31:31–34," 12–21.

146. Fensham, "The Marriage Metaphor," 77. Compare Bauer, *Gender in the Book of Jeremiah*, 147.

147. Leviticus 19:23–25 indicates fruit from newly planted vineyards cannot be used in the first three years, and the fourth year is set aside for the Lord. This implies at least five years of peace and prosperity in the land. As Carroll says, "this future is danced and sung, and what the villages produce they enjoy. No longer does the shadow of the invader frustrate their work." Carroll, *Jeremiah*, 590. For the same idea, see Mackay, *Jeremiah*, 2:210; Thompson, *Jeremiah*, 567; Lundbom, *Jeremiah 21–36*, 418.

watchmen in verse 5 are looking for the signal from Jerusalem that it is time to begin a new moon festival.[148]

In 31:10–14 the gathering of the people to Zion is a time of great joy, singing and feasting. Reminiscent of the wilderness tradition in Isa 40–55, the people of Israel will be brought back to a land which is overflowing with abundance. The verb נהר is usually taken as "radiant" (II נהר), but in the light of Isaiah, perhaps I נהר (to "gush, overflow") is a better translation. Like the entry into Canaan, the exiles will return to a land which is flowing with grain, wine, oil, flocks and herds. These exiles will eat and be satisfied (like a well-watered garden). Jeremiah 31:21–22 is a call for the virgin Israel to return from the wilderness. She is to mark well the path she takes, recalling language similar to the Isa 40:3 ("make straight the paths").

The marriage metaphor appears clearly in the New Covenant passage itself. After declaring that he will make a new covenant with the house of Judah and the house of Israel, the wilderness motif is invoked in 31:32 and the old covenant is described by the Lord in terms of a marriage: "I was like a husband to them."[149] Remarkably this sense of the text does is not favored in the commentaries, despite the consistent marriage metaphor in Jeremiah.[150] The old covenant was enacted at Sinai and immediately broken, the new covenant will be enacted in the future and it will not be broken. The Lord will enable is people to keep the covenant by engraving his Torah on his people's hearts. This new covenant will result in a restoration of the people to the position of God's people (31:33). The Lord says "I will be their God and they will be my people," reminiscent of the restoration of the marriage in Hos 2:25 [23]: the nation will no longer be "lo-Ami," "not by people."

Summary

Jeremiah's New Covenant is one of the most important texts used by Jesus therefore it is critical to the goals of this study that Jeremiah's description of the New Covenant uses a marriage metaphor to describe his present situation as well as his hope for a future restoration. Jeremiah reads the marriage metaphor of Hosea in the light of the fall of Jerusalem. The nation has been unfaithful and has experienced the complete

---

148. McKane, *Jeremiah* 2:785, following Duhm.

149. The verb בעל used in Jer 31:32 is related to the noun בַּעַל used in Hos 2:18. Lundbom therefore translates this verb as "I was their master" rather than husband, although he rightly states that the terms were virtually interchangeable. Lundbom, *Jeremiah 21–36*, 467. Similarly, Winkel sees this line as fitting well within the book of Jeremiah (ch. 3 especially) as well as the Hosean tradition. Winkel, *Jeremiah in the Prophetic Tradition*, 198.

150. For example, McKane follows Duhm and considers the phrase "obscure," translating the phrase as "though I have not abandoned my responsibility towards them." McKane, *Jeremiah* 2:189. Bright translates the phrase as "though I was their Lord," but accepts the possibility that "husband" is better in the light of the marriage metaphor. Bright, *Jeremiah* 283. Smend, however, finds Hos 2:25 as influential for this image, primarily for the words "not my people." Smend, "Die Bundesformel," 11–39. Cf., Buis, "La Nouvelle Alliance," 1–15.

destruction of the relationship she once enjoyed with the Lord. But like Hosea, Jeremiah also looks forward with the marriage metaphor to a time with the Lord will work a miracle to restore Israel to her former position of the "faithful bride." It is this restoration of the relationship Jesus' points in his ministry.

Jeremiah develops the marriage metaphor by blending it with the Wilderness tradition. Like Isa 40–55, there is an invitation to leave the wilderness and join the celebration (Jer 31:6, 21–22). The land itself will be fruitful, providing good food and drink for all (Jer 31:12–13). This gathering for a wedding feast is consistent with the eschatological banquet in Isa 25:6–8. While there is no direct reference to a formal wedding banquet using מִשְׁתֶּה, Jer 31 describes the future celebration of the New Covenant as a return from the wilderness to celebrate a renewed marriage.

Given the importance of Jer 31 in the synoptic Gospels, it is not at all surprising to find Jesus taking up the image of a bridegroom calling his wayward bride to repent and return to her husband in the Synoptic gospels. Based on Hays's criteria for identifying allusions as described in chapter 2, it is almost certain that Jesus had this stream of tradition in mind when he described himself as a bridegroom and his ministry as an ongoing wedding banquet. The metaphor is clearly used in texts often cited by Jesus and the popularity of the marriage metaphor would have made Jesus' meaning clear to all his listeners. For example, when Jesus described the present generation as "adulterous" (Mark 8:38), he called to mind the unfaithfulness of Israel Judah as spiritually adulterous. Yet Jesus continued to call on that adulterous generation to join him to celebrate restoration of Israel and Judah in his table fellowship. Jesus hosted these joyous celebrations and invited people to respond and join with him as the bridegroom (Mark 2:18–22).

Marriage Metaphor in Isaiah 40–55

Introduction

As observed in chapter four, Isaiah made extensive use of Exodus and Wilderness traditions to describe a New Exodus after the fall of Babylon. But Isaiah also regularly used feminine imagery to describe Jerusalem or Zion. In Isa 54–55 Jerusalem is like a woman who has lost her husband and her children. But the New Exodus will result in the restoration of Lady Jerusalem to her husband and a return of her children.

Isaiah 40–55 contains more female imagery than any other section of the Hebrew Bible.[151] Jerusalem / Zion is personified as a woman a number of times in these chapters and the same themes found in Hosea and Ezekiel are present here as well. Israel has been an unfaithful wife, she has been punished, and now is the time of her

---

151. Darr, *Isaiah's Vision*, 165. Exum, "Of Broken Pots, Fluttering Birds and Visions in the Night: Extended Simile and Poetic Technique in Isaiah," 331–52. Dille, *Mixing Metaphors: God as Mother and Father in Deutero-Isaiah*.

restoration. While Hosea and Ezekiel had a great deal more detail on the sin of the bride, Isa 40–55 focuses on the restoration of the relationship.

This section will briefly survey several of the relevant sections of Isaiah in order to trace development and application of the marriage metaphor in the post-exilic world of the writer. We have already seen that Isa 40–55 developed the idea of an eschatological banquet into an image of the end of the exile. The marriage metaphor receives a similar development and application to the hope for a return from Exile. In addition, the writer seems to consciously draw on Jeremiah re-applying that pre-exilic prophecy to the new, post-exilic situation.[152]

Isaiah 49:14–26

This section combines elements of Lamentations and Jer 2 into a complaint song.[153] In Isa 49:14 Lady Zion complains that her husband has forsaken her. Since אֲדֹנָי appears in parallel to יהוה, most translations render the noun as Lord, but given the context of abandoning and forgetting it is better to translate אֲדֹנָי as "husband."[154] The substance of this complaint appears to draw on Lam 5:20: the Lord has forsaken Israel. "Forsaken" is עזב, which most commonly simply means to leave or abandon, but in Isa 54:5, 60:15 and 62:4 for abandoning a wife or husband. The Akkadian cognate *ezêbu* includes the idea of divorce.[155] The metaphor seems to be that of a marriage which has come to an end. The wife accuses the husband of abandoning her, perhaps by quoting the husband's own words (Lam 5:20).

The Lord protests, however, stating that he has in no way forgotten his bride. The rhetorical question in verse 15 emphasizes the Lord's devotion to his bride by comparing his devotion to that of a nursing mother. In fact, he cannot forget Zion because her

---

152. Isaiah 47:3–4 could be included in this survey as well since there an implicit contrast between Israel as the Lord's redeemed people and Babylon. Both are portrayed as a woman. In chapter 47 Babylon is violated in a grotesque fashion; she is no longer the virgin Babylon, young and tender, but a woman who has been raped by her enemies, humiliated and dishonored. Darr notices an ironic turn here. The description of Babylon as "young and tender" (רַכָּה וַעֲנֻגָּה) appears in Deut. 28:56–57. This part of the curses for violating the covenant describes the horrific act of the wife who intends to cannibalize her own children. This very thing happened in the Babylonian siege of Jerusalem (Lam 2:20, 4:10), but now the "tables are turned" and Babylon herself is the delicate and tender woman who is forced into humiliation. Darr, *Isaiah's Vision*, 172. She is unveiled, skirts raised, no longer the queen of the nations. In vv. 5–6 Babylon is a wanton creature lounging in security. Babylon thought she would never be a widow or without children, yet now show is both in a single day (vv. 8–9). Even her magic and astrology cannot help her now, she will be destroyed and there is none who can save her (v. 15). In contrast, Israel thought she was a childless widow, but in chapters 54–55 we will learn that she was never widowed, nor was she divorced. Her husband desires to redeem her out of her slavery and he tents will need to be expanded for all of her children.

153. Goldingay and Payne, *Isaiah 40–55*, 2:180; Willey, "The Servant of YHWH and Daughter Zion: Alternating Visions of YHWH's Community," 267–303.

154. Goldingay and Payne suggest that אֲדֹנָי has been misvocalized. *Isaiah 40–55*, 2:185.

155. See Soden, *Akkadisches Handwörterbuch*, 267b.

name is "inscribed on his palms." Further, he says that "your walls are always before me." The commentaries normally explain these metaphors by pointing to the outline of a Sumerian city in the lap of King Gudea.[156] This is possible, but Isa 49:16 says that Lady Zion is inscribed in the Lord's hand, not that the city is engraved on his lap.[157]

Perhaps it is more consistent to read this statement as a part of the marriage metaphor. While the vocabulary is different, "inscribing on the arm" is an indication of love in Song 8:6. Fox sees a parallel between Song 8:6 and the *Cairo Love Songs* (COS 1.150) in which a young man expresses his desire to always be near his beloved: "If only I were her little seal-ring, the keeper of her finger! I would see her love each and every day." A signet-ring would be elaborately engraved with the name of the owner. To wear the ring would be a sign of a special relationship.[158] In Isa 49:16 the Lord uses similar language: Lady Zion is always before the Lord's eyes. It might be objected that in Isaiah the beloved is engraved on the palm, while in Song of Solomon the beloved is engraved on a ring worn on the arm, but as Pope points out, anatomical descriptions in poetry are quite flexible. An "arm wearing a ring" in Song 8:6 should likely be understood as a hand.[159]

That Lady Zion's walls are before the Lord seems to favor the Sumerian city view, but just a few lines later in Song of Solomon, the strength of the bride is described as a wall (Song 8:9–10). While the point of the metaphor is obscure,[160] it is not insignificant that the writer of the Song uses the noun טִירָה. This is a rare noun used for walls, pillars and ornaments in the Temple in Zion, implying great beauty and strength.[161] One additional detail should be mentioned. While Song 8:5 seems to be detached from 8:6–8, the fact that it describes the groom coming up out of the wilderness with his bride is yet another blending of the marriage metaphor with a Wilderness tradition.[162]

In Isa 49:18, the Lord swears an oath that Zion will adorn herself as a bride once again as her children return to Jerusalem. These verses are likely an allusion to Jer 2:32, "can a girl forget her ornaments?" Choo shows that four words in Isaiah are drawn from Jer 2:32: שׁכח, forget (Isa 48:14–15), עֲדִי, ornaments, כַּלָּה, bride and

156. Baker compares this to an architectural drawing of the palace of Nur Adad in Larsa, Baker, "Isaiah," 4:163.

157. *2 Baruch* 4:1–3 uses Isa 49:16 to describe a heavenly Jerusalem which was revealed to Adam, Abraham and Moses, but it is not the city of Jerusalem which was destroyed in 586 BCE or 70 CE.

158. Snaith, *The Song of Songs*, 120.

159. Pope, *Song of Songs*, 666. It is also possible to read the ring as a bracelet of some kind, but the text describes it as a seal, so a ring is more likely correct.

160. Pope suggests the wall is defensive, and therefore a symbol of inaccessibility. But the wall has a door, suggesting that the girl may allow someone to enter.

161. 1 Kgs 6:36, 7:2, 20, 42, 2 Chron 4:13. The word described ornaments in the tabernacle (Exod 28:17–20; 39:10–13) and in the future, eschatological temple (Ezek 46:23).

162. Pope cites the Targum which connects this verse in SoS to the resurrection of the dead at the beginning of the eschatological age. The Targumist alludes to Isaiah 49: "At that hour, Zion, mother of Israel, shall bear her children and Jerusalem will receive her captive children" (Pope, *Song of Solomon*, 665).

קִשֻׁרִים, band.[163] Before the exile, Jeremiah asked how a bride could possibly forget her wedding ornaments. After the exile Isaiah says that the Lord has not forgotten these things at all. He will in fact remember his wedding day and restore his bride to himself, thus ending the exile.

In summary, this text is an example of the benefits of an intertextual method as described in chapter 2.[164] There is a development of the marriage metaphor from a pre-exilic text in order to apply the metaphor to a new situation. In Jeremiah the marriage metaphor was used to condemn the Judah as spiritually adulterous, warning the nation of an impending separation or divorce. In the case of Isa 49, the separation is in the past and the bride should expect the restoration of her marriage. At the end of the exile, she will be dressed once again as a bride and her marriage to her Lord will be restored.[165]

Isaiah 54

Isaiah 54 is the climax of the marriage metaphor in Isa 40–55. Darr has called Isa 54 a "great love poem."[166] So too Kauffmann, who describes the chapter as an "allegory of Zion the Abandoned wife," corresponding to the previous allegory of Zion as an abandoned mother.[167] Lundbom argues that Isa 54:4–5 employs the same sort of metaphor as Hos 2 and Ezek 16: "Israel is Yahweh's young bride"[168] Dumbrell sees that Isa 54–55 takes up the image of a marriage for the relationship between God and Israel, especially emphasizing the idea of חֶסֶד.[169] Isaiah seems to allude to the marriage metaphor as found in Jeremiah. For example, the verb בעל appears in 54:1, 5 and Jer

---

163. Choo, "Mother Zion and her Children: Deutero-Isaiah's Use of a Prophetic Metaphor in the Context of Zion Theology," 107.

164. Isaiah 49 also points out a pitfall of my method. The development of a tradition must assume priority of texts. That Hosea preceded Jeremiah is fairly secure, but it is possible to date Isa 40–55 before or after Jeremiah. As I expressed in the introduction to chapter 4, I am of the opinion that Isa 40–55 was written after the exile and my explanation of Isa 49 is built on that view. If Isa 40–55 predates Jeremiah, then my intertextual method simply reverses the direction of development. Issues such as this will not be a problem in chapter 6 or 7 since there is no question that the Second Temple Period writers and Jesus postdate the prophets.

165. Perhaps Isa 50:1–3 ought to be included here as well. In this short section, the personified Zion is described as sold into slavery on account of her iniquities. While verse one mentions a certificate of divorce, it is not clear that the writer is saying that the marriage is dissolved. Goldingay, for example, reads verse one as a reference to the legal grounds for the divorce. (For example, Goldingay and Payne, *Isaiah 40–55*, 2:101; Westermann, *Isaiah 40–66*, 225; Koole, *Isaiah III*, 2:89). But other commentators understand this as a separation rather than a divorce. Choo points out several examples where the verb שלח does not refer to a divorce but a physical and social separation. Choo, "Mother Zion," 96. But neither of her examples are drawn from marriage. Tamar begs Amnon not to "send her away" (2 Sam 13:16) and Sarah demands that Hagar be "sent away." Neither case is a marriage, so the situation is not analogous to Isaiah 50.

166. Darr, *Isaiah's Vision*, 184.

167. Kaufmann, *The Babylonian Captivity and Deutero-Isaiah*, 93, 126–28.

168. Lundbom, *Jeremiah 1–20*, 253.

169. Dumbrell, *Covenant and Creation*, 194.

3:14 (often translated as "master") and Jer 31:32. The noun appears in Hos 2:18 [16] in parallel to the more common word for husband, אִישׁ.

The childlessness of Lady Zion is a shame to her (54:1–4). While this recalls several stories of infertile wives in the Hebrew Bible (Isa 51:2 alluded to Sarai, for example), other ancient Near Eastern literature describes a defeated city as a defeated god and therefore a humiliation in the eyes of surrounding nations.[170] When Zion was destroyed, it became like a desolate woman. Sawyer observes the word שׁוֹמֵמָה ("to be desolate") is used of Tamar, who is raped and humiliated by Amnon her brother (2 Sam 13:20).[171]

Holmgren sees this text as the Lord playing the role of the brother-in-law in a Levitrate marriage.[172] Redeemer and husband are brought into direct parallel and the shame of her youth will be forgotten. The verb כלם in v. 4 has the sense of shame as well and is used in the context of prostitution (Jer 3:3, 8:12, Ezek 16:27, 54, 61). Isaiah is describing the exile is as a childless widowhood. This is the same language we find in Lam 1:1, for example, the one who was a queen among the nations is now a widow and a slave. Babylon had no one to help her when she was attacked, therefore she became a widow and slave (whore?), so too did Israel become a widow and slave because of her sins, but she has a redeemer who will pay the price and bring her out of slavery and restore the marriage relationship she once enjoyed.

The reversal of Lady Zion's fortunes in Isa 54:5–8 are perhaps the most important verses for developing the idea of Zion as the Lord's bride. There are four titles used for God in verse five, the creator, the Lord of hosts, the Holy One of Israel, and the God of all the earth. In this verse God is called both husband (בעל)[173] and redeemer (גאל). Since the two nouns are in parallel, this is perhaps another hint at a Levirate marriage.[174]

Zion is like a wife who was abandoned in her youth. The Qal passive participle of עזב is used here for a divorce and the parallel verb מאס has the connotation of rejection. But the noun נְעוּרִים can be used for a young woman and betrothed virgin. In two important marriage metaphor texts, the word refers to the virginal state of Israel in the wilderness (Hos 2:17, Jer 2:2).[175] In fact, 54:10 indicates that this restoration is

---

170. Westermann, *Isaiah 40–66*, 273.

171. Sawyer, "Daughters of Zion and Servant of the Lord in Isaiah: A Comparison," 89–107, 95. The verb appears in Lam 5:18 to describe Mount Zion after 586.

172. Holmgren, *With Wings as Eagles*, 90. In further support of a levirate marriage in this text, the noun אַלְמָנוּת only appears in three places in the Hebrew Bible. In Gen 38:14, 19 the word describes Tamar, who was a childless widow to whom the son of Judah was promised in a levirate marriage. 2 Samuel 20:3 describes ten women in David's harem who were kept as widows because of their participation in Absalom's rebellion.

173. Cf. Isa 62:4, Gen 20:3, Deut 22:22.

174. Citing the story of Ruth, Goldingay and Payne, *Isaiah 40–55*, 2:346.

175. The wilderness period is likely in mind in Ezekiel's allegory of Israel's history (Ezek 16:22, 43, 60). There the word is used to describe the early years of Israel's history when she was a young and pure virgin, in contrast to her present status as a whore. In Lev 22:13 the woman is single, and not yet betrothed. In Mal 2:14 and Prov 5:18 it refers to a woman who is married, but she was faithful at

based on the covenant faithfulness of the husband (חֶסֶד). He will establish a covenant of peace (בְּרִית שְׁלוֹמִי) because he has compassion (רחם) on his wife. Both words are foundational for the restoration of the wife in Hosea. A "covenant of peace" appears first in Num. 25:12.[176] This same phrase appears in Ezekiel to describe the New Covenant in the last days (34:25; 37:26 cf. Mal. 2:5). The phrase is therefore thematically the same as the New Covenant in Jer 31:31–33.

The restoration of the city is described in 54:11–13 as a woman "adorned like a bride."[177] The noun פּוּךְ refers to eye-makeup, although the only other use in the Hebrew Bible refers to the onyx stones of the Temple (1 Chron 29:2). The stones which make up this rebuilt city are difficult to identify with certainty, but they are all precious stones which would be used as jewelry. For example, חֵפֶץ (v.12) is a generic word for precious stones (Prov 3:15, 8:11). The word is often translated as "joy" or "delight" (1 Sam 15:22, Job 22:28). In Sir 45:11 it is used for the exceedingly beautiful stones which adorned the high priest's garments.[178] It is possible that these precious stones are a part of the ornaments worn by a bride (cf. Jer 2:32).[179] In keeping with the earlier use of the marriage metaphor, 54:11 describes the woman as formerly "not-comforted" (Hos 1:6).

In summary, Isa 54 describes a restoration of the marriage between the Lord and his people. Lady Zion is told to anticipate the return of the exiles (her children) and to prepare for herself for a celebration marking the restoration of her marriage. There are clear allusions throughout this chapter to previous marriage metaphor texts (Hosea, Jer 2–4) yet they are applied to a new situation, the return of exiles to Jerusalem after 538 BCE.

Isaiah 62

While this survey has been bounded by Isa 40–55, the poem found in Isa 62 is important because it is perhaps the clearest example of the marriage metaphor being used for the eschatological age. In fact, Isa 62 certainly echoes the use of the marriage metaphor from Isa 40–55, but re-applies the metaphor to a renewed hope for the end of the exile.[180] Darr observed that there three principle motifs in Isaiah 62: renaming,

---

the time of marriage. Goldingay and Payne draw attention to parallels with both Hosea and Ezek 23. Goldingay and Payne, *Isaiah 40–55*, 3:347.

176. Numbers 25:12 may reflect a marriage metaphor as well. In Numbers the word is sued to describe Phineas' appointment to a "perpetual priesthood." What is important here is that the Covenant of Peace was given because Phineas defended the jealousy of God. Israel committed spiritual adultery in the wilderness and aroused the Lord to jealousy.

177. Biddle, "The Figure of Lady Jerusalem," 173–94.

178. 4Q164 Isaiah Pesher interprets the precious stones as a reference to the chief priests of the community who will be appointed as rulers in the last days.

179. This text is likely a source for the description of the New Jerusalem in Rev 21.

180. Westermann says that nearly every sentence of Isa 62 recalls Deutero-Isaiah. Westermann,

coronation and marriage imagery. These three interweave to create a scene of joy, reconciliation, and possibilities of new life. God and Zion are not just to be reconciled, the family is to be restored and the Lord will rejoice over his bride.[181]

Anderson drew attention to the renaming and wedding imagery in the chapter.[182] He observes that in Isa 62:4, Zion, personified as a woman, is renamed. Lady Zion will no longer be called Forsaken or Desolate, but rather Hephzibah and Beulah. Both are actual names of women in the Hebrew Bible, but here are to be taken in contrast to the former names.[183] Renaming is often associated with a covenant relationship[184] and in Isa 4:1 a renaming occurs in a marriage context in order to take away the reproach of the woman's poverty and desolation. While it is possible that the renaming ceremony envisioned here is a coronation, it is better to see this as a wedding ceremony. Andersen assembles evidence that Isa 62 describes the marriage of Zion to the Lord. He draws on many of the texts already surveyed in this chapter which employ the marriage metaphor to describe the relationship of God and his people.

Summary and Conclusion

Isaiah 40–55 combines the wilderness tradition with the marriage metaphor found Hosea in order to apply these texts to the return from Exile. Israel, as the wife of the Lord, has been unfaithful and has been punished. But now she is summoned once again into the wilderness where she will receive good things from the hand of her husband. The end of the exile is therefore described as a restoration of marriage with all of the joyous celebration expected at a marriage celebration. As Darr concludes,

---

Isaiah 40–66, 373. Isaiah 62:10–12 is a virtual "catena of quotations from Second Isaiah." Westermann, *Isaiah 40–66,* 378, citing Muilenberg. A way is prepared for the salvation of the Lord (cf. Isa 40:1–3) and the people of God are told to prepare to meet their salvation. The Lord brings his "reward and recompense" (62:11), a quotation from Isa 40:10. Isaiah 62 itself is developed by Zech 9:9. Both texts "behold, your salvation comes," although in Isa 62:11 it is salvation which is coming, but in Zech 9:9 it is the king who is coming, bringing with him salvation. In both cases the a announcement is made to the "daughter of Zion" and in both cases the announcement of the arrival of salvation is followed by the slaughter of the nations (Isa 63:1–6; Zech 9:14–15). What is more, both passages describe the people of God as jewels in his crown (Isa 62:3; Zech 9:16).

181. Darr, *Isaiah's Vision,* 203.

182. Andersen, "Renaming and Wedding Imagery in Isaiah 62," 75–80. Whybray agrees that "the restoration of Zion and her new status are described in familiar terms of marriage." Whybray, *Isaiah 40–66,* 247.

183. This is not unlike Naomi ("pleasant") renaming herself Mara ("bitter") when she lost her children (Ruth 1:20, cf. 4:13–17).

184. In Gen 17 Abram and Sarai are renamed in the context of a covenant renewal. In Gen 35:28 and 35:10 Jacob is renamed as Israel. It is possible that Nebuchadnezzar renames Mattaniah as Zedekiah in 2 Kgs 24:17 in order to demonstrate Zedekiah's new loyalties. Andersen, "Renaming and Wedding Imagery in Isaiah 62," 76.

Jesus the Bridegroom

"Once a widow bereaved of her children, Zion will raise offspring in a paradisiacal age-a fitting fate for the beloved bride of Isaiah 62."[185]

This observation is significant because of the importance of Isaiah in the teaching of Jesus as well as other Second Temple period writers. Jesus is described as reading from Isaiah 61 (Luke 4:16–21) and regularly alluding to other texts from Isaiah in the synoptic gospels. Jesus described the Kingdom of God as a wedding banquet in at least three parables (Matt 22:1–4, 25:1–12, Luke 14:12–24) and himself as a bridegroom hosting a joyous celebration (Mark 2:18–22). Isaiah described the restoration of Israel from exile as a new wilderness experience (chapter 4). The wilderness experience was to be a restoration of the covenant relationship between Israel and her husband, the Lord (this chapter). It is not at all surprising that Jesus would use these same vivid metaphors to describe his own call to Israel to join his celebration of the coming eschatological age.

Psalm 45: The Marriage of a King

Psalm 45 seems to be the best candidate for potential source material for the idea of the eschatological age as a wedding in the psalter.[186] The psalm is clearly describing the king of Israel as a bridegroom. In verse 7 the king appears to be called אֱלֹהִים and he is "anointed by God" (מְשָׁחֲךָ אֱלֹהִים) in verse 8 (7 ET). Both verses are cited in the New Testament as referring to Jesus as messiah and God (Heb 1:8–9).[187] Psalm 45 may also be

---

185. Darr, *Isaiah's Vision*, 224.

186. Before the rise of form criticism, the king in Psalm 45 was routinely identified as the Messiah by both Christian and Jewish interpreters. For example, Morison stated that "there is not, perhaps in the entire book of Psalms a more direct or sublime prediction of Christ and the church than the one embodied in this beautiful ode." Plumer agrees, *Psalms*, 514. Plumer's commentary on Ps 45 is a treasury of citations from nineteenth-century commentaries on the messianic nature of this psalm. The Targum on the Psalms understands Ps 45 eschatologically. The title "the lilies" is interpreted in the light of Hos 14:6 and therefore concerns the "time to come." Braude, *The Midrash on Psalms*, 1:450. The Targum on 45:3 reads "your beauty King Messiah is better than men." Edwards provides a fresh translation of Targum Ps 54 along with some commentary on the Messiah in the Psalm. *Exegesis in the Targum of the Psalms,* 185–92; 232–34. These allegorical interpretations are difficult because the separate the psalm from the historical context (a royal wedding) and the original intention of the Psalm. For the development of the psalm in the LXX, see Ausloos, "Psalm 45, Messianism and the Septuagint," 239–51.

187. In the opening verses of Hebrews the author brings together a number of texts from the Hebrew Bible and applies them to Jesus. Psalm 2 and 2 Sam 7:14 were clearly understood as messianic in the Second Temple period, the inclusion of Ps 45 in this context may imply that this psalm was also considered messianic in the first century. A few have taken this psalm as a reference to a pagan or polytheistic sacred marriage between the king and the goddess of love as part of a Mesopotamian New Year celebration (*hieros gamos*). Keel comments on this possibility, but concludes that there is very little in Psalm 45 which requires this sort of interpretation. Keel, *The Symbolism of the Biblical World*, 285; cf. Kraus, *Psalms 1–59*, 453. Lipinski connects Ps 19:5–6 and Ps 45 with the sacred marriage motif: "Le troisième moment important du ritual de la fete aurait été le mariage sacré. Selon Widengren, l'existence de ce rite est attestée par le Ps 19:5–6, que identifie 'tente' et 'chambre nuptiale' et ferait ainsi allusion au sanctuaire hiérogamique. Ce passage déterminerait le *Sitz im Leben* du Ps 45

the basis for Rev 19:6–8.[188] It is difficult to know how early this messianic interpretation is since there is little use of the psalm in the intertestamental literature.[189] A potential pre-Christian use of Psalm 45 to describe a messianic expectation is *T.Judah* 24, although this short compilation of messianic texts does not rely heavily on Psalm 45.[190]

This is also a good example of a psalm which seems to have a clear function in the life of the kings of Israel or Judah which was included in the Psalter because it continued to speak to Jews at a later time. J. McCann, for example, explains that psalms 45–49 "assisted the community to face the disorienting reality of exile and also to affirm the hope that was still possible."[191] Their function in the completed psalter went beyond the original context (a royal wedding) to a hope for a restored kingdom with the Lord himself ruling. In short, "the king represents the royal presence of God on earth."[192]

The King as God

That the king is called God in verse seven is a point of contention in the commentaries.[193] The main problem is the assumption that a king of Israel would accept the title of "God." This is theologically unacceptable in the Hebrew Bible, although Pss 2 and 110 describe the king as God's son.[194] There are several options for understanding the syntax

---

et des dialogues enflamimés du Cantique des Cantiques" (Lipinski, *La royauté de Yahwé dans la poésie et le culte de l'ancien Israël*, 64–65).

188. Zimmerman lists seven thematic and linguistic connections between Rev 19:6–8 and LXX Ps 44 (ET Ps 45) and concludes that there is an "intertextual relationship" between the two songs. Zimmermann, "Nuptial Imagery in the Revelation of John," 153–83.

189. Weiser states that the psalm had an early messianic interpretation prior to application of the text to Jesus made in Hebrews 1, but offers no evidence. Weiser, *Psalms*, 365.

190. Despite the implication of McKee, "Testament of the Twelve Patriarchs," 1:801na.

191. McCann, "Books I-III and the Editorial Purpose of the Hebrew Psalter," 102.

192. Kraus, *Psalms*, 1:457.

193. For a summary of commentaries prior to 1970, see Mulder, *Studies on Psalm 45*, 33–80. It is possible that the objection to the theology of v. 7 is misplaced because the line is not addressed to the king, but rather to God himself. That vv. 2–6 are addressed to the king are certain; v. 10 is addressed to the bride. Perhaps the solution is to see verse 7 as addressed to God in the performance of the psalm. Broyles, *Psalms*, 207. This solution preserves the obvious syntax of the line without resorting to re-pointing or emending the text. A second possible interpretation is to read אֱלֹהִים as the subject of the verb and translating "God will be your throne forever." According to Muldar, Barnes is perhaps the only commentator to accept this reading of the text. That the subject should be placed second in a verbless clause seems unlikely. A more attractive variation on אֱלֹהִים as a subject is to see the "throne of God" as the subject, translating "The throne of your God is forever." Mulder, *Studies in Psalm 45*, 49. A third possibility is to read אֱלֹהִים as the predicate of the verb and translate the phrase "your throne is God forever." There are several close parallels (Ps 82:6, for example), but none are precisely parallel since they do not use אֱלֹהִים or אֵל to refer to "God" but rather "gods." Mulder finds ample parallels in Egyptian and Mesopotamian texts, but nothing quite like this construction in the rest of the Hebrew Bible. Nevertheless, this is the way Ibn Ezra rendered the phrase and it is found in numerous modern commentaries. Ibid., 62–63.

194. Broyles, *Psalms*, 207.

Jesus the Bridegroom

of this verse, but the simplest is to take אֱלֹהִים as a vocative. A noun in apposition to a second person pronoun can be described as a vocative in a verbless clause.[195] Although this reading is the easiest, it does cause the theological problem of calling the king a "god." Yet the earliest history of interpretation of the verse in the LXX, takes אֱלֹהִים as a nominative (ὁ θεός) in apposition to ὁ θρόνος. Hebrews 1:8 quotes the verse from the LXX without variation. The vocative reading is also supported by other early translations such as Aquila, Symmachus, Theodotion, and the Peshitta and the Vulgate.[196]

The verse therefore refers to the anointed king as God. While the theology of this reading is more difficult, it does seem to be the plain reading of the text. That the king can be called a son of God in Pss 2 and 110 may help to understand the use of אֱלֹהִים in Ps 45.[197] This reading enhances the grandiose language and points to a larger messianic application for the bridegroom king of the Psalm.

Beyond a Royal Wedding

That Ps 45 was taken eschatologically from a very early time is evident from the echoes of the language of the psalm in later prophetic texts which are clearly messianic. Zephaniah 3:14–20 seems to echo Ps 45. In v. 14 Israel is called a daughter (בַּת, of Zion and Jerusalem), as in 45:9–10. The command "Sing O Daughter of Zion" in the NIV is a bland translation of רנן, which has the connotation of loud rejoicing or jubilation.[198] The parallel word in Zeph 3:14 is רוע normally used for a war cry, but in the hifel is often used for loud rejoicing. In a close verbal parallel to Zeph 3:14, Zech 9:9 uses both גיל and רוע as parallel commands to the daughter of Zion and daughter of Jerusalem. Zephaniah expands the exultation with a second couplet with two additional terms for loud rejoicing and triumph.[199] Both Zephaniah and Zechariah are commands to a young woman to rejoice as in the presence the mighty king.

---

195. GKC 126de; Joüon, 137. Waltke and O'Connor, *Biblical Hebrew Syntax*, 77, 196. The main objection to the vocative is that there is no definite article for אֱלֹהִים as might be expected in a vocative construction. Typically אֱלֹהִים does not take the definite article, so this objection is not critical. A more significant problem is the lack of a preposition for the predicate עוֹלָם וָעֶד, a unique construction in the Hebrew Bible. Mulder, *Studies in Psalm 45*, 47. There are some manuscripts with the preposition לְ, however, according to the apparatus of the BHS, and all translations take עוֹלָם וָעֶד as the predicate of an implied verb. If the exegete takes אֱלֹהִים as a vocative then the line is often interpreted as not referring to the king as a god. Weiser translates the phrase "O divine king," explaining that the function of the king as a divine ruler implies his righteous rule. Weiser, *Psalms*, 363. Goulder also translates the phrase "O divine one," avoiding a direct declaration that the king is thought of as a god. Goulder, *The Psalms of the Sons of Korah*, 129.

196. Mulder, *Studies in Psalm 45*, 34.

197. For this view, see Wilson, *Psalms*, 1:700.

198. In Ps 84:3 the word is in parallel to כסף ("to long greatly for") and כלה ("to languish or to pine away").

199. עלז is used only 16 times in the Hebrew Bible. Isa 23:12 uses the word in an inversion—the daughter of Sidon is told not to rejoice because she has been judged. In 2 Sam 1:20 the daughters of the Philistines rejoice over the death of Saul. Jeremiah 11:15 also uses the verb with Jerusalem personified

common יָפְיָ does appear in Ps 45:12 referring to the bride (cf. Ezek 16:14, 25, Prov 6:25). Zech 9:17 describes young men (בָּחוּר, vigorous unmarried man), flourishing by eating and drinking new wine. Third, both texts describe the young women using בְּתוּלָה. This is a common word for virgin found in Ps 45:14 for the entourage of the bride as well as in Zech 9:17. Fourth, in both Ps 45 and Zech 9:9 the king is riding to meet someone.[211] An obvious difference is that the king in Psalm 45:4 "rides forth" into battle, "the poet who desires to represent the king in all his glory bids him ascend his war chariot and ride forth."[212] Again, most commentaries see the king mounted on a donkey as a symbol of peace rather than a bridegroom coming for his bride. A final parallel cited by Mitchell is that both texts describe the king as coming in righteousness and justice.[213] Here Mitchell is on solid ground since there is a clear verbal parallel between the two texts, צֶדֶק appears in 45:8 and 9:9, but this cannot be decisive since it is a relatively common word for describing the king.

Summary and Conclusions

While it is possible Ps 45 provided Zech 9:9–10 with some imagery of the bridegroom-king as Messiah, it is better to see Ps 45 as part of a network of texts that describe the coming of the messiah in marriage-like terms. By drawing Zeph 3:16–17, Isa 62, and Jer 31 into this network of texts, then the evidence for the eschatological age as a wedding of the Messiah to the Daughter of Zion is strengthened. By reading Ps 45 as the marriage metaphor applied the eschatological age, the possibility of the metaphor of the eschatological banquet as a wedding celebration becomes more viable as a description of Jesus' ministry in the synoptic Gospels.

If Ps 45 and Zech 9:9 are indeed an example of an intertextual relationship, it is difficult to state with certainty which is the earlier text. Within the canon of the Hebrew Bible, either may have been the foundation for the other, or both could be intertextual readings of a third text (Song of Solomon, for example). But this is not a problem for the ultimate goal of this study since Jesus' use of a "messiah as bridegroom" metaphor is drawn from the web of texts under consideration. But if Zech 9:9 indeed refers to the messiah as a bridegroom, the Jesus' entry into Jerusalem on a donkey in Matt 21:1–11 could be interpreted as a conscious evocation of a messiah-as-bridegroom metaphor. Jesus acted out the words of Zech 9:9 as the son of David coming to accept his kingdom, just as Solomon did in 1 Kgs 1:38–40.[214]

---

211. Mitchell, *The Message of the Psalter*, 249.
212. Keel, *The Symbolism of the Biblical World*, 280.
213. Mitchell, *The Message of the Psalter*, 249.
214. See chapter 2 for a discussion of the celebration in this text.

Conclusion: Marriage as a Metaphor for God's Relationship with Israel

This chapter has shown that beginning with Hosea, the restoration of Israel from exile could be described in terms of a restoration of the marriage of Israel and her God. The marriage was threatened by the unfaithfulness of the nation. In fact, her covenant unfaithfulness resulted in the exile. When the exile ends, the bride will be recalled from the wilderness, her shame will be removed, and she will be restored to her position as the bride. This restoration will be marked by a joyous time of celebration and feasting naturally accompanying a marriage.

The marriage metaphor develops from the Wilderness tradition as surveyed in chapter 4 since it was in the wilderness that God's relationship with his people began. But it was also in the wilderness that the bride's unfaithfulness began. At the end of the exile the Lord will call his bride back to the land and he will act decisively to end this bride's shame. Despite the fact that the technical terminology for a banquet (מִשְׁתֶּה) does not appear, the end of the exile as a restored wedding has all the elements of a wedding celebration: joy, food, drink, music, and dancing. As with the eschatological banquet in Isa 25:6–8 and the new Exodus of Isa 40–55, there is a clear invitation issued to Israel to participate as well as the hope of a reversal of the nation's shame and the resultant joyous celebration.

There are several implications this data for an intertextual study of the wedding banquet in the synoptic Gospels. First, because the invitation to join in a celebration is an important element of the marriage metaphor, it not surprising that Jesus combined these two ideas in his teaching concerning the Kingdom of heaven as a wedding banquet. As I will show in chapter 7, the gospel of Matthew describes the Kingdom of Heaven as a wedding banquet to which people have been invited (Matt 22:1–14, 25:1–12), although not all participate in the banquet. Some will reject that invitation but others will replace these unresponsive guests and accept the invitation to enter into the celebration of the Kingdom of God.

Second, Jesus' table fellowship with sinners is described as a wedding celebration. When questioned about his Jesus describes himself as a bridegroom hosting a time of joyous celebration where mourning would simply be inappropriate (Mark 2:18–22). Just as LXX Jer 3:18 describes the gathering of Israel and Judah in the eschatological age, so too does Jesus gather the people of Israel to provide food for them in the wilderness (both texts use συνέρχομαι. Matthew 8:11 describes a pilgrimage of people from the "east and west" to celebrate the eschatological banquet. In addition, Jesus describes "this generation" as adulterous because they are not responding properly to his invitation to join his celebration (Mark 8:38). To describe the nation as "adulterous" evokes a stream of tradition from Hosea, Jeremiah and Isaiah.

Third, if Jesus is described in terms of the bridegroom hosting a wedding banquet at the end of the age, then imagery from the Hebrew Bible which originally described God is re-applied to Jesus. But this is not unusual. There are a number of examples of

Israel as the Wife of the Lord

Jesus applying language which originally applied to God to himself.[215] In the Gospels Jesus is the bridegroom calling his bride Israel out of the wilderness to celebrate renewed marriage, or as Jeremiah puts it, a new covenant. The fact that Jesus specifically cites Jer 31 at the Last Supper raises the question of his use of the marriage metaphor as described in this chapter.

Fourth, since others h read Hosea, Isaiah, Jeremiah or Ps 45 in this way, it is not unexpected to find that a Jewish teacher like Jesus would see the end of exile as a restoration of a marriage to be celebrated with joyous feasting.[216] This anticipates the next chapter in which I will survey the developments of the three traditions in the literature of the Second Temple period. One of the benefits of an intertextual method as described in chapter 2 is that the method expects traditions and metaphors to overlap and blend into one another in new and surprising ways. This blending of eschatological banquet, Wilderness traditions and the marriage metaphor would be just the sort of intertextual creation expected of a Jewish teacher like Jesus.

---

215. Payne, "The Authenticity of the Parables," 338–41. Payne collects data on a number of images for God drawn from the Hebrew Bible which are applied to Jesus in the Synoptic Gospels including shepherd, master of the harvest, sower, Lord, bridegroom, and king.

216. This reading of the material is supported by later rabbinic readings of wilderness texts in the prophets. The wilderness period is sometimes viewed in terms of marriage in the midrashic texts. The cloud of Glory greeted Israel like a groom who builds a canopy at the entrance of his bride's home. Mekhilta of Rabbi Simeon ben Yohai, 33, Midrash HaGadol (Margoliot) 2:214, 2:251cf. Targum Ps-Jonathan to Ex 13:20 and Nun 33:5. Rubenstein, *The History of Sukkot in the Second Temple and Rabbinic Periods*. See also Ulfgard, *The Story of Sukkot: The Setting, Shaping, and Sequel of the Biblical Feast of Tabernacles*. Isaiah 4:5 describes the future as a time when God builds a canopy on Zion, representing his presence, using word *chuppah* for canopy. Rubenstien reports an Amorite Midrash which goes further: the canopy will be the "world to come," and will be a "new creation" or a New Eden. The *chuppah* will be made of precious stones, with four rivers (flowing with milk, honey, wine, and balsam), adorned with jewels in Eden. Rubenstein, *The History of Sukkot*, 282n23.

6

From the Hebrew Bible to the Historical Jesus

*Banquet and the Marriage Metaphor
in the Second Temple Period Judaism*

Introduction

In the preceding chapters, I have shown that the eschatological age is described as a time of great feasting in the Hebrew Bible, whether that feasting is an inaugural banquet (Isa 25:5–6) or an ongoing time of bounty in the wilderness (Isa 40–55). In addition, the restoration of Israel at the end of the age is sometimes described as a restoration of a marriage, combining the joyous meal with a return from the wilderness (Hos 2, Jer 31). According to L. Schiffman, the idea of a messianic banquet was "quite widespread in Second Temple Judaism and continued in rabbinic aggadic tradition."[1] The purpose of this chapter is to survey the Second Temple period literature normally cited as evidence of a messianic banquet in order to determine how the metaphor might have functioned in a first-century Jewish context. As with material from the Hebrew Bible, the idea of the eschatological age as a new Exodus merges with the metaphor of a banquet. In addition, there are a number of texts which employ the marriage metaphor (or, at the very least, a personification of Israel / Jerusalem / Zion as a woman). After surveying the various texts which may fit these three sets of imagery, I will conclude with some comments on how these three metaphors play off one another in the Second Temple period to describe the end of the exile.

---

1. Schiffman, "Rule of the Congregation," 798.

Messianic Banquet in the Pseudepigrapha

Introduction

There are a number of texts in the literature of the Second Temple period which refer to the eschatological age as a time of eating and drinking. Like Isa 25:6–8, this banquet is sometimes described as the inauguration of a coming age of peace and prosperity. But in other texts the coming age is described in terms of an on-going time of prosperity during which God's people enjoy plentiful food in an Edenic restoration of creation. What is important for the goals of this study is that the writers of the Second Temple period picked up on the eschatological banquet drawn from texts like Isa 25:6–8 or Isa 40–55 and developed it in order to apply the tradition to the new situation of the Second Temple Period.

There are two problems with using the Pseudepigrapha as a source for studying first-century Judaism.[2] The first is the problem of the date of the documents. Some texts come to us in translations dated centuries later than the period under investigation. For example, *2 Enoch* (*The Slavonic Apocalypse of Enoch*) may date to the late first century AD, but there are no manuscripts which date earlier than the fourteenth century and any "supposed Greek composition need not have been produced before A.D. 1000."[3] Because of this, scholars date the original composition of *2 Enoch* anywhere from pre-Christian times into the late medieval period. Given this ambiguity, it is probably best not to use *2 Enoch* as the centerpiece of a description of Second Temple period theology.

A second problem concerns the influence any one book may have had on the theology of "common Judaism" in the first century. We may confidently date a book such as the *Psalms of Solomon* to "about 50 B.C." and even posit a Pharisaical context for the book, but how we know with any measure of confidence the book was read in the first century widely enough to impact the way people thought? It is difficult to state with confidence that any given Second Temple period book reflects a broad consensus of opinion. The book may have been written and circulated in among a very small community and was virtually unknown to readers outside of that community. Similarly, the book may have been the work of an individual maverick thinker who was out of touch with the rest of Judaism and received virtually no recognition until Christians began to use the text in the second or third centuries.

With these two caveats in mind, this chapter will survey several major books which can be dated to the Second Temple period with some measure of confidence. Texts which appear in the library at Qumran present no problems with respect to date since they clearly represent the period, but they may not represent abroad consensus

---

2. For a similar warning, see Davila, "The Old Testament Pseudepigrapha as Background to the New Testament," 53–57.

3. Anderson, "2 Enoch," in *OTP*, 1:94.

The Enoch Literature

There are several references to an eschatological meal in the Enoch literature.[4] In general, these texts look forward to a final judgment in which the righteous or elect will be vindicated and the unrighteous or non-elect will be punished. This is God's judgment, but an intermediary is sometimes included (as in *1 En.* 62, cf. Dan 7). The period after this judgment for the elect is described as a restoration of Paradise. Of primary importance is *1 En.* 62 since it describes eating a meal after the judgment of the Son of Man. The context is clearly an eschatological judgment (62:3, "on the day of judgment"). After the kings of this world experience pain compared to birth pangs (62:4) they will see the Son of Man sitting on his throne of glory (62:5). This Son of Man will execute judgment, vindicating the righteous "elect ones" and separating the unrighteous kings of this world for judgment (62:8–12).[5] Then "the Lord of Spirits will abide over them, and with that Son of Man shall they eat, and lie down and rise up for ever and ever" (62:14). The elect experience a form of eternal life: their garments will never wear out, nor will their glory ever come to an end.

1 Enoch 62:14 may also describe a meal of sorts. The text reads "because the Lord of Spirits shall rest upon them and his sword (shall obtain) from them a sacrifice." Isaac comments that the word translated "sword" is literally "a memorial meal."[6] This is a particularly gruesome metaphor in Isa 34:6–7: the sword of the Lord is engorged with the blood of Edom. The verb דשׁן in the piel has the connotation of "becoming fat" in a positive sense (Sir 26:13, for example).[7] As we will see below, the verb is associated with eschatological banquet texts at Qumran. The three other occurrences of the root in the pual all have sense of prosperity (Prov 11:25, 13:4, 28:25). Watts notes the enormity of the sacrifice described in 34:7, "sacrifice greater than any that has ever been offered."[8] If Isaac's alternative reading is adopted in the light of Isa 34:6–7, then it is possible the sacrifice is "memorial meal," albeit a rather gruesome version of the eschatological banquet.

However, *1 En.* 62 is not an inaugural "banquet" even if it might be implied from the text. Like Isa 25:6–8, the meal in *1 En.* 62 follows a judgment. What is clear from the

---

4. For Enoch, see also Knibb, *The Ethiopic Book of Enoch*; Olson, *Enoch: A New Translation*; Nickelsburg, *1 Enoch: A Commentary on the Book of 1 Enoch*.

5. The unrighteous are the oppressors of the elect ones and are delivered to the angels for judgment (62:11).

6. Isaac cites Charles who emends the text and translates the line "and His sword is drunk with their blood" as an allusion to Isa 34:6–7. Isaac, "1 Enoch," 1:44nr.

7. The verb in Isa 34:6 appears in the hotpa'el, intensifying the image.

8. Watts, *Isaiah 34–66*, 11.

text is the meal is ongoing fellowship with the Son of Man in the period following the vindication of the elect ones. Charles notes the similarity of this text to Zeph 3:13, the remnant of Israel will live in peace, "they will eat and lie down and no one will make the afraid."[9] After the judgment when the wicked are separated from the righteous, "eating" has the idea of a peace and prosperity. However, I would suggest that the description of the eschatological feast in *1 Enoch* 62 is based on the Wilderness traditions I described in chapter 4. The description of eating with the Son of Man in 62:14 is similar to Exod 24:11, although in *1 Enoch* all the elect eat and drink. Clothing which does not wear out is an allusion to the Wilderness period (Deut 8:4; cf. Neh 9:21).

Several texts in *1 Enoch* describe a period prosperity after the judgment without reference to a messiah. This period is a restoration of paradise where there will be plentiful eating for all, and a restoration of the tree of life.[10] In *1 En.* 24–25 the writer describes the throne of God "on which he will sit when he descends to judge the earth with goodness" (25:3) as well as a great tree from which the righteous will eat and live long lives. In *1 En.* 10:18–19 the fate of the righteous is described in terms of long life and plentiful food.

The Enoch literature is not consistent in its view of the end of the age. *1 En.* 90:28–29 is the climax of the "animal apocalypse," a thinly veiled allegory using various animals to tell the story of Israel down to the Maccabean period. Like Dan 7:9–10, *1 En.* 90:20–27 describes a future great throne set up in the pleasant land (Israel, cf. 89:49). We are told "Lord of the Sheep" who struck the earth with his rod will sit upon this throne and begin the judgment of the sheep and their shepherds (Ezek 34:1–10, "the Lord will judge the shepherd of Israel"). In 90:20 the books are opened and seven shepherds are punished for killing more sheep that they were ordered to (vs. 22).[11] These are cast into the fiery abyss (vs. 24), the seventy shepherds are found guilty as well and cast into the abyss to the right of the house (vs. 26, presumably Gehenna, to the east of the Temple). In 90:28–29 the Lord of the Sheep then renovates the old house (the Temple, or the city of Jerusalem) into a new, greater house. The old Temple is torn apart[12] and replaced with a more beautiful building and ornaments, recalling Ezek 40–48.[13] All of this is reminiscent of the judgment of *1 En.* 62, but there is no

---

9. *APOT* 2:228.

10. For the restoration of Eden, see also *2 En.* 8–9, *3 En.* 23:18.

11. Perhaps this refers to the various nations who have oppressed Israel: Assyrian, Babylon, Persia, Ptolemies, Seleucids, etc. In Nahum, for example, Assyria is not judged for their role in the destruction of Samaria since this was ordained by the Lord, but rather for going far beyond the decreed destruction by killing and torturing more victims than necessary. The same theme may be found in Obadiah, concerning Edomite atrocities in 586 BCE.

12. Literally the old house is "folded up." Knibb, *The Ethiopic Book of Enoch*, 214; Nickelsburg, *1 Enoch*, 403. Olson suggests the language of a tent / tabernacle is used to emphasize the temporary nature of the earthly temple. An important Ethiopic manuscript of *1 En.* (Tana 9, fifteenth century) has "transformed" here. Olson, *Enoch: A New Translation*, 208.

13. This cannot refer to the early second temple, which was not at all a beautiful building. Perhaps this is a prophecy of a restored Solomonic temple, or perhaps a reference to the Herodian renovations. It

indication of a period of prosperity following the restoration of neither the Temple nor any sort of victory celebration. At the point where one might expect a messianic banquet, the temple is restored to glory and all the sheep.[14]

To summarize, the Enoch literature is perhaps the best example of apocalyptic literature from the early Second Temple Period, yet there is only the barest hint of an eschatological banquet in this material. Taken as a whole, the Enoch literature looks forward to an eschatological age which is compared to a restoration of Eden-like prosperity and peace. In this respect, *1 Enoch* is working the same imagery as Isa 40–55. The meal described in *1 En 62* stands within the banquet motif as found in Isa 25:6–8 since there is an ongoing meal in an eschatological age shared by the elect of God. Because this section of *1 Enoch* is not preserved in Greek or Hebrew it is impossible to find any clear verbal allusions to Isaiah or any other text in the Hebrew Bible.

Second Baruch

The most commonly cited text to support the idea of a Second Temple period eschatological banquet is *2 Bar.* 29:1–8. While the Enoch literature dates prior to the first century, *2 Bar.* is undoubtedly written after the fall of Jerusalem in 70 CE, likely in the final decade of the first century.[15] The two books therefore provide a line of continuity which runs through the period of Jesus' ministry, showing that the idea of an eschatological age as an ongoing banquet was current in the early first century.

2 Baruch 29:1–8 is the climax of a series of great calamities on the earth (26–28), but those living in the land will be spared from them (29:2). After these apocalyptic signs, the Anointed One will be revealed (29:3). Nothing is said about what this Anointed One does, but the very next verse says Leviathan and Behemoth[16] will be

---

would seem odd, however, for the Herodian temple to be praised so highly. In a similar way, the *Apocalypse of Weeks* describes the final age of the world as a time when the "first heaven shall depart and pass away" and a "new heaven" will appear (*1 En.* 91:16, cf. the conclusion to the *Apocalypse of Weeks*, 106:13).

14. Perhaps there is a hint of a banquet at the end of the *Animal Apocalypse*. Enoch is brought into the restored Temple (90:31) where he witnesses the restoration of the sheep. In 90:39 Enoch "became satiated in their midst." This is thin evidence since two manuscripts have "I slept" rather than "became satiated." Charles translates "slept" (*The Book of Enoch*, 78) Isaac translates "became satiated," *OTP* 1:71.

15. Klijn, "2 (Syriac Apocalypse of) Baruch," 1:616–52. *2 Baruch* appears to have been written in the late first century, probably around 100 CE. *4 Ezra* and *2 Bar.* share many similarities, although the direction of the influence is hard to determine. Klijn is inclined to see *2 Bar.* as dependent on *4 Ezra* and therefore dates the book to the first part of the second century. Collins argues for a date a bit earlier based on the fall of Jerusalem in the twenty-fifth year of king Jeconiah in the first verse of *2 Bar.* This is not historically accurate, so it is possible the author is referring to the fall of Jerusalem in 70 CE, twenty-five years in the past. The book was written in Palestine and most likely in Hebrew. The book is closely related to the rabbinic literature and seems to be exhorting diaspora Jews from the perspective of Palestinian Jews. Collins, *Apocalyptic Imagination*, 212–13.

16. Leviathan and Behemoth are said to have been created on the fifth day of creation and preserved for this very time. See *4 Ezra* 6:47–52 for a similar creation story. Leviathan and Behemoth have been kept "to be eaten by whom you wish, and when you wish."

released at that time to be nourishment for those who are left. The text then expands this meal to include a fantastic amount of fruits and vegetables (v. 5),[17] and finally a heavenly supply of manna.[18]

2 Baruch 29 may be a meditation on several texts in the Hebrew Bible which feature a victory over Leviathan as part of the Exodus events. Isaiah 27:1 describes the Lord destroying Leviathan by his powerful sword. In Ps 74:14 the great salvation of the Exodus is described as a judgment on Leviathan—the Lord crushed the heads of Leviathan and gave the body to animals as food.[19] In Isa 51:9–11 Rahab is cut to pieces in an obvious reference to the passage through the Red Sea.[20] Isaiah 51 begins with a promise to comfort Zion by making her deserts and wastelands like Eden. The prophet looks forward to a new Exodus when the redeemed of the Lord will return to an Eden-like Zion in gladness and joy (51:11). This new Exodus will include release for prisoners who will never lack for bread (51:14). Thematically, there are several parallels to Isa 25:6–8. While Leviathan or Rahab are not mentioned in Isaiah, the Lord "consumes death." As observed in chapter 3, it is possible that the reference is to Mot, the Canaanite god representing death.

To summarize, *2 Baruch* 29 is therefore an example of combining various traditions drawn from the Hebrew Bible (Exodus and wilderness, primordial monsters, creation)[21] in order to create a new application of those traditions to the present situ-

---

17. This description is found in early Christian writings. Irenaeus, *Haer.* (5.33.3–4), cites Papias as the source, although the wording is virtually synonymous with *2 Bar.* Most scholars feel *2 Bar.* is the source for the saying. Charles, *The Apocalypse of Baruch*, 54. *1 Enoch* 10:19 has a similar description of the bounty of the messianic age. This text is used in *Apoc. Dan* 10, although in this ninth-century CE text the days of the Antichrist are described in terms of great abundance. Zervos is more cautious, stating that which text served as the source is impossible to know with certainty. Zervos, "Apocalypse of Daniel," 1:760.

18. The return of manna is a frequent image of the messianic age, see *Sib.Or.* 7:149, although the text may date as late as the second century CE. As Meyer observed, "in the age of salvation men will enjoy the same miraculous food and drink as did the wilderness generation." Meyer, "Μάννα," 4:465. For summaries from the rabbinic literature on the idea of manna, see Claassens, *The God Who Provides*, 1–22. Psalm 78:17–29 is an unexplored connection to the time of messianic plenty. The Psalmist recounts the wilderness wanderings when the people were given all the water they could drink and were fed all the manna they could eat. Though they complained, they were given so much meat that "it rained down like dust" and the people ate all that they craved. The pattern of an exodus followed by a time of miraculous plenty is clear, although it is a dark reminder of the rebellion of the people of God in the wilderness.

19. Compare to Job 26:12–13 where the sea monster Rahab is cut to pieces, cf. Ps 89:10 (ET), *1 En.* 60:7–9, 24. See also Day, "Leviathan," 4:295–26.

20. Ackroyd, *Exile and Restoration*, 129.

21. There are several texts in *2 Bar.* that have this new creation language. In *2 Bar.* 31–32, the prophet explains his vision to the elders of the people, urging them not to forget Zion, which will be soon taken from them and destroyed (31:1–5). If the people prepare their minds by "sowing into them the fruits of the law" they will be preserved in the coming disaster (32:1–2). The Mighty One will shake creation, destroy the temple, but it will be "renewed in glory" and "perfected into eternity" (32:4–5). After a time of great evil and trial, the Mighty One will renew his creation (32:6.) Similarly, *2 Bar.* 44 describes a coming time after the judgment of the Mighty One and the consolation of Zion (44:7–8)

ation (the fall of Jerusalem). It is impossible to know if the writer of *2 Baruch* had one particular text in mind, but it is likely he used several traditions rather than a specific text. Like the Enoch literature, *2 Baruch* contains some clear allusions to an eschatological banquet motif. The writer consciously alludes to the first Exodus by describing a future victory over Leviathan and a victory banquet which begins with consuming the destroyed enemy but eventually includes manna. The coming age is once again described as a restoration of Eden-like conditions of prosperity and peace. *2 Baruch* is particularly important for the goals of this study since the book was written in the last decade of the first century, demonstrating that the eschatological banquet motif is consistent throughout the Second Temple period.

Fourth Ezra

Like *2 Baruch*, *4 Ezra* is a meditation on the fall of Jerusalem dating to the end of the first century CE. *4 Ezra* provides additional evidence that the idea of the eschatological age as a banquet was current at the end of the first century. While chapters 1–2 and 15 are clearly a Christian framework, chapters 3–14 come from a Jewish writer.[22] There are several potential references to an eschatological banquet in this book.[23] *4 Ezra* 9:1–13 describes a series of cataclysmic signs followed by a final judgment and punishment of the wicked including a description of the coming age as a time of an

---

when there is a "new world" which does not carry corruption (44:12). That which is corruptible will pass away; the present will be forgotten because it is polluted by evils. One participates in this coming world by "preserving the truth of the Law" (44:14). The connection between coming judgment and a new creation is also found in 57:2. An angelic guide interprets Baruch's vision concerning "the hope of the world which will be renewed" and the "promise of life that will come later."

22. The Jewish apocalypse (chapters 3–14) was probably written about 100 CE based on the opening verse which states the book was written thirty years after Jerusalem was destroyed. The Christian framework was added in the second half of the third century. Collins states there is a "consensus" the Jewish apocalypse was written in Palestine at the end of the first century. Collins, *Apocalyptic Imagination*, 196. On the other hand, Metzger understands the reference to Babylon in 3:1 as Rome and concludes that the book is the product of Diaspora Jews. Metzger, "4 Ezra," 1:517. See also Stone, "Coherence and Inconsistency in the Apocalypses: The Case of 'The End' in 4 Ezra," 229–43.

23. The clearest text for messianic banquet is *4 Ezra* 2:38–41, but the date of the text makes this uncertain evidence of a pre-Christian banquet idea. This section is almost certainly Christian since it declares that the Kingdom of Jerusalem will be taken away from Israel and given to "my people," presumably Christians. God has rejected the nation of Israel as his people, and according to this text, he has turned to the gentiles. In 2:33–41 Ezra calls to the nations because Israel has rejected God: "O nations, await your true shepherd." The editor of *OTP* inserts "Ezra turns to the Gentiles" as a section heading for 2:33–41, which is far more than the text says—there is no conversion of the Gentiles in the text. The nations are then commanded to see "at the feast of the Lord the number of this age who has been sealed" (2:38). While the number of close parallels to Revelation make certain that this is a Christian composition, it is possible the idea of a "feast of the Lord" is drawn on earlier Jewish imagery of a messianic banquet. Those who are present at the feast of the Lord are described as wearing white garments, unlike the improperly dressed guest in Matt 22:10–14 (cf. Rev 3:4, 6:11, 7:1).

"unfailing table" (9:19). Charles argues that "the reference is to Paradise and its marvelous fruits ("an unfailing table") which its trees bear without cessation."[24]

In *4 Ezra* 8:52–54 the future age of righteousness is described as a time when "paradise is opened, the tree of life is planted, the age to come is prepared, plenty is provided, a city is built, rest is appointed, goodness is established and wisdom perfected beforehand" (NRSV). Several now familiar themes are found here, including a time of plenty and a return of Eden, but a strong emphasis on spiritual blessings is found here in contrast to *2 Baruch*. This text is more like Isa 25:6–8 since illness and death are done away with and even Hades "has fled" and sorrows are passed away.[25]

The Apocryphon of Ezekiel

The first fragment of the *Apocryphon*[26] contains a parable used by Epiphanes to discuss the relationship of the body and the soul. A king drafted his entire population into the army so there were no civilians except a blind man and a lame man.[27] The king then gave a wedding banquet for his son and invited the entire kingdom except the two civilians. They were insulted at this snub and made a plan to work together to enter the king's garden. The blind man helps the lame man walk; the lame man led the blind man.[28] When the king discovers what the men have done, he questions them, but they deny responsibility. Neither man could have entered the garden (the blind cannot see, the lame cannot walk). In Epiphanes' version the king flogs the men

---

24. Charles, *APOT*, 2:600. The NRSV reads "an inexhaustible pasture." Note the Latin versions have mistaken νομός (pasture) for νόμος, (law). Some translations therefore read "unfailing law."

25. The return of paradise motif appears in *4 Ezra* 7:26–44 which describes a time when a city appears and Israel will be delivered from the dangers of this world. "My son the Messiah" will appear and people will rejoice with him for 400 years (7:28). After that time he will die (7:29) and the world will return to primeval silence. As in the first creation, after seven days the world will be roused from primeval silence and all corruptible will perish. The dead will be raised to life and the Most High will be seated on the seat of judgment in order to pass judgment. The unrighteous will go down into the "furnace of hell" while the righteous into the "paradise of delight." This is no victory banquet, but it is a clear image of eschatological "plenty." After a long lament over the few who are judged as righteous, Ezra asks the angel about the state of the soul after death, the time when God will renew creation (7:75).

26. The *Apocryphon of Ezekiel* is a lost work known only through a fragment preserved in Epiphanes (*Against Heresies* 64.70, 5–17), b. Talmud Sanhedrin 91a, a fragment preserved in 1 Clement 8:3, a number variations of a saying Tertullian attributed to Ezekiel, a fragment in Justin Martyr (*Dialogue* 47), and a fragment in Clement of Alexandria (*Paedagogus* 1:9). A late date for the larger work can be set by 1 Clement is normally dated to 95 CE. Josephus seems knows of Ezekiel (*Ant.* 10.5.1 mentions two books.) Dates for Ezekiel's work range from 50 BCE to 50 CE. Mueller and Robinson, "The Apocryphon of Ezekiel," 1:487–95. Bregman, "The Parable of the Lame and the Blind: Epiphanius' Quotation from an Apocryphon of Ezekiel," 125–38. Cook, "The Five Fragments of the Apocryphon of Ezekiel: A Critical Study," 532–34; Stone, Wright, and Satran, *The Apocryphal Ezekiel*.

27. Jeremiah 31:8 uses the blind and the lame who will be gathered into the restored kingdom.

28. The version in the Talmud is slightly different in that the two men simply enter the garden and steal new figs without the wedding banquet.

to discover the truth—the one blames the other. In both versions of this parable the point is to illustrate the relationship of the soul and the body.

While there is no eschatology in this parable at all, it is an obvious parallel to two versions of the Parable of the Wedding Feast in Matt 22:1–14 and Luke 14:15–35.[29] In both the biblical version and the *Apocryphon* version a king gives a banquet and invites many guests. But in the biblical version the invited guests do not come to the banquet and are replaced by the blind, lame, etc. In the *Apocryphon*'s version the guests all accept the invitation and the two "outsiders" are not among those who should be at the banquet. It is too much to say this fragment had an impact on the thinking of Second Temple period Judaism, although it is clear from the writers who preserved them that early Christians read and used the *Apocryphon of Ezekiel*. While Christians used texts which could be applied to Jesus as the Messiah, it is almost impossible to know how a Jewish reader would have taken these same texts. This fragment at best indicates the currency of the metaphor of a wedding banquet.

Sibylline Oracles

The Sibylline literature is not a single collection from any one time. They range from Jewish works of the first century to late Christian theologies. To complicate matters, there are many sections which are Christian interpolations into a Jewish oracle. The problem we face in using this material is distinguishing the Jewish from the Christian. Sometimes this is obvious since the writer is clearly referring to Jesus, but other times the text is a vague reference to a messianic figure or the messianic age which could be either Jewish or Christian. Many times these "either/or" sections are not really important (praise of God, for example), but in eschatological contexts it is very difficult to tell the Jewish from the Christian.

Reference to eating a heavenly meal appears in the earliest of the Oracles.[30] In *Sib.Or.* 5:260–85 there is a reference to Jews returning to the land. The Greeks will be driven from Judea (264) and everyone in the land will glory in the Law of the Lord (265). The righteous will "attend table with devout music," sacrifices and prayers (267). While the pagan world endures famine caused by God's judgment, the "holy land of the pious ones" will enjoy honey streaming from rocks and springs and heav-

---

29. These two parables are probably independent, but are both parables based on a king giving a wedding banquet and use the theme of guests refusing the invitation.

30. The Fifth Sibylline Oracle cannot be dated earlier than 70 CE because of the numerous references to the Nero Myth in all but the very first section, but not much later than 80 CE. The first section has favorable comments about Hadrian, which Collins uses to argue for a date for the first section prior to the Bar Kokhba rebellion of 132 CE. There are a number of references to destroying pagan temples, possibly a reference to the Jewish Diaspora revolt of 115 CE. That the book originated in Egypt is clear from line 53 (the Sibyl is a friend of Isis) and the interest in Cleopatra found throughout the book. Collins comments that despite the similarities to the third Sibylline oracle, the eschatological perspective is quite different. Collins, "Sibylline Oracles," 1:391.

enly milk flowing for all the righteous (5:282–83, cf. Joel 4:18, ET 3:18). The Third Oracle describes a similar scene.[31] In the *Sib.Or.* 3:601–23, the world is judged with various pestilence, but after a great king comes up out of Asia God will give great joy to men and "true fruit," wine, sweet honey, white milk and corn (620–23). Virtually the same language appears in *Sib.Or.* 8:211.[32]

A "Return to Eden" Motif

The more general motif of a return of Eden and a time of plenty is found in other literature of this period without reference to banquet imagery. The restoration of the Land to an Eden-like state was a part of the Banquet in the Wilderness motif discussed in chapter 4.[33] In *PsSol.* 14:2–3 the devout will live forever in the Lord's paradise as "trees of life." In *4 Ezra* 8:51–52 the coming restoration is described as Paradise. The Tree of Life will be planted, plenty of food will be provided for the city and there will be rest from labor. *T.Levi* 18.10–11 describes the rise of an eschatological priest / king who will "shine forth like the sun in all the earth" (18:4).[34] During the reign of this priest, "sin shall cease" and the righteous "will find rest in him" (18:9), and he will "remove the gates of paradise" as well as the "sword which has threatened since Adam" (18:10) and "all the saints will be clothed in righteousness" (18:14). In the *Apoc. Elij.* 5:6 righteous will eat from tree of life, will not thirst.[35]

---

31. Collins argues for an Asian origin the Third Sibylline based on the frequent mention of Asian locations and (more importantly), the prediction that an Asian king will invade Egypt. Lines 367–80 predicted this Asian king will usher in a time of bliss for Egypt, then again in lines 601–23 an Asian king invades and God intervenes in the world. He concludes the author was a Jewish inhabitant of the Roman province of Asia. Collins agrees the "oracles against the nations" need to be dated a bit later, likely before the battle of Actium in 31 BCE, but the main section of the book, in Collins opinion, is earlier. Collins, "Sibylline Oracles," 1:360.

32. Collins considers lines 1–216 to be Jewish in origin although there is little that is distinctively Jewish or Christian. Based on animosity towards Hadrian in lines 50–59, the book must have been written after135 CE. Collins, "Sibylline Oracles," 1:416.

33. Commenting on Isaiah 40–55, Seitz states that the way out of exile "erupts in the desert" where God makes the wasteland into Eden. See Seitz, "Isaiah," 335.

34. Since many fragments of the *Testaments of the Twelve Patriarchs* are found at Qumran, a mid- to late-second century BCE date seems plausible. As with any of this literature, we must also deal with the probability there are Christian interpolations in the text. These are especially problematic when the text refers to the Messiah. Kee estimates ten of these references are Christian. For example, *T.Levi* 4:1, 14:2, both referring to violence towards the Son and refer to him as "savior of the world." Kee, "Testament of the Twelve," 1:777.

35. Since the book is clearly dependent on Revelation and appears to quote 1 John 2:18, a date of the mid-second century seems probable. If the book was a Christian re-working of a Jewish original, then some material may be still older. The book may reflect an Egyptian Christianity, but this is far from clear. There is a Hebrew *Apoc. El.* which may stand in the background of the book, but no one has systematically studied the possibility of a Hebrew to Greek to Coptic translation. Kee, "Testament of the Twelve," 1:730.

Summary and Conclusion

While the Pseudepigrapha has several allusions to an eschatological banquet, but varied and infrequent. Nevertheless, the examples collected above indicate that the tradition of an eschatological banquet was current in the Second Temple period and that this banquet could be combined with other traditions and applied to new situations. *1 Enoch* and *2 Baruch* both combine eschatological banquet, Wilderness tradition and creation language in ways which are consistent with Isa 40–55.

Messianic Banquet at Qumran

Introduction

The scrolls discovered at Qumran provide a wealth of material for the study of the Second Temple period. Since there are a number of methodological problems associated with the Qumran literature, it is necessary to make a few statements concerning my assumptions before approaching the scrolls. First, while there are a number of theories which make a distinction between the scrolls, the Essenes, and the purpose of the buildings at Qumran, I am going to assume the standard thesis that the scrolls represent the library of the Qumran community.[36] Whether that community represents the Essenes or not does not matter for this study. At the very least the community which lived at Qumran was a Jewish sect which separated from the Temple after the Maccabean revolt.[37] Second, while it is possible to study the scrolls chronologically, this study will view them as a whole. For example, for my purposes, it matters little if 1QSa pre-dates the *Community Rule*. Third, the scrolls represent a sub-group of Judaism in the first century, which was not representative of the mainstream of Jewish thinking in the first century. With these caveats in mind, I will now survey the texts in the scrolls which describe an eschatological banquet.

---

36. The most recent expression of the standard view of the scrolls is Schiffman, *Qumran and Jerusalem*. See also VanderKam, *The Dead Sea Scrolls Today*; Charlesworth, *The Dead Sea Scrolls and the Qumran Community*; Stegemann, *The Library of Qumran*. On the archaeology of Qumran, see Magness, *The Archaeology of Qumran and the Dead Sea Scrolls*.

37. Commenting on the origin of the Essenes, VanderKam states that "something may have happened around 150 BC that triggered the exile of the Teacher and his disciples." VanderKam, *The Dead Sea Scrolls Today*, 133. Similarly, Schiffman argues that 4QMMT indicates that the Essenes broke away from the Jerusalem establishment sometime after the Maccabean Revolt. Schiffman, *Qumran and Jerusalem*, 31–32.

Messianic Rule (1QSa)

The importance of 1QSa was recognized early by M. Burrows[38] and F. M. Cross,[39] although the most recent in-depth study of the document is L. Schiffman.[40] The text is sometimes called *Messianic Rule* or *Rule of the Community* because it was appended to a scroll containing the *Community Rule*. It is nevertheless a separate work and can be dated to 100–175 BCE.[41] Initially the text caused a stir because it was thought 2.11 said the "God will beget the messiah."[42] This reading is now rejected in favor of "the messiah shall assemble."[43] The fact that 1QSa describes the messiah as blessing both bread and wine generated, many early articles suggested that this was a "liturgical meal" similar to the Christian Eucharist. As with the so-called "birth of the messiah" text, most scholars now reject the implication that the meal in 1QSa is a liturgical meal.[44]

---

38. Burrows, *More Light on the Dead Sea Scrolls*, 300. Others early studies of 1QSa include Richardson, "Some Notes on 1QSa," 108–22; Yadin, "A Crucial Passage in the Dead Sea Scrolls: 1QSa 2:11–17," 238–41; Sutcliffe, "Rule of the Congregation (I QS a) II, 11–12: Text and Meaning," 541–47; Priest, "Messiah and the Meal in 1QSa," 95–100; Stegemann, "Some Remarks to 1QSa, to 1QSb, and to Qumran Messianism," 479–505.

39. Cross, *The Ancient Library of Qumran and Modern Biblical Studies*. The third edition does not modify the material on the messianic banquet, with the exception that Cross removes the word "liturgical" from his description of the meal.

40. Schiffman, *The Eschatology of the Dead Sea Scrolls Community*, which expands on his earlier article, "Communal Meals at Qumran," 45–56. Schiffman made several clarifications in his work in *Reclaiming the Dead Sea Scrolls*, 333–39. The most recent summary of his view is the short article "Rule of the Congregation," 797–99. For a recent assessment of the 1QSa, see Puech, "Préséance sacerdotale et Messie-Roi dans la Règle de la Congrégation (1QSa ii 11–22)," 351–65. Puech's article also includes the most recent photographs of the fragment. Smith briefly summarizes the 1QSa in his "Meals," 2:530–32.

41. Schiffman, "Rule of the Congregation," 797.

42. For a review of the initial interest in this line of 1QSa, see Smith, "'God's Begetting the Messiah' in 1QSa," 218–24.

43. Burrows, *More Light*, 302–3; Cross, *The Ancient Library*, 64n67. Cross reexamined the text with infrared photography and declared that the text "unquestionably read יוליד. Smith, "'God's Begetting the Messiah' in 1Qsa", 219. Smith then suggests יוליד is correct, but suggests a large gap be filled with text based on Lev 13 (for example), which describes a "blemish arising" using יולד. This makes sense since the context is purity before a meal, but there is nothing on the fragment itself to imply the nine words added by Smith were originally there. Nor is the verb ילד used in this way in the Hebrew Bible. Schiffman follows the suggestion of Licht, who suggested that the scribe first wrote הל, but erased it and wrote ויחד. Schiffman, "Communal Meals at Qumran," 50n23, citing Licht, *The Rule Scroll (1QS, 1QSa, 1QSb*. Barthélemy states that the reading of יוליד is "pratiquement certaine," but does refer to Milik's suggestion that the scribe mis-copied יוליך, an imperfect form of הלך, although this form does not appear in the Hebrew Bible. He translates the key phrase as "au cas où Dieu mènerait le Messie avec eux" ("where God would lead the Messiah with them"). Barthélemy and Milik, *Qumran Cave I*, 117. More recently, Peuch states that it is impossible to read the word at all, so it is impossible to render the word "begetting." Puech, "Préséance sacerdotale," 351–65. Martínez and Tigchelaar, however, retain the earlier reading of "when God begets the messiah." *The Dead Sea Scrolls: Study Edition (Translations)*, 103.

44. Although this point was made in 1957 by van der Ploeg, the idea that Essenes had sacred meals like Christians persists. Van der Ploeg, "Meals of the Essenes," 163–75. For example, Yadin argued that the communal meal at Qumran took the place of sacrifices in *The Scroll of the War of the Sons of Light against the Sons of Darkness*, 300.

F. M. Cross understood this meal as a messianic banquet, specifically citing Isa 25:6–8 and Isa 55:1–5 as examples of the motif of an eschatological banquet in the Hebrew Bible.[45] The Community believed the advent of the messianic age would include a banquet over which the priestly messiah himself would preside.[46] But 1QSa appears to describe a meal in which the members of the community ate frequently. The community is to do this whenever ten men have gathered for a meal (2:21–22). This meal is described with language similar to the daily meals in the *Community Rule* 6:2-3-6 which specifies that when ten members live together, they ought to eat together. A priest should preside over the meal and bless the first fruits of the bread and the wine. In both the *Community Rule* and 1QSa the word used for "new wine" is תִּירוֹשׁ rather than יַיִן. This is likely an allusion to Num 18:12 which uses תִּירוֹשׁ to describe the best wine set aside for the priests in the first fruits offering (cf. Deut 12:17, 18:4, 2 Chron 31:5). New wine ( ) appears in eschatological contexts as well (Isa 65:8, MT Joel 2:19, 24, Zech 9:17). This meal is eaten by individuals who consider themselves to be in a priestly state of purity.

The key line for the messianic banquet is 2.11, which Schiffman translates as "[The ses]sion of the men of renown, [invited to] the feast for the council of the community when [at the end] (of days) the messiah [shall assemble] with them."[47] The noun translated "feast" by Schiffman is מוֹעֵד, a "set time" or "appointed time." The noun is regularly used in the Hebrew Bible for a fixed or scheduled event (such as Passover or other appointed feasts (Num 9:2, Hos 2:13 [MT]) or an appointed place, such as the "tent of the assembly" (Exod 30:36). That the meal in 1QSa is described as מוֹעֵד is therefore additional evidence that the community thought of the meal as participation in a sacrificial, priestly meal.

If the meal described in 1QSa is a priestly meal, is it possible there were sacrifices at Qumran? The community at Qumran deposited animal bones outside the buildings, either covered in potsherds or in jars. The bones were carefully taken apart and were placed in the jars after the flesh was removed.[48] Magness points out that since meat was rarely eaten as part of a regular meal, the presence of these careful buried animal bones at Qumran may indicate that they are the remains of some sort of sacred meal, but she doubts the animals had been sacrificed.[49] No evidence of an altar has been found at Qumran and Philo said that the Essenes did not offer sacrifices.[50]

---

45. I argued in chapter 4 that these two texts were related thematically. Cross does not offer any explanation why he draws the two texts together.

46. Schiffman, *The Eschatology of the Dead Sea Scrolls Community*, 67.

47. Schiffman, *Reclaiming*, 333.

48. Magness, *Archaeology of Qumran*, 117. Magness comments on the work of Zeuner. Zeuner examined 39 deposits of bones, concluding that there were about 500 specimens represented, including goats, sheep, and oxen. These bones were clean, although some were charred, indicating they were remains of meals. Zeuner, "Notes on Qumrân," 27–36.

49. Magness, *Archaeology of Qumran*, 118.

50. That Philo was describing the community at Qumran is an open question.

Schiffman agrees that the bones are not an indication of sacrifices, since there is no command to bury bones in any Jewish sacrificial practice.⁵¹ F. M. Cross, on the other hand, thought the carefully preserved bones were evidence for some sort of a sacrifice at Qumran, despite the lack of an altar. He considers the fact that the community saw itself as an enactment of the camp in the wilderness during the original wilderness period as a rationale for sacrifice away from the Temple.⁵² Given the fact that there is no evidence of an altar at Qumran, it seems likely that the consensus view that these bones were not the remains of a sacrifice is correct. But the preserved bones do indicate the remains of a special meal of some sort eaten periodically by the community.⁵³

It is therefore clear from literary and archaeology evidence that there was in fact a communal meal at Qumran.⁵⁴ The meaning of this meal is less clear. Cross and Schiffman see this meal as a pre-enactment of the future messianic banquet.⁵⁵ Priest

---

51. Schiffman, *Qumran and Jerusalem*, 87.

52. Cross, *The Ancient Library at Qumran*, 86. Cross comments in note 2 that the practice of sacrifice away from the Temple is not without precedent. According to Josephus, Onias established a temple at Leontopolis at the time of the Maccabean revolt (*J.W.* 1.31–33, 7.422–35).

53. While it is impossible to know for certain, it is possible that the type of meal represented by the bones was associated with the celebration of Sukkot. The 500 specimens of animals cataloged by Zeuner included goats, sheep and oxen, the very animals specified by Num 29:13–38 for sacrifice at the Feast. While there are few texts from Qumran concerning Sukkot, see the section below on 4Q502.

54. Josephus and Philo also describe this communal meal among the Essenes. Josephus indicates that the initiated members of the Essene community eat a meal in a state of ritual purity (*J.W.* 2.129–31). Josephus uses both ἁγνεία and καθαρός to describe the participants in the meal. The noun appears elsewhere in Josephus for ritual purification (*Ap.* 2.198). The LXX normally uses καθαρός for ritual purity, although ἁγνεία is used for ritual purity in Num 6:2, 21 (the Nazarite), 2 Chron 30:19 and 1 Macc 14:36. The participants change into white garments, bathe themselves in cold water, and enter a private chamber "as if a sacred shrine." The noun δειπνητήριον is a civic-banquet hall. Moulton and Milligan, 139, citing the inscription of the time of Vespasian (AD 69–79). A priest blesses the meal and then individuals are given a single plate of food which is eaten in silence. After the meal a second prayer is given and the participants remove their linen clothing and return to their work. Magness considers this description to be focused on Qumran, based on the archaeology of the site (Magness, *The Archaeology of Qumran*, 131). Philo describes the Essenes as "priestlike" (ἱεροπρεπής) and calls them both pious and holy. *Every Good Man*, 75. 4 Macc uses this noun twice to describe the holiness of young men about to be martyred rather than give up traditional Jewish boundary markers. Moulton and Milligan indicate that the meaning "employed in sacred service" is found in an inscription. Philo describes them as "preparing their minds" Philo is clear, however, that these Essenes do not practice sacrifices. Rather than sacrificing, Philo describes the Essenes as preparing their minds for holiness and purity, using the verb κατασκευάζω. It is perhaps not coincidental that this verb is used in Mark 1:2 and Luke 1:17 for the ministry of John the Baptist, preparing the way for the messiah.

55. Schiffman, *The Eschatology of the Dead Sea Scrolls Community*, 70. Schiffman makes the point that there is no way to know how often these communal meals occurred. Schiffman, "Communal Meals at Qumran," 56. An additional line of evidence comes from 11Q Psalmsa (11Q5, Psalm, 154). This apocryphal Psalm is an invitation to join an assembly for the purpose of studying the Torah. Line 13 the worshipers "eat to bursting" and they "drink in unison." As in other messianic banquet texts, the verbs אכל and שתה appear, although the context is not eschatological. Sanders, *The Dead Sea Psalms Scroll*; Flint, *The Dead Sea Psalms Scrolls and the Book of Psalms*; Charlesworth and Sanders, "More Psalms of David," 2:617–19.

disagrees, arguing that this meal is purely eschatological.[56] He accepts the original reading of יוליד and translates the phrase "when God begets the Messiah." This he understands as the arrival of the royal messiah. The priest who blesses the bread and wine is the messiah even though he is only described as a priest. For Priest, this indicates that 1QSa pre-dates 1QS, the *Community Rule*, which expects both a royal and priestly messiah. The final line of column 2 does not mean that the current community participates in the meal, but that the eschatological community will eat and drink with the messiah in the future era. Puech, on the other hand, has re-examined new photographs from the Department of Antiquities in Jordan and suggests that there in an intra-linear correction to the word and a gimel has been inserted. The word should be read therefore as a hitpael form of גלה "to be revealed."[57]

Is it possible that 1QSa describes a meal which was never really a part of the daily life of the Community? Assuming a connection between the scrolls and the community which lived at Qumran, Schiffman argues that the large room identified as the "refectory" by DeVaux is evidence that meals were shared by the community. The proximity of a large *mikveh* to the room indicates that the Community prepared by the meal with ritual cleansing. Taken along with *Community Rule* 6:2–3–6, it seems certain that the community ate together and the meal was an anticipation of the messianic age.

In summary, 1QSa indicates that at least one Jewish group in the Second Temple period looked forward to an inaugural meal at the beginning of the eschatological age. Unlike Isa 25:6–8, this meal excluded the Gentiles and was restricted to only those individuals who were ritually pure and prepared for the coming age. While it is impossible to prove that the community at Qumran anticipated the eschatological age at every meal, it seems reasonable that at least the meal described in 1QSa was in fact an anticipation of a future inaugural banquet.

There are a number of remarkable parallels between the description of the banquet in 1QSa 2.11–22 and the banquets described in Luke 14 and Matt 22, but also a number of key differences to which we will return to in the analysis of these parables. Unlike Luke 14:7–11, the community is seated by rank (2.13) and those unfit for temple service are not permitted to participate.[58] While both of the parables in the gospels are inclusive (all are invited regardless of social class), the meal at Qumran is exclusive. No one who is paralyzed in his hands or feet, lame, blind, deaf, dumb or otherwise defiled in the flesh, nor may any "tottering old man" participate in these meals (1QSa 2.5–7). 1QSa will be of importance, therefore, for the development of

---

56. Priest, "Messiah and the Meal in 1QSa," 97.

57. "En conséquence, le verbe doit être le un toute certitude YT<G>LH, à la forme hitpaeël de GLH . . . la lecture YWLYD que l'on croyait assureé est totalement exclue" (Puech, "Préséance sacerdotale et Messie-Roi," 359–60). Puech cites a similar expression in *Pesiqla Rabbati* 36, 162a.

58. No one who is paralyzed in his hands or feet, lame, blind, deaf, dumb or otherwise defiled in the flesh, nor may any "tottering old man" participate in these meals (1QSa 2.5–7).

eschatological banquet ideas in the parables of Jesus since in the parable of the Great Banquet the blind and the lame are specifically included in the banquet (Luke 14:13) in contrast to 1QSa.

4Q171, 4Q pPs 37

F. M. Cross commented briefly on the possibility that this *pesher* on Ps 37:11 is another reflection of the messianic banquet.[59] Indeed, there are several significant allusions to eschatological banquet themes form the Hebrew Bible in this interpretation of Ps 37, although it is couched in a struggle between the Teacher of Righteousness and his enemy the Man of Lies (1.26). Like 1QSa, this fragment attracted attention because of the close parallel to the beatitude in Matt 5:5, the "meek shall inherit the earth" (2.9).

In the Hebrew Bible, Ps 37 is an acrostic poem which meditates on the fate of the wicked in contrast to that of the righteous.[60] It is not surprising that the Qumran community would select this Psalm and apply it to their struggles against the Man of Lies. The first column is badly damaged, but column 2-4 are reasonably well preserved. Those who "hope in the Lord" in Ps 37:10 are the community. They are the "meek who will possess the land" in 37:11. This verse is explained as predicting a time of great struggle before the wicked are cut off and the ones who possess the land will "grow fat with everything enjoy[able to] the flesh."[61] The noun דֶּשֶׁן is rare in the Hebrew Bible, but it appears in Jer 31:14 and Isa 55:2, clear eschatological banquet texts.[62] The cognate verb appears in Deut 31:20 to describe the results of the eating the good things of the land: the next generation will grow satisfied (שׂבע) and fat (דֶּשֶׁן), just as the banquet scene in Jer 31:14 where the people were satisfied (שׂבע) with rich foods. This provision of food is for those who have returned from the wilderness in a time of famine (4Q171 3.1).[63] This line therefore represents another example of a combination of eschatological banquet and Wilderness tradition.

---

59. Cross, *Ancient Library*, 78n7. Cross is among the many who saw the similarity to the beatitude, and therefore suggests that Luke 6:21 be taken as an allusion to the messianic banquet. Other studies on 4QpPs37 include Allegro, "A Newly Discovered Fragment of a Commentary on Psalms XXXVII," 69-75; Stegemann, "Weitere Stücke von 4QpPsalm 37, 193-210; Horgan, *Pesharim: Qumran Interpretations of Biblical Books*, 192-226; Coote, "MW'D HT'NYT in 4Q171 (Pesher Psalm 37) fragments 1-2, col. II, line 9," 81-85; Pardee, "A Restudy of the Commentary on Psalm 37 from Qumran Cave 4," 163-94.

60. Craigie, *Psalms 1-50*, 297.

61. Martinez and Tigchelaar, *Dead Sea Scrolls Study Edition: Translations*, 1:344.

62. Pardee comments that "fat as a blessing is well known in the Old Testament," citing Isa 55:2, although Isa 25:6-8 could have been cited as well. Pardee, "Restudy of the Commentary on Psalm 37," 166. Job 36:16 describes the wicked that allure the righteous with a table of rich foods: דֶּשֶׁן מָלֵא. In Ps 22:30 [ET 22:29], the cognate דָּשֵׁן is used ("all the "prosperous of the land.") The noun דֶּשֶׁן appears in Ps 36:9, 63:6 and 65:2. See above on *1 En.* 61:13.

63. Pardee observes that in 1QM I, 3 the exiles (the community) are in the "desert of the nations" and will return to the "desert of Jerusalem." Pardee, "Restudy of the Commentary on Psalm 37," 183.

In 3.11 the poor will inherit the "the high mountain of Israel" where they will "delight in his holy mountain." Both Cross and Pardee read this line as "banquet on the holy mountain,"[64] although Allegro translates the phrase as "and in his holy place luxuriate." The hitpael verb ענג may be drawn from Ps 37:4 and 11, although this interpretation is based on 37:21. The word has the connotation of enjoying oneself and appears in Isa 55:2 (a banquet passage) and 66:11 (a marriage metaphor).[65]

The phrase "and on a mountain of height" (בְּהַר מְרוֹם) occurs in Ezek 20:40 in parallel with "my holy mountain" (בְהַר־קָדְשִׁי). In Ezek 17:23 the reference seems to be Zion and in Ezek 34:14 the Lord brings the exiles back to the high mountain of Israel where he will feed them as the sheep of his pasture. While Ezek 34 is usually overlooked as a potential eschatological banquet text there is certainly a joyous meal served on God's mountain, even if the image is of a shepherd and his sheep. That the messianic feast should take place on the mountain of Zion is likely an allusion to traditions drawn from Isa 25:6–8 or Jer 31:12.

An additional indication that Ps 37 is being read eschatologically is that the next psalm column IV is Ps 45.[66] This wedding Psalm for a king was frequently interpreted as referring to the Messiah, although the scroll is too fragmentary to state that any pesher on Ps 45 was in fact messianic.[67] It is possible that these columns represent the interpretation of Psalms, applying them to the struggle of the Teacher of Righteousness and the Man of Lies. If this is true, then this scroll indicates that the hope of the community was to gather at Zion as promised in Isa 25:6–8.

4Q171 is significant because there are allusions to both Jer 31 and Isa 55, texts which I have already shown to be part of the eschatological banquet tradition. In addition, this banquet takes place on the "holy mountain," a possible allusion to Isa 25:6–8. While there is not enough evidence to state with certainty that the scroll also alludes to the marriage metaphor, it is possible that the interpretation of Ps 37 in this scroll blends eschatological banquet with the marriage metaphor to describe a future vindication of the community and a restoration of God's people to a restored Zion.

Other Fragments

There are number of fragments that may refer to a banquet in an eschatological age. The texts surveyed in this section are often so small that context is impossible to determine. They are included here in order to be as complete as possible.

64. Cross, *The Ancient Library*, 78n7; Pardee, "Restudy of the Commentary on Psalm 37," 168.
65. In four cases the verb is used for delighting in the Lord (Job 22:26, 27:10, Ps 37:4, Isa 58:14).
66. Stegemann, "Weitere Stücke von 4QpPsalm 37," 209.
67. The fragments of column IV contain the first two verses of Ps 45. That this was also an interpretation applied to the Teacher of Righteousness is clear, but no more can be said. Fragments 12 and 13 of column V are an interpretation of Ps 60:8–9, which is interpreted as referring to the gathering of the of the tribes of Gilead. That this Psalm refers to as Judah as the Lord's scepter (cf. Num 24:17–19) may indicate that this text had a messianic interpretation as well.

The Words of the Luminaries (4Q504, 4QDibHama), fragments 1–2, blends the wilderness motif with the restoration of Israel after a long exile.[68] Column II clearly refers to the wilderness period, but the fragment ends with "for our faults we were sold," a reference to the exile. Column III describes the Lord's punishment of Israel because of her covenant disloyalty. Column IV appears to describe the restoration of Israel after their time of punishment. This column begins with a reference to God's choice of Jerusalem and Judah, the place where he established his covenant and appointed David as a shepherd over God's people, "sitting on the throne of Israel forever" (lines 7–8). In lines 9–10 the nations will acknowledge the glory of the Lord and bring him offerings of silver, gold and precious stones at Zion, the Lord's house. Finally, line 14 says that "they ate and drank and were replete."[69] Similar vocabulary to 4Q171 appears once again (אכל, שבע, דָּשֵׁן). The end of line 13 is missing, so it is not completely clear if it is Israel or the nations who are eating and drinking. Unfortunately the fragment breaks off at this point, but there is room for five or six more lines on the scroll. It is certain, however, that the fragment describes the nations honoring God and possibly eating and drinking with Israel in Zion after a return from the wilderness.

4Q Messianic Apocalypse (4Q521) is a remarkable text which draws on Isa 61 to describe the beginnings of the messianic age.[70] In fragment 2, column II, the anointed one will honor the devout, free prisoners, give sight to the blind, and straighten out the twisted (lines 7–8), heal the badly wounded and make the dead alive (line 12). The final line of the fragment states that he anointed one will "give lavishly to the needy, lead the exiled and enrich the hungry..." (line 13). The noun יעשר (rich) appears occasionally in the Hebrew Bible, but it is always used for a wealthy person, never metaphorically for "rich foods." It appears here paired to רעבים, a common word for those enduring a famine. This is clearly an eschatological context, but there is no real "banquet." As Novakovic observes, any conclusions must be tentative due to the fragmentary nature of his text.[71]

4QPsalmsf (4Q88) is collection of psalms biblical and apocryphal psalms published in 1998.[72] The scroll contains Ps 107 and 109, but column 5 is missing and

---

68. So identified in Martínez and Tigchelaar, 2:1015. Puech identified this as column XV. Puech, "Review of DJD VII," 404–11; Puech, *La Croyance des Esséniens en la Vie Future*, 563–68.

69. This is likely an allusion to Ps 36:10–11 (ET 8–9). There are several verbal allusions to Ps 36 in the *Words of the Luminaries*. Column IV line 14 uses the verb דָּשֵׁן. Column V begins with "source of living water." Both texts use מַיִם חַיִּים מָקוֹר. Jeremiah 2:13 and 17:13 refer to the Lord as a spring of living water, using only מָקוֹר. The noun can be used metaphorically for a wife (cf. Prov 5:18).

70. Puech, "Une apocalypse messianique (4Q521)"; Puech, *La croyance des Esséniens*, 627–92; Novakovic, "4Q521: The Works of the Messiah or the Signs of the Messianic Time?" 208–31. This text clearing uses Isa 61 to describe events at the inauguration of the messianic age, the question which remains is the agent of these miracles. Does the Messiah do these things, or does God do them through the Messiah? Novakovic concludes that the activities listed in this fragment are only indirectly related to the messianic figure mentioned in line 1.

71. Novakovic, "4Q521: The Works of the Messiah," 209.

72. Skehan, Ulrich, and Flint, "A Scroll Containing 'Biblical' and 'Apocryphal' Psalms: A

there is sufficient space for the end of Ps 107, Ps 108, and the beginning of Ps 109. Following three canonical Psalms are three additional Psalms: Apostrophe to Zion, Eschatological Hymn, and Apostrophe to Judah. In addition, there are three small fragments which may contain Ps 22:15–17.

Of interest here is column IX which contains the Eschatological Psalm. After describing a time when the earth will produce Eden-like food, lines 13–14 state that "the lowly will eat and be filled, those who fear the Lord . . ."[73] Garcia-Martinez translates the line, "the poor will eat, and those who fear YHWH will be replete," taking the phrase "those who fear YHWH" as the subject of the verb שׂבע. Skehan, on the other hand, connected the two verbs in the line and made "the lowly" the subject of both. While the line is not unlike *The Words of the Luminaries* line 14 and Ps 36:8–9, it is more likely that this line alludes to Ps 22:27 (ET 22:26).[74] All four of these texts share אכל, שׂבע and דֶּשֶׁן; Ps 22:27 and 4Q88 line 14 both include עָנָו, (poor).[75] In addition, this collection of Psalms has two fragments of Ps 22:15–17 which appear to begin the scroll.[76] While this is not an eschatological banquet based on Isa 25:6–8, the fact that the poor will eat their fill from a restored creation is not unlike what we have already encountered in Isa 40–55.

The context of this eschatological psalm is also important. It is part of a conclusion to a collection of psalms which includes Ps 107. This Psalm is a description exiles dispersed throughout the world that will now be gathered and restored Land of Israel. They are described as "redeemed" (גאל) by the Lord and they are gathered from the nations because of his steadfast love (חֶסֶד).[77] Both terms are key words in the theology of Isa 40–55 and Israel's return from Exile. The conclusion of the Psalm describes the end of the exile as a new Exodus and a reversal of the curse of the covenant. The Land will burst forth with food and water in abundance (vss. 33–38). This eschatological psalm therefore resonates with the end-of-exile themes found in Isa 40–55. Once again, these fragments indicate that the end of the age was conceived of as a period of on-going celebration and feasting.

Summary and Conclusions

There appears to be a great deal of material describing the eschatological age as in terms of eating and drinking in the literature of the Second Temple period, whether it

---

Preliminary Edition of 4QPsf (4Q88)," 267–82. For an earlier summary of 4Q88, see Starcky, "Psaumes apocryphes de la grotte 4 de Qumrân, 4QPsf VII-X," 353–71.

73. Skehan, Ulrich, and Flint, "A Scroll Containing 'Biblical' and 'Apocryphal' Psalms," 281.

74. Ibid., 280.

75. This noun appears to two other important texts, Isa 61:1 and Ps 37:11. Both texts are of importance for the study of Jesus' proclamation in the Gospels.

76. Skehan, Ulrich, and Flint, "A Scroll Containing 'Biblical' and 'Apocryphal' Psalms," 269.

77. Allen describes this psalm as "a postexilic communal hymn praising God for immigration to the homeland." Allen, *Psalms 101–50 (Revised)*, 86.

is described as a banquet or not. The writers during this period allude to material from the Hebrew Bible and adapt that material to their own context in both traditional and unorthodox ways. Three elements of the banquet image should be highlighted before moving into the wilderness texts.

First, the period of the messianic age is characterized by "plenty." People will eat until they are filled. Just as God provided in Eden or the wilderness, so too will he provide plenty for the righteous in the eschatological age. This is not to be taken as sensual excess, but rather an indication of the peace and prosperity of the period as well as the close fellowship between God and man in the age to come. The coming age is not simply inaugurated by a banquet; the participants will always eat and drink with their Lord.

Second, the eschatological age is characterized by great joy for the righteous.[78] A time of feasting is naturally a time for great joy for those who participate. Just as Isa 25:6–8 described the feast on Zion as a time when the Lord would wipe away tears, so to the whole age is described in terms of joy and delight. The New Testament image of a wedding banquet is therefore not unanticipated since a wedding was typically a time of great feasting marked by joy and happiness.

Third, the eschatological age is described as a new Exodus and a New Creation. Primordial beasts which were present at creation and in the re-tellings of the Exodus story will be killed and consumed just as death itself is consumed in Isa 25:6–8. The great chaos monsters will be ultimately subdued and consumed. Eden itself will be restored and all will eat from the tree of life, just as the Israelites ate manna in the wilderness after the Exodus. Since this motif is present in a number of texts which do not include feasts, I will now survey a number of Second Temple period texts which develop the wilderness motif.

Wilderness Tradition in Second Temple Period Literature

Introduction

A text like *4Q Messianic Apocalypse* (4Q521) demonstrates how difficult it is to distinguish between the metaphor of an eschatological banquet and the metaphor of the return from exile as a new Exodus. The following texts use the wilderness journey as a typology for a future return of Israel to the land. As with Isa 40–55, the people of Israel are called to return to the Land with language that resonates with the first Exodus story.

---

78. Sim, *Apocalyptic Eschatology in the Gospel of Matthew*, 49–50.

Jesus the Bridegroom

Wisdom of Solomon

An example of a late Second Temple period use of the wilderness tradition is Wis 16.[79] This text may be described as a Midrash on the Exodus tradition since it draws a contrast between the plagues on the Egyptians and the provision of food for the Israelites.[80] While he was punishing the Egyptians, God prepared excellent food for Israel (16:2).[81] The writer uses the verb εὐεργετέω which has the connotation of benefaction.[82] In 16:20 God provide manna ("food of the angels") for the people. The verb used in this case, ψωμίζω, is associated with the giving of manna in LXX Deut 8:3, 16, Ps 79:6, 80:17. The verb appears in prophetic contexts relating to the wilderness. In contrast to the good food provided in the first time in the wilderness, God will now feed the nation wormwood because of their unfaithfulness (Jer 9:14 and 23:15). More striking is Ezek 16:19. In this allegory the Lord provides excellent food to his wife, but she misuses them in her adulteries. It is clear in Ezekiel's allegory that the provided foods include manna and that the prophet is reflecting on the wilderness as a very brief "ideal time" in the relationship between God and Israel. The Wisdom of Solomon goes on to describes creation itself punishing the wicked while at the same time bestowing kindness (εὐεργεσία) on the righteous (Wis 16:24).

The Wisdom of Solomon plays on themes found in the Wilderness tradition in order to bring the Wilderness tradition to bear on the current situation of the author. As the story appears in the Hebrew Bible, manna and quail are not welcomed as "food of angels" or "fine delicacies." In fact, the people complain about the food and long for the better foods of Egypt. The author of *Wisdom* reverses this comparison and makes

---

79. For an introduction to Wisdom of Solomon, see Winston, *Wisdom of Solomon* as well as his summary in "Wisdom of Solomon," 6:120–27; Kolarcik, "The Book of Wisdom," 5:435–600; deSilva, *Introducing the Apocrypha*. While there is virtual unanimity on Alexandria as a provenance for the book, suggested dates range from 220 BCE to 100 CE. It is clear that the author used LXX Isaiah, Job and Proverbs, implying a date after 200 BCE. Less clear is the use of Wisdom by the authors of the New Testament. DeSilva lists a number of potential parallel texts, the most striking being 2 Cor 5:1–4 and Wis 9:15. *Introducing the Apocrypha*, 150. Reider argues the New Testament writers presuppose the existence of Wisdom. Reider, *The Book of Wisdom*, 14. On the other hand, Grant is willing to agree that concepts found in Wisdom are present in Paul; he does not think that Paul knew the book itself. Grant, *After the New Testament*, 70. Since the book reflects clear anti-Egyptian rhetoric, scholars usually date the book to reign of Caligula, citing the persecution of the Jews under Flaccus in Alexandria (cf. Philo, *Against Flaccus*).

80. DeSilva, *Introducing the Apocrypha*, 139; Kolarcik, 577. In Wis 16 the plagues Egypt suffered are set in contrast to the blessings Israel enjoyed in the wilderness, although with no interest in the chronology of the two periods. For example, while the Egyptians suffer fire from heaven, Israel receives bread from heaven which fire cannot destroy. This bread appears as snow or ice (cf. Nu 11:7 LXX, the manna appears as ice), yet the first cannot destroy it. deSilva points out the similarities between the use of Exodus material in this text and *T.Levi* 2–5.

81. Excellent food is ὀρέξεως ξένην γεῦσιν and τροφὴν . This is almost always translated as "a rare and delicious food." See for example Bullard, *A Handbook on the Wisdom of Solomon*, 262. For example, the NAB renders the phrase "a novel dish."

82. The verb appears only 10x in the LXX; compare this use with 2 Macc 10:38 which describes the "great things done by God."

the food Israel received the finest imaginable and contrasts God's beneficence toward Israel with his judgment on Egypt. This is an adaptation of the story from the Hebrew Bible in order to make the point that while Egypt is still oppressing the Jews, God has judged them already and he will once again provide graciously for his righteous people once again.

Qumran

That the wilderness was an important theme at Qumran seems certain, given the location of the community in the desert and the importance of Isa 40:3 in the *Manual of Discipline*.[83] The idea of the "wilderness" does not often appear in the Qumran literature, when it does it seems connected to the view of wilderness in Isa 40–55.[84] Talmon argued that the wilderness normally has a negative connotation, but the exception is Isa 40–55.[85] In Isaiah, the wilderness is the place from which the faithful remnant is called. They will be invited to return to Zion, led by the Lord himself.[86] The Qumran community took Isa 40:3 to be a mandate. "For sectarians, the redemption from Egypt and the period of desert wandering, crowned by the revelation at Sinai, served as a paradigm of the future."[87]

The reference to the wilderness in 4Q171 has already been discussed, but there is more in this pesher on Ps 37 which draws from the wilderness tradition. In 2.7, the interpreter indicates that the community will have "forty years" of struggles before the wicked are finally judges. This clearly evokes the wilderness generation who endured forty years in the desert before entering the land. This forty year period is applied to the present suffering of the community.[88] In 3.1 the community is described as "having come out of the wilderness" and living for a thousand generations in safety.[89]

---

83. That the community thought it ought to live in the desert is based on 1QS 8:14. This has been a consensus opinion although it has not gone unchallenged. Golb, "The Problem of the Origin and Identification of the Dead Sea Scrolls," 1–24. For an assessment of Golb, see Brooke, "Isaiah 40:3 and The Wilderness Community," 117–32. Brooke concludes that Golb may be correct in suggesting that some of the community did not see the necessity of a "literal journey to the wilderness," the use of Isa 40:3 in 1QM and other texts make it clear an actual wilderness sojourn was part of the experience of the community (132).

84. Cross, *Canaanite Myth and Hebrew Epic*, 109n57. Cross points out that a "new conquest" motif is found in the DSS, see 1QS 8:12–14 (cf. Is 40), 1 QS 6:2 (cf. Ezek 20:38), 1 QM 1:3 (cf. Ezek 20:35).

85. Talmon, "The 'Desert Motif; in the Bible and Qumran Literature," 57.

86. Compare this to 4QpPsa 3:1 (4Q171), which describes those in the wilderness as "penitent" (Brooke's translation) and 1QM 1:2–3 which describes the community in the wilderness as "exiles" and "exiled sons of light." 4Q171 merits further study since column 3 lines 13–17 describe the Teacher of Righteousness in terms which seem borrowed from Isa 40:3 (his path was "straightened") while commenting on Ps 37:23–34. Column 2 has several elements which might be described as a wilderness motif, lines 8–9 refer to a forty year period after which the righteous will enter the land and enjoy peace and plenty. See also Brooke, "Psalms 105 and 106 at Qumran," 267–92.

87. Schiffman, *Reclaiming*, 339.

88. Pardee, "Restudy of the Commentary on Psalm 37," 175.

89. 4QIsaiah Pesher (4Q161) lines 14–15 refer to a return from the wilderness led by the "Prince

Jesus the Bridegroom

Summary and Conclusion

The Wilderness tradition is present in the literature of the Second Temple period, although it is muted compared to the eschatological banquet. The importance of the Wilderness tradition to the Qumran community should not be overlooked because they enacted a "return to the wilderness" to prepare for the eschatological age. In the wilderness the Community anticipated the coming age by means of an exclusive communal meal. This is "metaphor enacted" will be important for understanding Jesus' own retreat to a wilderness in the Synoptic Gospels since it is in the wilderness that Jesus hosted an inclusive meal (Mark 6:30–43).

Marriage Metaphor in the Second Temple Period

Introduction

Unlike the eschatological banquet and Wilderness tradition, the marriage metaphor is rare in the Second Temple period. For the most part it appears only when Zion or Jerusalem is personified as a woman. As Humphrey observed, "Whenever the City is given personality in writings later than the Hebrew Bible, the feminine is adopted, in accord with the prophetic literature."[90] Despite the rarity of the metaphor, it does appear in the later New Testament, especially in Revelation. For example, Rev 21:9 describes the New Jerusalem as "the Bride, the wife of the Lamb." Books like *4 Ezra* follow the classic prophetic tradition in describing a restoration of Israel as a woman restored to her husband.

Psalms of Solomon and Baruch

Psalms of Solomon 11 and Baruch 5:1–9 parallel passages which personify Zion / Jerusalem as a woman adorning herself with beauty to greet the returning exiles.[91] In both texts the pronouns are feminine. Jerusalem is told to stand on a high place and keep watch for her returning children (*PsSol* 11:2, Baruch 4:36–37). In both texts Jerusalem is told to adorn herself in beauty and holiness. The noun εὐπρέπεια usually associated with the splendor of the Temple (Ps 25:8, 49:2, 2 Macc 1:3) or the majesty of God (Ps 92:1, 103:1).[92] However, in Ezek 16:14 the word is used to describe the splendor given

---

of the Congregation." The fragment is badly damaged and details are missing.

90. Humphrey, *The Ladies and the Cities*, 23.

91. The date of Baruch (1 Baruch) is complicated by the fact that there is no Hebrew text of Baruch, although 1:1—3:8 appear to be a translation from Hebrew. In addition, the book is a compilation from two sources (1:1—3:8, 3:9—5:9). The second part of the book is dependent on *PsSol* 11, implying a date at least in the first century CE. That the book appears in the LXX may be an indication that it was written before the first century BCE. On the other hand, 4:37 may be taken as a reference to the diaspora after 70 CE (children gathered from the east and the west). Mendals, "Baruch," 1:618–20; deSilva, *Introducing the Apocrypha*, 198–213.

92. The noun is used in *PsSol* 17:42 to describe the "beauty of the king of Israel," a clear messianic

to the bride of the Lord. Lamentations 1:6 also uses the word to describe the state of the daughter of Zion in exile: she has put aside her splendor.

In Baruch 5:2, personified Zion is told to place a "diadem of glory" on her head. The noun μίτρα refers to a head covering, without which a woman was not considered "properly covered" (Jdth 10:3, 16:8). The word appears in Isa 61:10, one of the clearest examples of wedding language associated with the eschatological age.[93] A close parallel to these texts appears in *PsSol* 2. Jerusalem is personified as a woman who sets aside her glory in the exile. In language which is reminiscent of Lam 1:6, Jerusalem exchanged her royal clothes (εὐπρέπεια) for sackcloth and removed her crown of glory (μίτρα).

In these examples there is only a muted marriage metaphor. Lady Jerusalem or Lady Zion is stripped of her royal clothing when she went into exile, but the writer looks forward to the time when she will be restored to her former glory. When she is restored, her children will return to her from their exile. While she is stripped of her marriage clothes and bereft of her children, the future restoration is never explicitly described as a restoration of Zion's marriage to her husband, as in Hosea or Isa 40–55.

Joseph and Aseneth

Joseph and Aseneth is a romance describing Joseph's marriage to Aseneth, the daughter of Potiphera (called Pentephres in the book). Like *Jubilees*, *Jos. Asen.* attempts to answer questions concerning Joseph's marriage to the daughter of a pagan priest.[94] The first half of the book explains how Aseneth converted to Judaism and therefore a worthy wife for Joseph. Since the book concerns a marriage, there is much to illustrate wedding practices. In *Jos. Asen.* 18.5 Aseneth is clothed in a beautiful wedding garment which has been "ordained from all eternity" (cf. 21:1–3). She adorns herself with

---

text. In Sir 47:10 the word is used to describe the splendor of religious festivals during David's reign.

93. Zimmerman comments that Baruch 5:1–2 and PsSol 11 appear to follow directly on Isa 61:10. Zimmerman, "Nuptial Imagery in the Revelation of John," 172.

94. The book was written in Greek and seems to have been a Jewish book, although there are Christian interpolations. Collins states that the book has no unequivocal Christian elements, and that the praise for women in chapter 1 as well as the lack of a baptism at the time of Aseneth's conversion weighs strongly in favor of a Jewish origin of the book. Collins, "Joseph and Aseneth: Jewish or Christian?," 112. The book was known in the fourth century CE since it is mentioned in the *Pilgrimage of Etheria*. It is probable that the book uses the LXX, making for a date of no earlier than 100 BCE. If the work is from Alexandria (the scholarly consensus), then it is unlikely to have been written much after the Jewish revolt under Trajan, 115–17 CE. A major argument in favor of Egypt is that Aseneth is the heroine, the only convert to Judaism from Egypt. If it was from Palestine, then Ruth or Rahab might have been better examples of pagan conversions. This argument weakens if the book is an apologetic explaining why Joseph married an Egyptian, or an explanation of how Joseph married a gentile without punishment, aimed at Diaspora Jews tempted to marry gentiles. Like Reuben or Judah in *Jubilees*, the story may be intended to explain that just because Joseph was not punished for marrying an Egyptian. Burchard, "Joseph and Aseneth," 2:177–201; Fekkes, "'His Bride has Prepared Herself:' Revelation 19–21 and Isaian Nuptial Imagery," 269–87; Lieber, "I Set a Table before You," 63–77; Portier-Young, "Sweet Mercy Metropolis: Interpreting Aseneth's Honeycomb," 133–57.

jewelry, including golden bracelets (ψέλιον). This word appears rarely in the LXX (7x), but is included in the gifts given to Rebekah by the servant of Abraham when arranging Isaac's marriage (Gen 24:22). More significantly, the Lord gives his bride golden bracelets in Ezek 16:11. In both contexts bracelets can be described as wedding gifts from the groom to his bride.[95] In *Jos. Asen.* 18:6 Aseneth takes up a "scepter." Burchard reads the Greek as θέριστρον (sickle, cf. 1 Kgs 13:20), but more likely this is θέριστρον is a "light summer garment." The word is rare in the LXX, but the other four occurrences refer to clothing worn by a woman meeting a potential husband. In LXX Gen 24:65, Rebekah wears a θέριστρον when she first meets Isaac. Tamar removes her mourning clothes and puts on a θέριστρον before she meets Judah (Gen 38:14, 19). Finally, in Song 5:7 the woman seeks her lover wearing a θέριστρον. The word therefore refers to a beautiful veil worn by a bride when she meets her husband. Joseph is amazed by her beautiful wedding garment (19:4).

When Aseneth's father arrives, they eat and drink to celebrate the engagement (20.1–10). While Lieber takes this meal as a close parallel to Exod 24:11, (the elders of Israel saw God, then "ate and drank"), it is more likely that this meal simply celebrates the engagement of Joseph and Aseneth.[96] As observed in chapter 3, meals are associated with a variety of covenants in the Hebrew Bible, including a marriage covenant. Although there is no reference to a dowry, Aseneth's father promises to give a wedding feast for all of the nobility of Egypt. In *Jos. Asen.* 21:6, the Pharaoh himself celebrates the marriage of Joseph and Aseneth is celebrated by a week-long feast for the whole land, during which no work is permitted. This feast is described as a γάμος (wedding feast, cf. Matt 22:1), a δεῖπνον (dinner, cf. Luke 14:16), and a πότος (a drinking party).[97] All three terms refer to the joyous feasting associated with the marriage.

Is the marriage between *Joseph and Aseneth* eschatological? E. Stauffer thought so,[98] although interest in messianic elements in the novella has waned.[99] Stauffer observed that the marriage sequence in *Jos. Asen.* is between Messiah (Joseph) and the City of Refuge (Aseneth). While it is unlikely that Joseph is intended to be a messiah, there are several indications that the marriage was intended to be more than an entertaining romance story. First, Joseph is described as a heavenly figure (5:4–8, 6:2). While the account of Joseph's first arrival at Aseneth's home is modeled after Gen 41:42–45, the language of *Jos. Asen.* 5:4–8 is much more cosmic than the original. Joseph is accompanied by four snow-white horses with golden bridles. The noun χρυσοχάλινος only appears twice in the LXX. In 2 Macc 10:29 the word is used to

---

95. The word appears in the description of the beauty of Judith's outfit in Jdt 10:4.

96. Lieber, "I Set a Table before You," 77.

97. Xenophon used ποτός as a synonym for κλῆσις, banquet (BDAG). In LXX Job 1:4 the word is used to translate מִשְׁתֶּה, feast.

98. Stauffer, "γαμέω," 1:657.

99. For example, commenting on Aseneth as a City of Refuge, Fekkes states that "little or no eschatological significance in attached to this image." Fekkes, "His Bride Has Prepared Herself," 285.

describe five horsemen who appear from heaven to be leading the armies of Israel.[100] The ἅρμα (chariot) is the same as Gen 42, but in *Jos. Asen.* the chariot is made of pure gold. His crown is adorned with twelve chosen stones. While the twelve stones evoke the twelve sons of Jacob, the phrase λίθοι ἐκλεκτοί is associated with the choice stones in the New Jerusalem (Isa 54:12, LXX Jer 38:39).[101] Like Daniel's vision of a heavenly being (Dan 10:2–6) Joseph is clothed in white lined with a gold sash and he too shines like the sun (*Jos. Asen.* 5:5–6). Joseph carries a σκῆπτρον (scepter), a symbol of authority. Aseneth's reaction to meeting Joseph is described in terms reminiscent of Daniel's encounter with a heavenly being (Dan 10) or other reactions to apocalyptic visions (*4 Ezra* 10:28–30). Aseneth is "cut to the heart" when she first sees Joseph. The verb κατανύσσομαι appears only 16 times in the LXX, but twice to describe Daniel's reaction to seeing the heavenly being (Dan 10:9, 15).[102] Her soul is crushed, her knees are paralyzed[103] and she was filled with a great fear. She wants to hide from Joseph since he is "the son of God" (6:3, 5). In fact, the angelic being in 14:9–12 is described as "in every respect similar to Joseph." Once again, Aseneth falls to the ground in fear.

Second, Joseph is described as the "Powerful One of God" (3:4, 4:7, 18:1–3, 21:21). The title "powerful one" appears in LXX Ps 44:4 [ET 45:3] in a context which is usually taken as messianic. This Psalm is of interest here because it is a wedding song which describes the bridegroom with divine qualities. LXX Psalm 44:7 [ET 45:7] famously describes the groom-king as God who will rule forever.[104] The rod in LXX Ps 44:7 is ῥάβδος rather than σκῆπτρον, but the two words are near synonyms (*T.Jud* 24:5–6 employs the two words in parallel).

Third, Joseph is called the "firstborn Son of the Lord God of Heaven" (21:3, 21:20).[105] The Greek Version of *Jos. Asen.* is ὁ υἱὸς τοῦ θεοῦ ὁ πρωτότοκος While the phrase "son of God" might be taken from Psalm 2, πρωτότοκος may be a Christian interpolation. On the other hand, the love of God for Israel is sometimes described as love for a child (Hos 11). The phrase therefore is does not necessarily indicate a Christian interpolation. Both *PsSol* 18:4 and *4 Ezra* 6:58 use the term to describe Israel. When Aseneth meets Jacob on 22:3–7, he too is described in angelic / divine terms.

Fourth, Aseneth is described as a "City of Refuge" (17:4–6, 19:5) and a "bride of God" (νύμφην θεοῦ, 4:2) for all eternity (21:21).[106] After her marriage to Joseph,

---

100. The other occurrence is In 1 Esdras 3:6 to describe the magnificent honors associated with the greatest of Darius' bodyguards.

101. Schrenk, "ἐκλεκτός," 4:182.

102. LXX Isa 6:5, 47:5 uses the word to describe a person who is stunned to silence. Sirach uses the word three times in the context of feeling guilty for sin (12:12, 14:1, 20:21, cf. *T.Job* 21:3, Acts 2:37). The word also appears in Susanna 10 to describe the men who were "overwhelmed with passion" for Susanna.

103. This would be better translated "weak in the knees."

104. See chapter 5 for a discussion of this text.

105. The title could refer to his position as viceroy to Pharaoh.

106. As additional evidence for a messianic interpretation, I would point out that Fekkes makes a case for an allusion to *Jos. Asen.* in description of the New Jerusalem in Rev 21–22. Although both *Jos.*

Aseneth is called ἡ θυγάτηρ τοῦ ὑψίστου ("daughter of the most high," 21:3). The title "city of Refuge" naturally evokes the biblical Cities of Refuge (Num 35:9–15, Josh 20, 1 Chron 6).[107] Since no other text in the rest of Hebrew Bible or Second Temple period literature which use the cities of refuge as a metaphor in any way, let alone eschatologically, it is likely that this title is drawn from texts which describe Zion as a refuge.[108] For the present text, Isa 4 is the most important since the text refers to the cleansing of the daughters of Zion.[109] Like Aseneth, the daughters of Zion were haughty and proud (Isa 3:16–17) and are humbled by the Lord (Isa 3:18—14:1). In the future, however, they will be cleansed and Zion will become a refuge from oppression. As observed in chapter 5, the canopy which the Lord creates over Mount Zion is חֻפָּה, a nuptial tent. While there is no explicit reference to a restored marriage in Isa 4, the author of *Jos. Asen.* may have had in mind the idea that Zion would become a refuge for the returning exiles. Last, the marriage of Joseph and Aseneth was ordained since eternity (21:1–3), just as Aseneth's bridal clothes were created (15:10, 21:2–3). She is therefore a bride prepared from the foundation of the world. Joseph will be her husband for all eternity (Ἰωσὴφ ἔσται σου νυμφίος εἰς τὸν αἰῶνα χρόνον).

The description of Aseneth as a "City of Refuge" is intended to represent Jerusalem/Zion. This is consistent with the image of Zion as a bride/wife in the Hebrew Bible. However, there is little here which could be described as messianic. It is not even clear that the marriage of Joseph and Aseneth was intended to function at a typological or allegorical level to describe Israel's salvation history. The story of the marriage Joseph and Aseneth does however show that the marriage metaphor may be developed in a cosmic sense rather than as a typology for Israel's relationship with God.

Fourth Ezra

Fourth Ezra 9:26—10:59 is perhaps the best example of a marriage metaphor in the Second Temple period, although this allegory takes the motif a completely different direction.[110] Ezra is in a field meditating on the recent fall of Jerusalem. Beginning

---

Asen. and Rev 21–22 are probably both dependent in Isa 54:11–12, a city described as "adorned like a bride" is an eschatological motif at the very least.

107. Spencer, "Refuge, Cities of," 5:657–58; Auld, "Cities of Refuge in Israelite Tradition," 26–40.

108. For example, Isa 14:32 and Joel 4:16 [ET 3:16]. The fragmentary 4Q550e describes Zion as a refuge for the poor.

109. See also Ps 2:6, 12, 14 6–7; Isa 14:32, 30:2; 28:16–16; Joel 4:16 [ET 3:16]; Zeph 3:12–14.

110. The Jewish apocalypse (chapters 3–14) was probably written about 100 CE, with a Christian framework added in the second half of the third century. This is based on the opening verse which states the book was written thirty years after Jerusalem was destroyed. Since this verse claims to be the words of the main character in the story, Ezra, at the time of the destruction of Jerusalem in 586 BCE there is a clear historical anachronism. Since the book discusses the problem of the fall of Jerusalem it is applicable to either the destruction in 70 or 135 CE, but Metzger finds it unlikely a Jewish book would find popularity in the post-Bar Kokhba world, so probably the central section was not written

with the wilderness period, he describes Israel as squandering their opportunity to reap the harvest of the Law (9:29–37). Ezra's thoughts are disturbed by a despondent woman who explains that she is mourning the death of her son (9:88—10:4). She had been barren for thirty years, but the Lord finally gave her a son. She carefully raised him and when he was ready to marry she made a wedding banquet for him, but he died when he entered the bridal chamber. Ezra berates the woman for mourning for her son when Jerusalem is in ruins (10:5–24). The woman is then transformed into a great city with massive foundations (10:25–27). Ezra is shocked and paralyzed with fear. The angel Uriel comforts him and explains the meaning of the allegorical vision (10:28–59). The woman is Zion and the thirty years of childlessness were there 3000 years prior to Solomon's temple. The years she carefully raised her child were the years of Jerusalem's habitation and the death as the son enters the bridal chamber is the fall of Jerusalem in 586 BCE.

This allegory draws from the Hebrew Bible in several ways. First, Zion is personified as a woman and the fall of Jerusalem is imagined as the loss of her child. As we have seen, the prophets regularly portray Israel as the wife of God. The exile was the loss of her children; the restoration from exile will be the return of her children from the four corners of the world (Isa 54–55). Second, there is a hope of restoration for Zion in the future. The new city of Jerusalem will be established securely and glorious beyond imagination. This may reflect the fact that while Jerusalem was rebuilt after the exile, it was neither particularly impressive nor secure from enemies. The new Zion can be described beautiful, splendorous and secure (10:55).

However, there are several unique items in this allegory. Lady Zion is not the subject of the marriage metaphor. It is not her wedding which is celebrated nor is the restoration of the city pictured as a restored marriage. In fact, the husband is only mentioned in passing and the bride is missing entirely from the allegory. The son represents Israel and is not a messianic figure. Second, the wedding feast is the destruction of Jerusalem, not a banquet celebrating God's victory of Israel's enemies. In fact, the wedding feast is not important to the overall meaning of the allegory since Uriel does not give a meaning for the feast itself, only the entry into the bridal chamber. Not everything in an allegory must have a meaning and it is best to only interpret the items which the text explicitly are said to be allegorical. With this in mind, the bride and groom are not important, only that the child of Zion who died represents the exile.

What is important for this study is that the writer of *4 Ezra* has developed a theology of history around the idea of a marriage, although the consummation of the marriage never happens. Prior to his encounter with the grieving woman, Ezra was thinking about Israel's failure to respond properly to the Law of God during the

---

after even 120 CE. Collins states there is a "consensus" the Jewish apocalypse was written in Palestine (Collins, *Apocalyptic Imagination*, 196). Metzger, on the other hand, takes the reference to Babylon in 3:1 as Rome and sees the book is therefore the product of Diaspora Jews (*OTP* 1:520). Metzger, "The Fourth Book of Ezra," 1:516–59; Stone, "Esdras, Second Book of," 2:611–14.

wilderness period. The woman's experience confirms this observation during the kingdom as well. From Solomon until Jerusalem's destruction, Israel failed to keep the covenant. As a result, the son of Zion dies in the bridal chamber and the new age never occurs. From the perspective of the end of the first century, this allegory is not about the history of Israel up to 586 BCE., but rather through 70 CE. Since Zion has been destroyed again, will there be a future glorious restoration?[111] *4 Ezra* seems to think there will be, albeit with very few participants.

To anticipate the last chapter of this study, it is important that the marriage metaphor in *4 Ezra* is re-worked as a history of salvation using the marriage metaphor. As early as Hosea, God's relationship with his people could be described as a faithful husband longing to restore an unfaithful wife to her former status of purity. From the perspective of the end of the first century, that restoration did not occur and the spouse is not only still unfaithful, the spouse has died. The author of *4 Ezra* therefore may be calling on his readers to repent in the wake of the destruction of Jerusalem (the end of the marriage). Similarly, Jesus claims that the "kingdom of heaven is like a wedding banquet" and he invites true Israel to participate in the ongoing feast celebrating the restoration of the marriage. Like *4 Ezra*, very few truly respond to that invitation to participate in the feast.

The Maccabean Literature

Two related texts in First and Third Maccabees employ the marriage metaphor in the context of persecution of the Jews. 1 Maccabees reports the reaction of the Jews to the looting of the Temple by Antiochus. In order to demonstrate the outrageousness of this act, the writer says that "every bridegroom took up the lament, she who sat in the bridal chamber (παστός) was mourning" (1 Macc 1:27). The ones who ought to be celebrating with joy mourned because of the desecration of the Temple. Similarly, 3 Macc 1:19 describes brides who were prepared for their wedding tent neglecting proper modesty. 3 Macc 4:6 is a close parallel to 1 Macc 1:27. Women who had just entered their bridal chamber "exchanged joy for wailing, their myrrh-perfumed hair sprinkled with ashes, and were carried away unveiled, all together raising a lament instead of a wedding song."

These texts may be patterned after LXX Joel 2:16 (MT 3:16). When the Day of the Lord arrives, a fast will be declared in Zion and all people will assemble, from the elderly and the infant. "Let the bridegroom leave his bedroom (κοιτών) and the bride her canopy (παστός). The joy of the bride is turned to mourning in Jer 7:34, 16:9, 25:10, and in 33:11 the restoration of Israel is described as the restoration of the voice

---

111. Zion may be understood as either an eschatological, restored Jerusalem or the idealized, heavenly Jerusalem. Stone thinks that the text sees the restoration of Zion as ambiguous, it is both eschatological and heavenly. Stone, *Fourth Ezra*, 335.

of the bride and groom returning to the cities of Judah.[112] As I showed in chapter 5, the reversal of mourning to joy is a characteristic of the New Covenant in Jer 31, a text foundational to the Jesus' teaching at the Last Supper. Sorrow and joy is found in Matt 11:16–19, contrasting John the Baptist (who came mourning) and Jesus (who came rejoicing). These two texts from the Maccabean literature indicate this use of the marriage metaphor to illustrate a reversal of joy and mourning was current in the Second Temple period.

Marriage Metaphor in the Qumran Literature

There are only a few texts in the Qumran literature which may employ the marriage metaphor. Each of the examples surveyed in this section are so fragmentary that it is difficult to draw firm conclusions. Yet in the three texts I will examine here there is the same sort of combination of the marriage metaphor with Exodus and Wilderness traditions found in Isa 40–55. While there is no line which can be described with certainty as eschatological, this small sample once again confirms the blended of marriage and wilderness traditions.

4Q Tanhumin (4Q176)

4Q Tanhumin (4Q176) is a collection of texts mostly from Isa 40–55.[113] Stanley contrasted this scroll with *4Q Testimonia,* which collects scripture around a topic. For Stanley, 4Q176 is not a "thematic conglomeration" or a running commentary on a portion of scripture (like the *pesherim*), but rather a "written record of one person's progressive reading through a limited portion of scripture."[114] These texts are gathered to provide comfort for the community while looking forward to a "future restoration of an even more glorious state."[115] Column 1 calls on God to "perform your marvel." This phrase (עֲשֵׂה פֶלֶא) describes the Exodus in the Song of the Sea (Exod 15:11) and two reflections on the wilderness tradition in Ps 77:15 and 78:12.[116] The only other occurrence of the phrase in the Hebrew Bible is in the introduction to the eschatological banquet (Isa 25:1).

---

112. As I will argue in the next chapter, this contrast between the expected behaviors of the wedding party stands behind Jesus' words in Mark 2:18–22 and possibly in Matt 11:16–19.

113. Stanley, "The Importance of 4QTanhumim (4Q176)," 569–82. Stanley is more interested in the fact that some reader has taken notes on a reading of scripture than the theology of the collection itself. On the other hand, Nebe uses 4Q502 to comment on the text of *Jubilees.* Nebe, "Ergänzende Bemerkung zu 4Q176, Jubiläen 23:21," 129–30.

114. Stanley, "The Importance of 4QTanhumim (4Q176)," 576.

115. Wise, Cook, and Abegg, *The Dead Sea Scrolls: A New Translation*, 231; "The Importance of 4QTanhumim (4Q176)," 577.

116. The noun פֶלֶא only appears 13 times in the Hebrew Bible, almost always to describe God's miraculous deeds.

Jesus the Bridegroom

What is important for the marriage metaphor in the Qumran literature is that the three of the four fragments which remain cite texts which refer to Zion as a woman, including Isa 54:4–10, "your husband will be your maker." In fact, this collection of texts from Isaiah includes the texts surveyed in chapter 4 of this study as a part of the "banquet in the wilderness" motif and chapter 5 as a part of the marriage metaphor in Second Isaiah.

4Q502 Ritual of Marriage?

4Q502 is an extremely fragmentary text initially identified as a marriage ritual although two recent studies have brought this title into question.[117] Baillet considered the use of the use of both the verb and noun forms of שמח as evidence that the document preserves a wedding description (cf. Tobit 8). In fragments 7–10, line 5 describes the celebration as the "time of our happiness" (קץ שמחה) and in line 10 a "feast of our happiness" (מועד לשמחתנו). For Baillet, both phrases are appropriate to a wedding celebration. In addition, fragments 1–3 mention a man and his wife, procreation, and friends who accompany the couple. Fragments 7–10 resonate with the creation story. Fragment 24 is an exchange of blessings asking for a long and peaceful life. Fragment 34 describe "old men and women," presumably members of the wedding party.

J. Baumgarten disagrees with the identification of the 4Q502 as a wedding ritual and describes the text as a "Golden Age Ritual," or a celebration of the elderly members of the congregation.[118] He points out that the noun מועד is not a feast, but an "appointed time." Unless weddings were restricted to a certain time of year, Baumgarten thinks this may refer to a joyous gathering of the community rather than a wedding.[119] The fragments give a prominent place to both elderly men and women at a joyous celebration at a fixed time. Rather than a marriage ritual, Baumgarten argues this text represents the first day of the celebration of Sukkot known as *simhat bet ha-so-'ebah*, citing *Tosephta Sukkah* 4:2 in which the elderly are praised for their long lives. Since both 4Q502 and Philo describe a festive meal which includes elderly men and women, Baumgarten compares this joyous festival with the Theraputae (Philo, *Comptempl.* 66).[120]

M. L. Satlow agrees with Baumgarten that the identification of 4Q502 as a marriage ritual is errant, but finds Baumgarten's comparison to the Theraputae to be weak.[121] Since מוֹעֵד is used for the celebration, it cannot be a wedding but some other fixed

---

117. Baillet, *Qumran grotte 4. III (4Q482–4Q520)*, 81–105; García Martínez and Tigchelaar, *The Dead Sea Scrolls Study Edition (Translations)*, 2:995. The 344 fragments which constitute 4Q502 are in a poor state of preservation, but Baillet dated the document to the first century BCE. It is possible that the collection of fragments represent multiple documents. Baillet, *DJD* 7:81.

118. Baumgarten, "4Q502, Marriage or Golden Age Ritual?," 125–35.

119. Ibid., 128.

120. Ibid., 129–30.

121. Satlow, "4Q502 A New Year Festival?," 57–68.

festival. While Sukkot is a possibility based on the use of שִׂמְחָה, joy, Satlow suggests that these fragments describe a New Year festival on the first of Nisan.[122] Satlow points out that the only other time that the two phrases which describe the celebration appear together in the DSS is 4Q503, frag. 49.[123] Since Qumran followed a Solar calendar of 364 days divided into four quarters of 91 days, each new quarter was marked by a "turning day." These days were marked by special events in the Hebrew Bible and associated with joyous feasting.[124] Satlow understands the references to creation as a part of restorative eschatology at Qumran.[125] Assuming that fragments 1–3 do in fact precede 6–10, then the allusions to the creation story are in reverse (humans, livestock, creeping things, birds, produce, water).

J. Davila re-examined 4Q502 and concluded that the suggestions of Baumgarten and Satlow are possible, but the simplest solution is that the fragments describe a wedding ritual.[126] Davila agrees that the reference to לולבים in fragment 99 tends to confirms Baumgarten's theory that the document described a Sukkot celebration; he considers Baumgarten's use of the Theraputae as "ad hoc speculation."[127] In favor of a wedding, Davila points out that the blessing fragment 20 includes both "length of days" and "fruit of womb" and is reminiscent of Tobias' blessing in Tobit 8.[128] Since later marriage customs included bringing myrtle branches into the wedding chamber, it is possible that לולבים in fragment 99 refer to this practice.[129] Even the reference to "seven days" in frag. 97 could refer to equally to a festival or a wedding. Finally, Baumgarten and Satlow both argued that the use of מוֹעֵד (appointed time) is inappropriate for a wedding. But *m.Ketub* 1.1 states that the appointed day for the marriage of a virgin was Wednesday.[130] Davila therefore concludes that 4Q502 is in fact a wedding document of some kind, although the fragmentary nature of the scroll makes conclusions tentative.

---

122. In addition, fragments 94–100 mention sisters and a seven day festival. For Satlow, these could allude to Sukkot or a festival beginning on the first of Nisan. Satlow, "4Q502 A New Year Festival?," 59, 66–67.

123. In fact, these two collections of fragments may be related, as Baillet observed in the initial publication of 4Q503, "Il peut ainsi y en avoir qui appartiennent aux Prieres quotidiennes et l'on s'est parfois demande si les deux rouleaux n'en formaient pas un seul" (Baillet, *DJD* 7.81).

124. Satlow, "4Q502 A New Year Festival?," 61–62. The best example is that on the first of Nisan, Noah "made a feast and celebrated with great rejoicing" (*Jub.* 7.:3) 1QapGen 12:15 describes Noah celebrating a feast (מִשְׁתֶּה) on the first day of the new year. Compare also celebrations on the first day of Nisan in Josephus *Ant.* 1:81.

125. Satlow, "4Q502 A New Year Festival?," 64.

126. Davila, *Liturgical Works*, 181–207.

127. Ibid., 206.

128. Ibid., 198.

129. Ibid., citing Weinfeld, "Prayer and Liturgical Practice in the Qumran Sect," 241–58.

130. Ibid., 193.

4Q434a Grace after Meals

Based on parallels to 4QDeutj, 4QDeutn and *m.Ber* 6:8, Weinfeld identified this fragment as a prayer after a meal in a home which is in mourning.[131] The allusion to Isa 66:13 is found in later rabbinic blessings in the context of mourning.[132] Because of the nature of the blessing, the verb נחם (comfort, console) appears frequently l.1, 4 and 6. Davila treats this fragment briefly and agrees that this is a "Grace after Meal" and that the specific context is that of comfort for a house in mourning.[133]

Despite this text being a blessing after a meal, there are several elements of the blessing which resonate with the texts covered in chapters 4 and 5. Line 1 and Isa 54:11 both describe the personified city as afflicted (עָנִי) and therefore needing comfort. Line 3 alludes to a new creation as Eden-like feasting (cf. Isa 65:17–18). The phrase "eating the good fruit" (פריה וטובה לאכול) in line 4–5 appears in Jer 2:7 and Neh 9:36, both prophetic reflections on the wilderness traditions. Like this blessing, these prophetic texts look back to the time when Israel first came into the land and enjoyed eating the good produce of the Land.

In chapter 5 I argued that Jer 2–4 mixes both wilderness and nuptial imagery. Line 6 also combines the imagery stating that "he (God) will console Jerusalem as a bridegroom consoles his bride." The term נחם (comfort) is a key motif in Isa 40–55, framing Isa 40–55 (Isa 40:1, 54:11). Both 4Q434a l.6 and Isa 62:5 describe Jerusalem Zion as a bride (כַּלָּה). Isa 61:10 describes the anointed one as clothed with righteous like a bride (כַּלָּה). Line 7 of the blessing may allude to Ps 45:7 [ET 45:6]. Line 7 has כסאו לעולם; Ps 45:7 has the same words but inserts אֱלֹהִים between the two words.[134]

Is there a "messianic feast" in lines 4–5? Weinfeld points out that *b.Ber.* 48b indicates that the "messianic element is indispensable in a grace after meals."[135] While it is tempting to read l.4 ורב טוב as a bountiful meal since the final word of the line is לאכול, Weinfeld correctly takes this as a title for God, "the one abounding in goodness."[136] Cook, on the other hand, translates the phrase as the instrumental object of the verb:

---

131. Weinfeld, "Grace after Meals in Qumran," 427–40.

132. Weinfeld provides the text of a traditional "Grace after Meal in the Mourner's House" as an appendix to his article. Weinfeld, "Grace after Meals in Qumran," 438–39.

133. Davila, *Liturgical Works*, 175. So also Seely, "4Q437: A First Look at an Unpublished Barki Nafshi Text," 147–60.

134. Weinfeld points out similar wording in the Davidic covenant 2 Sam 7:16 / 1 Chron 17:14. Weinfeld, "Grace after Meals," 433. These are not likely allusions since the throne in 2 Sam 7:16 is the object of the verb ("will be established") and עַד־עוֹלָם appears rather than לעולם. In Ps 93:2 God's throne is forever מֵעוֹלָם. Finally, Lam 5:19, God endures forever (לעולם), but his throne endures to all generations (לְדֹר וָדֹר).

135. "Whoever did not mention the kingdom of David in the Benediction over Jerusalem did not fulfill his obligation" (Weinfeld, "Grace after Meals in Qumran," 436).

136. Ibid., 432. The phrase never describes a meal, in the Hebrew Bible. Rather, it is used several times to describe God's abundant, good gifts (Isa 63:7, Ps 31:20 [ET 19], 145:7. Only Neh 9:35 refers to the abundance of the land.

"he will console them with abundant goodness."[137] In either case, it is difficult to make this phrase an eschatological feast. Nevertheless, in the context of comfort for a mourning family, this blessing uses scripture which looks forward to a future time when God will comfort his people like a bridegroom comforts a bride.

Summary and Conclusions

There is little at Qumran which can be described as using a marriage metaphor to describe the eschatological age. That time will be a time of comfort for Israel and that comfort can be described as a bridegroom's comfort for his bride, but the writers of these fragmentary documents do not explicitly make describe the future age as a wedding feast. It is also significant that each of the text in this section also use wilderness language, giving evidence for a blending of marriage and marriage traditions. While it is tempting to follow Satlow's suggestion that 4Q502 reflects "restorative eschatology,"[138] there is not enough clear evidence in the fragments to form that conclusion.

Summary and Conclusions: The End of the Exile in the Second Temple Period

As conclusion to this chapter I want to return to the idea of the Exile in Second Temple period Judaism. This topic has been covered in by a number of detailed studies;[139] my intention here is only to show how the three metaphors (banquet, wilderness, marriage) converge as an "end of the Exile." The idea that many Jews in the Second Temple period believed they were still in some form of Exile was popularized by N. T. Wright. Wright argues that the return from Babylon was not the glorious restoration of the nation envisioned by Isa 40–55 because the Land was still occupied by foreigners and the nation was living in dispersion throughout the nations.[140] While this assertion has been criticized,[141] it appears that the main contours of Wright's thesis can be shown from the literature of the Second Temple period.[142]

137. Wise, Cook, and Abegg, *A New Translation*, 395.

138. Satlow, "4Q502 A New Year Festival?," 64.

139. The "idea of the exile" was first described by P. Ackroyd, *Exile and Restoration*, 237–47. Knibb contributed two essays on the idea of the exile in the Second Temple Period: Knibb, "The Exile in the Intertestamental Period," 253–72, reprinted in Knibb, *Essays in the Book of Enoch*; Knibb, "Exile in the Damascus Document," 213–31.

140. Wright, *New Testament and the People of God*, 268–69.

141. Casey, "Where Wright Is Wrong: A Critical Review of N.T. Wright's *Jesus and The Victory Of God*," 95–103; Marsh, "Theological History? N.T. Wright's *Jesus and the Victory of God*," 77–94. Wright responded to these criticisms in "Theology, History and Jesus: A Response to Maurice Casey and Clive Marsh," 105–12.

142. Evans collects an impressive number of Second Temple Period texts which support Wright's contention, concluding with the comment "in my opinion the evidence fully justifies N. T. Wright's emphasis on Exile theology in Jesus and his contemporaries." Evans, "Jesus and the Continuing Exile

M. Knibb follows Ackroyd's view that by the time Dan 9:24–27 was written, the "exile is understood as a state that is to be ended only by the intervention of God and the inauguration of the eschatological era."[143] Knibb surveys a number of texts written in the Second Temple period and makes several points concerning this ongoing state of exile.[144] First, the post-exilic period is characterized as a sinful period. For example, in the *Animal Apocalypse* (*1 En.* 89–90)[145] the writer describes the shepherds in the post-exilic period as "blind" (89:74), "exceedingly deaf and dim-sighted (90:7). In 90:17 the final 12 twelve shepherds are responsible for the "great destruction." In the *Apocalypse of Weeks* (*1 En.* 93:1–10, 91:11–17), the seventh week describes the events of the post-exilic period: "its deeds shall be many, and all of them criminal" (90:9). The fact that the writer of this apocalypse does not even mention the rebuilding of the Temple implies that for him, "the second Temple was of no consequence in relation to God's plan for Israel."[146]

Second, the writers of this material see themselves as still living in the exile.[147] The best evidence for this contention comes from *4 Ezra* and *2 Baruch*, two documents which were written near the end of the first century CE and both use exilic characters as pseudonyms. For Knibb, this alone implies that the authors saw themselves as "living in a more or less permanent state of exile" since Jerusalem fell.[148] In fact, Baruch 3:8 describes his generation as "we are today in our exile where you have scattered us" (cf. Dan 9:8–15). Along with Dan 9, Knibb observes that there are several interpretations of the 70 years of Jer 25:11–12 which lengthen the period considerably. The *Letter of Jeremiah*, for example, indicates that they exile would last seven generations rather than seventy years (v. 3).

Third, the exile ends when God intervenes in history and establishes a messianic age.[149] Returning the *Animal Apocalypse*, the sheep remain blind and deaf until the Lord of the Sheep destroys the enemy of the flock and "a throne is erected in the pleasant land" in order to render judgment (*1 En.* 90:14–21). The Lord of the Sheep will restore the sight and hearing of the sheep and they will live in a magnificent new Temple (*1 En.* 90:35–26). The *Damascus Document* claims to be written some 390 years since the exile began. The event which ends the period is the advent of the Teacher of Righteousness, whom God "raised up" to lead the community.[150]

---

of Israel," 77–100.

143. Knibb, "The Exile in the Literature," 194; Ackroyd, *Exile and Restoration*, 242–43.

144. Knibb, "The Exile in the Literature," 196; cf. the seventh week is "categorically described as a time of sin." Stuckenbruck, *1 Enoch 91–108*, 123.

145. Tiller, *A Commentary on the Animal Apocalypse (1 En. 85–90)*.

146. Stuckenbruck, *1 Enoch 91–108*, 122. An additional text is *As. Mos.* 7 which describes the people after the exile as "imperious hypocrites" who love feasts and "luxurious wining and dining."

147. Knibb, "The Exile in the Literature," 208.

148. Ibid., 211.

149. Ibid., 194–95; Ackroyd, *Exile and Restoration*, 242–43.

150. *CD* I, 5–11; Knibb, "The Exile in the Literature," 200; Knibb, "Exile in the Damascus Document,"

These three elements of the "idea of the exile" can be observed in the metaphorical matrix of the eschatological banquet, wilderness, marriage surveyed in the previous chapters. We have observed that a major feature of the eschatological banquet is an invitation to return to Zion from the wilderness. In Isa 40–55 the writer calls to Israel to participate in a new Exodus and return to Zion where they will enjoy the ongoing bounty of the Lord's feast in the wilderness. The exiles are like Hosea's wife, driven into exile because of their sin, waiting for her husband to recall her and restore her to her former role as wife and mother.

The passages surveyed in the previous chapters indicate that the writers lived in exile, but looked forward to a final, decisive act of God which would restore Zion. In all three of these metaphors the restoration is an act of God which initiates a new age. The new age may be a return to Eden (Isa 40–55) or a marriage restored to its original joy (Hos 2, Isa 55:1–5), or God's final decisive victory over death itself (Isa 25:6–8). As we turn to the New Testament use of these themes, I swill show how the writers of the Synoptic Gospels developed these motifs into an invitation to participate in Jesus' ministry as an ongoing banquet as the bridegroom invites all Israel to join in the end of the exile.

228.

7

The Wedding Banquet in the Synoptic Gospels

Introduction

Summary of the Study

I BEGAN THIS STUDY with the observation that New Testament scholars often state that writers of the Second Temple period conceive of the end of the age as a messianic banquet, but never as a wedding banquet. The Synoptic Gospels, on the other hand, describe Jesus as claiming that the kingdom of Heaven "like a wedding banquet" and he refers to himself as a bridegroom. This is therefore a problem for some scholars because it is assumed that Jesus would have used metaphors which were current in the first century in order to communicate his message clearly. If no one was describing the messianic age as a wedding banquet, it is highly unlikely that Jesus would choose to use that particular metaphor for his messianic ministry.[1] How did the eschatological banquet at the end of the age come to be a description of Jesus' ministry? How did a banquet motif transform into a wedding banquet in the Synoptic Gospels?

In order to explore this problem, I proposed to use an intertextual methodology in order to explore how the Gospel writers applied the metaphor of a messianic banquet. In my second chapter, I adapted Hays's method for detecting allusions to include both texts and traditions found in earlier documents. In an oral culture it was not always possible for an audience to "read" a text. Rather, they heard a story which employed common tradition known to all. The first step of my method is to "hear an echo" in the Gospel text. For example, in Matt 8:11–12 Jesus describes the kingdom in terms of a messianic banquet ("many from the east and west reclining at the table with

---

1. This is perhaps a problem with the so-called Criterion of Dissimilarity. While some scholars insist on a double-dissimilarity (Jesus is neither like Second Temple Period Judaism nor the later church), recent historical Jesus research has emphasized Jesus' Jewishness. Since the "wedding banquet" metaphor is judged as "not Jewish," it is rejected as a later addition by the early (Matthean) church.

Abraham"). In Mark 2:19–20 Jesus describes himself as a bridegroom and his ministry as an on-going wedding banquet characterized by feasting. In these examples a listener might "hear an echo" of traditions from the Hebrew Bible.

The second stage of my method was to gather texts which might have been used by the Gospel writers. I therefore reviewed data from the Hebrew Bible and Second Temple period that describes the beginning eschatological age as a banquet (chapter 3) or the return from exile as a new Exodus and an ongoing banquet with the Lord in the Wilderness (chapter 4). Since there are a number of texts which describe the end of the age as a restoration of the marriage between Israel and her God, I examined the marriage metaphor in Hosea, Jeremiah and Isaiah (chapter 5). Frequently the Wilderness period was used to describe the initial marriage of Israel and their God. These three related sets of imagery overlap and blend together, creating various combinations of joyous celebration of a renewed marriage at the end of the exile. One of the ways a future age could be described was as an invitation to join in the joyous celebration which accompanies the marriage of Israel.

These three traditions appear in various combinations in the literature of the Second Temple period. In chapter 6 I observed that the literature of the period conceived of the exile as ongoing and therefore looked forward to the end of the age. In some texts, there is a great feast at the beginning of new age, but in other texts the next age is characterized by an ongoing feast sometimes characterized as a return to the conditions of Eden. The new age will be a time when humans eat abundant food in the presence of God. Like Isaiah 40–55, the exiles are in the wilderness and are invited to return to a restored Zion. That this new age is a like a wedding is a muted theme, appearing primarily in *4 Ezra* as a wedding which went badly.

The task of the present chapter is the last part of the intertextual method described in chapter 2. It remains to demonstrate that how these three traditions are combined in the Synoptic Gospels as a part of Jesus' teaching and practice. Jesus is presented as a bridegroom who is hosting an ongoing feast which celebrates the beginning of the new age. In fact, Jesus describes the "kingdom of heaven" as a "wedding banquet" (Matt 22:1). This chapter will examine the ways in Jesus developed and adapted these overlapping traditions in order to describe his own mission.

Assumptions and Limitations

Before examining the motif of a wedding banquet in the Synoptic Gospels, I need to clarify several methodological assumptions. It is not possible to argue at length these assumptions as part of this dissertation. For the most part, there is nothing radical here. These are issues which are the subject of continuing dialogue among scholars, making it impossible to treat them with the sort of thoroughness expected in a study such as this. I will merely state my convictions within these ongoing discussions among New Testament scholars.

First, this chapter will proceed with the working assumption of Markan priority and the so-called two source hypothesis for the development of Matthew and Luke. Alternative theories are entirely possible, but I find that Markan priority answers more questions and creates less problems than Matthean priority. Despite the fact that Matthew and Luke knew and used both Mark and a Sayings source of some kind, I will not be overly concerned with questions of redaction.[2] The sayings of Jesus will be treated within the context of the individual Gospel itself. This has the advantage of "staying within the story world" of the writer and giving full weight to their skills as an author.[3]

Second, I will not argue for or against the authenticity of individual sayings. There are several reasons for this methodological decision. First, within the narrative world of the Synoptic Gospels, Jesus makes these statements and they are "authentic" within the world of the individual Gospels. The recognition that the Gospels are literary creations has freed scholarship from the often fruitless search for sources, proto-Gospels, or layers of traditions. While it is certain that the gospel writers used sources and traditions, these early layers are not what matter in this dissertation. Mark, Matthew and Luke are therefore treated as authors who presented Jesus with all sorts of assumptions and prejudices.[4]

A second reason for suspending judgment on the words of Jesus is that studies which seek to authenticate the words of Jesus tend to be concerned only with methods for authenticating the words and less interested in what is actually said in the Gospels. These types of studies fall into three categories. Some reject virtually everything the gospels report as words of Jesus.[5] The classic example of this historical skepticism is R. Bultmann, who famously said that we can know little more than the fact that Jesus lived and died. His "Jesus of History" and "Christ of Faith" dichotomy is not particularly helpful and yields very little in the way of historical insight. Others accept the words of Jesus as presented in the gospels with no attempt to sort out the voice of the Gospel writer from the voice of Jesus. This is problematic for the simple reason that we do not have the words of Jesus at all. He taught in Aramaic, we read the remembrance of those words recorded in Greek many years after they were first spoken.

Most scholars who work in the field of Historical Jesus research attempt to find a place between these two extremes.[6] This approach to the words of Jesus would use the tools of the scholarship to weigh sayings of Jesus less skeptically than the first group,

---

2. Dunn, *Jesus Remembered*, 254.

3. Hatina, *In Search of a Context*.

4. I will use the names of the traditional authors of the gospels without arguing for or against the traditional authorship for the Gospels. Since I will be discussing all three of the Synoptic Gospels I will need to distinguish between the three rather than using the scholarly convention of "the Evangelist" or "the Author."

5. For example, Crossan, *The Historical Jesus*; Lüdemann, *Jesus After 2000 Years: What He Really Said and Did*.

6. For example, Meyer, *The Aims of Jesus*; Meier, *A Marginal Jew*, vol. 1; Wright, *Jesus and the Victory of God*; Pitre, *Jesus, the Tribulation, and the End of the Exile*.

but also less naively than the second. While it is obvious that we do not have the actual words of Jesus, we have access to the "voice of Jesus" as reported by the evangelists. In this view, various criteria of authenticity are favored over others, producing differing results. As is typically the case for middle positions, the skeptics find this approach to be inadequate (or worse, faith-based) and the conservative finds them too restrictive (or worse, liberal).

This is not to say that I am skeptical of the sayings of Jesus in the Synoptic Gospels. On the contrary, I am convinced that the Synoptic Gospels accurately record the "voice of Jesus." The work of N. T. Wright, for example, attempts to read Jesus within the story of the Jewish people and treats the words of Jesus within that narrative world.[7] Similarly, J. D. G. Dunn argues that the synoptic traditions were shaped by an oral tradition repeatedly performed by disciples interested in what Jesus actually said or did.[8] However, this study simply cannot argue for the authenticity of the words of Jesus at every point.

This chapter will begin by Jesus' table fellowship in all three gospels. The reason for beginning with table fellowship is that there is little doubt that Jesus did in fact eat with sinners.[9] Frequently Historical Jesus studies begin with the words rather than the activities of Jesus. Sayings judged as authentic are then used to decide which things Jesus might have actually done. In his monograph on the relationship of Jesus and Judaism, E. P. Sanders suggested that this method is backwards.[10] Rather than beginning with the sayings of Jesus, Sanders created a list of activities which we can be certain Jesus did then used this list to evaluate the words of Jesus.[11] For Sanders, Jesus' activity in the Temple becomes the starting point for his study, but any certain activity might be chosen.[12] Since my interest is in Jesus' claim to be "the bridegroom"

---

7. Wright, *The New Testament and the People of God* and *Jesus and the Victory of God*. Wright borrows "critical realism" from Meyer as a historical method, but also recognizes the value of understanding the meta-narrative of the Hebrew Bible as a basis for reading the New Testament. This is not a simplistic "Jesus was a Jew" method. Wright identifies the world view of Jewish people in the first century, then shows that Jesus' words and deeds are perfectly at home within that world view.

8. Dunn, *Jesus Remembered*, 335–36.

9. This is true for even the most skeptical Jesus scholars. For example, Crossan sees Jesus' eating with sinners as a cornerstone the "broker-less" kingdom of God. Crossan, *The Historical Jesus*, 422. Borg considers table fellowship to be "one of the central characteristics" of Jesus' movement. Borg, *Jesus: A New Vision*, 131.

10. Sanders, *Jesus and Judaism*. Sanders is building in the foundation Fuchs, *Studies of the Historical Jesus*. Citing the work of Smith and Harvey, Sanders points out that these two scholars came to radically different conclusions about Jesus while agreeing on a common pool of facts about the life of Jesus. Smith, *Jesus the Magician*; Harvey, *Jesus and the Constraints of History*.

11. His list includes: Jesus was baptized by John the Baptist; he was a Galilean who preached and healed; he had disciples known as "the twelve"; he confined his activity to Israel; he engaged in controversy of the Temple; he was crucified by Roman officials; his followers were persecuted by Jews at least until the end of Paul's career. Sanders, *Jesus and Judaism*, 11. This list is more expansive than Bultmann, but not by much.

12. Sanders, *Jesus and Judaism*, 61. By way of method, Sanders examines the reports of the so-called

and his use of wedding banquet language to describe his ministry, table fellowship becomes the historical ground on which the sayings within the synoptic gospels can be examined.

Table Fellowship

Meals in Second Temple Period Judaism

Food and sharing meals was a major issue in the first century, especially for the Pharisees.[13] With respect to table fellowship, it is true Pharisees did not eat with people "lower" than themselves since they saw table fellowship as "eating with God."[14] A lay-Pharisee would gladly accept an invitation to eat with a priest, since he would know for certain the priest would be eating as pure as the Pharisee (or more so). On the Sabbath, however, it is likely Pharisees ate together. This is the view of E. P. Sanders although he contradicts scholars such as Neusner and Jeremias. Neusner and Jeremias have, in Sanders' opinion, confused the Qumran Community with the Pharisees.[15] Neusner states "if someone were to set out to organize a "Mishnah" before 70, "his single operative category would have been making meals."[16] In fact, according to Neusner, "the primary mark of Pharisaic commitment was the observance of the laws of ritual purity outside the Temple, and this ritual purity extended primarily to food.[17] He demonstrates that of the 341 rulings that go back to the Pharisees, 229 are related to table fellowship. For this reason, he says that the Pharisees might be considered an "eating club."[18] Sanders disagrees, arguing this does not "tally with the evidence" since

---

"cleansing of the Temple" and tries to explain why Jesus would have made accusations against the Temple administration. In doing so, he compares Jesus to the criticisms found in the DSS and *PsSol* (ibid., 65), and then compares Jesus' sayings about the destruction of the Temple with the Second Temple Period views on the Temple, a New Temple (ibid., chap. 2), and the restoration of Israel (ibid., chap. 3). In the end, Sanders is able to state "on the basis of facts" that Jesus hoped for the restoration of Israel and that fact becomes the basis for his study of the kingdom sayings of Jesus (ibid.,118).

13. Bartchy,"Table Fellowship," 796–800; Smith, "Table Fellowship as a Literary Motif in the Gospel of Luke," 613–28; Smith, "Table Fellowship," 6:302–3; Smith, "Table Fellowship and the Historical Jesus," 135–62. Neusner contributes several articles on Pharisees and food laws in Neusner and Chilton, *In Quest of the Historical Pharisees*.

14. Sanders, *Judaism: Practice and Belief 63 BCE–66 CE*, 440–41. Sanders notes this is not particularly unusual; Methodists often have dinners were only Methodists are present. We normally eat with whatever social group we associate with, although not for reasons of purity in most cases.

15. Sanders, *Judaism: Practice and Belief*, 442–43, points out Neusner recognized there is no evidence for a Pharisaic eating ritual ("making a rather big point of it") and he never wrote that Pharisees hated and despised other Jews (as did Jeremias). "[W]here he disagreed with Jeremias, he was completely right."

16. Cited by Sanders, *Judaism: Practice and Belief*, 443.

17. Neusner, *The Rabbinic Traditions about the Pharisees Before 70*, 3:288. Neusner is referring to the post-Hillel for of Judaism.

18. Neusner, *From Politics to Piety: The Emergence of Pharisaic Judaism*; Neusner, "Two Picture of the Pharisees: Philosophical Circle or Eating Club," 525–57.

The Wedding Banquet in the Synoptic Gospels

the earliest strata of the Mishnah, like the Pharisaic rules, "cover almost the entirety of the Bible and a good deal more."[19] The meals at Qumran seem to have gone beyond even the Pharisees. As described in chapter 6, the Qumran community took their communal meals seriously, attempting to eat them in a state of ritual purity normally reserved for priests in the temple. These meals were exclusive, restricted to only qualified members of the community.

Jesus and Open Table Fellowship

Jesus' practice was nothing like that of the Pharisee or Qumran Community. If there is anything that is certain about Jesus' ministry it is that Jesus ate and drank with sinners.[20] This was controversial enough among the Pharisees, but even some of the followers of John the Baptist question this regular practice of Jesus. Wright, for example, considers the fact that Jesus welcomed "sinners" into table-fellowship a "fixed point."[21] Jesus' reputation for feasting with disreputable people is well known in the New Testament. For example, in Matt 11:19 / Luke 7:34, for example, Jesus is described as a "glutton and drunkard" as well as a friend of "tax-collectors and sinners." This description of Jesus is undoubtedly authentic since it is unlikely that such a description would be created by a later Christian community.

This table fellowship is frequently associated with the messianic banquet in New Testament studies. For example, D. Allison states that "the present table fellowship around Jesus is only an anticipation of the coming messianic banquet."[22] So too Dunn, who observes that table fellowship is related to Jesus' use of the "already familiar imagery of the banquet or wedding feast as an image for life in the coming kingdom."[23] W. Lane goes so far as to say that "the basis of table-fellowship was messianic forgiveness, and the meal itself was an anticipation of the messianic banquet."[24] Likewise, J. Nol-

---

19. Sanders, *Judaism: Practice and Belief*, 443. The Pharisees were meticulous in their definition of the law and precise in their obedience to it. The precision of their definition is often attacked as "casuistry," attempts to be precise in a definition so as to avoid the point of the commandment in the first place. But casuistry is not really what the Pharisees (and their rabbinical descendants) intended when they set about precisely defining the law. They were not dishonest and trying to find a way around the law, rather their intent was to keep the law fully in a new situation historically and theologically (the temple is destroyed, how do we sacrifice?). The law can be kept precisely, and everyone is benefitted. The ultimate motive, then, is living a life in closeness to God. The *shema*, recited twice a day is a reminder of what God is and what he has done and the eighteen benedictions emphasize repentance, grace, thanksgiving, election and redemption.

20. Modica, "Jesus as Glutton and Drunkard: The 'Excesses' of Jesus," 50–73; Crossan, *Jesus: A Revolutionary Biography*, 69.

21. Wright, *Jesus and the Victory of God*, 267. Wright points out that the definition of a rebellious son in Deut 21:18–21 is "a drunkard and glutton." This pair of words appears in Prov 23:20–21 and 28:7, defining a "fool." LXX Deut 21:20 has the noun οἰνοφλυγέω; Matt 11:19 has οἰνοπότης.

22. Allison, *The End of the Ages Has Come*, 102.

23. Dunn, *Jesus Remembered*, 601.

24. Lane, *Mark*, 106.

land considers table fellowship in Luke as "potentially an anticipatory experience of this eschatological banquet."[25] M. Bird calls Jesus' table fellowship the "*hors d'oeuvres* of the messianic feast" which foreshadow "exactly who would be vindicated in the renewed Israel he was creating around himself."[26] This consensus opinion is certainly clear in the Gospel of Mark.

Mark highlights Jesus table fellowship with tax-collectors and sinners in a series of conflict stories in chapter 2. This sequence of stories appears in Matthew and Luke with very little variation. The miraculous feeding stories in Mark 6:30–44 and 8:1–10 also appear in each of the synoptic gospels (although Luke only has one feeding story). Mark and Matthew portray Jesus' Galilean ministry as characterized by hosting meals to which everyone is invited. In the central section of Luke (9:51—19:27) inclusion and exclusion in the messianic movement is a major motif. Luke describes Jesus as participating in table fellowship with both sinners and Pharisees. Jesus' table fellowship defies social distinctions. As Crossan observes, the meals are "a microcosm of societal discrimination" which Jesus reverses in his ministry.[27]

The meal described in Mark 2:13–17 (Luke 5:27–32 / Matt 9:9–13) is typical of Jesus' open fellowship. After calling Levi as a disciple, Jesus hosts a meal attended by Levi and other "tax-collectors and sinners." The meal is set ambiguously at "his house." This is likely Levi's home, but Jesus is functioning as the host since he is the one sitting with the guests. The invited guests are there to listen to him during the meal, not Levi. Jesus reclined (κατάκειμαι) for the meal, a word which describes a formal banquet.[28] In the next line, the guests "recline with him" (συνανάκειμαι), another verb which can describe a formal banquet. While the word is used to describe Herod's banquet in Matt 14:9 / Mark 6:22, the word does not necessarily mean that this was a formal Greco-Roman banquet, although some of the elements of a formal banquet may be present.[29] More significant however is the presence of this word in Luke 14:15, a clear reference to an eschatological banquet. At the very least, Jesus is sharing an excellent meal with Levi and the other sinners gathered.

The Pharisees observe this open fellowship and question Jesus' disciples. Likely as not the Pharisees question the disciples because they cannot get to Jesus without coming into contact with impurity. Jesus' response highlights another eschatological

---

25. Nolland, *Luke 9:21—18:34*, 755. Stein contrasts those who consider "God's kingdom is a distant abstraction" with Jesus' teaching of the kingdom as a "present reality brought about by his coming." Stein, *Luke*, 392.

26. Bird, *Are You the One Who is to Come?*, 111.

27. Crossan, *Jesus: A Revolutionary Biography*, 69. Smith describes table fellowship a exemplifying "group identity and solidarity." Smith, "Table Fellowship as a Literary Motif," 633. Cf., Smith, "Table Fellowship and the Historical Jesus," 469–70, for sociological studies of ancient meals.

28. Xenophon, *Anabasis* 6.1.4; *Symp.* 1.14; Plato, *Symp.* 177d.

29. France, *The Gospel of Mark*, 132. France suspects Mark chose this word to highlight the implications of messianic banquet in Jesus' meal. Lane agrees: "[T]he meal itself is an anticipation of the messianic banquet" (Lane, *Mark*, 106).

banquet theme. He has not come to call the righteous, but rather sinners. Since the verb καλέω is common in banquet / wedding contexts, Mann suggests that Jesus is describing himself as the host of a messianic banquet.[30] The next pericope in each of the synoptic gospels is on fasting in the presence of the bridegroom.[31] This saying will be examined below, but it is important to at least observe the connection between Jesus eating with all who respond to his call and his role as the bridegroom. The meal shared with Levi is described as a wedding feast because it is hosted by the bridegroom.

What is the point of Jesus' table fellowship? First, these meals were inclusive of all Jews who responded to his invitation. Certainly the meals are inclusive of all Jews, not restricted to the ritually pure as at Qumran. However, while Jesus' meals were an invitation to sinners, these sinners were still Jewish, albeit on the very fringe of Jewish society. For example, he eats with tax collectors (Levi, Zacchaeus). In the case of Zacchaeus, Jesus says that "Salvation has come to this house, since he is also a son of Abraham." (Luke 19:9). There is no example of Jesus extending table fellowship to Gentiles.[32] This will be an important observation understanding the Wedding parables in Matthew.

Second, in most cases, participation in the meal is an indication of repentance.[33] This is certainly the case in Mark 2:17, a saying which specifically associates repentance with the meal. Zacchaeus is another example of a sinner who repents and then shares table fellowship with Jesus. While it is not a literal meal in the ministry of Jesus, the celebration in the parable of the Prodigal Son is another example of a festive meal celebrating repentance. As I will show below, the parable of the Prodigal Son describes what is happening in Jesus' ministry.

Third, the meals hosted by Jesus are joyous occasions. This is implied by the description of the meal as a wedding feast as well as the contrast to the fasting of the Pharisees. The saying in Matt 11:17–18 / Luke 7:32–33 contrasts the ministry style of Jesus and John. Jesus came celebrating a feast with music and dancing. The return of

30. Mann, *Mark*, 232. The verb καλέω in banquet contexts is covered below with respect to Matt 22:1–14.

31. France comments that the two stories do not necessarily follow one another, but Mark has placed one story on feasting alongside of a story on fasting. France, *Mark*, 136.

32. A few commentaries suggest that "sinners" in Mark 2:16 includes Gentiles and that the story is a creation of the church after the controversy over table fellowship with Gentiles (Gal 2:11–14). This stretches the definition of sinners too far, given that the Pharisees use the description. Certainly Levi is a Jew and the fellow sinners who attend his feast are likely Jewish as well. Gundry, *Mark*, 128. The lack of Gentiles at the meals of Jesus makes it highly unlikely that these stories were creations of a later church. Since one of the earliest controversies of the church was table fellowship with Gentiles (Gal 2, Acts 15) these meals would be ideal opportunities to create a story which spoke to that problem directly, either by including gentiles in Jesus' banquets or by clearly separating from Gentiles during a meal. The fact that Gentiles are not even mentioned in Jesus' table fellowship therefore gives weight to the historicity of these meals.

33. In Luke, however, there are a few meals when Jesus is not the host. In Luke 7:36–50 Jesus shares a Sabbath meal with Simon, a Pharisee who does not seem to be a follower of Jesus. That same is true for the meal shared in Luke 14.

the Prodigal is also celebrated by a joyous feast with plenty of food accompanied by music. In Jer 31 music and dancing accompanies the New Covenant (31:4, 13).

That Jesus should use a joyous meal to call true Israel to repent and return to their God invokes a stream of tradition which begins with Isa 25:6–8 and was developed in Isa 40–55.[34] With Jesus' ministry the end of the exile has come and the eschatological age is dawning. Just as Isaiah called Israel to return to their God and re-travel the wilderness to Zion, Jesus is calling on Israel to repent and join with him in an ongoing feast of celebration.

Summary and Conclusions

From this brief survey of Jesus' practice of table fellowship, it is clear that his ministry was characterized by sharing meals with those he intended to reach. First, Jesus functions as the host of many of these meals. Second, as host, Jesus invites people to participate his banquet. Some of those invited join him, other do not. Those who are gathered for the meal are a mixed group since some are followers, others are not. Third, Jesus' meals are open to all without respect to ritual purity. While Jesus undoubtedly ate with his disciples privately, Jesus' regular practice was to eat with people who were "sinners" but also with those who were more interested in ritual purity, such as Pharisees. Fourth, Jesus intended there to be a connection between his meals and the Kingdom of God. To eat and drink with Jesus was to identify oneself with his ministry of kingdom-initiation, but also to anticipate the kingdom which was coming in the future. In this, Jesus' meals look much like an open-to-all version of the meals closed meals shared in the Qumran community. Fifth, evidently these meals were joyous feasts. That Jesus is called a drunkard and glutton implies that good food and wine was plentiful at these meals. This is in contrast to the somber, silent meals described in 1QS and 1QSa. The metaphor of a wedding feast, in contrast to a funeral fast, is therefore appropriate. Lastly, since the Hebrew Bible described the eschatological age as either inaugurated with a victory banquet or as an on-going time of feasting, Jesus intentionally evokes the stream of tradition described in chapters three and four of this study. But these meals are more than an inauguration of a kingdom, they are a celebration of a new covenant with the house of Israel and a restoration of the marriage of the Lord and his people, evoking the tradition described in chapter 5. The point of table fellowship is therefore to blend the eschatological banquet and marriage motifs to declare to Israel the exile is over and the wedding celebration has begun.

Having described the importance of table-fellowship in the ministry of Jesus in all three synoptic Gospels, I will now turn to specific instances in each gospel which

---

34. This point is made by J. Ernst in the context of Luke 6:21. He states that Luke sees the historical experience of Jesus' table fellowship in the light of the traditions found in Isaiah, citing 25:8 specifically. Ernst, *Das Evangelium nach Lukas*, 218.

The Wedding Banquet in the Synoptic Gospels

describe Jesus as not only eating and drinking, but as presenting himself as a bridegroom or describing the kingdom in terms of a wedding banquet.

Wedding Banquet in Mark

Introduction

As the earliest of the synoptic gospels, Mark contains several potential allusions to the eschatological feast including the main text which describes Jesus as a bridegroom. Since I used this meal shared with Levi and other sinners in the previous section as a model for Jesus' table fellowship in the previous section, I return to it here in order to examine the bridegroom metaphor more closely. Mark also includes two miracles which involve the feeding of large crowds. Since these are often regarded as anticipations of the messianic banquet I will examine these meals as well, although they are not banquets in a formal sense. Since there is a brief hint of a marriage metaphor in Mark 8:38, I will include brief note on Jesus' description of the present age as "adulterous." This section concludes with the Last Supper, a Passover meal during which Jesus refers to eating in the Kingdom of God.

Beginning with Mark is also important because the second Gospel is sometimes described as using a New Exodus motif to present the story of Jesus. R. E. Watts, for example, argues at length that Jesus ministry was "the inauguration of the fulfillment of Isaiah's long awaited New Exodus."[35] Beginning with the introductory citation in Mark 1:1–2, Watts shows that Mark has intentionally blended texts from Isaiah, Malachi and Exodus to show that the "long-awaited coming of Yahweh as King and Warrior has begun"[36] and that Jesus is "to be identified in some way with the personal manifestation of Yahweh's judging presence."[37]

The view that Mark describes Jesus as in some way bringing the long Exile of Israel to an end is likely correct and Watts develops this well in his monograph. But as I have shown in chapter 4 and 5 of this study, a new Exodus implies a new period in the wilderness. Hosea saw a return from the wilderness as a restoration of the marriage covenant between God and Israel. Jeremiah 2–4 describes the marriage of Israel and her God broken, but it will be restored in the future return from Exile. Likewise, Isa 40 calls on Israel to make the way straight in the wilderness as the Lord himself leads the people out of the Exile. But by Isa 54–55 that return is also a restoration of the marriage between Israel and her God. If Mark employed a new Exodus theme to

---

35. Watts, *Isaiah's New Exodus in Mark*, 383. Wright is usually credited with popularizing the view that the Exile did not end with the decree of Cyrus

36. Ibid., 90.

37. Ibid., 135. Hatina appreciates Watts's argument, but cautions that the Exile as a metanarrative "threatens to overshadow whatever narrative might be latent in the gospel itself." Hatina, "Exile," 350.

describe Jesus and the initiation of a Kingdom for Israel, then it is not at all surprising to find other elements of Wilderness and Marriage traditions in the Gospel.

Mark 2:18–22: Jesus as the Bridegroom

In Mark 2:18–22 (Luke 5:34 / Matt 9:14–15) Jesus refers to himself as the bridegroom and his own ministry as a wedding banquet.[38] This saying appears early in all three gospels and indicates the ministry Jesus was different than two other forms of Second Temple Period Judaism, the ministry of John the Baptist and the Pharisees. In 2:13–15 Levi has responded to the call of Jesus and hosts a joyous celebration and meal which includes Jesus, tax collector and sinners. When the Pharisees question Jesus' behavior in eating with sinners and failing to fast as they do, Jesus simply points out that he has not come to call the righteous to repentance, but sinners (2:16–17). The people ask Jesus why he does not fast like the Pharisees or disciple of John, leading to Jesus' claim that the it is inappropriate for the "sons of the bridegroom" to fast while the groom is still with them (2:18–20). The unit ends with a brief analogy concerning new wine (2:21–22).

In this section Jesus describes his table fellowship as a joyous wedding feast. Fasting is associated with mourning, so the natural contrast to a fast of mourning is a wedding feast. Other than the Day of Atonement, the Law does not require fasting. However, Zech 7:5, 8:19 indicates that Israel observed fasts to commemorate the fall of Jerusalem (the tenth of Tebeth) and destruction of the Temple (the ninth of Ab).[39] Jeremiah described this coming destruction as a silencing of joy and mirth of weddings (Jer 7:34, 16:9, 25:10). But when the Lord restores the fortunes of Israel, the joy of the bride and groom will be restored (Jer 33:11).

---

38. This saying is regularly dismissed as a creation of Mark reflecting the situation of the Church in the latter half of the first period. Funk and Hoover, *The Five Gospels*, 47–49. There are three primary reasons for this. First, the text clearly predicts the death of Jesus, and it is assumed that Jesus did not expect to die. Second, the saying appears to be a justification for fasting after the resurrection. When the bridegroom is taken away, then it is appropriate to fast. Third, the use of the metaphor of a bridegroom reflects later Church theology. Christ as the Bridegroom coming for his Bride is indeed found in late first-century texts (Rev 19:6–8). In response, there is no evidence that Jesus did not expect his death other than an a priori dismissal of such predictions. The saying in Mark 2:20 is far from a detailed prediction created by the later Church. Rather, it is vague and does not clearly indicate how the bridegroom will be removed. Second, it is not at all clear why anyone in the later Church would need a justification to fast. By the end of the first century, as *Didache* 8 makes clear, Christians did in fact fast. But there is no justification given for the practice in *Didache* or any early Church writing based on Jesus' words in Mark 2:20. If the saying was created to justify fasting, it seems to have been poorly received. In addition, all evidence for regular Christian fasting comes from the post-apostolic era. Gundry, *Mark*, 133, 137. The third objection is based on a lack of "messiah is the bridegroom" texts in the Second Temple Period. But Jesus is not claiming to be the messiah here, but rather the bridegroom. He is the one inviting people into a joyous feast which celebrates the coming of the kingdom of God at the end of the age. The metaphor of a bridegroom is appropriate in this case, and invokes the marriage metaphor so common on the Hebrew Bible (chapter 5).

39. Lane, *Mark*, 108n57. Hare suggests that the fasting of John the Baptist and the Pharisees ought to be seen in the light of national repentance. Hare, *Mark*, 41.

The Wedding Banquet in the Synoptic Gospels

Using the same metaphor, Jesus says that it is inappropriate to fast and mourn because the bridegroom is still present.[40] Jesus places himself in the role of bridegroom and his disciples are the "friends of the bridegroom." While the groom is present, the appropriate behavior is joy and feasting.[41] It is important to observe here that Jesus is not necessarily equating his role as messiah with the metaphor of bridegroom, as is frequently assumed.[42] He is making a contrast between his ministry and that of John the Baptist.

This saying emphasizes the contrast between Jesus' present ministry and a future time when the bridegroom will be taken from his disciples. This is usually taken as an allegorical hint of the death and resurrection and therefore not something Jesus would have said. The most common way of treating this saying is to assume the early church created the saying as a prediction of the resurrection and a justification for Christian fasting. There are several problems with this view. First, as recent studies of parables have shown, allegorical elements can be included in parables in the Second Temple Period. Rejection of allegory had more to do with the literary sense of the interpreter than a solid understanding of the genre in a Jewish, first-century context. Second, fasting is not a particularly controversial issue in the first few generations of the church. It is unlikely that the early church would create a saying to justify a widely accepted practice. Third, while the image of messiah as bridegroom is indeed unknown in Second Temple Period literature, the idea that a re-gathered Israel will travel through the wilderness to renew her (marriage) covenant with her God is an

---

40. Luke 7:33 contrasts John the Baptist and Jesus. In Luke 7:18 two messengers from John arrive in order to ask Jesus if he is "the one who is to come." Jesus responds by pointing to his messianic signs and the messengers depart. Jesus then addresses the crowd on the topic of John's ministry (7:24–28). Verse 29 is the key for understanding this pericope. After Jesus explains that John is the greatest of this age, but the "least of the Kingdom of God" is greater than John. The tax-collectors rejoice because they had been baptized by John, but the Pharisees and scribes had not been. Here is the familiar contrast between the tax-collector and sinner who has repented and the Pharisee and scribe who has not yet repented.

41. 1 Macc 9:37–39 is one of the few descriptions of a wedding celebration in the Second Temple Period. The procession is described as "tumultuous" (θρόος), a term which includes musical instruments, "tambourines and musicians" (μετὰ τυμπάνων καὶ μουσικῶν). This wedding party was ambushed and the sounds of the wedding turned to mourning, the musicians began to play a funeral dirge (θρῆνος). The cognate verb is used in Matt 11:17 / Luke 7:32, describing the contrast John the Baptist and Jesus.

42. Anderson makes this point, saying that Jesus is merely making a contrast between his disciples (who are feasting) and the disciples of John (who are fasting). H. Anderson, *Mark*, 107. Cranfield suggests that the disciples of John the Baptist are fasting because of the recent death of John. This would explain the contrast between wedding and funeral imagery in the saying without assigning the saying to the later church. Cranfield, *The Gospel According to St. Mark*, 111. But as Gundry comments, this trivializes the issue since the main problem is regular fasts, not an occasional fast in at the time of a death. Gundry, *Mark*, 135. Taylor sees the bridegroom as messianic language, but Jesus only silently implies that he is the messiah. Taylor, *The Gospel According to Mark*, 210. For the view that Jesus is equating the messiah and the bridegroom, see Swete, *The Gospel According to St. Mark*, 44. Commenting on the Lukan version of this saying, Green says that the bridegroom "draws on an eschatological symbol for divine visitation," citing Isa 54:5–6, 62:4–5 and Jer 2:2. Green, *The Gospel of Luke*, 249. See also Ebeling, "Die Fastenfrage (Mark 2.18–22)," 382–96.

important image in the Hebrew Bible. Jesus is not necessarily saying that he is the bridegroom-messiah, but that his ministry is in some way celebrating that renewal of the original relationship between God and his people. Based on chapters 3–5 of this study, if table fellowship is in fact part of Jesus' kingdom initiation, then it is not at all unusual that he would describe that table fellowship as a wedding celebration.[43]

However, if this saying is eschatological, then Jesus is placing himself in the place of the Lord as bridegroom, calling Israel to repentance.[44] H. Riesenfeld argues that the image of Jesus as a bridegroom in Mark 2:20 may very well go back to Jesus himself since the metaphor of a marriage is common in the Hebrew Bible (citing Ps 45, Hos 2 and Ezek 16).[45] Riesenfeld's topic is the use of allegory in the Parables, specifically the parable of the Ten Virgins (Matt 25:1–14). Like many other writers in the late twentieth century, Riesenfeld is reacting against the idea that parables do not have any allegorical context at all. Jeremias, for example, rejected the authenticity of Mark 2:20 because the bridegroom is an allegory of Jesus.[46] Since he assumed that Jesus did not use allegory he denied the saying could come from a historical Jesus. Riesenfeld points out that in Mark 2:1–12 Jesus forgave sin, which only God can do. In Mark 2:20 he applies a metaphor from the Hebrew Bible which is associated with God to himself to explain his ministry of table fellowship.[47] The implicit claim to be the bridegroom from the Hebrew Bible is therefore part of the description of who Jesus is in the greater context of Mark's gospel.[48]

Mark 2:21–22 forms a conclusion to the larger unit of 2:13–22. While there is no grammatical reason to see a break between verse 20 and 21, scholars rarely relate the bridegroom saying and the new wine saying.[49] Gundry, on the other hand, describes Jesus as using three metaphors to reply to the question of fasting, a wedding, a cloth, and new wine.[50] In fact, the metaphor of a wedding is extended to proper clothing for the wedding and abundant wine. It is inappropriate for a person to patch clothing or

---

43. Although the *Gospel of Thomas* post-dates Mark, it is worth observing that Logion 104 also makes a reference to a bridegroom in the context of fasting. "They said to [Jesus] 'Come, let us pray and fast today!' Jesus said: 'What sin is it that I have committed, or wherein have I been overcome? But when the bridegroom comes out of the wedding chamber, then let (us) fast and pray'" (Bethge, *Evangelium Thomae Copticum*, 543).

44. Swete thought Jesus is alluding to Hosea. Swete, *Gospel According to St. Mark*, 44. Mann also hears echoes of Hosea, Isa 54:4, 62:4 and Ezek 16. Mann is not sure, however, if Jesus is explicitly proclaiming himself to be the Messiah. Mann, *Mark*, 233.

45. Riesenfeld, *The Gospel Tradition*, 153. Cf. Dunkerley, "The Bridegroom Passage," 303–4.

46. Jeremias, "νύμφη," 4:1101.

47. Riesenfeld, *The Gospel Tradition*, 153–54.

48. Trocmé misses this point because he the only this saying is either a metaphor or an allegory. By looking at the statement as intertextually drawing on the marriage metaphor, there is no need for a "messiah 'bridegroom'" allegory. Trocmé, *L'évangile Selon Saint Marc*, 76.

49. For example, Taylor, *The Gospel According to Saint Mark*, 212.

50. Gundry, *Mark*, 131; cf. Funk and Hoover, *The Five Gospels*, 49.

store wine in these ways, the result will ruin the clothing or wine-skin. Likewise, one who mourns at a wedding celebration ruins the celebration.[51]

The saying in v. 21–22 is has often been taken to mean that Christianity is superior to Judaism and will replace it.[52] This supersessionist reading is not at all what Jesus is saying in his use of this metaphor. First, the contrast is not necessarily between Jesus and the Pharisees. The disciples of John the Baptist are also questioning Jesus on fasting. The point of the metaphor is not replacement of old things with new, but rather appropriate behavior when the bridegroom is present.[53] Second, the image of new wine is suggested by the context of a feast at the beginning of a new age. When Hosea describes the restoration of the marriage of Israel, the wife is given vineyards (2:16–17 [ET14–15]) and the Lord will cause the earth to produce grain and תִּירוֹשׁ, "new wine." New wine is associated with the eschatological age in Joel 2:24 and is the wine served in the messianic banquet in 1QSa. In chapter 6 I suggested that תִּירוֹשׁ was used in 1QSa because this is the wine set aside for the priests in the first fruits offering.[54]

In summary, in the bridegroom saying in Mark 2:19 Jesus describes his practice of open fellowship as like a wedding banquet which he hosts as the bridegroom. His emphasis on the joy of feasting in contrast to gloom of fasting stands on the foundation of the New Covenant (Jer 33:11). The people participating in this joyous meal are celebrating the restoration of Israel's marriage at the end of the Exile.

Mark 6:31–44: The Feeding of Multitudes[55]

The feeding of the 5000 is a symbolic miracle in which Jesus departs to a lonely place and provides a crowd with miraculous food in the wilderness (cf. Matt 14:13–21 / Luke 9:12–17). Everyone eats until they are satisfied and there is a great quantity which remains.[56] As early as A. Schweitzer, this event has been seen as an anticipation of the

---

51. *GThomas* 47 has a similar saying, although the point is that new wine ought to go into new wineskins, old wine into old wineskins.

52. Jeremias, *Parables*, 117–18. So too Hurtado, who sees the metaphors as pointing out how "inappropriate the beliefs and practice of the past are not when the kingdom of God is already approaching." Hurtado, *Mark*, 46. To a lesser extent, Allison sees this saying as a clear indication that "Jesus was conscious of a changing in the times." Allison, "Jesus and the Covenant," 71. Edwards agrees with Drury that these two parables refer to the relationship "of Jesus, of Christianity indeed, with traditional Judaism." Edwards, *Mark*, 92.

53. Gundry, *Mark*, 138.

54. Brooke argued that Jesus was arguing against the practice of the Qumran community in 11Q19 (Temple) 19:11–21. Certainly the scroll mentions new wine (19.14, יין חדש) but it is in the context of the first-fruits celebration rather than a wedding celebration. Brooke, "The Feast of New Wine and the Question of Fasting," 175–76.

55. The feeding of the 4000 appears in Mark 8:1–10 and Matt 15:32–39. This miracle is less an allusion to the eschatological banquet that first feeding, likely because it is a miracle outside of Galilee.

56. The Gospel of John records several details which may explain the story as it appears in Mark and Matthew. For example, John 6:15 says that the crowd sought to make Jesus king, hinting at that the crowd in Galilee understood Jesus in a political sense. Dunn, *Jesus Remembered*, 646, France,

eschatological feast.⁵⁷ Many commentators see this miracle is an anticipation of the messianic banquet. France, for example, says that "for those with eyes to see it, this will be a foretaste of the messianic banquet."⁵⁸ Similarly, Dunn says that a shared meal in a desolate place "would probably carry strong messianic overtones to those with even half an ear."⁵⁹ Davies and Allison see an allusion to Jesus as a new Moses, who leads the people into the wilderness where God provides them with food.⁶⁰

Gundry, on the other hand, points out that the disciples do not eat in this pericope; therefore it cannot be an anticipation of either a Eucharist meal or the messianic banquet.⁶¹ The disciples simply do not share food with Jesus or the crowds. In fact, Gundry sees the presence of fish in the story sufficient reason to reject an allusion to the Last Supper and Elisha's miracle (2 Kgs 4:42–44)⁶² and the lack of wine indicates that this cannot be the messianic banquet.⁶³ The force of this objection is limited since the focus in the story is not on the disciples eating with Jesus, but on the crowd's participation in the meal. In fact, there is nothing in the pericope which states the disciples did not share in the meal.

While Gundry's observations are important, there seem to be a number of elements of banquet in this miraculous feeding that make it likely that Mark (and Matthew) intended this event to be seen as an anticipation of the messianic banquet. In fact, the miracle is an example of an intertextual blending of Wilderness tradition and eschatological banquet texts.

Mark, 261.

57. Schweitzer thought that the "messianic feast therefore played a dominant part in the conception of blessedness from Enoch to the Apocalypse of John." Schweitzer, *Quest for the Historical Jesus*, 377. An early proponent of Mark 6:31–44 as a messianic meal was Stauffer. He was among first to use 1QSa 2:11–22 to illustrate the messianic banquet idea in this miracle story. Stauffer, "Zum apokalyptischen Festmahl in Mc 6:34ff," 264–66.

58. France, *Mark*, 260. France also thinks there may be hints of the Last Supper as well, but since Mark 14:15 is also a foreshadowing of the messianic banquet, it is difficult to separate the two meals. France, *Mark*, 262.

59. Dunn, *Jesus Remembered*, 646. Dunn suggests parallels to both Israel's wilderness wandering and the communal meals at Qumran. See also O'Neill, "The Silence of Jesus," 153–67. Twelftree believes that Matthew is more intentional in presenting the feeding of the 5000 as a messianic banquet, although his arguments are equally valid for Mark. Twelftree, *Jesus the Miracle Worker*, 129. Mann sees this miracle as an anticipation of the messianic feast "looking ahead to the future consummation of the reign of God." Mann, *Mark*, 300.

60. Davies and Allison, *Matthew*, 2:482. They draw attention to the *Sipre* on Numbers 11:22 which indicates that Israel ate fish in the wilderness, cf. Wisd 19:12, the quail "came up from the sea."

61. Gundry, *Mark*, 328. Much of the secondary literature on this miracle deals with the possibility that Jesus is anticipating the Last Supper while little attention is paid to the details which point to an allusion to the eschatological banquet.

62. Gundry, *Mark*, 330.

63. Gundry, *Mark*, 331. While συμπόσιον (Mark 6:39) can mean "drinking party," that cannot be the meaning in Mark 6. See Masuda, "The Good News of the Miracle of the Bread: The Tradition and its Markan Redaction," 195.

The Wedding Banquet in the Synoptic Gospels

First, the miracle enacts the expectations of Isa 40–55, that Israel would re-gather in the wilderness and re-experience the wilderness events, including the provision of food at the hand of their God. The event occurs in the wilderness or a "lonely place." Mauser thought this was a reference to wilderness tradition[64] but Gundry rejects the allusion because the phrase ἔρημον τόπον does not appear in the LXX with reference to the Wilderness period.[65] I would point out that an allusion to the wilderness tradition does not rely solely on the use of the term ἔρημος. It is the fact that the people are being fed in the wilderness that calls to mind the Wilderness tradition. Wright, for example, correctly points out that not only is the location of this even significant, but also the fact that the people are fed in the wilderness and immediately after the feeding the Lord works a great miracle at the Red Sea, just as Jesus will do a great miracle on the sea.[66]

There are other allusions to Wilderness tradition here. When Jesus sees the great crowd he is move with compassion and observes that they are "like sheep without a shepherd." This is an allusion to Num 27:15–23.[67] Just prior to Moses death, he asks the Lord to appoint a leader over the people, so that they will not be like sheep without a shepherd. Moses calls Israel the congregation of the Lord (ἡ συναγωγὴ κυρίου). The people "recline" (ἀνακλίνω) on the green grass. While this word is used for reclining at a banquet (Luke 12:37), the word used in Matt 9:11 / Luke 13:29 specifically for the eschatological banquet. They are seated in συμπόσιον, "eating parties." The word can refer to "drinking parties," although there is nothing in this miracle which indicates wine was served with the meal. The groupings are in of fifty and a hundred evokes the wilderness tradition as well. In Exod 18:21, 25 Moses divides the people up into groups of "thousands, hundreds, fifties and tens."[68] Like Hosea, these allusions look back to the beginning of the relationship of God and Israel in the wilderness.

Second, after the crowd eats the food, they are described as satisfied, (Mark 6:42). Eating bread in the wilderness naturally recalls, manna, although only the gospel of John makes this allusion explicit.[69] The verb χορτάζω (to "be satisfied"), however, appears in the Psalms several times in clear wilderness tradition. In LXX Ps 80:17 [ET 16] the word is used to describe the food provided in the wilderness (honey from the rock). In Ps 106:9, the psalmist describes the satisfaction of the people when the Lord fed them in the wilderness at the end of the exile. This Psalm begins with a gathering of the people after the exile from every direction. Some have passed through the wilderness yet the Lord led them on a straight path back to the Land where he "satisfies their

---

64. Mauser, *Christ in The Wilderness*, 104–5.

65. Gundry, *Mark*, 328. The phrase only appears in LXX Jer 13:24 (Cod. A), 40:12 (not in Cod. A) and Dan 4:25.

66. Wright, *Jesus and the Victory of God*, 193.

67. Gundry, *Mark*, 323.

68. Compare to Num, 31:14, 1QSa 1:14–15, 27–22:1, 1QM 4:1—5:16, CD 13:1. Trocmé rejects this parallel on the basis that there is no Mark does not include thousands and tens of thousands, or clan chiefs in his description. Trocmé, *L'évangile Selon Saint Marc*, 183.

69. Chapman, *The Orphan Gospel: Mark's Perspective on Jesus*, 55–67.

soul." In Ps 131:15 χορτάζω appears in the context of the restoration of Zion. Zion is personified as a woman who will have abundant provisions, her poor "will be satisfied with bread." The word also appears in a marriage metaphor context in Jer 5:7. While the Lord has fed his people completely (χορτάζω), they have committed adultery. It is significant that this word appears in LXX Jer 38:14 [ET 31:14], a text described earlier in this study as combining Wilderness tradition and eschatological banquet motifs as well as the marriage metaphor (31:32).[70] In addition, the verb ἐμπίπλημι, a close synonym for χορτάζω, is used in the Johannine version of the feeding miracle (John 6:12). In Luke 6:21 and 25 the two verbs are used in parallel to describe those who will be satisfied with food in the Kingdom of God. This verb is also associated with the wilderness tradition,[71] and there are a number of places in the LXX where this word describes the abundance of the eschatological age.[72] The reverse appears in Hos 4:10, which describes Israel as eating and not being satisfied as a result of her adultery.[73]

Third, the placement of the miracle is significant as well. In the Gospel of Mark, the feeding follows immediately after the mission of the Twelve (Mark 6:7–13, 30). It is likely this preaching which generates the huge crowd in 6:31–33. This miracle then is a symbolic action in which Jesus hosts a meal in the wilderness, declaring that he is in fact the new Moses, the eschatological shepherd, or messiah. This conclusion is confirmed by a series of miracles in the following chapters concluding with Peter's confession of Jesus as the Messiah (8:27–29). At that point, Jesus begins to predict his crucifixion in Jerusalem (8:31–34, 9:30–32, 10:32–34). Following the first prediction is the story of the Transfiguration (9:28–36). Whatever this story means, it is certainly the climax of a sequence of events which are all associated with the revelation of the Kingdom of God. This sequence is repeated in each of the synoptic gospels with little variation. Mark has designed his gospel to slowly reveal who Jesus is, with the climax in Peter's confession and the Transfiguration. The meal in the wilderness is a key component of that design.

In the gospel of Matthew the feeding miracle functions similarly. After observing Jesus for some time, the Pharisees finally conclude that Jesus is not the messiah and declare that he casts out demons by the power of Beelzebub (12:22–32). Jesus refuses to show the Pharisees a sign (12:38–42), leading to Jesus' declaration that his family are those who do his will. In fact, the "new family" of Jesus more or less frames the parables in chapter 13 (12:46–50, 13:53–58). Immediately after this break with the

---

70. For Jer 31:14 and the wilderness tradition, see chapter 4. For Jer 31:32 as marriage metaphor, see chapter 5.

71. Translating שבע with χορτάζω, Deut 31:20, Ps 103:5, 105:40 107:9.

72. Isaiah 33:5, 58:10–11, 65:20, 66:11, LXX Jer 26:10 [ET 46:10]; LXX 38:14, 25, 31:14, 25; Ezek 39:20. Ezekiel 32:4–6 also describes an eschatological banquet, but in this feast the birds of the air engorge themselves on the flesh and blood of the enemies of Israel.

73. ἐμπίπλημι also appears in Ruth 2:13, translating שבע. In the Talmud Ruth's meal is taken as a reference to the messianic banquet: "In a Tannaite statement it was repeated: '"she ate"—in this world; "and had enough"—in the days of the Messiah. "And some left over"—in the age to come'" (*b. Shabb.* 113b).

Pharisees, Jesus begins to teach in parables in order to explain the "mysteries of the kingdom of Heaven" (13:1–50). The parables in chapter 13 have a strong apocalyptic undertones, including a great separation at future fiery judgment (13:48–50 especially). Perhaps more important for the feeding miracle, there are two short parables which describe the kingdom as something small, yet it grows in order to provide for many. After these parables, Matthew picks up the sequence of events from Mark, beginning with the death of John through the confession of Peter. Matthew has therefore placed the miraculous feeding after the parables of growth in order to highlight the "mystery of the kingdom" at work in the miracle of Jesus.

In conclusion, the miraculous feeding in the wilderness is in fact an allusion to the tradition of an eschatological banquet, despite Gundry's protests. In all four Gospels Jesus reveals his messianic intentions by hosting a meal in wilderness for a "new Israel." In each of the Synoptic Gospels the miraculous feeding is an important piece of evidence which brings Peter to his confession that Jesus is the Messiah. This presentation is a blending Wilderness tradition with messianic banquet motifs to reveal Jesus as the Messiah. While the event itself lacks a marriage component, the blending of two of the three motifs in this miracle indicates that the earliest traditions saw Jesus hosting a messianic banquet in the wilderness.

Mark 8:38: An Adulterous Generation

An overlooked use of the marriage metaphor is Jesus' description of his generation as "adulterous" in Mark 8:38.[74] The noun μοιχαλίς is used texts which employ the marriage metaphor to describe Israel's relationship with God (Hos 3:1, Ezek 16:38, 23:45). LXX Jer 3:8 uses the verb μοιχάω to describe Judah's unfaithfulness.[75] The context of the phrase in Mark's gospel is important. The confession of Peter in Mark 8:27–30 is the climax of the first half of the gospel. In the first eight chapters Mark slowly reveals who Jesus is, until Peter finally expresses his belief that Jesus is the Messiah. After this, Jesus "begins to teach" his disciples that the Son of Man must suffer, be rejected, die, and rise again (8:31). Peter expresses confusion over this and Jesus rebukes him for not fully understanding the mission of the Messiah (8:32–33). After this, Jesus calls the crowd and tells them that it is now time to decide if they are going to follow him to Jerusalem or be ashamed of him (8:34–37). Jesus says that this adulterous generation will fall under judgment when "the Son of Man comes in the glory of his father with the holy angels." The context is both messianic and apocalyptic. It seems clear that Jesus alludes to Dan 7:13–14, even if the wording is not quite the same.[76]

---

74. A few commentaries notice an allusion to Hosea or Jeremiah. See Brooks, *Mark*, 183; France, *Mark*, 342; Mann, *Mark*, 350.

75. LXX Jeremiah 36:23 (ET 29:33).

76. Dan 7:13 has an aorist subjunctive of ἔρχομαι, the LXX has imperfect, Theodotion has a participle. The title "Son of Man" in Mark 8:38 is articular, in Dan 7:13 it is not. For Dan 7:13 as an

Only Mark includes the phrase "this adulterous generation" at this point in the narrative, although a similar phrase occurs in twice in Matthew (12:39, 16:4, cf. Luke 11:29).[77] In both cases Matthew has γενεὰ πονηρὰ καὶ μοιχαλίς, substituting πονηρὰ for Mark's ἁμαρτωλός. Luke 12:29 drops μοιχαλίς, retaining only "an evil generation." In it possible that Matthew shaped the saying after LXX Isa 57:3 since both words appear there, but the order is reversed and σπέρμα is used rather than γενεὰ.

To describe the nation as a wicked generation is an allusion to the wilderness period (Deut 1:35, 32:5, *Jub.* 23:14).[78] But to also describe a generation as "adulterous" evokes the traditional marriage metaphor from the Hebrew Bible, especially the book of Hosea. But as we have seen, there is significant overlap of those two streams of tradition already in the Hebrew Bible. Since Jesus has already described himself as the bridegroom in Mark 2:18, this declaration that the nation is still in a state of adultery is a condemnation on those who have already rejected Jesus. They are in the same adulterous spiritual state as the kingdom of Israel in Hosea.

The Last Supper (Mark 14:17–25)

While it is undoubted Jesus often ate with his disciples, the only meal in the Synoptic gospels shared with only his disciples is the Last Supper.[79] This Passover meal is shared with his closest disciples just prior to his arrest and crucifixion. Since this is a Passover meal the Exodus events are automatically highlighted. The group is "reclining" and eating. While ἀνάκειμαι is used to describe any meal, it is the verb used in Mark 6:26 for those who share in the miraculous feeding as well as Matt 22:10 for the guests at the wedding banquet.[80]

In Mark 14:25 Jesus states that he will not drink again from the fruit of the vine until he drinks it anew in the Kingdom of God. Since the emphasis is on drinking wine when the kingdom comes, this should be taken as an allusion to an eschatological banquet which celebrates the final victory.[81] C. Blomberg states that the Last Supper was a "foreshadowing of the messianic banquet" and connects the event to Isa 25:6–9.[82]

---

influence on Jesus, see Dunn, *Jesus Remembered*, 747–54.

77. Similar phrases appear in Matt 17:17 / Luke 9:41, a "faithless generation" and Matt 12:45, an "evil generation." In Acts 2:40 Peter uses the phrase "crooked generation," cf. Phil 2:15. James 4:4 refers to his readers as "adulterous" (μοιχαλίδες). *ApocSed* 6:4 uses the noun to describe Adam's rebellion.

78. Davies and Allison, *Matthew*, 2:354.

79. The literature on the Last Supper is vast. For a lengthy bibliography, see Beasley-Murray, *Jesus and the Kingdom*, 258–73; Evans, *Mark 8:27—16:20*, 379–85. Much of this secondary literature concerns the details of the meal, the type of meal, and the historicity of the words of Jesus.

80. The verb appears in Matthew's version of Levi's banquet (Matt 9:10), Mark has the cognate συνανάκειμαι.

81. Gundry, *Mark*, 834.

82. Blomberg, *Contagious Holiness*, 29. Dunn includes the Last Supper in his section on "heavenly banquet." Dunn, *Jesus Remembered*, 427. Taylor sees the meal as eschatological and describes verse 25 as an allusion to the messianic banquet: Jesus' "messianic consciousness is manifest." *Mark*,

The Wedding Banquet in the Synoptic Gospels

Similarly, Allison says "Jesus announces that he will feast at the messianic banquet."[83] But what is there in this saying which implies a connection to the eschatological feast I described earlier in chapter 3?

First, the description of the meal is laced with allusions to the sorts of texts surveyed in the previous chapters. For example, Gundry suggests that Jesus is blending Exod 24:8, Isa 53:12, and Jer 31:31.[84] The "blood of the covenant" in Exod 24:8 is followed by a meal on Sinai in which Moses, Aaron and the seventy elders eat and drink before God. This meal at the establishment of the first covenant is the foundation on which the meal at the establishment of the new Covenant is built in Isa 25:6–8. As I have already observed, rather than a meal restricted to only the leaders of Israel at Sinai, the eschatological banquet includes all people at Zion.

Second, Jesus clearly alludes to the new covenant text (Jer 31:33). Jeremiah 31 combines both an eschatological meal and a marriage metaphor to describe the restoration of Israel's relationship with her God at the end of the Exile. That a covenant was ratified with the blood of a sacrifice is commonplace in the Hebrew Bible, but of primary importance is the sacrifice which accompanied the first covenant in Exod 24:8.

Third, Evans suggests that the broken piece of bread which Jesus distributes is the *afikoman* (ἀφικόμενος, אפיקומן). At the beginning of the Seder, a small portion of bread is broken off, to be consumed at the end of the meal. The bread represented the whole of the Jewish people and the broken portion represented "what the Messiah will eat when he returns to celebrate with Israel."[85] If the breaking of the bread does reflect the *afikoman* tradition, then it explains how Jesus could say that bread somehow represented him and his body.[86] The bread already represented something, the Messiah. Jesus is making a claim that he is in fact the Messiah when he breaks the bread. This is how the disciples understood breaking of bread in Luke 24 as well.[87] If the breaking of bread was a messianic self-revelation then it would be strong evidence in favor of the Last Supper as a messianic banquet. Unfortunately there is no solid evidence that this traditional use

---

547. Mann describes the section as "thoroughly Jewish" and contains an allusion to the messianic banquet (Isa 25:6–8). Mann, *Mark*, 580.

83. Allison, *The End of the Ages*, 138. Gundry thinks that this saying is a prediction that Jesus will return to "transform the Passover meal into the messianic banquet." Gundry, *Mark*, 843. Cf. Higgins: "Jesus looked forward and would have his disciples took forward to the greater banquet of the Kingdom of God, when all the Passover promises of eschatological joy, of redemption, and of the glorious Messianic age should be fulfilled" (Higgins, *The Lord's Supper in the New Testament*, 48).

84. Gundry, *Mark,* 843; cf. Evans, *Mark 8:27—16:20*, 393; Taylor, *Mark*, 545–47.

85. Evans, *Mark 8:27—16:20*, 390. Evans is following Daube, *He That Cometh*; Carmichael, "David Daube on the Eucharist and the Passover Seder," 45–67. The earliest suggestion that Jesus was referring to the *afiko* is Eisler, "Das Letzte Abendmahl," 161–92. Carmichael finds additional support for this understanding of the bread in Melito of Sardis, a second-century writer who creates a "Christian Haggadah." Melito uses the term ἀφικόμενος twice with reference to Jesus as the coming Messiah.

86. Carmichael, "David Daube on the Eucharist," 55.

87. Ibid., 56.

of the bread was current in the first century, so Evans suggestion may not be helpful in showing that the bread is an allusion to messianic themes.

Fourth, the messianic banquet text in 1QSa sheds some light on the Last Supper as an anticipation of the eschatological meal. As I argued in chapter 6, 1QSa was initially thought to describe a Eucharist-like meal, although this has been (rightly) abandoned for the most part in recent scholarship. However, there are still remarkable comparisons and contrasts between the two meals. The participants in the meal in 1QSa are seated according to their rank, with the Messiah of Israel at their head. After the Messiah blesses the food, they drink new wine and eat the first-fruits of the bread. At the last supper Jesus eats with his twelve disciples, a number invoking the twelve tribes of a reconstituted Israel. Jesus indeed blesses the bread and wine, although there is no reference to sharing these among the participants at Qumran. The meal at Qumran was to celebrate the coming of the Messiah, so also here in the Last Supper. Jesus declares to his disciples that the New Covenant in imminent and that he will not drink wine again until he drinks it "new" in the Kingdom of God. Like the Qumran community, Jesus' celebration of Passover is an anticipation of the coming eschatological age.

In summary, the Last Supper is an anticipation of the messianic banquet. As such, it is an intertextual blending of several traditions beginning with the covenant meal in Exod 24 and the restoration of the marriage of Israel and her God in Jer 31. Because discussion of the Last Supper is usually laden with theological questions about later Christian practice, the Jewish eschatological implications can be overlooked. Jesus finally reveals himself as the one who will initiate the New Covenant and restore Israel to her rightful place.

Summary and Conclusions

Mark describes Jesus as hosting meals at three important points in his ministry. At the beginning of his public ministry he hosts a meal at the home of Levi, eating and drinking with sinners. Jesus describes this joyous celebration as a wedding and himself the bridegroom. At the midpoint of the Gospel of Mark Jesus hosts a meal in the wilderness in which a huge crowd shares bread and fish miraculously provided. This meal evokes the wilderness tradition, but also eschatological banquet texts. Finally, Jesus hosts a final meal Passover meal just before his crucifixion during which he refers to eating in the coming Kingdom of God. All three synoptic Gospels include these events with very little variation. While Mark refers to Jesus as a bridegroom in 2:19–20, the marriage metaphor is less important in the Gospel of Mark than in Matthew. There are several theological and pastoral emphases in Mark's use of these traditions.

First, Mark presents Jesus as hosting meals as a regular part of his ministry. This table fellowship was open to all without regard to social standing or ritual purity. In doing so he confused the disciples of John and angered the Pharisees. Yet this part of his ministry was so important that he develops a reputation as a "drunkard and glutton." Perhaps this is the most pastoral element of Mark's banquet theme. Just as Jesus was inclusive, so too the Church of Mark's day should welcome those on the fringes of society.[88]

Second, the feeding of the 5000 in the wilderness evokes the wilderness tradition. Jesus is calling Israel back to her beginnings in the wilderness, the place where her relationship with God began. This is consistent with the wilderness tradition in Isa 40–55 as well as the book of Hosea described in chapter 4. If the first wilderness period was the honeymoon, the second was like a divorce. Second Isaiah declared that the exile was over and the marriage restored. Jesus too declares that the time in the wilderness is over and the time of renewal is present.

Third, there is certainly an eschatological element to the banquet metaphor in Mark's gospel. Jesus' words at the Last Supper are built on Jer 31, a text shown in chapter 5 to use the wilderness tradition, the eschatological banquet, and the marriage metaphor. Jesus takes this well-known text and applies to what he is about to do in the crucifixion and resurrection.

Mark's gospel therefore demonstrates the value of the intertextual method proposed in chapter 2. By hearing the echo of earlier traditions (such as banquet, wilderness, marriage traditions), the interpreter can use the Hebrew Bible to illuminate the later text. As a creative author, Mark blends three strands of tradition to describe Jesus' practice of eating with outsiders as well as with his inner circle. For Mark, Jesus' practice of table fellowship is a demonstration of how Jesus saw himself and his mission. Jesus is the host of the eschatological banquet at the inauguration of the New Covenant. This blending of traditions becomes the foundation for development in both the gospels of Matthew and Luke.

Wedding Banquet in Matthew

Introduction

Matthew takes up several of the banquet themes found in Mark's gospel and develops them by emphasizing the marriage metaphor. He retains Mark's bridegroom saying but develops it in a pair of wedding parables. As J. M. Ford observes, "all three evangelists refer to Christ as the bridegroom but it is St. Matthew who appears to bring this theme to a climax."[89] The wilderness tradition is less important, although Matthew includes the feeding of the five thousand. I will first discuss the saying in Matt 8:11 / Luke 13:30 which describes an eschatological feast since it seems reasonably clear that Matthew intended this saying to be understood in the same context as the two parables.

---

88. If the traditional view of Mark's gospel as the preaching of Peter has any merit, it may not be coincidental that Peter is described as reaching out to the fringes of Judaism in Acts 9–12 (Tabitha, Aeneas, Simon the Tanner, and Cornelius the God-Fearer). He is continuing the type of table fellowship he shared during the ministry of Jesus.

89. Ford, "The Parable of the Foolish Scholars," 121.

Jesus the Bridegroom

Matthew 8:11: Many from the East and West

This brief logion states that "Many will come from the east and west to recline at the table with Abraham, Isaac and Jacob in the kingdom of heaven." The verb ἀνακλίνω appears here to describe a banquet or feast at the beginning of the eschatological age not unlike Isa 25:6–8.[90] It appears that Abraham is the host of this banquet, although it is possible the messiah hosts the banquet which Abraham and the patriarchs also attend. In the literature of the Second Temple Period, Abraham appears in an eschatological context several times.[91] It therefore seems likely that Jesus has in mind an eschatological feast in Matt 8:11. The fate of those not included in the feast in 8:11 is identical to the man cast out of the wedding banquet in Matt 22:13 and similar to the virgins who are not admitted to the wedding feast in 25:12.

The context of the saying in Matthew is important. The saying is embedded in a story concerning a Gentile who expresses greater faith than anyone in Israel (8:10). This act of faith prompts Jesus to compare the "many from the east and west" who will participate in the eschatological feast with those "sons of the kingdom" are cast outside of the banquet. Those who do not participate in the banquet are "outside, where there is weeping and gnashing of teeth."[92] This saying is part of a series of miracle stories following the Sermon on the Mount in which Jesus encounters outcasts from mainstream Judaism. After the people declare that Jesus is not like any teacher they have ever heard before, Jesus first encounters a leper (8:1–4) and then a Gentile (8:5–10). Both of these men express remarkable faith in Jesus and receive healing as a result. The third story concerns the healing of Peter's mother-in-law from a fever (8:14–16). The verb πυρέσσω and the cognate verb πυρετός are rare in the New Testament and the only the verb appears in the LXX. In Deut 28:22 it translates the Hebrew noun קַדַּחַת as a part of the curse of the Law (Lev 26:16). These first three miracles, therefore, concern people who would be excluded from worship at the temple and would certainly not be the sort of people expected to express faith in a Jewish teacher like Jesus.

It is clear that Jesus is making a contrast between the "sons of the kingdom" who will not participate in the eschatological feast and those who will. The ones who do recline at the table with Abraham are "many from the east and the west." The identity of those who enter is a matter of discussion in recent scholarship. Since Jeremias, the majority opinion is that the included "many" are believing Gentiles and that the

---

90. Nolland, *The Gospel of Matthew*, 357n44.

91. Abraham is the subject of revelatory visions in *The Testament of Abraham*, and *The Apocalypse of Abraham*. Both *2 Baruch* 4:3–5 and *4 Ezra* 3:13–15 describe Abraham as a prophetic figure to whom a vision of the heavenly Jerusalem was given. In *Pseudo-Philo* 18:5 the Lord says that he has revealed everything he does to Abraham. Benedikt, "Den apokalyptiske Abraham: patriarken i den antikke jødiske litteratur," 2–13.

92. This phrase appears in Matt 22:13 to describe the man who is expelled from the wedding banquet as well as Matt 13:42, 50, once again indicating the fate of those who are outside of the kingdom of God. The other two occurrences in Matthew are 24:51 and 25:30. Both passages describe eschatological separation.

excluded "sons of the kingdom" are unbelieving Jews.[93] Jeremias gives five features of Jesus' view of the eschatological pilgrimage of the Gentiles.[94] First, God reveals himself to all humanity (Isa 2:2; 40:5). Second, God calls everyone to Zion (Isa 45:20–22). Third, the journey of the Gentiles to Zion, from Egypt and Assyria (Isa 2:3, 19:23). Fourth, the nations will worship at the "world-sanctuary" (Isa 56:7, 66:18). Last of all is the messianic banquet on the world-mountain (Isa 25:6–8). Matthew 8:11 is, for Jeremias, an interpretation of Mal 1:11 highlighting the in-gathering of the Gentiles.[95]

D. Allison challenged this consensus opinion by arguing that the "many from the east and the west" are Jews from the Diaspora rather than Gentiles replacing Jews at the eschatological feast.[96] Allison points out that there is no text in the Hebrew Bible or the Second Temple Period which describes Gentiles as coming from the east and west.[97] Isaiah 59:19 describes a pilgrimage from the east and west when the Redeemer comes to Zion for those in Jacob who have turned from transgression. Psalm 107:3 describes Israel coming from the east, west, north and south. Philo (*Spec. Leg.* 1.69) uses this language ("from the east and west") to describe the return of Diaspora Jews from Alexandria and Babylon to Jerusalem for festival days.[98] *Psalms of Solomon* 11 combines the gathering of the children of Zion (*PsSol* 11:2, cf. Isa 54:1–4) with the voice of one bringing good news to Zion (*PsSol* 11:1–2, Isa 52:7). The Zion is to clothe herself with garments of glory (*PsSol* 11:7, cf. Isa 52:1) because the way through the wilderness has been prepared by leveling the path and turning the desert into paradise (*PsSol* 11:4–5, cf. Isa 40:4, 41:17–18). This pilgrimage only concerns Jews scattered throughout the world as they return to Zion and Jerusalem.

Allison also states that even if there is an allusion to an eschatological pilgrimage of the nations to Zion, it cannot be assumed that the original hearers would have thought

---

93. Jeremias, *Jesus' Promise to the Nations*, 51. Jeremias takes πολλοί as referring to Gentiles based on the contrast with "sons of the kingdom."

94. Ibid., 57–60.

95. Ibid., 62. Jeremias contrasts his view of Jesus' thinking with the rabbinic interpretation of Mal 1:11 as a reference to the Torah and evening prayers. He recognizes that Isa 25:6–8 was read as judgment for the nations in the rabbinic literature, but Jesus reversed this interpretation in Matt 8:11 to Gentile salvation. Aside from the fact that the rabbinic sources cited by Jeremias are much later than the first century, it seems anachronistic to think that Jesus interpreted Mal 1:11 and Isa 25:6–8 in a way which anticipated a Gentile church.

96. Allison, "Who Will Come from East and West?," 158–70. Much of this material is summarized in Davies and Allison, *Matthew*, 2:27–28. While he does not interact with Allison's article, Nolland agrees, saying that a re-application of the gathering of Israel to the gathering of the Gentiles is to claim too much." Jewish eschatological thinking always allowed for Gentile participation in the Jewish eschatological gathering. Nolland, *Matthew*, 357. See also Dupont, "'Beaucoup viendront du levant et du couchant . . .': (Matt 8:11–12; Lk 13:28–29)," 153–67.

97. Cf. Schlosser: "Dans l'AT l'expression 'du levant et du couchant' se rencontre principalement in des textes annoçant le reassemblement de dispersés d'Israel et en des textes protant sur la reconnaissance universellle de Jahvé" (Schlosser, *Le règne de Dieu dans les dits de Jésus*, 2:621).

98. For other texts describing a pilgrimage from the "east and west, north and south," see LXX Ps 106:2–3 (ET 107:2–3), Isa 43:5–6; Zech 8:7–8, *1 Enoch* 57:1.

of this pilgrimage as universal salvation of Gentiles.[99] Allison cites a number of Second Temple Period texts which indicate that the Gentile pilgrimage in the future will be one of judgment, not salvation. As early as Ezek 39 the nations come to Israel but instead of finding salvation at an eschatological banquet, they are utterly destroyed and become the food for the banquet (Ezek 39:17–20).[100] Allison is correct that at least some streams of Second Temple Period Judaism did not envision a future conversion of the nations, but rather their destruction. As I observed in chapter 3, the source for this diversity is the ambiguity found the foundation eschatological banquet text, Isa 25:6–8. In fact, this is the only text in the Hebrew Bible which may connect the pilgrimage of the nations to Zion with the messianic feast. In every other text, the nations travel to Zion to pay homage to the God of Israel, but the feast is celebrated only by Israel.[101] Allison concludes that Jesus would not have turned the metaphor of the messianic banquet upside down by replacing Israel with the Gentiles. Rather, he was indicating that the Jews who thought they ought to be sharing in the messianic banquet will be replaced by other Jewish guests, perhaps even those from the Diaspora.[102]

While agreeing with many of Allison's points, M. Bird nevertheless maintains that the consensus view is essentially correct.[103] Bird points out that the book of Isaiah has both a "pilgrimage of the Gentiles" (Isa 2:2–4) and an eschatological banquet (Isa 25:6–8). Allison does not think that Jesus' audience would have read the two texts together since there is no pilgrimage and conversion of the nations in the eschatological feast. Following C. Keener, Bird disagrees and argues that Jesus and other Second Temple Period thinkers frequently read Isaiah synthetically. "Even if he drew on only a single text, [Jesus] understanding of that text would be informed by the others."[104] Similarly, W. Carter is convinced that Allison is correct about inclusion of the Diaspora, but does not see this as a non-inclusion of the Gentiles.[105] The context of

99. Allison, "Who Will Come From the East and West?," 163.

100. Allison cites 4 *Ezra* 13, *The War Scroll* (1QM) as examples of judgment on the nations. While Jub. 20 and 1QSa are also cited, they do not include a Gentile pilgrimage or eschatological judgment. Allison, "Who Will Come From the East and West?," 163.

101. This point is made by Beasley-Murray, *Jesus and the Kingdom*, 170. Compare Chilton, who sees Zechariah 8 as the background for this saying. Chilton says that Jesus "did not articulate that vision by claiming-in the Pauline manner-that the distinction between Israel and the nations no longer existed." Chilton, *Pure Kingdom: Jesus' Vision of God*, 82.

102. Allison, "Who Will Come From the East and West?," 165. In his later commentary, Allison suggests that there does not have to be a literal, geographic pilgrimage of Jews or Gentiles to Zion. Rather, he suggests that Matthew had in mind a re-creation of the world rather than a literal banquet in a "millennial kingdom." Davies and Allison, *Matthew*, 2:29.

103. Bird, "Who Comes from the East and the West?," 441–57.

104. Keener, *The Gospel of Matthew*, 270n26. Keener also comments that even if Jesus meant Diaspora Jews, Matthew intends this saying to refer to Gentile inclusion.

105. Carter, *Matthew and the Margins*, 203. Turner has a similar evaluation of Allison's view, calling it "doubtful." Turner, *Matthew*, 233. Luz reads the saying through the lens of an author who "has experienced both Israel's no to Jesus and the destruction of Jerusalem" and is living in at a time when many Gentiles have in fact turned to Jesus. Luz, *Matthew 8–20*, 11.

Matt 8:8–10 is the compelling factor for Carter. Matthew has placed this saying into a context which highlights Gentile conversion.

If the saying was inserted only into the story of the healing of the centurion's servant, then perhaps Bird and Carter have a valid point. But the literary unit of Matt 8–9 should be considered as a whole. This section is a series of miracles and conflict stories between two teaching sections (Matt 5–7 and 10).[106] In this larger section Jesus comes into contact with various outsiders: a leper, the demon-possessed, tax collectors, the blind and lame, as well as a Gentile. The faith of the Gentile centurion stands as part of a series of events which demonstrate that Jesus extends mercy to the outsiders.[107] When read within the context of Matthew's gospel, this saying about an eschatological banquet does not so much refer to geographical Diaspora Jews, but rather a sort of sociological Diaspora. An additional factor is the placement of the saying in Luke 13:29, where there is no hint of Gentile salvation in Luke. In fact, read within the context of Luke-Acts, the "many from the east and west" are in fact Diaspora Jews gathered at Pentecost who hear the preaching of the Apostles and receive the Holy Spirit.[108]

In summary, this saying is a clear reference to the eschatological banquet. But the banquet is expanded to include those who are on the very fringes of the Jewish faith. The saying is less about a future banquet than Jesus' ongoing ministry of table fellowship.[109] Only a chapter later many do in fact come to sit with Jesus and celebrate with him as a bridegroom (Matt 9:9–13).

Matthew 22:1–14: The Kingdom of Heaven as Wedding Banquet

Introduction to Matthew's Wedding Parables

The Parables of the Wedding Banquet and the Ten Virgins are intended as extended similes. In Matt 22:1 and 25:1 both use the word ὁμοιόω, "to make something or someone like something else" (BDAG), to describe the "kingdom of heaven." The use of the word ὁμοιόω signals the presence of an extended metaphor.[110] But the observation

---

106. That there are three sets of three miracles in these two chapters is seen as an allusion to Moses and the plagues on Egypt which have a similar pattern. Like Moses, Jesus comes down from the mountain (8:1) and does a series of signs. Keener, *Matthew*, 258.

107. In fact, there is nothing in 8:5–13 which anticipates the sort of Gentile mission which would have been the case when Matthew finally wrote his Gospel. If Matthew were creating a story to show that Jesus was extending salvation to the Gentiles, then Jesus should have shared a meal with the Gentile as he did the (Jewish) tax-collectors and other sinners in Matt 9:9–13. The fact that the centurion knows that it is not proper for Jesus to enter his home may imply that this man was a God-fearing Gentile not unlike Cornelius (Acts 10:28). In the Lukan parallel the Centurion is described as a patron of the Synagogue at Capernaum (Luke 7:4–5).

108. This is suggested by Johnson, who considered this "proleptically fulfilled in Acts 2:5–13." Johnson, *The Gospel of Luke*, 217.

109. Dodd, *The Parables of the Kingdom*, 55.

110. Commenting on this word, Schneider says "in the comparison a thought is clarified by associating with it a statement or story which is similar but which belongs to a field directly known to the

that this parable is an extended metaphor has sometimes encouraged commentators to allegorize elements of the parable.[111] It is improbable that a king "in the real world" would give a banquet on this scale and have all of his subjects rejected his invitation. This is shocking hyperbole which Jesus used to surprise the listener. It is not necessary to resort to a fully allegorical interpretation of these elements nor to completely reject the idea of metaphor (specifically, hyperbole) in reading parables. In fact, by reading the Parable of the Wedding Banquet as an extended-metaphor rather than allegory we are liberated from some of the more difficult problems of interpretation which vex the commentators (such as the identity of the servants, the identity of the unprepared guest, the lack of a bride, etc.) It is best to stay within the world of the story when reading the Parables and try to hear the story as Jesus told it.[112]

This parable is an excellent illustration of the benefit of the intertextual method described in chapter two. The reader first must hear the echoes of earlier tradition, but what echoes are present in this parable? At least three elements are present in these parables which are intended to create a relationship with earlier tradition in the minds of the reader. First, the "Kingdom of Heaven" sets this parable in an eschatological context. The restoration of the kingdom to Israel such an important issue in

---

listeners." Schneider, "ὁμοιόω," 5:187, cf. Louw and Nida, 64.4 and 64.5, the semantic domain of "comparison." While he does not state the word is used to mean "a metaphor," the definition he provides is remarkably similar to modern definitions of metaphor. Carson detects a bit more theology in the use of the word to introduce parables by noting the tense of the verb. When there is an eschatological focus Matthew uses a future passive form, when the focus is on the "inaugurated kingdom" an aorist is used. If Carson is correct in this observation, then we are dealing with extended metaphors which treat the kingdom as a present kingdom in 22:1, but as a future event in 25:1. This has the potential to clear up some of the more troublesome aspects of the Wedding Banquet parable. Carson, "The *Homoios* Word-Group," 277–82.

111. There are potential problems with reading the parable of the Wedding Banquet or the Parable of the Wise Virgins even with this limited allegorical approach. Blickenstaff, for example, is rather disturbed by the common interpretation of the Wedding Banquet which makes the king "equal" God in an allegory of salvation history. Her motivation in this case is the image of God as a violent king who avenges his honor by destroying a whole city and killing all of the citizens of the town. She argues this is an inappropriate description for God based on Jesus' peaceful teaching in the Sermon on the Mount. How can this king "represent" God, she wonders, if he can get away with hatred, anger, and murder, the very things Jesus spoke so passionately against in Matt 5? Blickenstaff, *"While the Bridegroom is With Them,"* 41. Blickenstaff is correct in resisting an allegorical interpretation of the parable, but seems to ignore some important elements of the literary form of parables. Parables tell "real world" stories yet not every element has to make perfect sense "in the real world." That a king would burn a whole city and kill everyone in it while his wedding banquet is being prepared is a hyperbole intended to shock the listeners with the violence of the response. Extreme violence is present in the conquest of Canaan and the destruction of Jericho, Samson's response to the Philistines in Judg 11, and even the curses of the Deuteronomic covenant (Lev 26:14–26 and Deut 28:15–68). The vivid descriptions of the fall of Jerusalem in 586 BC are examples of violent judgments of a just God who acts with righteous wrath in punishing his rebellious people. Rather than a hyperbole, the destruction of the city in Matt 22 may be a reflection on the rather sad history of Israel and the punishment it has already received. For a survey of interpretation of this parable, see Beare, "The Parable of the Guests at the Banquet," 1–7.

112. Snodgrass argues that the reader ought to "at least attempt to hear his voice and not assume that the only situation addressed is that of the Evangelist's church." Snodgrass, *Stories with Intent*, 310.

The Wedding Banquet in the Synoptic Gospels

Second Temple Judaism that it is unlikely that anyone in the Passover crowds gathered around Jesus would not have a clear idea of what "kingdom" meant, even if they disagreed among themselves about the details. Second, the parable describes a feast which inaugurates this eschatological kingdom. I have already shown that the image of a feast at the beginning of the eschatological age is common in the Second Temple Period. If the kingdom has been restored to Israel, then Israel's enemies have been destroyed and the nation can recline at a victory feast in peace. Third, this feast is a celebration of a marriage. Again, I have already argued that the image of a marriage was common in the Hebrew Bible for God's relationship with Israel. Although this motif is muted in the literature of the Second Temple Period, it is certainly present in Matthew's gospel (9:11, 25:1). Reading this parable as an intertextual blending of these three well-known motifs will help to understand some of the problems commentaries usually detected in the parable.

Within the world of Matthew's gospel, Jesus teaches this parable as the third of three parables which answer a challenge to his authority (21:23–27). The brief Parable of the Two Sons (21:28–32) contrasts two types of responses to Jesus' invitation to participate in the kingdom. The one who have responded to Jesus' invitation are the tax-collectors and sinners. These outsiders are entering the kingdom before the chief priests and elders of the people. Since προάγω is a present tense verb it is likely that Jesus is talking about his practice of table fellowship as Matthew has described it earlier in his gospel (for example, Matt 9:11). Because there is an association of table fellowship and a wedding celebration in that pericope, it is not surprising to find an association in this series of three parables. The second parable in the series is the rather pointed story of tenants who not only fail to respond properly to the call of the owner of the vineyard; they abuse his messengers and ultimately kill his son "outside the vineyard." The owner therefore destroys the first tenants and replaces them with new tenants. Jesus then cites Ps 118:22–23 as a conclusion to this parable in order to draw an explicit connection between the rejection of his invitation and what the chief priests are about to do to him in the crucifixion. Matthew tells the reader that it was clear to everyone that this parable is spoken against the chief priests and Pharisees (21:45–46). The third parable of the series picks up on these themes and describes the kingdom of Heaven as a wedding banquet to which the subjects of that King are invited. As in the first two parables, there are two groups described; those who enter the wedding feast and those who do not.

The Invitation

Perhaps the most important feature of the banquet highlighted in both the Wedding Banquet and the Ten Virgins is that of an invitation. Both of these parables concern themselves with who is invited to the feast and who eventually enters the feast rather than the feast itself. Matthew uses forms of καλέω in the parable analogous to first-century wedding invitation as evidenced in the papyri.¹¹³ The word is, however, more theological in other contexts in Matthew. In Matt 9:13, for example, Jesus states that he has come to "call sinners." The word is also used in conjunction with δεῦτε, "come," in Matt 4:19–21 when Jesus calls his first disciples. While it is tempting to find a fully theological "calling" in this "invitation," this was not Jesus' point at all.¹¹⁴ If there is to be a wedding banquet, there must be an invitation.

That a king might give a banquet and send out invitations is a common feature found in other uses of banquet imagery. For example, in the *Apocryphon of Ezekiel* a king gives a banquet and invites many guests.¹¹⁵ In this parable the invited guests all accept the king's summons. The plot of the story concerns two "outsiders," a blind man and a lame man, who were not invited. Those whom the king invites might have been expected socially to attend the banquet, but the two outsiders are socially unacceptable at such an event. In the version of the biblical parable found in Luke 14:21 the invited guests do not come to the banquet and are replaced by the poor, cripple and blind, while in Matt 22 the replacement guests come from the margins of society.¹¹⁶ As Allison and Davies state, "perhaps Jesus mined one folk tale for two parables."¹¹⁷

---

113. Llewellyn, "Invitation to a Wedding," in *NewDocs* 9, 63. Invitations use either a form of ἐρωτάω or καλέω, the invitation is to come "into the wedding feast," εἰς τοὺς γάμους as in Matt 22:3. In a similar context, Tobit 9:5 (Sinaiticus) has καλεῖ αὐτὸν εἰς τὸν γάμον. The singular for "wedding feast" appears regularly in Tobit, rather than Matthew's plural. While the word is not used in Parable of the Wise Virgins, the women are certainly invited to the wedding banquet since they are part of the bridegroom's wedding party.

114. See, for example, Lenski, *The Interpretation of St. Matthew's Gospel*, 859. Lenski reads the final verse of the parable with a rather Calvinistic lens.

115. Bauckham argues that the *Apocryphon* dates from 50 BC to AD 50. Bauckham, "The Parable of the Royal Wedding Feast," 471–88.

116. *Midrash Rabbah Lamentations* 4:2 is sometimes cited as an example the practice of sending two invitations to guests, but as Bailey points out the text is irrelevant to the banquet parables of Jesus. Bailey's argument is that the double-invitation is the standard tradition of the Middle East and therefore does not need to be supported by a late rabbinic saying. The saying is however similar to Philo, who says "those who make a feast do not invite their guests to the entertainment before they have provided everything for festivity" (*On Creation* 78). The point of a double-invitation was quite practical. A host would send out invitations to potential guests before the date of the banquet. Based on the response to this invitation, the host would prepare enough food for the guests who indicated they would attend. The host would then butcher and cook a sufficient amount of meat to feed the guests who had indicated they would come since "once the countdown was started, it could not be stopped." When the food was nearly ready servants would be sent to gather the guests into the banquet. In the ancient world the food served at a banquet of this sort would have to be eaten that night or it would be wasted. Therefore anyone who refused the second invitation would have been especially rude. Since the food was prepared on the basis of the first invitation, the original listener would have been struck by the absolute lack of social manners demonstrated by the invited guests. Bailey, *Through Peasant Eyes*, 94. This observation frees the parable from the temptation to allegorize the two sets of servants.

117. Allison and Davies, *Matthew*, 3:203. Another close parallel parable is found in *y. Sanh* 6.23c. In this parable two righteous men ate together and studied the Torah for many years. One of the righteous men died but was not properly mourned. When a tax collector named Bar Ma'jan died the whole town turned out to mourn him. The first pious man was disturbed by this inequity, so his friend came to him in a dream and told him it was just because he had done one evil deed in his life.

The Wedding Banquet in the Synoptic Gospels

Rejecting the Invitation

An important corollary to the idea of the invitation is the rejection of the invitation. Most commentators notice the improbability that anyone would reject the invitation of the king to a wedding banquet. The meal is likely to be the best meal imaginable and the occasion of the wedding of a prince would be a socially important event. In addition, to miss the wedding hosted by the king would be a politically dangerous choice which would be interpreted as not only disrespectful but as treasonous. Not only are the first invited guests unwilling, but they abuse the second set of servants, killing some of them. Often commentators wonder about the possibility of guests rejecting an invitation of this sort, usually taking the rejection as an allegorical gloss from Matthew. Again, this is not necessary because what is unlikely or impossible in the real world can occur in the world of the extended metaphor. The charge of unreality could be leveled against the wicked tenants or the unwilling son, but in both of those cases Jesus rather clearly identifies the negative character as the Pharisees and teachers of the Law. That ought to be the case in the Wedding Banquet parable as well.

A banquet of this type would be expected to be a village-wide event. Blickenstaff reports a papyri invitation which invites the whole village to attend the celebration (κῶμος) of a wedding.[118] Matthew 22 does not emphasize feasting, although the description of the meal leads us to believe this is a very large banquet. Typically a calf would feed 35–75 people,[119] yet 22:4 indicates that at least two bulls have been slaughtered along with at least two fatted calves. At a minimum, this banquet would feed two hundred people.[120]

There are two types of guests in the Wedding Banquet parable: those who enter the banquet and those who do not. In Matt 22, the "proper guests" are the ones who could reasonably be expected to be invited to the wedding of a king's son yet do not enter the banquet because of their own unwillingness (imperfect of θέλω to indicate an ongoing

---

Because he had put his phylacteries on in the wrong order he was not honored at his death. The tax collector never did anything good, except once. He gave a breakfast for the leading men of the city, but no one came. He therefore invited the poor to eat the meal rather than have it go to waste. The image of a man hosting a special meal for the social elite, having the invited guests fail to arrive and then filling the meal with the poor are all close parallels to Matt 22. Despite questions of dating material in the Talmud, many commentators consider this a solid parallel for Matt 22 and Luke 14. Neusner, *The Talmud of the Land of Israel*, 23:145–46.

118. Blickenstaff, "*While the Bridegroom is With Them*," 57n40, citing P.Oxy 33.2678. The invitation is δειπνῆσαι εἰς γάμους τοῦ υἱοῦ. P.Giss 33 contains an invitation to the wedding of a daughter, εἰς γάμ(ον) θυγατ(ρὸς) αὐτ(οῦ). Josephus mentions a wedding procession in *Antiq.* 13.18–21, describing it as "splendid and costly" (λαμπρὰν καὶ πολυτελῆ). The use of λαμπρός ("shining, glistening") is reminiscent of the bridesmaids in Matthew 25 who were to carry λαμπάς to accompany the bridegroom into the banquet.

119. Bailey, *Through Peasant Eyes*, 94. Cf. Josephus, *Antiq.* 6.339, the witch of Endor slaughters a calf for Saul and his men, an act praised by Josephus as "generous."

120. Compare to Tobit 8:19, also a rather large banquet: "many loaves of bread," two steers and four rams.

past action).¹²¹ Matthew uses the same verb in two other places in the immediate context which are important for understanding the refusal of the guests. First in the parable of the Two Sons, one son is not willing to obey the father, (using θέλω), but eventually does obey (21:19). In the Parable of the Two Sons it is the chief priests and Pharisees are ones who say they are willing, but refuse the father. The second use of θέλω in close context to the Wedding Banquet is in the polemic against the Pharisees in chapter 23. In Matt 23:4 the Pharisees are described as tying heavy loads for others to carry, but they themselves "are not willing to lift a finger to move them" (NIV).

The invited guests pay no attention to the invitation and some go off to their field or business.¹²² The word used for the careless attitude of the invited guests (ἀμελέω) appears four times in the New Testament. More importantly, the word appears two contexts in Jeremiah which employ the marriage metaphor. In LXX Jer 4:17 the word appears as a translation of the Hebrew מרה, to be "recalcitrant or rebellious" (HALOT). The use of the verb in LXX Jer 38:32 (MT 31:32) is more troublesome. The saying clearly describes Israel's unfaithfulness in the wilderness period, but the marriage metaphor found in the MT is lost in the LXX translation. In the MT, the Hebrew reads וְאָנֹכִי בָּעַלְתִּי בָם, "I was a husband to them" (MT Jer 31:32). The same phrase appears in Jer 3:14 to describe the relationship of Israel and their Lord in the wilderness. But in LXX Jer 38:32 the word is used with the Lord as the subject, Israel as the object ("I neglected them"), probably taking the MT בָּעַלְתִּי בָם ("I was their husband") as בָם בחלהי ("I despised them"). It is also possible the ב was mistaken as a ג resulting in געל, to "loathe, despise" (Cf. Ezek 16:45). An adverbial form of ἀμελέω appears in LXX Jer 31:10 (ET 48:10), ἀμελῶς, translating רְמִיָּה, "indolence, looseness" (HALOT).

In either case, the word was chosen because of the willful disregard for the king's invitation.¹²³ It appears, therefore, that the language used to describe the rejection of the first invitation was guided by wilderness and marriage texts in Jeremiah.

---

121. BDF 327; Wallace, *Greek Grammar beyond the Basics*, 543. This is often called a progressive or descriptive imperfect.

122. The Luke version of the parable gives three excuses, *GThomas* has four. Bailey comments these excuses are not simply lame, but rather bold-faced lies. For example, no one in the Middle East would purchase land without thoroughly investigating it. Bailey says this would be begging off from a dinner invitation because you just closed on a house and now you need to go visit it for the first time— no one would believe such a lie. The need to examine oxen is "transparent fabrication" and the need to go spend time with one's new wife is "intensely rude" in a Middle East context. Often this is softened by citing Deut 20:7, which exempts a man from war for one year after marrying, but this cannot apply here since he is being invited to a wedding banquet, not a war! Bailey, *Through Peasant Eyes*, 95–98.

123. In the *Wisdom of Solomon* 3:10 the ungodly "disregard righteousness" and in 2 Macc 4:14 the word is used to describe the priests who ignored their service at the altar during the period of Jason's high priesthood. The word appears in a letter with the sense of neglecting a duty, see Horsley, *NewDocs* 1, 62, Moulten and Milligan describe the word as common in the papyri, citing numerous examples.

The King's Response

When the prophet described the nation as unconcerned with their relationship with God, he also predicted the destruction of Jerusalem as result of their unfaithfulness. In the Parable, the response of the king is exaggerated. He becomes angry and orders soldiers to burn the city with fire. The majority of commentaries on the parable of the Wedding Feast assume verses 6–7 are a reference to the fall of Jerusalem in AD 70 (which was in fact burned with fire).[124]

As with other elements often allegorized as a "history of salvation," there is no need for this destruction of a city to necessarily be the fall of Jerusalem in AD 70. A violent end awaits most of the negative characters in the parables (cast out into the darkness where there is weeping and gnashing of teeth, the weeds are thrown on the fire, etc.) Boring warns that the burning of the city may well be a reflection on texts such as Isa 5:24–25 just as much as a reference to the fall of Jerusalem.[125] Blickenstaff does not take the burning of Jerusalem as an allegory reference to the fall of Jerusalem because it makes God the author of great violence, wrath and evil, an inappropriate description of God given the peacefulness of the Sermon on the Mount.[126] The source for Jesus' description of the destruction of the city is the Hebrew Bible concerning the end of the first kingdom.

The Replacement Guests

The king is now faced with a dilemma. He has prepared an enormous banquet, but those who were invited were not worthy to enter. He therefore sends out a second set of servants to gather whomever they should find to fill the wedding feast. The second group is those who were not the sort of people who would have been invited at all. They are "outsiders" in the kingdom of the parable. The noun διέξοδος has the sense of the edges of society, but is used in the LXX for the borders of the Land (for example, Num 34:4). These are not outsiders in the sense that they are drawn from outside of the King's domain, but outsiders in the sense that they live on the fringe of society.

124. This idea is found as early as Eusebius, *HE* 2.5. Usually the commentaries assume Matthew added these verses to the original parable of Jesus in order to "update the allegory." Many note that the idea that a king who was setting up a wedding feast should delay the feast while his soldiers waged a military campaign against a city is ludicrous, therefore it must be an exaggerated allegorical element. As we have already noted, we are not in the "real" world, but in the world of an extended metaphor where things can happen which are not normally the case. In this case a king's honor has been challenged; therefore his response is not unusual, albeit violent.

125. Boring, "Matthew," 418. This observation is strengthened by the presence of θέλω in LXX Isa 5:24. As Israel was not willing to keep the Law of the Lord in Isaiah's day, so too the first invited guests are unwilling to respond to the invitation to the wedding. Hasler considers verses 7–8 as a polemic against the Jews. Hasler, "Die königliche Hochzeit, Matth. 22, 1–14," 25–35.

126. Blickenstaff interprets the burning of the city consistently with her thesis that the king is "earthly powers" who are unjustly treating Christian missionaries. *'While the Bridegroom is With Them'*, 63–64.

Jesus the Bridegroom

This second set of invitations is routinely taken as an allegory of Christian mission,[127] usually as the gentile mission,[128] although this allegorical interpretation is not at all necessary given the parallel to the Bar Ma'jan parable mentioned above. Snodgrass categorically denies this interpretation, calling it "merciless allegorizing."[129] If this parable is consistent with the other two in the context of Matthew's gospel, then the replacement guests must be those who have responded to Jesus' invitation and have been eating and drinking wand "sinners" are people who indeed live on the fringe of society and they are the very people who have been "filling the banquet" hosted by Jesus.

The Bride and Groom

There are some features of a wedding which are missing in this parable. For example, the bride is not mentioned in this parable and the bridegroom is not a particularly important factor.[130] While the bridegroom is featured significantly in the parable of the Wise Virgins, the bride is unmentioned. Many who comment on this parable take the bridegroom as Jesus (a reasonable assumption given Jesus' own words in Matt 9:15) and the bride as the Church. This is unwarranted allegorizing since the bride is not featured in either parable at all. To include the bride in these parables introduces a character into the parable in order to make a theological point based on texts like Eph 5:25–33. By avoiding the allegorical reading, we are not forced into finding a bride in a parable where one is not mentioned. The point is not the marriage of the bride and groom, but the king's invitation to enter into the wedding feast.

Many Are Called, Few are Chosen

This cryptic line is usually assigned to a later layer of tradition which sought to apply the parable to a new situation in the early church. For example, Dodd thought the line was added by Matthew to "guard against the reception of the Gentiles into the Church on too easy terms."[131] Linnemann warned that we ought to read this verse as "a piece of preaching" the parable acquired at some point in the life of the Church.[132]

---

127. Hultgren, *Parables of Jesus*, 345.

128. Gundry, *Matthew*, 437–38; Lenski, *Matthew*, 853–54; Plummer, *Luke*, 301; Swete, *Parables*, 79; Hunter, *Interpreting the Parables*, 57; Wenham, *The Parables of Jesus*, 135.

129. Snodgrass, *Stories with Intent*, 315.

130. That the bride is not mentioned causes some to wonder who the bride might be. Commonly the disciples are identified as the bride, or the church in a more allegorical approach to the parable. See Stauffer, "γαμέω," 1:663–65.

131. Dodd, *Parables of the Kingdom*, 122.

132. Linnemann, *Parables of Jesus: Introduction and Exposition*, 97.

Like the image of a wedding feast for an eschatological kingdom, the idea of the "elect" is a powerful image in Second Temple Period Judaism. Of critical importance is the election of Israel as God's people and the covenant he made with them.[133] Philo says "Yet out of the whole human race He chose as of special merit and judged worthy of pre-eminence over all, those who are in a true sense men, and called them to the service of Himself, the perennial fountain of things excellent" (*Spec. Laws* 1.303). Similar statements of Israel's election are common in nearly all the literature of the second temple. Equally common are statements about the covenant God sought to initiate with the people he had chosen. For example, Pseudo-Philo says "I will give my light to the world and illume their dwelling places and establish my covenant with the sons of men and glorify my people above all the nations" (*Bibl. Antiq.* 11.1f). Romans 9 is another clear example of the theology of the election of Israel. Gundry comments that "the center of gravity in the notion of election had shifted from God's choice of the whole nation of Israel to that of the righteous remnant."[134]

If my reading of the Wedding Banquet parable is correct, then perhaps the cryptic aphorism plays on the idea of Israel's election in general, and Jesus' followers in particular. The line would therefore mean "not all of the elect Israel are chosen to enter the kingdom." The first guests are "all Israel," the second guests are the outsiders who have participated in table fellowship with Jesus and have entered into the Kingdom of Heaven. As Snodgrass concludes, while some Jews have rejected Jesus as Messiah, "other Jews will respond."[135] This suggestion avoids the implicit anti-Semitic conclusion that the Gentiles have replaced God's people.

Summary and Conclusion

If we take seriously Jesus' role as host at table-fellowship, then Jesus must be the king in this parable rather than the bridegroom. He is inviting people to enter into the wedding banquet and participate in the feast. In fact, the feast itself is not the main point of the parable. While there is an anticipation of great feasting in Matt 22, the feast itself is not the important element of the story. The response to the invitation is the main topic of the parable.

Jesus therefore develops the eschatological banquet (Isa 25:6–8) by combining it with a Marriage metaphor. This adaptation of well-known traditions highlights something new about the Kingdom of Heaven. When the Kingdom arrives there will be a joyous celebration. But rather than a victory banquet in which the enemies of God are slaughtered and consumed (2 Baruch 28, for example), the eschatological banquet will be a joyous celebration of the restoration of God's people. Since this restoration

---

133. Davies and Allison cite a saying of Rabbi Hertzberg: "The essence of Judaism is the affirmation that the Jews are the chosen people. All else is commentary" (*Matthew*, 3:208n77).

134. Gundry, *Matthew*, 441. As evidence, Gundry lists Wisd 3:9, 4:15, *1 Enoch* 5:1–9, *ApocAbr* 29.

135. Snodgrass, *Stories with Intent*, 321.

is described in terms of a restored marriage in the Hebrew Bible, Jesus used a wedding celebration to describe his practice of calling and inviting people to join in his ministry as a celebration of the present and coming Kingdom. Matthew 22:1–12 is therefore consistent with other the material in the Synoptic gospels surveyed earlier in this chapter.

Rather than an allegorical commentary of salvation history from the cross to the gentile mission, Jesus is looking back at his own ministry in Galilee.[136] The point of the parable of the Wedding Banquet in Matt 22 is to describe Jesus' ministry. Those who were invited to the wedding banquet rejected the invitation (already) and are replaced with "outsiders" from the margins of society (already). In the narrative context of Matthew's gospel it is difficult not to see the invited guests who do not respond as the religious leaders of Israel who have in fact rejected Jesus' invitation already.[137] Consistent with Matt 8:11, those who have "enter into" the kingdom are not the ones initially invited. The expected invited guests are not only unwilling to come to the banquet, they are actively antagonistic toward the invitation and will kill the messengers of the king. As N. T. Wright has observed, Jesus "spoke of himself as the bridegroom. His kingdom-banquets were foretastes of the messianic banquet, but also of the great feast that YHWH and Israel would celebrate together once more, following the new wilderness wooing."[138] This "wilderness wooing" is drawn from Hos 2:14–15, Jer 2–4 and other texts. From the desert God will recall his bride and woo here once again to himself. The combined metaphors of messianic banquet and wedding banquet powerfully draw the imagery together at the climax of Jesus' ministry in the book of Matthew.

Matthew 25:1–12: The Wise and Foolish Virgins

For J. M. Ford, this parable "reflects a theme common to all three evangelists, namely, Jesus as bridegroom," but in Matthew the parable of the Wise and Foolish Virgins "comes as the climax of the Exodus motif. Jesus comes like God on Mount Sinai on the 'day of espousals.'"[139] Like the Wedding Banquet Parable, Matthew includes this parable to emphasize his theme that those who are invited to the Kingdom may not actually enter the feast. The parable, however, is not particularly popular among New Testament scholars.[140] It is generally dismissed as a creation of Matthew attempting to explain the delay of the Parousia.[141]

---

136. Hultgren, *The Parables of Jesus*, 349. Cf. Chilton, who thinks that this parable shows that the "invitations have already been issued" and can "either be accepted or rejected." Chilton, *Pure Kingdom*, 76.

137. Turner, *Matthew*, 522.

138. Wright, *Jesus and the Victory of God*, 645.

139. Ford, "Ten Foolish Scholars," 118.

140. Snodgrass, *Stories with Intent*, 505.

141. Hunter, *Interpreting the Parables*, 86. The parable of the Ten Virgins is frequently assumed to be a creation of Matthew. For example, Dodd described this parable influenced Luke's Parable of the

The Wedding Banquet in the Synoptic Gospels

Parable or Allegory?

The parable of the Ten Virgins has been subjected to allegorical interpretation throughout church history. The identity of the bridegroom and the virgins is discussed, as well as the meaning of the lamps, the oil, and the door that shuts the virgins out of the wedding feast.[142] A more modern example of creative allegory is J. M. Ford, who argues that the ten virgins are rabbinical scholars, the lamps represent the Law, but because they do not practice good deeds they are shut out of the "Chamber of Instruction."[143] Jeremias on the other hand attempted to strip the parable of any allegorical additions. He argues that the parable was not an allegory when Jesus taught it, but that it developed into an allegory in its use by the early church. The original parable was an accurate description of wedding traditions at the time of Jesus, and was a simple narrative used to teach that the time of the wedding banquet had come, and that it may already be too late to participate in the kingdom. For Jeremias, there is no eschatology present in the parable.[144]

R. Zimmerman has recently suggested that the parable should not be read as an allegory at all since the elements of the parable are explained as part of Hellenistic wedding ritual.[145] For Zimmerman, the parable is not about the delay of the Parousia at all, but rather a exhortation to the church to be the light of the world (Matt 5:16). Zimmerman concludes that the meaning of the parable is not to be found in symbolic

---

Watchmen or that there was a third form that Matthew and Luke both knew and adapted into a new form. Dodd, *Parables of the Kingdom,* 173. Gundry states that the parable is a creation of Matthew, a combination of Luke 12:36, 13:25–28 and Mark 13:33–37. According to Gundry, Matthew changes the lamps of Luke 12:35 into torches to match the outdoor setting of his parable, and takes the number of virgins from Luke 19:11–27, the parable of the Minas. Because he used the number ten in the parable of the virgins, Matthew omits it from the parable of the Talents beginning in 25:14. Gundry, *Matthew,* 497. While it is certain that there are parallels between the parable of the Watchman and the parable of the Ten Virgins, there are enough significant differences that the parables represent two teachings by Jesus. The Parable of the Watchman has only one person waiting, and they are waiting on the inside of the house, ready to admit the master when he returns. The virgins are waiting to join the master as he enters the wedding banquet, and only the foolish are shut out. The themes are similar but the method of teaching those themes is vastly different.

142. Trench's often-reprinted commentary on parables is an example of this allegorizing approach to the parable. He discusses the lamps at length, and concludes that the lamps represent an outward Christian profession, and the oil represents an inward and spiritual Christian expression (Trench, *The Parables of Our Lord,* 253). The midnight cry of the bridegroom is the return of the Lord (ibid., 259) and the sellers of oil are the church as "dispensers of heavenly grace" (ibid., 264). The door that is shut is Christ (ibid., 265).

143. Ford, "The Parable of the Foolish Scholars," 107–23.

144. Jeremias, *The Parables of Jesus,* 161.

145. Zimmermann, "Das Hochzeitsritual im Jungfrauengleichnis: sozialgeschichtliche Hintergründe zu Mt 25.1–13," 48–70. Zimmerman compares what little information we have on Jewish weddings with more abundant literary descriptions of Greek wedding ritual and concludes that the wedding described in Matt 25 follows the pattern of Greek weddings. This evidence includes amphora depicting a wedding procession, including young women with torches accompanying the bridegroom (ibid., 64).

codes, but rather in the real and tangible world of experience.¹⁴⁶ Zimmerman is correct to ground the parable in the real world in order to avoid allegorizing the elements of the parable. As with the parable of the Wedding Feast, the reader must "stay within the word of the story." Whether the wedding is more Greek or Jewish does not matter since both have bridesmaids who await the arrival of the wedding part. The bridesmaids are present in the parable because they are always a part of a wedding and nothing more needs to be made of them.

While Zimmerman is correct to look to the social world of the first century to interpret the parable, he fails to consider the possibility that this parable reflects on earlier traditions. This is another example of the benefit of an intertextual methodology as described in chapter 2. As with the Parable of the Wedding Feast, there are echoes of tradition drawn from the Hebrew Bible. The marriage metaphor is the most important here since the parable includes the bridegroom, but the eschatological age as a feast is important as well. There is nothing in the parable which is inconsistent with the collection of texts surveyed in the previous chapters. Jesus stands on traditions drawn from the Hebrew Bible and blends them in order to highlight the need for preparation for a longer-than-expected interim period. As such, the parable fits well within the teaching of Jesus as it is presented in Matthew and is consistent with the teaching found in the rest of Matt 24–25. There is a clear contrast between those who enter the wedding feast and those who do not. Those who find themselves on the outside assume that they ought to have been included in the feast (7:21), but they will remain outside in the darkness (Matt 22:13).

The Wise and the Foolish in Matthew

Jesus compares the Kingdom of Heaven to ten virgins who go out to meet a bridegroom. These women all brought lamps in order to escort the bridegroom to the wedding feast.¹⁴⁷ The arrival of the bridegroom was at night, accompanied by torch bearers who light his path to the bride's house. The main contrast of the parable is between the two sets of virgins. They are described as μωραὶ and φρόνιμοι based on their preparation for a long wait. While it is true that the root meaning of the word μωρός is "dull witted,"¹⁴⁸ the word has more theological overtone in biblical literature. In the LXX the word is used for people who do not have the true knowledge of God and therefore must face the justice of God.¹⁴⁹ The fool (μωρός) is not ignorant, but one that chooses not to act wisely.

---

146. Ibid., 70.

147. Jeremias argues convincingly that this is a common feature of the climax and conclusion of wedding celebrations at the time of Jesus. Jeremias, *The Parables of Jesus*, 173.

148. Bertram, "μωρός," 4:832.

149. For example, in Jer 5:21 the people are foolish because they have eyes but do not see, ears but do not hear. The reject God their creator and are therefore under God's punishment (5:29).

This parable must be understood along with the Parable of the Builders (Matt 7:24–27). There Jesus says that the one that hears his words and does them is like a wise builder; the one that hears the words and does not do them is a foolish builder. The same terms are used for the wise and the foolish, but the distinction there is the reaction to the words of Jesus. The one that reacts by changing his life is called a wise man; the one that rejects the words is the fool. The two parables both begin with a future passive form of ὁμοιόω, the only occurrences of this form in the New Testament. The response of the foolish virgins in 25:11 is also found in 7:22 on the lips of the "evil doers" in the parable of the Builders. In addition, the response of the Lord is the same in both passages. It is significant that these warnings coming at the end of the Sermon on the Mount, the first major teachings section in Matthew, are echoed here in the last major teaching section, also a sermon delivered on a mount. Matthew is therefore concluding two major teaching sections with a contrast between those who hear and respond to the word of the Lord and those who do not.

The Ten Women

As detailed in chapter 5, one of the features of the marriage metaphor is a group of women waiting the coming bridegroom or king to arrive. There are at least thirty examples of the phrase "daughters of Zion" in the Hebrew Bible, many in texts where they are part of the entourage of a king. Song of Solomon 3:11 includes the daughters of Zion in a description of King Solomon arriving from the wilderness in glory. Psalm 45:14 describes the beauty of the bride awaiting her groom, accompanied by "virgin companions." In Isa 3:18—14:6 the daughters of Zion are faithless brides who are called to purify themselves and return to Zion under the "canopy" the Mountain. "Hearing the echo" of the marriage traditions from the Hebrew Bible help to understand the point of this group of women. The whole group is invited to enter the wedding feast but only some are prepared when the bridegroom arrives. The whole group is Israel, but not all Israel was prepared to welcome the bridegroom when he finally arrived.

The Long Delay

The "crisis" of the parable is an unusually long wait for the bridegroom to arrive.[150] In the second section of the parable a cry wakens the sleeping girls. The unknown speaker commands the women go out and meet the bridegroom. The noun ἀπάντησις

---

150. The English translation of "midnight" is deceptive since this is a specific time in our culture. "Midnight" in Western cultures is a particularly climatic time and often has a connotation of the end of the present period in popular teaching. But the Greek text simply has "middle of the night," indicating a time well after the sun has gone down, yet also well before dawn. The phrase is μέσης νυκτὸς, an anarthrous attributive construction with the genitive being used in a partitive sense, see BDF 270.2. Matthew might have used μεσονύκτιον, although even this term has the sense of "when the night is half over" (Luke 12:15; L&N 67.75).

is used of the civic custom of going out of the city to meet an important visitor and bring them into the city.[151] The unprepared women are not present then the bridegroom arrives and do not enter the wedding feast. The door shut to the feast is shut and no one else may gain entrance to the wedding. When the foolish virgins have arrived at the wedding they find themselves locked out. They knock on the door and ask the master to open the door (κύριε κύριε, ἄνοιξον ἡμῖν). These words appear in Matt 7:22 with reference to the final judgment at the end of the age. The same response is given to these foolish virgins; the Lord does not know them now that the door to the wedding has been closed. As in the Wedding Banquet Parable, the foolish Virgins remain outside in the darkness, outside of the wedding feast.[152]

Summary and Conclusion

What makes the bridesmaids "wise" or "foolish"? It is not that they were asleep since both get drowsy and fall asleep. The delay was so long that normal life had to go on. The issue is that the foolish five are unprepared for the long wait. The type of lamp that they used would have had to be refueled when the groom arrived. They did not think ahead and prepare for a lengthy wait. By preparing themselves, the five wise bridesmaids are allowed to join the groom and enter into the wedding feast. The unprepared virgins are under a final judgment since there is no way for them to get into the kingdom. The groom says that he does not even know them. In Matt 7:21–23 Jesus says that not everyone that cries out "Lord Lord" will be in the kingdom, the same words are used here, the virgins cry out "Lord Lord". The implication is that they had the same opportunity to be ready, and that since they were not ready at the right time, they will have no part in the kingdom. They remain outside, in the dark.

Like the parable of the wedding banquet, Jesus uses a wedding and the late arrival of the bridegroom to explain the course of his ministry. The bridegroom was indeed long in coming to call his people to join him in the eschatological feast celebrating the restoration of Israel's reunion with her God.

Summary and Conclusions

Applying an intertextual method to the wedding banquet texts in Matthew's gospel enables the interpreter to "hear the echoes" of traditions drawn from the Hebrew Bible. The Kingdom is in some ways "like a banquet," but more specifically, it is like a "wedding banquet." Building on the foundation of table fellowship as an anticipation of the coming age from Mark's gospel, Matthew's Jesus develops the kingdom of God

---

151. Peterson, "ἀπάντησις," 1:380–81. While this is the word used in 1 Thess 4:17 for the believers "meeting the Lord in the air," there is no "hint" of rapture in this parable.

152. Compare this to *GThomas* 75: "Many are standing before the door, but it is the solitary ones who will enter the wedding hall" (Bethge, *Evangelium Thomae Copticum*, 538).

as a wedding banquet by combining these two traditions. While Mark's wilderness tradition is not developed further in Matthew's presentation, he retains the miraculous feeding in the wilderness.

The final step of an intertextual methodology is to use the echoes of tradition to illuminate the texts under examination. "Hearing the echoes" of the Hebrew Bible in the teaching of Jesus in Matthew will help to highlight several contributes to the eschatological banquet tradition as it is merged with the marriage metaphor. First, the emphasis in both of the Matthean parables is on the invitation to join in the wedding banquet. While the parables are built around the traditional elements of the eschatological banquet and the marriage metaphor, the highlighted feature is the response to the invitation. Some respond properly to this call, others do not. The "many from the east and west" will enter the Kingdom, while others do not respond are cast into the "outer darkness" (Matt 8:11). Some guests who respond to the invitation are unprepared to enter the kingdom (Matt 22:11–14, 25:1–14). Like Isa 40–55, Jesus is calling people to come out of the exile and into his kingdom feast.

Second, there is a reversal of expectation in the two wedding parables. Certainly the "sons of the kingdom" should expect to recline at the table in the kingdom, yet they are the ones "cast into outer darkness" (Matt 8:11). In the Wedding Banquet parable, people who were not expected to enter the banquet are the ones who find themselves the recipients of the gracious invitation of the King. In the parable of the Ten Virgins, five of the women expected that their relationship with the bridegroom ensured their entry, but because they were not prepared they were not allowed into the celebration.

Third, in the Wedding Banquet parable, the first guests reject the invitation and are killed. In the Ten Virgins the foolish women are left outside in the darkness. Likewise, the "sons of the kingdom" are cast out into darkness. There is finality to this separation which points to a future, eschatological judgment. Like the harvest parables (Matt 13:24–30, 47–50), there is coming a time when all those who call on the name of the Lord will be sorted and only those who were actually prepared to enter into the wedding banquet will do so. That this sorting includes Jesus' followers who have been participating in the banquet is the point of the perplexing sequel to the Wedding Banquet (Matt 22:11–13). Those who eat and drink with Jesus are not guaranteed a place in the eschatological banquet. This emphasis on separation within the supposed insiders is an application of Jesus' parables to the Matthean community.[153]

More than the other Synoptic Gospels, Matthew's Jesus combines the marriage metaphor with the eschatological banquet, creating a unique image of the coming age as a wedding banquet. The point in the resulting metaphor is that the eschatological age has already begun with Jesus' invitation to join him in celebrating the renewal of

---

153. From a pastoral perspective, it is probable that there were many in Matthew's churches who believed that they were followers but they have not really prepared themselves for the wedding feast. The parables of the Wedding feast are warnings to half-hearted members of Matthew's churches.

Jesus the Bridegroom

God's covenant with Israel. There is great danger in ignoring this invitation and there is a further responsibility of preparing oneself to participate in the wedding banquet.

Wedding Banquet in Luke

Introduction

In this final section I will examine Luke's contribution to the eschatological banquet image in the synoptic gospels. Just as Matthew picked up themes from Mark and developed them to highlight his own theological and pastoral agenda, so too does Luke. Luke includes Mark's use of the wilderness tradition, although he only includes one miraculous feeding and he includes the bridegroom saying. Rather than reexamine these, I will highlight Luke's unique contribution to the idea of the eschatological banquet. My assumption here is that Matthew and Luke independently develop the banquet traditions as they found them in Mark and adapt them from their own gospels. Chronologically, I assume the two are writing about the same time. That the section on Matthew precedes Luke in this study does not imply that Luke developed Matthew's thinking in a new direction. These are parallel developments which both use Mark's gospel along with their own traditions and meditations on the Hebrew Bible.

There are many references to eating in Luke's Travel Narrative (9:51—19:10) and it is well known that Luke places Jesus in a number of banquet-scenes, the most important being Luke 14:1–24.[154] It is necessary to examine Luke's version of the Wedding Banquet parable (Matt 22) in detail since the context of the parable is rather different than in Matthew. Luke's parable of the Great Banquet can be described as the "center" of the so-called travel narrative of Luke. In addition, there are two pericopes which seem to have the traditions similar to Matt 25:1–14 in a slightly different context.[155] First, however, it is necessary first to examine the Lukan Beatitudes since there is a general consensus that at least the second and third sayings reflect an eschatological banquet perspective not present in the Matthew forms.

Luke 6:21: Blessed Are You Who Hunger, You Will Be Filled

Possible eschatological features of the Beatitudes have generated interest recently, although the focus is primarily on the presence of the "Son of Man" in Luke 6:22.[156] The

---

154. Luke 5:29–37, 7:36–50, 9:10–17, 10:38–48, 11:37–54, 14:1–24, 19:1–10, 22:7–38, 24:13–35. Of these, three are with Pharisees, 7:36–60 (Simon), 11:37–54, 14:1–24, three are with sinners, 5:29–37 (Levi), 15:1–2 (tax collectors and sinners), 19:1–10 (Zacchaeus) and three are with disciples (10:38–48 (Mary and Martha), 22:7–38 (the Last Supper), 24:13–35 (the disciples at Emmaus). We should add the feeding of the 5000 to this list as well (9:10–17).

155. It is possible that there was an original form of the Wise Virgins parable which Matthew and Luke adapted in different contexts. For an assessment of this issue, see Fitzmyer, *Luke X–XXIV*, 1021.

156. Neirynck, "Q 6,20b–21; 7,22 and Isaiah 61," 27–64; Charlesworth, "The Qumran Beatitudes

two blessings in Luke 6:21 are often considered to reflect a messianic banquet motif. Dunn, for example, includes this text as a description of eschatological banquet.[157] F. M. Cross suggested that there is a hint of an eschatological banquet in the beatitude based on similar language in 4QpPs 37.[158] J. Green sees the beatitude as part of Luke's motif of eschatological reversal, but also as an allusion to the messianic banquet.[159] G. Meadors calls this beatitude a "cryptic allusion to the messianic banquet."[160] That the hungry are eating and the mourners are rejoicing with Jesus indicates that his ministry of table-fellowship is a foreshadowing of this beatitude.[161]

There are several reasons for taking Luke 6:21 as a eschatological banquet. First, the verbs in the second and third beatitudes in Luke 6:20–22 are future, the first and fourth are present.[162] Second, the inclusion of the phrase "Son of Man" in 6:22 sets the beatitudes in an eschatological context.[163] Third, the verb χορτάζω appears the Miraculous Feeding (Mark 6:42, Matt 14:20, Luke 9:17, cf. John 6:26), a story which alludes to the eschatological feast. Revelation 19:21 uses the verb to describe the birds who gorge themselves at the "great supper of God."

Fourth and most significantly, like other eschatological feast texts survey in this study, the "reversal" described in Luke's beatitudes from fasting and mourning to feasting and joy. There are several linguistic connections between this saying and feasting texts in Jeremiah. In LXX Jer 38:12 (ET 31:12), the hungry will hunger no longer (using the same verb as Luke 6:21, πεινάω) because the Lord himself will provide food for his people. In the next verse in Jeremiah there is a description of joyful dancing when mourning is turned into joy (using forms of χαίρω rather than Luke's γελάω).

(4Q525) and the New Testament (Mt 5:3–11, Lk 6:20–26)," 13–35; Di Luccio, "'The 'Son of Man' and the Eschatology of the Q Beatitudes: the Case of Lk 6,22c," 553–70; Di Luccio, "Son of Man, Sons of the Woman, and Teachers of the Law," 337–53.

157. Dunn, *Jesus Remembered*, 426.

158. Cross, *The Ancient Library of Qumran*, 67n81.

159. Green, *The Gospel of Luke*, 267. Green specifically cites Isa 25:6–8 and 49:10–13. Similarly Fitzmyer sees this as an allusion to the eschatological banquet and cites the same texts. Fitzmyer, *Luke I-IX*, 634. Sim points out that the state of the righteous in the eschatological age is described in the beatitudes as fully sated (no longer hungry or thirsty) and comforted (mourning is turned to rejoicing), motifs certainly present in the eschatological banquet tradition. Sim, *Apocalyptic Eschatology in the Gospel of Matthew*, 141. Culpepper agrees, calling this beatitude an echo of "Old Testament expectations of an eschatological banquet for the elect (Ps 107:9, Isa 25:6)." Culpepper, "Luke," 9:144.

160. Meadors, "The 'Messianic' Implications of the Q Material," 267. Similarly, Wiefel: "Wenn dem Hunger im jetzigen Augenblick die kommende Sattigung gegenubergestellt wird, so is damit auf das eschatologische Mahl als Mitte der Gottesherrschaft hingedeutet" (Wiefel, *Das Evangelium nach Lukas*, 131).

161. As Ernst says, "die Vorstellung von der eschatologischen Mahlgemeinschaft nimmt dem Bild die materialistisch-sinnenhaften Züge und ordnet es in den grosseren Rahmen der Reich-Gottes-Verkündigung ein." He goes on to state that Luke sees the historical experience of Jesus' table fellowship in the light of the traditions found in Isaiah, citing 25:8 specifically. Ernst, *Das Evangelium nach Lukas*, 218.

162. Green, *The Gospel of Luke*, 265.

163. Di Luccio, "The 'Son of Man' and the Eschatology of the Q Beatitudes: the Case of Lk 6,22c," 569.

Jesus the Bridegroom

As I suggested in chapter 5, Jer 31 describes a reversal from mourning to joy, a funeral to a wedding celebration. LXX Jer 38:25 (ET 31:25) refers to those who hunger and thirst, using forms of πεινάω and διψάω (used in Matthew's form of the saying). As F. Bovon points out, comfort for those who cry is similar to the eschatological banquet in Isa 25:6–8 is the "drying of tears."[164] Jeremiah described the joy and celebration which will accompany the return from Exile and the establishment of a New Covenant with Israel and Judah. Jesus is taking that language and describing a coming reversal of fortunes for his followers as they participate in that New Covenant.

In summary, it seems that the sayings in Luke 6:21 should be taken as at least a muted allusion to an eschatological feast. From an intertextual perspective, there is enough evidence to suggest that the saying is an intertextual reflection on earlier tradition well known to Jesus and his original listeners. The language of the sayings is based on texts drawn from Jeremiah which employ a marriage metaphor to describe the restoration of Israel at the time of the New Covenant. Since Jesus alludes to Jer 31 on other occasions, it seems likely that he is doing so in the saying in Luke 6:21.

Luke 12:36–40: Eating at the Master's Table

This short parable-like saying has affinities with the Wise and Foolish Virgins (Matt 25:1–12).[165] Certainly the theme of preparation for the return of a master from the wedding banquet is the same, although it is not clear if the master is the bridegroom. But there is no reference to a set of foolish servants who are unprepared for the return of the master in these verses. Luke may have separated the foolish servants from the original form of the parable and moved them to verse 45–47. There is simply not enough evidence to decide if Luke and Matthew are using the same parable in this case. My inclination is to take Luke's parable as unrelated to the Wise Virgins, despite similar themes.

In this parable the wise servants are alert for the coming of the master and open the door for him. As a result are invited to eat at the master's table where they are served by the master himself. While this might simply be a warning to use one's time wisely, there are several elements in the story which point to an eschatological reading.[166] In addition, the sayings in this section are intertextual reflections of earlier traditions including the wilderness tradition as well as eschatological feast texts.

---

164. "Derriere cette troisième béatitude, il y a la theologie vétérotestamentaire de Dieu consolateur" (Bovon, *L'Évangile selon saint Luc. 1, 1–9*, 295). Bovon warns there is no eschatological gathering of all people in these beatitudes. Bovon, *Luke 1*, 226nn40 and 42.

165. Plummer thought that this is a condensed form of the Ten Virgins parable. Plummer, *Luke*, 330; Fitzmyer considers this suggestion "far-fetched," citing the different word used for lamps, the fact that servants have the lamps in Luke, not wedding attendants, and that the master in Luke is not a bridegroom. Fitzmyer, *Luke X–XXIV*, 988. Marshall makes a similar point based on the differing words used for lamps. Marshall, *The Gospel of Luke*, 535.

166. Deterding sees this pericope as drawing heavily on the Passover to describe a "second

First, the command in 12:35 to be dressed and ready clearly evokes the Passover events from the wilderness tradition.[167] The phrase ὑμῶν αἱ ὀσφύες περιεζωσμέναι appears in LXX Exod 12:11. Deterding thinks the lighting of the lamps is an allusion to the Passover based on Exod 12:14–20 and *m.Pesachim* 1:1.[168] Second, the servants are to be like men "waiting for the master." While the verb προσδέχομαι (v. 36) appears rarely in the New Testament, it is used to describe Joseph of Arimathea as "awaiting the Kingdom of God" (Mark 15:43, Luke 23:51).[169] Third, the servants recline (ἀνακλίνω) at the table. This word appears in Luke 13:39, a clear reference to the eschatological banquet (cf. Matt 8:11, 14:19).[170] Fourth, the saying which concludes the Wise Virgins parable commands watchfulness using the same verb in Luke 12:37 (γρηγορέω). Watchfulness is a common theme in eschatological contexts.[171] Fifth, 12:39 refers to the sudden arrival of a thief, another clear reference to the Parousia (Matt 24:43, 1 Thess 5:2).

Last, the master is returning from a "wedding feast" (ἐκ τῶν γάμων). This is not the expected phrase if there is an allusion to the eschatological banquet, since the master ought to be coming to the wedding feast rather than from the feast. For this reason, Marshall considers the possibility of an allusion to the eschatological banquet "completely excluded."[172] He tales γάμων as a royal feast, as in Esth 2:18 (מִשְׁתֶּה, LXX γάμους). While it is true that both words can refer to a royal feast or a wedding feast, every other occurrence of γάμος in the New Testament refers to a wedding feast. But as shown in chapter 4, a feast can be a description of the eschatological age as a whole as well as an inauguration. Thus the timing of the feast is not as defining a factor as Marshall implies. While the plural form seems to be against this, it is possible to take ἐκ τῶν γάμων as "from the wedding chamber." In this case, the master is returning home after the consummation of his marriage. For Bovon, the unexpected arrival of the master and the "wedding atmosphere" is enough to suggest an eschatological interpretation.[173]

---

exodus." Deterding, "Eschatological and Eucharistic Motifs," 85–94. Bovon, *L'Évangile selon saint Luc 9,51—14,35,* 291.

167. Green, *The Gospel of Luke,* 500. Green points out that in 12:1 Jesus warned of the "leaven of the Pharisees." Culpepper, "Luke," 9:263.

168. Deterding, "Eschatological and Eucharistic Motifs," 85. Deterding detects several allusions to Passover, although many are drawn from *m.Pesachim* and the Midrash Rabbah on Exodus rather than the text of Exodus.

169. The word also describes the return of the Lord in Titus 2:13 and Jude 21.

170. Leaney, *A Commentary on the Gospel According to St. Luke,* 201.

171. Fitzmyer points out that watchfulness and the Day of the Lord are commonly associated in the Hebrew Bible (Isa 13:6, Ezek 30:3, Joel 1:15, 2:1, Amos 5:18, Obad 15, Zeph 1:14–18). Fitzmyer, *Luke X–XXIV,* 987. Cf. Kümmel, *Promise and Fulfillment,* 55.

172. Marshall, *The Gospel of Luke,* 536. Cf. Ernst, who thinks that it is unlikely that the master could be both the guest of the wedding feast and the host at the same time. Ernst, *Das Evangelium nach Lukas,* 408.

173. "L'arrivée inopinée du maitre suggere la Parousia; l'atmosphère nuptiale enfin pressentir le

If this parable refers to eschatological watchfulness, then a unique element is the service of the master to the slaves. Deterding takes this as a "great reversal" in which alludes to the messiah serves the banquet to the people.[174] Perhaps, but his evidence is thin. He cites *1 Enoch* 62:13–14 as an example of this service, but there is nothing there which indicates the Son of Man will serve those who attend the feast. In addition, this reversal functions differently than the other parables. In the Wedding Banquet and Great Banquet parables, the reversal concerns insiders and outsiders. If this parable had followed the pattern of the others, then the contrast would have been between wise and foolish servants.

Deterding's point could be better made by looking back to the eschatological feast traditions surveyed in this study, especially Isa 25:6–8. There it is the Lord himself who "makes the banquet on Zion" and invites the people to gather for the feast. Deterding also suggest that this service is a prediction of the Last Supper.[175] Clearly Jesus serves his disciples in that final meal, which, as I have already shown, is packed with allusions to the eschatological banquet.

In summary, given the likely parallels to Matt 22:1–14 and 25:1–12, it is best to see Jesus' teaching in Luke 12:36–40 as eschatological and intertextual reflections on both wilderness and messi9anic banquet traditions. That two titles associated with the messiah are used to describe the master helps identify him as a messianic figure. He is the "coming one" (v. 37) and the Son of Man (v. 40). Luke's contribution to the image of a wedding banquet is to merge the image of a feast with a master who will serve his servants. He will return to this motif in his version of the Last Supper (22:24–30).

Luke 13:22–29: The Narrow Door

The parable of the Narrow Door in Luke 13:24–30 seems to indicate that Jesus understood his table fellowship as an ongoing feast in the kingdom. Like Luke 12:36–40, there are affinities to Matthean banquet texts, primarily the Wise Virgins parable and the saying found in Matt 8:11–12.[176] The judgment of those outside of the banquet is the same as the unprepared guest in Matt 22:13: the servants are cast out into darkness, "where there is weeping and gnashing of teeth."[177]

Royaume." In addition, Bovon points out the frequency of the image of a sudden arrival for the Parousia. Bovon, *L'Évangile selon saint Luc 9,51—14,35*, 292.

174. Deterding, "Eschatological and Eucharistic," 90. Johnson points out that Jesus says that he serves his disciples in Luke 22:27. Johnson, *The Gospel of Luke*, 206.

175. Deterding, "Eschatological and Eucharistic Motifs," 92.

176. Ernst things that the image is drawn from Matthew 25:1–13: "Das bild vom himmlischen Festsaal, das aus Mt 25, 1–13 abgeleitet, muss im Zusammenhang mit V. 23.24 gesehen werden: war dort die Tur noch geoffnet, so is sie jetzt geschlossen" (Ernst, *Das Evangelium nach Lukas*, 428).

177. Johnson points out the similarity to the woe-saying in Luke 6:25: "You will mourn and weep." Johnson, *The Gospel of Luke*, 217.

While there is language reminiscent of Matthean banquet passages, there is no direct reference to a feast or wedding. The narrow door may be the entrance to a banquet-hall, but that is only an implication from the cry of those left outside ("we ate and drank with you").[178] That those who are on the outside see Abraham and the patriarchs reclining (ἀνακλίνω) with "many from the east and west"[179] implies an eschatological banquet (Matt 8:11–12), but the feast is still only implied from the context. Yet for Meadors, this is a clear example of messianic banquet in Q.[180]

The section begins with a question which may have been common in Second Temple Period Judaism.[181] An anonymous voice asks if "those who are saved will be few." There is a discussion of who will participate in the world to come in *m.Sanh.* 10. The section begins with the statement that "all Israelites will share in the world to come." But this sweeping statement is narrowed in the discussion which follows (no Sadducees, Epicureans, no one who pronounced the divine name, several villains from the Hebrew Bible, the generation of the flood, etc.) Defining who will participate in the eschatological age is a preoccupation of the Qumran Community. Only those who are spiritual prepared will participate in the eschatological war as the Sons of Light against the Sons of Darkness (1QSa 2:11–22, 1QM 7). In *4 Ezra* 8:1 the world to come is only for a few.

Remarkably, Jesus agrees with this sort of thinking by saying that those who are saved are the ones who have entered through a "narrow gate" which will be closed at some point. The metaphor of a narrow door is used in *4 Ezra* 7:3 to describe the difficult troubles the righteous will endure in order to enter the heavenly city. Rather than creating a list of who will be at the eschatological banquet, Jesus warns his listeners that they need to worry about themselves, entering in through the narrow door before it is forever closed. This is not far from the sequel to the Wedding Banquet parable in Matt 22:11–13. There a man gets into the banquet, but he is unprepared and is ejected into the darkness. Similarly, the foolish virgins ask to enter through the closed door of the wedding banquet with similar words (Matt 25:11, Luke 13:25).

178. Fitzmyer, *Luke X–XXIV*, 1022.

179. That these are Gentiles is the consensus opinion among Lukan scholars. For example, Fitzmyer, *Luke X–XXIV*, 1023. While this can be challenged on the same grounds reviewed above on the Matthean version of this saying, it is difficult to not read Luke along with Acts and the Gentile mission. Johnson reads the saying in the light of Acts 2:5–13 where Diaspora Jews hear the message of the Kingdom and receive the Holy Spirit. Johnson, *The Gospel of Luke*, 217. In Luke 13:28–29, however, the saying is not associated with the healing of the Centurion's servant, but it is connected with a series of sayings on the exclusiveness of Jesus' following. Culpepper points out that even though it is impossible to resolve the issue using just this text, Gentile salvation is an important issue for Luke. Culpepper, "Luke," 9:278. From the perspective of Jesus in this story, Gentiles are not in view; from the perspective of Luke, Gentiles may very well be in view. Wiefel does not come to a conclusion: "Ob diese Aussage bestimmt ist durch die Vorstellung von der "eschatologischen Völkerwallfahrt zum Gottesberg" is umstritten vor allem ist die Verbindung von Völkerwallfahrt und Heilsmahl (Jes 25, 6–8) ungewöhnlich." Wiefel, *Evangelium nach Lukas*, 262.

180. Meadors, "The 'Messianic' Implications of the Q Material," 267.

181. Leaney, *A Commentary on the Gospel According to St. Luke*, 208.

Like the other eschatological banquet texts surveyed, the main point of this saying is inclusion or exclusion from the banquet. When the banquet finally arrives, there will be people on the outside who assumed they ought to be included. A unique element in this pericope is that not all who shared table-fellowship with Jesus will enter through the narrow door. This is therefore a warning to Jesus' followers that they too must be prepared to enter the banquet.[182] Merely associating with Jesus is not enough to guarantee participation in the eschatological age, one must act now and actually enter through the door before it is closed. After the door to the banquet is closed, those left outside cannot enter.

Luke 14: The Great Banquet

Introduction

That Luke 14 is the result of "a rather sophisticated compositional planning" is assumed in scholarly writing on this chapter.[183] Stein, for example, sees Luke as drawing together three episodes critical of the Pharisees around the theme of eating.[184] Marshall accepts chapter 14 as a clear unit, "but the unity is probably secondary; it is not certain whether the unity was created by Luke."[185] Some scholars understand this banquet scene as a Greco-Roman symposium[186] while others see the whole chapter

---

182. Johnson makes repentance the main theme of the pericope. Johnson, *The Gospel of Luke*, 220. Manson sees this as a warning against "belated repentance." Manson, *The Gospel of Luke*, 167. A similar idea is found in *m.Aboth* 4.16: "[P]repare yourself in the vestibule that you may enter the banquet hall."

183. For example, Braun, *Feasting and Social Rhetoric in Luke 14*, 176. In another article, Braun says "Evidence of deliberate collation of these units into a coherent episode is difficult to miss" (Braun, "Symposium or Anti-Symposium?," 72).

184. Stein, *Luke*, 385.

185. Marshall, *The Gospel of Luke*, 577.

186. There are several scholars who argue Luke as created a scene along the lines of a Greco-Roman symposium. Perhaps the first to make this suggestion was Meeûs in 1961. Meeûs identifies a number of elements of symposia which Luke appears to employ (invitation, announcement of issue for debate, dialogue in the form of table-talk, typical guests and uninvited guests, etc.). Meeûs, "Composition De Lc 14 Et Genre Symposiaque," 847–70. Steele argued that Luke employed the form of symposium in order to demonstrate Jesus' superiority over the other guests at the banquet, just as Plato showed Socrates to be superior to those who ate with him. Steele, "Luke 11:37–54-a Modified Hellenistic Symposium," 379–94. The various elements of a symposium are demonstrated in all three such meals in Luke (7:36–50, 11:37–54, 14:1–24) to varying degrees. Smith argues Luke only used symposium as a genre as far as it supported his overall purpose of critiquing the rich. Smith, "Table Fellowship as a Literary Motif," 617. It is possible to argue that Luke has taken a setting which was quite Jewish and re-cast it for a Hellenistic Jewish context which might have expected a more "Greek Jesus," or for Gentiles who would have missed the whole point of a messianic banquet altogether. There are other examples of this in Luke. Steele uses this text to show that Luke has adapted the story found in Matthew and Mark along the lines of a Greco-Roman symposium. Steele, "Luke 11:37–54-a Modified Hellenistic Symposium," 390.

as a *chreia* based on a general banquet motif.[187] In either case, the blessing given by a fellow-banqueter concerning the one who eats at the feast in the Kingdom of Heaven (14:15) seems consistent with the other references to eschatological banquet found in Mark and Matthew. It is likely that this man firmly believed that he would be one of those blessed by sharing in the messianic feast.[188] Jesus' response to this blessing implies a common understanding the eschatological as inaugurated by great banquet. Stein comments that the "great banquet" in the parable is "a clear allusion to the Jewish hope for the time when the Messiah would come and share a great feast with Israel's devout."[189]

Jesus uses the common banquet motif to give a response to the beatitude in 14:15. That Luke has adapted that parable along Greco-Roman lines in order to make the Jewish Jesus appeal a gentile readership is not a problem since the elements of an eschatological banquet are still clear. This mixing of Jewish source and Greco-Roman genre could account for the struggle to describe the material precisely: both potential backgrounds are in fact present in Luke.

Context of the Parable of the Great Banquet

The parable of the Great Banquet is placed in the so-called "travel narrative" of Luke.[190] While the section is widely recognized, it is not at all clear what Luke's overall purpose

---

187. Having rejected the suggestion that Luke 14 is a symposium, Braun describes this chapter as *chreia* (a brief statement, thesis, or an "instructive anecdote") and parable. Aphthonius of Antioch defined chreia in the late fourth to early fifth century as "a concise reminiscence aptly attributed to some [specific] character" and generally useful [for living]." Cameron, "'What Have You Come out to See?,'" 46. After expanding the definition of this rhetorical device, Braun argues Luke 14 is also built around a "*chreia* pattern" or an "elaboration pattern" as found in *On the Chreia* by Hermongenes of Tarsus. Malherbe collects several *chreiai* in the New Testament, all from Luke (6:5 in Codex Bezae, 12:13–14, 17:20–21). Malherbe, *Moral Exhortation: A Greco-Roman Sourcebook*, 111. This pattern includes "maxims, pronouncements, contraries, analogies and exempla to construct an argument on an issue embedded in a *chreia*," precisely the pattern Braun finds in Luke 14. Luke 14 begins with the story of the healing of the man with dropsy (14:1–6), in which the householder seeks to find honor at the expense the poor and concludes with the parable of the Great Banquet in which a wealthy man becomes a benefactor for the poor. There is therefore a sustain series of statements and examples in which Jesus reverses common thinking by exalting the poor. See also the brief introduction by Watson, "Chreia/Aphorism," 104–6.

188. Ernst, *Das Evangelium nach Lukas*, 442, citing Isa 25:6–8; cf. Stöger, *Luke*, 2:25, 27.

189. Stein, *Luke*, 393. Stein then cites as evidence of this "widespread messianic expectation" a series of texts in the Hebrew Bible (Isa 25:6; 65:13–14; Ps 81:16) and the intertestamental period (2 *Esdras* 2:38; *1 Enoch* 62:14; 1QSa 2:11–13) along with Luke 13:28–29; 22:15–20, 30; 1 Cor 11:23–26 and Rev 19:9. Cf. Evans, *Saint Luke*, 559, citing the same apocalyptic texts. For a similar list, see Just, *The Ongoing Feast*, 167–68.

190. While the travel narrative obviously begins at 9:51 with the words " Jesus resolutely set out for Jerusalem," the conclusion is less certain. The end of the unit could be the triumphal entry (19:28–44), which functions as a transition to Jesus' ministry in Jerusalem, completing the "journey" signaled in 9:51. Blomberg, however, ends the travel section in 18:34 based on his overall chiastic scheme for the section in which 18:31–34 are parallel to 9:51–62, and introduction and conclusion to following

was for the unit.[191] The "travel narrative" is not really about travel since Luke does not describe a real journey from Galilee to Jerusalem in travelogue fashion. The journey is not the key to the section, but rather the destination (Jerusalem) and what will happen at that destination (the crucifixion). A major indication of the importance of the destination is found in 13:29–30 which states that people will be gathered from around the world to share in the messianic banquet.

J. A. Sanders has picked up the suggestion first made by C. F. Evans that the travel narrative is a Midrash on the book of Deuteronomy.[192] Sanders works very hard to show that Deut 14 is roughly parallel to the Great Banquet parable, although the best evidence is found in the nature of the excuses given by those invited to the banquet. Regardless of whether one is swayed by the midrash-theory of the central section of Luke, the importance of the Great Banquet is once again highlighted.

Within the central section of the travel narrative (13:10—15:32) several motifs appear. Feasting is obviously a major factor, but in the table fellowship scenes Luke seems to be contrasting insiders with outsiders, specifically Pharisees and the "underclass" or sinners. This contrast works itself out in a series of "reversals" in which the expected positive role model is replaced by a negative model, one which the original hearer would never have guessed.[193] This is certainly the case in the reversal of guests in the Great Banquet as well as the Prodigal Son. In order to enter the Banquet, there must be an invitation (καλέω). There are some who are invited and refuse, others who are invited and enter. Once one has entered the banquet, there is great joy. This is true for the Lost Son parable in Luke 15. The lost son enters the celebration banquet where

---

Jesus, with the individual steps of the chiasm found in the parable material distributed throughout the section. Blomberg, "Midrash, Chiasmus, and the Outline of Luke's Central Section," 245. The details of this chiasm are sometimes difficult to see, but Blomberg's work highlights the importance of the Parable of the Great Banquet in chapter 14 as the "center" of the Travel Narrative. Stein runs the Travel Narrative from 9:51 through 19:27, but declines to even attempt to identify a structure for the subunits, other than to break the section into three parts based on the three mentions of Jerusalem (9:51, 13:22, 17:11). Stein, *Luke*, 295. Green ends the Travel Narrative in 19:48, noting the transitional nature of 19:28–48, although he observes the ending of the section is not a particularly critical point in the interpretation of the middle section of Luke. Green, *The Gospel of Luke*, 399.

191. Nolland has a very helpful excursus on the travel narrative with bibliography. Nolland, *Luke 9:21—18:34*, 525–31. See also Blomberg, "Midrash, Chiasmus"; Moessner, *Lord of the Banquet*; Marshall, *Luke: Historian and Theologian*, 148–53.

192. Sanders, "The Ethic of Election in Luke's Great Banquet Parable," 245–71. This article was revised and included as chapter 8 in Evans and Sanders, *Luke and Scripture: The Function of Sacred Tradition in Luke-Acts*. See p. 121 of this volume above for a chart comparing Deuteronomy and Luke. Deut 11–14 is roughly equivalent to the central section in this scheme.

193. The "good" Samaritan, for example, is something a Jew of the first century would have thought impossible (Luke 10:25–37), that a tax collector might go up to the temple to pray at the same time as a Pharisee yet come away justified would have been a ridiculous suggestion (18:9–14), that a sinful woman would burst into a banquet held by a Pharisee and weep all over a rabbi's feet yet leave forgiven of her sins would have been completely unexpected (Luke 7:36–50). In each of these examples, it is a Pharisee or teacher of the Law who comes out on the wrong side of the illustration.

there is great joy at his return. His brother receives a similar invitation, but he does not enter into the celebration.

Chapter 14 begins a new Sabbath, all the sub-pericopes in the chapter are at a Sabbath-dinner. Like the previous section, the series of stories begins with a healing on the Sabbath (14:1–6). In 14:7–14 Jesus gives a brief teaching on seating at a wedding feast or banquet. One of those at the banquet comments "Blessed is the man who will eat at the feast in the kingdom of God" (14:17). Jesus responds with the parable of the Great Banquet (14:18–24) in which those who think they will be at the banquet are not in fact going to be there. This is a classic "reversal of fortunes" since it is the poor and impure who will enter the banquet instead of those initially invited. In addition, the rejection of the invitation is most clearly highlighted in this parable. Perhaps the parable is less about a great banquet but about the lameness of the excuses for not participating. Since the issue is still table fellowship, Luke 15 must be seen as an extension of chapter 14.

If this analysis of 13:10—15:32 is correct, then there are several themes which revolve around the banquet motif in Luke's travel narrative. First, the banquet is a time of great joy and celebration for those who are in attendance. Second, and perhaps key to this motif, is the invitation to participate in the banquet. Those to whom the invitation was first given have rejected the summons and have been replaced by others. Third, those who expect to be in the banquet will find themselves excluded by their own choice. Lastly, those who find themselves attending the banquet are the "underclass," the least likely of all to be there at all.

The Parable as Allegory

As with the parables of the Wedding Banquet or Wise Virgins, there are problems with the assumption the parable in Luke 14 was intended as an allegory, either by Jesus or by Luke. Often the servants sent to invite the guests are seen as allegorical of the prophets.[194] D. Smith sees the banquet scene, which was originally a comment on the ministry of Jesus, adapted by Luke to comment on the contemporary state of the church.[195] As Marshall comments, "difficulty is caused by attempting to take all the details of the story in too literal a sense in order to construct a coherent allegory."[196]

---

194. Hultgren lists several possible allegorical interpretations of the two sets of servants who are unsuccessful when delivering the invitation: the former and latter prophets (Gundry, *Matthew*, 437); the prophets of Israel and John the Baptist (Hagner, *Matthew 14–28*, 630). The prophets and the Christian missionaries (Lüz, *Matthew 21–28*, 3:240); John the Baptist, Jesus his disciples and the Christian missionaries (McNeile, *Matthew*, 314–15); There is no correlation, it simply means that God has sent a lot of prophets to Israel without much effect. Hultgren, *Parables of Jesus*, 344–45.

195. "The church is to follow Jesus' lead by extended its fellowship (or its meal invitation) to society's outcasts, just as Jesus did (and will do at the end time)" (Smith, "Table Fellowship as Literary Motif," 637). This is certainly an appropriate application, but to what extent this is the intention of Luke is unclear.

196. Marshall, *The Gospel of Luke*, 586. His warning is wise for reading the Wedding Banquet

Derrett argues there is nothing in the story which is implausible once the proper background to the parable is set.[197] Marshall does not work this out consistently himself, since he understands the second invitation in v. 23 as potentially including the gentiles.[198] Stein also rejects allegorizing, but cannot resist in the case of the second invitation: "the second sending is unique to Luke and speaks of the entrance of the Gentiles into God's kingdom."[199] Derrett is consistent, however, noting that there is no reference to the Gentiles in the parable.[200] If we reject the "parable as Church-created allegory" hermeneutic and stay within the story Luke is telling, then the parable is a response to the banquet-goer's comment about a particular messianic expectation.

The Invitation and Excuses

In the Lukan version of the parable the invited guests do not come to the banquet and are replaced by the poor, cripple and blind, while in Matt 22 the replacement guests come from the margins of society. The Luke version of the parable gives three excuses, while *GThomas* 64 has four. The differences are minor. Bailey comments that these excuses[201] are not simply lame, but rather bold-faced lies.[202] For example, no one in the Middle East would purchase land without thoroughly investigating it. Derrett, on the other hand, seeks a legal basis for this excuse,[203] but Bailey dismisses these as unnecessary since banquets are normally held in the late afternoon, after the day's work is over.[204] The need to examine[205] oxen is "transparent fabrication" since no man would buy oxen without first seeing them pull a load first.[206] Sometimes the offense

---

parable in Matt 22:1–14 as well.

197. Derrett, *Law in the New Testament*, 127.

198. Marshall, *The Gospel of Luke*, 590. He does not explicitly connect the second invitation to the gentile mission in Acts, however. So to Fitzmyer, *Luke(X-XXIV,* 1053, who states that Luke has allegorized the original parable of Jesus in terms of Luke's view of salvation history. The people in the "highways and hedges" are Jews of less noble status. Acts 13:46 is of critical importance for Fiztmyer's view—the gospel much be preached to the Jews first, then after it is rejected, to the Gentiles. However, it is hard to see the parable reaching into the book of Acts since there are three such rejections in Acts (18:6, 28:23–28). If Luke were inclined toward allegory, he might have done a better job and had three opportunities for the first invited guests to join the banquet, rather than one.

199. Stein, *Luke*, 394.

200. Derrett, *Law in the New Testament*, 127.

201. The verb παραιτέομαι is found a dozen times in the New Testament and is used in classical Greek as a euphemism for declining an invitation (BDAG, citing Polybius 5, 27, 3). The word can be used for asking for someone's release from execution (Acts 25:11), See also *EDNT* 3:23; Schönweiss, *DNTT* 2:858–59; Stählin, *TDNT* 1:195. There is no negative connotation inherent in the word.

202. Bailey, *Through Peasant Eyes*, 95–98.

203. Derrett, *Law in the New Testament*, 137.

204. Bailey, *Through Peasant Eyes*, 96.

205. The verb δοκιμάζω (to test) here means "to look them over." He is not going to simply "look them over" but rather examine them closely.

206. Bailey says that the need to go spend time with one's new wife is "intensely rude" in a Middle

is softened by citing Deut 20:7, which exempts a man from war for one year after marrying, but this cannot apply here since he is being invited to a banquet, not a war![207]

The Replacement Guests

The host of the banquet became angry and ordered his servants to go out a second time in order to replace the guests who had given lame excuses.[208] They are told to go first to the "streets and the alleyways" (εἰς τὰς πλατείας καὶ ῥύμας τῆς πόλεως) and then later to "roads and country lanes" (εἰς τὰς ὁδοὺς καὶ φραγμοὺς). These are locations are all places where one might potentially encounter beggars, especially φραγμός, "hedge or fence" where beggars normally take refuge.[209] This fits well with the description of the new guests as "poor, crippled, blind and lame," a list which recalls Jesus' advice on who to invite to a banquet rather than the privileged (14:10-12). The πτωχός "designates the person wholly without possessions who must acquire the necessities of life through petition."[210] While proper treatment of the poor was an important part of Jewish religion in the first century, one did not typically ask the poor to join them at a banquet. Likewise, the ἀνάπειρος are the maimed and mutilated, perhaps as a result of war (cf. 2 Mac 8:24). The "blind and the lame" are something of a stock image of decrepitness in both the Hebrew Bible and the New Testament.[211] The eschatological age is often pictured as a time with the blind and the lame will be restored to sight and full strength (Isa 29:18-20, 35:56, Jer 31:8). These newly invited guests are similar to those who were excluded from communal meals at Qumran. 1QSa 2:5-9 excludes "everyone who is defiled in his flesh, paralyzed in his feet or in his hands, lame, blind, deaf, dumb or defiled in his flesh with a blemish visible to the eyes, or the tottering old man."[212]

Should anything be made of a first and second sending? Frequently this is taken as a Lukan allegorical touch in which the first sending is Jesus' ministry and

---

East context since men do not discuss women in a formal setting. Bailey, *Through Peasant Eyes*, 97.

207. Derrett, *Law in the New Testament*, 126–55; Ballard, "Reasons for Refusing the Great Supper," 347. Stein comments this is far too obscure for Luke's readers to understand. Stein, *Luke*, 393,

208. A passive participle of ὀργίζω, which only appears in the passive voice twice in Luke, the second time is in the conclusion to the Prodigal Son when the older brother becomes angry with the father for hosting a banquet for this worthless brother.

209. Marshall, *The Gospel of Luke*, 589.

210. Merklein, "πτωχός," *EDNT* 3:193. Cf. Bammel, "πτωχός," 6:884–915. The earliest use of the word has the sense of "destitute" and "mendicant."

211. See 2 Sam 5:6–8; Job 29:15; Jer 31:8, for example. Recall the *Apocryphon of Ezekiel* concerns two outsiders, a blind man and a lame man.

212. The second sets of guests are compelled (ἀναγκάζω) to come into the banquet. This aorist imperative ought not to be taken as forcing the guests "against their will," but rather as a reflection of the custom of politely refusing an invitation until one is pressed to accept it. Marshall, *The Gospel of Luke*, 590. On the other hand, Stein attempts to soften this word by saying that the command is to help the poor overcome their shyness and feelings of unworthiness. Stein, *Luke*, 693.

the second is the gentile mission of Acts. For example, Stein states "this detail would almost certainly have been interpreted allegorically by Luke's readers as an indication that Gentiles also were invited to partake of the messianic banquet."[213] It is better, however, to ground this parable in the ministry of Jesus and these multiple invitations as Jesus' ongoing ministry calling Israel to repentance. As Bailey says, the task in the parable is fulfilled in the ministry of Jesus: the banquet is in fact filled with the outcasts of Israel, "the details of the parable as it now stands precisely fit Jesus' own historical ministry."[214]

The parable ends with a somewhat enigmatic statement that the original guests will not even taste the food from the banquet. Derrett tries to explain this as a reference to taking food to those who are unable to attend the banquet on the basis of Neh 8:10–12,[215] but perhaps it is better take in the context of 15:1–2 where Jesus is eating once again with "tax collectors and other sinners." Jesus has gathered the spiritually poor and needy who are responding to his message and is eating with them in an enactment of the messianic banquet described in the Great Banquet parable. Clearly neither the Pharisee who hosted the meal in Luke 14 nor any of the other participants of the meal were in attendance at the "banquet" in 15:1–2 where Jesus ate with sinners. The final line of the parable may not be the voice of the host of the banquet in the parable, but rather the voice of Jesus, excluding those who reject his message from the eschatological feast.

Summary and Conclusion

It is important to notice that Jesus heeds his own teaching in this chapter—this is the last time in Luke he dines with a rich man or Pharisee. From this point in his ministry, Jesus will fellowship with the underclass of society.[216] Crossan makes the same point; Jesus lived out his parable in Luke 14 by eating with tax-collectors and other sinners despite accusations from his opponents.[217]

This observation highlights the centrality of the banquet in the parable of Luke 14. The parable is a turning point in the central section and may represent Luke's official statement that the breach between Jesus and the Pharisees is irreparable. It is the Pharisees who have made the lame excuses to the master of the banquet (Jesus)

---

213. Stein, *Luke*, 393. Similarly, Ernst states that this parable has been transformed into a theology for church mission: "[D]as gleichnis is in der jetzt vorliegenden Form vielschichtig: Aus der prophetischen Verheissung und Warnung is gedeutete Geschichte geworden. Die eschatologische Spannung wird auf eine kirchliche und missionstheologische Ebene transponiert" (Ernst, *Das Evangelium nach Lukas,* 446).

214. Bailey, *Through Peasant Eyes,* 101. Bailey correctly observes that Jesus did not carry out major Gentile ministry during his earthly ministry. Cf. Jeremias, *Jesus' Promise to the Nations*, 26.

215. Derrett, *Law in the New Testament*, 141.

216. Braun, *Feasting*, 175.

217. Crossan, *Revolutionary Biography*, 69.

and as a result they are being replaced with those who are in the outside (Jesus' disciples, the crowds, the repentant sinners, etc.) Yet they have the audacity to complain about not being in the banquet. As with the "other brother" in Luke 15, they need to be reminded that they have always had the opportunity to enter the banquet and celebrate with the father, but they have chosen to exclude themselves. The Pharisees have presumed upon an invitation to the messianic banquet, but miss out because of pride and arrogance.[218]

Luke 15: The Celebration of the Prodigal's Return

Luke 15 needs to be taken as an extension of chapter 14 since the issue is still table fellowship with tax-collectors and other sinners. I have already pointed out several linguistic connections between the two parables which imply that Luke intended to read the three parables of lostness along with the parable of the great banquet. What is morenT. Wright has suggested that this parable is the "story of Israel," specifically the exile and restoration of the nation.[219] Wright's reading of this parable is consistent with his view that many Jews in the Second Temple Period believed they were still living in the exile and the that the coming kingdom of God would put an end to that exile. It is not necessary to examine the details of the parable; of interest for this study is Luke's conscious placement of the parables of Lostness after the parable of the Great Banquet.

In Luke 15:1–2, the Pharisees complain that Jesus eats with sinners, thereby breaking table fellowship taboos which they think are important. Both Jesus and the Pharisees agree that the people Jesus is eating with are in fact lost; Jesus however believes that they can be "found." The proper course of action for a Pharisee would be to shun the sinner and have nothing to do with them,[220] but Jesus refuses to do this. He treats these outsiders with respect and fellowships with them as equals.[221]

The three parables which follow all revolve around the attitude of the Pharisees toward those who are coming to Jesus. In response to the "muttering" of the Pharisees Jesus teaches three parables of lostness: the lost sheep, the lost coin, and the lost son. The first two parables can be simply summarized: Someone has lost an item, a small

218. If Luke's community is a diaspora Jewish community, they too may be in danger of missing out on the messianic banquet as did their cousins in Jerusalem because they cannot accept the gentile sinners who have repented. This tension between Jew and Gentile is found in Acts, although it is developed more sharply in the book of Galatians and 1 Corinthians. The whole section calls into question "the confidence of those who take it for granted that they will be present at the great eschatological banquet." Nolland, *Luke 9:21—18:34*, 758.

219. Wright, *Jesus and the Victory of God*, 126. Bailey has written two monographs on Luke 15. He says he developed the idea that the Prodigal Son tells the story of Israel from Wright's brief comment. Bailey, *Jacob & the Prodigal: How Jesus Retold Israel's Story*; Bailey, *The Cross & the Prodigal: Luke 15 Through the Eyes of Middle Eastern Peasants*.

220. Hultgren, *The Parables of Jesus*, 61.

221. This is a clear theme in the Synoptic Gospels, but especially in Luke, cf. 5:29–32, 7:36–50; 17:11–19, 19:1–9.

percentage of whole (1% of the sheep, 10% of the coins); they will not rest until the lost item is found and returned; after restoring the lost item, there is much rejoicing. Jesus is describing his ministry as aimed at restoring those "lost" members of the nation of Israel, those who have fallen through the cracks of the religious establishment. Each of these parables teaches God's unrelenting search for the lost (a sheep, a coin, a son). In each parable there is a demonstration of great joy (expressed in hyperbolic terms) when the lost is found, a joy expressed as a celebration to which the neighbors are invited. This is remarkably similar to the set of messianic banquet motifs present in the previous chapter. The final movement of the final parable is critical—the "other brother" is on the outside of the great celebration. The reader does not know if he enters in and participates or not. This is the ultimate reversal of fortune since the proper, obedient son does not celebrate with his father yet the disobedient son is treated with honor. This parable might be better to call this the Parable of the other Brother since the real goal of the parable is not necessarily to teach that God will always be there for the wanton sinner, but rather to teach the religious establishment that they are in danger of missing out on the kingdom since they, like the older brother, choose to remain outside the celebration.

Summary and Conclusions

Luke develops the idea of a banquet by highlighting the present aspects of that banquet in Jesus' ministry. He certainly does not downplay eschatological aspect in the Last Supper, but the coming eschatological age is not as important for him as the banquet as present in Jesus' ministry. There are several aspects of the eschatological banquet which are highlighted in Luke's gospel.

First, the invitation to the eschatological banquet has already been issued and many have responded positively to it. The sinners who are fellowshipping with Jesus in Luke 15:1–2 are those who were invited from the "highways and byways" (Luke 14:23). But there are others who have rejected that invitation, and they have done so with lame, insulting excuses. Like the older brother, the Pharisees think that they are doing the father's will, but they are not. In fact, they are insulting the father by refusing to rejoice over the repentance of the sinner.

Second, the invitation to join in the banquet is still open, but it will not be open forever. Jesus says that the door to the banquet will close and there will be people on the outside. In fact, there are some within Jesus' followers who may find themselves on the outside when the door is shut. Luke has a pastoral motivation by highlighting this aspect of the eschatological banquet. Not all of those who are sharing table fellowship with Jesus are in fact prepared for the closing of the door.

Third, unlike Matthew, the banquet as a wedding is less important in Luke. Although the language appears several times in the gospel, Luke assumes the image of a wedding celebration but does not develop it to the extent that Matthew did. It may be that Luke's audience was not as aware of the marriage metaphor in the prophets of the Hebrew Bible. They would not have "heard the echo" as clearly as Matthew's audience; therefore Luke mutes that aspect of Jesus' teaching.

Summary and Conclusions

Having surveyed the texts in the synoptic gospels, it is possible to offer a few concluding remarks on the eschatological / wedding banquet in the synoptic gospels. Three overlapping strands of tradition appear over and over again in the synoptic gospels. There was a widespread belief in the Second Temple Period that the eschatological age would be inaugurated by grand feast hosted by the messiah himself. The eschatological age would be a restoration from exile, beginning with the invitation for Israel to travel through the wilderness once again and gather at Zion. Here the feast is ongoing as God provides food in the wilderness for his people. But this eschatological age is also described as a restoration of the marriage covenant between God and his people. The Lord will call his wife from the wilderness and restore the relationship on Zion. The Gospel writers emphasize all three aspects of this tradition drawn from the Hebrew Bible, weaving them in unique ways to highlight aspects of Jesus and his ministry. Several emphases emerge.

First, in his table fellowship and other shared meals, Jesus presented his ministry has an ongoing banquet in anticipation of the eschatological banquet. This is consistent with the meals at Qumran, although in many ways quite different. Rather than exclusive table fellowship with members defined by purity, Jesus' meals are open to everyone without concern for purity.

Second, at these banquets, Jesus is inviting everyone to join him in the celebration. While John was the "voice crying in the wilderness," Jesus is the one who invites people to eat and drink with him in the wilderness. This invitation appears to have been a part of Jesus' mission from the beginning and especially characterized his ministry in Galilee. This aspect of Jesus' ministry caused concern among the disciples of John since they prepared for the coming new age by fasting. Since Jesus did not concern himself with the traditions of the Pharisees with respect to purity during meals, the Pharisees were angered with Jesus' table fellowship.

Third, this celebration is sometimes described as a wedding banquet, with Jesus as the host. In one case he describes himself as bridegroom, other times he is simply the honored guest at a meal. It goes beyond the evidence to claim that the image of a bridegroom was a metaphor for the Messiah. Rather, the bridegroom is in fact God as he reconciles with his bride, Israel.

Fourth, Jesus invited people to join a celebration which inaugurates a new age. That new age was the hope of the prophets and is aptly described as a reunion true Israel and her God. Those who join Jesus celebrate the restoration of the covenant between God and his people. Like the symbol of twelve disciples, a celebration of an eschatological feast was intended to play on the current hopes of the Second Temple Period.

Fifth, those who participate with Jesus in his ongoing celebration of the dawning eschatological age are new Israel; those who reject the invitation will find themselves outside of the coming kingdom, unable to ever enter the eschatological feast. In the ministry of Jesus, those who accept his teaching are the least likely candidates for the kingdom, while those who reject his teaching are exactly those most in the Second Temple world would have expected to enter the kingdom feast first.

8

Conclusions and Suggestions For Further Research

THIS STUDY HAS SHOWN that Jesus' description of his ministry as a wedding banquet is consistent with several well-known traditions from the Hebrew Bible. Jesus combined eschatological banquet with Wilderness and Marriage traditions in order to describe the end of the Exile and the role of his mission in the reunion of Israel. What is unique in the Second Temple Period is his application of the marriage metaphor to himself. Jesus described himself as a bridegroom who is inviting Israel to return from the Wilderness and join with him in celebration of the end of the age. Several conclusions can be drawn from this study.

First, the intertextual methodology described in chapter 2 can be used to study traditions from the Hebrew Bible in the Gospels. In the case of this dissertation, I "heard the echo" of several traditions in the teaching of Jesus. These echoes became more clear as I surveyed the material in the Hebrew Bible and Second Temple Period, which might contribute to Jesus' unique combination of the eschatological banquet with Wilderness Tradition and marriage metaphor drawn from the Hebrew prophets. By applying this wealth of material to the actions and sayings of Jesus, it became clear that Jesus' use of these traditions was intentional. Jesus wanted to place himself and his mission within the world of the Hebrew Bible in order to call Israel to repentance. A banquet in the Wilderness that celebrates the restoration of the bride Israel to her God is a development of these strands of tradition in order to apply them to the new circumstance of Jesus' life and mission.

Potentially this method could be applied to any tradition that may be drawn from the Hebrew Bible. Several scholars have already examined the Exodus tradition or shepherd metaphors, but this intertextual method could be employed to study any echo of earlier tradition. There are many agricultural metaphors for the end of the age in Jesus' teaching. It is possible this intertextual method could illuminate a number of Jesus' parables by examining the traditions from the Hebrew Bible, which uses harvest language. This method could be applied to the epistles as well. Paul makes use of election language in his epistles. By "hearing an echo" from the Hebrew Bible, it may be possible to understand Paul's use of this language in a way that is more consistent with the canon of Scripture rather than imposing modern theological questions on the text.

Second, it is clear from this dissertation that Second Temple Period Judaism often conceived of the end of the age in terms of a glorious banquet. This may be an inaugural victory feast shared after the defeat of Israel's enemies, or an ongoing banquet of sumptuous food. The eschatological age is like a return to Eden and a time when all people will eat and be satisfied. Jesus enacts this tradition in his table fellowship. Just as Isa 25:6–8 anticipated a celebration on Mount Zion, Jesus celebrates the coming age by eating and drinking with his followers as a restored Israel.

Third, it is equally clear that the end of the age could be understood as a restoration of Israel to her place as the bride of the Lord. While this tradition is muted in the literature of the Second Temple Period, the marriage metaphor was a powerful and moving description of the Lord's love for his people despite their disobedience. By combining these two traditions Jesus was able to use the eschatological message of the Hebrew Bible to describe his mission as well as the current state of Israel. They are still "in the Wilderness" of the Exile and need to return to their husband.

Fourth, a common element in both of these conceptions of the end of the age is an invitation to return from the Wilderness and enjoy this renewed relationship with God. That both John the Baptist and the Qumran community used Isa 40:1–5 is an important indication that the Wilderness figured prominently in Jewish messianic hope. Because the place where Israel first encountered her God was the Wilderness, both Hosea and Isaiah use the Wilderness as a way of describing a new Exodus in the coming age. Jesus evokes that tradition as well. The Synoptic Gospels portray Jesus as feeding the multitude in the Wilderness as a re-enactment of the original Exodus. Since the end of the exile did not happen as some expected, many writers continued to think of Israel as still in exile.

Fifth, Jesus' table fellowship can be said with confidence to be a historically accurate reminiscence of Jesus' ministry. Certainly Jesus' participation in meals is found in every layer of tradition and is unlikely to be a creation of the apostolic community. On the one hand, the later church would not create stories that made Jesus look soft on sin (eating with sinners, etc.). Even assuming that Matthew represents a Jewish Diaspora community in Antioch, it is unlikely that Matthew would not redact Mark's presentation of Jesus as eating with unclean people. The accusation that Jesus was a "drunkard and glutton" is also unlikely to be a creation of a later church that increasingly held Jesus to be sinless.

From these five conclusions, several questions for further study emerge. First, if Jesus really did "come eating and drinking," then it is at least possible that he described himself in terms of a bridegroom and presented his ministry as a kind of ongoing wedding celebration. This would explain the importance of table fellowship among

Conclusions and Suggestions For Further Research

the disciples of Jesus after the resurrection (Acts 2:42–44). Peter continues to reach to the fringes of Judaism in Acts, sharing hospitality with Simon the Tanner (Acts 9:43).

Second, since the idea of the end of the age as a banquet and as a marriage celebration was likely current in the first century, it may very well be that Jesus himself is responsible for the combination of the ideas to describe his ministry. If this is the case, then the case for the authenticity of the parables in Matt 22 and 25 as well as Luke 14 is strengthened. These parables are congruent with the traditions of the Hebrew Bible and are expressed in ways that are consistent with the eschatological thinking of the Second Temple Period. There is no need to see the use of a marriage metaphor as a sign of an allegorizing Gospel writer since it was very much a part of Second Temple Period Judaism. Jesus created the parables himself out of these existing traditions. While there is no clear statement in the Synoptic Gospels in which Jesus explicitly states "my ministry is like a wedding banquet," it is implied. This also strengthens the case for the historicity of the wedding parables. If they were the creation of later Christian writers then the connection would have been more explicit. Later texts developed what was only implicit in the teachings of Jesus.

Third, the image of Israel as a bride persists and develops further in Judaism as well as in Christianity, although in different directions. There is nothing in the Pauline corpus that picks up on the eschatological banquet, nor is his use of the Wilderness Tradition in 1 Cor 10 eschatological. His scant use of a marriage metaphor for the Church (2 Cor 11:2; Eph 5:25–33) has nothing to do with the tradition as found in Hosea, Jeremiah, or Jesus, and there is certainly no eschatology in these passages. Christianity developed the metaphor and applied it to the church, perhaps as a result of early replacement theology. If Israel was the bride of the Lord, then the church must now be the bride of Christ.[1] The development of a union between the church and Christ occurs early, perhaps as early as the Gospel of John and the Apocalypse. It should be possible to trace the trajectory of the marriage metaphor in second-century Christian works such as *Shepherd of Hermas*, which equates the bride image with the Church. What is missing, however, is the invitation to return from Exile, travel the Wilderness once again, and come to Zion to meet with the Lord. As the marriage metaphor develops, it is divorced from the eschatological banquet and transformed into the mystical union of Christ and the Church. This post-biblical theological development should not be read back into the Gospels and the teaching of Jesus. Jesus' use of traditions drawn from the Hebrew Bible is part of the Second Temple Period discussion, not the later Christian developments.

---

1. For example, Huber understands the metaphor of the Bride in Rev 21 as indicating that the Christian Community is a renewed Israel and the New Jerusalem, the bride of the Lamb. Huber, *Like a Bride Adorned: Reading Metaphor in John's Apocalypse*, 168.

Bibliography

Aageson, J. W. "Typology, Correspondence, and Application of Scripture in Rom 9–11." *JSNT* 31 (1987) 51–72.
Abma, R. *Bonds of Love: Methodic Studies of Prophetic Texts with Marriage Imagery (Isaiah 50: 1–3 and 54:1–10, Hosea 1–3, Jeremiah 2–3)*. Studia Semitica Neerlandica 40. Assen: Van Gorcum, 1999.
Achtemeier, E. "Typology." In *IDBSup*, 926–27.
Ackroyd, P. R. *Exile and Restoration: A Study of Hebrew Thought of the Sixth Century B.C.* OTL. Philadelphia: Westminster, 1968.
Addinall, P. "The Wilderness in Pedersen's Israel." *JSOT* 20 (1981) 75–83.
Adler, E. J. "The Background for the Metaphor of Covenant as Marriage in the Hebrew Bible." PhD diss., University of California, Berkeley, 1990.
Ahearne-Kroll, S. P. "The Suffering of David and the Suffering of Jesus: The Use of Four Psalms of Individual Lament in the Passion Narrative of the Gospel of Mark." PhD diss., University of Chicago, 2005.
Aichele, G. and G. Phillips. *Intertextuality and the Bible*. Semeia 69–70. Atlanta: Society of Biblical Literature, 1995.
Albertz, R. *A History of Israelite Religion in the Old Testament Period*. 2 vols. OTL. Louisville: Westminster John Knox, 1994.
Allegro, J. M. "A Newly Discovered Fragment of a Commentary on Psalms XXXVII." *PEQ* 86 (1954) 69–75.
Allen, L. C. *Ezekiel 20–48*. WBC 29. Dallas: Word, 1990.
———. *Psalms 101–50 (Revised)*. WBC 21. Waco: Word, 2002.
Allison, D. C., Jr. *The End of the Ages Has Come*. Philadelphia: Fortress, 1985.
———. *The Intertextual Jesus: Scripture in Q*. Valley Forge, PA: Trinity, 2000.
———. "Jesus and the Covenant." In *Studies in the Historical Jesus*, edited by C. A. Evans and S. E. Porter, 61–82. Sheffield: Sheffield Academic, 1995.
———. *The New Moses: A Matthean Typology*. Minneapolis: Fortress, 1993.
———. "Who Will Come from East and West? Observations on Matt 8.11–12/Luke 13.28–29." *IBS* 11 (1989) 158–70.
Amsler, S. "Des visions de Zacharie à l'apocalypse d'Esaïe 24–27." In *Book of Isaiah—Le livre d'Isaïe*, edited by J. Vermeylen, 263–73. Leuven: Leuven University, 1989.
Andersen, T. D. "Renaming and Wedding Imagery in Isaiah 62." *Bib* 67 (1986) 75–80.
Andersen, F. I., and D. N. Freedman. *Amos*. AB 24A. New York: Doubleday, 1989.
———. *Hosea*. AB 24. New York: Doubleday, 1986.
Anderson, A. A. *2 Samuel*. WBC 11. Dallas: Word, 1989.

Bibliography

Anderson, B. W. "Exodus and Covenant in Second Isaiah and Prophetic Tradition." In *Magnalia dei*, 339–60. Garden City, NY: Doubleday, 1976.

———. "Exodus Typology in Second Isaiah." In *Israel's Prophetic Heritage: Essays in Honor of James Muilenburg*, edited by B. W. Anderson and W. J. Harrelson, 177–95. New York: Harper, 1962.

Anderson, H. *The Gospel of Mark*. NCB. Grand Rapids: Eerdmans, 1976.

———. "The Old Testament in Mark's Gospel." In *The Use of the Old Testament in the New and Other Essays: Studies in Honor of William Franklin Stinespring*, edited by J. M. Efird, 280–306. Durham, NC: Duke University, 1972.

Anderson, R. T. "The Role of the Desert in Israelite Thought." *JBR* 27 (1959) 41–44.

Anderson, B. W., and W. J. Harrelson, editors. *Israel's Prophetic Heritage: Essays in Honor of James Muilenburg*. New York: Harper, 1962.

Archer, G. L. *A Survey of Old Testament Introduction*. Chicago: Moody, 1964.

Argall, R. A., B. A. Bow, and R. A. Werline. *For a Later Generation: The Transformation of Tradition in Israel, Early Judaism, and Early Christianity*. Harrisburg, PA: Trinity, 2000.

Auld, A. G. "Cities of Refuge in Israelite Tradition." *JSOT* 10 (1978) 26–40.

Aune, D. E. *Revelation 1–5*. WBC 52A. Nashville: Nelson, 1997.

Ausloos, H. "Psalm 45, Messianism and the Septuagint." In *Septuagint and Messianism*, 239–51. Leuven: Leuven University, 2006.

Bailey, K. E. *The Cross & the Prodigal: Luke 15 Through the Eyes of Middle Eastern Peasants*. 2nd editor. Downers Grove, IL: InterVarsity, 2005.

———. *Jacob & the Prodigal: How Jesus Retold Israel's Story*. Downers Grove, IL: InterVarsity, 2003.

———. *Poet & Peasant and Through Peasant Eyes*. Grand Rapids: Eerdmans, 1983.

———. *Through Peasant Eyes: More Lucan Parables, Their Culture and Style*. Grand Rapids: Eerdmans, 1980.

Bailey, L. R. *Biblical Perspectives on Death*. Philadelphia: Fortress, 1979.

Bailey, K. E., and W. L. Holladay. "Young Camel and Wild Ass in Jer 2:23–25." *VT* 18 (1968) 256–60.

Baillet, M. "Qumran grotte 4. III (4Q482–4Q520)." In *DJD* 7, 81–105.

Baker, D. "Isaiah." In *ZBBCOT*, 4:2–227.

Baker, D. L. "Typology and the Christian Use of the Old Testament." *SJT* 29 (1976) 137–57.

Ballard, P. H. "Reasons for Refusing the Great Supper." *JTS* (1972) 341–50.

Baltzer, K. *Deutero-Isaiah*. Hermeneia. Minneapolis: Fortress, 2001.

Balz, H., and G. Schneider. *Exegetical Dictionary of the New Testament*. 3 vols. Grand Rapids: Eerdmans, 1993.

Barnett, R. D. "Bringing the God into the Temple." In *Temples and High Places in Biblical Times*, edited by Avraham Biran, 10–20. Jerusalem: Nelson Glueck School of Biblical Archaeology of Hebrew Union College, 1981.

Barstad, H. M. *A Way in the Wilderness: The "Second Exodus" in the Message of Second Isaiah*. JSS Monograph 12. Manchester: University of Manchester, 1989.

Bartchy, S. S. "Table Fellowship." In *Dictionary of Jesus and the Gospels*, edited by J. B. Green, S. McKnight, and I. H. Marshall, 796–800. Downers Grove, IL: InterVarsity, 1992.

Barth, C. *Die Errettung vom Tode in den individuellen Klage und Dankliedern des Alten Testamentes*. Zollikon: Evangelischer, 1947.

Barthélemy, D., and J. T. Milik, editors. *Qumran Cave I*. DJD 1. Oxford: Clarendon, 1964.

Batey, R. A. "Jewish Gnosticism and the 'hieros gamos' of Eph 5:21–33." *NTS* 10 (1963) 121–27.

———. "The *mia sarx* Union of Christ and the Church." *NTS* 13 (1967) 270–81.

———. *New Testament Nuptial Imagery*. Leiden: Brill, 1971.

Bauckham, R. *The Climax of Prophecy: Studies on the Book of Revelation*. Edinburgh: T. & T. Clark, 1993.

———. "The Parable of the Royal Wedding Feast (Matthew 22:1–14) and the Parable of the Lame Man and the Blind Man (Apocryphon of Ezekiel)." *JBL* 115 (1996) 471–88.

Bauer, A. *Gender in the Book of Jeremiah: A Feminist-literary Reading*. Studies in Biblical Literature 5. New York: Lang, 1999.

Baumann, G. *Love and Violence: Marriage as a Metaphor for the Relationship between YHWH and Israel in the Prophetic Books*. Translated by L. Maloney. Collegeville, MN: Liturgical, 2003.

Baumgarten, J. M. "4Q502, Marriage or Golden Age Ritual?" *Journal of Jewish Studies* 34 (1983) 125–35.

———. "1QSa 1:11: Age of Testimony or Responsibility?" *Jewish Quarterly Review* (1959) 157–61.

———. *Studies in Qumran Law*. Studies in Judaism in Late Antiquity 24. Leiden: Brill, 1977.

Beale, G. K. "A Response to Jon Paulien on the Use of the Old Testament in Revelation." *AUSS* 39 (2001) 23–34.

———. *The Right Doctrine from the Wrong Texts? Essays on the Use of the Old Testament in the New*. Grand Rapids: Baker, 1994.

———. *The Use of Daniel in Jewish Apocalyptic Literature and in the Revelation of St. John*. Lanham, MD: University Press of America, 1984.

Beale, G. K., and D. A. Carson. *Commentary on the New Testament Use of the Old Testament*. Grand Rapids: Baker, 2007.

Beare, F. W. "The Parable of the Guests at the Banquet: A Sketch of the History of Its Interpretation." In *The Joy of Study: Papers on the New Testament and Related Subjects*, edited by S. E. Johnson, 1–7. New York: Macmillan, 1951.

Beasley-Murray, G. R. *Jesus and the Kingdom of God*. Grand Rapids: Eerdmans, 1986.

Beaucamp, E. "'Chant nouveau du retour' (Isa 42:10–17) un monstre de l'exégèse moderne." *Revue des sciences religieuses* 56 (1982) 145–58.

Beaudet, R. "La typologie de l'Exode dans le Second-Isaïe." *Laval théologique et philosophique* 19 (1963) 11–21.

Begrich, J. *Studien zu Deuterojesaja*. Theologische Bucherei 20. Munich: Kaiser, 1938.

Beker, J. C. "Echoes and Intertextuality: On the Role of Scripture in Paul's Theology." In *Paul and the Scriptures of Israel*, edited by C. A. Evans and J. A. Sanders, 64–69. JSNTSup 83. Sheffield: JSOT, 1993.

Ben-Barak, Z. "The Legal Background to the Restoration of Michal to David." In *Studies in the Historical Books*, edited by J. A. Emerton, 15–27. Leiden: Brill, 1979.

Benedikt, O. "Den apokalyptiske Abraham: patriarken i den antikke jødiske litteratur." *Dansk teologisk tidsskrift* 69 (2006) 2–13.

Benoit, P., and J. T. Milik. *DJD* 2. Oxford: Clarendon, 1961.

Ben-Porat, Z. "The Poetics of Literary Allusion." *PTL: A Journal for Descriptive Poetics and Theory of Literature* 1 (1976) 105–28.

Bibliography

Ben Zvi, E. "Observations on the Marital Metaphor of YHWH and Israel in Its Ancient Israel Context: General Conclusions and Particular Images in Hosea 1.2." *JSOT* 28 (2004) 363–84.

———. *Utopia and Dystopia in Prophetic Literature*. Göttingen: Vandenhoeck & Ruprecht, 2006.

Bergen, R. D. *1, 2 Samuel*. NAC 7. Nashville: Broadman & Holman, 1996.

Berges, U. "Der zweite Exodus im Jesajabuch: Auszug oder Verwandlung?" In *Manna fällt auch heute noch*, edited by E. Zenger, 77–95. Freiburg: Herder, 2004.

———. *Jesaja 1–12*. Freiburg: Herder, 2003.

———. *Jesaja 13–27*. Freiburg: Herder, 2007.

———. *Jesaja 40–48*. Freiburg: Herder, 2008.

Bethge, H. *Evangelium Thomae Copticum*. Stuttgart: Deutsche Bibelgesellschaft, 1963.

Beuken, W. A. M. "Isa. 55, 3–5: The Reinterpretation of David." *Bijdragen* 35 (1974) 49–64.

Biddle, M. E. "The City of Chaos and the New Jerusalem: Isaiah 24–27 in Context." *Perspectives in Religious Studies* 22 (1995) 5–12.

———. "The Figure of Lady Jerusalem: Identification, Deification and Personification of Cities in the ANE." In *The Biblical Canon in Comparative Perspective*, edited by W. Hallo, 173–94. Lewiston, NY: Mellen, 1991.

Bienaimé, G. "Un retour du Paradis dans le désert de l'Exode selon une tradition juive." In *Création dans l'Orient ancient*, 429–29. Paris: Cerf, 1987.

Biran, A., editor. *Temples and High Places in Biblical Times*. Jerusalem: Nelson Glueck School of Biblical Archaeology of Hebrew Union College, 1981.

Birch, B. C. "First and Second Samuel." In *NIB*, 2:947–1383.

Bird, M. *Are You the One Who Is to Come? The Historical Jesus and the Messianic Question*. Grand Rapids: Baker, 2009.

———. "Who Comes from the East and the West? Luke 13.28–29/Matt 8.11–12 and the Historical Jesus." *NTS* 52 (2006) 441–57.

Bird, P. "'To Play the Harlot': An Inquiry into an Old Testament Metaphor." In *Gender and Difference in Ancient Israel*, edited by P. Day, 75–94. Minneapolis: Fortress, 1989.

Birks, T. R. *Commentary on the Book of Isaiah*. London: Rivingtons, 1871.

Bisschops, R. "Are Religious Metaphors Rooted in Experience? On Ezekiel's Wedding Metaphors." In *The Bible Through Metaphor and Translation: A Cognitive Semantic Perspective*, edited by K. Feyaerts, 113–51. Oxford; New York: Lang, 2003.

Blenkinsopp, J. "The Family in First Temple Israel." In *Families in Ancient Israel*, edited by L. Perdue, 48–103. Louisville: Westminster John Knox, 1997.

———. *Isaiah 1–39*. AB 19. New York: Doubleday, 2000.

———. *Isaiah 40–55*. AB 19A. New York: Doubleday, 2000.

———. "Scope and Depth of the Exodus Tradition in Deutero-Isaiah, 40–55." *Concilium* 20 (1966) 41–55.

Blickenstaff, M. *"While the Bridegroom Is With Them": Marriage, Family, and Violence in the Gospel of Matthew*. JSNTSup 292. London: T. & T. Clark, 2005.

Block, D. I. *Judges, Ruth*. NAC 6. Nashville: Broadman & Holman, 1999.

Blomberg, C. *Contagious Holiness: Jesus' Meals with Sinners*. NSBT 19. Downers Grove, IL: InterVarsity, 2005.

———. *Interpreting the Parables*. Downers Grove, IL: InterVarsity, 1990.

———. *Matthew*. NAC 22. Nashville: Broadman & Holman, 1992.

———. "Midrash, Chiasmus, and the Outline of Luke's Central Section." In *Gospel Perspectives,* edited by R. T. France and D. Wenham, 3:217–61. Sheffield: JSOT, 1983.
Bloom, H. *The Anxiety of Influence.* New York: Oxford University, 1973.
———. *A Map of Misreading.* New York: Oxford University, 2003.
Bock, D. L. *Proclamation from Prophecy and Pattern: Lucan Old Testament Christology.* JSNTSup 12. Sheffield: Sheffield Academic, 1987.
Bonnard, P. E. *Le second Isaïe, son disciple et leurs éditeurs: Isaïe 40–66.* Paris: Gabalda, 1972.
———. "La Signification du desert, selon le Nouveau Testament." In *Hommage et reconnaissance: Recueil de travaux publiés à l'occasion du 60e anniversaire de Karl Barth,* 9–18. Paris: Delachaux & Niestle, 1946.
Boomershine, T. E. "Jesus of Nazareth and the Watershed of Ancient Orality and Literacy." In *Semeia* 65, edited by J. Dewey, 7–36. Atlanta: Society of Biblical Literature, 1994.
Bordreuil, P. "Les 'graces de David' et 1 Maccabees 2:57." *VT* 31 (1981) 73–76.
Borg, M. *Jesus: A New Vision.* San Francisco: HarperSanFrancisco, 1987.
Boring, E. M. "Matthew." In *NIB,* 8:87–505.
———. "A Proposed Reconstruction of Q 13:28–29." In *SBLSP* 28, 1–22. Atlanta: Scholars, 1989.
Bosman, H. J., and H. W. M. van Grol. *Studies in Isaiah 24–27.* Oudtestamentische studiën 43. Leiden: Brill, 2000.
Bovon, F. *L'Évangile selon saint Luc. 1, 1–9.* Commentaire du Nouveau Testament. Geneva: Labor et fides, 1991.
———. *L'Évangile selon saint Luc 9,51—14,35.* Commentaire du Nouveau Testament. Geneva: Labor et Fides, 1996.
———. *L'Évangile selon saint Luc 15,1—19,27.* Commentaire du Nouveau Testament. Geneva: Labor et Fides, 2001.
———. *L'Évangile selon saint Luc 19,28—24,53.* Commentaire du Nouveau Testament. Geneva: Labor et Fides, 2009.
———. *Luke 1.* Hermeneia. Minneapolis: Fortress, 2002.
———. *Luke the Theologian: Fifty-five Years of Research (1950–2005).* Waco: Baylor University, 2005.
Boyarin, D. *Intertextuality and the Reading of Midrash.* Indiana Studies in Biblical Literature. Bloomington: Indiana University, 1994.
Boyce, R. N. "Isaiah 55:6–13." *Interpretation* 44 (1990) 56–60.
Boyd, M. L. "Translation, Origin, and Meaning of Isaiah XXIV–XXVII." PhD diss., Southern Methodist University, 1931.
Braude, W. G. *The Midrash on Psalms.* Yale Judaica Series 13. New Haven: Yale University, 1959.
Braun, W. *Feasting and Social Rhetoric in Luke 14.* SNTSMS 85. Cambridge: Cambridge University Press, 1995.
———. "Symposium or Anti-Symposium? Reflections on Luke 14:1–24." *TJT* 8 (1992) 70–84.
Brawley, R. L. "Canon and Community: Intertextuality, Canon, Interpretation, Christology, Theology and Persuasive Rhetoric in Luke 4:1–13." In *SBLSP* 33, 419–34. Atlanta: Scholars, 1992.
———. *Text to Text Pours Forth Speech: Voices of Scripture in Luke-Acts.* Bloomington: Indiana University, 1995.

Bibliography

Bregman, M. "The Parable of the Lame and the Blind: Epiphanius' Quotation from an Apocryphon of Ezekiel." *JTS* 42 (1991) 125–38.

Breneman, M. *Ezra, Nehemiah, Esther.* NAC 10. Nashville: Broadman & Holman, 1993.

Brewer, D. I. "Three Weddings and a Divorce: God's Covenant with Israel, Judah and the Church." *TynBul* 47 (1996) 1–25.

Briggs, C. A., and E. G. Briggs. *Psalms, II.* ICC. Edinburgh: T. & T. Clark, 1906.

Bright, J. *A History of Israel.* Philadelphia: Westminster, 1959.

———. *Jeremiah.* AB 21. Garden City, NJ: Doubleday, 1965.

Broadribb, D. "Thoughts on the Song of Solomon." *Abr-Nahrain* 3 (1963) 11–36.

Brooke, G. J. "The Feast of New Wine and the Question of Fasting." *ExpTim* 95 (1984) 175–76.

———. "Isaiah 40:3 and the Wilderness Community." In *New Qumran Texts and Studies*, edited by G. F. Brooke and F. García Martínez, 117–32. Studies on the Texts of the Desert of Judah 15. Leiden: Brill, 1994.

———. "Psalms 105 and 106 at Qumran." *RevQ* 14 (1989) 267–92.

Brooke, G. J., and F. García Martínez. *New Qumran Texts and Studies.* STDJ 15. Leiden: Brill, 1994.

Brooks, J. A. *Mark.* NAC 23. Nashville: Broadman, 1991.

Brown, C., editor. *The New International Dictionary of New Testament Theology.* 4 vols. Grand Rapids: Zondervan, 1980.

Brownlee, W. H. *The Meaning of the Qumrân Scrolls for the Bible: With Special Attention to the Book of Isaiah.* New York: Oxford University, 1964. "

———. Messianic Motifs of Qumran and the New Testament." *NTS* (1956) 12–30.

———. *The Midrash Pesher of Habakkuk.* Society of Biblical Literature Monograph 11. Philadelphia: Society of Biblical Literature, 1959.

Broyles, C. C. *Psalms.* NIBCOT 11. Peabody, MA: Hendrickson, 1999.

Broyles, C. C., and C. A. Evans. *Writing and Reading the Scroll of Isaiah: Studies of an Interpretive Tradition.* 2 vols. VTSup 70. Leiden: Brill, 1997.

Bruce, F. F. *Biblical Exegesis in the Qumran Texts.* Grand Rapids: Eerdmans, 1959.

Brueggemann, W. *Isaiah 1–39.* Louisville: Westminster John Knox, 1998.

———. "Isaiah 55 and Deuteronomic Theology." *ZAW* 80 (1968) 191–203.

———. *To Pluck Up, To Tear Down: A Commentary on the Book of Jeremiah 1–25.* ITC. Grand Rapids: Eerdmans, 1988.

———. "Unity and Dynamic in the Isaiah Tradition." *JSOT* 29 (1984) 89–107.

Brunson, A. C. *Psalm 118 in the Gospel of John: An Intertextual Study on the New Exodus Pattern in the Theology of John.* WUNT 2/158. Tübingen: Mohr/Siebeck, 2003.

Buchanan, G. W. *Introduction to Intertextuality.* Lewiston, NY: Mellen Biblical, 1994.

———. "Isaianic Midrash and the Exodus." In *Function of Scripture in Early Jewish and Christian Tradition*, edited by C. A. Evans and J. A. Sanders, 89–109. JSNTSup 154. Sheffield: Sheffield Academic, 1998.

———. *Jesus, the King and His Kingdom.* Macon, GA: Mercer, 1984.

Bugge, C. A. *Die Haupt-Parabeln Jesu.* Giessen: Ricker, 1903.

Buis, P. "La Nouvelle Alliance." *VT* 18 (1968) 1–15.

Bullard, R. A. *A Handbook on the Wisdom of Solomon.* New York: United Bible Societies, 2004.

Bultmann, R. *The Gospel of John.* Translated by G. R. Beasley-Murray. Oxford: Blackwell, 1971.

———. *The History of the Synoptic Tradition.* New York: Harper & Row, 1963.

———. "Ursprung und Sinn der Typologie als Hermeneutischer Methode." *TLZ* 5 (1950) 205–12.

Burchard, C. "Joseph and Aseneth." In *OTP* 2:177–201.

Burden, T. L. "The Wilderness Traditions in the Hebrew Bible: Kerygma and Community of Faith." PhD diss., Southern Baptist Theological Seminary, 1992.

Burrows, M. *More Light on the Dead Sea Scrolls: New Scrolls and New Interpretations.* New York: Viking, 1958.

Cadbury, H. J. *The Making of Luke-Acts.* New York: Macmillan, 1927.

Cadoux, A. T. *The Parables of Jesus, Their Art and Use.* London: Clarke, 1930.

Cameron, R. "'What Have You Come out to See?' Characterizations of John and Jesus in the Gospels." *Semeia* 49 (1990) 34–69.

Campbell, A. F. "Psalm 78: A Contribution to the Theology of Tenth Century Israel." *CBQ* 41 (1979) 51–79.

Caquot, A. "Cinq Observations sur le Psaume 45." In *Ascribe to the Lord,* 253–64. Sheffield: JSOT Press, 1988.

———. "Les 'grâces de David' à propos d'Isaïe, 55/3b." *Sem* 15 (1965) 45–59.

———. "Remarques sur le "banquet des nations" en Esaïe 25:6–8." *RHPR* 69 (1989) 109–19.

Carlston, C. E. *The Parables of the Triple Tradition.* Philadelphia: Fortress, 1975.

Carmichael, D. B. "David Daube on the Eucharist and the Passover Seder." *JSNT* 42 (1997) 45–67.

Carr, G. L. "The Old Testament Love Songs and Their Use in the New Testament." *JETS* 24 (1981) 97–105.

Carroll, R. P. "Eschatological Delay in the Prophetic Tradition." *ZAW* 94 (1982) 47–58.

———. *Jeremiah.* OTL. Philadelphia: Westminster, 1986.

Carson, D. A. "The Homoios Word-Group as Introduction to Some Matthean Parables." *NTS* 31 (1985) 277–82.

Carter, W. *Matthew and the Margins: A Sociopolitical and Religious Reading.* Maryknoll, NY: Orbis, 2000.

Carter, W., and J. P. Heil. *Matthew's Parables: Audience-Oriented Perspectives.* CBQMS 30. Washington, DC: Catholic Biblical Association, 1998.

Carson, D. A., and H. G. M. Williamson. *It Is Written—Scripture Citing Scripture: Essays in Honour of Barnabas Lindars, SSF.* Cambridge: Cambridge University Press, 1988.

Casey, M. "Where Wright Is Wrong: A Critical Review of N. T. Wright's *Jesus and The Victory Of God*." *JSNT* 69 (1998) 95–103.

Cassuto, U. *A Commentary on the Book of Exodus.* Jerusalem: Magnes, 1967.

Catchpole, D. R. "Tradition History." In *New Testament Interpretation: Essays on Principles and Methods*, edited by I. H. Marshall, 165–80. Grand Rapids: Eerdmans, 1977.

Ceresko, A. R. "The Rhetorical Strategy of the Fourth Servant Song (Isaiah 52:13—53:12) Poetry and the Exodus-New Exodus." *CBQ* 56 (1994) 42–55.

Chae, Y. S. *Jesus as the Eschatological Davidic Shepherd.* WUNT 2/216. Tübingen: Mohr/Siebeck, 2006.

Chapman, D. W. *The Orphan Gospel: Mark's Perspective on Jesus.* Biblical Seminar 16. Sheffield: JSOT Press, 1993.

Charles, R. H. *The Apocalypse of Baruch.* Dublin: Trinity College, 1896.

———. *The Apocrypha and Pseudepigrapha of the Old Testament in English.* Oxford: Oxford University Press, 1913.

Bibliography

Charlesworth, J. H., editor. *The Dead Sea Scrolls and the Qumran Community.* Waco: Baylor University, 2006.

———. *Old Testament Pseudepigrapha.* 2 vols. New York: Doubleday, 1985.

———. "The Qumran Beatitudes (4Q525) and the New Testament (Mt 5:3-11, Lk 6:20-26)." *Revue d'histoire et de philosophie religieuses* 80 (2000) 13-35.

Charlesworth, J. H., and J. A. Sanders. "More Psalms of David." In *OTP,* 2:609-24.

Chavesse, C. *The Bride of Christ.* London: Religious Book Club, 1939.

Childs, B. S. *The Book of Exodus.* OTL. Philadelphia: Westminster, 1974.

———. "Critique of Recent Intertextual Canonical Interpretation." *ZAW* 115 (2003) 173-84.

———. "Deuteronomic Formulae of the Exodus Traditions." In *Hebräische Wortforschung; Festschrift zum 80 Geburtstag von Walter Baumgartner,* 30-39. Leiden: Brill, 1967.

———. *Introduction to the Old Testament as Scripture.* Philadelphia: Fortress, 1979.

———. *Isaiah.* OTL. Louisville: Westminster John Knox, 2001.

Chilton, B. *A Galilean Rabbi and His Bible: Jesus' Use of the Interpreted Scripture of His Time.* Wilmington, DE: Glazier, 1984.

———. *Jesus and the Ethics of the Kingdom.* Grand Rapids: Eerdmans, 1988.

———. "Jesus within Judaism." In *Jesus in Context: Temple, Purity and Restoration,* edited by B. Chilton and C. A. Evans. Leiden: Brill, 1997.

———. *Pure Kingdom: Jesus' Vision of God.* Grand Rapids: Eerdmans, 1996.

Chilton, B., and C. A. Evans. *Jesus in Context: Temple, Purity and Restoration.* Leiden: Brill, 1997.

Chisholm, R. B., Jr. "The Christological Fulfillment of Isaiah's Servant Songs." *Bibsac* 163 (2006) 387-404.

———. "The 'Everlasting Covenant' and the 'City of Chaos': Intentional Ambiguity and Irony in Isaiah 24." *CTR* 6 (1993) 237-53.

Cho, T. Y. "The Son of Man Came Eating and Drinking (Matthew 11:19) A Study of the Table Fellowship in Qumran and Q." PhD diss., Drew University, 1992.

Choo, M. S. S. "Mother Zion and Her Children: Deutero-Isaiah's Use of a Prophetic Metaphor in the Context of Zion Theology." PhD diss., Union Theological Seminary, 2009.

Christensen, D. L. *Deuteronomy 1:1—21:9.* WBC 6A. Nashville: Nelson, 2001.

———. *Deuteronomy 21:10—34:12.* WBC 6B. Nashville: Nelson, 2002.

Claassens, L. J. M. *The God Who Provides: Biblical Images of Divine Nourishment.* Nashville: Abingdon, 2004.

Clements, R. E. *Prophecy and Covenant.* SBT 43. Naperville, IL: Allenson, 1965.

———. "The Unity of the Book of Isaiah." *Int* 36 (1982) 117-29.

Clifford, R. *The Cosmic Mountain in Canaan and the Old Testament.* Cambridge, MA: Harvard University, 1972.

———. *Fair Spoken and Persuading: An Interpretation of Second Isaiah.* New York: Paulist, 1984.

———. "Isaiah 55: Invitation to a Feast." In *The Word of the Lord Shall Go Forth: Essays in Honor of David Noel Freedman in Celebration of His Sixtieth Birthday,* edited by C. L. Meyers and M. O'Connor, 27-35. Winona Lake, IN: Eisenbrauns, 1983.

Clines, D. J. A., and D. M. Gunn. "You Tried to Persuade Me and Violence Outrage in Jeremiah 20:7-8." *VT* 28 (1978) 20-27.

Coats, G. W. "Conquest Traditions in the Wilderness Theme." *JBL* 95 (1976) 177-90.

———. "History and Theology in the Sea Tradition." *ST* 29 (1975) 53-62.

———. "Tradition Criticism (OT)." In *IDBSup,* 912-14.

———. "Wilderness Itinerary." *CBQ* 34 (1972) 135–52.
Collins, J. *The Apocalyptic Imagination*. 2nd ed. Grand Rapids: Eerdmans, 1998.
———. *Between Athens and Jerusalem: Jewish Identity in Hellenistic Diaspora*. 2nd ed. Grand Rapids: Eerdmans, 2000.
———. "The Expectation of the End in the Dead Sea Scrolls." In *Eschatology, Messianism and the Dead Sea Scrolls*, edited by C. A. Evans and P. W. Flint, 74–90. Grand Rapids: Eerdmans, 1997.
———. "Joseph and Aseneth: Jewish or Christian?" *JSOP* 14 (2005) 97–112.
Collins, R. F. "Marriage (New Testament)." In *ABD* 4:569–72.
Collins, T. "The Literary Context of Zechariah 9:9." In *The Book of Zechariah and Its Influence*, edited by C. M. Tuckett, 29–40. Hampshire, UK: Ashgate, 2003.
Conzelmann, H. *The Theology of St. Luke*. New York: Harper, 1961.
Cook, S. L. "The Five Fragments of the Apocryphon of Ezekiel: A Critical Study." *JBL* 115 (1996) 532–34.
Cooper, L. E. *Ezekiel*. NAC 17. Nashville: Broadman & Holman, 1994.
Coote, R. B. "Additional Remarks on rhmyh (Amos 1:11)." *JBL* 90 (1971) 206–8.
———. "MW'D HT'NYT in 4Q171 (Pesher Psalm 37) fragments 1–2, col. II, line 9." *RevQ* 8 (1972) 81–85.
Coppens, J. "La nouvelle alliance en Jer 31:31–34." *CBQ* 25 (1963) 12–21.
Couffignal, R. "Les Structures Figuratives du Psaume 45." *ZAW* 113 (2001) 198–208.
Craigie, P. C. *Psalms 1–50*. WBC 19. Waco: Word, 1983.
Craigie, P. C., P. H. Kelley, and J. F. Drinkard. *Jeremiah 1–25*. WBC 26. Dallas: Word, 1991.
Cranfield, C. E. B. *The Gospel According to Saint Mark*. Cambridge: Cambridge University Press, 1959.
Cremer, F. G. *Die Fastenaussage Jesu: Mk 2,20 und Parallelen in der Sicht der patristischen und scholatischen Exegese*. Bonner biblische Beiträge 23. Bonn: Hanstein, 1965.
———. "Die Söhne des Brautgemachs (Mk 2,19 parr) in der griechischen und lateinischen Schrifterklärung." *BZ* 11 (1967) 246–53.
Crenshaw, J. L. *Essays in Old Testament Ethics*. New York: KTAV, 1974.
Crockett, L. C. "The Old Testament in the Gospel of Luke: With Emphasis on the Interpretation of Isaiah 61, 1–2." PhD diss., Brown University, 1966.
Cross, F. M. *The Ancient Library of Qumran*. 3rd ed. Sheffield: Sheffield Academic, 1995.
———. *The Ancient Library of Qumran and Modern Biblical Studies*. Garden City, NY: Doubleday, 1961.
———. *Canaanite Myth and Hebrew Epic*. Cambridge, MA: Harvard University, 1973.
Crossan, J. D. *Cliffs of Fall: Paradox and Polyvalence in the Parables of Jesus*. New York: Seabury, 1980.
———. *The Historical Jesus: The Life of a Mediterranean Jewish Peasant*. San Francisco: HarperSanFrancisco, 1991.
———. *In Parables: The Challenge of the Historical Jesus*. San Francisco: Harper & Row, 1973.
———. *Jesus: A Revolutionary Biography*. San Francisco: HarperSanFrancisco, 1994.
Crossan, J. D., and J. L. Reed. *Excavating Jesus*. San Francisco: HarperSanFrancisco, 2001.
Culpepper, R. A. "Luke." In *NIB*, 9:3–490.
Curtis, E. L., and A. A. Madsen. *The Books of Chronicles*. ICC. Edinburgh: T. & T. Clark, 1910.
Dahmen, U. "רחם." In *TDOT*, 13:437–54.
Dahood, M. *Psalms I, 1–50*. AB 16. New York: Doubleday, 1966.
———. *Psalms II, 51–100*. AB 17. New York: Doubleday, 1968.

Bibliography

———. *Psalms III, 101–50.* AB 17A. New York: Doubleday, 1970.

Daniélou, J. *Études d'exégèse judéo-chrétienne (les Testimonia).* Théologie historique 5. Paris: Beauchesne, 1966.

Daniels, D. R. *Hosea and Salvation History: The Early Traditions of Israel in the Prophecy of Hosea.* BZAW 191. Berlin: de Gruyter, 1990.

Darr, K. P. *Isaiah's Vision and the Family of God.* Louisville: Westminster John Knox, 1994.

Daube, D. *The Exodus Pattern in the Bible.* London: Faber & Faber, 1963.

———. *He That Cometh.* London: Council for Christian-Jewish Understanding, 1966.

———. *The New Testament and Rabbinic Judaism.* London: Athlone, 1956.

Davidovitch, D. *The Ketuba: Jewish Marriage Contracts through the Ages.* Tel-Aviv: Lewin-Epstein, 1979.

Davidson, R. M. *Typology in Scripture.* Berrien Springs, MI: Andrews University, 1981.

Davies, G. I. "The Destiny of the Nations in the Book of Isaiah." In *Book of Isaiah*, edited by J. Vermeylen, 93–120. Leuven: Leuven, 1989.

———. "Wilderness Wandering." In *ABD* 6:912–14.

Davies, P. R. "The Wilderness Years: Utopia and Dystopia in the Book of Hosea." In *Utopia and Dystopia in Prophetic Literature*, edited by E. Ben Zvi, 160–74. Göttingen: Vandenhoeck & Ruprecht, 2006.

Davies, W. D., and D. C. Allison. *A Critical and Exegetical Commentary on the Gospel According to Saint Matthew.* 3 vols. ICC. Edinburgh: T. & T. Clark, 1997.

Davila, J. R. *Liturgical Works.* Grand Rapids: Eerdmans, 2000.

———. "The Old Testament Pseudepigrapha as Background to the New Testament." *ExpTim* 117 (2005) 53–57.

Davis, E. W. "Inheritance Rights and the Hebrew Levirate Marriage, Part 1." *VT* 31 (1981) 138–45.

———. "Inheritance Rights and the Hebrew Levirate Marriage, Part 2." *VT* 31 (1981) 257–68.

Day, J. *God's Conflict with the Dragon and the Sea.* Cambridge: Cambridge University Press, 1985.

———. "Rahab (Dragon)." In *ABD* 5:610.

Day, P. "Metaphor and Social Reality: Isaiah 23.17–18, Ezekiel 16.35–37 and Hosea 2.4–5." In *Inspired Speech*, 63–71. London: T. & T. Clark, 2004.

De Lacey, D. R. "In Search of a Pharisee." *TynBul* 43 (1992) 353–72.

de Meeûs, X. "Composition De Lc 14 Et Genre Symposiaque." *Ephemerides theologicae lovanienses* 37 (1961) 847–70.

De Roche, M. "Jeremiah 2:2–3 and Israel's Love for God during the Wilderness Wanderings." *CBQ* 45 (1983) 364–76.

———. "The Reversal of Creation in Hosea." *VT* 31 (1981) 400–409.

de Winkel, H. *Jeremiah in the Prophetic Tradition.* 26. Leuven: Peeters, 2000.

Deissler, A. "Das 'Echo' der Hosea-Verkundigung im Jeremiabuch." In *Künder des Wortes: Beiträge zur Theologie der Propheten*, edited by L. Ruppert, 61–75. Würzburg: Echter, 1982.

Delcor, M. "Festin d'immortalité sur la montagne de Sion a l'ère eschatologique en Isaïe 25:6–9, à la lumière de la litterature ugaritique." In *Mesianismo y escatologia*, edited by L. Arnaldich, 89–98. Salamanca, Spain: Universidad Pontificia, 1976.

Derrett, J. D. M. *Law in the New Testament.* London: Darton, Longman & Todd, 1970.

DeSilva, D. A. *Introducing the Apocrypha.* Grand Rapids: Baker, 2002.

Deterding, P. E. "Eschatological and Eucharistic Motifs in Luke 12:35–40." *Concordia Journal* 5 (1979) 85–94.

Di Luccio, P. "The 'Son of Man' and the Eschatology of the Q Beatitudes: The Case of Lk 6,22c." *EstEcl* 82 (2007) 553–70.

———. "Son of Man, Sons of the Woman, and Teachers of the Law: Eschatological Features of the Gospel Beatitudes, with a Selected Bibliography on the 'Son of Man.'" *EstEcl* 84 (2009) 337–53

Diamond, A. R. P. "Desert." In *NIDOTTE*, 4:520–28.

Diamond, A. R. P., and K. M. O'Connor. "Unfaithful Passions: Coding Women Coding Men in Jeremiah 2–3 (4:2)." *BibInt* 4 (1996) 288–310.

Diaz, M. "I Will Speak to Their Hearts." *SEDOS Bulletin* 28 (1996) 271–76.

Dibelius, M. *From Tradition to Gospel.* New York: Scribners, 1935.

Dieissler, A. "Das 'Echo' der Hosea-Verkundigung im Jeremiabuch." In *Künder des Wortes: Beiträge zur Theologie der Propheten*, edited by L. Ruppert, P. Weimar, and E. Zenger, 61–75. Würzburg: Echter, 1982.

Dillard, R. B. "Joel." In *The Minor Prophets*, edited by T. E. McComiskey, 1:239–314. Grand Rapids: Baker, 1992.

———. *2 Chronicles.* WBC 15. Waco: Word, 1987.

Dille, S. J. *Mixing Metaphors.* JSOTSup 398; Gender, Culture, Theory 13. London: T. & T. Clark, 2004.

Dimant, D., editor. *The Dead Sea Scrolls: Forty Years of Research.* Leiden: Brill, 1992.

Dodd, C. H. *According to the Scriptures: The Sub-Structure of New Testament Theology.* London: Nisbet, 1952.

———. *The Old Testament in the New.* London: Athlone, 1952.

———. *The Old Testament in the New.* Philadelphia: Fortress, 1963.

———. *The Parables of the Kingdom.* New York: Scribners, 1935.

Doeve, J. W. *Jewish Hermeneutics in the Synoptic Gospels and Acts.* Assen: Van Gorcum, 1953.

Dorsey, D. A. *The Roads and Highways of Ancient Israel.* Baltimore: Johns Hopkins University, 1991.

Douglas, M. *In the Wilderness: The Doctrine of Defilement in the Book of Numbers.* JSOTSup 158. Sheffield: Sheffield Academic, 2004.

Doyle, B. *The Apocalypse of Isaiah Metaphorically Speaking: A Study of the Use, Function, and Significance of Metaphors in Isaiah 24–27.* BETL 151. Leuven: Peeters, 2000.

Dozeman, T. B. *God on the Mountain: A Study of Redaction, Theology and Canon in Exodus 19–24.* Atlanta: Scholars, 1989.

———. "Horeb/Sinai and the Rise of Law in the Wilderness Tradition." *SBLSP* 28 (1989) 282–90.

———. "Hosea and the Wilderness Wandering Tradition." In *Rethinking the Foundations*, edited by S. L. McKenzie and T. Romer, 55–70. Berlin: de Gruyter, 2000.

———. "The Wilderness and Salvation History in the Hagar Story." *JBL* 117 (1998) 23–43.

Draisma, S. *Intertextuality in Biblical Writings: Essays in Honour of Bas van Iersel.* Kampen: Kok, 1989.

Drazin, N. *History of Jewish Education from 515 B.C.E. to 220 C.E.* Baltimore: Johns Hopkins University, 1940.

Drews, A. *Hat Jesus gelebt?* Berlin: Deutschen Monistenbundes, 1910.

Dreytza, M. "זְרוֹעַ." In *NIDOTTE*, 1:1146–47.

Drury, J. *Tradition and Design in Luke's Gospel.* Atlanta: Knox, 1976.

Bibliography

Duhm, B. *Das Buch Jesaia*. HKAT. Göttingen: Vandenhoeck & Ruprecht, 1892.

Dumbrell, W. J. *Covenant and Creation: A Theology of Old Testament Covenants*. Nashville: Nelson, 1984.

Dunkerley, R. "The Bridegroom Passage." *ExpTim* 64 (1953) 303–4.

Dunn, J. D. G. *Jesus Remembered*. Grand Rapids: Eerdmans, 2003.

Dupont, J. "'Beaucoup viendront du levant et du couchant . . .': (Matt 8:11–12; Lk 13:28–29)." *ScEccl* 19 (1967) 153–67.

———. *Études sur les Actes des apôtres*. Lectio divina 45. Paris: Cerf, 1967.

Durham, J. I. *Exodus*. WBC 3. Nashville: Nelson, 1987.

Ebeling, H. J. "Die Fastenfrage (Mark 2.18–22)." *TSK* 108 (1937) 382–96.

Eco, U. *Semiotics and the Philosophy of Language*. Bloomington: Indiana University, 1984.

Edwards, J. *Mark*. PNTC. Grand Rapids: Eerdmans, 2009.

Efird, J. M., editor. *The Use of the Old Testament in the New and Other Essays: Studies in Honor of William Franklin Stinespring*. Durham, NC: Duke University, 1972.

Eichrodt, W. *Ezekiel*. OTL. Philadelphia: Fortress, 1970.

———. "Is Typological Exegesis an Appropriate Method?" In *Essays on Old Testament Interpretation*, edited by C. Westermann, 224–45. London: SCM, 1963.

Eidevall, G. *Grapes in the Desert: Metaphors, Models, and Themes in Hosea 4–14*. ConBOT 43. Stockholm: Almqvist & Wiksell, 1996.

Eisler, R. "Das Letzte Abendmahl." *ZAW* 24 (1925) 161–92.

Eissfeldt, O. "Promises of Grace to David in Isaiah 55:1–5." In *Israel's Prophetic Heritage: Essays in Honor of James Muilenburg*, 196–207. New York: Harper, 1962.

Elliger, K. *Deuterojesaja*. BKAT 11/1. Neukirchen-Vluyn: Neukrichener Verlag des Erziehungsvereins, 1978.

Ellis, E. E. "Midrash, Targum and New Testament Quotations." In *Neotestamentica et Semitica: Studies in Honour of Matthew Black*, 61–69. Edinburgh: T. & T. Clark, 1969.

———. "Midrashic Features in the Speeches of Acts." In *Mélanges bibliques en hommage au R. P. Béda Rigaux*, edited by Albert Descamps and André de Halleux, 303–12. Gembloux, Belgium: Duculot, 1970.

———. *Prophecy and Hermeneutic in Early Christianity: New Testament Essays*. WUNT 1/18. Tübingen: Mohr/Siebeck, 1978.

———. *The Old Testament in Early Christianity: Canon and Interpretation in the Light of Modern Research*. WUNT 1/54. Tübingen: Mohr/Siebeck, 1991.

Emmerson, G. I. *Hosea: An Israelite Prophet in Judean Perspective*. Sheffield: JSOT Press, 1984.

Epstein, L. M. *The Jewish Marriage Contract: A Study in the Status of the Woman in Jewish Law*. New York: Jewish Theological Seminary of America, 1927.

Ernst, J. *Das Evangelium nach Lukas*. RNT. Regensburg: Pustet, 1977.

Eshel, E., and A. Kloner. "An Aramaic Ostracon of an Edomite Marriage Contract from Maresha, Dated 176 BCE." *IEJ* (1996) 1–22.

Eslinger, L. "Inner-Biblical Exegesis and Inner Biblical Allusion: The Question of Category." *VT* 42 (1992) 47–58.

Evans, C. A. "Jesus and the Continuing Exile of Israel." In *Jesus & the Restoration of Israel: A Critical Assessment of N.T. Wright's Jesus and the Victory of God*, edited by C. Newman, 77–100. Downers Grove, IL: InterVarsity, 1999.

———. "Listening to Echoes of Interpreted Scripture." In *Paul and the Scriptures of Israel*, edited by C. A. Evans and J. A. Sanders, 47–57. JSNTSup 83. Sheffield: JSOT, 1993.

———. *Mark 8:27—16:20*. WBC 34B. Nashville: Nelson, 2001.
Evans, C. A., editor. *From Prophecy to Testament: The Function of the Old Testament in the New.* Peabody, MA: Hendrickson, 2004.
Evans, C. A., and S. E. Porter. *Dictionary of New Testament Background.* Downers Grove, IL: InterVarsity, 2000.
———. *New Testament Backgrounds.* Biblical Seminar 43. Sheffield: Sheffield Academic, 1997.
———. *Studies in the Historical Jesus.* Sheffield: Sheffield Academic, 1995.
Evans, C. A., and J. A. Sanders. *Luke and Scripture: The Function of Sacred Tradition in Luke-Acts.* Minneapolis: Fortress, 1993.
Evans, C. A., and W. R. Stegner. *The Gospels and the Scriptures of Israel.* JSNTSup 104. Sheffield: Sheffield Academic, 1994.
Evans, C. A., and W. F. Stinespring editors. *Early Jewish and Christian Exegesis: Studies in Memory of William Hugh Brownlee.* Atlanta: Scholars, 1987.
Evans, C. F. *Saint Luke.* London: SCM, 1990.
Evans, S. A., and S. Talmon editors. *The Quest for Context and Meaning: Studies in Biblical Intertextuality in Honor of James A. Sanders.* Leiden: Brill, 1997.
Fabry, H.-J. "מִרְזֵחַ." TDOT, 9:10–14.
Fairbairn, P. *The Typology of Scripture: Viewed in Connection with the Entire Scheme of the Divine Dispensations.* 2nd ed. Edinburgh: T. & T. Clark, 1854.
Falk, Z. *Hebrew Law in Biblical Times.* Winona Lake, IN: Eisenbrauns, 2001.
Fekkes, J. "'His Bride Has Prepared Herself': Revelation 19–21 and Isaian Nuptial Imagery." *JBL* 109 (1990) 269–87.
———. *Isaiah and Prophetic Traditions in the Book of Revelation: Visionary Antecedents and Their Development.* JSNTSup 93. Sheffield: JSOT, 1994.
Feldman, A. *The Parables and Similes of the Rabbis, Agricultural and Pastoral.* Cambridge: Cambridge University Press, 1924.
Fensham, F. C. "Neh 9 and Pss 105, 106, 135 and 136: Post-exilic Historical Traditions in Poetic Form." *JNSL* 9 (1981) 35–51.
———. "The Marriage Metaphor in Hosea for the Covenant Relationship between the Lord and His People (Hos 1:2–9)." *JNSL* 12 (1984) 71–78.
Fewell, D. N. *Reading Between Texts: Intertextuality and the Hebrew Bible.* Literary Currents in Biblical Interpretation. Louisville: Westminster John Knox, 1992.
Fiebig, P. *Altjüdische Gleichnisse und die Gleichnisse Jesu.* Tübingen: Mohr/Siebeck, 1904.
Finley, T. J. *Joel, Amos, Obadiah: An Exegetical Commentary.* Chicago: Moody, 1990.
Fischer, G. "Die Redewendung דבר על־לב im AT—Ein Beitrag zum Verständnis von Jes 40, 2." *Bib* 65 (1984) 244–50.
Fischer, J. "Das Problem des neuen Exodus in Isaias c. 40–55." *TQ* 110 (1929) 111–30.
Fishbane, M. "Additional Remarks on *rhmyh* (Amos 1:11)." *JBL* 91 (1972) 391–92.
———. *Biblical Interpretation in Ancient Israel.* Oxford: Clarendon, 1985.
———. *The Garments of Torah: Essays in Biblical Hermeneutics.* Bloomington: Indiana University, 1989.
———. "Revelation and Tradition: Aspects of Inner-Biblical Exegesis." *JBL* 99 (1980) 343–61.
———. *Text and Texture: Close Readings of Selected Biblical Texts.* New York: Schocken, 1979.
———. "Treaty Background of Amos 1:11 and Related Matters." *JBL* 89 (1970) 313–18.

Bibliography

Fisher, E. J. "Cultic Prostitution in the Ancient Near East? A Reassessment." *BTB* 5 (1976) 225–36.

Fisher, F. L. "New and Greater Exodus: The Exodus Pattern in the New Testament." *SwJT* 20 (1977) 69–79.

Fitzmyer, J. A. *The Genesis Apocryphon of Qumran Cave I*. 2nd rev. ed. Biblica et orientalia 18a. Rome: Biblical Institute 1971.

———. *The Gospel According to Luke I–IX*. AB 28. Garden City, NY: Doubleday, 1981.

———. *The Gospel According to Luke X–XXIV*. AB 28A. New York: Doubleday, 1985.

Flint, P. W. *The Dead Sea Psalms Scrolls and the Book of Psalms*. Studies on the Texts of the Desert of Judah 17. Leiden: Brill, 1997.

Flusser, D. *Die rabbinischen Gleichnisse und der Gleichniserzähler Jesus*. Judaica et Christiana 4. Bern: Lang, 1981.

Ford, J. M. "The Parable of the Foolish Scholars (Matt. XV 1–13)." *NovT* 9 (1967) 107–23.

Fox, M. V. "Jeremiah 2:2 and the Desert Ideal." *CBQ* 35 (1973) 441–50.

France, R. T. *The Gospel of Mark*. NIGTC. Grand Rapids: Eerdmans, 2002.

———. *Jesus and the Old Testament: His Application of Old Testament Passages to Himself and His Mission*. Grand Rapids: Baker, 1982.

Franklin, E. *Christ the Lord: A Study in the Purpose and Theology of Luke-Acts*. Philadelphia: Westminster, 1975.

Fretheim, T. E. *Jeremiah*. Macon, GA: Smith & Helwys, 2002.

Friedman, M. A. "Israel's Response in Hosea 2:17b : 'You Are My Husband.'" *JBL* 99 (1980) 199–204.

———. *Jewish Marriage in Palestine: A Cairo Genizah Study*. 2 vols. Tel-Aviv: Tel-Aviv University, 1980.

Fritz, V. *Israel in der Wüste*. Marburg: Elwert, 1970.

Fuchs, E. *Studies of the Historical Jesus*. SBT 42. Naperville, IL: Allenson, 1964.

Funk, R. W. "The Wilderness." *JBL* 78 (1959) 205–14.

Funk, R., and R. Hoover. *The Five Gospels: The Search for the Authentic Words of Jesus*. New York: Macmillan, 1993.

Galambush, J. *Jerusalem in the Book of Ezekiel: The City as Yahweh's Wife*. Atlanta: Scholars, 1992.

Galling, K. *Die erwählungstraditionen Israels*. ZAW 48. Giessen: Töpelmann, 1928.

García-Martínez, F., and E. J. C. Tigchelaar. *The Dead Sea Scrolls Study Edition (Translations)*. Leiden: Brill, 1998.

Garrett, D. A. *Hosea, Joel*. NAC 19A. Nashville: Broadman & Holman, 1997.

———. *Proverbs, Ecclesiastes, Song of Songs*. NAC 14. Nashville: Broadman & Holman, 1993.

Gaster, T. H. "Psalm 45." *JBL* 74 (1955) 239–51.

Geller, M. J. "Elephantine Papyri and Hosea 2,3." *JSJ* 8 (1977) 139–48.

Gerhardsson, B. "Illuminating the Kingdom: Narrative *meshalim* in the Synoptic Gospels." In *Jesus and the Oral Gospel*, edited by H. Wansbrough, 266–309. JSNTSup 64. Sheffield: Sheffield Academic, 1991.

———. *Memory and Manuscript*. Uppsala: Gleerup, 1961.

Gese, H. "Tradition and Biblical Theology." In *Tradition and Theology in the Old Testament*, edited by D. A. Knight and W. J. Harrelson, 301–26. Philadelphia: Fortress, 1977.

Gesenius, Wilhelm, E. Kautzsch, and A. E. Cowley. *Gesenius' Hebrew Grammar*. 2nd English ed. Oxford: Clarendon, 1910.

Ginsberg, H. L. "The Arm of YHWH in Isaiah 51–63 and the Text of Isa 53:10–11." *JBL* 77 (1958) 152–56.
Glazier-McDonald, B. "Intermarriage, Divorce, and the *bat'-el-nekar*: Insights into Mal 2:10–16." *JBL* 106 (1987) 603–11.
Golb, N. "The Problem of the Origin and Identification of the Dead Sea Scrolls." *Proceedings of the American Philosophical Society* 124 (1980) 1–24.
Goldingay, J. *Isaiah*. NIBCOT 13. Peabody, MA: Hendrickson, 2001.
———. *Old Testament Theology: Israel's Faith*. Downers Grove, IL: InterVarsity, 2003.
———. *Old Testament Theology: Israel's Gospel*. Downers Grove, IL: InterVarsity, 2003.
Goldingay, J., and D. Payne. *Isaiah 40–55*. 2 vols. ICC. Edinburgh: T. & T. Clark, 2006.
Goppelt, L. *Typos, The Typological Interpretation of the Old Testament in the New* Translated by D. H. Madvig. Grand Rapids: Eerdmans, 1982.
Gordis, R. "Hosea's Marriage and Message: A New Approach." *HUCA* 25 (1954) 9–35.
———. "The Jewish Concept of Marriage." *Judaism* 2 (1953) 225–38.
———. "A Wedding Song for Solomon." *JBL* 63 (1944) 263–70.
Goulder, M. D. *Midrash and Lection in Matthew*. London: SPCK, 1974.
———. *The Psalms of the Sons of Korah*. JSOTSup 20. Sheffield: JSOT, 1982.
———. "The Social Setting of Book II of the Psalter." In *The Book of Psalms: Composition and Reception*, edited by P. W. Flint and P. D. Miller, 349–67. Leiden: Brill, 2005.
Grant, R. M. *After the New Testament*. Philadelphia: Fortress, 1967.
Gray, G. B. *Isaiah I–XXXIX*. ICC. Edinburgh: T. & T. Clark, 1912.
Green, J. B. *The Gospel of Luke*. NICNT. Grand Rapids: Eerdmans, 1997.
———. "The Problem of a Beginning: Israel's Scriptures in Luke 1–2." *BBR* 4 (1994) 61–85.
Green, J. B., S. McKnight, and I. H. Marshall. *Dictionary of Jesus and the Gospels*. Downers Grove, IL: InterVarsity, 1992.
Grimm, W. *Weil ich dich liebe: Die Verkündigung Jesu und Deuterojesaja*. Arbeiten zum Neuen Testament und Judentum 1. Bern: Lang, 1981.
———. "Zum Hintergrund von Mt 8:11f/Lk 13:28f." *BZ* 16 (1972) 255–56.
Gross, W., and G. A. Hunold. "Die Ehe im Spiegel biblischer und kulturgeschichtlicher Überlieferungen." *TQ* 167 (1987) 82–95.
Guelich, R. A. "The Beginning of Mark's Gospel." *BR* 27 (1982) 5–15.
Guenther, A. "A Typology of Israelite Marriage: Kinship, Socio-Economic, and Religious Factors." *JSOT* 29 (2005) 387–407.
Gundry, R. H. *Mark: A Commentary on His Apology for the Cross*. Grand Rapids: Eerdmans, 1993.
———. *Matthew: A Commentary on His Literary and Theological Art*. Grand Rapids: Eerdmans, 1982.
———. *The Use of the Old Testament in St. Matthew's Gospel with Special Reference to the Messianic Hope*. NovTSup 18. Leiden: Brill, 1975.
Gundry, S. N. "Typology as a Means of Interpretation: Past and Present." *JETS* 12 (1969) 233–40.
Hagelia, H. *Coram deo: Spirituality in the Book of Isaiah*. ConBNT 49. Stockholm: Almqvist & Wiksell, 2001.
———. "Meal on Mount Zion—Does Isa 25:6–8 Describe a Covenant Meal?" *Svensk exegetisk årsbok* 68 (2003) 73–95.
Hagner, D. A. *Matthew 1–13*. WBC 33A. Dallas: Word, 1993.
———. *Matthew 14–28*. WBC 33B. Dallas: Word, 1995.

Bibliography

Hall, G. "The Marriage Imagery in Jeremiah 2 and 3: A Study of Antecedents and Innovations in Prophetic Metaphor." PhD diss., Union Theological Seminary, 1982.

———. "Origin of the Marriage Metaphor." *HS* 23 (1982) 169–71.

Hallo, W. editor. *Canonical Compositions from the Biblical World*. Vol. 1 of *The Context of Scripture*. Leiden: Brill, 1997.

Ham, C. A. *The Coming King and the Rejected Shepherd: Matthew's Reading of Zechariah's Messianic Hope*. Sheffield: Phoenix, 2006.

Hamilton, V. "Marriage, Old Testament." In *ABD* 4:560–69.

Hanson, A. T. *Jesus Christ in the Old Testament*. London: SPCK, 1965.

Hare, D. R. A. *Mark*. Louisville: Westminster John Knox, 1996.

Harner, P. B. "Creation Faith in Deutero-Isaiah." *VT* 17 (1967) 298–306.

Harrison, R. K. *Introduction to the Old Testament*. Grand Rapids: Eerdmans, 1969.

Harvey, A. E. *Jesus and the Constraints of History*. Philadelphia: Westminster, 1982.

Harvey, J. "La typologie de l'Exode dans les Psaumes." *ScEccl* 15 (1963) 383–405.

Hasel, G. F. *Understanding the Book of Amos*. Grand Rapids: Baker, 1991.

Hasler, V. "Die königliche Hochzeit, Matth. 22, 1–14." *TZ* 18 (1962) 25–35.

Hatina, T. R. "Exile." In *Dictionary of New Testament Background*, edited by C. A. Evans and S. E. Porter, 348–51. Downers Grove, IL: InterVarsity, 2000.

———. *In Search of a Context: The Function of Scripture in Mark's Narrative*. JSNTSup 232. London: Sheffield Academic, 2002.

———. "Intertextuality and Historical Criticism in New Testament Studies: Is There a Relationship?" *BI* 7 (1999) 28–43.

Hayes, J. H. *Amos*. Nashville: Abingdon, 1988.

Hays, R. B. *Echoes of Scripture in the Letters of Paul*. New Haven: Yale University, 1989.

Head, P. M. "A Further Note on Reading and Writing in the Time of Jesus." *EQ* 75 (2003) 343–45.

Hengel, M. *The Charismatic Leader and His Followers*. Edinburgh: T. & T. Clark, 1996.

Heskett, R. *Messianism within the Scriptural Scroll of Isaiah*. LOTS 456. New York: T. & T. Clark, 2007.

Hibbard, J. T. *Intertextuality in Isaiah 24–27: The Reuse and Evocation of Earlier Texts and Traditions*. FAT 16. Tübingen: Mohr/Siebeck, 2006.

Higgins, A. J. B. *The Lord's Supper in the New Testament*. SBT 6. London: SCM, 1952.

Hoffman, L. A. "The Jewish Wedding Ceremony." In *Life Cycles in Jewish and Christian Worship*, 129–53. South Bend, IN: University of Notre Dame, 1996.

Hoffmeier, J. K. "The Arm of God Versus the Arm of Pharaoh in the Exodus Narratives." *Bib* 67 (1986) 378–87.

Holladay, W. L. *Jeremiah 1*. Hermeneia. Philadelphia: Fortress, 1986.

———. W. L. *Jeremiah 2*. Hermeneia. Minneapolis: Fortress, 1989.

Hollander, J. *The Figure of Echo: A Mode of Allusion in Milton and After*. Berkeley: University of California, 1981.

Holmgren, F. *With Wings as Eagles*. New York: Biblical Scholars, 1973.

Hooke, S. H., and A. M. Blackman. *Myth and Ritual: Essays on the Myth and Ritual of the Hebrews in Relation to the Culture Pattern of the Ancient East*. London: Oxford University, 1932.

Hooker, M. D. "Mark." In *It is Written—Scripture Citing Scripture: Essays in Honour of Barnabas Lindars*, edited by D. A. Carson and H. G. M. Williamson, 220–30. Cambridge: Cambridge University Press, 1988.

Hooker, P. K. *First and Second Chronicles*. Louisville: Westminster John Knox, 2001.
Horgan, M. P. *Pesharim: Qumran Interpretations of Biblical Books*. CBQMS 8. Washington, D.C.: Catholic Biblical Association of America, 1979.
Horsley, G. H. R. *New Documents Illustrating Early Christianity 1*. North Ryde, Australia: Macquarie University, 1981.
Hosein, F. "The Banquet Type-Scene in the Parables of Jesus." PhD diss., Andrews University, 2001.
Houtman, C. *Exodus*. 3 vols. Leuven: Peeters, 2000.
Hubbard, D. A. *Joel and Amos*. Downers Grove, IL: InterVarsity, 1989.
Huber, L. R. *Like a Bride Adorned: Reading Metaphor in John's Apocalypse*. New York: T. & T. Clark, 2007.
Hugenberger, G. P. *Marriage as a Covenant: Biblical Law and Ethics as Developed from Malachi*. Grand Rapids: Baker, 1998.
Hultgren, A. J. *The Parables of Jesus: A Commentary*. Grand Rapids: Eerdmans, 2002.
Humphrey, E. M. *The Ladies and the Cities: Transformation and Apocalyptic Identity in Joseph and Aseneth, 4 Ezra, the Apocalypse and the Shepherd of Hermas*. JSOPSup 17. Sheffield: Sheffield Academic, 1995.
Hunter, A. M. *Interpreting the Parables*. Philadelphia: Westminster, 1961.
———. *The Parables Then and Now*. Philadelphia: Westminster, 1971.
Hurtado, L. W. *Mark*. NIBCNT 2. Peabody, MA: Hendrickson, 1989.
Ibn Ezra, A. *The Commentary of Ibn Ezra on Isaiah*. London: Trübner, 1873.
Ishida, T., editor. *Studies in the Period of David and Solomon and Other Essays*. Winona Lake, IN: Eisenbrauns, 1982.
Jacob, I., and W. Jacob. "Flora." In *ABD* 2:803-17.
Japhet, S. *I & II Chronicles*. OTL. Louisville: Westminster John Knox, 1993.
Jauhiainen, M. *The Use of Zechariah in Revelation*. WUNT 2/199. Tübingen: Mohr/Siebeck, 2005.
Jeremias, J. *The Book of Amos*. OTL. Louisville: Westminster John Knox, 1998.
———. *Jesus' Promise to the Nations*. SBT 24. London: SCM, 1958.
———. "νύμφη." In *TDNT* 4:1099-1106.
———. *The Parables of Jesus*. Translated by S. H. Hooke. New York: Scribners, 1955.
Johnson, D. G. *From Chaos to Restoration: An Integrative Reading of Isaiah 24-27*. JSOTSup 61. Sheffield: JSOT, 1988.
Johnson, L. T. *The Gospel of Luke*. Sacra Pagina 3. Collegeville, MN: Liturgical, 1991.
Juel, D. *Messianic Exegesis: Christological Interpretation of the Old Testament in Early Christianity*. Philadelphia: Fortress, 1988.
Jülicher, A. *Die gleichnisreden Jesu*. 2 vols. Freiburg: Mohr/Siebeck, 1899.
Junker, H. "Die literarische Art von Isa 5:1-7." *Bib* 40 (1959) 259-66.
Just, A. A. *The Ongoing Feast: Table Fellowship and Eschatology at Emmaus*. Collegeville, MN: Liturgical, 1993.
Kaiser, O. *Introduction to the Old Testament*. Translated by John Sturdy. Rev. ed. Oxford: Blackwell, 1975.
Kaiser, W. C., Jr. "The Unfailing Kindnesses Promised to David: Isaiah 55:3." *JSOT* (1989) 91-98.
———. *The Uses of the Old Testament in the New*. Chicago: Moody, 1985.
Kakkanattu, J. P. *God's Enduring Love in the Book of Hosea*. FAT 2/14. Tübingen: Mohr/Siebeck, 2006.

Bibliography

Kallai, Z. "The Wandering-Traditions from Kadesh-Barnea to Canaan: A Study in Biblical Historiography." *JJS* 33 (1982) 175–84.

Kaufmann, Y. *The Babylonian Captivity and Deutero-Isaiah*. New York: Union of American Hebrew Congregations, 1970.

Keck, L. E., editor. *New Interpreter's Bible*. 12 vols. Nashville: Abingdon, 2002.

Kee, H. C. "Function of Scriptural Quotations and Allusions in Mark 11–16." In *Jesus und Paulus: Festschrift für Werner Georg Kümmel*, edited by E. Earle Ellis and Erich Grässer, 165–88. Göttingen: Vandenhoeck & Ruprecht, 1975.

Keefe, A. A. *Women's Body and the Social Body in Hosea*. JSOTSup 338; Gender Culture, Theory 10. Sheffield: Sheffield Academic, 2001.

Keel, O. *The Symbolism of the Biblical World*. Translated by T. J. Hallet. New York: Seabury, 1978.

Keener, C. S. *The Gospel of Matthew: A Socio-Rhetorical Commentary*. Grand Rapids: Eerdmans, 2009.

Keil, C. F., and F. Delitzsch. *Commentary on the Old Testament*. 10 vols. Edinburgh: T. & T. Clark, 1886–91.

Kelle, B. E. *Hosea 2: Metaphor and Rhetoric in Historical Perspective*. Academic Biblica 20. Atlanta: Society of Biblical Literature, 2005.

Keown, G. L. *Jeremiah 26–52*. WBC 27. Waco: Word, 1995.

Kertelge, K. "The Messianic Banquet Reconsidered." In *Future of Early Christianity*, edited by B. A. Pearson, 64–73. Minneapolis: Fortress, 1991.

Kiesow, K. *Exodustexte im Jesajabuch: literarkritische und motivgeschichtliche Analysen*. Göttingen: Vandenhoeck & Ruprecht, 1979.

Kimball, C. A. *Jesus' Exposition of the Old Testament in Luke's Gospel*. JSNTSup 94. Sheffield: JSOT Press, 1994.

Kissane, E. J. *The Book of Isaiah*. 2 vols. Dublin: Browne & Nolan, 1960.

Kistemaker, S. J. *The Parables of Jesus*. Grand Rapids: Baker, 1980.

Kittel, G., and G. Friedrich, editors. *Theological Dictionary of the New Testament*. Translated by G. W. Bromiley. 10 vols. Grand Rapids: Eerdmans, 1964.

Klein, D. J. "Proving and Provision at Marah: Exodus 15:22–27." *Kerux* 15 (2000) 24–29.

Klein, R. W. *1 Chronicles*. Hermeneia. Minneapolis: Fortress, 2006.

Knauf, E. "Kedar (Person)." In *ABD* 4:9–10.

Knibb, M. A. *Essays on the Book of Enoch and Other Early Jewish Texts and Traditions*. SVTP 22. Leiden: Brill, 2009.

———. *The Ethiopic Book of Enoch*. Oxford: Clarendon, 1978.

———. "Exile in the Damascus Document." In *Essays in the Book of Enoch*, 213–31. Leiden: Brill, 2009.

———. "The Exile in the Intertestamental Period." *HJ* 17 (1976) 253–72.

———. "The Exile in the Literature of the Second Temple Period." In *Essays in the Book of Enoch*, 190–212. Leiden: Brill, 2009.

Knight, D. A. *Rediscovering the Traditions of Israel*. SBLDS 9. Missoula, MT: Scholars, 1975.

———. "Tradition History." In *ABD* 6:633–38.

Knight, D. A., and W. J. Harrelson, editors. *Tradition and Theology in the Old Testament*. Philadelphia: Fortress, 1977.

Knight, G. *Deutero-Isaiah: A Theological Commentary on Isaiah 40–55*. New York: Abingdon, 1965.

———. *Servant Theology: A Commentary on the Book of Isaiah 40–55*. Rev. ed. ICC. Grand Rapids: Eerdmans, 1984.
Koester, C. R. *Symbolism in the Fourth Gospel: Meaning, Mystery, Community*. Minneapolis: Fortress, 1995.
Kolarick, M. "The Book of Wisdom." In *The New Interpreter's Bible*, edited by L. Keck, 5:435–600. Nashville: Abingdon, 1997.
Koole, J. L. *Isaiah II*. Kampen: Kok Pharos, 1997.
———. *Isaiah III*. Kampen: Kok Pharos, 1997.
Kornfeld, W. "L'adultere dans l'orient antique." *RB* 57 (1950) 92–109.
Kraus, H.-J. *Psalms 1–59*. Translated by H. C. Oswald. Minneapolis: Augsburg, 1988.
———. *Psalms 60–150*. Translated by H. C. Oswald. Minneapolis: Augsburg, 1989.
Kristeva, J. *Desire in Language: A Semiotic Approach to Literature and Art*. New York: Columbia University, 1980.
Kruger, P. "The Hem of the Garment in Marriage: The Meaning of the Symbolic Gesture in Ruth 3:9 and Ezek 16:8." *JNSL* 12 (1984) 79–86.
———. "Israel, the Harlot (Hos 2:4–9)." *JNSL* 11 (1983) 107–16.
———. "'I Will Hedge Her Way with Thornbushes' (Hosea 2,8) Another Example of Literary Multiplicity?" *BZ* (1999) 92–99.
———. "The Marriage Metaphor in Hosea 2:4–17 Against Its Ancient Near Eastern Background." *Old Testament Essays* 5 (1992) 7–25.
———. "Promiscuity or Marriage Fidelity: A Note on Prov 5:15–18." *JNSL* 13 (1987) 61–68.
Kugel, J. L., and R. A. Greer. *Early Biblical Interpretation*. Philadelphia: Westminster, 1986.
Kümmel, W. G. *Promise and Fulfillment*. SBT 23. London: SCM, 1961.
Lakoff, G., and M. Johnson. *Metaphors We Live By*. Chicago: University of Chicago, 1980.
Lampe, G. W. H., and K. J. Woollcombe. *Essays on Typology*. SBT 22. Naperville, IL: Allenson, 1957.
Lane, W. L. *The Gospel according to Mark*. NICNT. Grand Rapids: Eerdmans, 1974.
Le Donne, A. *Historical Jesus: What Can We Know and How Can We Know It?* Grand Rapids: Eerdmans, 2011.
Leal, R. B. *Wilderness in the Bible: Toward a Theology of Wilderness*. Studies in Biblical Literature 72. New York: Lang, 2004.
Leaney, A. R. C. *A Commentary on the Gospel According to St. Luke*. BNTC. London: Adam & Black, 1958.
Lemcio, E. E. "The Parables of the Great Supper and the Wedding Feast: History, Redaction and Canon." *HBT* 8 (1986) 1–26.
Lenski, R. C. H. *The Interpretation of St. Matthew's Gospel*. Minneapolis: Wartburg, 1943.
Leslie, E. A. *Isaiah*. New York: Abingdon, 1963.
Leveen, A. *Memory and Tradition in the Book of Numbers*. New York: Cambridge University Press, 2008.
Levenson, J. D. "Zion Traditions." In *ABD* 6:1098–1102.
Levine, B. A. *Numbers 1–20*. AB 4A. New York: Doubleday, 1993.
Levine, E. "The Land of Milk and Honey." *JSOT* 87 (2000) 43–57.
Lewis, T. J. "Mot." In *ABD* 4:922–24.
Licht, J. *The Rule Scroll (1QS, 1QSa, 1QSb)*. Jerusalem: Bialik Institute, 1965.
Lieber, A. "I Set a Table before You: The Jewish Eschatological Character of Aseneth's Conversion Meal." *JSOP* 14 (2005) 63–77.

Bibliography

Lindars, B. *New Testament Apologetic: The Doctrinal Significance of the Old Testament Quotations.* London: SCM, 1961.
Linnemann, E. *Parables of Jesus: Introduction and Exposition.* London: SPCK, 1966.
———. "Überlegungen zur Parabel vom grossen Abendmahl: Lc 14 15–24/Mt 22 1–14." *ZNW* 51 (1960) 246–55.
Lipinski, E. *La royauté de Yahwé dans la poésie et le culte de l'ancien Israël.* Brussels: Paleis der Academien, 1965.
———. "Marriage and Divorce in the Judaism of the Persian Period." *Transeuphratène* 4 (1991) 63–71.
———. "A Woman's Right to Divorce in the Light of Ancient Near Eastern Tradition." *Jewish Law Annual* 4 (1981) 9–27.
Litwak, K. D. *Echoes of Scripture in Luke-Acts: Telling the History of God's People Intertextually.* London: T. & T. Clark, 2005.
Llewelyn, S. R. *New Documents Illustrating Early Christianity.* Vol. 9. Grand Rapids: Eerdmans, 2002.
Longenecker, R. N. *Biblical Exegesis in the Apostolic Period.* Grand Rapids: Eerdmans, 1977.
———. *The Challenge of Jesus' Parables.* Grand Rapids: Eerdmans, 2000.
Lövestam, E. *Son and Saviour: A Study of Acts 13, 32–37.* ConBNT 18. Lund: Gleerup, 1961.
Lüdemann, G. *Jesus After 2000 Years: What He Really Said and Did.* London: SCM, 2000.
Lundbom, J. R. *Jeremiah 1–20.* AB 21A. New York: Doubleday, 1999.
———. *Jeremiah 21–36.* AB 21B. New York: Doubleday, 2004.
———. *Jeremiah 37–52.* AB 21C. New York: Doubleday, 2004.
Luz, U. *Matthew 1–7.* Hermeneia. Minneapolis: Fortress, 2007.
———. *Matthew 8–20.* Hermeneia. Minneapolis: Fortress, 2001.
———. *Matthew 21–28.* Hermeneia. Minneapolis: Fortress, 2005.
Lys, D. "J'ai deux amours, ou l'amant jugé: Exercise sur Osée 2, 4–25." *ETR* 51 (1976) 59–77.
Mace, D. *Hebrew Marriage: A Sociological Study.* London: Epworth, 1953.
Macintosh, A. A. *Hosea.* ICC. Edinburgh: T. & T. Clark, 1997.
Mackay, J. L. *Jeremiah.* 2 vols. Fearn: Mentor, 2004.
Magness, J. *The Archaeology of Qumran and the Dead Sea Scrolls.* Grand Rapids: Eerdmans, 2003.
Malherbe, A. J. *Moral Exhortation: A Greco-Roman Sourcebook.* LEC 4. Philadelphia: Westminster, 1986.
Manek, J. "The New Exodus in the Books of Luke." *NovT* 2 (1957) 8–23.
Mann, C. S. *Mark.* AB 27. New York: Doubleday, 1986.
Manning, G. T. *Echoes of a Prophet: The Use of Ezekiel in the Gospel of John and in Literature of the Second Temple Period.* JSNTSup 270. London: T. & T. Clark, 2004.
Manson, T. W. *The Teaching of Jesus: Studies of Its Form and Content.* Cambridge: Cambridge University Press, 1931.
Manson, W. *The Gospel of Luke.* MNTC 3. New York: Harper, 1930.
Marcus, J. *The Mystery of the Kingdom of God.* SBLDS 90. Atlanta: Scholars 1986.
———. *The Way of the Lord: Christological Exegesis of the Old Testament in the Gospel of Mark.* Louisville: Westminster John Knox, 1992.
Mare, W. H. "Serpent's Stone." In *ABD* 5:1116–17.
Marmion, J. C. "The Parable of the Banquet." *Epiphany* 4 (1984) 27–29.
Marsh, C. "Theological History? N.T. Wright's *Jesus and the Victory of God*." *JSNT* 69 (1998) 77–94.

Marshall, I. H. *Commentary on Luke*. Rev. ed., NIGTC. Grand Rapids: Eerdmans, 1974.

———. *Luke: Historian and Theologian*. Exeter: Paternoster, 1970.

Marshall, I. H., editor. *New Testament Interpretation: Essays on Principles and Methods*. Grand Rapids: Eerdmans, 1977.

Martin-Achard, R. "'Il engloutit la mort à jamais': remarques sur Esaïe, 25, 8a." In *Mélanges bibliques et orientaux en l'honneur de M Mathias Delcor*, 283-96. Kevelaer, Germany: Butzon & Bercker, 1985.

Mason, R. "The Use of Earlier Biblical Materials in Zechariah 9-14: A Study in Inner Biblical Exegesis." In *Bringing Out the Treasure: Inner Biblical Allusion in Zechariah 9-14*, edited by M. Boda and M. Floyd, 1-209. JSOTSup 370. London: Sheffield Academic, 2003.

Masterman, E. W. G. "Serpent's Stone." In *ISBE*, 4:419.

Masuda, S. "The Good News of the Miracle of the Bread: The Tradition and Its Markan Redaction." *NTS* 28 (1982) 119-219.

Matera, F. J. *The Kingship of Jesus: Composition and Theology in Mark 15*. Chico, CA: Scholars, 1982.

Mathews, K. A. *Genesis 11:27—50:26*. NAC 1B. Nashville: Broadman & Holman, 2005.

Matura, T. "Les invités à la noce royale: Mt 22,1-14." *AsSeign* 59 (1974) 16-27.

Mauser, U. *Christ in the Wilderness: The Wilderness Theme in the Second Gospel and Its Basis in the Biblical Tradition*. SBT 39. London: SCM, 1963.

Maximiliano, G. C., editor. *Mesianismo y escatologia*. Bibliotheca Salmanticensis 16 Estudios 14. Salamanca, Spain: Universidad Pontificia, 1976.

May, H. G. "The Fertility Cult in Hosea." *AJSL* 48 (1932) 73-98.

McArthur, H. K., and R. M. Johnston. *They Also Taught in Parables: Rabbinic Parables from the First Centuries of the Christian Era*. Grand Rapids: Zondervan, 1990.

McCann, J. "Books I-III and the Editorial Purpose of the Hebrew Psalter." In *Shape and Shaping of the Psalter*, 93-107. Sheffield: JSOT Press, 1993.

McCarter, P. K. "The Ritual Dedication of the City of David in 2 Samuel 6." In *The Word of the Lord Shall Go Forth: Essays in Honor of David Noel Freedman in Celebration of His Sixtieth Birthday*, edited by C. L. Meyers and M. O'Connor, 276-77. Winona Lake, IN: Eisenbrauns, 1983.

McCarthy, D. J. *Old Testament Covenant: A Survey of Current Opinions*. Richmond, VA: Knox, 1972.

———. "Social Compact and Sacral Kingship." In *Studies in the Period of David and Solomon and Other Essays*, edited by T. Ishida, 77-79. Winona Lake, IN: Eisenbrauns, 1983.

McKane, W. *Jeremiah*. ICC. Edinburgh: T. & T. Clark, 1986.

McKeating, H. *The Book of Jeremiah*. London: Epworth, 1999.

McKee, H. C. "Testament of the Twelve Patriarchs." In *OTP* 1:775-828.

McKnight, S., and J. B. Modica. *Who Do My Opponents Say I Am? An Investigation of the Accusations against Jesus*. LNTS 327. London: T. & T. Clark, 2008.

McNeile, A. H. *The Gospel according to St. Matthew*. London: Macmillan, 1928.

McWhirter, J. *The Bridegroom Messiah and the People of God: Marriage in the Fourth Gospel*. Cambridge: Cambridge University Press, 2006.

Meadors, E. P. *Jesus, the Messianic Herald of Salvation*. Peabody, MA: Hendrickson, 1997.

———. "The 'Messianic' Implications of the Q Material." *JBL* 118 (1999) 253-77.

Meier, J. P. *A Marginal Jew: Rethinking the Historical Jesus*. 4 vols. ABRL. New York: Doubleday, 1991-2001; New Haven: Yale University Press, 2009.

Melugin, R. *The Formation of Isaiah 40-55*. BZAW 141. Berlin: de Gruyter, 1976.

Bibliography

Mendals, D. "Baruch." In *ABD* 1:618-20.
Mendenhall, G. E., and G. A. Herion. "Covenant." In *ABD* 1:1179-1202.
Mercer, S. A. B. *The Tell el-Amarna Tablets*. Toronto: Macmillan, 1939.
Merendino, R. P. *Der Erste und der letzte: eine Untersuchung von Jes 40-48*. VTSup 31. Leiden: Brill, 1981.
Merrill, E. H. *Deuteronomy*. NAC 4. Nashville: Broadman & Holman, 1994.
Mettinger, T. N. D. *King and Messiah: The Civil and Sacral Legitimation of the Israelite Kings*. Coniectanea biblica 8. Lund: Gleerup, 1976.
Metzger, B. M. "The Fourth Book of Ezra." In *OTP* 1:516-59.
Meyer, B. F. *The Aims of Jesus*. London: SCM, 1979.
Meyer, R. "Μάννα," In *TDNT* 4:464-65
———. "Many (=All) Are Called, but Few (=Not All) Are Chosen." *NTS* 36 (1990) 89-97.
Meyers, C. L. "Of Drums and Damsels: Women's Performance in Ancient Israel." *BA* 54 (1991) 16-27.
Meyers, C. L., and E. M. Meyers. *Zechariah 9-14*. AB 25C. New York: Doubleday, 1992.
Meyers, C. L., and M. O'Connor. *The Word of the Lord Shall Go Forth: Essays in Honor of David Noel Freedman in Celebration of His Sixtieth Birthday*. Winona Lake, IN: Eisenbrauns, 1983.
Meyers, J. *Ezra—Nehemiah*. AB 14. New York: Doubleday, 1965.
Mickelsen, A. B. *Interpreting the Bible*. Grand Rapids: Eerdmans, 1963.
Milgrom, J. *Cult and Conscience: The Asham and the Priestly Doctrine of Repentance*. SJLA 18. Leiden: Brill, 1976.
———. *Leviticus 23-27*. AB 3B. New York: Doubleday, 2001.
———. *Numbers*. The JPS Torah Commentary. Philadelphia: Jewish Publication Society, 1990.
Millar, W. R. *Isaiah 24-27 and the Origin of Apocalyptic*. Missoula, MT: Scholars, 1976.
Millard, A. R. *Reading and Writing in the Time of Jesus*. Biblical Seminar 69. Sheffield: Sheffield Academic, 2000.
Miller, D., and P. Miller. *The Gospel of Mark as Midrash on Earlier Jewish and New Testament Literature*. Lewiston, NY: Mellen, 1990.
Miller, G. "Isaiah 25:6-8." *Int* 49 (1995) 175-78.
Miller, S. R. *Daniel*. NAC 18. Nashville: Broadman & Holman, 1994.
Miscall, P. D. "Isaiah: New Heavens, New Earth, New Book." In *Reading Between Texts: Intertextuality and the Hebrew Bible*, edited by D. N. Fewell, 41-56. Louisville: Westminster John Knox, 1992.
Mitchell, D. C. *The Message of the Psalter: An Eschatological Programme in the Book of Psalms*. JSOTSup 252. Sheffield: Sheffield Academic, 1997.
Modica, J. B. "Jesus as Glutton and Drunkard: The 'Excesses' of Jesus." In *Who Do My Opponents Say I Am? An Investigation of the Accusations against Jesus*, edited by S. McKnight and J. B. Modica, 50-73. LNTS 327. London: T. & T. Clark, 2008.
Moessner, D. P. *Lord of the Banquet: The Literary and Theological Significance of the Lukan Travel Narrative*. Harrisburg, PA: Trinity, 1998.
Moo, D. J. *The Old Testament in the Gospel Passion Narratives*. Sheffield: Almond, 1983.
Moore, G. F. *Judaism in the First Centuries of the Christian Era*. Reprint [3 vols. in 2] editor. 2 vols. New York: Schocken, 1971.
———. *Judges*. ICC. Edinburgh: T. & T. Clark, 1895.

Moore, S. D. *Poststructuralism and the New Testament: Derrida and Foucault at the Foot of the Cross*. Minneapolis: Fortress, 1994.
Moran, W. L. *The Amarna Letters*. Baltimore: Johns Hopkins University, 1992.
———. "Ancient Near Eastern Background of the Love of God in Deuteronomy." *CBQ* 25 (1963) 77–87.
Morganstern, J. "A Chapter in the History of the High Priesthood." *AJSL* 40 (1938) 1–24.
Moseley, N. A. "A Critical Evaluation of the Methods and Motifs in the Polemic against Baalism in Hosea." PhD diss., New Orleans Baptist Theological Seminary, 1987.
Motyer, J. A. *The Prophecy of Isaiah*. Downers Grove, IL: InterVarsity, 1993.
Moulton, J. and G. Milligan. *Vocabulary of the New Testament*. Grand Rapids: Eerdmans, 1930.
Mowinckel, S. *The Psalms in Israel's Worship*. New York: Abingdon, 1962.
Moyise, S. "Authorial Intention and the Book of Revelation." *AUSS* 39 (2001) 35–40.
———. "Can We Use the New Testament in the Way Which the New Testament Authors Use the Old Testament?" *die Skriflig* 36 (2002) 643–60.
———. "Does the Author of Revelation Misappropriate the Scriptures?" *AUSS* 40 (2002) 3–21.
———. "Intertextuality and the Study of the Old Testament in the New Testament." In *The Old Testament in the New Testament: Essays in Honour of J. L. North*, edited by S. Moyise. JSNTSup 189, 14–41. Sheffield: Sheffield Academic, 2000.
———. *The Old Testament in the Book of Revelation*. JSNTSup 115. Sheffield: Sheffield Academic, 1995.
———. *The Old Testament in the New: An Introduction*. Continuum Biblical Studies Series. New York: Continuum, 2001.
———. *The Old Testament in the New Testament: Essays in Honour of J .L. North*. JSNTSup 189. Sheffield: Sheffield Academic, 2000.
———. "The Wilderness Quotation in Mark 1.2–3." In *Wilderness: Essays in Honour of Frances Young*, edited by R. S. Sugirtharajah, 78–87. London: T. & T. Clark, 2005.
Moyise, S., editor. *Studies in the Book of Revelation*. Edinburgh: T. & T. Clark, 2001.
Muilenburg, J. "Isaiah 40–66." In *IB* 5:381–773.
Mulder, J. S. M. *Studies on Psalm 45*. Oss, The Netherlands: Witsiers, 1972.
Mulder, M. J. *Mikra: Text, Translation, Reading & Interpretation of the Hebrew Bible in Ancient Judaism & Early Christianity*. Peabody, MA: Hendrickson, 2004.
Murihead, I. A. "The Bride of Christ." *SJT* 5 (1952) 175–87.
Musurillo, H. A. "'Many Are Called, but Few Are Chosen': Matthew 22:14." *TSK* 7 (1946) 583–89.
Myers, J. M. *II Chronicles*. AB 13. Garden City, NY: Doubleday, 1965.
Navarro, E. F. *El desierto transformado: una imagen deuteroisaiana de regeneración*. Rome: Pontificio Istituto Biblico, 1992.
Navone, J. "The Parable of the Banquet." *The Bible Today* (1964) 923–29.
Nebe, G. W. "Ergänzende Bemerkung zu 4Q176, Jubiläen 23:21." *RevQ* 14 (1989) 129–30.
Neher, A. "Le symbolisme conjugal: Expression de l'historie dans l'Ancien Testament." *SJLA* 34 (1954) 30–49.
Neirynck, F. "Q 6,20b–21; 7,22 and Isaiah 61." In *Scriptures in the Gospels*, edited by C. M. Tuckett, 27–64. Leuven: Leuven University, 1997.
Neubrand, M. "Die Wüste: Zur Theologischen Deutung in der Bibel." In *Jericho und Qumran*, 89–110. Regensburg: Pustet, 2000.

Bibliography

Neusner, J. *From Politics to Piety: The Emergence of Pharisaic Judaism.* Englewood Cliffs, NJ: Prentice-Hall, 1972.

———. *The Halakah: Historical and Religious Perspectives.* BTLJ 8. Leiden: Brill, 2002.

———. *Rabbinic Literature and the New Testament.* Valley Forge, PA: Trinity, 1990.

———. *The Talmud of the Land of Israel.* Atlanta: Scholars, 1999.

———. "Two Picture of the Pharisees: Philosophical Circle or Eating Club." *AThR* 64 (1982) 525–57.

Neusner, J., and B. Chilton. *In Quest of the Historical Pharisees.* Waco: Baylor, 2007.

Newell, J. E., and R. R. Newell. "Parable of the Wicked Tenants." *NovT* 14 (1972) 226–37.

Newman, C. *Jesus & the Restoration of Israel: A Critical Assessment of N.T. Wright's Jesus and the Victory of God.* Downers Grove, IL: InterVarsity, 1999.

Newsom, C. A., and S. H. Ringe, editors. *The Women's Bible Commentary.* London: SPCK, 1992.

Neyrey, J. H. "Ceremonies in Luke-Acts: The Case of Meals and Table-Fellowship." In *Social World of Luke-Acts,* 361–87. Peabody, MA: Hendrickson, 1991.

Nicholson, E. W. "Antiquity of the Tradition in Exodus 24:9–22." *VT* 25 (1975) 69–79.

———. "Interpretation of Exodus 24:9–11." *VT* 24 (1974) 77–97.

———. "Origin of the Tradition in Exodus 24:9–11." *VT* 26 (1976) 148–60.

Nickelsburg, G. W. E. *1 Enoch: A Commentary on the Book of 1 Enoch.* Minneapolis: Fortress, 2001.

Ninow, F. *Indicators of Typology within the Old Testament: The Exodus Motif.* Friedensauer Schriftenreihe 4. Frankfurt: Lang, 2001.

Noël, T. "The Parable of the Wedding Guest: A Narrative-Critical Interpretation." *PRSt* 16 (1989) 17–27.

Nolland, J. *The Gospel of Matthew.* NIGTC. Grand Rapids: Eerdmans, 2005.

———. *Luke 9:21—18:34.* WBC 35B. Nashville: Nelson, 1993.

Noth, M. *Exodus.* OTL. Philadelphia: Westminster, 1962.

———. *A History of Pentateuchal Traditions.* Englewood Cliffs, NJ: Prentice-Hall, 1972.

Novakovic, L. "4Q521: The Works of the Messiah or the Signs of the Messianic Time?" In *Qumran Studies: New Approaches, New Questions,* edited by M. T. Davis and B. A. Strawn, 208–31. Grand Rapids: Eerdmans, 2007.

Nwaoru, E. O. *Imagery in the Prophecy of Hosea.* Ägypten und Altes Testament 41. Wiesbaden: Harrassowitz, 1999.

Nyberg, H. S. "'Speak Tenderly to Jerusalem': Second Isaiah's Reception and Use of Daughter Zion." *PSB* (1999) 281–94.

———. *Studien zum Hoseabuche.* Uppsala Universitets Årsskrift 6. Uppsala: Lundequistska, 1935.

O'Callaghan, J. "Dos retoques antioquenos: Mt 10:10; Mc 2:20." *Bib* 68 (1987) 564–67.

Ochs, C. "The Desert, Biblical Spirituality, and Creation." *STRev* 36 (1993) 493–508.

———. "The Presence of the Desert." *Cross Currents* 43 (1993) 293–306.

O'Connor, K. M. "'Speak Tenderly to Jerusalem': Second Isaiah's Reception and Use of Daughter Zion." *PSB* (1999) 281–94.

———. "The Tears of God and Divine Character." In *Troubling Jeremiah,* edited by A. R. Diamond, K. M. O'Connor, and L. Stulman, 387–401. Sheffield: Sheffield Academic, 1999.

Oesterley, W. O. E. *The Gospel Parables in the Light of Their Jewish Background.* London: SPCK, 1936.

Oestreich, B. *Metaphors and Similes for Yahweh in Hosea 14:2–9 (1–8)*. Friedensauer Schriftenreihe 1. Frankfurt: Lang, 1998.
O'Kane, M. "Isaiah: A Prophet in the Footsteps of Moses." *JSOT* 69 (1996) 29–51.
Olmstead, W. G. *Matthew's Trilogy of Parables: The Nation, the Nations, and the Reader in Matthew 21.28–22.14*. Cambridge: Cambridge University Press, 2003.
Olson, D. C. *Enoch: A New Translation*. North Richland Hills, TX: BIBAL, 2004.
O'Neill, J. C. "The Silence of Jesus." *NTS* 15 (1968) 153–67.
———. "The Source of the Parables of the Bridegroom and the Wicked Husbandmen." *JTS* 39 (1988) 485–89.
Oropeza, B. J. "Echoes of Isaiah in the Rhetoric of Paul: New Exodus, Wisdom, and the Humility of the Cross in Utopian-Apocalyptic Expectations." In *Intertexture of Apocalyptic Discourse in the New Testament*, edited by D. F. Watson, 87–112. Atlanta: Society of Biblical Literature, 2002.
O'Rourke, J. J. "Possible Uses of the Old Testament in the Gospels: An Overview." In *The Gospels and The Scriptures of Israel*, edited by C. A. Evans and W. R. Stegner, 15–25. Sheffield: Sheffield Academic, 1994.
Orton, D. E. *The Understanding Scribe: Matthew and the Apocalyptic Ideal*. Sheffield: Sheffield Academic, 1989.
Osborne, G. "The Evangelical and Traditionsgeschichte." *JETS* 21 (1978) 117–30.
Osiek, C. "The Bride of Christ (Ephesians 5:22–33) A Problematic Wedding." *BTB* 32 (2002) 29–39.
Oswalt, J. *The Book of Isaiah: Chapters 1–39*. NICOT. Grand Rapids: Eerdmans, 1986.
———. *The Book of Isaiah: Chapters 40–66*. NICOT. Grand Rapids: Eerdmans, 1998.
———. "Isaiah 24–27: Songs in the Night." *CTJ* 40 (2005) 76–84.
Otzen, B. "Traditions and Structures of Isaiah 24–27." *VT* 24 (1974) 196–206.
Pagenkemper, K. E. "Rejection Imagery in the Synoptic Parables." *BibSac* 153 (1996) 308–31.
Pao, D. W. *Acts and the Isaianic New Exodus*. Grand Rapids: Baker, 2002.
Paolantonio, M. "God as Husband." *The Bible Today* 27 (1989) 299–303.
Pardee, D. "As Strong as Death." In *Love and Death in the Ancient Near East: Essays in Honour of Marvin H. Pope*, edited by J. H. Marks and R. M. Good, 65–69. Guilford, CT: Four Quarters, 1987.
———. "A Restudy of the Commentary on Psalm 37 from Qumran Cave 4." *RevQ* 13 (1973) 163–94.
Parker, S. B. "The Marriage Blessing in Israelite and Ugaritic Literature." *JBL* 95 (1976) 23–30.
Parunak, H. V. D. "Semantic Survey of *nhm*." *Bib* 56 (1975) 512–32.
Patai, R. "Hebrew Installation Rites." In *HUCA* 20, 143–225. New York: KTAV, 1947.
Patterson, R. D. "A Multiplex Approach to Psalm 45." *Grace Theological Journal* 6 (1985) 29–48.
Paulien, J. *Decoding Revelation's Trumpets: Literary Allusions and Interpretation of Revelation 8:7–12*. AUSDS 11. Berrien Springs, MI: Andrews University, 1988.
———. "Dreading the Whirlwind: Intertextuality and the Use of the Old Testament in Revelation." *AUSS* 39 (2001) 5–22.
Payne, P. J. "The Authenticity of the Parables." In *Gospel Perspectives 2: Studies of History and Tradition in the Four Gospels*, edited by R. T. France and D. Wenham, 329–44. Sheffield: JSOT Press, 1981.
Pedersen, J. *Israel, Its Life and Culture*. South Florida Studies in the History of Judaism 28. Atlanta: Scholars, 1991.

Bibliography

Phillips, A. "Another Look at Adultery." *JSOT* 20 (1981) 3–25.

———. "'Double for All Her Sins.'" *ZAW* 94 (1982) 130–32.

———. "Some Aspects of Family Law in Pre-Exilic Israel." *VT* 23 (1973) 349–61.

Piper, O. A. "Unchanging Promises: Exodus in the New Testament." *Int* 11 (1957) 3–22.

Pitre, B. J. *Jesus, the Tribulation, and the End of the Exile: Restoration Eschatology and the Origin of the Atonement.* Grand Rapids: Baker, 2005.

Ploeg, J. P. M. van der. "Meals of the Essenes." *JSS* 2 (1957) 163–75.

Plumer, W. S. *Psalms.* Edinburgh: Banner of Truth, 1867.

Plummer, A. *A Critical and Exegetical Commentary on the Gospel According to St. Luke.* 5th editor. ICC. Edinburgh: T. & T. Clark, 1922.

Polaski, D. C. *Authorizing an End: The Isaiah Apocalypse and Intertextuality.* Biblical Interpretation Series 50. Leiden: Brill, 2001.

Pope, M. H. *Song of Songs.* AB 7C. Garden City, NY: Doubleday, 1977.

Porter, J. R. "The Interpretation of 2 Samuel 6 and Psalm 132." *JTS* (1954) 161–73.

Porter, S. E. *Hearing the Old Testament in the New Testament.* Grand Rapids: Eerdmans, 2006.

———. "The Use of the Old Testament in the New Testament: A Brief Comment on Method and Terminology." In *Early Christian Interpretation of the Scriptures of Israel: Investigations and Proposals*, edited by C. A. Evans and J. A. Sanders, 79–96. JSNTSup 14. Sheffield: Sheffield Academic, 1997.

Portier-Young, A. E. "Sweet Mercy Metropolis: Interpreting Aseneth's Honeycomb." *JSOP* 14 (2005) 133–57.

Prabhu, G. M. S. *The Formula Quotations in the Infancy Narrative of Matthew: An Enquiry into the Tradition History of Mt 1–2.* AnBib 63. Rome: Biblical Institute, 1976.

Pressler, C.J. "Achor." In *ABD* 1:56.

Priest, J. "Ben Sira 45:25 in the Light of the Qumran Literature." *RevQ* 5 (1964) 111–18.

———. "*Mebaqqer, paqid,* and the Messiah." *JBL* 81 (1962) 55–61.

———. "Messiah and the Meal in 1QSa." *JBL* 82 (1963) 95–100.

———. "A Note on the Messianic Banquet." In *The Messiah: Developments in Earliest Judaism and Christianity*, edited by J. H. Charlesworth, 222–38. Minneapolis: Fortress, 1992.

Pritchard, J. B., editor. *Ancient Near Eastern Texts Relating to the Old Testament.* 3rd ed. Princeton: Princeton University, 1969.

Propp, W. H. "Is Psalm 45 an Erotic Poem?" *BR* 20 (2004) 33–37, 42.

———. *Water in the Wilderness: A Biblical Motif and Its Mythological Background.* Atlanta: Scholars 1987.

Provan, I. W. *1 and 2 Kings.* NIBCOT. Peabody, MA: Hendrickson, 1995.

Puech, É. *La croyance des Esséniens en la vie future.* EBib 21. Paris: Gabalda, 1993.

———. "Préséance sacerdotale et Messie-Roi dans la Règle de la Congrégation (1QSa ii 11–22)." *RevQ* 16 (1994) 351–65.

———. "Review of DJD VII." *RB* 95 (1988) 414–17.

———. "Une apocalypse messianique (4Q521)." *RevQ* 15 (1992) 475–522.

Puig i Tàrrech, A. *La Parabole des Dix Vierges: Mt 25, 1–13.* AnBib 102. Rome: Biblical Institute, 1983.

Quarles, C. L. "Midrash As Creative Historiography: Portrait of a Misnomer." *JETS* 39 (1996) 457–64.

———. *Midrash Criticism: Introduction and Appraisal.* Lanham, MD: University Press of America, 1997.

Rad, G. von. *The Message of the Prophets.* New York: Harper & Row, 1967.

———. *Old Testament Theology*. Translated by D. Stalker. New York: McGraw-Hill, 1966.
———. *The Problem of the Hexateuch and Other Essays*. Translated by D. Stalker. New York: Harper, 1966.
———. "Typological Interpretation of the Old Testament." In *Essays on Old Testament Interpretation*, edited by C. Westermann, 17–39. London: SCM, 1963.
Raisanen, H. *Jesus, Paul and Torah: Collected Essays*. Translated by D. E. Orton. JSNTSup 42. Sheffield: Sheffield Academic, 1992.
Rallis, I. "Nuptial Imagery in the Book of Hosea: Israel as the Bride of Yahweh." *SVQT* 34 (1990) 197–219.
Ramm, B. L. *Protestant Biblical Interpretation*. Complete rev. ed. Boston: Wilde, 1956.
Rashi. *Rashi's Commentary on Psalms*. Edited by M. I. Gruber. BRLJ 18. Leiden: Brill, 2004.
Redditt, P. L. "Isaiah 24–27: A Form Critical Analysis." PhD diss., Vanderbilt, 1972.
———. "Once Again, the City in Isaiah 24–27." *Hebrew Annual Review* 10 (1986) 317–35.
Reider, J. *The Book of Wisdom*. New York: Harper, 1957.
Rese, M. *Alttestamentliche Motive in der Christologie des Lukas*. SNT 1. Gütersloh: Mohn, 1969.
Reymond, P. *L'eau, sa vie, et sa signification dans l'Ancien Testament*. Leiden: Brill, 1958.
Rice, G. "Dining with Deutero-Isaiah." *JRT* 37 (1980) 23–30.
Richards, K. H. "Death, Old Testament." In *ABD* 2:108–10.
Richardson, H. N. "Some Notes on 1QSa." *JBL* 76 (1957) 108–22.
Riemann, P. A. "Desert and Return to Desert in the Pre-exilic Prophets." PhD diss., Harvard University, 1964.
Riesenfeld, H. *The Gospel Tradition*. Philadelphia: Fortress, 1970.
Riesner, R. *Jesus als Lehrer: eine Untersuchung zum Ursprung der Evangelien-Überlieferung*. WUNT 2/7. Tübingen: Mohr/Siebeck, 1981.
———. "Jesus as Preacher and Teacher." In *Jesus and the Oral Gospel*, edited by H. Wansbrough, 185–210. JSNTSup 64. Sheffield: Sheffield Academic, 1991.
Ringgren, H. "The Marriage Motif in Israelite Religion." In *Ancient Israelite Religion*, edited by P. D. Miller, P. D. Hanson, and S. D. McBride, 421–28. Philadelphia: Fortress, 1987.
———. "Some Observations on Style and Structure in the Isaiah Apocalypse." In *ASTI* 9, 107–15. Leiden: Brill, 1974.
Robert, A. "La paix eschatologique dans le Cantique des Cantiques." In *Actas el XXXV Congreso Eucaristico Internacional*, 335–37. Barcelona: Sesiones de Estudio, 1954.
Robertson, A. T. *A Grammar of the Greek New Testament in the Light of Historical Research*. Nashville: Broadman, 1914.
Rogers, J. B., Jr. "Jeremiah 31:7–14." *Int* 42 (1988) 281–91.
Ross, J. P. "Jahweh Sebaôt in Samuel and Psalms." *VT* 17 (1967) 76–92.
Roth, M. T. *Babylonian Marriage Agreements: 7th-3rd Centuries B.C.* AOAT 222. Neukirchen-Vluyn: Neukirchener, 1989.
Rowley, H. H. "The Marriage of Hosea." *BJRL* 39 (1956) 200–223.
Rubenstein, J. L. *The History of Sukkot in the Second Temple and Rabbinic Periods*. BJS 302. Atlanta: Scholars, 1995.
Rudolph, W. *Hosea*. KAT 13/1. Gütersloh: Mohn, 1966.
Ruprecht, E. "Exodus 24:9–11 als Beispiel lebendiger Erzähltradition aus der Zeit des babylonischen Exils." In *Werden und Wirken des Alten Testaments*, 138–73. Göttingen: Vandenhoeck & Ruprecht, 1980.

Bibliography

Russell, D. S. *The Method and Message of Jewish Apocalyptic, 200 B.C.-A.D. 100*. OTL. Philadelphia: Westminster, 1964.

Rütersworden, U. "Erwägungen zur Metaphorik des Wassers in Jes 40ff." *SJOT* (1989) 1–22.

Ryken, L. *The Literature of the Bible*. Grand Rapids: Zondervan, 1974.

Safari, S. "Elementary Education, Its Religious and Social Significance in the Talmudic Period." in *Jewish Society Through the Ages*, edited by H. H. Ben-Sasson and S. Ettinger, 11:148–68. London: Vallentine Mitchell, 1971.

Sailhamer, J. "The Canonical Approach to the OT: Its Effect on Understanding Prophecy." *JETS* 30 (1987) 307–15.

Sanders, E. P. *The Historical Figure of Jesus*. New York: Penguin, 1996.

———. *Jesus and Judaism*. Philadelphia: Fortress, 1985.

———. "Jesus and the Sinners." In *Studies in the Historical Jesus*, edited by C. A. Evans and S. E. Porter. 29–60. Sheffield: Sheffield Academic, 1995.

———. *Judaism: Practice and Belief, 63 BCE-66 CE*. Philadelphia: Trinity, 1994.

Sanders, J. A. "Banquet of the Dispossessed." *USQR* 20 (1965) 355–63.

———. *The Dead Sea Psalms Scroll*. Ithaca, NY: Cornell University, 1967.

———. "The Ethic of Election in Luke's Great Banquet Parable." In *Essays in Old Testament Ethics*, edited by J. L. Crenshaw, 245–71. New York: KTAV, 1974.

———. "Isaiah 55:1–9." *Int* 32 (1978) 291–95.

Sandmel, S. "Parallelomania." *JBL* (1962) 1–13.

Sapaugh, G. P. "A Call to the Wedding Celebration: An Exposition of Matthew 22:1–14." *Journal of the Grace Evangelical Society* 5 (1992) 11–34.

Satlow, M. L. "4Q502: A New Year Festival?" *DSD* 5 (1998) 57–68.

———. *Jewish Marriage in Antiquity*. Princeton: Princeton University, 2001.

Sawyer, J. F. A. "Daughters of Zion and Servant of the Lord in Isaiah: A Comparison." *JSOT* 44 (1989) 89–107.

Schiffman, L. H. "Communal Meals at Qumran." *RevQ* 10 (1979) 45–56.

———. *The Eschatological Community of the Dead Sea Scrolls: A Study of the Rule of the Congregation*. SBLMS 38. Atlanta: Scholars, 1989.

———. *Qumran and Jerusalem: Studies in the Dead Sea Scrolls and the History of Judaism*. Grand Rapids: Eerdmans, 2010.

———. *Reclaiming the Dead Sea Scrolls*. ABRL. New Haven: Yale University, 2007.

———. "Rule of the Congregation." In *Encyclopedia of The Dead Sea Scrolls*, edited by L. H. Schiffman and J. VanderKam, 2:797–99. Oxford: Oxford University, 2000.

Schlosser, J. *Le règne de Dieu dans les dits de Jésus*. 2 vols. Paris: Gabalda, 1980.

Schmauch, W. *Orte der Offenbarung und der Offenbarungsort im Neuen Testament*. Göttingen: Vandenhoeck & Ruprecht, 1956.

Schmitt, J. J. "The City as Woman in Isaiah 1–39." In *Writing and Reading the Scroll of Isaiah: Studies of an Interpretive Tradition*, edited by C. C. Broyles and C A. Evans, 1:95–120. VTSup 70. Leiden: Brill, 1997.

———. "The Motherhood of God and Zion as Mother." *RB* 92 (1985) 557–69.

———. "The Wife of God in Hosea 2." *BR* 34 (1989) 5–18.

———. "Yahweh's Divorce in Hosea 2—Who Is That Woman?" *SJOT* 9 (1995) 119–32.

Schoors, A. "L'eschatologie dans la prophéties du Deutéro-Isaïe." In *Recherches bibliques VIII*, 107–18. Bruges: Desclée de Brouwe, 1967.

———. *I Am God Your Saviour: A Form-Critical Study of the Main Genres in Is. XL-LV*. VTSup 24. Leiden: Brill, 1973.

Schweitzer, A. *The Mystery of the Kingdom of God: The Secret of Jesus' Messiahship and Passion.* New York: Macmillan, 1957.

———. *Quest for the Historical Jesus.* London: A. & C. Black, 1931.

Seely, D. R. "4Q437: A First Look at an Unpublished Barki Nafshi Text." In *Provo International Conference on the Dead Sea Scrolls*, edited by D. Parry and E. C. Ulrich, 147-60. Leiden: Brill, 1999.

Seitz, C. R. "Isaiah." In *NIB*, 6:309-552.

———. *Isaiah 1-39.* Louisville: John Knox, 1993.

Selbie, W. B. "The Parable of the Marriage Feast (Matt. XXII. 1-14)." *ExpTim* 37 (1925) 267.

Selms, A. van. "The Best Man and the Bride: From Sumer to St. John with a New Interpretation of Judges, Chapters 14 and 15." *JNES* 9 (1950) 65-75.

———. *Marriage and Family Life in Ugaritic Literature.* Pretoria Oriental Series 1. London: Luzac, 1954.

Seow, C. L. *Myth, Drama, and the Politics of David's Dance.* HSM 44. Atlanta: Scholars, 1989.

Setel, T. D. "Prophets and Pornography: Female Sexual Imagery in Hosea." In *Feminist Interpretation of the Bible*, edited by L. Russell, 86-95. Philadelphia: Westminster, 1985.

Sheriffs, D. "'A Tale of Two Cities': Nationalism in Zion and Babylon." *TynBul* 39 (1988) 19-57.

Sherwood, Y. *The Prostitute and the Prophet: Hosea's Marriage in Literary-Theological Perspective.* JSOTSup 212. London: T. & T. Clark, 2004.

Shields, M. E. *Circumscribing the Prostitute: The Rhetorics of Intertextuality, Metaphor, and Gender in Jeremiah 3.1-4.4.* JSOTSup 387. London: T. & T. Clark, 2004.

Sigal, P. *The Halakah of Jesus of Nazareth According to the Gospel of Matthew.* Lanham, MD: University Press of America, 1986.

Sim, D. C. *Apocalyptic Eschatology in the Gospel of Matthew.* Cambridge: Cambridge University Press, 1996.

———. "The Man without the Wedding Garment (Matthew 22:11-13)." *HeyJ* 31 (1990) 165-78.

———. "Matthew 22:13a and 1 Enoch 10:4a: A Case of Literary Dependence?" *JSNT* (1992) 3-19.

Simian-Yofre, H. "Exodo en Deuteroisaias." *Bib* 61 (1980) 530-53.

Skehan, P. W., E. C. Ulrich, and P. W. Flint. "A Scroll Containing 'Biblical' and 'Apocryphal' Psalms: A Preliminary Edition of 4QPsf (4Q88)." *CBQ* 60 (1998) 267-82.

Slotki, I. W. *Isaiah: Hebrew Text & English Translation.* Rev. editor. London: Soncino, 1983.

Smend, R. "Die Bundesformel." In *Die Mitte des Alten Testaments*, 11-39. Munich: Kaiser, 1986.

Smith, D. E. *From Symposium to Eucharist: The Banquet in the Early Christian World.* Minneapolis: Fortress, 2005.

———. "Meals." In *Encyclopedia of the Dead Sea Scrolls*, edited by L. H. Schiffman and J. VanderKam, 2:530-32. Oxford: Oxford University, 2000.

———. "Messianic Banquet." In *ABD* 4:788-91.

———. "The Messianic Banquet Reconsidered." In *Future of Early Christianity*, edited by B. A. Pearson, 64-73. Minneapolis: Fortress, 1991.

———. "Table Fellowship." In *ABD* 6:302-3.

———. "Table Fellowship and the Historical Jesus." In *Religious Propaganda and Missionary Competition in the New Testament World*, 135-62. Leiden: Brill, 1994.

———. "Table Fellowship as a Literary Motif in the Gospel of Luke." *JBL* 106 (1987) 613-28.

Bibliography

Smith, D. E., and H. Taussig. *Many Tables: The Eucharist in the New Testament and Liturgy Today.* Philadelphia: Trinity, 1990.

Smith, G. V. *Isaiah 1–39.* NAC 15A. Nashville: Broadman & Holman, 2007.

Smith, H. P. *The Books of Samuel.* ICC. Edinburgh: T. & T. Clark, 1899.

Smith, M. "'God's Begetting the Messiah' in 1QSa." *NTS* 5 (1959) 218–24.

———. *Jesus the Magician.* San Francisco: Harper & Row, 1978.

Smith, M. S. "The Psalms as a Book for Pilgrims." *Int* 46 (1992) 156–66.

Smith, R. H. "Exodus Typology in the Fourth Gospel." *JBL* 81 (1962) 349–92.

Smith, R. L. *Micah-Malachi.* WBC 32. Waco: Word, 1984.

Snaith, J. G. *The Song of Songs.* NCB Commentary. Grand Rapids: Eerdmans, 1993.

Snaith, N. H. *Five Psalms: (I, XXVII, LI, CVII, XXXIV) A New Translation with Commentary & Questionary.* London: Epworth, 1938.

———. *Studies on the Second Part of the Book of Isaiah.* VTSup 14. Leiden: Brill, 1967.

Snodgrass, K. "Common Life with Jesus: The Parable of the Banquet in Luke 14:16–24." In *Common Life in the Early Church: Essays Honoring Graydon F. Snyder*, edited by J. V. Hills, 186–201. Harrisburg, PA: Trinity, 1998.

———. "From Allegorizing to Allegorizing: A History of the Interpretation of the Parables." In *The Challenge of Jesus' Parables*, edited by Richard Longenecker, 3–29. Grand Rapids: Eerdmans, 2000.

———. *The Parable of the Wicked Tenants.* WUNT 1/27. Tübingen: Mohr (Paul Siebeck), 1983.

———. "Recent Research on the Parable of the Wicked Tenants: An Assessment." *BRB* 8 (1998) 187–216.

———. *Stories with Intent: A Comprehensive Guide to the Parables of Jesus.* Grand Rapids: Eerdmans, 2008.

———. "Streams of Tradition Emerging from Isaiah 40:1–5 and Their Adaptation in the New Testament." *JSNT* 8 (1980) 24–45.

———. "The Use of the Old Testament in the New." In *New Testament Criticism and Interpretation*, edited by D. A. Black and D. S. Dockery, 425–56. Grand Rapids: Zondervan, 1991.

Soden, W. von. *Akkadisches Handwörterbuch.* Wiesbaden: Harrassowitz, 1965.

Soggin, J. A. *Introduction to the Old Testament: From Its Origins to the Closing of the Alexandrian Canon.* Translated by J. Bowden. Rev. ed. OTL. Philadelphia: Westminster, 1980.

Sommer, B. D. "Allusions and Illusions: The Unity of the Book of Isaiah in Light of Deutero-Isaiah's Use of Prophetic Tradition." In *New Visions of Isaiah*, edited by R. F. Melugin and M. A. Sweeney, 156–86. Sheffield: Sheffield Academic, 1996.

———. *A Prophet Reads Scripture: Allusion in Isaiah 40–66.* Stanford, CA: Stanford University, 1998.

Soskice, J. M. *Metaphor and Religious Language.* London: Oxford University, 1985.

Spencer, B.J. "The 'New Deal' for Post-exilic Judah in Isaiah 41,17–20." *ZAW* 112 (2000) 583–97.

Spencer, J. R. "Refuge, Cities of." In *ABD* 5:657–58.

Sprinkle, J. "Old Testament Perspectives on Divorce And Remarriage." *JETS* 40 (1997) 529–50.

———. "Sexuality, Sexual Ethics." In *Dictionary of the Old Testament: Pentateuch*, edited by T. D. Alexander and D. W. Baker, 741–53. Downers Grove, IL: InterVarsity, 2003.

Spykerboer, H. C. "Isaiah 55:1–5: The Climax of Deutero-Isaiah: An Invitation to Come to the New Jerusalem." In *Book of Isaiah—Le livre d'Isaie*, 357–59. Leuven: Leuven University, 1989.

Stallman, R. C. "Divine Hospitality in the Pentateuch: A Metaphorical Perspective on God as Host." PhD diss., Westminster Theological Seminary, 1999.

Stanley, C. D. "The Importance of 4QTanhumim (4Q176)." *RevQ* 15 (1992) 569–82.

Starbuck, S. R. A. "Theological Anthropology at a Fulcrum: Isaiah 55:1–5, Psalm 89, and Second Stage Traditio in the Royal Psalms." In *David and Zion: Biblical Studies in Honor of J. J. M. Roberts*, edited by B. F. Batto and K. L. Roberts, 247–65. Winona Lake, IN: Eisenbrauns, 2004.

Starcky, J. "Psaumes apocryphes de la grotte 4 de Qumrân, 4QPsf VII–X." *RB* 73 (1966) 353–71.

Staudigel, H. "Hermeneutische Überlegungen zu einer triumphalen Glosse in Jesaja 25,6–8." in *Theologische Versuche 1*, 9–13. Berlin: Evangelische Verlagsanstalt, 1989.

Stauffer, E. "Zum apokalyptischen Festmahl in Mc 6:34ff." *ZNW* 46 (1955) 264–66.

Steele, E. S. "Luke 11:37–54—A Modified Hellenistic Symposium." *JBL* 103 (1984) 379–94.

Steffen, D. S. "The Messianic Banquet as a Paradigm for Israel-Gentile Salvation in Matthew." PhD diss., Dallas Theological Seminary, 2001.

Stegemann, H. "Some Remarks to 1QSa, to 1QSb, and to Qumran Messianism." *RevQ* 17 (1996) 479–505.

———. "Weitere Stücke von 4QpPsalm 37." *RevQ* 6 (1967) 193–210.

Stein, R. H. *Luke*. NAC 24. Nashville: Broadman & Holman, 1992.

Stek, H. O. "Zion als Gelände und Gestalt: Überlegungen zur Wahrnehmung Jerusalems als Stadt und Frau im Alten Testament." *ZTK* 86 (1989) 261–81.

Stendahl, K. *The School of St. Matthew and Its Use of the Old Testament*. Uppsala: Gleerup, 1954.

Stern, P. D. "The 'Bloodbath of Anat' and Psalm xxiii." *VT* 44 (1994) 120–25.

Stevenson, G. M. "Communal Imagery and the Individual Lament: Exodus Typology in Psalm 77." *ResQ* 39 (1997) 215–29.

Stienstra, N. *Yahweh Is the Husband of His People*. Kampen: Kok Pharos, 1993.

Stinespring, W. F. "No Daughter of Zion: A Study of the Appositional Genitive in Hebrew Grammar." *Encounter* 26 (1965) 133–41.

Stock, A. *Saint Matthew*. Saint Andrew Bible Commentary 28. Conception, MO: Abbey, 1960.

———. *The Way in the Wilderness: Exodus, Wilderness, and Moses Themes in Old Testament and New*. Collegeville, MN: Liturgical, 1969.

Stoebe, H. J. "רחם." In TLOT 3:1225–30.

Stöger, A. *The Gospel According to St Luke*. 2 vols. New York: Herder & Herder, 1969.

Stone, M. E. "Coherence and Inconsistency in the Apocalypses: The Case of 'The End' in 4 Ezra." *JBL* 102 (1983) 229–43.

———. "Esdras, Second Book of." In *ABD* 2:611–14.

———. *Fourth Ezra*. Hermeneia. Minneapolis: Fortress, 1990.

———. "Reactions to Destructions of the Second Temple: Theology, Perception and Conversion." *JSJ* 12 (1981) 195–204.

Stone, M. E., B. G. Wright, and D. Satran. *The Apocryphal Ezekiel*. Atlanta: Society of Biblical Literature, 2000.

Bibliography

Strack, H. L., and P. Billerbeck. *Kommentar zum Neuen Testament aus Talmud und Midrasch.* Munich: Beck, 1928.

Strong, J. T. "Zion: Theology of." In *NIDOTTE*, 4:1314–21.

Stuart, D. K. *Hosea-Jonah.* WBC 31. Waco: Word, 1987.

Stuckenbruck, L. T. *1 Enoch 91–108.* Commentaries on Early Jewish Literature. Berlin: de Gruyter, 2007.

Stuhlmueller, C. *Creative Redemption in Deutero-Isaiah.* AnBib 43. Rome: Biblical Institute, 1970.

———. "Deutero-Isaiah: Major Transitions in the Prophet's Theology and in Contemporary Scholarship." *CBQ* 42 (1980) 1–29.

Suhl, A. *Die Funktion der alttestamentlichen Zitate und Anspielungen im Markusevangelium.* Gütersloher: Mohn, 1965.

Sutcliffe, E. F. "Rule of the Congregation (1QSa) II, 11–12: Text and Meaning." *RevQ* 2 (1960) 541–47.

Swaeles, R. "L'orientation ecclésiastique de la parabole du Festin Nuptial en Mt 22:1–14." *ETL* 36 (1960) 655–84.

Swanson, D. M. "Serpent's Stone." In *Eerdmans Dictionary of the Bible,* edited by D. N. Freedman, 1188. Grand Rapids: Eerdmans, 2000.

Sweeney, M. A. *Isaiah 1–39.* FOTL 16. Grand Rapids: Eerdmans, 1996.

———. "Textual Citations in Isaiah 24–27: Toward an Understanding of the Redactional Function of Chapters 24–27 in the Book of Isaiah." *JBL* 107 (1988) 39–52.

———. "The Wilderness Traditions of the Pentateuch: A Reassessment of Their Function and Intent in Relation to Exodus 32–34." *SBLSP* 28 (1989) 291–99.

Swete, H. B. *The Gospel according to St. Mark.* 3rd ed. Grand Rapids: Eerdmans, 1951.

Talmon, S. "The 'Desert Motif' in the Bible and Qumran Literature." In *Biblical Motifs,* edited by A. Altmann, 31–63. Cambridge: Harvard University, 1966.

———. "Wilderness." In *IDBSup,* 946–49.

Tan, S. S. "A Double Reading of the "Wilderness" Narratives: Implications for Old Testament Theology." *RestQ* 42 (2000) 155–68.

Tasker, R. V. G. *The Gospel according to St. Matthew.* Grand Rapids: Eerdmans, 1961.

Taylor, V. *The Gospel according to St. Mark.* London: Macmillan, 1952.

Terrien, S. "Amos and Wisdom." In *Israel's Prophetic Heritage: Essays in Honor of James Muilenburg,* edited by B. W. Anderson and W. J. Harrelson, 108–15. New York: Harper, 1962.

Terrien, S. L. *The Psalms: Strophic Structure and Theological Commentary.* ECC. Grand Rapids: Eerdmans, 2003.

Theissen, G., and D. Winter. *The Quest for the Plausible Jesus: The Question of Criteria.* Louisville: Westminster John Knox, 2002.

Thomas, R. L., and F. D. Farnell, editors. *The Jesus Crisis: The Inroads of Historical Criticism into Evangelical Scholarship.* Grand Rapids: Kregel, 1998.

Thompson, J. A. *The Book of Jeremiah.* NICOT. Grand Rapids: Eerdmans, 1980.

Thompson, M. *Clothed with Christ: The Example and Teaching of Jesus in Romans 12.1–15.13.* JSNTSup 59. Sheffield: JSOT Press, 1991.

Thoulock, A. *The Book of Psalms.* Translated by J. Isidor Mombert. Philadelphia: Martien, 1858.

Tidwell, N. L. "No Highway! The Outline of Semantic Description of *mesillā.*" *VT* 45 (1995) 251–69.

Tiller, P. A. *A Commentary of the Animal Apocalypse of I Enoch*. Early Judaism and Its Literature 4. Atlanta: Scholars, 1993.

Törnkvist, R. *The Use and Abuse of Female Sexual Imagery in the Book of Hosea: A Feminist Critical Approach to Hos 1–3*. Uppsala: Uppsala Library, 1998.

Townsend, J. T. "Ancient Education in the Time of the Early Roman Empire." In *The Catacombs and the Coliseum*, edited by S. Benko and J. J. O'Rourke, 139-63. Valley Forge, PA: Trinity, 1971.

———. "Education (Greco-Roman)." In *ABD* 2:312–17.

Trench, R. C. *The Parables of Our Lord*. London: Macmillian, 1877.

Trocmé, E. *L'évangile selon saint Marc*. Geneva: Labor et Fides, 2000.

Turner, D. L. *Matthew*. BECNT. Grand Rapids: Baker, 2008.

Twelftree, G. H. *Jesus the Miracle Worker: A Historical & Theological Study*. Downers Grove, IL: InterVarsity, 1999.

Ulfgard, H. *The Story of Sukkot: The Setting, Shaping, and Sequel of the Biblical Feast of Tabernacles*. BGBE 34. Tübingen: Mohr/Siebeck, 1998.

Unterman, J. *From Repentance to Redemption: Jeremiah's Thought in Transition*. JSOTSup 54. Sheffield: JSOT, 1987.

Van Aarde, A. G. *God-with-us: The Dominant Perspective in Matthew's Story and Other Essays*. HvTSt 5. Pretoria: Nederduitsch Hervormde Kerk van Afrika, 1994.

———. "A Historical-Critical Classification of Jesus' Parables and the Metaphoric Narration of the Wedding Feast in Matthew 22:1–14." In *God-with-Us: The Dominant Perspective in Matthew's Story and Other Essays*, edited by A. G. Van Aarde, 229–47. HvTSt 5. Pretoria: Nederduitsch Hervormde Kerk van Afrika, 1994.

———. "Matthew and Apocalypticism as the 'Mother of Christian Theology': Ernst Käsemann Revisited." *HvTSt* 58 (2002) 118–42.

———. "Plot as Mediated Through Point of View: Mt 22:1–14—A Case Study." In *South African Perspective on the New Testament*, edited by P. J. Hartin and J. H. Petzer, 62–75. Leiden: Brill, 1986.

van der Woude, A. S. "זְרוֹעַ." In *TLOT*, 1:392–93.

Van Seters, J. "Law and the Wilderness Rebellion Tradition: Exodus 32." *SBLSP* 29 (1990) 583–91.

Van Wijk-Bos, J. W. H. *Ezra, Nehemiah, and Esther*. Louisville: Westminster John Knox, 1998.

van Wolde, E. "Trendy Intertextuality?" In *Intertextuality in Biblical Writings: Essays in Honour of Bas van Iersel*, edited by S. Draisma, 43–50. Kampen: Kok, 1989.

VanderKam, J. C. *The Dead Sea Scrolls Today*. 2nd ed. Grand Rapids: Eerdmans, 2010.

Vanhoozer, K. J. *Is There a Meaning in This Text? The Bible, the Reader, and the Morality of Literary Knowledge*. Grand Rapids: Zondervan, 1998.

Vannorsdall, A. O. "The Use of the Covenant Liturgy in Hosea." PhD diss., Boston University, 1968.

Vegge, T. "The Literacy of Jesus the Carpenter's Son: On the Literary Style in the Words of Jesus." *ST* 59 (2005) 19–37.

Vermès, G. *Scripture and Tradition in Judaism: Haggadic Studies*. Studia post-biblica 4. Leiden: Brill, 1961.

Vermeylen, J. "Composition littéraire de l'"apocalypse d'Isaïe" (Is 24–27)." *ETL* 50 (1974) 5–38.

Bibliography

Vögtle, A. *Gott und seine Gäste: das Schicksal des Gleichnisses Jesu vom grossen Gastmahl (Lukas 14, 16b–24, Matthäus 22, 2–14).* Biblisch-theologische Studien 29. Neukirchen-Vluyn: Neukirchener, 1996.

Vorster, W. S. "The Function of the Use of the Old Testament in Mark." *Neot* 14 (1980) 62–72.

Wacker, M.-T. *Figurationen des Weiblichen im Hosea-Buch.* Freiburg: Herder, 1996.

Wagenaar, J. A. "The Cessation of Manna: Editorial Frames for the Wilderness Wandering in Exodus 16,35 and Joshua 5,10–12." *ZAW* 112 (2000) 192–209.

Wagner, J. R. *Heralds of the Good News: Isaiah and Paul "in Concert" in the Letter to the Romans.* NovTSup 101. Leiden: Brill, 2002.

Wakeman, M. K. *God's Battle with the Monster: A Study in Biblical Imagery.* Leiden: Brill, 1973.

Waldow, H.-E. von. "Anlass und Hintergrund der Verkuendigung des Deuterojesaja." ThD diss., Rheinische Friedrich Wilhelms-Universität, Bonn, 1953.

Wallace, D. B. *Greek Grammar beyond the Basics: An Exegetical Syntax of the New Testament.* Grand Rapids: Zondervan, 1996.

Waltke, B. K. *An Introduction to Biblical Hebrew Syntax.* Winona Lake, IN: Eisenbrauns, 1990.

Waltke, B. K., and Yu C. *An Old Testament Theology: An Exegetical, Canonical, and Thematic Approach.* Grand Rapids: Zondervan, 2007.

Walton, J. H., editor. *Zondervan Illustrated Bible Backgrounds Commentary.* 5 vols. Grand Rapids: Zondervan, 2009.

Wansbrough, H. *Jesus and the Oral Gospel.* JSNTSup 64. Sheffield: Sheffield Academic, 1991.

Watson, D. F. "Chreia/Aphorism." In *Dictionary of Jesus and the Gospels*, edited by J. B. Green, S. McKnight, and I. H. Marshall, 104–6. Downers Grove, IL: InterVarsity, 1992.

Watson, P. L. "The Death of 'Death' in the Ugaritic Texts." *JAOS* 92 (1972) 60–64.

Watts, J. D. W. *Isaiah 1–33.* Rev. ed. WBC 24. Nashville: Nelson, 2005.

———. *Isaiah 34–66.* Rev. ed. WBC 25. Nashville: Nelson, 2005.

Watts, R. E. "Consolation or Confrontation: Isaiah 40–55 and the Delay of the New Exodus." *TynBul* 41 (1990) 31–59.

———. "Echoes from the Past: Israel's Ancient Traditions and the Destiny of the Nations in Isaiah 40–55." *JSOT* 28 (2004) 481–508.

———. *Isaiah's New Exodus in Mark.* WUNT 2/88. Tübingen: Mohr/Siebeck, 1997.

———. *Isaiah's New Exodus in Mark.* Grand Rapids: Baker, 2000.

Weems, R. J. "Gomer: Victim of Violence or Victim of Metaphor?" *Semeia* 47 (1989) 87–104.

Weinfeld, M. "Grace after Meals in Qumran." *JBL* 111 (1992) 427–40.

———. "Prayer and Liturgical Practice in the Qumran Sect." In *The Dead Sea Scrolls: Forty Years of Research*, edited by D. Dimant, 241–58. Leiden: Brill, 1992.

Weisberg, D. "The Widow of Our Discontent: Levirate Marriage in the Bible and Ancient Israel." *JSOT* 28 (2004) 403–29.

Weiser, A. *The Psalms: A Commentary.* OTL. Philadelphia: Westminster John Knox, 1962.

Welch, A. C. *Post-Exilic Judaism.* Edinburgh: Blackwood, 1935.

Welten, P. "Die Vernichtung des Todes und die Königsherrschaft Gottes: eine traditionsgeschichtliche Studie zu Jes 25:6–8; 24:21–23 und Ex 24:9–11." *TZ* 38 (1982) 129–46.

Wenham, D. *The Parables of Jesus.* Downers Grove, IL: InterVarsity, 1989.

Wenham, G. J. "Marriage and Divorce in the Old Testament." *Didaskalia* 1 (1989) 6–17.

———. "The Restoration of Marriage Reconsidered." *JJS* 30 (1979) 36–40.

Westbrook, R. "Adultery in Ancient Near Eastern Law." *RB* 97 (1990) 542–80.

Westermann, C. *Isaiah 40–66*. OTL. Philadelphia: Westminster, 1969.

———. *The Parables of Jesus in the Light of the Old Testament*. Minneapolis: Fortress, 1990.

Westermann, C., editor. *Essays on Old Testament Interpretation*. London: SCM, 1963.

Wetzstein, J. G. "Die Syrische Dreschtafel." *Zeitschrift für Ethnologie* 5 (1873) 270–302.

Whitt, W. D. "The Divorce of Yahweh and Asherah in Hos 2:4–7,12ff." *SJOT* 6 (1992) 31–67.

———. "The Jacob Traditions in Hosea and Their Relation to Genesis." *ZAW* 103 (1991) 18–43.

Whitters, M. "Taxo and His Seven Sons in the Cave (Assumption of Moses 9–10)." *CBQ* 72 (2010) 718–31.

Whybray, R. N. *Isaiah 40–66*. NCB. Grand Rapids: Eerdmans, 1981.

Wiefel, W. *Das Evangelium nach Lukas*. Leipzig: Deichert, 1987.

Wildberger, H. "Das Freudenmahl auf dem Zion: Erwägungen zu Jes 25, 6–8." *Theologische Zeitschrift* 33 (1977) 373–83.

———. *Isaiah 13–27*. CC. Minneapolis: Fortress, 1997.

Willey, P. T. *Remember the Former Things: The Recollection of Previous Texts in Second Isaiah*. SBLDS 161. Atlanta: Scholars, 1997.

———. "The Servant of YHWH and Daughter Zion: Alternating Visions of YHWH's Community." In *SBLSP*, 34, 267–303 Atlanta: Scholars, 1995.

Williamson, H. G. M. *Ezra, Nehemiah*. WBC 16. Waco: Word, 1985.

———. *1 and 2 Chronicles*. NCB. Grand Rapids: Eerdmans, 1982.

———. "The Messianic Texts in Isaiah 1–39." In *King and Messiah in Israel and the Ancient Near East*, 238–70. Sheffield: Sheffield, 1998.

———. "Sure Mercies of David: Subjective or Objective Genitive." *JSS* 23 (1978) 31–49.

———. "Word Order in Isaiah xliii. 12." *JTS* 30 (1979) 499–502.

Willis, J. T. "Psalm 1: An Entity." *ZAW* 91 (1979) 381–401.

Willis, T. M. "Yahweh's Elders (Isa 24,23) Senior Officials of the Divine Court." *ZAW* 103 (1991) 375–85.

Willoughby, B. "Amos, Book of." In *ABD* 1:203–12.

Wilson, A. *The Nations in Deutero-Isaiah*. Ancient Near Eastern Texts and Studies 1. Lewiston, NY: Mellen, 1986.

Wilson, G. H. *Psalms*. NIV Application Commentary. Grand Rapids: Zondervan, 2002.

Wineman, A. "Wedding-Feasts, Exiled Princes and Hasidic Parable-Traditions." *HS* 40 (1999) 191–216.

Winger, M. "Why Didn't Jesus Write?" *ExpTim* 111 (2000) 259–61.

Winston, D. *The Wisdom of Solomon*. AB 43. New York: Doubleday, 1979.

———. "Wisdom of Solomon." In *ABD* 6:120–27.

Wise, M. O., M. G. Abegg, and E. M. Cook. *The Dead Sea Scrolls: A New Translation*. San Francisco: HarperSanFrancisco, 1996.

Wodecki, B. "The Religious Universalism of the Pericope Is 25:6–9." In *Goldene Äpfel in Silbernen Schalen*, 35–47. Frankfurt: Lang, 1992.

Wolff, H. W. "The Hermeneutics of the Old Testament." In *Essays on Old Testament Interpretation*, edited by C. Westermann, 160–99. London: SCM, 1963.

———. *Hosea*. Translated by G. Stansell. Hermeneia. Philadelphia: Fortress, 1974.

———. *Joel and Amos*. Translated by W. Janzen. Hermeneia. Philadelphia: Fortress, 1977.

Wright, D. P. "Music and Dance in Second Samuel Six." *JBL* 121 (2002) 201–25.

Wright, G. E. *God Who Acts: Biblical Theology as Recital*. SBT 8. London: SCM, 1952.

Bibliography

Wright, N. T. *Jesus and the Victory of God*. Vol. 2 of *Christian Origins and the Question of God*. Atlanta: Fortress, 1996.

———. *The New Testament and the People of God*. Vol. 1 of *Christian Origins and the Question of God*. Atlanta: Fortress, 1992.

———. "Theology, History and Jesus: A Response to Maurice Casey and Clive Marsh." *JSNT* 69 (1998) 105–12.

Yadin, Y. "A Crucial Passage in the Dead Sea Scrolls: 1QSa 2:11–17." *JBL* 78 (1959) 238–41.

———. *The Documents from the Bar Kokhba Period in the Cave of Letters*. Jerusalem: Israel Exploration Society, 1989.

———. "Expedition D—The Cave of the Letters." *IEJ* 12 (1962) 227–57.

———. *The Scroll of the War of the Sons of Light against the Sons of Darkness*. London: Oxford, 1962.

Yamauchi, E. M. "Cultural Aspects of Marriage in the Ancient World." *BibSac* 135 (1978) 241–52.

Yaron, R. "The Restoration of Marriage." *JJS* 17 (1966) 1–11.

Yates, G. E. "Jeremiah's Message of Judgment and Hope for God's Unfaithful 'Wife.'" *BibSac* 167 (2010) 144–65.

Yee, G. *Poor Banished Children of Eve*. Minneapolis: Fortress, 2003.

Young, B. *Jesus and His Jewish Parables: Rediscovering the Roots of Jesus' Teaching*. Theological Inquiries. New York: Paulist, 1989.

———. *The Parables: Jewish Tradition and Christian Interpretation*. Peabody, MA: Hendrickson, 1998.

Yonge, C. D. *The Works of Philo: Complete and Unabridged*. Peabody, MA: Hendrickson, 1995.

Young, E. J. *The Book of Isaiah*. NICOT. Grand Rapids: Eerdmans, 1969.

Zeitlin, S. "Midrash: A Historical Study." *JQR* 44 (1953) 21–36.

Zeller, D. "Das Logion Mt 8:11f/Lk 13:28f und das Motiv der "Völkerwallfahrt." *BZ* 16 (1972) 84–93.

Zeman, F. "Le statut de la femme en Mesopotamie d'après les sources juridiques." *Science et Espirit* 43 (1991) 69–86.

Zenger, E. "The God of Exodus in the Message of the Prophets as Seen in Isaiah." In *Exodus, A Lasting Paradigm*, edited by B. Iersel, A. G. Weiler, and M. Lefébvre, 22–33. Edinburgh: T. & T. Clark, 1987.

Zervos, G. T. "Apocalypse of Daniel," In *OTP* 1:775–72.

Zeuner, F. E. "Notes on Qumrân." *PEQ* 92 (1960) 27–36.

Ziesler, J. A. "The Removal of the Bridegroom: A Note on Mark II, 18–22 and Parallels." *NTS* 19 (1972) 190–94.

Zillessen, A. "Der alte und der neue Exodus." *Archiv für Religionwissenschaft* 6, no. 4 (1903) 289–304.

Zimmerli, W. "Le nouvel "exode" dans le message de deux grands prophètes de l'exil." In *Maggel Shagdeh: Hommage à Wilhelm Vischer*, edited by Jean Cadier, 216–27. Montpellier: Causse, Graille, Castelnau, 1960.

Zimmermann, J. *Messianische Texte aus Qumran: königliche, priesterliche und prophetische Messiasvorstellungen in den Schriftfunden von Qumran*. WUNT 2/104. Tübingen: Mohr/Siebeck, 1998.

Zimmermann, R. "Das Hochzeitsritual im Jungfrauengleichnis: sozialgeschichtliche Hintergründe zu Mt 25.1–13." *NTS* 48 (2002) 48–70.

———. *Geschlechtermetaphorik und Gottesverhältnis: Traditionsgeschichte und Theologie eines Bildfelds in Urchristentum und antiker Umwelt.* WUNT 2/122. Tübingen: Mohr/Siebeck, 2001.

———. "Nuptial Imagery in the Revelation of John." *Bib* 84 (2003) 153–83.

———. "Die Virginitäts-Metapher in Apk 14:4–5 im Horizont von Befleckung, Loskauf und Erstlingsfrucht." *NovT* 45 (2003) 45–70.

Zipor, M. A. "'Scenes from a Marriage'—According to Jeremiah." *JSOT* 65 (1995) 83–91.

Zobel, H.-J. "Die Zeit der Wüstenwanderung Israels im Lichte prophetischer Texte." *VT* 41 (1991) 192–202.

www.ingramcontent.com/pod-product-compliance
Lightning Source LLC
Chambersburg PA
CBHW081417230426
43668CB00016B/2264